ABRAHAM LINCOLN
The Southern View

THE LOCHLAINN SEABROOK COLLECTION

AMERICAN CIVIL WAR
Abraham Lincoln Was a Liberal, Jefferson Davis Was a Conservative: The Missing Key to Understanding the American Civil War
Confederacy 101: Amazing Facts You Never Knew About America's Oldest Political Tradition
Confederate Blood and Treasure: An Interview With Lochlainn Seabrook
Everything You Were Taught About African-Americans and the Civil War is Wrong, Ask a Southerner!
Everything You Were Taught About the Civil War is Wrong, Ask a Southerner!
Give This Book to a Yankee! A Southern Guide to the Civil War For Northerners
Heroes of the Southern Confederacy: The Illustrated Book of Confederate Officials, Soldiers, and Civilians
Lincoln's War: The Real Cause, the Real Winner, the Real Loser
The Great Yankee Coverup: What the North Doesn't Want You to Know About Lincoln's War!
The Ultimate Civil War Quiz Book: How Much Do You Really Know About America's Most Misunderstood Conflict?
Women in Gray: A Tribute to the Ladies Who Supported the Southern Confederacy

CONFEDERATE MONUMENTS
Confederate Monuments: Why Every American Should Honor Confederate Soldiers and Their Memorials

CONFEDERATE FLAG
Confederate Flag Facts: What Every American Should Know About Dixie's Southern Cross
What the Confederate Flag Means to Me: Americans Speak Out in Defense of Southern Honor, Heritage, and History

SECESSION
All We Ask Is To Be Let Alone: The Southern Secession Fact Book

SLAVERY
Everything You Were Taught About American Slavery is Wrong, Ask a Southerner!
Slavery 101: Amazing Facts You Never Knew About America's "Peculiar Institution"

CHILDREN
Honest Jeff and Dishonest Abe: A Southern Children's Guide to the Civil War
Saddle, Sword, and Gun: A Biography of Nathan Bedford Forrest For Teens

NATHAN BEDFORD FORREST
A Rebel Born: A Defense of Nathan Bedford Forrest - Confederate General, American Legend (winner of the 2011 Jefferson Davis Historical Gold Medal)
A Rebel Born: The Screenplay (film about N. B. Forrest)
Forrest! 99 Reasons to Love Nathan Bedford Forrest
Give 'Em Hell Boys! The Complete Military Correspondence of Nathan Bedford Forrest
I Rode With Forrest! Confederate Soldiers Who Served With the World's Greatest Cavalry Leader
Nathan Bedford Forrest and African-Americans: Yankee Myth, Confederate Fact
Nathan Bedford Forrest and the Battle of Fort Pillow: Yankee Myth, Confederate Fact
Nathan Bedford Forrest and the Ku Klux Klan: Yankee Myth, Confederate Fact
Nathan Bedford Forrest: Southern Hero, American Patriot - Honoring a Confederate Icon and the Old South
Saddle, Sword, and Gun: A Biography of Nathan Bedford Forrest For Teens
The God of War: Nathan Bedford Forrest As He Was Seen By His Contemporaries
The Quotable Nathan Bedford Forrest: Selections From the Writings and Speeches of the Confederacy's Most Brilliant Cavalryman

QUOTABLE SERIES
The Alexander H. Stephens Reader: Excerpts From the Works of a Confederate Founding Father
The Quotable Alexander H. Stephens: Selections From the Writings and Speeches of the Confederacy's First Vice President
The Quotable Jefferson Davis: Selections From the Writings and Speeches of the Confederacy's First President
The Quotable Nathan Bedford Forrest: Selections From the Writings and Speeches of the Confederacy's Most Brilliant Cavalryman
The Quotable Robert E. Lee: Selections From the Writings and Speeches of the South's Most Beloved Civil War General
The Quotable Stonewall Jackson: Selections From the Writings and Speeches of the South's Most Famous General
The Unquotable Abraham Lincoln: The President's Quotes They Don't Want You To Know!

CIVIL WAR BATTLES
Encyclopedia of the Battle of Franklin - A Comprehensive Guide to the Conflict that Changed the Civil War
Nathan Bedford Forrest and the Battle of Fort Pillow: Yankee Myth, Confederate Fact
The Battle of Franklin: Recollections of Confederate and Union Soldiers
The Battle of Nashville: Recollections of Confederate and Union Soldiers
The Battle of Spring Hill: Recollections of Confederate and Union Soldiers

CONSTITUTIONAL HISTORY
America's Three Constitutions: Complete Texts of the Articles of Confederation, Constitution of the United States of America, and Constitution of the Confederate States of America
The Articles of Confederation Explained: A Clause-by-Clause Study of America's First Constitution
The Constitution of the Confederate States of America Explained: A Clause-by-Clause Study of the South's Magna Carta

VICTORIAN CONFEDERATE LITERATURE
Rise Up and Call Them Blessed: Victorian Tributes to the Confederate Soldier, 1861-1901
Support Your Local Confederate: Wit and Humor in the Southern Confederacy
The God of War: Nathan Bedford Forrest As He Was Seen By His Contemporaries
The Old Rebel: Robert E. Lee As He Was Seen By His Contemporaries
Victorian Confederate Poetry: The Southern Cause in Verse, 1861-1901

ABRAHAM LINCOLN
Abraham Lincoln: The Southern View - Demythologizing America's Sixteenth President
Lincolnology: The Real Abraham Lincoln Revealed in His Own Words - A Study of Lincoln's Suppressed, Misinterpreted, and Forgotten Writings and Speeches
Lincoln's War: The Real Cause, the Real Winner, the Real Loser
The Great Impersonator! 99 Reasons to Dislike Abraham Lincoln
The Unholy Crusade: Lincoln's Legacy of Destruction in the American South
The Unquotable Abraham Lincoln: The President's Quotes They Don't Want You To Know!

NATURAL HISTORY
North America's Amazing Mammals: An Encyclopedia for the Whole Family
The Concise Book of Owls: A Guide to Nature's Most Mysterious Birds
The Concise Book of Tigers: A Guide to Nature's Most Remarkable Cats

PARANORMAL
Carnton Plantation Ghost Stories: True Tales of the Unexplained from Tennessee's Most Haunted Civil War House!
UFOs and Aliens: The Complete Guidebook

FAMILY HISTORIES
The Blakeneys: An Etymological, Ethnological, and Genealogical Study - Uncovering the Mysterious Origins of the Blakeney Family and Name
The Caudills: An Etymological, Ethnological, and Genealogical Study - Exploring the Name and National Origins of a European-American Family
The McGavocks of Carnton Plantation: A Southern History - Celebrating One of Dixie's Most Noble Confederate Families and Their Tennessee Home

MIND, BODY, SPIRIT
Autobiography of a Non-Yogi: A Scientist's Journey From Hinduism to Christianity (Dr. Amitava Dasgupta, with Lochlainn Seabrook)
Britannia Rules: Goddess-Worship in Ancient Anglo-Celtic Society - An Academic Look at the United Kingdom's Matricentric Spiritual Past
Christ Is All and In All: Rediscovering Your Divine Nature and the Kingdom Within
Christmas Before Christianity: How the Birthday of the "Sun" Became the Birthday of the "Son"
Jesus and the Gospel of Q: Christ's Pre-Christian Teachings As Recorded in the New Testament
Jesus and the Law of Attraction: The Bible-Based Guide to Creating Perfect Health, Wealth, and Happiness Following Christ's Simple Formula
Seabrook's Bible Dictionary of Traditional and Mystical Christian Doctrines
Sea Raven Press Blank Page Journal: For Reflections, Notes, and Sketches
The Bible and the Law of Attraction: 99 Teachings of Jesus, the Apostles, and the Prophets
The Book of Kelle: An Introduction to Goddess-Worship and the Great Celtic Mother-Goddess Kelle, Original Blessed Lady of Ireland
The Goddess Dictionary of Words and Phrases: Introducing a New Core Vocabulary for the Women's Spirituality Movement
The Great Martian Mystery: Did an Advanced Race Once Live on Mars?
Vintage Southern Cookbook: Delicious Dishes From Dixie

WOMEN
Aphrodite's Trade: The Hidden History of Prostitution Unveiled
Princess Diana: Modern Day Moon-Goddess - A Psychoanalytical and Mythological Look at Diana Spencer's Life, Marriage, and Death (with Dr. Jane Goldberg)
Women in Gray: A Tribute to the Ladies Who Supported the Southern Confederacy

REPRINTS
A Short History of the Confederate States of America (author Jefferson Davis; editor Lochlainn Seabrook)
Prison Life of Jefferson Davis (author John J. Craven; editor Lochlainn Seabrook)
Life of Beethoven (author Ludwig Nohl; editor Lochlainn Seabrook)
The New Revelation (author Arthur Conan Doyle; editor Lochlainn Seabrook)

Lochlainn Seabrook does not author books for fame and fortune, but for the love of writing and sharing his knowledge.

SeaRavenPress.com

ABRAHAM LINCOLN
THE SOUTHERN VIEW

Demythologizing America's Sixteenth President

LOCHLAINN SEABROOK
JEFFERSON DAVIS HISTORICAL GOLD MEDAL WINNER

Foreword by Clint Johnson

Diligently Researched and Generously
Illustrated for the Elucidation of the Reader

2007

SEA RAVEN PRESS, NASHVILLE, TENNESSEE, USA

ABRAHAM LINCOLN: THE SOUTHERN VIEW

Published by
Sea Raven Press, Cassidy Ravensdale, President
PO Box 1484, Spring Hill, Tennessee 37174-1484 USA
SeaRavenPress.com • searavenpress@gmail.com

Copyright © 2007, 2009, 2010, 2013, 2016, 2021 Lochlainn Seabrook
in accordance with U.S. and international copyright laws and regulations, as stated and protected under the Berne Union for the Protection of Literary and Artistic Property (Berne Convention), and the Universal Copyright Convention (the UCC). All rights reserved under the Pan-American and International Copyright Conventions.

1st SRP paperback ed., 1st printing, October 2007, ISBN: 978-0-9827700-0-9 • 2nd SRP paperback ed., 1st printing: November 2009
3rd SRP paperback ed., 1st printing, June 2010 • 4th SRP paperback ed., 1st printing, February 2013; 2nd printing, February 2021; 3rd printing, October 2021
1st SRP hardcover edition, 1st printing, January 2016, ISBN: 978-1-943737-21-5; 2nd printing, February 2021; 3rd printing, October 2021

ISBN: 978-0-9827700-0-9 (paperback)
Library of Congress Control Number: 2010928626

This work is the copyrighted intellectual property of Lochlainn Seabrook and has been registered with the Copyright Office at the Library of Congress in Washington, D.C., USA. No part of this work (including text, covers, drawings, photos, illustrations, maps, images, diagrams, etc.), in whole or in part, may be used, reproduced, stored in a retrieval system, or transmitted, in any form or by any means now known or hereafter invented, without written permission from the publisher. The sale, duplication, hire, lending, copying, digitalization, or reproduction of this material, in any manner or form whatsoever, is also prohibited, and is a violation of federal, civil, and digital copyright law, which provides severe civil and criminal penalties for any violations.

Abraham Lincoln: The Southern View - Demythologizing America's Sixteenth President, by Lochlainn Seabrook. Foreword by Clint Johnson. Includes an introduction, footnotes, illustrations, a bibliography, appendices, and an index.

Front & back cover design & art, book design, layout, & interior art by Lochlainn Seabrook
All images, image captions, graphic design, & graphic art copyright © Lochlainn Seabrook
All images selected, placed, manipulated, and/or created by Lochlainn Seabrook
Image cleaning, coloration, & tinting by Lochlainn Seabrook
Cover image and design by Lochlainn Seabrook copyright © 2021
Poster art, design, & text on page ten © Lochlainn Seabrook
Cover photo: (L-R) Allan Pinkerton, Abraham Lincoln, Union Gen. John A. McClernand, Antietam, Maryland, Fall 1862
Portions of this book have been excerpted from the author's other works

All persons who approve of the authority and principles of Colonel Lochlainn Seabrook's literary work, and realize its benefits as a means of reeducating the world about the South and the Confederacy, are hereby requested to avidly recommend his books to others and to vigorously cooperate in extending their reach, scope, and influence around the globe.

THE VIEWS ON THE AMERICAN "CIVIL WAR" DOCUMENTED IN THIS BOOK ARE THOSE OF THE PUBLISHER.

PRINTED & MANUFACTURED IN OCCUPIED TENNESSEE, FORMER CONFEDERATE STATES OF AMERICA

DOCUMENTED FACTS ABOUT
ABRAHAM LINCOLN
That You Will Learn In This Book

- Lincoln was selected as the Republican presidential candidate in 1860 by slave-trading Yankee tycoons; not because he was an abolitionist, but because he was a white supremacist who promised not to interfere with slavery.
- Lincoln funded the "Civil War" and his two presidential campaigns using profits from Northern slavery, financed by the same people, the "Wall Street Boys," who put him into office.
- Though a Republican, Lincoln was an ultra left-wing liberal who was obsessed with big government, big business, big spending, and Big Brother politics, the antithesis of the Confederacy's conservative, small government, Democratic President Jefferson Davis.
- Though not technically a socialist, Left-wing Lincoln had strong socialistic tendencies, which is why he packed his administration and army with socialists and communists—two groups who still adore him to this day. Indeed, the term "New Deal" dates from the Lincoln administration, when it was used to describe the president's socialist domestic policies.
- In his day Lincoln was voted the worst president in American history.
- In 1860 America did not want Lincoln to be president: only 39 percent of the country voted for him in his first election.
- As with his first, Lincoln won his second election by rigging the polls, bribery, intimidation, patronage, and coercion, and by restricting free speech and freedom of the press.
- Lincoln did not preserve the Union, he destroyed it.
- Lincoln's Emancipation Proclamation freed no slaves.
- It was not the South, but Lincoln who started the War.
- Secession is legal, therefore the South had every right to secede, making the "Civil War" illegal and Lincoln a war criminal.
- Lincoln did not fight the South over slavery, as he himself said repeatedly. It was about money (the tariff), a fact he clearly articulated in his First Inaugural Address; further proof of this is that it would have cost ten times less to simply free America's slaves than to go to war.
- Due to his Left-wing belief that justice is a "Higher Law" than the U.S. Constitution, Lincoln subverted it, eventually drastically altering it from the original version created by the Founding Fathers—all of this in defiance of his presidential oath.
- Lincoln had to be pushed, cajoled, and pressured for years by abolitionists to issue the Emancipation Proclamation.
- If Lincoln had not become president, slavery would have been abolished sooner.

8   ABRAHAM LINCOLN: THE SOUTHERN VIEW

- Lincoln openly supported the proposed 1861 Corwin Amendment, which would have allowed slavery to continue indefinitely in both the North and the South.
- Lincoln committed thousands of unlawful acts, not only against the South, but against the North as well.
- Lincoln ordered or sanctioned the illegal arrest, imprisonment, torture, and murder of hundreds of thousands of Southerners and Northerners, soldiers and civilians, whites, blacks, coloreds, and Native-Americans.
- President Lincoln, an amoral and avaricious brute who hired spies, detectives, "secret agents," and armed vigilante gangs to do his "dirty work," was the leader of what could only be called a true thugocracy.
- The American abolition movement started in the South, not in the North.
- Both the American slave trade and American slavery began in the North, not in the South.
- White slavery in early America laid the groundwork for the introduction of black slavery.
- Lincoln was a white racist, a white supremacist, and a white separatist who campaigned throughout his entire political career for American apartheid, and who helped create and pass laws designed to restrict blacks.
- Lincoln and his cabinet referred to blacks as "niggers," Native-Americans as "savages," and Mexicans as "mongrels."
- As a lawyer Lincoln defended not slaves, but slave owners.
- Lincoln hated abolitionists and believed that abolition would cause more problems than slavery.
- As many as 1,000,000 blacks fought for the Confederacy, 80 percent more than fought for Lincoln and the North.
- While only 6 percent of Lincoln's military was black, up to 50 percent of the Confederate military was black.
- Lincoln's Emancipation Proclamation was unlawful, a point he himself acknowledged.
- Lincoln never intended his Emancipation Proclamation to be permanent; it was meant to be only a temporary "war measure."
- Lincoln issued the Emancipation Proclamation primarily because his armies were dwindling and he needed more men, which is why, for once being completely honest, he called it a "military emancipation."
- In a private conversation Lincoln once told former Northern slave Sojourner Truth that he would not have issued the Emancipation Proclamation if Southerners had "behaved themselves."
- Lincoln's main goal pertaining to slavery was not to end it, but to prevent it from spreading North and West.
- Lincoln wanted to restrict the institution to the South because he did not want Northern and Western whites to have to compete with slaves for jobs and

housing.
- Lincoln had little interest in true civil rights for blacks, or any other minority, including women and children.
- Lincoln was wholly against interracial marriage, black citizenship, and black suffrage.
- One of Lincoln's closest black "friends," former Northern slave Frederick Douglass, said that the president's policies regarding African-Americans were "missing the genuine spark of humanity."
- Lincoln was an anti-Christian atheist who wrote a book denying the divinity of Christ, denouncing miracles as "impossible," and declaring the Bible to be false.
- Lincoln's soldiers burned down some 1,200 Southern churches and turned millions of innocent Southern men, women, and children (of all races and creeds) into homeless starving refugees. Why? To "preserve the Union"?
- Socialistic Lincoln stole Southern land and wealth and redistributed it, giving most of it to affluent Yankee businessmen and industrialists.
- One of Lincoln's lifelong goals was black colonization: ridding the U.S. of all "persons of African descent," as he phrased it, an obsession that—according to one of his own military officers—lasted right up until the day he died.
- Lincoln was a leader in the American Colonization Society, a Yankee organization whose stated mission was to ship all blacks back to Africa in order to make America "white from coast to coast."
- If colonization proved unworkable, Lincoln wanted to corral all African-Americans into their own black-only state.
- Of the South's 3,500,000 black servants, only 500,000 (just 14 percent) were imported from Africa between 1607 (the settling of Jamestown, Virginia) and 1861. (The other 3,000,000, that is, the remaining 86 percent, were all American-born, the result of natural reproduction.)
- There were tens of thousands of Africa-American and Native-American slave owners in the North and in the South before and up to the "Civil War."
- Percentage wise, there were far more black slave owners than white, and on average Indian slave owners owned more slaves than white slave owners.
- Lincoln was hated in the South for being a Northerner and was hated in the North for being a Southerner.
- The South is still recovering from Lincoln's War and his Reconstruction and Northernization policies.

If you are interested in discovering the true Lincoln rather than the false one portrayed by pro-North historians and revisionist writers, then you will find Lochlainn Seabrook's comprehensive well documented book, *Abraham Lincoln: The Southern View*, an invaluable addition to your library.

WANTED!

ABRAHAM LINCOLN
DICTATOR

★ For War Crimes Against Humanity
★ For Treason Against the United States of America
★ For Suspension of Habeas Corpus,
Freedom of Speech, & Freedom of the Press
★ For Usurpation of the U.S. Constitution & The Bill of Rights

His Many Outrages Include: Racism, Sexism, Rapine, False Arrest, False Imprisonment, Torture, Murder, Initiating War Without Congressional Approval, Inciting Riots, Racial Divisiveness, Establishing A Naval Blockade Without Declaring War, Issuing An Emancipation Proclamation In A Foreign Country, Numerous Violations Of The 1863 Geneva Convention, Abuse Of Women & Children, Mass Execution of Native-Americans, The Ordered Killing Of Civilians, & Unarmed Noncombatants, & The Invasion Of The Southern Confederacy—A Sovereign Nation!

DEAD OR ALIVE!

Praise For Lochlainn Seabrook's
ABRAHAM LINCOLN
THE SOUTHERN VIEW

"From the symbolic cover photo to the brilliant research and writing, powerful, eye-opening, jaw-dropping! Destined to become a classic." — NEIL, ALABAMA

"*Abraham Lincoln: The Southern View* should be required reading in every American school." — CLIVE, TENNESSEE

"A mind-bending exploration of our 16th President that will overturn everything that's been written about him. Filled with little known riveting facts, this is a provocative read, with thousands of footnotes and a huge bibliography!" — SKEET, KENTUCKY

"Mr. Seabrook provides ironclad evidence that Lincoln was not who we were taught he was." — JESSIE, LOUISIANA

"I have African-American ancestors who fought for the Confederacy. Very happy to see someone finally giving them the recognition they deserve!" — TERRELL, FLORIDA

"If I had a nickel for every time I heard someone say that 'Lincoln was our greatest president,' I'd be a millionaire. If I could, I'd give a copy of this book to each and every one of them. The American people need to know the truth, the '*Southern* truth,' as the author puts it." — MITSUKO, MASSACHUSETTS

"Lochlainn Seabrook calls it like it is in this amazing book about the Lincoln that has been virtually ignored by history. Rather than the Great Emancipator, we find out that he was a white supremacist. Rather than a humanitarian, we discover that he was a cruel butcher. Rather than a law-abiding civil servant, we learn that he was a criminal and demagogue who thought nothing of walking over the Constitution." — SADIE, OREGON

"Who was the real Lincoln? The infallible granite-like deity of Northern myth, or the weak, depressed, power-hungry, uneducated, all-too-human bully of Mr. Seabrook's work *Abraham Lincoln: The Southern View*? Read the book and decide for yourself." — CAROL, VIRGINIA

"Be prepared to have your favorite president chewed up and tossed out with the morning trash. It's about time!" — LEONARD, NEW YORK

"People need to pay more attention to books like this. Seabrook knows what he's talking about. Here in the South we've known about this stuff for decades. Now we just have to educate the rest of the country! This book will help." — MATT, MISSISSIPPI

"I had never known about any of this before. Clear, hard-hitting, well researched writing made the bitter truth easier to accept." — TIA, NEVADA

12 ABRAHAM LINCOLN: THE SOUTHERN VIEW

"Our educational system has deceived us: 'Honest Abe' actually turns out to be a scoundrel, an autocrat, and a crook of the worst kind, and *Abraham Lincoln: The Southern View* proves it." — AIDAN, MONTANA

"For those who think they know Lincoln, think again. Author Lochlainn Seabrook offers a *tour de force* in American history, undoing a century and a half of what he calls 'Yankee mythology' surrounding Lincoln. In light of the facts disclosed here, we need to completely rewrite our text books, if not American history itself." — HAROLD, ARIZONA

"Loved, loved, loved this book! Will be handing out copies as gifts for birthdays, Christmas, Confederate Memorial Day, Robert E. Lee Day, etc." — RITA, TEXAS

"I always thought Lincoln was too good to be true. After reading *Abraham Lincoln: The Southern View*, now I know he was!" — GISÈLE, ALBERTA, CANADA

"As a Native American I've had enough of the lies about American history. We say good for Mr. Seabrook. This book is long overdue. Lincoln was no friend of the red man and the author has the guts to talk about it." — TAKODA, KANSAS

"The 'Great Emancipator' of history is dead and gone, replaced by a more believable, everyday Lincoln . . . but still not anyone I'd want to have a cup of coffee with!" — CHUCK, ARKANSAS

"Suspicious of the old hackneyed stories about Abraham Lincoln? How he "freed the slaves," "saved the Union," "healed the nation"? If you're like me, you're probably hungering for authentic history. If so, Lochlainn Seabrook's *Abraham Lincoln* is for you. Much of it taken from Lincoln's own writings and speeches, we finally get an inside look at the genuine man. Jarring, refreshing, enlightening, recommended." — MICHELLE, VERMONT

"Those who worship at the feet of Lincoln won't like this book. But that's exactly why they need to read it. I understand the author has another work on Lincoln coming out. Can't wait." — SAMMY, FLORIDA

"I'm already going through Seabrook's book on Lincoln a second time. There's a lot to take in. It took me the whole first read just to get used to the idea that the Lincoln I knew is not the Lincoln who was." — JOYCE, WASHINGTON, D.C.

"A wonderful read about a terrible man." — EDUARDO, MICHIGAN

"Here in the South we've always hated Lincoln, and always will. Seabrook's book explains why!" — LYLE, SOUTH CAROLINA

"We believe the pro-North books on Lincoln at our peril." — GARY, OKLAHOMA

"After reading *Abraham Lincoln: The Southern View*, I wrote to my congressman and asked him to take old Abe's face off our state license plate. This is not a man anybody should be venerating!" — VIC, ILLINOIS

Dedication

To the

1,000,000 European-Americans
300,000 African-Americans
70,000 Native-Americans
60,000 Latin-Americans
50,000 foreigners
12,000 Jewish-Americans
10,000 Asian-Americans

who donned Confederate gray and fought for the South in the cause of freedom, self-determination, the Constitution, and the original Confederate States of America, the U.S.A.

Epigraph

That the career of Mr. Lincoln was one of the most remarkable recorded in history, and that he must have had some element of character which made that career possible, no one will deny. But that he was the pious and exemplary Christian, the great and good man, "the prophet, priest and kind," the "Washington," the "Moses," the "Second to Christ," now being portrayed to the world by some of his prejudiced and intemperate admirers, we unhesitatingly deny, and we think it our duty, both to ourselves and to our children, to correct some of the false impressions attempted to be made about this man's character and career . . .

We have no right to do so, and we do not object, in the least, that Mr. Lincoln shall be put forward as the representative man and ideal of the North; but we do object to, and protest against, his being proclaimed to the world as the exemplar and representative of the South and its people. We proclaim George Washington, Patrick Henry, James Madison, James Monroe, Jefferson Davis, Robert E. Lee, "Stonewall" Jackson, Joseph E. Johnston, Albert Sydney Johnston, Wade Hampton, Jeb Stuart, and such like men, as our heroes and ideals and as the exemplars for our children and our children's children.

George Llewellyn Christian
OCTOBER 29, 1909, RICHMOND, VIRGINIA

Contents

Documented Facts About Abraham Lincoln - 7

Praise for Abraham Lincoln: The Southern View - 11

Notes to the Reader - 17

Foreword, by Clint Johnson - 27

Preface, by Lochlainn Seabrook - 29

Introduction, by Lochlainn Seabrook - 31

Section One
CONFEDERATION, SECESSION, & STATES' RIGHTS

1 Roots of the Southern Confederacy - 37
2 Lincoln Sets the Stage for War - 57
3 The Truth About Secession - 85
4 Trickery at Fort Sumter & the Call to Arms - 107

Section Two
SLAVERY, PROPAGANDA, & RACISM

5 Uncle Tom & the Whip - 139
6 African Slavery, Yankee Slave Trade - 163
7 Southern Abolition, Northern Racism: Part One - 191
8 Southern Abolition, Northern Racism: Part Two - 217
9 Lincoln, White Separatism, & Black Deportation - 243

16   ABRAHAM LINCOLN: THE SOUTHERN VIEW

SECTION THREE
ELECTIONS, WAR CRIMES, & EMANCIPATION

10   LINCOLN'S WAR AGAINST THE NORTH - 265

11   LINCOLN: WAR CRIMINAL - 295

12   BLACKS IN LINCOLN'S ARMY: PART ONE - 321

13   BLACKS IN LINCOLN'S ARMY: PART TWO - 349

14   LINCOLN'S VIEWS ON BLACKS, SLAVERY, & EMANCIPATION: PART ONE - 373

15   A BRIEF STUDY OF THE TRUE ORIGINS OF SLAVERY - 387

16   LINCOLN'S VIEWS ON BLACKS, SLAVERY, & EMANCIPATION: PART TWO - 413

SECTION FOUR
INVASION, SUBJUGATION, & RECONSTRUCTION

17   SOUTH-HATING IN VICTORIAN AMERICA - 427

18   DESTRUCTION OF THE UNION & UNPLANNED EMANCIPATION - 455

19   SOUTHERN & NORTHERN VIEWS OF LINCOLN: PART ONE - 475

20   SOUTHERN & NORTHERN VIEWS OF LINCOLN: PART TWO - 497

21   RECONSTRUCTION: LINCOLN'S FINAL CRIME: PART ONE - 521

22   RECONSTRUCTION: LINCOLN'S FINAL CRIME: PART TWO - 547

Appendix A: Lincoln, Washington, and Nero - 573

Appendix B: Marx's 1864 Letter to Lincoln (complete text) - 575

Bibliography - 581

Index - 619

A Note on John Wilkes Booth - 649

Meet the Author - 651

Learn More - 653

🍃 Notes to the Reader 🍃

☛ 1. The original spelling and punctuation of most of the individuals quoted have been left intact, resulting in various grammatical peculiarities that will be unfamiliar to most modern readers. This is intentional; an effort to preserve the style and mood of the day.

☛ 2. Throughout this work I use such terms as federal, federated, confederal, and confederacy. Unfortunately, for the student of history, the meanings of these words have changed numerous times over the centuries, with some even taking on the opposite meaning from the original. In the 1800s, for instance, the word federal was often used to describe what today we would call a confederate form of government, while today the word federal is used mainly as a synonym for "national" (actually, we now define a federal government as one made up of both the state governments and the national government).[1]

The result has been that these words are now used to mean different things by different individuals. To add to the lingual chaos, some of these words, while still quite relevant, are considered "archaic" and not used anymore.

Words like confederate and federate actually began as the same word, the latter being simply an abbreviation of the former. As such, many of the Founding Fathers, as Hamilton did in *The Federalist*, used them interchangeably.[2]

Even before the War for Southern Independence, however, these words were beginning to take on different meanings, not only from the original one ("to form a compact"), but meanings that sharply opposed one another. By 1861, for example, we have Lincoln, the head of a *federate* government, and his political opposite, Jefferson Davis, who called himself a *confederate*; this despite the fact that these two words were originally identical in meaning.

For clarification, and to avoid further confusion, below I provide the definitions of these words, and others, as I interpret and use them in this book, and in my other works.[3]

---

[1]. Burns and Peltason, p. 81.
[2]. Nivola and Rosenbloom, p. 70.
[3]. My definitions, to some extent, coalesce with *Webster's Ninth New Collegiate Dictionary*. See Mish. See also Hacker, pp. 238-239.

ANTIFEDERALISM: same as confederalism; similar to today's libertarianism; in Thomas Jefferson's day known as Republicanism. Along with the Federalists, the Antifederalists (Republicans) were America's first modern political parties.[4]

ANTIFEDERALIST: same as confederalist, similar to today's libertarian. Antifederalists, like Thomas Jefferson, opposed the original U.S. Constitution as giving too much power to the central government.[5] Antifederalists were originally called Republicans, and, along with the Federalists, made up the first modern political party in the U.S.[6]

CONFEDER: This obsolete word derives from the Latin *confoederare*, meaning "to league together."[7]

CONFEDERACY: from the Middle English and Old French word *confederacie*.[8] Not a nation, but a union of states formed under a confederal government; the opposite of a federacy. A body of states united to form a league,[9] in which the states retain all sovereign power, while the central government is completely legally dependent on the will of the states.[10] Example: the original United States of America, known as the "Confederacy," or "Confederate States of America,"[11] which operated from 1781 to 1789[12] under the Articles of Confederation.[13]

CONFEDERAL: (from Latin *com*, "jointly," and Latin *foeder*, a "compact"; from *foedus*, "faith";[14] thus meaning a "joint compact") a union in which strong, sovereign political units (typically nations, states, or nation-states)[15] form a compact or treaty with a weak, central government; the opposite of federal. Note: for those interested, what follows is an in-depth etymological discussion of the word confederal. As mentioned above, confederal derives from the Old Latin *com* (Latin *cum*), meaning "jointly," "with," or "together," and the Latin *foeder*, meaning "compact." The original root of *com* is from the Indo-European etymon *kom*, "closely," "next to"; related to the Greek

---

4. Bernhard, p. 15.
5. Mish, s.v. "anti-federalist."
6. Bernhard, pp. 8, 15.
7. Ox. E.D., s.v. "confeder."
8. Neufeldt, s.v. "confederacy."
9. Mish, s.v. "confederacy."
10. Nivola and Rosenbloom, p. 67.
11. For more on this topic, see Seabrook, C101, passim.
12. See Jensen, NN and AC, passim.
13. Ox. E.D., s.v. "confederal."
14. Nivola and Rosenbloom, p. 70.
15. See Hamilton, Madison, and Jay, p. 21.

word *koinos*, meaning "common." Federal began as an abbreviation of confederal, some say by way of aphesis (the loss of a short unaccented vowel). Why then is confederal now spelled with the prefix *con* when the original prefix was *com*? According to Webster, modern grammatical rules ordain that the prefix *com* ("with," "together," "jointly") is to be used only when coming before the letters "b," "p," or "m" (e.g., commingle). *Com* becomes *col* before the letter "l" (e.g., collinear). *Com* becomes *con* before all other sounds and letters, including "c," "d," "f," "g," "j," "n," "q," "s," "t," and "v" (e.g., concentrate; confederacy).[16] Finally, *com* becomes *co* before the letter "h" or a vowel (e.g., cohost).[17] Thus, despite the strangeness of these rules to the modern mind, confederal and federal were once the same words. The original Latin may have been *comfoeder*, *comfoedus*, or *confoeder*, meaning "joint compact" (*com* = "joint"; *foedus* = "compact"). The Late Latin spelling was *confoederatus*, a part participle of *confoederare*: to "unite" by a "league."[18] Similarly, the Latin word *confero* means "to bring together," while *confertim* means "shoulder to shoulder."[19]

CONFEDERALISM: a principle describing the distribution of power between strong independent states and a weak central government; sometimes also known as Jeffersonianism (after Thomas Jefferson) or Antifederalism; the opposite of Federalism. It is similar to what we now call the Republican party, with many elements of libertarianism.

CONFEDERALIST: a member of a confederation;[20] one who advocates confederalism; an antifederalist; the opposite of a federalist. Notable early Confederalists, then known as Antifederalists, include Thomas Jefferson, Patrick Henry, George Mason, James Monroe, Richard Henry Lee, George Clinton, John Lansing, Robert Yates, Elbridge Gerry, Samuel Adams, Samuel Chase, and Luther Martin.

CONFEDERALIZATION: the act of confederalizing (i.e., the formation of a confederal government); the state of being confederalized; the opposite of federalization.

CONFEDERALIZE: the act of creating, or uniting under, a confederal government; the opposite of federalize.

CONFEDERANCE: this obsolete word has the same meaning as

---

16. Mish, s.v. "com-."
17. Mish, s.v. "co-."
18. Neufeldt, s.v. "confederate."
19. Traupman, s.v. "confero"; "confertim."
20. Ox. E.D., s.v. "confederalist."

confederacy, or alliance.[21]

CONFEDERATE: the creation of a confederal government; the act of joining a confederation; one who espouses confederal ideals (i.e., one who is *against* federation); the opposite of federate.

CONFEDERATED: "leagued," "allied," "joined in confederacy."[22]

CONFEDERATELY: "like confederates."[23]

CONFEDERATESHIP: same meaning as "confederacy."[24]

CONFEDERATING: the action of the verb confederate.[25]

CONFEDERATION: from the Middle English word *confederacion*, from the Late Latin word *confoederatio*, from *com* ("united") and *foeder* ("league").[26] A confederal government; a union of states, with the central government receiving its power solely from the states, with no direct authority over the people; the opposite of a federation.[27] Technically, a confederation (i.e., a confederacy) is not a nation. It is a freely formed, voluntary league of states.

CONFEDERATISM: the political idea, system, or practice of confederates.[28]

CONFEDERATIVE: of or relating to confederates or a confederation.[29]

CONFEDERATOR: one who confederates with others.[30]

CONFEDERY: this obsolete word has the same meaning as confederacy.[31]

DEMOCRAT: same as a Federalist.

FEDERACY: a union under a federal government (same as a federation); a nation; the opposite of a confederacy. Example: today's United States of America.

FEDERAL: (from the Latin *foeder*, a "compact") a union in which weak dependent political units (typically nations, states, or nation-states)[32] form a compact or treaty with a strong central government; similar to the

---

21. Ox. E.D., s.v. "confederance."
22. Ox. E.D., s.v. "confederated."
23. Ox. E.D., s.v. "confederately."
24. Ox. E.D., s.v. "confederateship."
25. Ox. E.D., s.v. "confederating."
26. Neufeldt, s.v. "confederation."
27. I follow the tradition here of defining a confederation as separate from, and opposed to, a federation, with a confederation being a constitutional compact between states and a central government, in which the latter lacks the power to regulate the conduct of individuals, and exists and operates only through the sufferance of the state governments. Burns and Peltason, p. 80.
28. Ox. E.D., s.v. "confederatism."
29. Neufeldt, s.v. "confederative."
30. Ox. E.D., s.v. "confederator."
31. Ox. E.D., s.v. "confedery."
32. See Hamilton, Madison, and Jay, p. 21.

meaning of national; the opposite of confederal. Note: some political scientists consider a federal government to be a combination of both confederal (power is solely with the states) and national (power is solely with the central government) systems.[33] Webster, for example, gives the traditional 21st-Century definition of federal as "a compact between political units that surrender their individual sovereignty to a central authority but retain limited residuary powers of government."[34] This is the standard modern definition, but not everyone uses it.

FEDERALISM: a principle describing the distribution of power between a strong central government and weak dependent states;[35] sometimes also known as Hamiltonianism (after Alexander Hamilton); the same as nationalism; the opposite of confederalism, Federalism has some distant affinities with socialism and even monarchism, and is similar to what we now call the Democratic party.

FEDERALIST: one who advocates federalism (a strong central government);[36] a nationalist; the opposite of a confederalist. Jefferson called the Federalists of his day an "Anglican, monarchical, and aristocratical party."[37] Notable early Federalists include Alexander Hamilton, John Adams, John Marshall, and Fisher Ames. Along with the Antifederalists (Republicans), the Federalists were America's first modern political parties.[38]

FEDERALIZATION: the act of federalizing (i.e., the formation of a federal government); the state of being federalized;[39] same as nationalization; the opposite of confederalization.

FEDERALIZE: the act of creating, or uniting under, a federal government;[40] same as nationalize; the opposite of confederalize.

FEDERATE: the creation of a federal government; the act of joining a federation; one who espouses federal ideals (i.e., one who is *for* federation);[41] the opposite of confederate.

FEDERATION: a federal government (same as a federacy); the opposite of

---

33. Nivola and Rosenbloom, pp. 67-68.
34. Mish, s.v. "federal."
35. See Mish, s.v. "federalism."
36. Mish, s.v. "federalist."
37. Smucker, p. 392.
38. Bernhard, p. 15.
39. Mish, s.v. "federalization."
40. Mish, s.v. "federalize."
41. Mish, s.v. "federate."

a confederation. A union of people, with both the state governments and the central government receiving their power from the people, over which both types of government have direct authority.[42] A federation is, in other words, a nation. Here, the central government possesses all sovereign power while the states are legally dependent upon its will.[43]

HAMILTONIANISM: named for liberal, monarchical, big government advocate Alexander Hamilton; the same as federalism and nationalism, and later, the Democratic party. A Hamiltonian believes in a strong central government, a broad (as opposed to a strict) interpretation of the U.S. Constitution, a preference for a commercial and industry based economy, and a distrust of the political capacity or wisdom of the common man and woman.[44] Federate (Union) President Abraham Lincoln was a Hamiltonian.

JEFFERSONIANISM: named for conservative, small government advocate Thomas Jefferson; the same as confederalism, antifederalism and, originally, republicanism. A Jeffersonian believes in a weak central government, a strict (as opposed to a broad) interpretation of the U.S. Constitution, a preference for an agrarian based economy, and a trust in the political capacity or wisdom of the common man and woman. Confederate President Jefferson Davis was a Jeffersonian. Today the same as, or similar to, the Republican party, with strong affinities with libertarianism.

NATIONALISM: same a Federalism and Hamiltonianism; similar to monarchism and the modern Democratic party.

REPUBLICAN: same as an Antifederalist or Confederalist.

SCALAWAG/SCALLYWAG: a Southerner who embraces anti-South Northern beliefs, myths, and ideas; in other words, a Northernized Southerner, one who has turned their back on their own region, culture, traditions, heritage, and history. In many parts of the traditional South scallywags are still considered "traitors" and are greatly disliked.

YANKEE: this word has different meanings around the world. In the United Kingdom, for example, it is used to mean all Americans. In the American North it refers to New Englanders specifically. In the American South, however, it has long been used to designate anyone from states that were not part of the old Southern Confederacy; i.e., someone from the Northeastern and Midwestern states, and to some extent the Western states and territories. Throughout this book it is this last definition that will be

---

42. See Burns and Peltason, p. 80.
43. Nivola and Rosenbloom, pp. 67-68.
44. Mish, s.v. "Hamiltonianism."

used, just as it was used by Victorian Southerners.[45]

☛ 3. Another topic that needs clarification is the matter of the two main political parties during the War for Southern Independence: the Republican and Democratic parties. At the time, the two held views that were completely opposite of those they hold today, a cause of much confusion for many students of American history.

In the 20th Century the two parties had wildly divergent perspectives in most areas, the Republicans eschewing a conservative standpoint, the Democrats promoting a liberal perspective. The difference was overt and easy for the populace to see and understand. One has only to think of men like Ronald Reagan (conservative Republican) and Jimmy Carter (liberal Democrat).

However, today in the 21st Century, the two parties have continued to moderate their views and platforms to such an extent that there are less and less real differences between them. Both are so determined to stay in power that in order to appeal to the widest number of people possible, they are willing to say and do whatever is necessary. As a result, in many areas the two parties are now quite similar and are often difficult to tell apart.

Contrast this with the situation in Thomas Jefferson's time. His Antifederalist or Republican party, the Jeffersonians (also confusingly known as the Democratic-Republican party), and the opposition Federalist party, the Hamiltonians, were as different as black and white. The result is that today, what were the 18th-Century Antifederalists (the Jeffersonians) would now be what we call the Republican party (or even more correctly, the ultraconservative branches known as paleoconservatives, libertarians, and the National Tea Party), while the 18th-Century Federalists (the Hamiltonians) would now be what we call the Democratic party,[46] or by some, even the Socialist party.

By the time of Lincoln, nearly a century later, however, the parties had switched platforms, so that the conservative Republicans of Jefferson's day were by then called Democrats, while the liberal Federalists (Democrats) of Jefferson's day became known as Republicans.[47] Hence,

---

45. See e.g., Pollard, LC, p. 139.
46. Napolitano, pp. 28-29; DeGregorio, s.v. "John Adams" (p. 27).
47. The Jacksonian Republicans (named after President Andrew Jackson) assumed the name Democrats after 1840, while after 1860, the Whigs took on the name Republicans. Hacker, p. 339; Faust, s.v. "Republican party." For a 19th-Century view on this topic see Seabrook, TAHSR, pp. 401, 549-550, 551.

during the presidential campaign of 1860, traditional Southerners were Democrats (in that period, conservatives, as they called themselves), while Lincoln and most Northerners were Republicans (in that period, liberals, as they referred to themselves).[48]

Lincoln, in his usual highly sectional manner, described the confusing situation in a letter from Springfield, Illinois, on April 6, 1859:

> Bearing in mind that about seventy years ago two great political parties were first formed in this country, that Thomas Jefferson was the head of one of them and Boston the headquarters of the other, it is both curious and interesting that those supposed to descend politically from the party opposed to Jefferson should now be celebrating his birthday in their own original seat of empire, while those claiming political descent from him have nearly ceased to breathe his name everywhere.
>
> Remembering, too, that the Jefferson party was formed upon its supposed superior devotion to the personal rights of men, holding the rights of property to be secondary only, and greatly inferior, and assuming that the so-called Democracy of to-day are the Jefferson, and their opponents the anti-Jefferson, party, it will be equally interesting to note how completely the two have changed hands as to the principle upon which they were originally supposed to be divided. The Democracy of to-day hold the liberty of one man to be absolutely nothing, when in conflict with another man's right of property; Republicans, on the contrary, are for both the man and the dollar, but in case of conflict the man before the dollar.[49]

While the two parties have remained the same, since Lincoln's day they have since switched back to their original platforms—though, as mentioned above, in highly diluted forms. Modern paleoconservatism and libertarianism are both attempts to retain the original conservative, republican doctrines and beliefs of the Southern Founding Fathers.

On this topic Dr. Thomas E. Woods Jr. writes that in the 1790s, when the first American party system was launched, it pitted the small government, states' rights Republicans against the big government Federalists. Our nation's second party system arose as a result of divisions

---

48. See e.g., Pollard, LC, p. 178; J. H. Franklin, pp. 101, 111, 130, 149; Nicolay and Hay, ALCW, Vol. 1, p. 627.
49. Nicolay and Hay, ALCW, Vol. 1, p. 532.

surrounding Andrew Jackson's presidency (1829-1837).[50] It was similar to the first, but in this case the Whigs took over the Federalist tradition while the Democrats took over the Republican tradition.[51]

In essence, Lincoln, though a Republican, was a liberal, as were most Northerners. His opponents in the 1860 and 1864 elections, though Democrats, were conservatives, as were most Southerners.[52]

The widespread misunderstanding surrounding the history of the two parties has resulted in various strange phenomena. For example, many conservative Southerners today, wanting to remain true to the South's 19th-Century political heritage (the Democratic party), wrongly vote Democrat. What they do not realize is that the Democrats of the 19th Century espoused a platform (conservatism) that was the opposite of today's Democratic party (liberalism). Thus, modern conservative Southerners should vote Independent, Republican, or Libertarian; not Democrat.

Also, today in the North, where democratic liberalism reigns supreme, many Yankees enjoy boasting of their party's 19th-Century progressive ideology, not realizing that in Lincoln's day the Democratic party was conservative.

In short, while Lincoln was indeed a Republican, it is important to bear in mind that the Republicans (mainly Northerners) of his day were more akin to today's liberal Democrats, while his opposition, the Democrats (mainly Southerners), were more akin to today's conservative Republicans. For a complete discussion and history on this complex but vital topic see my book, *Abraham Lincoln Was a Liberal, Jefferson Davis Was a Conservative: The Missing Key to Understanding the American Civil War*.

☛ 4. Finally, we need to look at the maddening and confusing use of the words liberal and conservative. Remarkably, various writers, scholars, and historians use these two words interchangeably, so that liberal can sometimes mean conservative while conservative can sometimes mean liberal. In this way I have seen Hamilton (an unswerving liberal) described as a conservative, and Jefferson (a staunch conservative) described as a liberal!

The confusion comes from both a biased perception and a lack of familiarity with the dictionary. Take the term *laissez-faire* as an example.

---

50. Website: www.whitehouse.gov/about/presidents/andrewjackson.
51. Woods, p. 47.
52. Grissom, pp. 149-150.

Meaning "to let do" in French, *laissez-faire* is a philosophy opposing intervention of any kind, be it from a person, organization, or government. It is usually applied to issues involving money, and in this case refers to the concept of allowing economic matters to "run their own course."[53]

In essence, *laissez-faire* is a doctrine proposing that the government should refrain from interfering in the commercial marketplace.

Is this a liberal philosophy or a conservative one?

Some would term this a liberal idea, since it seems to call for a lackadaisical, do-as-you-please approach to economic issues. However, to the true conservative and libertarian this is most certainly a conservative idea, for *laissez-faire* asks the government to *conserve* itself in financial areas; i.e., to act in a hands-off, cautious, and frugal way—i.e., in a *conservative* way.

Similarly, during Lincoln's War, the North pushed for action on the part of the central government. Such intervention is a liberal act. At the same time, the South called for no action. This is a conservative act.[54]

As a final clarification, Webster defines a liberal as one who is open to change, is not literal or strict, and who is not constrained by tradition.[55] He defines a conservative as one who is not receptive to change, is literal and strict, and who adheres to traditional methods, views, ideas, or institutions.[56]

It is Webster's definitions—conservatively (i.e., strictly) interpreted—that I use throughout this book.

L. S.

---

53. Mish, s.v. "Laissez-faire."
54. See Simpson, p. 75.
55. Mish, s.v. "liberal."
56. Mish, s.v. "conservative."

FOREWORD

To the Second Edition

With the 200th birthday of President Abraham Lincoln rapidly approaching in February 2009, the bookstores are already filled with scores of volumes dissecting every aspect of Lincoln's life. There are books about his depression, his speeches, his writings, his skills as a military leader, even one odd book that speculates that the 16th president was a homosexual because he once slept in a bed with another man. Of course, that book scarcely mentions that sharing beds was a common practice during the 19th century since beds were expensive commodities in those days, but injecting reality into the Lincoln life story is often difficult to get into print.

An artist's rendering of Charleston, South Carolina, after Lincoln's War, complete with "Sherman's Sentinels" (smoke-scarred, lone-standing chimneys). For Lincoln's crimes one Confederate officer, Captain Alfred Bell, echoed Southern sentiment when he insisted that the Northern president "ought to be burnt in a hell ten thousand times hotter than fire."

Lincoln has become an unassailable icon, a marble man, a statue, the cover man for the five-dollar bill, a man who never committed any wrong against anyone in his entire life. According to most of the books praising Lincoln, the single term Congressman from Illinois, who the state rejected in his bid to become its United States Senator in 1858, became the perfect president just two years later.

Struggling to get attention during 2009, the designated year of Lincoln worship, will be those books that look at Lincoln's whole political life and career, not just his actions that fit into the mold of "Honest Abe, The Man Who Saved The Union." This indepth book by Lochlainn Seabrook, *Abraham Lincoln, The Southern View - Demythologizing America's Sixteenth President*, is one of those books that gives readers another view of Lincoln, the man, the president, the politician. Seabrook has found historical references that show that Lincoln wasn't as kind as many people have been led to believe. He wasn't as willing to

welcome black people into roles as equal citizens as many have been led to believe. He wasn't quite as "Honest Abe" as many have been led to believe.

There is no doubt that Lincoln was one of the greatest politicians who ever lived. Witness the hero worship that is about to explode over the nation on his 200th birthday. Any man who has been dead since 1865 who still controls his image as well as Lincoln is the very definition of a marvelous politician.

Was Lincoln the nation's greatest president as we have been told? Read all of the books on the man, including this one, before making up your mind.

Clint Johnson
Jefferson, North Carolina, USA
Winter 2008
clintjohnsonbooks.com

Lincoln, who suffered from chronic depression, megalomania, prophetic dreams, low self-esteem, and Marfan Syndrome, towered over his officers, his top hat adding to the effect.

PREFACE
To the Fourth Edition

Much has transpired since I wrote the first edition of this book in 2007. On November 4, 2008, Lincoln worshiping, Constitution loathing, big spending socialist Barack Hussein Obama was made U.S. president.

Elected for a second term in 2012, Obama's eight year, ultra liberal "reign of terror" has given us Southerners a glimpse of what life must have been like between 1861 and 1865, living under the dictatorial thumb of his tyrannical and oppressive idol.

Those familiar with my work will recall that Liberal Lincoln publicly stated that he did not like the U.S. Constitution then repeatedly trampled over it, while his followers referred to our nation's most sacred manuscript as "a covenant with death, and an agreement with hell." As I write this, a federal appeals court is overturning one of Obama's more recent unconstitutional acts, his 2012 recess appointments—this after he declared the Constitution "an imperfect document." Meanwhile, his followers are campaigning to throw out the *entire* Constitution, calling it "old, outdated, and useless." And while only the Southern states seceded after Lincoln's election in 1860, since Obama entered the White House, *all* fifty states have sent secession petitions to Washington.

Yes, it's the ghost of Lincoln haunting us all over again.

Second, the year 2011 ushered in the 150th anniversary of the War for Southern Independence. The "Civil War Sesquicentennial," as it is more generally known, has brought Lincoln back into the spotlight and focused new attention on his War.

As expected, industrious and devout members of the Church of Lincoln (mainly Northerners, Liberals, and scallywags) have been hard at work cranking out as many books, articles, documentaries, and films as possible on their favorite American president. Though, while brimming with anti-South propaganda, Yankee mythology, and the usual absurd cardboard stereotypes—and thus nearly all wildly inaccurate—they care little. For the point is not precise history. It is to blanket the world with the North's image of "Honest Abe" and its version of the American "Civil War." Why is this so important to them?

As I have pointed out in my other three books on the individual my Southern ancestors called "Stinkin' Lincoln," it is because exposing the real man would also expose both his many war crimes and the unconstitutionality of Lincoln's War itself. This, in fact, is the same reason the U.S. government refused to allow the illegally imprisoned Jefferson Davis and Alexander H. Stephens to testify on the stand before a jury of their peers after the War—even though they, along with numerous other Confederate officials, literally begged to be put on trial.

Since the anti-South movement bases its opinions, beliefs, writings, and movies about Dixie on self-serving fairy tales, junk research, opinion, wishful thinking, and outright intellectual fraud, few of us in the South take such nonsense seriously. What we *do* take seriously is the manner in which the North's great Lincoln Myth negatively impacts the South. For as long as this lie is promoted as "fact" across the country, the Southern people will continue to be attacked and slandered, their history will continue to be suppressed, perverted, and rewritten, and their heritage, traditions, heroes, cemeteries, and monuments will continue to be besmirched, defaced, slandered, and defamed.

On the positive side, since *Abraham Lincoln: The Southern View* first came out, hundreds of new outlets around the world have begun carrying it—from bookstores, Civil War sites, historic homes, Websites, and museums, to gun shops, convenience stores, general stores, gas stations, and airports—helping to fight the insidious Lincoln Myth while spreading the Truth about him and his War.

Social media, which has provided a wonderful new outlet for Southern, Confederate, Traditionalist, Conservative, Libertarian, and Tea Party thought, has also assisted my publisher in bringing this book, as well as my many other titles, before a broader public. New pro-South groups spring up everyday online, giving voice to an entire culture that has long been silenced by both the East and West Coast Elites and the Bill of Rights-hating Liberal Establishment.

Few things are more vital to the survival of traditional Southern culture than disseminating the Truth about Abraham Lincoln. For once he is exposed, the rest of the thousands of ridiculous Northern myths surrounding him fall like a house of cards.

You see, what modern pro-North Civil War writers call "fact" is all paper maché; smoke and mirrors; reflected light. If they would stop copying each other's error-filled mythological works, and instead read Lincoln's actual words, they would realize their self-delusion. In this book I provide exactly that: the president's own statements. For without knowing the real Lincoln, a true understanding of his insane and unnecessary war on the Constitution and the American people is impossible.

I am honored to be at the forefront of the campaign to preserve authentic Southern history, which is why, as a Lincoln scholar, I have written four books on our nation's most duplicitous chief executive—the man I call the "Great Impersonator." For us in the South, the more people who know the facts about the big government, atheistic, bigoted, liberal-outlaw from Illinois, the better.

Lochlainn Seabrook, SCV
Franklin, Tennessee, USA
February 2013
Gospel of Luke 17:21 (KJV)

🕮 INTRODUCTION 🕮
To the First Edition

Most of what we know about Lincoln today has been invented by Northern folklorists, many who were, and are, adversaries of the South. In fact, nearly every one of the books in the Lincolnian hagiography have been penned by pro-North writers, published by pro-North publishers.

Can we honestly expect to get a true and unbiased picture of who Lincoln really was from such uncritical works?

My book on Lincoln—not an anti-Lincoln work, but a pro-truth one—addresses this problem by looking at the president from the South's point of view. From this perspective we learn that he was almost nothing like what we have been taught.

Abraham Lincoln, America's most polarizing president: a god in the liberal, industrial North, a devil in the conservative, agrarian South.

For example, far from being the "Great Emancipator," as a lawyer Lincoln defended slave owners, helped create laws in Illinois that limited black civil rights, and throughout his entire life lobbied to have all Americans of African descent expelled from the U.S. He was even a manager of the Illinois chapter of the American Colonization Society, a Northern organization whose stated mission was to make America white from coast to coast.

Like the true demagogue he was, Lincoln carefully tailored his speeches to specific audiences, changing his wording to match current political trends, as Stephen A. Douglas and others frequently pointed out. Behind closed doors, however, he was always diligently working on his own private agenda: the installation of big government, the destruction of states' rights, and the deportation of all African-Americans.

During his two terms in office, Lincoln also committed countless crimes, among them: starting a war without congressional approval, subverting the Constitution, illegally suspending *habeas corpus*, rigging elections, bribing associates, shutting down over 300 Northern newspapers, and harassing, intimidating, arresting, imprisoning, deporting, and even torturing, fellow Northerners who advocated peace. And this is just a partial list.

Under President Lincoln's auspices black slaves worked on the still uncompleted U.S. Capitol Building in Washington, D.C., where he allowed slavery to continue until April 1862, one and a half years after he was elected.

Even his Emancipation Proclamation is not what is generally taught. Actually a cynical and vindictive political ploy, Lincoln himself said it was illegal and called it, not a black civil rights measure, but a "necessary war measure." For by 1863, with his army desperately in need of more manpower and an upcoming bid for reelection, its primary purpose was to maintain abolitionist support in the North and help him recruit an additional 180,000 black soldiers (whom he had previously banned from serving), along with their votes. This kept him in office for a second term while enabling him to continue his War long enough to grind down the South and institute his lifelong liberal dream: big government.

As I point out in the following pages, Lincoln's proclamation, or what he termed his "military emancipation," did not even free any slaves, for he made it active only in the Southern Confederacy, now a foreign nation, where he had no legal authority. In truth, and contrary to Northern mythology, most Southern blacks (95 percent) voluntarily remained in the South during the War, as many as 1,000,000 serving (in one capacity or another) in the Confederate army in the valiant fight against "Honest Abe" and his invaders. Thousands more fled further South to try and escape Lincoln's soldiers, well-known for their racist and barbaric treatment of African-Americans.

Despite the passage of 150 years, the man portrayed on this 1920s U.S. postage stamp is still detested by millions of Southerners as a war criminal, an enemy of civil liberties, and America's first dictator.

These and many other seldom-discussed facts are recounted here in the traditional South's take on the United States' most overly mythologized and least accurately understood leader. I promise that you will never look at America's sixteenth president, his War, or the South, the same way again.

Lochlainn Seabrook, SCV
Franklin, Tennessee, USA
October 2007
Gospel of Thomas: 77:1-2

ABRAHAM LINCOLN
The Southern View

Demythologizing America's Sixteenth President

"Books invite all; they constrain none."
Hartley Burr Alexander (1873-1939)

SECTION ONE

CONFEDERATION, SECESSION, & STATES' RIGHTS

The whole story of Lincoln's career from beginning to end is so dreary, so wretched, so shabby, such a tissue of pitiful dodging and chicanery, so unrelieved by anything pure, noble, or dignified, that to even follow it as far as we have done, has well-nigh surpassed our limits of endurance; and when, putting all partisan feeling aside, we look back at the men who once were chosen by their countrymen to fill the places that this man has occupied—a Washington, a Jefferson, a Madison, an Adams, or later, a Webster, a Clay, or a Calhoun—men of culture and refinement, of honor, of exalted patriotism, of broad views and wise statesmanship—and measure the distance from them to Abraham Lincoln, we sicken with shame and disgust.

William Hand Browne (1828-1912)
September 1872

ROOTS OF THE SOUTHERN CONFEDERACY

IF WE ARE TO BELIEVE Northern mythology, then the "Civil War" was fought over slavery and the victorious hero, Abraham Lincoln, the Great Emancipator, "freed the slaves" and "preserved the Union." At least this is what the Lincolnian hagiography—the 16,000 books reverently written about him—claim.

Like the rest of Yankee folklore, however, these beliefs are false and it is time to rid our history books of them, for as Judge George L. Christian correctly stated to a Confederate group on October 29, 1909, the entire Lincoln story "amounts to a patent perversion of the truth, and a positive fraud on the public."[57]

The fraud begins with the very name of the great American conflict Lincoln inaugurated in 1861. Here in the South we do not call it the "Civil War" (as Lincoln did)[58] or the "War Between the States" (as Lincoln also did),[59] for these terms are incorrect. According to Webster, the definition of a civil war is "a war between opposing groups of citizens of the *same* country."[60] Lincoln's War started on April 12, 1861. However, on February 8, 1861, after a number of Southern states had already legally and constitutionally seceded from the U.S.A., the C.S.A.

---

57. Christian, p. 4.
58. Nicolay and Hay, ALCW, Vol. 2, p. 7.
59. Nicolay and Hay, ALCW, Vol. 1, p. 505. His actual phrase was "conflict between the states," which has the same meaning as "war between the states."
60. Mish, s.v. "civil war." Italics are mine.

(Confederate States of America) was formed.[61] This was a full two months before the War was launched. The C.S.A. was now a sovereign nation, in relation to the U.S.A. as foreign as England, France, or Germany.

The conflict then was "a war between opposing groups of citizens of *different* countries," for the South was an independent country at the time it began. Since it is inaccurate to refer to it as a civil war or even as the war between the states, in Dixie it is known by many other names, most commonly the "War for Southern Independence," or the "War Against Northern Aggression."

In my opinion, however, the most precise historical term is "Lincoln's War." For, though he at first tried to call it "the people's war,"[62] as we will see, not only did Lincoln himself intentionally start the conflict,[63] in essence it was primarily his personal fight to kill off states' rights in the South and install big government in the North.[64]

While this book will examine many of the Northern myths surrounding Lincoln and his War, it is only meant to serve as an introduction to this important, seldom discussed, and often misunderstood topic. Further illumination on the real Lincoln may be found in my other works on him, listed in my Bibliography.[65]

Traditional Southerners will be quite familiar with much of what follows. Northerners, non-Southerners, New South Southerners, and non-Americans, however, may find some of this material discomforting, shocking, even unbelievable. Rest assured that all of it has been well chronicled over the past 150 years and comes from authentic, heavily researched, well documented sources, much of it from Lincoln's own mind, mouth, and pen.

Lincoln was what today we would call an ultra, left-wing, liberal, big government, big business, big spending Democrat, or as Thomas Jefferson would have referred to him in 1820s parlance, one of the "high

---

61. Denney, p. 25.
62. C. Adams, p. 208.
63. Ashe, p. 24.
64. K. L. Hall, s.v. "Civil War."
65. Lincoln was so complex, and his mythology is so elaborate and deeply ingrained in the American psyche, that I believe a full treatment of the authentic man is not humanly possible. It would require countless researchers and writers, numberless volumes of text, and numerous lifetimes to complete. Here we can only hope to scratch the surface. My other three books on him, particularly *Lincolnology*, provide material that is beyond the scope of the present work.

priests of Federalism."[66] It is true that Lincoln was a Republican, but since the 1860s the two parties have exchanged platforms, so that the Republicans of Lincoln's day (mainly Northerners) were what we now know as Democrats, while the Democrats of his day (mainly Southerners) are what we now call Republicans. As an added point of reference, men like Jefferson, one of the Southern Founding Fathers, would now be described as a paleoconservative (as opposed to the Democrat-like neoconservatives), or more accurately, as a libertarian.[67]

Lincoln—the first president born outside the boundaries of the original thirteen colonies[68]—started life in the South (Kentucky) but later moved with his family to the North (Indiana, then Illinois), and for good reason: emotionally, mentally, and politically he and his parents were innate Northerners.[69] As Lincoln himself proudly said during a speech before the House of Representatives on July 27, 1848: "I am a Northern man . . ."[70]

Being psychologically wired as a Yankee explains why he got along so famously with other Illinoisans, and why he gave $100 to Yankee John Brown, the infamous South-loathing murderer from Connecticut.[71] In fact, Lincoln typified the region in every way.[72]

The North as a whole was seen by 19th-Century Southerners as American, industrial, nationally-controlled, materialistic, liberal, atheistic, publicly-schooled, conformist, Catholic, progressive, discourteous,

---

66. Smucker, p. 348.
67. For more on this topic, see Seabrook, ALWALJDWAC. Also, Hacker, p. 247; Napolitano, pp. 28-29.
68. Sobel, s.v. "Lincoln, Abraham."
69. Despite both having been born in Virginia, Lincoln's parents, Thomas Lincoln and Nancy Hanks, continued to move northward and westward throughout their lives.
70. Nicolay and Hay, ALCW, Vol. 1, p. 138.
71. Ashe, p. 32.
72. Lincoln's Southern roots haunted him for the rest of his life, even causing his patriotism for the North and the Union to be repeatedly questioned. His wife, Mary (Todd) Lincoln, being from the South (like Lincoln, also from Kentucky), only complicated the situation further for the president. Mary's brother George Rogers Clark Todd was a surgeon in the Confederate army; her half-brother, Samuel Briggs Todd, was a Confederate soldier who was killed at the Battle of Shiloh; her half-brother David H. Todd, a Confederate officer, died from injuries received at Vicksburg; another half-brother, Alexander H. Todd, was killed at the Battle of Baton Rouge. Confederate General Ben Hardin Helm, the husband of Mary's half sister Emilie Todd, died at the Battle of Chickamauga. Brooks, p. 47. Finally, two of Mary's other brothers-in-law also fought for Confederate Cause. For the president, things got so serious that he finally felt compelled to confront the Committee on the Conduct of the War, to whom he said: "I, Abraham Lincoln, President of the United States, appear on my own volition before the committee of the Senate, to say I, of my own knowledge, know that it is untrue that any of my family hold treasonable relations with the enemy." Kane, p. 185; Faust, s.v. "Lincoln, Abraham."

reserved, greedy, cold, inhumane, fast-paced, and business oriented; a region that interpreted the Constitution broadly and favored a strong central government.

The South saw itself, in stark contrast, as European, agricultural, state-controlled, spiritual, conservative, home-schooled, nonconformist, highly religious, Protestant, traditional, well mannered, generous, warm, humanitarian, leisurely, and family oriented; a region that interpreted the Constitution strictly and favored a weak central government.

The two regions even approached combat differently: while Northern men were considered cool and passive in temperament, Southrons (as we like to be called)[73] were seen as hot-blooded and aggressive, quick to anger, and even quicker to fight. This is why the Southern belief that "a fighter is a hero" absolutely horrified Victorian Northerners.[74]

Midway through Lincoln's War, on November 26, 1863, the Mobile *Register* put the situation like this: the belief is commonplace that the current conflict has its origins in Southern slavery. This is completely false, however. True, slavery was an issue of contention, but it was never the cause. The real cause derived from the deep and insurmountable differences between the South and the North, differences in everything from character and habits to political and religious ideas; even the manner of thinking. These dissimilarities, the *Register* went on to say, have long created an overwhelming sense of alienation between the two sections, with the Southron eyeing the Yankee with distrust and disdain, and the Yankee viewing the Southron with jealousy and hatred.[75]

These pronounced differences produced ongoing tensions between the two regions that spanned centuries, even dating back to the very beginning of European-American settlement, the rise of the American colonies, and the formation of the United States. Indeed, mutual animosities between South and North were already brewing at the

---

73. The term Southron (pronounced SUTH-ren) is a Scottish word, originally applied to the English (who live *south* of Scotland). The term was eventually carried over to also mean "one who lives in the American South." Southron derives from the Late Middle English word *sothron*, a dialectic variation of southern, "one who lives to the south," or "one from the south." Neufeldt, s.v. "southron"; Mish, s.v. "Southron."
74. McWhiney and Jamieson, p. 171. Similarly, the South's centuries-old love of firearms continues to frighten and disturb many Northerners today.
75. See Durden, p. 42.

Constitutional Convention at Philadelphia in 1787,[76] and in 1798, only eight years after the U.S. Constitution became fully operative, Southerner Thomas Jefferson was complaining of the North's domination of the South, and even hinted at the possible secession of several Southern states because of it. It is, Jefferson wrote that year,

> not unusual now to estimate the separate mass of Virginia and North Carolina with a view to their separate existence. It is true that we are completely under the saddle of Massachusetts and Connecticut, and that they ride us very hard, cruelly insulting our feelings as well as exhausting our strength and substance. Their natural friends, the three other [north] eastern States, join them from a sort of family pride, and they have the art to divide certain other parts of the Union so as to make use of them to govern the whole. This is not new. It is the old practice of despots to use part of the people to keep the rest in order, and those who have once got an ascendency and possessed themselves of all the resources of the nation, their revenues and offices, have immense means for retaining their advantages.[77]

Jefferson, whose grandson George Wythe Randolph later served as the Southern Confederacy's first secretary of war,[78] is only hinting at what has been a long and bitter rivalry between South and North.[79] Little wonder that an Englishman who visited the colonies in 1759 believed that if something was not done to resolve this contention, there would soon be a bloody civil war stretching from one end of America to the other.[80]

One of the factors that drove the built-in wedge between the two regions even deeper was the Missouri Compromise of 1820, much hated by Antifederalists like Jefferson, who predicted that it would rile up sectional hatreds and instigate a North-South "schism."[81] Wrote America's third president of the "Missouri question":

> . . . this momentous question, like a fire-bell in the night, awakened and filled me with terror. I considered it at once as the

---

76. Collier and Collier, p. 202.
77. Bergh, Vol. 17, pp. 206-207.
78. Warner, GG, s.v. "George Wythe Randolph."
79. Grissom, pp. ii-iii.
80. Morgan, p. 6.
81. Foley, p. 565.

[death] knell of the Union. It is hushed, indeed, for the moment. But this is a reprieve only, not a final sentence.[82]

Pushed through by Lincoln's political idol Henry Clay, the Missouri Compromise of 1820 essentially split the U.S. in half, the Northern half becoming a slavery-prohibited region, the Southern half a slavery-optional region. Jefferson's prognostication came true.[83] This artificial demarcation aroused further hostilities and misunderstandings between South and North, an enmity that carried well into the future, when, in 1854, the Kansas-Nebraska Act was passed.[84]

This congressional statute effectively overturned the Missouri Compromise of 1820 by reestablishing self-government within the states, allowing each to decide for itself whether to allow slavery or not. Left-wing progressives responded to this check on their attempt to turn the U.S. government into an empire by forming the Republican party (today known as the Democratic party). Their first major victory? Rigging elections to get their presidential candidate, arch liberal Abraham Lincoln, into the White House in 1860, the beginning of the end for small government, civil liberties, and states' rights.[85] ("Old Hickory," Federalist Andrew Jackson, had begun the erosion of Jefferson's Republic thirty years earlier by transforming the U.S. into a democracy.)[86]

In short, when it came to the South and the North, there could not have been two more divergent cultures living side by side. "A continent of almost distinct nations," Frances Trollope called them in 1829, for by then Dixie was already being referred to as America's "other province."[87] In fact many, then as now, considered the South and North to be two completely different civilizations.[88] When we add their enormous political, religious, and economic differences, it is little wonder that these two "civilizations" reached an impasse in 1861.

Money matters were particularly irritating to the South, for as Jefferson feared, the North was slowly but surely turning industry and

---

82. Bergh, Vol. 15, p. 249.
83. Rozwenc, p. 55.
84. Rosenbaum and Brinkley, s.v. "Missouri Compromise."
85. L. Johnson, pp. 123-124.
86. Jackson was the last man to have fought in the Revolutionary War to become president. He was also the only American president to have been a prisoner of war. DeGregorio, s.v. "Andrew Jackson" (p. 109).
87. Coit, p. 205.
88. Simpson, p. 72.

finance from the servants of agriculture and commerce into their masters, the opposite of what the Founders had intended.[89] In 1813, forty-eight years before Lincoln's War, James Madison commented on this growing and disturbing phenomenon:

> The great road of profitable intercourse for New England . . . lies through . . . the Cotton . . . fields of her Southern . . . Confederates.[90]

In 1851, just ten years before Lincoln's War, Northern interests were still treating the South like a Yankee milk cow. That year Southern Senator Thomas Hart Benton complained of how the North "redirected" Dixie's wealth to support itself, giving literally nothing in return:

> Under Federal Legislation, the exports of the South have been the basis of the Federal Revenue. Virginia, the two Carolinas, and Georgia, may be said to defray three fourths of the annual expense of supporting the Federal Government; and of this great sum, annually furnished by them, nothing or next to nothing is returned to them, in the shape of Government expenditures. That expenditure flows in an opposite direction—it flows north, in one uniform, uninterrupted and perennial stream. This is the reason why wealth disappears from the south and rises up in the north. Federal Legislation does this.[91]

"The result," an irritated Calhoun said in 1850, ". . . is to give the Northern section a predominance in every department of the Government,"[92] as well as in the North's many financial, commercial, and manufacturing groups.[93]

Northerners like Lincoln naturally supported such tactics, which is why the North voted him into office and why the South viewed him as the vile epitome of Yankeedom: a radical, progressive, demagogue operating out of self-interest, avarice, and political expediency instead of out of concern for the welfare of both the Southern and Northern people,

---

89. Coit, p. 175.
90. Madison, Vol. 2, pp. 561-562.
91. Semmes, p. 58.
92. Crallé, Vol. 4, p. 545.
93. Rosenbaum and Brinkley, s.v. "Jeffersonian Republican Party."

the true and only function of a president. For while liberal Lincoln and the North wanted to change America's government, the conservative South wanted to retain what was left of the one they already had. This is why Southerners, like Frank Lawrence Owsley, could say that as far as Dixie was concerned at the time, "the philosophy of the North [was] the religion of an alien God."[94]

Decades earlier, Calhoun, Jefferson's spiritual and political heir, said that all Southerners had ever wanted was to maintain the "primitive purity" of the original government and Constitution,[95] whose framework had been laid out by two Southerners (James Madison of Virginia, and Charles Pinckney of South Carolina) and a Scotsman (James Wilson).[96]

And here was the flashpoint for a war from which America will never completely recover, one that left emotional wounds from which our nation will never totally heal;[97] a heritage, as historian Louis M. Hacker writes, that "still survives to plague us."[98]

That this awful heritage was unnecessarily created, in great part by Lincoln, is easily illustrated.

America was first formed as a confederacy and was indeed first known as "the Confederacy" by the Founders, and her first Constitution was called "the Articles of Confederation." Additionally, many Americans and foreigners referred to the original U.S.A. as "the Confederate States of America," an important topic we will return to throughout this work.[99] A confederacy has a small, weak, decentralized government that is supported by a voluntary group of strong and wholly independent nation-states,[100] whose power, authority, and sovereignty rests on the bedrock of the separation of powers, the right of secession, and states' rights.

According to the confederate ideals of the Founders, the central government was to deal with foreign issues, state governments with local ones. It was only by way of a weak limited central government, Confederalists believed, that liberty could be preserved.[101] After all, they

---

94. Simpson, p. 67.
95. Coit, p. 218.
96. C. Johnson, p. 104.
97. J. C. Bradford, p. 93.
98. Hacker, p. 584.
99. Seabrook, C101, passim.
100. In *The Federalist* John Jay referred to the separate American colonies or states as "distinct nations." Hamilton, Madison, and Jay, p. 21.
101. Hacker, p. 339.

had only recently fought an acrimonious and bloody war of independence against a strong central government: Britain's.[102]

Our eighth president, Martin Van Buren, summarized the concept nicely:

> All communities are apt to look to Government for too much. Even in our own country, where its powers and duties are so strictly limited, we are prone to do so, especially at periods of sudden embarrassments and distress. But this ought not to be. The framers of our excellent constitution, and the people who approved it with calm and sagacious deliberation, acted at the time on a sounder principle. They wisely judged that the less Government interferes with private pursuits, the better for general prosperity. It is not its legitimate object to make men rich, or to repair, by direct grants of money or legislation in favor of particular pursuits, losses not incurred in the public service. This would be substantially to use the property of some for the benefit of others. But its real duty—that duty the performance of which makes a good Government the most precious of human blessings—is to enact and enforce a system of general laws commensurate with, but not exceeding, the objects of its establishment, and to leave every citizen and every interest to reap, under its benign protection, the rewards of virtue, industry, and prudence.[103]

In other words, as Thomas Paine so adroitly put it: "That government is best which governs least." Most of the Founders agreed with this view, along with Paine's belief that government is a "necessary evil."[104] Indeed, "if men were angels," Alexander Hamilton wrote in *The Federalist*, "no government would be necessary."[105]

Thus, forming our nation on the concept of confederation was no accident, for it was the least of the different forms of governmental evils. The doctrine of states' rights itself, just one aspect of Confederalism, was inspired by gentlemen farmers like George Washington, Thomas Jefferson, and James Madison, who envisioned an agrarian America built around the farmer[106]—a figure who formed the vast majority of the

---

102. Jensen, NN, p. 347.
103. Coe, pp. 267-268.
104. Putnam, p. 410.
105. Lodge, Vol. 12, p. 44.
106. Jefferson once referred to farmers as "the chosen people of God." Foley, p. 323.

population in the late 1700s.[107]

As such, Southerners as a whole desired a defensive bulwark against the North's industrial and commercial encroachments. The Yankees' intrusive policies included protective tariffs, a nationalized bank, ship subsidies, and internal improvements,[108] all which hurt the *laissez-faire*, agricultural South,[109] and intolerably infringed upon her innate individualism (as embodied in Southern hero Andrew Jackson).[110] Confederalism then was Dixie's primary shield.[111]

On March 4, 1801, in his First Inaugural Address, Southerner Thomas Jefferson laid out what he deemed "the essential principles of our Government, and consequently those which ought to shape its Administration." Among them was the concept of states' rights, the very ideal for which the South fought Lincoln in 1861. According to Jefferson, the best approach to preserving American freedom is

> . . . the support of the State governments in all their rights, as the most competent administrations for our domestic concerns and the surest bulwarks against anti-republican tendencies . . .[112]

Confederalism was preferred by the predominantly Southern Founding Fathers for another reason: it was the best solution for halting (and later preventing) the excesses and abuses the early American colonies were suffering from under British rule, with its despotic king, George III, and his country's tyrannical monarchy. The American Founders' exact words are instructive. On May 15, 1776, Virginia delegates convened to prepare a document declaring the colonies independent of Great Britain. They wrote:

> . . . Congress should declare that these United colonies are . . . to be free and independent states, that they are absolved from all allegiance to the British crown . . . [and that] a Confederation be

---

107. Collier and Collier, pp. 49-50, 65.
108. P. M. Roberts, p. 195.
109. Thornton and Ekelund, p. 16.
110. See Ward, pp. 149, 188, 190, 210, 212-213.
111. Simpson, pp. 87-89. Modern cliometric research has proven the South correct: high protective tariffs reduced the price of cotton (by imposing a 20 percent tax on the profits of Southern planters), while raising both the income and the profits of Yankee labor and manufacturers. See Fogel, p. 296.
112. Bergh, Vol. 3, p. 321. In my interpretation, the word "antirepublican" is the same as anti-Confederal.

formed to bind the colonies more closely together.[113]

Later, after repeatedly referring to this Confederation as "the Confederacy," the document goes on to record the appointment of several individuals who were to "prepare a plan of confederation for the colonies."[114]

In his notes on the Articles of Confederation (America's first constitution), Jefferson wrote of the importance of forming a confederacy:

> All men admit that a confederacy is necessary. Should the idea get abroad that there is likely to be no union among us, it will damp the minds of the people, diminish the glory of our struggle, and lessen its importance; because it will open to our view future prospects of war and dissension among ourselves. If an equal vote be refused, the smaller states will become vassals to the larger; and all experience has shown that the vassals and subjects of free states are the most enslaved.[115]

Jefferson then expresses his hope that "in the present enlightened state of men's minds we might expect a lasting confederacy . . ."[116]

"A lasting Confederacy." These words will burn throughout this book like a beacon of traditional light in the vast darkness of progressive liberalism.

The original "Confederate States of America," the American Confederacy (1781 to 1789), was later renamed the "United States of America" and her first constitution, the Articles of Confederation, was later reformulated and renamed the "United States Constitution." However, the idea that America was created to be a Confederacy did not change, and was not intended to change.[117] And it would not completely change, until Lincoln entered the picture eighty-four years later.[118]

The Founding Fathers, such as Samuel Adams, referred to the U.S. as a "Confederation" as early as 1776,[119] while in *The Federalist* (1787-

---

113. Bergh, Vol. 1, p. 175.
114. Bergh, Vol. 1, p. 26.
115. Bergh, Vol. 1, p. 47.
116. Bergh, Vol. 1, p. 48.
117. Napolitano, p. 118.
118. Ashe, pp. 21-22.
119. Banks, p. 186.

1788) Hamilton called the U.S. the "American Confederacy"[120] and Madison called it "the present Confederation of the American States."[121] In the same series of essays John Jay referred to the Southern states as the "Southern Confederacy"[122] and Hamilton referred to the Northern states as the "Northern Confederacy."[123]

Jefferson talked of "our confederated fabric" in 1820,[124] and was still referring to the U.S. as "our confederacy" in 1823, just three years before his death.[125] Missouri Senator Thomas Hart Benton made mention of the U.S. "confederacy" in 1831[126] and again in 1844;[127] and in 1836 future U.S. President John Tyler referred to his country as "the Confederacy."[128]

Nine years later, in 1845, President James Knox Polk mentioned "our Confederacy" and "our confederation" in his First Inaugural Address,[129] and in 1848 the future president of the Southern Confederacy, Jefferson Davis (named after Thomas Jefferson),[130] spoke of the U.S. as "this glorious Confederacy," only twelve years prior to Lincoln's election.[131] In 1849 Robert A. Toombs of Georgia referred to "this Confederacy" on the floor of the House.[132] And it was not just 19th-Century Southerners.

Most Northerners too correctly called the U.S. "the Confederacy."[133] In a December 24, 1847, letter Governor Lewis Cass of Michigan used the phrase "the people of the Confederacy,"[134] and during his First Inaugural Address in 1853 American President Franklin Pierce of New Hampshire made reference to "this Confederacy."[135] During his

---

120. Hamilton, Madison, and Jay, p. 106.
121. Hamilton, Madison, and Jay, p. 89. See also M. D. Peterson, JM, pp. 102-103; Hacker, p. 213.
122. Hamilton, Madison, and Jay, p. 21.
123. Hamilton, Madison, and Jay, p. 65.
124. Bergh, Vol. 15, p. 297.
125. M. D. Peterson, TJ, p. 1482.
126. Hacker, p. 420.
127. Ransom, p. 96.
128. Tyler, LTT, Vol. 3, pp. 67, 68.
129. DeGregorio, s.v. "James K. Polk" (p. 168).
130. During his presidency, Davis often worked out of the Confederate Capitol at Richmond, Virginia, designed by his namesake Thomas Jefferson. Channing, p. 168.
131. W. Davis, JD, p. 177.
132. Ransom, p. 99.
133. Litwack, NS, p. 49.
134. Nicolay and Hay, ALCW, Vol. 1, p. 143.
135. DeGregorio, s.v. "Franklin Pierce" (p. 203).

seventh and final debate with Lincoln on October 15, 1858, Illinois Senator Stephen A. Douglas referred to the U.S. as "a confederacy of sovereign and equal states."[136]

Lincoln himself, a self-professed "northern man,"[137] labeled the nation "the Confederation" during this same debate with Douglas at Alton, Illinois, and as the "Confederacy," both during his New York address at the Cooper Institute on February 27, 1860,[138] and as president-elect during his speech at Independence Hall, Philadelphia, Pennsylvania, on February 22, 1861.[139]

Even the U.S. Constitution refers to our country, in its original form, as a Confederacy. In Article 6, it reads:

> All debts contracted and engagements entered into, before the adoption of this Constitution, shall be as valid against the United States under this Constitution, as under the Confederation.[140]

Alexis de Tocqueville and many others captured the true nature of the U.S.A. when they referred to it as "the Confederate States of America."[141]

How then did our American Confederacy, with its republic-styled government,[142] become a democratized empire?

Lincoln was obsessed with his political hero, slave owner Henry Clay, a man he called "my *beau ideal* of a statesman, the man for whom I fought all my humble life."[143] Lincoln, who campaigned for Clay during the 1844 presidential election, was infatuated with his idol's beliefs and ideas.[144] One of these was what Clay held to be the perfect form of government, one known as the "American System."

Devised and promoted by Clay,[145] the American System was a

---

136. Nicolay and Hay, ALCW, Vol. 1, p. 487.
137. Nicolay and Hay, ALCW, Vol. 1, p. 138.
138. Nicolay and Hay, ALCW, Vol. 1, p. 606. Lincoln actually used the word Confederacy many dozens of times throughout his political career. See e.g., Nicolay and Hay, ALCW, Vol. 1, pp. 143, 168, 181, 345, 346, 487, 501, 611, 616, 624, 627, 628.
139. Nicolay and Hay, ALCW, Vol. 1, p. 691.
140. Findlay and Findlay, pp. 182-183.
141. Seabrook, C101, passim.
142. A republic is here defined as a form of government with the following characteristics: 1) sovereign power belongs to the people; 2) all laws are made by representatives of the people; 3) the powers of the government are defined and limited by a written constitution. Findlay and Findlay, p. 169.
143. Nicolay and Hay, ALCW, Vol. 1, p. 299.
144. See Ashworth, Vol. 2, p. 212.
145. DeGregorio, s.v. "John Quincy Adams" (p. 97).

nationalist program in which there was to be a single sovereign authority, the president, who was to assume the role of a kinglike ruler with autocratic powers. Likewise, the government at Washington, D.C. was to be federated, acting as a consolidated superpower that would eventually control the money supply, offer internal improvements,[146] intervene in foreign affairs, nationalize the banking system,[147] issue soaring tariffs, grant subsidies to corporations, engage in protectionism, and impose an income tax,[148] all hints of Lincoln's coming empire.[149]

In essence, what the American System proposed was a federal government that was the polar opposite of a confederal government. Under federation, its proponents, the Federalists, Monarchists, or Hamiltonians (after Alexander Hamilton), as they were variously called,[150] not only sought to create a large, domineering, all-powerful, nationalized government to which all interests (from private to business) were subordinate,[151] but they also proposed that the states be largely stripped of their independence and authority, then placed in an inferior role. Hamilton himself wanted to get rid of the states completely.[152] Jeffersonianism was to be abolished and replaced with the Hamiltonian or American system.

As in a true empire, those in the highest positions stood to reap the most power, privilege, and money. This, after all, is one of the core motivations of dictators: lining the pockets of close supporters in exchange for their allegiance.

Naturally everything about Clay's American System was repugnant to traditional Southerners—a group that we will call the Confederalists (i.e., those "against federalism"),[153] but one that referred to itself as the Antifederalists or Jeffersonians (after Thomas Jefferson).[154]

---

146. Like all liberals, Lincoln liked the idea of the government bailing out mismanaged, bankrupt, and corrupt businesses, an idea then known as "internal improvements," but which we now more honestly refer to as "corporate welfare." See e.g., Lincoln's comment on, and support of, the internal improvement idea in Nicolay and Hay, ALCW, Vol. 1, p. 8.
147. Simpson, p. 75.
148. Rosenbaum and Brinkley, s.v. "American System."
149. Weintraub, pp. 48-49.
150. Today we would refer to the Federalists and Hamiltonians as Democrats; in other words, liberals.
151. Woods, p. 34.
152. A. Cooke, ACA, p. 140.
153. For more on my use of this term, see "Notes to the Reader."
154. Today we would refer to the Antifederalists or Jeffersonians as Conservative Republicans, or in some cases Libertarians.

Calhoun prophetically referred to the American System as "a dangerous and growing disease,"[155] one that would someday bring about the ruin of a delicately designed nation.[156]

Why was the American System anathema to the Jeffersonians? Because it went counter to the ideas set forth by the Founders in their formation of the American Confederacy, the system of government favored by the South. Jefferson, for instance, a man who put his faith in ordinary people rather than in institutions,[157] had intended for America to be built on the farmer, its economy on agriculture, and its government on republicanism (then nearly akin to what we now call libertarianism). He distrusted the world of manufacturing, banking and foreign trade, believing that it led to class divisions, economic chaos, and mob rule.[158] Instead, he preferred an agrarian economy built around a simple equalitarian republic, even if it meant slowing the growth of the national economy.[159]

The Hamiltonians, on the other hand, wanted to replace the farmer with the merchant, agrarianism with industrialism, republicanism with socialism.[160] Their emphasis was on capitalism, even if it meant economic inequality in American society.[161] They also wanted to dilute sectional differences between North and South and establish a strong permanent national army, both hostile ideas in the South.[162]

Tragically, the Founders' agriculturally-based Confederacy, with its small, weak central government, would soon be completely destroyed by Lincoln's industrially-based, federated American System, with its massive, all-powerful central government. The liberalizing process toward empire was already well underway long before Lincoln, however.

After the Constitutional Convention of 1787, the ink had not even dried on the first draft of the new pre-Bill of Rights Constitution when liberal-minded Federalists and monarchists, like Hamilton, were moving mountains to consolidate power in Washington, D.C. in an

---

155. Crallé, Vol. 2, p. 224.
156. Coit, p. 249.
157. Shorto, p. 124.
158. Hacker, pp. 247, 264.
159. Bernhard, p. 18.
160. Hacker, p. 583.
161. Bernhard, p. 18.
162. DeGregorio, s.v. "George Washington" (pp. 8-9).

attempt to form an omnipotent national government.[163]

This was carried forward, to a great extent, by manipulation of the words in the Constitution: Federalists had given Congress nearly unlimited power, along with control over taxation, the military, and the judicial branch. And not only did they squeeze in dangerous phrases like "necessary and proper," "general welfare," and "supreme law of the land" (all three to be used later for the most evil and destructive purposes by Lincoln), but they had even managed to leave out any clause reserving powers.[164]

At this point in the political development of the United States, consolidation of the central government was heading toward complete nationalization, with the states certain to end up in relation to Washington, D.C., as counties are to a state.

Virginian and Confederalist (i.e., Antifederalist) George Mason was horrified. Before the Virginia Convention he condemned the liberal direction that the Constitution was moving in:

> . . . whether the Constitution be good or bad, the present clause clearly discovers that it is a national government, and no longer a Confederation. I mean that first clause which gives the first hint of the general government laying direct taxes. The assumption of this power . . . does . . . entirely change the confederation of the states into one consolidated government.[165]

Many Northerners too understood the inherent danger of unreserved powers. One of these, Thomas Wait of Portland, Maine, wrote:

> The vast Continent of America cannot be long subjected to a Democracy if consolidated into one Government. You might as well attempt to rule Hell by Prayer.[166]

Massachusetts politicians put it even more bluntly:

---

163. Stonebraker, pp. 14-15.
164. See Main, pp. 119-127.
165. Elliot, Vol. 3, p. 29.
166. Harding, p. 39.

> The Constitution took too much power from the State and gave it to the nation.[167]

With the new Constitution favoring the consolidating Federalists, Confederalists like Mason fought back, demanding a bill of rights (or what Jefferson called a "declaration of rights")[168] that would reign in the powers of the central government and establish individual human liberties.[169] Why was this so important to them?

Confederalists respected and even feared what they understood to be the essence of human nature. "Every man has a natural propensity to power," they accurately declared, power that would end in the oppression of the American people if it got into the wrong hands.[170] For as Thomas Hart Benton observed, in the basest sense "it is the principle of money to favor money."[171]

Southerners in particular, conservative by nature, were anxious to speak their minds on this topic. North Carolinian William Goudy said:

> We know that private interest governs mankind generally. Power belongs originally to the people; but if rulers be not well guarded, that power may be usurped from them. People ought to be cautious in giving away power.[172]

William Lenoir, also from the Tar Heel State, observed:

> It is natural for men to aspire to power—it is the nature of mankind to be tyrannical.[173]

Jefferson put it like this: "Bribery corrupts them. Personal interests lead them astray from the general interests of the constituents . . .,"[174] while Calhoun noted that

---

167. Stebbins, p. 133.
168. See e.g., Foley, pp. 35, 38, 52, 54, 89, 90, 91, 159, 186, 187, 188, 192, 229, 241, 395, 451, 452, 579, 581, 743, 746.
169. A. Cooke, ACA, p. 140.
170. Main, p. 127.
171. Benton, Vol. 1, p. 193.
172. Elliot, Vol. 4, p. 10.
173. Elliot, Vol. 4, p. 203.
174. Foley, p. 377.

government, although intended to protect and preserve society, has itself a strong tendency to disorder and abuse of its powers, as all experience and almost every page of history testify.[175]

In short, while Federalists were displeased with the new Constitution (a remake of the original, the Articles of Confederation) because it failed to grant the government enough power,[176] Confederalists were upset because it gave the government too much power, and because it failed to protect even the most basic of human rights and liberties against the "tyrannical tendencies" inherent in all men.

From this conflict was created the Bill of Rights, the first ten amendments of the Constitution. Influenced by Southerner George Mason and the European Enlightenment, introduced by Southerner James Madison in 1789, and ratified in 1791, the Bill of Rights established the fundamental American freedoms that we are now so familiar with, such as freedom of religion, the right to bear arms, and the guarantee of a speedy public trial and an impartial jury.

But, just as it has not stopped today's liberals, like President Barack Obama, from trying to enlarge the central government (hundreds of new departments, bureaus, and programs have been created since he took office),[177] even this sweeping human rights document did not halt the monarchical activities of the Federalists in the 1700s.

Preaching that the states were a result of a compact with the central government (meaning, in their opinion, that the central government possessed nearly unlimited powers), in 1798 the Federalists pushed through the Alien and Sedition Acts.[178] The sedition portion of these statutes threatened punishment for those who spoke "with intent to defame" the central government, an overt attempt to silence Antifederalists like Jefferson,[179] along with other Republican

---

175. Crallé, Vol. 1, p. 7.
176. Napolitano, pp. 2-4.
177. In his first year in office alone President Obama appointed as many as fifty "czars" (special White House advisors), far more than any other president has during his entire term (President George W. Bush, for example, chose only eighteen during his two terms). The practice of appointing czars (which began with Franklin Delano Roosevelt) is not illegal. However, appointing them without approval of the Senate is. A number of Obama's czars have not gone through this process, making their appointments unconstitutional. September, 16, 2009, "Happening Now," FOX News.
178. Hacker, p. 246.
179. C. Johnson, p. 114.

(conservative) critics.[180]

Jefferson, now vice president of the U.S. (under President John Adams), and James Madison responded with the Kentucky and Virginia Resolutions, which were passed respectively by the legislatures of these two states in 1798 and 1799.[181] Jefferson and Madison's resolutions not only declared the Alien and Sedition Acts illegal,[182] but more importantly they emphasized individual civil rights and reasserted the original Confederate concept that the central government was, in fact, the result of a compact between the states. Thus, if the central government assumed powers that had not been specifically granted to it by the states, such as issuing acts against the wishes of the people, the states could declare these acts unconstitutional.[183] Calhoun would later use his predecessor's Kentucky and Virginia Resolutions to support the constitutional right of secession against Clay and other antebellum Federalists and progressives. (Sadly for Dixie, Calhoun, staunch defender of Southern interests, died ten years before Lincoln entered the Oval Office. Had he lived long enough it is possible that he may have been able to help avert the coming war.)[184]

The modern etymology of the words federation and confederation, as we will define and use them, now becomes clear: the North wanted to *federate* (i.e., consolidate, strengthen, and expand) governmental power; the South wanted to *confederate* (i.e., diffuse, decentralize, and reduce) governmental power.[185] Hence, the rise of the original American Confederacy, established through the First Revolutionary War for Independence (1775-1783), and its daughter, the Southern Confederacy, established in what traditional Southerners still call the Second Revolutionary War for Independence; i.e., the "Civil War" (1861-1865).

Next time you see a Starry Cross (the Confederate battle flag), on

---

180. Bernhard, p. 18.
181. Hacker, p. 246.
182. Jefferson wrote the Kentucky Resolutions, Madison wrote the Virginia Resolutions. See DeGregorio, s.v. "Thomas Jefferson" (p. 45); "James Madison" (pp. 60-61).
183. Weintraub, p. 53.
184. Calhoun died on March 31, 1850, a mere eleven years before Lincoln's War. His last words were prophetic: "The South, the poor South." Sobel, s.v. "Calhoun, John C."
185. Although my interpretations and definitions of the words federate and confederate do not exactly correlate with their original meanings, as these have changed numerous times over the centuries, mine are easier for the modern mind to grasp. Again, for more on this topic, see my "Notes to the Reader."

display, its meaning will now be apparent: purposefully designed on Scotland's flag, St. Andrew's Cross, and on Ireland's flag, St. Patrick's Cross, it is an archetypal Christian symbol of both heritage (the South) and small government and states' rights (Jeffersonianism). As such, it is an American patriotic emblem, one that has nothing to do with racism, or even sectionalism (South versus North). Indeed, the neo-Confederate organization to which I belong, the Sons of Confederate Veterans, whose symbol is the Confederate battle flag, is comprised of members of all races, from every part of the U.S.[186]

Jeffersonianism, with its adherence to the conservative, confederate ideals of the Founding generation, knows no racial or regional boundaries. Some of the greatest supporters of American neo-Confederate ideals today live outside the U.S., in regions such as Canada, Europe, Oceania, South America, Africa, and Asia, where "rebels" continue the struggle to break away from their own dictatorial central governments.

---

186. For more on the topic of the Confederate battle flag, see Seabrook, CFF, passim.

Lincoln Sets the Stage for War

WHAT DOES ALL OF THIS tell us? A republic confederation is America's true, traditional form of nationhood, not a democratic federation, as we have today. While the Old North was federate, liberal, and progressive, the Old South was confederate, conservative, and traditional. And so it clung to the old ways, which included the Confederacy of the Framers,[187] a group that feared not just big government, but government itself, whatever its size.[188]

In 1860, however, Lincoln openly campaigned on a platform promoting Clay's anti-South, federating American System. From his very first day as a politician, Lincoln made it clear that he stood front and center with the Hamiltonian federalists, monarchists, and socialists. The following is from his first speech as a candidate for the Illinois Legislature in 1832:

> Fellow citizens, I presume you all know who I am. I am humble Abraham Lincoln. I have been solicited by many friends to become a candidate for the Legislature. My politics are short and sweet, like the old woman's dance. I am in favor of a national bank. I am in favor of the internal improvement system, and a high protective tariff. These are my sentiments and political principles. If elected, I shall be thankful; if not, it will be all the same.[189]

---

187. Ashe, pp. 21-22.
188. Burns and Peltason, p. 31.
189. F. T. Miller, p. 112.

With Lincoln's twenty-eight year record as an anti-South, socialistic liberal, is it any wonder that on the day of his election to president, November 6, 1860, the conservative Southern states began to hastily secede to form their own nation?[190] On December 20, just a few weeks later, the first Southern state, South Carolina, did just that. Mississippi, Florida, Alabama, Georgia, Louisiana, and Texas quickly followed, and on February 8, 1861, the new Southern Confederacy was officially formed.[191]

An unwavering left-wing war monger, Lincoln stuck to his guns, ignoring the existence of the new nation to his south. Arrogantly considering it nothing more than a pesky "rebellion" made up of "persons engaged in disorderly proceedings,"[192] in his First Inaugural Address on March 4, 1861, he promised to invade any state that did not collect his new, exorbitantly high tariff rate:

> The power confided to me will be used to hold, occupy, and possess the property and places belonging to the government, and to collect the duties and imposts; but beyond what may be necessary for these objects, there will be no invasion . . . In doing this there needs to be no bloodshed or violence; and there shall be none, unless it be forced upon the national authority.[193]

The South refused to "pay up," and the always money-minded Lincoln invaded.

It was Southerner Thomas Jefferson who said of Northerners: "They are avaricious and venal, looking always for gain."[194] Thus it was the Yankee love of money, along with Northern greed and materialism, that led to the inevitable "violence" of the so-called "Civil War."[195] For clearly, as we will discuss in more detail shortly, the South did not "force bloodshed upon the national authority," as Lincoln put it. By placing cupidity above constitutional rights, it was he himself who was responsible.

Most in the North and West supported Lincoln's unwarranted

---

190. Harwell, p. 3.
191. Denney, p. 25. The other four states of the Confederacy, Virginia, Arkansas, North Carolina, and Tennessee, would secede later, after the Battle of Fort Sumter and Lincoln's call for troops in April 1861.
192. Pollard, LC, p. 176.
193. Nicolay and Hay, ALAH, Vol. 3, pp. 333-334.
194. Oglesby, p. 34.
195. Thornton and Ekelund, p. xiv.

aggression: the War would be one concerned with money, not with morals, constitutional legalities, patriotism, or black civil rights. If the slavery issue were to be brought into it at all, as the New York *Times* asserted, it will not be about "conscience and religion," but about "social and industrial economy." Lincoln's party members concurred as well, stating that the War had nothing to do with abolition. Instead, where slavery was concerned, it was about protecting free white labor against the "degrading" effects of the institution. A Western newspaper editor spoke for the vast majority of Lincolnites when he said: I'm not against slavery because it hurts blacks, but because it hurts whites.[196]

Many Southern abolitionists used the same argument. One of these, Kentucky aristocrat Cassius M. Clay (a cousin of Lincoln's idol, Henry Clay), stated that his own personal emancipation plans were created

> to seek the highest welfare of the white, whatever may be the consequences of liberation of the African.[197]

For Clay, Lincoln, and most other emancipationists, slavery was objectionable because, they believed, it checked economic growth and competed with white labor. In 1841 Clay stood before the Kentucky legislature and said: there are many whites who

> would import slaves 'to clear up the forests of the Green River Country' . . . . [But] [t]ake one day's ride from this capital and then go and tell them what you have seen. . . . tell them of the houses untenanted and decaying: tell them of the depopulation of the country and consequent ruin of the towns and villages: tell them the white Kentuckian has been driven out by slaves, by the unequal competition of unpaid labor: tell them that the mass of our people are uneducated: tell them that you have heard the children of the white Kentuckian crying for bread, whilst the children of the African was clothed, and fed, and laughed! And then ask them if they will have blacks to fell their forests.[198]

Lincoln's own words on this topic are instructive. Southern

---

196. Foner, FSFLFM, p. 62.
197. Greeley, WCMC, p. 174.
198. Greeley, WCMC, pp. 73-74.

partisan, Albert Taylor Bledsoe, recorded the following infuriating conversation with the Yankee leader:

> When asked, as President of the United States, 'why not let the South go?' his simple, direct, and honest answer revealed one secret of the wise policy of the Washington Cabinet. 'Let the South go!' said he, *'where, then, shall we get our revenue?'* There lies the secret. The Declaration of Independence is great; the voice of all the fathers is mighty; but then they yield us no revenue. The right of self government is 'a most valuable, a most sacred right;' but in this particular case, it gives us no revenue. Hence, this 'most valuable, this most sacred right,' may and should shine upon every other land under heaven; but here it must 'pale its ineffectual fires,' and sink into utter insignificance and contempt in the August presence of the 'ALMIGHTY DOLLAR.'[199]

On April 19, 1861, only a few weeks after his First Inaugural Address, and only four days after his illegal announcement calling for 75,000 troops to invade the South[200] (according to the Constitution, only Congress can declare war),[201] the liberal Northern president issued his infamous proclamation calling for a blockade of the Confederacy's 3,600-mile coastline.[202] The edict was, as usual, unconstitutional, for Lincoln published it without congressional approval (under international law, blockades are unlawful unless war has been officially declared; it had not).[203]

Yet the contents of Lincoln's proclamation are revealing: the only purpose given is the collection of the tariff, or "the revenue," as he terms it. The opening paragraph reads:

> Whereas an insurrection against the Government of the United States has broken out in the States of South Carolina, Georgia, Alabama, Florida, Mississippi, Louisiana, and Texas, and the laws of the United States for the collection of the revenue cannot be effectually executed therein conformably to that provision of the

---

199. Bledsoe, IDT, pp. 143-144.
200. Nicolay and Hay, ALCW, Vol. 2, p. 34.
201. Findlay and Findlay, pp. 84-85; Napolitano, pp. 14-15.
202. Nicolay and Hay, ALCW, Vol. 2, pp. 35-36.
203. As the president, not Congress, had "declared war," it was not an official declaration, and was therefore illegal. See K. L. Hall, s.v. "Lincoln, Abraham"; "Civil War"; W. B. Garrison, CWC, p. 13; W. B. Garrison, CWTFB, p. 254.

Constitution which requires duties to be uniform throughout the United States . . .[204]

Lincoln's blockade proclamation was the butt of jokes across Europe. For one thing, it was widely understood that it would be physically impossible to block off every bay, channel, river mouth, lagoon, bayou, estuary, bottomland, and swamp that lay along the South's enormous coastline. And in fact, it was. Because of this, Lincoln's blockade, the largest one ever attempted, was far from being "fully effective," just one of the many reasons it was illegal.[205]

Meanwhile, on February 18, 1861, at Montgomery, Alabama, the president of the new Southern Confederacy, Jefferson Davis, gave his First Inaugural Address. Touching on the tariff issue, he emphasized the fact that any and all future conflicts that might occur between the South and the North would certainly be economically based. Why? Because a protective tariff raised the price of goods imported by the South.[206] Speaking of the Confederate states, Davis said:

> An agricultural people, whose chief interest is the export of commodities required in every manufacturing country, our true policy is peace, and the freest trade which our necessities will permit. It is alike our interest and that of all those to whom we would sell, and from whom we would buy, that there should be the fewest practicable restrictions upon the interchange of these commodities. There can, however, be but little rivalry between ours and any manufacturing or navigating community such as the Northeastern States of the American Union.
>
>   . . . Actuated solely by a desire to protect and preserve our own rights, and promote our own welfare, the separation of the Confederate States has been marked by no aggression upon

---

204. Nicolay and Hay, ALCW, Vol. 2, p. 35.
205. One of the requirements necessary for a *legal* blockade is that coverage of the area must be 100 percent secure. Due to the South's enormous and complex coastline, Lincoln's blockade never even came close to meeting this stipulation. See Faust, s.v. "blockade"; Owsley, pp. 229-267.
206. Northerners favored a protective tariff because they believed it helped protect Yankee businesses from foreign competition. Weintraub, p. 55. One of the most notorious governmental taxes was the Tariff of Abominations of 1828, which was placed on imported manufactured goods. Proposed by President John Quincy Adams of Massachusetts, he hoped the exorbitantly high duty would secure domestic industry which, at the time, was headquartered in the North. DeGregorio, s.v. "John Quincy Adams" (pp. 99-100). Obviously, Southerners were not happy. Vice President John C. Calhoun of South Carolina—who saw the tax as a direct attack on the South—rightly called the Tariff of Abominations, "unconstitutional, oppressive, and unjust." Tocqueville, Vol. 2, p. 450.

others, and followed by no domestic convulsion. Our industrial pursuits have received no check; the cultivation of our fields has progressed as heretofore, and even should we be involved in war, there would be no considerable diminution in the production of the great staple which constitutes our exports, and in which the commercial world has an interest scarcely less than our own. This common interest of producer and consumer can only be interrupted by external force, which would obstruct shipments to foreign markets—a course of conduct which would be detrimental to manufacturing and commercial interests abroad.

Should reason guide the action of the government from which we have separated, a policy so detrimental to the civilized world, the Northern States included, could not be dictated by even the strongest desire to inflict injury upon us; but, if the contrary should be proven true, a terrible responsibility will rest upon it, and the suffering of millions will bear testimony to the folly and wickedness of our aggressors.[207]

Three years later, in an 1864 interview with a Northern journalist, Davis said:

I tried all in my power to avert this war. I saw it coming, and for twelve years I worked night and day to prevent it, but I could not. The North was mad and blind; it would not let us govern ourselves, and so the war came, and now it must go on till the last man of this generation falls in his tracks, and his children seize his musket and fight our battle, *unless you acknowledge our right to self-government.* We are not fighting for slavery. We are fighting for Independence, and that, or extermination, we *will* have.[208]

... [Slavery] never was an essential element. It was only a means of bringing other conflicting elements to an earlier culmination.... There are essential differences between the North and the South, that will, however this war may end, make them two nations.[209]

In Alabama, an article in the November 26, 1863, issue of the Mobile *Register* pointed out, as Davis did above, that the North had already decided to conquer the South economically *prior* to Lincoln's War.

---

207. J. Davis, RFCG, Vol. 1, pp. 233, 235.
208. Seabrook, TQJD, p. 80.
209. F. Moore, Vol. 11, pp. 83, 84.

Therefore, the conflict could not have been over slavery. It was for the Constitution and our civil rights, not for the Negroes, that we fought, the writer asserted; it was not due to slavery, but because of the abuses and injustices the South suffered at the hands of the Yankee. Yet the institution of slavery continues to be held up as the cause of Lincoln's War by the uninformed.[210]

Sixteen years later, in 1879, Confederate General Richard Taylor wrote in his book *Destruction and Reconstruction*:

> During all these years the conduct of the Southern people has been admirable. Submitting to the inevitable, they have shown fortitude and dignity, and rarely has one been found base enough to take wages of shame from the oppressor and maligner of his brethren. Accepting the harshest conditions and faithfully observing them, they have struggled in all honourable ways, and for what? For their slaves? Regret for their loss has neither been felt nor expressed. But they have striven for that which brought our forefathers to Runnymede, the privilege of exercising some influence in their own government.[211]

Here we can begin to dismantle one of the North's greatest Lincolnian myths, that "the South's secession and the War were over slavery." The Anti-South movement considers this a "worn-out" topic, one they insultingly refer to as a piece of "revisionist Southern mythology." We strongly disagree, for we have, as will be shown, authentic facts on our side.

The truth is that as long as South-haters continue to promote the idea that slavery was the cause of the War, it is they themselves who are responsible for keeping this issue alive. It is the traditional South that has been trying, for a century and a half, to put it to rest.

To begin with, it is clear from what we have just examined alone that Lincoln's War did not spring from slavery, for why would the South's 95 percent non-slaving owning majority risk their lives for the 5 percent slave owning minority? To any thinking person this is illogical in the extreme. As English journalist Alistair Cooke notes, slavery alone could have never united the many different types of Southerners that existed in

---

210. See Durden, p. 43.
211. R. Taylor, p. 238.

Victorian Dixie, from mountaineers, merchants, and farmers, to poor whites, middle-class mulattos, and wealthy blacks.[212]

Besides, how could the War have been over slavery when abolition was not part of the platform of any of the primary political parties at the time, including Lincoln's? Indeed, Lincoln himself promised not to interfere with the institution in his First Inaugural Speech.[213] And if about slavery, why did the War not end with the Emancipation Proclamation? Instead, the conflict continued for another two long years.[214]

What are the facts then? Why did eleven Southern states (along with portions of Kentucky and Missouri) secede to form their own confederacy?

The South left the Union because a man hostile to everything Dixie held dear had risen to America's highest office;[215] a man—the first sectional (pro-North, anti-South) president in American history—who quite deliberately planned to impose his will on the South, dismantle her way of life, trample on her traditions, and overturn her right to self-government.[216]

On July 17, 1858, during a speech at Springfield, Illinois, Lincoln purposefully antagonized the South, openly hinting at the invasion, violence, and oppression that was to come:

> I believe that this government cannot endure permanently half slave and half free. It will become all one thing or all the other.[217]

But Lincoln was dead wrong. As Stephen A. Douglas countered:

> Why cannot this government endure, divided into Free and Slave States as our fathers made it? When this government was established by Washington, Jefferson, Madison, Jay, Hamilton, Franklin, and the other sages and patriots of that day, it was composed of Free States and Slave States, bound together by one common Constitution. We have existed and prospered from that

---

212. A. Cooke, ACA, p. 206.
213. See Nicolay and Hay, ALCW, Vol. 2, p. 1; Beard and Beard, Vol. 2, pp. 39-40.
214. See Stonebraker, p. 250.
215. J. M. McPherson, BCF, p. 254.
216. C. Adams, p. 89.
217. Lincoln and Douglas, p. 74.

> day to this thus divided, and have increased with a rapidity never before equalled, in wealth, the extension of territory, and all the elements of power and greatness, until we have become the first nation on the face of the globe. Why can we not thus continue to prosper? We can, if we will live up to and execute the government upon those principles upon which our fathers established it.[218]

Bizarrely, Lincoln himself admitted in the same speech that the U.S. had already "endured, half slave and half free, for eighty-two years."[219]

Why then bring up the topic of slavery at all? Why agitate things? Because, as he always did, Lincoln was attempting to obscure the real issue: the power struggle between Northern Federalists, who demanded centralization (governmental consolidation), and Southern Confederalists, who demanded states' rights (decentralization). What despot Lincoln could never see, acknowledge, or accept was that what was right, moral, and positive for the North, was wrong, immoral, and negative for the South.[220] Like the typical self-righteous Yankee of his day, he believed that what was best for the North was also best for everyone else.[221]

Southerners, of course, saw things quite differently. In 1863, the C.S.A.'s president, Jefferson Davis, declared:

> The people of the States now confederated became convinced that the Government of the United States had fallen into the hands of a sectional majority, who would pervert that most sacred of all trusts to the destruction of the rights which it was pledged to protect. They believed that to remain longer in the Union would subject them to a continuance of a disparaging discrimination, submission to which would be inconsistent with their welfare, and intolerable to a proud people. They therefore determined to sever its bonds and establish a new Confederacy for themselves.
>
> The experiment instituted by our revolutionary fathers, of a voluntary Union of sovereign States for the purposes specified in a solemn compact, had been perverted by those who, feeling power and forgetting right, were determined to respect no law but

---

218. Lincoln and Douglas, pp. 186-187.
219. Lincoln and Douglas, p. 74.
220. Simpson, pp. 74, 76.
221. To this day, many Southerners believe this sentiment is still very much alive across the North—and with good reason. The ongoing disrespect shown for the traditional South, toward her history, culture, icons, traditions, monuments, and society, as daily displayed in print, TV, radio, film, and on the Internet certainly substantiates this view.

their own will. The Government had ceased to answer the ends for which it was ordained and established. To save ourselves from a revolution which, in its silent but rapid progress, was about to place us under the despotism of numbers, and to preserve in spirit, as well as in form, a system of government we believed to be peculiarly fitted to our condition, and full of promise for mankind, we determined to make a new association, composed of States homogenous in interest, in policy, and in feeling.

True to our traditions of peace and our love of justice, we sent commissioners to the United States to propose a fair and amicable settlement of all questions of public debt or property which might be in dispute. But the Government at Washington [i.e., Lincoln], denying our right to self-government, refused even to listen to any proposals for a peaceful separation. Nothing was then left to do but to prepare for war.[222]

Thus, Davis asserted, the South was forced to take up arms against the North, not over slavery, but

to vindicate the political rights, the freedom, equality, and State sovereignty which were the heritage purchased by the blood of our revolutionary sires.[223]

After Lincoln's War, Southerner Lyon Gardiner Tyler, the son of America's tenth President, John Tyler,[224] put the matter this way:

The emancipation of slaves [in 1863] by the late war is the best evidence that the South never fought for slavery, but *against a foreign dictation and a sectional will*. Within the Union slavery was probably secure for many years to come. The war was nothing

---

222. F. Moore, Vol. 4, p. 201.
223. *ORA*, Ser. 2, Vol. 3, p. 153.
224. To his great credit, Virginian John Tyler (1790-1862), America's tenth president, was the only man of that office, former or future, to either join the Confederacy or serve in the Confederate government. Though he did not fight in Lincoln's "Civil War" (being too old at the time), he served as a member of the Provisional Congress of the Confederacy. He was later elected to the Confederate House of Representatives, but passed away before taking his seat. Tyler was an example of the overt anti-South bias that has long permeated the U.S. government: because of his devotion to the Confederate Cause, Northerners in his day regarded him as a traitor, his death in 1862 was ignored in Washington, and an official U.S. memorial was not placed over his grave until 1915, fifty-three years after he died. DeGregorio, s.v. "John Tyler" (pp. 158-159). In total, six men who would become U.S. presidents fought in the War for Southern Independence; unfortunately for history, all got it wrong by siding with liberal tyrant Lincoln and the North: Benjamin Harrison, James A. Garfield, Ulysses S. Grant, Rutherford B. Hayes, Chester A. Arthur, and William McKinley.

more than the outcome of a tyranny exerted for seventy-two years by the North over vital interests of the South.[225]

The common Rebel soldier knew exactly why he was defending Dixie, even if his description was not as elegant as Tyler's. A Yankee officer once asked a filthy, ragged, barefoot Confederate prisoner why in the world he was fighting. Looking him squarely in the eyes, Johnny Reb said: "Because y'all are down here."[226]

One Confederate officer who felt the same way was General Nathan Bedford Forrest. On April 12, 1864, during the Battle of Fort Pillow, the by now famous Forrest came upon a Yankee soldier. "What in hell are you doing down here?" he asked the terrified Federal, as minié balls whizzed by their ears. "I should kill you right here and now!" he continued. "If you goddamned Yanks had stayed home and minded yer own business, the war would have been over a long time ago!"[227]

As for the North itself, as we will see, Lincoln stated in no uncertain terms that he took up arms against the South to "preserve the Union," a position from which he never wavered.

It will become clear then that abolition was merely one of the many results of the War, not the cause;[228] a means by which Lincoln could achieve his goal of installing big government—not the end itself.[229]

Evidence of this took place at the Hampton Roads Conference on February 3, 1865. Here, Lincoln demanded restoration of the Union, while the Southern peace commissioners demanded independence. Neither side would budge and the War continued for another two months. If the conflict had been over slavery, as Northern mythology repeatedly

---

225. Tyler, LTT, Vol. 2, p. 567.
226. Strode, Vol. 2, p. xvii. There were some Southerners who claimed that secession and Lincoln's War originated over slavery; that slavery was in danger of being abolished. At the time, however, Southern slavery was not in danger (from outside forces, at least; in the South slavery was in more danger from the abolitionist majority), and no one, not even Lincoln, truly believed this view (indeed, slavery was more prosperous than ever in 1860—see Fogel and Engerman, pp. 38-106). In truth, those few Southerners, like Confederate Vice President Alexander Stephens, who declared that slavery was the "cornerstone" of the South, were engaging in a clever but reckless political ploy, one used to try and agitate other Southerners in the tariff conflicts with the North. C. Adams, p. 4. If slavery had truly been the "cornerstone of the Confederacy," then Lincoln's War would have ended with his Final Emancipation Proclamation on January 1, 1863. See Parker, p. 343.
227. Forrest ended up sparing the life of this very lucky Yank. See Seabrook, ARB, p. 485.
228. Garraty and McCaughey, p. 244; Faust, s.v. "slavery."
229. Napolitano, p. 75.

tells us, then it would have ended that day,[230] for Davis had already decided to emancipate Southern slaves and enlist them in the Confederate army (this decision was made official by the Confederate Congress just a few weeks later, in March).[231]

Finally, as Patrick J. Buchanan points out, at the time Lincoln declared war on the South, the vast majority of slave owners and their slaves were still part of the U.S. On April 12, 1861, the day the Battle of Fort Sumter began, Virginia, for example, one of the largest slave-holding states, had not yet seceded and was still in the Union. Obviously then, Lincoln's attack on the South was not an attack on slavery.[232]

In short, the "Civil War" was not a "crisis of abolition." It was what truly objective historians call a "crisis of constitutionalism."[233]

Another Yankee myth we must confront is that "the South created the idea of confederacy," and that a confederacy is somehow "evil" and anti-American.

First, confederacies existed in Europe long before 1861, or even 1776. Second, America herself was a land of confederacies dating back to prehistoric times: thousands of Native-Americans instituted and lived under confederacies right up into the late 19th Century.[234] New Indian confederacies continue to flourish in the 21st Century, such as, for example, the Confederation of Tennessee Native Tribes.[235]

Hence, there is nothing inherently negative, "rebellious," or Southern about this form of government. To the contrary, as we have seen, acting as an allied, mutual support system, one built on a "friendly compact" between separate and "distinct nations" or nation-states,[236] confederation is the very essence of what the American Founders had in mind for their new republic in 1776.[237]

As for the American South and the formation of its own Confederacy in 1861, this was merely the region's attempt to continue, and maintain, the Founding Fathers' original Confederacy, though under

---

230. Channing, p. 165.
231. McElroy, pp. 444-447.
232. Website: http://buchanan.org/blog/the-new-intolerance-3878.
233. Kelly, Harbison, and Belz, Vol. 2, p. xxiii.
234. Jefferson, NSV, pp. 128-132.
235. See Website: www.tennesseenativetribes.com/common.
236. Hamilton, Madison, and Jay, p. 21.
237. Collier and Collier, p. 4.

a new name: the Confederate States of America.[238] The founders of the Southern Confederacy knew well the words of one of their Southern heroes, Thomas Jefferson, who, in 1786, wrote of what would soon be called the United States of America:

> Our confederacy must be viewed as the nest from which all America, North and South is to be peopled.[239]

Thus, as Lincoln's War was about to open in the Spring of 1861, Southerners viewed themselves correctly as defending the principles of 1776;[240] i.e., of trying to preserve the original confederate government and Constitution of the Founding Fathers. As Robert E. Lee said five years later, in 1866:

> All that the South has ever desired was that the Union, as established by our forefathers, should be preserved, and that the government as originally organized should be administered in purity and truth.[241]

Again, that same year Lee wrote:

> ... I trust that the constitution may undergo no change, but that it may be handed down to succeeding generations in the form we received it from our forefathers.[242]

It is little wonder that Southerners felt so strongly about these issues on the eve of Lincoln's inauguration March 4, 1861. Before even stepping foot in the White House Lincoln had made it patently clear what his opinions were on the topic.

In February 1861, while meeting with a Southern peace commission at Willard's Hotel in Washington, D.C., the president-elect was asked by New York businessman William E. Dodge what he was going to do to prevent war with the South. Lincoln's response is chilling. When I get to the Oval Office, he said,

---

238. Ashe, pp. 21-22.
239. Foley, p. 699.
240. M. Davis, p. 39.
241. Lee Jr., p. 225.
242. F. L. Riley, GRELAA, p. 241.

> I shall take an oath to the best of my ability to preserve, protect, and defend the Constitution. This is a great and solemn duty. With the support of the people and the assistance of the Almighty I shall undertake to perform it. I have full faith that I shall perform it. *It is not the Constitution as I would like to have it*, but as it is that is to be defended.[243]

Reading between the lines, it is obvious that even prior to becoming president, Lincoln was plotting to alter, and even destroy, the Constitution of Washington, Jefferson, Madison, Franklin, Mason, Pinckney, and the other Founders.[244] Under such circumstances the Constitution-loving Southern states then had every reason, and right, to secede.

Even more disturbing, after the Southern states did secede, Lincoln declared the act a "rebellion" against the Union. But this was technically impossible. Jefferson Davis pointed out the obvious, something Lincoln knew perfectly well but would not acknowledge: the Southern states were "the sovereign parties to the compact of union," and thus they "had the reserved power to secede from it whenever it should be found not to answer the ends for which it was established."[245] In other words, sovereigns cannot rebel because there is nothing to rebel against. They are free entities, with the power to come and go as they please.[246]

In one sense, however, the South did "rebel." But not against the

---

243. Coffin, p. 235. Emphasis added. Lincoln-worshiper President Obama recently made a similar statement, calling the U.S. Constitution "an imperfect document." "Glenn Beck," FOX News, September 17, 2009 (Constitution Day, 222nd anniversary).
244. A note on South Carolinian Charles Pinckney: many continue to believe that he had little or nothing to do with helping to shape or found the United States. Recent research, however, has uncovered that this is quite false and that it was James Madison who is largely responsible for this historical oversight. Pinckney, in fact, contributed much to the founding documents and to the manner in which our government operates. For example, he came up with the idea of the president's annual State of the Union address; he recommended that the president should also function as the commander-in-chief of the military; and he thought up the terms "president," "House," and "Senate," along with numerous other concepts that are still in use. Most importantly, the U.S. Constitution contains at least twenty-one provisions that came from Pinckney, and a total of forty-three original contributions of one kind or another. Out of personal distaste and rivalry, Madison—the only man who thought to record the events of the Constitutional Convention of 1787 (these can be found in his *Notes of the Debates in the Federal Convention*)—ignored or suppressed much of Pinckney's writings and ideas, even labeling his brilliant plan for the new U.S. government a "forgery." Fortunately for American history's sake, modern scholars have been able to reconstruct much of Pinckney's contributions and work from contemporaneous documents. For more on this fascinating Southerner, see R. S. Phillips, s.v. "Charles Cotesworth Pinckney"; Chambers, s.v. "Pinckney, Charles Cotesworth"; Collier and Collier, pp. 87-101; Neilson, s.v. "Pinckney, Charles Cotesworth"; Ellis, FB, pp. 92, 95.
245. J. Davis, RFCG, Vol. 2, p. 764.
246. See Cooper, JDA, p. 672.

Union. It rebelled against Lincoln's perverse and self-deluded idea of the Union. Almost every Southerner of note at the time was a unionist, not a disunionist, and was violently against the idea of breaking up the U.S. Such men included everyone from President Jefferson Davis, Vice President Alexander H. Stephens, Robert E. Lee, and Nathan Bedford Forrest, to John Singleton Mosby, Stephen R. Mallory, Robert A. Toombs, and Edmund Ruffin. After all, the American Union had been formed primarily by their own Southern ancestors, and thus was for them a sacred institution, one we will recall Southerner Jefferson said was meant to be "a lasting Confederacy."[247]

Indeed, this is one reason why, during the construction of the new Southern Confederacy, Southerners were so adamant about creating a national flag that retained elements of the old U.S. flag. (It was only after several months of War against a despotic, aggressive, cruel, and meddlesome U.S. that they began to change their minds and demand a flag that was as dissimilar to the U.S. flag as possible.)[248]

Constitutionally speaking, in fact, it was the North who "rebelled" and then "seceded." From what? From the real Union, the true and original one: the Confederacy created by the Founders. Lincoln, who advocated an all-powerful central government with he himself as its monarchical head, revealed an appalling ignorance of the ideals of the great and wise men who came before him.

This is no doubt why he revealingly referred to the conflict he started as "the War of Rebellion." Certainly, if it had been over slavery, as Northern mythologists, the politically correct, and New South Southerners (derogatorily known in Dixie as scallywags) claim, why did he not call it "the War of Slavery"?

The reason is simple. For Lincoln the War was about politics, power, economics, and ego. For the South it was about self-government and the protection of the right of secession. As President Davis put it:

> . . . the war was, on the part of the United States government, one of aggression and usurpation, and, on the part of the South, was for the defense of an inherent, unalienable right.[249]

---

247. Bergh, Vol. 1, p. 48.
248. Cannon, pp. 7, 11, 14.
249. J. Davis, RFCG, Vol. 2, p. 764.

This is why Lincoln had fellow Northerners arrested, tried, and sentenced (often to long prison terms and hard labor) for referring to his war as a "Nigger War." Not because the term insulted blacks, but because the conflict was not about slavery or abolition, and he did not want the idea to catch hold with the public.[250] This is also why the following Yankee newspaper headline was so popular across the North. White Union soldiers, it read, are

> WILLING TO FIGHT FOR UNCLE SAM BUT NOT FOR UNCLE SAMBO.[251]

Why, if Lincoln's War was over slavery, did the most famous Southerner of all, Robert E. Lee, say the following after the conflict came to an end?

> So far from engaging in a war to perpetuate slavery, I am rejoiced that slavery is abolished.[252]

Yes, Lincoln called it "the War of Rebellion." And, as mentioned, the South did "rebel." But not against the Union. It rebelled only against Lincoln's attempt to usurp the American Constitution and topple the Founders' confederated government. As Southern agrarian Andrew Nelson Lytle phrased it:

> If Lincoln loved the Union, he was responsible, more than any man, for its destruction, for he consciously violated the Constitution. . . . The war was not a war of slavery versus freedom; it was a war between those who preferred a federated nation to those who preferred a confederation of sovereign states. Slavery was the ink thrown into the pool to confuse the issue.[253]

There are other reasons we know that the War was not fought over slavery. Some come from comments made by Lincoln's own party members, even those among the most radically anti-South. One of these was the arch Dixie-hater, New Englander Charles Sumner, the leader of

---

250. Neely, p. 174.
251. Wright, s.v. "Uncle Sambo" (p. 309); K. C. Davis, p. 270.
252. *The Century Magazine*, Vol. 30, Ser. 8, May 1885 to October 1885, p. 167.
253. *The Virginia Quarterly Review*, October, 1931.

the Northern abolition party in the U.S. Congress. Standing before the Senate on February 25, 1861, he said:

> I take this occasion to declare most explicitly that I do not think that Congress has any right to interfere with slavery in a State.[254]

A few months later, on July 22, 1861, the U.S. Congress itself stated in no uncertain terms that Lincoln's War was not about slavery. A resolution passed that day read:

> That this war is not waged on our part in any spirit of oppression, or for any purpose of conquest or subjugation, or purpose of overthrowing or interfering with the rights or established institutions of those [Confederate] States; but to defend and maintain the supremacy of the Constitution, and to preserve the Union with all the dignity, equality, and rights of the several States unimpaired; and that, as soon as these objects are accomplished the war ought to cease.[255]

Nothing about slavery, abolition, or emancipation here. Instead, Congress promises not to interfere with the institution, asserting that the War would end, not when slavery ended, but when the Southern states returned to the Union.

Secretary of state William H. Seward, Lincoln's confidant and governmental mouthpiece, was certainly speaking for the president when he said:

> Experience in public affairs has confirmed my opinion that domestic slavery existing in any State is wisely left by the Constitution of the United States, exclusively to the care, management, and disposition of that state; and if it were in my power I would not alter the Constitution in that respect.[256]

In April 1861, in a letter to a Yankee diplomat then stationed in Paris, Seward reasserted his feelings on the matter, writing that for Lincoln to disturb "the system of slavery as it is existing under the Constitution and

---

254. J. Davis, RFCG, Vol. 2, p. 160.
255. J. Davis, RFCG, Vol. 2, p. 189.
256. Pollard, LC, p. 216.

laws . . . would be unconstitutional."[257]

Before, and even during his first year in office, Lincoln himself repeatedly promised not to interfere slavery. In fact, as president he not only pledged to continue to support the Fugitive Slave Law (which required runaway slaves to be returned to their owners), but he also admitted that it would be illegal to meddle with the institution itself,[258] prompting abolitionist Wendell Phillips to call him "that slavehound from Illinois."[259] All of this was in keeping with Lincoln's personal views on the matter, as the *Encyclopedia Britannica* states, "that the basic issue of the time was not the freedom of the slaves but the preservation of the ideal of democracy."[260]

As such, in the first year of the War, Lincoln's officers in the field were ordered to send runaway slaves back home, as well as stamp out any slave riots or insurrections that arose.[261] On May 26, 1861, Yankee General George B. McClellan issued a proclamation to the people of West Virginia that read:

> Notwithstanding all that has been said by the [Rebel] traitors to induce you to believe that our advent among you will be signalized by interference with your slaves, understand one thing clearly—not only will we abstain from interfering with your slaves, but we will, on the contrary, with an iron hand, crush any attempt at insurrection on their part.[262]

In late 1861, also under Lincoln's mandate, Henry W. Halleck, then Commander of the Military Department of the West, issued his infamous General Order No. 3, which denied runaway slaves admission into Union lines. As with most of the "slavehound's" actions, the edict infuriated abolitionists and black civil rights leaders alike. Frederick Douglass acidly observed that the president's soldiers "made themselves more active in kicking colored men out of their camps than in shooting rebels."[263]

---

257. Pollard, LC, p. 217.
258. Adams and Sanders, p. 183.
259. McGehee, p. 81; Meriwether, p. 159.
260. Encyc. Brit., s.v. "Lincoln, Abraham."
261. Quarles, p. 65.
262. *ORA*, Ser. 1, Vol. 2, pp. 48-49.
263. Douglass, LTFD, p. 293.

Standing his ground, on March 4, 1861, in his First Inaugural Address, the new U.S. commander-in-chief drove home his policies on slaves ("property") and slavery. Said Lincoln:

> Apprehension seems to exist among the people of the Southern States that by the accession of a Republican administration their property and their peace and personal security are to be endangered. There has never been any reasonable cause for such apprehension. Indeed, the most ample evidence to the contrary has all the while existed and been open to their inspection. It is found in nearly all the published speeches of him who now addresses you. I do but quote from one of those speeches when I declare that 'I have no purpose, directly or indirectly, to interfere with the institution of slavery in the States where it exists. I believe I have no lawful right to do so, and I have no inclination to do so.' Those who nominated and elected me did so with full knowledge that I had made this and many similar declarations, and had never recanted them.[264]

Four weeks later, Lincoln would conveniently forget these words and send 75,000 Yankee troops south to "subdue the Rebellion" he himself had recklessly created. He thus made a mockery of his Inaugural Address by doing everything in his power to "endanger the property, peace, and personal security" of Southerners. But it was not due to Southern slavery.

Indeed, on April 15, 1861, Lincoln issued a proclamation that included the following revealing statement regarding his War:

> . . . in every event the utmost care will be observed, consistently with the objects aforesaid, to avoid any devastation, any destruction of, or interference with, property, or any disturbance of peaceful citizens in any part of the country . . .[265]

The "property" he refers to here of course included black slaves, and by extension the institution of slavery itself. This was to remain untouched Lincoln said at the start of the conflict, for his fight had nothing to do with abolition.

In fact, one of the many reasons he gave for refusing to enlist

---

264. E. McPherson, PHUSAGR, p. 105.
265. F. Moore, Vol. 1, p. 63.

blacks for the first two years of the War was that he did not want the world to think that it was about African-Americans, civil rights, or abolition. This war is between Northern and Southern whites, the Lincoln administration continually maintained, and has absolutely nothing to do with the Negro, either bonded or free.[266] This is precisely why, in his May 19, 1862, announcement to annul General David Hunter's emancipation proclamation, Lincoln said that he would not free the slaves until "it shall have become a necessity indispensable to the maintenance of the Government . . ."[267]

If there are any doubts left as to Lincoln's true intentions, consider his words from August 1864:

> My enemies pretend I am now carrying on this war for the sole purpose of abolition. So long as I am President, it shall be carried on for the sole purpose of restoring the Union.[268]

These words are actually carved into the interior walls of the Lincoln Memorial in Washington, D.C. for all to see.

It is clear then that destroying slavery was never part of Lincoln's original intention to vanquish the South, and he was, at first, as unequivocal as he could be about it: I went to war against the Confederacy, he said repeatedly, to "preserve the Union." But even this was just a cover-up to conceal an element of his true plan: to demolish the concept of states' rights (which included the right of secession) in the South. If this is what Lincoln meant by "preserving the Union," it certainly was not for the benefit of the North *and* the South. It was for the benefit of the North only.

The question is, why did Lincoln want to extinguish the constitutional rights of secession and state sovereignty? Because he could not install the American System as long as these two ideas were alive in the South. Like oil and water, his Northern view and the Southern one were so incompatible that they could not exist side by side. One had to go, and Lincoln was prepared to use force, drain the treasury, and even expend lives in order to make sure his view came out on top.

---

266. Mullen, p. 18.
267. Greeley, AC, Vol. 2, p. 246.
268. Nicolay and Hay, ALCW, Vol. 2, p. 562.

The South just wanted to be allowed to go its own way, in peace, and it said so often, before, during, and after the War. It had no designs on the North, no intention to invade, no desire to conquer, no interest in taking over the U.S. government or in occupying its lands. "All we ask is to be left alone," Jefferson Davis pleaded in his message to the Confederate Congress, April 29, 1861.[269] But Lincoln was not interested in leaving the South alone, and so he never gave peace a chance. Why? Because war was part of his original scheme to begin with.

And what a scheme it was: he would lead the U.S., a country that had been founded on secession (from Britain), in a war against the Confederacy for seceding!

Even if Lincoln would not acknowledge his hypocritical, illogical, and illegal deception publicly, many Europeans would, and did. In the latter half of 1861, a sagacious British editor noted:

> . . . it does seem the most monstrous of anomalies that a government founded on the 'sacred right of insurrection' should pretend to treat as traitors and rebels six or seven million people who withdrew from the Union, and merely asked to be let alone.[270]

There were monetary aspects behind all this, of course, for all wars are ultimately rooted in economics. In Lincoln's case, he wanted and needed the support of special interest groups, most importantly, the "Wall Street Boys," robber barons, and Yankee industrialists; i.e., the Northern business establishment, which had bankrolled his first (and later his second) presidential campaign using money they had made primarily from the Yankee slave trade.[271]

If the South were allowed to go her own way, Northern businessmen would have been financially devastated, many even bankrupted, by Dixie's insistence on low tariffs, a *laissez-faire* economy, and a free trade system. There was also the certainty that secession would shift trade from the three great Northern ports, Boston, New York, and Philadelphia, to the Southern ports, resulting in an economic decline of

---

269. Kettell, p. 84.
270. *The Quarterly Review* (London, England), Vol. 111, January and April 1862, p. 256.
271. Curti, Thorpe, and Baker, p. 572; Rosenbaum and Brinkley, s.v. "Slavery."

the former.[272]

Finally, there were the tariffs, which amounted to 95 percent of the federal revenue. Through them the South by herself was financing 70 percent of the cost of the central government in Washington.[273] In short, an independent South would have spelled financial doom for the North.

Lincoln was not about to let this occur. He and his Northern business associates were thick as thieves, and together they were committed to recapturing the goose that laid the golden egg: the seceded Southern states.

Yankee abolitionist, individualist, and natural rights advocate, Lysander Spooner, saw right through Lincoln's tragicomedy, correctly referring to the president's Wall Street Boys as the "lenders of blood money." As Spooner saw it:

> . . . these lenders of blood money had, for a long series of years previous to the war, been the willing accomplices of the slave-holders in perverting the government from the purposes of liberty and justice, to the greatest of crimes. They had been such accomplices *for a purely pecuniary consideration*, to wit, a control of the markets in the South; in other words, the privilege of holding the slave-holders themselves in industrial and commercial subjection to the manufacturers and merchants of the North (who afterwards furnished the money for the [Civil] war). And these Northern merchants and manufacturers, these lenders of blood money, were willing to continue to be the accomplices of the slaveholders in the future, for the same pecuniary considerations. But the slaveholders, either doubting the fidelity of their Northern allies, or feeling themselves strong enough to keep their slaves in subjection without Northern assistance, would no longer pay the price these Northern men demanded. And it was to enforce this price in the future—that is, to monopolize the Southern markets, to maintain their industrial and commercial control over the South—that these Northern manufacturers and merchants lent some of the profits of their former monopolies for the [Civil] war, in order to secure themselves the same, or greater, monopolies in the future. These—and not any love of liberty or justice—were the motives on which the money for the [Civil] war was lent by the

---

272. C. Adams, p. 25.
273. Crocker, pp. 20, 31.

North.[274]

By subduing the South and forcing her to return to the Union, Lincoln was able to continue imposing high tariffs on his southern neighbors which, in turn, created huge corporate profits for Yankee businessmen (which included dozens of Northern slave traders), his biggest and most important financial backers. For not only did they finance both his campaigns, but, as is clear from Spooner's observations above, they also funded the War itself.[275] It was a self-serving symbiotic relationship that the wily Lincoln crafted and managed with the skill and finesse of a surgeon.

Besides tariffs, Lincoln's subjugation of the South benefitted the North financially in another way: Dixie's 3,549 miles of coastline, her innumerable port towns, inlets, rivers, immense fertile farmlands, abundant agricultural products, and her hardworking people, were all vital to Northern economic growth and stability. The South's major seaports alone—New Orleans, Louisiana; Mobile, Alabama; Pensacola, Florida; Fernandina, Florida; Savannah, South Carolina; Charleston, South Carolina; Wilmington, Delaware; New Bern, North Carolina; and Norfolk, Virginia—were worth untold billions of dollars to the North.

The South was so abundant in natural and manmade resources that in 1860, just prior to the start of Lincoln's War, not only was she far richer than the North,[276] but her economy was the third largest of any region or country in either Europe or the Americas.[277] As far as wealth, the Confederate States were the fourth richest nation in the world,[278] more affluent than any European country except England. Modern Italy did not reach the level of per capita income the antebellum South possessed until the beginning of World War II.[279]

Additionally, between 1840 and 1860, the per capita income of the South grew at an average annual rate of 1.7 percent, and was a third higher than in the North. This is a sustained long-term growth rate that

---

274. Spooner, NT, No. 6, p. 54.
275. Also see Pollard, LC, p. 154.
276. Pollard, LC, pp. 131-132.
277. Kennedy and Kennedy, SWR, p. 21.
278. Fogel, p. 87.
279. Fogel and Engerman, p. 249.

has been achieved by few nations.[280] And though the South possessed only 30 percent of America's population, 60 percent of America's wealthiest men were Southerners, a group that owned twice as much property as moneyed Northerners.[281]

In 1860, of the 7,000 U.S. families who possessed wealth of $111,000 or more, 4,500 of them (nearly 65 percent) lived in the South, while of the richest percentile that same year, 59 percent were Southerners.[282] So wealthy was the Confederacy that if she had been allowed to develop without interference from Lincoln, she would have become one of the world's major international powers, with a standing army many times bigger than the North's[283]—and this with a far smaller population than the North.[284]

The greedy, materialistic, commercially-minded North could not ignore such riches, power, and potential. For the Southern states, in essence, were seen by Yankees as vital elements in the creation of a nationwide domestic market that was to be controlled at the North.[285]

Based on economics alone then, Lincoln was not going to allow the South to secede. For the North the American "Civil War" was indeed, in great part, a conflict built around business and finance. While modern Yankee mythologists have tried hard to obscure this fact, Lincoln knew it and so did nearly everyone else, including most foreigners. In 1862, English novelist Charles Dickens exposed the truth behind America's "War Between the States":

> The Northern onslaught upon slavery is no more than a piece of specious humbug disguised to conceal its desire for economic control of the United States. Union means so many millions a year lost to the South; secession means loss of the same millions to the North. The love of money is the root of this as many, many other evils. The quarrel between the North and South is, as it stands, solely a fiscal quarrel.[286]

---

280. Fogel, pp. 87-88. Sadly, Lincoln's War destroyed much of the South's wealth. As just one example, it took Dixie another 100 years (into the 1960s) to reduce her income gap to the level she had enjoyed in 1860. Fogel, p. 89.
281. Current, TC, s.v. "Plantation."
282. Fogel, p. 436.
283. Fogel, pp. 414-415.
284. Collier and Collier, p. 71.
285. Hacker, p. 593.
286. "American Disunion," Charles Dickens, *All the Year Round*, December 21, 1861, p. 299.

The South was rich in countless resources. Therefore her "economic control" was absolutely vital to Northern interests. It is easy to see then why Lincoln and his Wall Street Boys considered Dixie the ultimate money prize, one they could not afford to lose.[287]

On July 1, 1861, in his Message to Congress, Lincoln drove the point home: the South *must* be forced to return to the Union, otherwise the North would suffer tremendous loss financially. Said the president:

> What is now combated, is the position that secession is consistent with the Constitution—is lawful, and peaceful. It is not contended that there is any express law for it; and nothing should ever be implied as law, which leads to unjust, or absurd consequences. The nation purchased, with money, the countries out of which several of these States were formed. Is it just that they shall go off without leave, and without refunding? The nation paid very large sums, (in the aggregate, I believe, nearly a hundred millions) to relieve Florida of the aboriginal tribes. Is it just that she shall now be off without consent, or without making any return? The nation is now in debt for money applied to the benefit of these so-called seceding States, in common with the rest. Is it just, either that creditors shall go unpaid, or the remaining States pay the whole? A part of the present national debt was contracted to pay the old debts of Texas. Is it just that she shall leave, and pay no part of this herself?
>
> Again, if one State may secede, so may another; and when all shall have seceded, none is left to pay the debts. Is this quite just to creditors? Did we notify them of this sage view of ours, when we borrowed their money? If we now recognize this doctrine, by allowing the seceders to go in peace, it is difficult to see what we can do, if others choose to go, or to extort terms upon which they will promise to remain.[288]

Money was clearly front and center in Lincoln's mind when he initiated war against Dixie: in this same speech he asked Congress for $400,000,000 (in today's currency about $10 billion) to pay for the men and supplies necessary to physically coerce the South back into the Union.[289]

This had to be one of the most preposterous plans ever laid before

---

287. Ashe, p. 24.
288. Nicolay and Hay, ALCW, Vol. 2, p. 63.
289. Nicolay and Hay, ALCW, Vol. 2, pp. 60-61.

Congress, for if enacted it would only put the U.S. further in debt (the national debt was one of Lincoln's chief complaints to begin with). Additionally, if in the future the North were to be victorious and the South were forced to pay back this sum, it would surely bankrupt her. Northern deficit, Southern insolvency, and all for what purpose?

Did Lincoln really believe that the South would willingly rejoin the Union after waging a bloody war against her, after bombing her into rubble, after exterminating nearly 25 percent of her population, after humiliating and occupying her, then bankrupting her? Diplomacy was certainly not one of his strong points.

Despite the extreme irrationality of Lincoln's congressional request, Northern pro-Lincoln journalists, magazine editors, and newspapers were quick to support his concerns over the potential loss of the South and her abundant wealth and resources. A month before the War, on March 2, 1861, the *New York Evening Post*, enunciated Lincoln's concerns perfectly, saying that the revenue from duties must be collected at the Southern ports, otherwise the sources that supply the treasury would dry up. This would leave the government without money. Unable to function, the *Evening Post* ranted on, it would go bankrupt, leaving nothing for the U.S. army, navy, or their officers' salaries.[290]

Lincoln's Wall Street Boys were also on board, of course, as were the Boston elite—the latter group, in particular, making it known that it was quite willing to make huge concessions to the South in the interest of making money.[291]

As for Lincoln's idea of "preserving the Union," the idea was laughable in the South. Southerners, nearly all who were well-versed in the Constitution, understood that there was no such concept in that document. In fact, the Declaration of Independence allows and even encourages individual states to break away from the Union if they feel it no longer meets their needs, or if it encroaches on their rights as small, self-governing nations. This is why the concept of secession was built into our Founding documents in the first place. Not to preserve the Union, but to preserve states' rights.

Secession was (and still is) perfectly legal, which makes Lincoln's

---

290. Perkins, Vol. 2, pp. 598-601.
291. Zinn, p. 185.

War on the South illegal and everything that the North inflicted on the Southern people between 1861 and 1877 (the year "Reconstruction" ended) a war crime. Pro-North and anti-South movements disagree. But based on what? On Lincoln's own self-serving fabrications concerning American history, of course.

To put Lincoln, the "Civil War," and the Confederacy in their proper perspective, let us establish, once and for all, the legality of secession and the illegality of Lincoln's War.

THE TRUTH ABOUT SECESSION

THE UNITED STATES OF AMERICA, what many early Americans and foreigners revealingly called "the Confederate States of America,"[292] is the literal offspring of secession: born in the cauldron of discontent, she was forged on the anvil of separation from the Mother Country (Britain), an act of political withdrawal (the American Revolutionary War) without which she would not exist today.

This is why secession is one of the original rights of states, and it is why states' rights are assured and openly declared in the Declaration of Independence, penned by Southern hero and Founding Father, Thomas Jefferson. Indeed, the Declaration of Independence, issued by the U.S. Congress on July 4, 1776, could rightly be called a "states' rights document," for from beginning to end it speaks of almost nothing else, as the following excerpt illustrates:

> When, in the course of human events, it becomes necessary for one people to dissolve the political bands which have connected them with another . . . a decent respect to the opinions of mankind requires that they should declare the causes which impel them to the separation.
> We hold these truths to be self-evident, that all men are created equal, that they are endowed by their Creator with certain unalienable rights, that among these are life, liberty and the pursuit of happiness. That, to secure these rights, Governments are instituted among men, deriving their just powers from the consent of the governed; that, whenever any form of government becomes

---

292. Seabrook, C101, passim; Seabrook, AWAITBLA, passim.

destructive of these ends, it is the right of the people to alter or to abolish it, and to institute new government, laying its foundation on such principles, and organizing its powers in such form, as to them shall seem most likely to effect their safety and happiness.

. . . We, therefore, the representatives of the United States of America, in general Congress assembled . . . do, in the name, and by the authority of the good people of these colonies, solemnly publish and declare, that these united colonies are, and of right ought to be, free and independent states . . . and that as free and independent states, they have full power to levy war, conclude peace, contract alliances, establish commerce, and to do all other acts and things which independent states may of right do.[293]

It is true that the Declaration of Independence was meant as a document officially separating the American colonies from Britain. However, its focus on states' rights, and the concomitant right of secession, was carried forward into the formulation of America's first constitution: the Articles of Confederation—proposed by Congress November 15, 1777, and ratified March 1, 1781.

In the Articles of Confederation the central government was given explicit limited powers, while the states retained all other powers.[294] This, the essence of states' rights, is plainly laid out in Article 2:

Each state retains its sovereignty, freedom, and independence, and every power, jurisdiction, and right, which is not by this Confederation expressly delegated to the United States, in Congress assembled.[295]

For various reasons, the first American Confederacy (i.e., the original thirteen colonies) eventually found the Articles of Confederation wanting,[296] which led to the creation of the Constitution of the United

---

293. Calvert, Vol. 8, pp. 1-5.
294. Jensen, NN, p. 25; Lancaster and Plumb, p. 197.
295. F. Moore, Vol. 2, p. 204.
296. The problems that arose from the Articles of Confederation dealt mainly with the issue of the balance of power between the states and the central government. By the mid 1780s, many, mainly Federalists (the Liberals of the day), came to believe that the Articles had formulated a central government that was too weak. It would need more power, they argued. But how much more? It was this issue that was addressed at the Constitutional Convention (May 25 to September 17, 1787) in Philadelphia, Pennsylvania. Unfortunately for the conservative Confederalists (Antifederalists), instead of merely re-weighing the delicate balance of powers, the convention members decided to create an entirely new government. In the process, the original Confederal government was diluted and the Articles of Confederation were largely abandoned.

States of America—proposed by convention, September 17, 1787, and made effective March 4, 1789. Again the Founders did not neglect states' rights. In fact, they considered them so important that they were included as a separate amendment in the Bill of Rights (the first ten Amendments), which went into effect in 1791. The Tenth Amendment is, in its entirety, solely devoted to states' rights[297]:

> The powers not delegated to the United States by the Constitution, nor prohibited by it to the States, are reserved to the States respectively, or to the people.[298]

In other words—based on John Locke's view that government is created by the people merely to protect already existing rights[299]—the national government was only allowed to exercise those powers bestowed on it by the people. What are these powers? They are explicitly defined in Article 4, Section 4:

> The United States shall guarantee to every state in this Union a republican form of government, and shall protect each of them against invasion; and on application of the Legislature, or of the executive (when the Legislature cannot be convened), against domestic violence.[300]

As laid out here, in essence, the only power originally granted to the national government by the people was the power to protect them against the formation of state dictatorships, foreign invasion, and internal disturbances (e.g., riots). Outside of these three obligations (basically, the defense of lives, rights, and property), all sovereign power was to remain in the hands of the people.[301]

Confederalists resisted. Federalists pushed and, to a great degree, got their way. With the ratification of the new Constitution in 1789, the U.S. Confederacy became a Confederate Republic, a compromise on the original pure Confederacy. See Stephens, CV, Vol. 1, pp. 504-505. As a political entity, the U.S. Confederacy had lasted a mere eight years, from 1781 to 1789. However, because the new government contained various important aspects carried over from the Confederacy, Americans would continue to refer to the U.S. as "the Confederacy" for many generations to come. See Jensen, NN, pp. 348, 421, passim; Collier and Collier, passim; Seabrook, TCOTCSAE, passim.
297. Napolitano, pp. 25, 63.
298. Calvert, Vol. 8, p. 37.
299. Bronowski and Mazlish, p. 213.
300. Calvert, Vol. 8, p. 33.
301. Findlay and Findlay, pp. 168-169. See also, pp. 215-217.

President James Madison put it this way:

> The powers delegated by the proposed constitution to the Federal Government are few and defined; those which are to remain in the State governments are numerous and indefinite; the former will be exercised principally on external objects, as war, peace, negotiation, and foreign commerce—with which last the powers of taxation will, for the most part, be connected. The powers reserved to the several States, will extend to all the objects which, in the ordinary course of affairs, concern the lives, liberties, and properties of the people, and the internal order, improvement, and prosperity of the State.[302]

In his First Inaugural Address, March 4, 1801, President Thomas Jefferson, spoke plainly about the states' right of secession:

> If there be any among us who would wish to dissolve the Union or to change its republican form, let them stand undisturbed as monuments of the safety with which error of opinion may be tolerated where reason is left free to combat it.[303]

In 1839, President John Quincy Adams, though an anti-Jeffersonian Federalist, gave a passionate speech at the fiftieth anniversary celebration of George Washington's inauguration. According to Adams:

> To the people alone is then reserved, as well the *dissolving* as the constituent power; and that power can be exercised by them only under the tie of conscience, binding them to the retributive justice of heaven. With these qualifications, we may admit the same right to be vested in the people of every State in the Union, with reference to the general government, which was exercised by the people of the United colonies with reference to the supreme head of the British Empire, of which they formed a part; and, under these limitations, have the people of each State in the Union a right to secede from the Confederated Union itself. Thus stands the right. But the indissoluble link of union between the people of the several States of this confederated nation is, after all, not in the right, but in the heart. If the day should ever come (may heaven avert it!) when the affections of the people of these States shall be

---

302. Greeley, HSSER, p. 17.
303. E. P. Powell, p. 128.

alienated from each other—when the fraternal spirit shall give way to cold indifference, or collisions of interest shall fester into hatred—the bands of political association will not long hold together parties no longer attracted by the magnetism of conciliated interests and kindly sympathies; and far better will it be for the people of the disunited States to part in friendship from each other, than to be held together by constraint.[304]

On March 11, 1861, seventy years after the Bill of Rights went into effect, the Southern states—now a sovereign nation called the Confederate States of America (CSA)—issued its own national charter. The C.S. Constitution, closely patterned on the U.S. Constitution, began with the following preamble:

> We, the people of the Confederate States, each State acting in its sovereign and independent character, in order to form a permanent federal government, establish justice, insure domestic tranquillity, and secure the blessings of liberty to ourselves and our posterity—invoking the favor and guidance of Almighty God do ordain and establish this Constitution for the Confederate States of America.[305]

Then, in Article 6, the C.S. Constitution uses the exact wording of the U.S. Constitution in its proclamation of states' rights, only substituting the words United States with Confederate States:

> The powers not delegated to the Confederate States by the Constitution, nor prohibited by it to the States, are reserved to the States, respectively, or to the people thereof.[306]

Though at the time (1860) Lincoln was not among them, a truly stunning number of Northerners agreed with both the Confederate Constitution and the "Cotton States" (i.e., the South) that secession was indeed lawful, and that, under the circumstances, it was entirely appropriate. One of these was Yankee abolitionist and New York *Tribune* owner Horace Greeley,[307] who, in the November 10, 1860 issue, wrote:

---

304. McHenry, pp. xliii-xliv.
305. F. Moore, Vol. 2, p. 321.
306. F. Moore, Vol. 2, p. 327.
307. Nicolay and Hay, ALAH, Vol. 9, p. 184.

And now, if the Cotton States consider the value of the Union debatable, we maintain their perfect right to discuss it. Nay, we hold with Jefferson to the inalienable right of communities to alter or abolish forms of government that have become oppressive or injurious; and if the Cotton States shall decide that they can do better out of the Union than in it, we insist on letting them go in peace. The right to secede may be a revolutionary one, but it exists nevertheless; and we do not see how one party can have a right to do what another party has a right to prevent. We must ever resist the asserted right of any State to remain in the Union and nullify or defy the laws thereof; to withdraw from the Union is quite another matter. And whenever a considerable section of our Union shall deliberately resolve to go out, we shall resist all coercive measures designed to keep it in. We hope never to live in a republic, whereof one section is pinned to the residue with bayonets.[308]

As we will see momentarily, Lincoln's predecessor, President James Buchanan, also understood the legal nature of secession, citing Southern Founding Father President James Madison as confirmation of his views.

In short, based on the preceding, if the individual states of the U.S. were intended to be sovereign nation-states, as these documents clearly assert they were, and are, then the rights of both accession (joining) and secession (leaving) are legal.

As the original function of the federal government was merely "protection" (from invasion and domestic violence), it is obvious that all other powers were to remain with the states. This system, part of what was known as the separation of powers, was intentionally built into the Constitution to prevent the very type of tyranny that Lincoln would later institute in 1861.[309]

States' rights then, which include secession, were legal across the U.S.A. in the mid-1800s, for they are clearly elucidated in the Declaration of Independence, the Articles of Confederation, and the United States Constitution. These rights rest, not on the authority of the national government, but on the authority derived from the will of the people, as noted in the Constitutions's Preamble and in Article 7.[310]

---

308. A. C. Gordon, p. 111.
309. Spaeth and Smith, p. 12.
310. Spaeth and Smith, p. 12.

While these facts were purposefully distorted by Lincoln for political gain, before 1861 the right of secession was once so well understood and accepted by all Americans that it was taught for years at New York's West Point Military Academy—by Northerners.[311] The textbook used, *A View of the Constitution of the United States of America*, was penned in 1829 by William Rawle, a Yankee appointed by President George Washington as U.S. District Attorney for Pennsylvania. In fact, many of both the North's and the South's future "Civil War" officers were taught Constitutional law, and the right of secession, from this very book. In a letter to his wife, one of these officers, Confederate General George E. Pickett, wrote:

> I, of course, have always strenuously opposed disunion, not as doubting the right of secession, which was taught in our textbook at West Point, but as gravely questioning its expediency.[312]

Rawle's statements, such as the following, were memorized by thousands of Northern and Southern military men like Pickett, and, handed down from generation to generation as an American tradition, were thus "mutually understood." For a state, Rawle wrote in his textbook, to withdraw from the Union

> is a solemn, serious act. Whenever it may appear expedient to the people of a state, it must be manifested in a direct and unequivocal manner. *If* it is ever done indirectly, the people must refuse to elect representatives, as well as to suffer their legislature to re-appoint senators.
> . . . But without plain, decisive measures of this nature, proceeding from the only legitimate source, the people, the United States cannot consider their legislative powers over such states suspended, nor their executive or judicial powers any way impaired . . .
> . . . This right [of secession] must be considered as an ingredient in the original composition of the general government, which, though not expressed, was mutually understood . . .
> . . . The states, then, may wholly withdraw from the

---

311. Ashe, pp. 6, 53, 63, 75; Woods, p. 64.
312. G. E. Pickett, p. 34.

Union . . .[313]

In 1803, Southern abolitionist, lawyer, and judge, St. George Tucker, gave perhaps the most concisely accurate interpretation of the constitutional right of secession:

> The Constitution of the United States, then, being that instrument by which the Federal Government hath been created, its powers defined and limited, and the duties and functions of its several departments prescribed, the Government, thus established, may be pronounced to be a Confederate Republic, composed of several Independent and Sovereign Democratic States, united for their common defence and security against foreign Nations, and for the purposes of harmony and mutual intercourse between each other; each State retaining an entire liberty of exercising, as it thinks proper, all those parts of its Sovereignty which are not mentioned in the Constitution, or Act of Union, as parts that ought to be exercised in common.
>
> In becoming a member of the Federal Alliance, established between the American States by the Articles of Confederation, she expressly retained her Sovereignty and Independence. The constraints, put upon the exercise of that Sovereignty by those Articles, did not destroy its existence.
>
> The Federal Government, then, appears to be the organ through which the united Republics communicate with foreign Nations, and with each other. Their submission to its operation is voluntary; its councils, its engagements, its authority, are theirs, modified and united. Its Sovereignty is an emanation from theirs, not a flame, in which they have been consumed, nor a vortex, in which they are swallowed up. Each is still a perfect State, still Sovereign, still independent, and still capable, should the occasion require, to resume the exercise of its functions, as such, in the most unlimited extent.
>
> But, until the time shall arrive, when the occasion requires a resumption of the rights of Sovereignty by the several States (and far be that period removed, when it shall happen), the exercise of the rights of Sovereignty by the States, individually, is wholly suspended or discontinued in the cases before mentioned; nor can that suspension ever be removed, so long as the present Constitution remains unchanged, but by the dissolution of the bonds of union; an event which no good citizen can wish, and

---

313. Rawle, pp. 296, 297, 305.

which no good or wise administration will ever hazard.[314]

Lincoln apparently never read any of Tucker's writings; or if he did, he disregarded them because they did not conform to his political views and agenda. In 1911, Confederate Captain Samuel A. Ashe, of Raleigh, North Carolina—the "last surviving commissioned officer of the Confederate States Army"—commented on the Illinois rail-splitter's level of knowledge pertaining to American history:

> . . . Lincoln says that no state ever was a state out of the Union; and that the Union was made in 1774. All untrue! He did not know what he was talking about![315]

The depth of Lincoln's ignorance pertaining to secession is highlighted by the fact that even many foreigners had a far better grasp of the Founding documents than he did. In his two-volume book, *Democracy in America*, for instance, published consecutively in 1835 and 1840, French aristocrat, Alexis de Tocqueville, displayed a clear understanding of the legal right of secession in America:

> The [American] Union was formed by the voluntary agreement of States; and, in uniting together, they have not forfeited their nationality, nor have they been reduced to the condition of one and the same people. If one of the States chose to withdraw its name from the contract, it would be difficult to disprove its right of doing so; and the Federal Government would have no means of maintaining its claims directly either by force or by right.[316]

As some have argued, it is true that, despite the inclusion of the Tenth Amendment, the Constitution of the United States does not refer directly to the right of secession. At the same time, however, it should be pointed out that it makes no mention of any governmental power to prohibit it.

The question is, why did the Founders not speak clearly about secession in the Constitution? Because they took this very important right

---

314. Stephens, CV, Vol. 1, pp. 504-505.
315. Ashe, p. 54.
316. Tocqueville, Vol. 2, p. 426.

so for granted that they did not feel it was necessary. As Rawle said, "though not expressed, [it] was mutually understood."[317] Actually, up until 1865, secession was the most frequently discussed political issue in both the United States and the Confederate States.[318] Thus to both the Framers and the general populace, it was just another common law that was universally recognized and accepted by every American citizen.

In 1840 Abel Parker Upshur (1790-1844), a Virginia judge, lawyer, politician, and both the secretary of the navy and secretary of state under U.S. President John Tyler, wrote the following concerning secession:

> But whether this check be the best or the worst in its nature, it is at least one which our system allows. It is not found *within* the Constitution but exists independent of it. As that Constitution was formed by sovereign States, they alone are authorized, whenever the question arises between them and their common government, to determine, in the last resort, what powers they intended to confer on it. This is an inseparable incident of sovereignty; a right which belongs to the States, simply because they have never surrendered it to any other power. But to render this right available for any good purpose, it is indispensably necessary to maintain the States in their proper position. If their people suffer them to sink into the insignificance of mere municipal corporations, it will be vain to invoke their protection against the gigantic power of the federal government. This is the point to which the vigilance of the people should be chiefly directed. Their highest interest is at home; their palladium is their own State governments. They ought to know that they can look nowhere else with perfect assurance of safety and protection. Let them then maintain those governments, not only in their rights, but in their dignity and influence. Make it the interest of their people to serve them; an interest strong enough to resist all the temptations of federal office and patronage. Then alone will their voice be heard with respect at Washington; then alone will their interposition avail to protect their own people against the usurpations of the great central power. It is vain to hope that the federative principle of our government can be preserved, or that any thing can prevent it from running into the absolutism of consolidation, if we suffer the rights of the States to be filched away, and their dignity and influence to

---

317. Rawle, p. 296.
318. Smelser, DR, p. 78.

be lost, through our carelessness or neglect.[319]

For such reasons alone, it is apparent to all thinking people that secession was legal in 1860, and that it remains a fundamental right of the fifty states to this day.

Still, no matter how we choose to interpret the Constitution, it is patently obvious what the Founders' intentions were concerning this issue 225 years ago. In June 1816, the man who authored the Declaration of Independence, now former President Thomas Jefferson, wrote a letter to William Crawford that read in part:

> If any state in the Union will declare that it prefers separation to a continuance in the Union, I have no hesitation in saying, 'Let us separate.'[320]

President Jefferson Davis, named after Thomas Jefferson, and an adept student of the U.S. Constitution, noted that in addition to the Tenth Amendment, several state Constitutions openly refer to the right of secession. Virginia's Constitution, for example, affirms that:

> the powers granted under the [U.S.] Constitution, being derived from the people of the United States, may be resumed by them, whensoever the same shall be perverted to their injury or oppression, and that every power not granted thereby remains with them and at their will.[321]

The Constitutions of New York and Rhode Island also include clauses regarding secession, stating that

> the powers of government may be resumed by the people whenever it shall become necessary to their happiness.[322]

As Davis points out in his brilliant pro-South book, *The Rise and Fall of the Confederate Government*:

---

319. Upshur, p. 131.
320. Randolph, p. 284.
321. J. Davis, RFCG, Vol. 1, p. 173.
322. J. Davis, RFCG, Vol. 2, p. 623.

By inserting these declarations in their ordinances, Virginia, New York, and Rhode Island formally, officially, and permanently declared their interpretation of the [U.S.] Constitution as recognizing the right of secession by the resumption of their grants. By accepting the ratifications with this declaration incorporated, the other states as formally accepted the principle which it asserted.[323]

When, beginning in 1860, the South began acting on this principal, of legal, peaceful "separation" and the resumption of "the powers of government," it was derogatorily called a "rebellion" by Lincoln, as if it were a great political sin.[324] However, here is what Thomas Jefferson, writing from Paris, France, to James Madison on January 30, 1787, said on this subject:

> The spirit of resistance to government is so valuable on certain occasions, that I wish it always to be kept alive. It will often be exercised when wrong, but better so than not to be exercised at all. I like a little rebellion now and then. It is [cleansing,] like a storm in the atmosphere.[325]

After decades of interference from the Northern states, the South finally decided to exercise her Constitutional right to foment "a little rebellion," a Jeffersonian act of secession that was both correct and legal according to every important, official document created by the U.S. government up to that time. Again, let us recall President Jefferson's words from his First Inaugural Address:

> If there be any among us who would wish to dissolve this union or to change its republican form, let them stand undisturbed as monuments of the safety with which error of opinion may be tolerated where reason is left free to combat it.[326]

If any states want to secede, Jefferson noted further:

> It is the elder and the younger son differing. God bless them both,

---

323. J. Davis, RFCG, Vol. 1, p. 173.
324. Nicolay and Hay, ALCW, Vol. 2, p. 60.
325. Forman, p. 354.
326. Foley, p. 894.

and keep them in the union, if it be for their good, but separate them, if it be better.[327]

It was from these very ideas that America's first and second Confederacies were created: the former, as we have seen, in 1776, to "throw off" the despotic government of Britain's King George; the latter, in 1861, to "throw off" the despotic government of America's "King Abraham."

In both cases, the Founders' intention was to form a government in which the Union was subservient to the individual states. In 1776 this succeeded because the colonies, which were considered individual nation-states[328]—a loose union of sovereign and independent "little republics," as Jefferson styled them,[329] or "distinct nations," as Jay referred to them[330]—did indeed create the Union. This is why, in 1781, Jefferson spoke of Virginia as "but one of thirteen nations, who have agreed to act and speak together."[331] It is because of this concept, state sovereignty, that there *cannot* be a Union without states. And it is why there *can* be states without a Union, contrary to what Lincoln believed and preached.

This is also why, during the First American War of Independence, the American colonies did not secede from Britain as a unified body. While independence was declared jointly, each state, a nation in its own right, declared itself independent individually.[332] Hence, when King George III signed an agreement recognizing the nation-states known as the "original thirteen colonies" as sovereign, he addressed each one individually, by name.[333] In Article 1 of the *Treaty With Great Britain*, we find the following passage:

> His Britannic Majesty acknowledges the said United States, viz., New Hampshire, Massachusetts Bay, Rhode Island and Providence Plantations, Connecticut, New York, New Jersey, Pennsylvania, Delaware, Maryland, Virginia, North Carolina, South Carolina, and Georgia, to be free, sovereign and independent States; that he

---

327. Foley, p. 513.
328. Collier and Collier, p. 4.
329. Foley, pp. 212, 797.
330. Hamilton, Madison, and Jay, p. 21.
331. H. A. Washington, p. 174.
332. Burns and Peltason, p. 41.
333. Ashe, pp. 17, 25.

treats with them as such, and for himself, his heirs and successors, relinquishes all claims to the Government, propriety and territorial rights of the same, and every part thereof.[334]

That the original thirteen American colonies began life as separate nation-states is the same reason early Americans pledged their allegiance to their native states rather than to the U.S.[335] Hence the majority of Southerners, like Robert E. Lee, literally referred to their home states as "my country." Though admitting that he was a citizen of the United States, Jefferson Davis observed that "my allegiance is first due to the State I represent."[336] Thomas Jefferson too called Virginia "my country."[337] John Randolph of Virginia took note of the North's desire to exact allegiance from the Southern states, saying:

> When I speak of my country, I mean the Commonwealth of Virginia. I was born in allegiance to [the English King] George III. . . . My ancestors threw off the oppressive yoke of the mother country, but they never made me subject to New England in matters spiritual or temporal; neither do I mean to become so voluntarily.[338]

Thus in the Old South one would refer to himself as a Tennessean, a South Carolinian, a Floridian, a Virginian, or a Texan, while a Northerner would refer to himself as a "citizen of the United States."[339]

If any doubts remain as to these facts, we need only examine the last paragraph of the Declaration of Independence. In breaking their ties with Great Britain, the leaders of the thirteen American colonies repeatedly refer to themselves as "Free and Independent States," each endowed with all the powers of a sovereign nation:

> We, therefore, the Representatives of the United States of

---

334. Rouse, pp. 78-79.
335. Rosenbaum and Brinkley, s.v. "Antifederalists."
336. Rowland, Vol. 1, p. 509.
337. See e.g., Foley, pp. 399, 900.
338. Garland, p. 103.
339. Henry, SC, p. 16. The question of loyalty to state or nation was debated as early as 1787, at the Constitutional Convention in Philadelphia. Collier and Collier, p. 264. While most Northerners pledged their allegiance to the nation, well into the 1800s most Southerners chose to give their allegiance to their home states. This tradition lives on across Dixie to this day.

America, in General Congress, Assembled, appealing to the Supreme Judge of the world for the rectitude of our intentions, do, in the Name, and by Authority of the good People of these Colonies, solemnly publish and declare, That these united Colonies are, and of Right ought to be Free and Independent States, that they are Absolved from all Allegiance to the British Crown, and that all political connection between them and the State of Great Britain, is and ought to be totally dissolved; and that as Free and Independent States, they have full Power to levy War, conclude Peace, contract Alliances, establish Commerce, and to do all other Acts and Things which Independent States may of right do. And for the support of this Declaration, with a firm reliance on the protection of Divine Providence, we mutually pledge to each other our Lives, our Fortunes, and our sacred Honor.[340]

Beneath these words, at the bottom of the Declaration of Independence, each nation-state was itemized, along with the signers from that particular colony. Note that the states were listed, not as a single nationalized people, as the "United States of America," but separately, as individual political bodies—each an autonomous nation unto itself. Here is the actual text showing the names of the signatories along with their home-countries (states):

> New Hampshire: Josiah Bartlett, William Whipple, Matthew Thornton
> Massachusetts: John Hancock, Samuel Adams, John Adams, Robert Treat Paine, Elbridge Gerry
> Rhode Island: Stephen Hopkins, William Ellery
> Connecticut: Roger Sherman, Samuel Huntington, William Williams, Oliver Wolcott
> New York: William Floyd, Philip Livingston, Francis Lewis, Lewis Morris
> New Jersey: Richard Stockton, John Witherspoon, Francis Hopkinson, John Hart, Abraham Clark
> Pennsylvania: Robert Morris, Benjamin Rush, Benjamin Franklin, John Morton, George Clymer, James Smith, George Taylor, James Wilson, George Ross
> Delaware: Caesar Rodney, George Read, Thomas McKean
> Maryland: Samuel Chase, William Paca, Thomas Stone, Charles Carroll of Carrollton

---

340. Rouse, p. 56.

Virginia: George Wythe, Richard Henry Lee, Thomas Jefferson, Benjamin Harrison, Thomas Nelson, Jr., Francis Lightfoot Lee, Carter Braxton
North Carolina: William Hooper, Joseph Hewes, John Penn
South Carolina: Edward Rutledge, Thomas Heyward, Jr., Thomas Lynch, Jr., Arthur Middleton
Georgia: Button Gwinnett, Lyman Hall, George Walton[341]

From such documents the conclusion is clear. The United States of America began as "the Confederate States of America": a confederation of thirteen individual nations with a weak central government, a Union that was subordinate to those states. After the Constitutional Convention of 1787, the Articles of Confederation were replaced by the U.S. Constitution. But our government remained a Confederate Republic, and each of the states retained all of the rights originally accorded to them as individual nation-states by the Declaration of Independence, the Articles of Confederation, the U.S. Constitution, and finally the Bill of Rights.[342]

In one of the more bizarre incidents in American history, in 1861 Lincoln dismissed all of this, as if none of it were true or had ever even existed. Since his erroneous thinking on this topic helped launch the War, let us examine it in more detail for a moment.

We have established that the U.S. began as a Confederacy, with the Union being inferior to the states. As mentioned, this obviously means that the Union *could not* exist without the states, but that the states *could* exist without the Union. Our nation at this time was seen then, not as the United States, but rather as the "States United,"[343] a vitally important distinction.

Lincoln reversed all of this by insisting, impossibly, that "the Union created the states," that they were indeed the "*United* States,"[344] even declaring, as he did in the Gettysburg Address, that:

> Four score and seven years ago our fathers brought forth on this continent, a new nation . . .[345]

---

341. Rouse, pp. 56-58.
342. Seabrook, C101, passim. For a full discussion of Southern secession see my book, AWAITBLA.
343. Henry, SC, pp. 12-13.
344. Ashe, p. 21.
345. Rouse, p. 320.

But by declaring its independence from Britain in 1776 a "new nation" was not "brought forth." What was eventually created was a confederacy made up of thirteen sovereign nations (today commonly referred to as colonies, or states).

Despite these facts, from his own twisted mind Lincoln extrapolated that there could be no states without the Union, and that the Union was meant to be "perpetual." Here, on March 4, 1861, is how he phrased these silly, confused, and ultimately dangerous ideas in his First Inaugural Address:

> I hold that, in contemplation of universal law, and of the Constitution, the Union of these States is perpetual. Perpetuity is implied, if not expressed, in the fundamental law of all national governments. It is safe to assert that no government proper ever had a provision in its organic law for its own termination. Continue to execute all the express provisions of our national Constitution, and the Union will endure forever—it being impossible to destroy it, except by some action not provided for in the instrument itself.
>
> Again, if the United States be not a government proper, but an association of States in the nature of contract merely, can it, as a contract, be peaceably unmade, by less than all the parties who made it? One party to a contract may violate it—break it, so to speak; but does it not require all to lawfully rescind it?
>
> Descending from these general principles, we find the proposition that, in legal contemplation, the Union is perpetual, confirmed by the history of the Union itself. The Union is much older than the Constitution. It was formed in fact by the Articles of Association in 1774. It was matured and continued by the Declaration of Independence in 1776. It was further matured, and the faith of all the then thirteen States expressly plighted and engaged that it should be perpetual, by the Articles of Confederation in 1778. And, finally, in 1787, one of the declared objects for ordaining and establishing the Constitution, was '*to form a more perfect Union.*'
>
> But if the destruction of the Union, by one, or by a part only, of the States, be lawfully possible, the Union is *less* perfect than before, the Constitution having lost the vital element of perpetuity.
>
> It follows, from these views, that no State, upon its own mere motion, can lawfully get out of the Union; that *resolves* and *ordinances* to that effect are legally void, and that acts of violence, within any State or States, against the authority of the United

> States, are insurrectionary or revolutionary, according to circumstances.
>
> I, therefore, consider that, in view of the Constitution and the laws, the Union is unbroken, and, to the extent of my ability, I shall take care, as the Constitution itself expressly enjoins upon me, that the laws of the Union be faithfully executed in all the States.[346]

The ignorance and arrogance behind these comments would not be so appalling if they had come from an illiterate, 19th-Century common laborer. What makes them truly shocking is that they came from an intelligent and successful lawyer, a man who should have known better; the man who became our sixteenth president.

Edward A. Pollard artfully expressed the conservative South's reaction to this liberal nonsense:

> In his message, Mr. Lincoln announced a great political discovery. It was that all former statesmen of America had lived, and written, and labored under a great delusion: that the States, instead of having created the Union, were its *creatures*; that they obtained their sovereignty and independence from it, and never possessed either until the Convention of 1787. This singular doctrine of consolidation was the natural preface to a series of measures to strengthen the Government, to enlarge the Executive power, and to conduct the war with new decision, and on a most unexpected scale of magnitude.[347]

Pollard was entirely correct. Lincoln went on to use his fictitious ideas to help justify crushing personal liberties across the country, both South and North, severely damaging civil rights, as John C. Breckinridge of Kentucky pointed out:

> The atrocious doctrine is announced by the President, and acted upon, that the States derive their power from the Federal Government, and may be suppressed on any pretence of military necessity. Everywhere the civil has given way to the military power.[348]

---

346. E. McPherson, PHUSAGR, p. 106.
347. Pollard, LC, p. 175.
348. Pollard, LC, p. 181.

Lincoln's personal beliefs, that the states could not exist without the Union and that the Union was meant to be "perpetual," must certainly rank as two of the most preposterous and historically inaccurate ideas ever put forth. Why? Because as any first-year student of American history knows, the Union did not exist prior to the states. It only came afterward as a result of its creation by those states, at which point the thirteen original colonies legally and voluntary joined it.

Why then, some counter, did the Founding Fathers begin the Preamble of the U.S. Constitution with the words "We the people of the United States . . ." if they did not intend to create a nation of one people?

The answer is quite simple: these were not the original opening words of the Preamble.[349] In his *Notes of the Debates in the Federal Convention*, James Madison reveals the introductory text of the Preamble as it was written (about August 1787) in the first draft of the U.S. Constitution. It read:

> We, the people of the States of New Hampshire, Massachusetts, Rhode-Island and Providence Plantations, Connecticut, New York, New Jersey, Pennsylvania, Delaware, Maryland, Virginia, North Carolina, South Carolina, and Georgia, do ordain, declare and establish, the following Constitution, for the government of ourselves and our posterity.[350]

In other words, in the earliest rough outline of the Constitution, the thirteen original nation-states were listed individually.

Why then were these dropped and replaced with the phrase "We the people"? This question was aptly answered in 1876 by lawyer, author, and legal scholar William O. Bateman:

> The change of this expression of the organic will, to that of 'We, the people of the United States,' etc., was proposed by a sub-committee on *style*. And wherefore? Because, it could not be foreknown, which of the States would accept and ratify the new constitution. If any *nine* of them should do so, they, at all events, *according to the last article of the instrument*, would thence become the *United States* of America. Hence the committee on style revised the language of the convention, and substituted 'the United States,' in

---
349. See Stonebraker, pp. 67-68.
350. J. B. Scott, pp. 84-85. See also pp. 86-87.

place of 'the States of New Hampshire, Massachusetts, Rhode Island,' etc.[351]

The change in wording then came because of a simple timing issue.

With that problem settled, it is plain to see that the right to voluntarily enter a union gives one the right to voluntarily leave a union as well. This idea, being the very marrow of the rights of both accession and secession, decimates Lincoln's conviction that the Union, and by extension the Constitution, were meant to be "perpetual."

Eighty years earlier, in his pamphlet *Notes on the State of Virginia* (authored during the years 1781 and 1782), Thomas Jefferson wrote of the formation of America's first government by the colonies, noting that

> . . . they organized the government by the ordinance entitled a Constitution . . . . it does not say, that it shall be perpetual; that it shall be unalterable . . .[352]

Jefferson goes on to refute those who had wrongly declared that both the Constitution and the Union were meant to be everlasting:

> Not only the silence of the instrument is a proof they [i.e., the legislatures] thought it would be alterable, but their own practice also: for this very convention, meeting as a House of Delegates in General Assembly with the new Senate in the autumn of that year, passed acts of assembly in contradiction to their ordinance of government; and every assembly from that time to this has done the same. I am safe therefore in the position, that the constitution itself is alterable by the ordinary legislature. Though this opinion seems founded on the first elements of common sense, yet is the contrary maintained by some persons: 1. Because, say they, the conventions were vested with every power necessary to make effectual opposition to Great-Britain. But to complete this argument, they must go on, and say further, that effectual opposition could not be made to Great-Britain, without establishing a form of government perpetual and unalterable by the legislature; which is not true. An opposition which at some time or other was to come to an end, could not need a perpetual institution to carry it on: and a government, amendable as its defects should be

---

351. Bateman, p. 179.
352. Bergh, Vol. 1, p. 167.

discovered, was as likely to make effectual resistance, as one which should be unalterably wrong. Besides, the assemblies were as much vested with all powers requisite for resistance as the conventions were. If therefore these powers included that of modelling the form of government in the one case, they did so in the other. The assemblies then as well as the conventions may model the government; that is, they may alter the ordinance of government.[353]

From this it is evident that, because of the right of secession, the Union was not, is not, and could not be perpetual. The same is true of the original Constitution: because of the right of legislative amendments, it was not and is not meant to be perpetual. And the Constitution now possesses twenty-seven Amendments added to it since its creation to prove it.[354] The only thing that *was* meant to be perpetual was the sovereignty of the states, the very thing that Lincoln despised, and tried to destroy.

---

353. Bergh, Vol. 1, pp. 167-168.
354. The twenty-seven amendments to the Constitution are: (Bill of Rights, first ten Amendments) First Amendment: freedom of religion, press, expression, assembly, petition (1791); Second Amendment: right to bear arms (1791); Third Amendment: quartering of soldiers (1791); Fourth Amendment: search and seizure (1791); Fifth Amendment: grand jury, double jeopardy, self-incrimination, due process (1791); Sixth Amendment: criminal prosecutions, jury trial, right to confront and to counsel (1791); Seventh Amendment: common law suits, trial by jury in civil cases (1791); Eighth Amendment: excessive bail or fines, cruel and unusual punishment (1791); Ninth Amendment: non-enumerated rights, construction of Constitution (1791); Tenth Amendment: states' rights (rights reserved to states), i.e., powers of the states and people (1791); Eleventh Amendment: suits against a state, judicial limits (1795); Twelfth Amendment: election of president and vice president (1804); Thirteenth Amendment: abolition of slavery (1865); Fourteenth Amendment: privileges and immunities, due process, equal protection, apportionment of representatives, Civil War disqualification and debt (1868); Fifteenth Amendment: rights not to be denied on account of race (1870); Sixteenth Amendment: status of income tax clarified (1913); Seventeenth Amendment: senators elected by popular vote (1913); Eighteenth Amendment: Prohibition, liquor abolished (1919); Nineteenth Amendment: women given the vote (1920); Twentieth Amendment: presidential term and succession (1933); Twenty-First Amendment: Eighteenth Amendment repealed (1933); Twenty-Second Amendment: two-term limit on president (1951); Twenty-Third Amendment: presidential vote for District of Columbia (1961); Twenty-Fourth Amendment: poll taxes barred (1964); Twenty-Fifth Amendment: presidential disability and succession (1967); Twenty-Sixth Amendment: voting age set to eighteen years (1971); Twenty-Seventh Amendment: compensation of members of Congress (1992). See K. L. Hall, s.v. "Constitutional Amendments."

Trickery at Fort Sumter & the Call to Arms

LINCOLN LIKED TO PRETEND THAT the Southern states were the first to desire secession from the Union, an act of "rebellion" for which he felt they should be punished. But the well-read politician knew full well that long before the formation of the Southern Confederacy in 1861, the New England states had been seriously discussing the idea, and were in fact the first to do so.

Yankee secessionist sentiment was born of infuriation over several legislative actions by then U.S. President Thomas Jefferson (who served from 1801 to 1809). These included the Louisiana Purchase (1803), the Embargo Act—which placed restrictions on Yankee merchants and exporters (1807), and the War of 1812 (caused, in part, by the embargo). These actions, and others that were felt to negatively impact the North, launched the fourteen-year, New England Secession Movement, led by Massachusetts Senator Timothy Pickering, George Washington's former adjutant general,[355] and later President John Adams' secretary of state.[356]

In a March 4, 1804, letter to fellow New Englander Rufus King (like most other Yankees, both a Federalist and an advocate of black colonization),[357] Jefferson-hating Pickering discussed the proposed secession plan of the Northern states:

---

355. C. Johnson, pp. 115-117.
356. For plotting with Alexander Hamilton against administration policy, Pickering was dismissed by Adams, the first and only secretary of state to be terminated in this manner. DeGregorio, s.v. "John Adams" (p. 28).
357. DeGregorio, s.v. "James Monroe" (p. 78).

> I am disgusted with the men who now rule us and with their measures. At some manifestations of their malignancy I am shocked. . . . I am therefore ready to say 'come out from among them and be ye separate.' . . . Were New York detached (as under his [Aaron Burr's] administration it would be) from the Virginian influence, the whole Union would be benefitted. [President] Jefferson would then be forced to observe some caution and forbearance in his measures. And, if a separation should be deemed proper, the five New England States, New York, and New Jersey would naturally be united. Among those seven States, there is a sufficient congeniality of character to authorize the expectation of practicable harmony and a permanent union, New York the centre. Without a separation, can those States ever rid themselves of negro Presidents and negro Congresses, and regain their just weight in the political balance? . . . As population is *in fact* no rule of taxation, the negro representation ought to be given up. If refused, it would be a strong ground of separation; tho' perhaps an earlier occasion may occur to declare it.[358]

The brewing issue finally culminated in the Hartford Convention, a secession conference held in December 1814 and January 1815.[359] Here, twenty-six Federalist delegates met secretly to not only propose amendments that would lessen the influence of the South,[360] but to discuss leaving the Union in order to form a new and separate confederacy, the "New England Confederacy," as they called it, one they hoped would eventually include New York, Pennsylvania, and even Nova Scotia.[361]

A furious, anti-South Pickering—who once called Southern hero Thomas Jefferson a "revolutionary monster," and accused him of cruelty, cowardice, turpitude, corruption, and baseness[362]—spoke for the convention's members:

> I will rather anticipate a new Confederacy, exempt from the corrupt and corrupting influence of the aristocratic Democrats of the South. There will be—and our children at farthest will see it—a separation. The white and black population will mark the boundary. The British Provinces, even with the assent of Britain,

---

358. C. King, Vol. 4, pp. 364-366.
359. C. Adams, p. 15.
360. DeGregorio, s.v. "James Madison" (p. 66).
361. Smelser, DR, p. 78.
362. H. Adams, p. 351.

will become members of the Northern confederacy. A continued tyranny of the present ruling sect will precipitate that event.[363]

With congressional ratification of the Treaty of Ghent on February 15, 1815, the War of 1812 soon came to an end.[364] New England then decided against secession, though only for economic reasons. The important point, however, is that had she desired to do so, New England could have seceded legally and peacefully—and unlike Lincoln's violent, militaristic reaction to Southern secession, the South would not have stood in New England's way.[365] Why?

There was never any doubt among Americans at the time that the individual states were independent nations, and that secession was therefore a constitutional right, as Southern President Woodrow Wilson would later confirm in his writings.[366] Indeed, this is why Lincoln's predecessor, President James Buchanan, allowed the first seven Southern states to leave the Union in peace in early 1861.[367] As Jefferson Davis noted of America's fifteenth president:

> Like all who had intelligently and impartially studied the history of the formation of the Constitution, he held that the federal government had no rightful power to coerce a state.[368]

Davis was referring to Buchanan's final annual message, which he gave on December 4, 1860, just before vacating his office to Lincoln. Unfortunately, the latter did not possess the former's firm knowledge of constitutional history, as is evident from the following excerpt from Buchanan's speech. Note that he refers to the U.S. as "the Confederacy" only five months before Lincoln's War:

> The question, fairly stated, is: Has the Constitution delegated to Congress the power to coerce a State into submission which is attempting to withdraw or has actually withdrawn from the

---

363. H. Adams, p. 338.
364. See Website: www.nps.gov/jela/the-treaty-of-ghent.htm.
365. During America's early history, in fact, Massachusetts threatened to secede from the Union on four different occasions, all without any violent resistance from any other state. Pollard, LC, p. 85.
366. DeGregorio, s.v. "Woodrow Wilson" (p. 411).
367. Pollard, LC, p. 96.
368. J. Davis, RFCG, Vol. 1, p. 54.

Confederacy? If answered in the affirmative, it must be on the principle that the power has been conferred upon Congress to declare and to make war against a State. After much serious reflection I have arrived at the conclusion that no such power has been delegated to Congress nor to any other department of the Federal Government. It is manifest, upon an inspection of the Constitution, that this is not among the specific and enumerated powers granted to Congress; and it is equally apparent that its exercise is not 'necessary and proper for carrying into execution' any one of these powers. So far from this power having been delegated to Congress, it was expressly refused by the Convention which framed the Constitution. It appears, from the proceedings of that body, that on the 31st May, 1787, the clause '*authorizing an exertion of the force of the whole against a delinquent State*' came up for consideration. Mr. Madison opposed it in a brief but powerful speech, from which I shall extract but a single sentence. He observed: 'The use of force against a State would look more like a declaration of war than an infliction of punishment, and would probably be considered by the party attacked as a dissolution of all previous compacts by which it might be bound.' Upon his motion the clause was unanimously postponed, and was never, I believe, again presented. Soon afterwards, on the 8th June, 1787, when incidentally adverting to the subject, he said: 'Any Government for the United States, formed on the supposed practicability of using force against the unconstitutional proceedings of the States, would prove as visionary and fallacious as the government of Congress,' evidently meaning the then existing Congress of the old Confederation.

Without descending to particulars, it may be safely asserted that the power to make war against a State is at variance with the whole spirit and intent of the Constitution. Suppose such a war should result in the conquest of a State, how are we to govern it afterwards? Shall we hold it as a province and govern it by despotic power? In the nature of things we could not, by physical force, control the will of the people, and compel them to elect Senators and Representatives to Congress, and to perform all the other duties depending upon their own volition, and required from the free citizens of a free State as a constituent member of the Confederacy.

But, if we possessed this power, would it be wise to exercise it under existing circumstances? The object would doubtless be to preserve the Union. War would not only present the most effectual means of destroying it, but would banish all hope of its peaceable reconstruction. Besides, in the fraternal conflict a vast amount of blood and treasure would be expended, rendering future reconciliation between the States impossible. In the meantime who can foretell what would be the sufferings and privations of the people during its existence?

The fact is, that our Union rests upon public opinion, and can never be cemented by the blood of its citizens shed in civil war. If it cannot live in the affections of the people, it must one day perish. Congress possesses many means of preserving it by conciliation; but the sword was not placed in their hand to preserve it by force.[369]

These brilliant words, spoken by a rank-and-file Northerner,[370] were words that every Southerner could truly appreciate, and hopes were high that when Lincoln—himself originally a Southerner—entered the White House, he would follow in Buchanan's footsteps.[371]

Secession is lawful, Lincoln himself once asserted. He even called it a "most sacred right." On January 12, 1848, in a speech before the U.S. House of Representatives, he said:

> Any people anywhere, being inclined and having the power, have the right to rise up, and shake off the existing government, and form a new one that suits them better. This is a most valuable, a most sacred right—a right which, we hope and believe, is to liberate the world. Nor is this right confined to cases in which the whole people of an existing government may choose to exercise it. Any portion of such people that can may revolutionize, and make their own of so much of the territory as they inhabit.[372]

When it was politically expedient to change his mind, Lincoln, of course, did just that.

As U.S. president thirteen years later, on July 4, 1861, in his "Message to Congress in Special Session," he called the new Southern Confederacy an "illegal organization,"[373] and the constitutional right of secession an "ingenious sophism," an "insidious debauching of the public

---

369. E. McPherson, PHUSAGR, pp. 49-50.
370. Buchanan was born in Pennsylvania.
371. On vacating the presidential chair for the last time, Buchanan told Lincoln: "My dear sir, if you are as happy on entering the White House as I on leaving it, you are a very happy man indeed." C. O'Brien, SLUSP, p. 83.
372. F. Moore, Vol. 7, p. 306.
373. Nicolay and Hay, ALCW, Vol. 2, p. 55.

mind," and a "sugar-coated invention" of the South.[374] Those who challenged these views were labeled "traitors" and "rebels." This is how Confederate soldiers got the epithet "Johnny Rebel," and how the name of Lincoln's War, "the War of Rebellion," came about. It is also why, after the War, Confederate officers were charged with "treason": for believing in, and acting on, the legal right of secession. Even the term Copperhead (meaning a Northerner who sympathized with the South) was anti-South: ridiculously and incorrectly, it likened such supporters to the deadly venomous snake of the same name.[375]

Semantics were just the start of Lincoln's premeditated plan to ignore, alter, and subvert the Constitution, then remake the South in the North's image (i.e., Northernize her), all for personal political gain. To achieve these goals, Lincoln would go on to commit a litany of crimes unlike anything the Western world had seen since the days of the ancient Roman emperors; men, as it turns out, with whom he had much in common.[376]

Such crimes would include everything from calling himself a "military hero" in the Black Hawk War ("I fought, bled, and came away," he fibbed to the House of Representatives on July 27, 1848)[377]—even though he actually never saw a single day of combat[378] or even a single Indian in that conflict,[379] to launching the largest and most bloody conflict on U.S. soil without congressional approval, violating Article 1, Section 8, Clause 11 of the U.S. Constitution, which states that only Congress can formally declare war.[380]

---

374. Nicolay and Hay, ALCW, Vol. 2, p. 61.
375. The height of irony is that while Lincoln referred to his critics as snakes, he was one himself. According to the ancient science of Chinese astrology, Lincoln was born under the sign of the "Snake." Chinese astrologers tell us that when angered, Snakes are fueled by a hatred that knows no bounds; yet they keep their antagonistic feelings well-hidden. Instead, using their devious calculating minds, they seek to totally destroy their enemies; but only when the time is just right. The Snake's vindictive spirit is second only to its lust for power, intrigue, and the limelight. Lau, pp. 119, 121. Besides being vengeful and power-hungry, Snakes are also known to be stealthy, secretive, stingy, jealous, possessive, stubborn, dishonest, lethargic, and procrastinating. At their worst, Snakes not only engage in bizarre and antisocial behavior, but they can also become criminals. Wu, p. 148. Whether one accepts Chinese astrology as valid or not, I know of no better description of our sixteenth president—as my book will show.
376. L. Johnson, pp. 123-128.
377. Nicolay and Hay, ALCW, Vol. 1, p. 142.
378. Woodworth, p. xi; Zinn, p. 129; Encyc. Brit., s.v. "Lincoln, Abraham"; Hendelson, s.v. "Lincoln, Abraham."
379. C. Johnson, pp. 119-120. Lincoln later "painfully" admitted that he was "not a military man." Nicolay and Hay, ALCW, Vol. 2, p. 218.
380. Findlay and Findlay, pp. 84-85.

Lincoln's nefarious mind was in evidence from the moment he was elected president on November 6, 1860. All available evidence points to the fact that he was determined to go to war against the South from that day forward, and that nothing would stand in his way. And he would use all means at his disposal, including engaging in any kind of criminal activity he felt was required.

As the days passed, a plan unfolded between Lincoln and several of his military officers; an outrageous lie so well kept that 150 years later it is still believed to be true by the majority of Americans.

The plot? To make it appear as if the South initiated the "Civil War"[381]—and so history has incorrectly recorded it.[382]

It all began on April 12, 1861, when Lincoln tricked the Confederacy into firing the first shot at Fort Sumter, South Carolina.[383] That day, the South, now an independent nation, was invaded by a foreign enemy (Fort Sumter clearly belonged to the C.S.A.: it is located on an island in Charleston Harbor, South Carolina, the first state to secede from the Union five months earlier on December 20, 1860). Lincoln sent a Federal ship to "reprovision" the Southern fort that was, by then, unlawfully occupied by Northern troops. This despite the facts that:

1) the Yankee soldiers stationed there did not actually need provisions[384] (for everyday "the people of Charleston sent to Sumter a boat load of food supplies, fresh meats, fowls, fruits, vegetables, etc.").[385]

2) three times Lincoln promised the Confederacy (through his secretary of state William H. Seward) that he would not resupply the fort.[386]

3) Lincoln had been sternly warned against reprovisioning the fort by both Southern leaders and his own cabinet members.[387]

---

381. W. B. Garrison, CWTFB, p. 101.
382. L. Johnson, pp. 279-280.
383. See Seabrook, TAHSR, pp. 627-633; C. Adams, pp. 202-203; Grissom, pp. 103, 108-109; Pollard, LC, p. 108.
384. Tilley, FHLO, pp. 38-47.
385. Meriwether, p. 263.
386. E. M. Thomas, p. 81; Pollard, LC, p. 108.
387. Henry, SC, p. 30; J. M. McPherson, ACW, p. 21.

As always, Lincoln ignored those who knew better. Instead of ordering his troops off the island, as he should have, he ordered the fake "reprovision"—complete with the arrival of an intimidating fleet of well-armed war ships and sailors he had no intention of using.[388] In 1867, six years later, Southern fire-eater Edward A. Pollard wrote of the situation in his extraordinary book, *The Lost Cause*:[389]

> The point of the [Northern] government was to devise some artifice for the relief of Fort Sumter, short of open military reinforcements, decided to be impracticable, and which would have the effect of inaugurating the war by a safe indirection and under a plausible and convenient pretence. The device was at last conceived.[390]

When Lincoln's "device" was unleashed, Dixie sincerely believed she had no choice but to defend herself. So she let loose her artillery on Sumter, at that moment completely unaware of the absolute guile and cunning of America's sixteenth president.

The fighting was so light that not a single Union or Rebel soldier was killed, let alone wounded, during the conflict.[391] Additionally, the ninety-man Yankee unit was not captured and held prisoner, but instead was permitted to simply walk out of the fort and go home.[392] Why? Because the South, having no interest in war, had not declared war.[393]

Yet, Lincoln used this insignificant skirmish to launch a massive invasion of the Confederacy, issuing, on April 15, 1861, a proclamation calling for 75,000 soldiers to invade and subdue the South. His public excuse for this madness was that the "rebellion" was "too powerful to be suppressed by the ordinary course of judicial proceedings . . ."[394] This

---

388. See Pollard, LC, p. 110.
389. Like all of Pollard's works, every Southern household should own a copy of *The Lost Cause*. Northerners especially would benefit tremendously from reading this book, one of the few complete histories of the "Civil War" written from the South's point of view. It is all the more valuable since Pollard lived through the conflict and even spent time in a Yankee prison.
390. Pollard, LC, p. 108.
391. Civil War Society, CWB, s.v. "Fort Sumter."
392. So magnanimous was the commanding Confederate officer at Sumter, General Pierre G. T. Beauregard, that not only were the surrendered Yankee soldiers allowed to salute the Union flag and march out of the fort to a band playing *Yankee Doodle*, but the Confederacy even provided a steamer to transport them to an awaiting U.S. ship. Tilley, FHLO, pp. 48-49. Lincoln never would have been, and never was, so generous with Southern soldiers.
393. C. Johnson, p. 151.
394. Nicolay and Hay, ALCW, Vol. 2, p. 34.

must rank as one of the most pitiful excuses for starting a full-scale war ever known.[395]

Not only that, it was an outright fabrication: even as Lincoln was uttering these words, the Confederacy was sending one peace commission after another to Washington, D.C., to try and prevent any bloodshed. Lincoln refused to see any of them, and often did not even acknowledge their presence or respond to their letters.[396] Instead, so badly did he want war that he finagled the South into firing the first shot at Sumter, then passed this falsehood onto the American public as fact. Again, Pollard writes:

> The battle of Sumter had been brought on by the Washington Government by a trick too dishonest and shallow to account for the immense display of sentiment in the North that ensued. The event afforded indeed to many politicians in the North a most flimsy and false excuse for loosing passions of hate against the South that had all along been festering in the concealment of their hearts.[397]

Even Lincoln's own authorized biographers, John G. Nicolay and John Hay, admitted that:

> When the President determined on war, and with the purpose of making it appear that the South was the aggressor, he took

---

395. Lincoln's preposterous request for troops went out to all states in both the Union and the Confederacy. All of the Southern states, of course, refused to oblige him. The governor of North Carolina, for instance, John Willis Ellis, telegraphed Lincoln's office the following reply: "Your dispatch is received, and, if genuine—which its extraordinary character leads me to doubt,—I have to say in reply that I regard the levy of troops made by the Administration, for the purpose of subjugating the States of the South, as in violation of the Constitution, and a usurpation of power. I can be no party to this wicked violation of the laws of the country, and to this war upon the liberties of a free people. You can get no troops from North Carolina." E. McPherson, PHUSAGR, p. 114. Similar, even less polite responses, were sent to Lincoln from the rest of the Southern governors. Governor Claiborne F. Jackson of Missouri sent Lincoln this curt reply: "Your requisition in my judgment is illegal, unconstitutional, and revolutionary, and, in its objects, inhuman and diabolical." Pollard, LC, pp. 121-122.
396. In fact, Lincoln did not meet with a single Confederate peace official until February 3, 1865, at Hampton Roads, Virginia. As he was well aware, by then his War was nearly over and the North was to be the victor. W. B. Garrison, CWTFB, p. 109. For Lincoln, the Hampton Roads Conference was what we would call today nothing more than a publicity stunt, one engineered to make the South look unreasonable and inflexible, the side responsible for continuing the conflict. The truth is that during the entire War, no attempts for a peaceful compromise ever came from Lincoln. All were suggested by the South; all were rejected by the North. Pollard, LC, p. 93.
397. Pollard, LC, pp. 111-112.

measures . . .[398]

These "measures" began just weeks after Lincoln was elected in November 1860.

On December 21 of that year, the day after South Carolina seceded, the Yankee president wrote a "confidential" letter to Elihu B. Washburne in which he said:

> Please present my respects to the General [Winfield Scott], and tell him, confidentially, I shall be obliged to him to be as well prepared as he can to either *hold*, or *retake*, the forts, as the case may require, at, and after the inauguration.[399]

It was clear what Lincoln was saying here: "Be prepared to retake the forts when I become president."[400] He was certainly thinking far ahead: he had not even been inaugurated yet and the War was still five months away!

Shrewd as he was, Lincoln cannot claim credit for the idea of tricking the Confederates; only for perpetrating the hoax.[401] It came from his secretary of the navy, Gideon Welles,[402] who slyly advised the president that "it is very important that the Rebels strike the first blow in the conflict."[403] Lincoln's assistant secretary of the navy, Gustavus Fox, then took Welles' idea and worked out the details of the plan. Writing to Montgomery Blair (soon to be Lincoln's postmaster general) on February 23, 1861, Fox said:

> I simply propose three tugs, convoyed by light-draft men-of-war. . . . The first tug to lead in empty, to open their fire.[404]

This was a no-win situation for the South: if she allowed Lincoln to "resupply" the fort, it would remain in the enemy's hands, humiliating the Confederacy. If the South attacked, she would be blamed for "starting the War." Lincoln had her right where he wanted.

---

398. Ashe, p. 56.
399. Tilley, LTC, p. 105; Oates, AF, p. 106.
400. Norwood, p. 353.
401. Harwell, p. 344.
402. Grissom, p. 108.
403. Scharf, pp. 129-130; Tilley, FHLO, p. 50.
404. *ORA*, Ser. 1, Vol. 4, pp. 224-225.

Fox's plan never materialized, however, because the Rebels, having been grossly misled and lied to, went ahead and bombed and captured the fort first. But either way, the end result was still what Lincoln had intended: the South appeared to the world to be the aggressor.[405] Now the onus of initiating war lay with the Confederacy.

On May 1, 1861, three weeks after his foul deed at Sumter had been committed, Lincoln acknowledged his devilish connivance in a letter to Fox. While Fox was disappointed that his and Welles' plan had not succeeded, Lincoln was elated:

> I sincerely regret that the failure of the attempt to provision Fort Sumter should be the source of annoyance to you . . .
> You and I both anticipated that the cause of the country would be advanced by making the attempt to provision Fort Sumter even if it should fail; and it is no small consolation now to feel that our anticipation is justified in the results.[406]

What "results?" The inauguration of a war he so desperately wanted!

The English perceived Lincoln's treachery at Fort Sumter, even if most of the Yankee populace did not. The Manchester *Guardian* wrote:

> The only plausible explanation of President Lincoln's account [of the Battle of Fort Sumter] is that he has thought that a political object was to be obtained by putting the Southerners in the wrong, if they could be maneuvered into firing the first shot.[407]

Thus, as Confederate army chaplain Robert Lewis Dabney so aptly observed, Lincoln's War was "conceived in duplicity, and brought forth in iniquity."[408]

Four years later, in his Second Inaugural Address, on March 4, 1865, Lincoln was still trying to keep up the pretense before the public. Here he had the nerve to say that both the South and the North had tried to avoid bloodshed,

> but one of them would *make* war rather than let the nation survive,

---

405. Tilley, FHLO, pp. 50-51.
406. Nicolay and Hay, ALCW, Vol. 2, p. 41.
407. Grissom, p. 108; Sandburg, ALWY, Vol. 3, p. 212; Maihafer, p. 40.
408. *Southern Historical Society Papers*, Vol. 1, January to June, 1876, p. 455.

and the other would *accept* war rather than let it perish; and the war came.[409]

The idea that the war simply "came," and that this was due to the aggressive actions of those he preposterously called the "Southern insurgents," is absurd, and an insult to all intelligent people. Yet it was in this exact way that the South has been held criminally responsible for a war it did not begin, or want.[410]

Lincoln, a lifelong lawyer, knew his War was unconstitutional and thus illegal. Indeed, this is why, in early April 1865, when it was clear that the Southern Cause was lost (prompting Jefferson Davis to flee west to join up with General Nathan Bedford Forrest in the hope of establishing a new confederacy),[411] Lincoln, along with fellow war criminal Grant, "wished and hoped" that Davis would not be captured, that he would, in fact, make good his escape.[412] For if Davis were ever put on trial for the crime of "treason" (i.e., for "leading the Southern secession movement"), there would not be a court in the world that would convict him.

Lincoln's fear was fully justified.

For one thing, far from calling for secession, Davis had strongly opposed it; nor was he one of the Confederacy's Founding Fathers, the noted Southerners who first framed the Confederacy at the Montgomery Convention held February 4-9, 1861.[413] Another problem: nothing Davis did met the definition of "treason" as given in the Constitution.[414] For example, he had never led the movement that caused the final break with the Union. Indeed, he had never even sought election; rather he was appointed president of the Confederacy, at first against his wishes.[415]

But Lincoln had a much larger and more important issue to deal with if he intended on bringing Davis to trial. Using the Declaration of Independence, the Articles of Confederation, and the U.S. Constitution, Southern attorneys would have easily and quickly shown that secession was legal, and Lincoln's War would have been exposed for what it was: the

---

409. W. Wilson, HAP, Vol. 9, p. 137.
410. Durden, p. 191.
411. J. Davis, RFCG, Vol. 2, pp. 696, 697.
412. Sandburg, SOL, pp. 412-414.
413. Denney, p. 25.
414. See Calvert, Vol. 9, pp. 133-134.
415. W. C. Davis, HD, pp. 384-385.

unlawful invasion of a non-hostile foreign nation, initiated without congressional approval or public support.

Revealingly, Davis, who was later captured near Irwinville, Georgia, was never brought to trial, even though he actually requested one. Indeed, the U.S. government itself asked three different prosecuting attorneys to try Davis. All three refused, deeming the case thoroughly unwinnable.[416] As one of them later said of Davis:

> Gentleman, the Supreme Court of the United States will have to acquit that man under the Constitution when it will be proven to the world that the North waged an unconstitutional warfare against the South.[417]

Southern commentators were quick to respond to Lincoln's underhanded assault on Fort Sumter (which the president repeatedly misspelled "Fort Sumpter").[418] Pollard, staunch Confederate editor of the Richmond *Examiner*, wrote:

> The fact was that the President had long ago calculated the result and effect, on the country, of hostile movements which he had directed against the sovereignty of South Carolina. He had procured the battle of Sumter; he had no desire or hope to retain the fort: the circumstances of the battle and the non-participation of his fleet in it, were sufficient evidences, to every honest and reflecting mind, that it was not a contest for victory, and that the 'sending provisions to a starving garrison' was an ingenious artifice to commence the war that the Federal Government had fully resolved upon, under the specious but shallow appearance of that government being involved by the force of circumstances, rather by

---

416. C. Adams, p. 186. After his capture on May 10, 1865, Davis was imprisoned at Fort Monroe, Virginia, for "treason" where, for two long years he was chained, treated inhumanely, and suffered numerous indignities in a cold, dark, damp cell. He became ill on several occasions and nearly lost his life. To the great relief of his family and supporters, President Davis survived the ordeal, and on May 14, 1867, he was "released on bond." This was an intelligent move on the part of the U.S. government, as a trial would have certainly exposed the illegalities of both the North's war on the South and Davis' imprisonment. Sobel, s.v. "Davis, Jefferson." Hoping to prove that secession was legal, numerous other Confederates demanded that they be tried for "treason" by the U.S. government. All were turned down—for obvious reasons. C. Johnson, p. 201.
417. Stonebraker, p. 75.
418. Donald, L, p. 286; Delbanco, p. 204. South-illiterate Northern newspapers, like the New York *Times*, also misspelled the word. See W. B. Garrison, CWTFB, p. 96.

its own volition, in the terrible consequence of civil war.[419]

After Sumter, even Judge John A. Campbell, a justice on the U.S. Supreme Court and a pre-war mediator between the North and the South, concluded that he had been the victim of Lincoln's criminal trickery and political treachery.[420] On April 13, 1861, in a letter to Lincoln's secretary of state Seward, Campbell said:

> I think no candid man, who will read over what I have written and consider for a moment what is going on at Sumter, but will agree that the equivocating conduct of the [U.S.] administration, as measured and interpreted in connection with these promises, is the proximate cause of the great calamity.[421]

Seward never replied (an unprofessional habit he picked up from his boss Mr. Lincoln).[422] On April 30, Campbell resigned from the Court in disgust and outrage, then fled to the Confederacy.[423] Soon after, the *Southern Literary Messenger* commented on Lincoln's role at Sumter:

> The annals of the world in its blackest and bloodiest periods, do not furnish an instance of more inhuman and fiend like policy.[424]

To this day, lovers of truth and liberty still gasp at this brazen display of political deviousness. By his own admission Lincoln intentionally set out to start an armed conflict with the South, then fooled her into initiating it. Despite his own confession, the North continues to pretend that "the South started the War." What this undisputedly proves, and what the North cannot hide, however, is the fact that it was Lincoln's election to the presidency that was the underlying spark that ignited the

---

419. Pollard, SHW, Vol. 1, p. 61.
420. M. Davis, p. 56.
421. F. Moore, Vol. 1, pp. 427-428.
422. Christian, p. 15.
423. Campbell was later named the Confederacy's assistant secretary of war by President Jefferson Davis. Boatner, s.v. "Campbell, John Archibald."
424. Robert R. Howison, "History of the War," *Southern Literary Messenger*, Vol. 34, July and August, 1862, p. 404.

"Civil War,"[425] for the Southern states did not begin seceding until shortly after his election in November 1860.

By the middle of Lincoln's War (late 1862), Northern support for his bloody military debacle was dying, reenlistments had decreased alarmingly, and the Federal army had lost hundreds of thousands of soldiers to disease, wounds, desertion,[426] defection, and death, as Lincoln himself acknowledged.[427]

Defeatism had set in.[428] The Northern populace was now revolted by the bloody debacle and wanted it brought to a speedy end. (Little wonder that Northern talk of assassinating Lincoln increased as the War drew on.) As Northerners saw it, if twenty million of them could not beat eight million Southerners after two years of total war using a scorched earth policy, Lincoln had failed, and failed miserably, and for this they would not give him a second chance at the presidency.

Yet, for "Honest Abe," the War was far from over, and victory (installing the American System) was not yet in his grasp. Therefore gaining a second term was absolutely vital. As he put it at the time, "God wills this contest, and wills that it shall not end yet."[429] (Since Lincoln was an atheist, what he was really saying was: "*I* will this contest, and will that it shall not end yet.")

The situation was bleak enough that Lincoln himself came to believe he could not get reelected, a sentiment he held all the way to late 1864, only months before the November election. On August 23, of that year, in one of his more bizarre political documents, he scribbled the following to his cabinet members on a crumbled up piece of paper:

> This morning, as for some days past, it seems exceedingly probable that this administration will not be re-elected. Then it will be my duty to so cooperate with the President-elect, as to save the Union between the election and the inauguration; as he will have secured his election on such grounds that he can not possibly save it

---

425. W. B. Garrison, CWTFB, p. 145. Lincoln was not only the instigator of the War, it was also he who was mainly responsible for setting off its first major conflict: the Battle of First Manassas. W. B. Garrison, CWTFB, p. 220.
426. Most authorities agree that some 200,000 Yanks deserted during Lincoln's War, about 4,166 soldiers a week. Alotta, p. 188; Wiley, LBY, p. 407; Zinn, p. 232.
427. See e.g., Nicolay and Hay, ALCW, Vol. 2, pp. 192-193.
428. Hacker, p. 584; C. Eaton, JD, p. 231.
429. Tarbell, Vol. 2, p. 221.

afterward.[430]

Written over a year and a half after issuing his Final Emancipation Proclamation, this document is revealing. Not only does Lincoln nearly admit defeat just before the election, it is clear that almost four years into his War his pretended intention was still to "preserve the Union," not abolish slavery.

Late 1862 was indeed a gloomy period for madman Lincoln and his sacred but imaginary "perpetual" Union. With his own people against him, his troop strength greatly decreased, and the Confederacy sending regular peace commissions to the White house in an attempt to negotiate an end to the bloodshed, all seemed lost for the North. What was Lincoln's response?

Desperately needing a major military triumph to execute his dastardly plan, he disregarded both his war-hating constituents and the Southern men of peace. He would find more soldiers and his War would go on, as he himself said, as long as it was "in his power to continue hostilities."[431] But how?

He would find a way. And he did: in black emancipation.

Lincoln had long been vehemently against enlisting blacks. On July 21, 1862, for instance, he met with his cabinet and stated: "I am averse to arming the negroes,"[432] just one of dozens of times in which, for obviously racist reasons, he flatly refused to even entertain the idea.

Despite his foolhardy resistance, at the start of the War thousands of blacks begged to be allowed to enlist to fight for the Union.[433] In April 1861, as just one example, Jacob Dodson, an experienced and well respected black soldier, offered himself and 300 other African-Americans for military service. Lincoln was not interested, however, and had his secretary of war, Simon Cameron, send back the following brusque reply to a stunned Dodson:

> This Department has no intention at present to call into the service of the Government any colored soldiers.[434]

---

430. Nicolay and Hay, ALCW, Vol. 2, p. 568.
431. Harwell, p. 309.
432. Tyler, PH, p. 12.
433. Faust, s.v. "black soldiers"; Quarles, p. 29.
434. ORA, Ser. 3, Vol. 1, p. 133.

On August 6, 1862, Lincoln's War Department sent a similar message to the governor of Wisconsin that read: "The President declines to receive Indians or negroes as troops."[435] Or as Cameron put it even more indelicately, the present conflict "forbids the use of savages."[436] And so tens of thousands of blacks (and Native-Americans) were turned away by Lincoln during the first two years of the War.

Blacks who managed to enlist without being noticed, were soon caught and "honorably discharged." White clergyman Moncure D. Conway wrote: "At Washington I found that the mere mention of a Negro made the President nervous . . ."[437] Thus, in Cincinnati, Ohio, a black recruiting office was shut down by police, who told the blacks who had shown up to fight for Lincoln: "This is the white man's war, and you damned niggers are not needed or wanted!"[438]

At the time, Lincoln's reasons for being "nervous" about bringing blacks into the military were numerous, but can be broken down into five basic items:

1) Believing that the conflict was a "white man's war,"[439] nearly the entire Northern populace, being highly Negrophobic, was strongly against black enlistment. Lincoln would lose potential votes for his reelection if he ignored this huge majority of the Yankee population.[440]

2) Black enlistment might subject the U.S. to the disrespect and disapproval of foreign nations.[441]

3) Black enlistment might stir up both white hostility and slave insurrections in the border states (Delaware, Kentucky, Maryland, and Missouri), whose support Lincoln was trying to win.[442]

4) It was believed that blacks, being an "inferior race," as Lincoln and his

---

435. Cornish, p. 73; D. Brown, pp. 179-180.
436. *ORA*, Ser. 3, Vol. 1, p. 184.
437. Conway, p. 108.
438. R. M. Reid, p. 2; Barney, pp. 127-128. My paraphrasal.
439. See Quarles, p. 31; Buckley, p. 81.
440. See Wiley, SN, pp. 300-301.
441. See Wiley, SN, p. 301.
442. Crocker, p. 59; Current, LNK, p. 220.

officers referred to them,[443] were not fit to fight; or more likely, being "natural cowards," would not fight. Yankee Colonel T. J. Morgan, for example, stated that the black man would not hold up on the battlefield because "he belonged to a degraded, inferior race, wanting in soldierly qualities . . . he was too grossly ignorant to perform intelligently the duties of a soldier."[444] Northern war hero General William T. Sherman declared:

> I would prefer to have this a white man's war . . . With my opinions of negroes and my experience, yea prejudice, I cannot trust them yet. Time may change this but I cannot bring myself to trust negroes with arms in positions of danger and trust.[445]

Union General Benjamin F. Butler, at first also very much opposed to colored enlistment, suggested that if blacks were to be enrolled, they should be employed as common laborers for cutting down trees.[446]

5) White Northern soldiers themselves had made it clear that they would not fight next to blacks on the battlefield. Sherman—who had long been against the idea of black enlistment, did not want runaway slaves allowed in Union camps, and believed that they should be surrendered immediately upon demand of their owners[447]—felt the very idea of it was "unjust to the brave [white] soldiers and volunteers." A U.S. senator said that white soldiers would feel "degraded" if forced to serve next to blacks.[448] One New York officer, Corporal Felix Brannigan, wrote his sister: 'We whites are the superior race. We will never fight alongside the nigger.'[449]

Being a white separatist, Lincoln understood, and agreed with, such sentiments, which is why he turned away thousands of willing would-be black recruits during the first forty-eight months of his War. But by the end of 1862, realizing that he was running out of time and options, the

---

443. See e.g., Nicolay and Hay, ALCW, Vol. 1, pp. 289, 370, 457, 458, 469, 539; Basler, ALSW, pp. 400, 402, 403-404; Stern, pp. 492-493; Holzer, pp. 189, 251.
444. J. T. Wilson, p. 290.
445. M. A. D. Howe, pp. 252-253.
446. ORA, Ser. 1, Vol. 15, p. 535.
447. McMaster, p. 250.
448. Wiley, SN, p. 302.
449. See Astor, p. 22; J. D. Smith, p. 6; J. W. McPherson, SE, p. 193. My paraphrasal.

president had a major "change of heart." The moment had come, as he put it, for "laying [a] strong hand upon the colored element."[450] And what a "strong hand" it would turn out to be!

By then, not only did Lincoln require a means of destroying the labor system (servitude) of thousands of white and black slave-owning Southern families, but he also needed manpower, warm bodies on the battlefield,[451] whatever their race or color—and the sooner the better.[452] By this time he was even willing to consider Mexicans, who he publicly called "greasers,"[453] "mongrels," and also inevitably, an "inferior race."[454]

Because of their sheer numbers, however, it was mainly blacks that Lincoln was interested in enrolling, a people who he was inclined to refer to using the "n" word, as he often did during his debates with Stephen A. Douglas in 1858.[455] At the Quincy, Illinois, debate on October 13, for instance, in countering one of his opponent's arguments, Lincoln made the following remarks:

> Mr. Douglas will insist that I want a Nigger wife [great laughter from the audience]; but never can he be brought to understand that there is any middle ground on this. Now I, for my part have lived some fifty years. And I have never had a negro slave or a negro wife [cheers from the crowd], and I think I can live for fifty centuries for that matter without having either . . . [cheers and laughter][456]

Lincoln's reluctance to enlist blacks in his military is all the more surprising in light of the fact that blacks fought side by side with their white brothers through all of America's previous wars, including the French and Indian War (1754-1763), the first Revolutionary War (1775-1783), the War of 1812, the Battle of New Orleans (1814),[457] and the Mexican-American War (1846-1848).[458] During the American Revolutionary War alone, some 5,000 blacks served, a number of them

---

450. Nicolay and Hay, ALCW, Vol. 2, p. 508.
451. Garraty and McCaughey, p. 254.
452. Mullen, p. 19.
453. See e.g., Nicolay and Hay, ALCW, Vol. 1, p. 524; Neely, p. 213.
454. See e.g., Nicolay and Hay, ALCW, Vol. 1, p. 449.
455. See Holzer, pp. 22-23, 67, 318, 361.
456. See Nicolay and Hay, ALCW, Vol. 1, pp. 292, 298, 483.
457. Wiley, SN, p. 147.
458. Mullen, pp. 9-17; Greenberg and Waugh, p. 391.

in every major battle from Lexington to Yorktown.[459]

Indeed, the first man to die in a major American conflict was a black sailor named Crispus Attucks. On March 5, 1770, at Boston, Massachusetts, Attucks was shot down while leading an attack against British soldiers during the Revolutionary War. Four whites died with Attucks in what came to be known as the Boston Massacre, martyrs for the cause of freedom from tyranny[460]—the same cause for which hundreds of thousands of white and black Southerners would fight ninety-one years later against Lincoln. For their service in Washington's Continental Army (about 15 percent which had been black),[461] Virginia's House of Burgesses granted black slaves their freedom in 1783,[462] years before most Northern states freed their slaves.

In the 1860s, there was no great resistance among the Northern people to enlisting Latin-Americans, or even those that Lincoln and the North derogatorily called "primitive savages"—i.e., Native-Americans (though Lincoln himself at first banned them from enlistment).[463] But when it came to African-Americans, there were several major problems.

First, free blacks could not be enrolled in Lincoln's military because they were not American citizens. Second, enslaved blacks could not be enrolled because they were considered "private property." Third, slaves, being seen as childlike subordinates, were not considered full-grown men in the proper legal sense.[464]

The political and legal barriers, however, were virtually

---

459. Garraty and McCaughey, p. 81.
460. Mullen, p. 9.
461. Buckley, p. xiii.
462. K. C. Davis, p. 11.
463. Cornish, p. 73. The U.S. government's general policy toward Native-Americans in Lincoln's day has been termed "genocide-at-law," for its primary goals at the time were "land acquisition and cultural extermination." K. L. Hall, s.v. "Native Americans." This brutal program was later warmly endorsed by one of Lincoln's more zealous admirers, Adolf Hitler, who was awed by the efficiency with which the U.S. extirpated its red population in the 1800s. Toland, p. 506. Yankee General William T. Sherman, who famously declared that "the only good Indian is a dead Indian," typified the Northern attitude toward Native-Americans. D. Brown, p. 170. (See also Custer, p. 119.) After Lincoln's death, the U.S. government continued its war against Indians. On April 9, 1866, for example, the Thirty-ninth Congress passed a civil rights act "to protect all persons in the United States." Unfortunately for Native-Americans, "all persons in the United States" did not include them. Kane, p. 193. The U.S. Civil Rights Act of 1866 also upheld state segregation. In fact, the U.S. allowed discrimination based on race until the mid 20th Century, when the Civil Rights Act of 1964 was passed. J. S. Bowman, ECW, s.v. "Civil Rights Acts of 1866 and 1875." This is certainly something that would not have occurred in the much more racially tolerant Southern Confederacy had Lincoln, in 1861, allowed her to remain a free and sovereign nation.
464. Cornish, p. 291.

meaningless compared to the true cultural and social issue: nearly all white Northerners at the time, including Lincoln, considered blacks to be subhuman, an alien creature that fell somewhere between ape and man. Respected Yankee historian, James Ford Rhodes, for instance, described slaves as "indolent and filthy," "stupid" and "duplicitous," with "brute-like countenances."[465]

Other Northerners were less kind. Famed Harvard scientist Louis Agassiz declared that "the negro race groped in barbarism and never originated a regular organization among themselves."[466] Agassiz, like his English associate, Charles Darwin (who originated the idea of natural selection, or "survival of the fittest"),[467] believed that blacks were so evolutionarily feeble that once freed from slavery they would eventually "die out" in the U.S.[468]

Yankees in general, even Northern Christian leaders, spared little sentimentality at the thought of the black race disappearing. In 1860, here is what the renowned Connecticut minister and theologian Horace Bushnell told his congregation about the "coming extinction" of African-Americans:

> I know of no example in human history where an inferior and far less cultivated stock has been able, freely intermixed with a superior, to hold its ground. . . . it will always be seen that the superior lives the other down, and finally quite lives it away. And indeed, since we must all die, why should it grieve us, that a stock thousands of years behind, in the scale of culture, should die with few and still fewer children to succeed, till finally the whole succession remains in the more cultivated race?[469]

Being of Puritan stock,[470] not surprisingly, much of this type of Yankee white racism was derived from the Bible. Here, Christian supporters of slavery could always turn to the book of Genesis and read of the idea that Africans bore the "mark of Cain,"[471] a people cursed by Noah

---

465. Rhodes, Vol. 1, pp. 307, 309.
466. Seligmann, p. 9.
467. See Darwin, p. 91.
468. Bailyn, Dallek, Davis, Donald, Thomas, and Wood, p. 29.
469. Bushnell, p. 12.
470. Haller, p. 191.
471. Philip Smith, Vol. 1, p. 30.

to be the "servants of servants," meaning the "lowest of slaves."[472] As the Old Testament text reads:

> And Ham, the father of Canaan, saw the nakedness of his father, and told his two brethren without. And Shem and Japheth took a garment, and laid it upon both their shoulders, and went backward, and covered the nakedness of their father; and their faces were backward, and they saw not their father's nakedness. And Noah awoke from his wine, and knew what his younger son had done unto him. And he said, Cursed be Canaan; a servant of servants shall he be unto his brethren. And he said, Blessed be the Lord God of Shem; and Canaan shall be his servant. God shall enlarge Japheth, and he shall dwell in the tents of Shem; and Canaan shall be his servant.[473]

Also known as the "curse of Ham" (actually the curse of Ham's son, Canaan, and his descendants), early Americans, like the Mormons, construed this passage to mean that Africans had inherited the "affliction" of black skin and a life of servitude under white rule. Polygamist and former Mason, Joseph Smith, the founder and first leader of the Mormon Church, thus wrote:

> . . . for behold the Lord shall curse the land with much heat, and the barrenness thereof shall go forth forever; and there was a blackness came upon all the children of Canaan, that they were despised among all people.[474]

Based on just such beliefs, early Mormons solved the "problem" of the presence of blacks by legalizing slavery in Utah and banning African-Americans from their priesthood.[475]

---

472. Genesis 4:1-15; 9:25. See Metzger and Coogan, s.v. "Slavery and the Bible."
473. Genesis 9:22-27.
474. J. Smith, p. 23 (Book of Moses).
475. The pseudo-Christian, non-Bible-based, Mason-inspired denomination, the Mormons, or the members of the Church of Jesus Christ of Latter-Day Saints (LDS), have long embraced a belief in the "mark of Cain," though understandably this fact has been largely kept from the general public. As such, early Mormon laws did not prohibit slavery; instead, they sanctioned them. Mormon leader Brigham Young, for example, not only welcomed white slave owners into the Church, he settled Utah's Salt Lake Valley using Mormon slave owners and their slaves. And in 1852, as the first territorial governor of the Beehive State, Young asked the Utah legislature to legalize slavery, making it the only territory west of the Missouri River and north of the Missouri Compromise line to allow the institution. B. H. Johnson, p. 140; Olson, p. 148. Mormons—who refuse to exhibit crosses or crucifixes anywhere inside or outside their churches—once held that blacks would

Lincoln was looking for his own answer to the great "racial problem" that haunted 19th-Century white America: how to get rid of slavery while keeping the country as white as possible.[476] For he, like most others antislavery advocates, believed that blacks would never assimilate into American society because of a mutual innate antagonism between the two races.[477]

Lincoln found a solution in what was then called black colonization:[478] the deportation of all blacks out of the country (in the North the words abolition and colonization meant virtually the same thing).[479] Once they were transported outside U.S. lines, they would no longer be his problem.[480] But how, he asked himself, could this be accomplished when a majority of African-Americans were considered "property" that belonged to private owners?

As president, Lincoln's "final solution" to all of these dilemmas was simple: end slavery in the South. This would have a number of immediate effects, he hoped. It would change the character of the war from a political one to a moral one; it would permit black colonization; it would "disrupt" the Southern economy; it would stir up slave insurrections across Dixie; it would win European support for the Union;

---

continue to be an "inferior race" in the "Next World." Blacks, being of the "lineage of Cain," were not allowed to join the Mormon priesthood or participate in Temple ordinances until 1978, 148 years after the Church's founding in 1830 by Yankee polygamist and ex-Mason Joseph Smith. The change only came after decades of severe criticism, condemnation, and charges of racism from around the world. Little wonder that in the early 1900s the Utah branch of the new KKK (distinct and separate from the original KKK of the 1860s) flourished with the membership of Mormon ministers. Wade, p. 173. Despite the Church's modern 1978 concession, the belief in the "Curse of Ham" survives among some individual Mormons and Mormon groups. The Church continues to embrace other unorthodox dogmas as well, such as a belief in both a Father-God and a Mother-Goddess (as well as a "plurality" of other deities); the secret ritual of baptism for the dead (condemned in 1 Corinthians 15:29 by St. Paul as a Pagan practice); the belief that Jesus and Satan are biological brothers; the belief that the ancient Aztec God Quetzalcoatl was actually Jesus; the posthumous attainment of self-godhood (in order to rule other planets after earthly death); and the continuance of male polygamy after death—a tenant particularly distressing to many modern female LDS members. For more on these topics from an LDS perspective, see the Church's excellent publication: *Encyclopedia of Mormonism*, by Daniel H. Ludlow, s.v. "Cain," "Race, Racism," "Blacks," "Devils," "Priesthood," "Mother in Heaven," "Godhood," "Baptism for the Dead," passim. For a non-Mormon *Christian* view of the LDS Church see: *Mormonism Unmasked*, by R. Philip Roberts. Also see books by Carr, Persuitte, Abanes, Decker and Matrisciana, and Decker and Hunt. Revealingly, the scandalous Joseph Smith, murdered in an Illinois jail by an angry Christian mob, was an admirer of the equally scandalous Abraham Lincoln of Illinois. See e.g., Nicolay and Hay, ALAH, Vol. 1, p. 182.

476. Quarles, p. 145.
477. Fogel, p. 251.
478. Tarbell, Vol. 3, p. 96.
479. Smelser, DR, p. 44.
480. Napolitano, p. 64.

and finally, and most importantly, it would lift the black enlistment ban, allowing both free and bonded blacks to become Union soldiers,[481] easily filling the enlistment quotas of Yankee governors.[482] With the needed extra soldiery, the North would achieve more victories, boasting popular support that would assure Lincoln of reelection in the fall of 1864. What an ingenious and devious plan this was!

Times indeed were desperate. With his white ranks shrinking ever more dramatically each day, Lincoln began reluctantly considering what many of his own white soldiers had been discussing for months. As one of them, John W. De Forest, wrote from camp in August of 1862: nearly everyone I know is starting to consider arming the Negro.[483]

Revealingly, however, even after haltingly inviting blacks to enlist for the first time (on August 25, 1862), the Lincoln government strove to hide the fact from the Northern populace: his authorization of black enlistment included an accompanying note that read, "must never see the light of day because it is so much in advance of [Northern] public opinion."[484]

Just as appalling, even after issuing his Emancipation Proclamation (on January 1, 1863), which for the first time *publicly* called for black enlistment, Lincoln would still not allow his new black recruits to become active combatants, or even American citizens. He even dragged his feet on acknowledging them, not creating a Bureau of Colored Troops until May 1863, over two years after the War started.[485] The question we must put to all of these actions is why?

The answer, as we will show, is that his main concern was never black civil rights.

The truth that the North and the New South will still not admit is that Lincoln, as we have touched on, would not have issued the Emancipation Proclamation at all if he had not needed to raise new troops in 1863. On August 17, 1864, the double-talking Yankee president himself conceded this fact in a letter to Charles D. Robinson:

---

481. L. Johnson, p. 133; Crocker, p. 59.
482. K. C. Davis, p. 276.
483. De Forest, p. 40.
484. H. Wilson, Vol. 3, p. 370.
485. Wiley, SN, p. 306.

> We can not spare the hundred and forty or fifty thousand [blacks] now serving as [Union] soldiers, seamen, and laborers. This is not a question of sentiment or taste, but one of physical force which may be measured and estimated as horse-power and steam-power are measured and estimated. Keep it and you can save the Union. Throw it away, and the Union goes with it.[486]

In Lincoln's own words, he makes it clear that he had allowed blacks to become soldiers, not because of "sentiment or taste" (i.e., out of sympathy for blacks or for the purpose of racial equality), but because of a need of "physical force," one, he assured Robinson, the North would need in order to subdue the South. (As with so many Northerners at the time, for Lincoln the War was all about numbers and dominance.)

In the final analysis, Lincoln's Emancipation Proclamation was the necessary product of a military emergency brought about by a war he himself had created.[487] Otherwise, why did he not abolish slavery the first day he entered the White House? Why wait over two years before moving to end the institution—and then only grudgingly, half-heartedly, and under enormous pressure from abolitionists, a group he openly despised? Throughout 1862 alone, numerous antislavery groups regularly called on Lincoln, week after week, pressing for emancipation.[488] He rejected every proposal, even when it was made by religious organizations and groups of clergymen.[489] Again, why?

Let us let the man answer these questions for himself.

Throughout his political career Illinoisan Lincoln was repeatedly challenged as to whether he was in favor of "negro citizenship," and he repeatedly gave the same answer, as he did at Charleston, Illinois, on September 18, 1858:

> . . . very frankly . . . I am not in favor of Negro citizenship. . . . Now, my opinion is that the different States have the power to make a negro a citizen, under the constitution of the United States, if they choose. . . . If the State of Illinois had that power, I should be against the exercise of it. That is all I have to say about it.[490]

---

486. Nicolay and Hay, ALCW, Vol. 2, p. 564.
487. Fogel, pp. 481, 484.
488. Nye, p. 175.
489. See e.g., McMaster, pp. 256-257.
490. Lincoln and Douglas, p. 187.

So much for black citizenship under the future Lincoln administration.

Another potential "bonus" of his scheme to free and then enlist black slaves was that, as Lincoln dearly hoped, emancipation would cause a great servile insurrection across the South, and that blacks would rise up, arm themselves, overturn the plantations, and kill their white owners, disrupting the fabric of Southern society. Shockingly, Lincoln thought this would be a convenient and efficient way to win, then end, the War.

On September 13, 1862, he himself admitted as much when he was questioned about the motivations behind the Emancipation Proclamation, his temporary "war measure," as he termed it.[491] In reply Lincoln said:

> . . . I have a right to take any measure which may best subdue the enemy; nor do I urge objection of a moral nature in view of possible consequences of insurrection and massacre at the South.[492]

Such icy, callous statements appalled and horrified Southerners, and for good reason. Lincoln's Emancipation Proclamation itself suggests an open invitation to Southern blacks to riot and murder their white brothers and sisters. Consider the following words, also from Lincoln's own pen:

> . . . the Executive Government of the United States, including the military and the naval authority thereof, will recognize and maintain the freedom of such [black] persons, and will do no act or acts to repress such persons, or any of them, in any efforts they may make for their actual freedom.[493]

The phrase "any efforts," of course, included the possibility of insurrection, mayhem, and the wanton murder of Southern whites, 96 percent who did not even own slaves.

Lincoln's stand on the issue of Southern black rebellion allows us to more fully understand the following incident. Once, when Stephen A. Douglas introduced a bill in the Senate calling for the punishment of anyone attempting to incite slave revolts in the South, Lincoln called it a

---

491. See Greenberg and Waugh, p. 355.
492. E. McPherson, PHUSAGR, p. 231.
493. E. McPherson, PHUSAGR, pp. 227-228.

"seditious speech," and his party members booed it down.[494]

Lincoln indeed had the backing of many of his constituents, and for good reason. As his secretary of the navy, Gideon Welles, wrote in his diary: the North was hoping for a slave insurrection in order to keep white Southerners preoccupied, and thus more easily conquerable.[495]

That Lincoln was of the same mind is indicated in a letter he wrote on September 28, 1862, to his first vice president, Hannibal Hamlin, just six days after issuing his Preliminary Emancipation Proclamation:

> The time for its effect southward has not come [yet]; but northward the effect should be instantaneous.[496]

The "effect Southward" Lincoln refers to here was the much anticipated revolt of the South's 3,500,000 slaves and the subsequent mass slaughter of their white owners.

But nothing ever happened.

When his Final Emancipation Proclamation also utterly failed to launch a single slave rebellion in January 1863, Lincoln and his officers connived to create their own, as the *Official Records* testify. Just four months later, in May 1863, a cowardly and despicable plan began passing between Union authorities.[497] According to its white Northern author, "Augustus S. Montgomery," Southern blacks were to be "induced" to

> make a concerted and simultaneous movement or rising, on the night of the 1ˢᵗ of August next, over the entire States in rebellion; to arm themselves with any and every kind of weapon that may come to hand, and commence operations by burning all railroad and country bridges and tear up railroad tracks and destroy telegraph lines, etc., and then take to the woods, the swamps, or the mountains, whence they may emerge as occasion may offer for provisions and for further depredations.[498]

The only reason this insane plot was not carried through was

---

494. Ashe, p. 46.
495. Ashe, p. 35.
496. Nicolay and Hay, ALCW, Vol. 2, p. 242. See also Ashe, pp. 35-36.
497. Ashe, pp. 36-37.
498. *ORA*, Ser. 1, Vol. 51, Pt. 2, p. 737.

because it was intercepted by vigilant Confederate soldiers. By July 18, Jefferson Davis' secretary of war, James A. Seddon, was in possession of it, copies of which he sent out to all of the Confederate governors.[499] When General Robert E. Lee read the insurrectionary cabal he rightly called it "a diabolical project."[500]

What Lincoln's exact role was in all of this will never be known. However, as he was commander-in-chief of the North's armed forces, and as a murderous slave rebellion across the South was one of his primary goals, we can be sure he knew about the cryptic scheme, and authorized it. How could he not have known? His officers' letters, reports, and dispatches pertaining to the affair ended up in the North's own chronicle of Lincoln's War, the voluminous 158-volume *Official Records*.

While such underhanded chicanery was all in a days's work for "Honest Abe," many fellow Northerners were astonished at his sordid crimes and cold-hearted inhumanity. As we will see, however, those who spoke out against his lawless savageries were soon silenced in the harshest and most inhumane ways, while the president, unfazed, moved forward with his plot to establish Clay's American System under the guise of "preserving the Union."

On September 22, 1862, Lincoln issued what he called his Preliminary Emancipation Proclamation. In it there is no mention of black civil rights, nothing about black suffrage, black citizenship, or enlisting blacks in the military, all issues desperately lobbied for by abolitionists and black leaders. He does refer to blacks, however. But the man who utters these words is not the false Abraham Lincoln, the one of Northern myth. For once he is the real Abraham Lincoln, the one of Southern reality.

After reasserting the nonsense that the purpose of the War was to "preserve the Union," and after promising those Southern states who rejoined the Union before January 1, 1863, that they would no longer have to free their slaves,[501] he proclaims that, "the effort to colonize persons of African descent . . . will be continued." Here are the words from his Preliminary Emancipation Proclamation in context:

> I, Abraham Lincoln, President of the United States of America, and

---

499. *ORA*, Ser. 1, Vol. 51, Pt. 2, pp. 736-737.
500. Ashe, p. 37.
501. M. Davis, p. 82.

Commander-in-Chief of the Army and Navy thereof, do hereby proclaim and declare that hereafter, as heretofore, the war will be prosecuted for the object of practically restoring the constitutional relation between the United States and each of the States, and the people thereof, in which States that relation is or may be suspended or disturbed.

That it is my purpose, upon the next meeting of Congress, to again recommend the adoption of a practical measure tendering pecuniary aid to the free acceptance or rejection of all slave-states, so called, the people whereof may not then be in rebellion against the United States, and which states may then have voluntarily adopted, or thereafter may voluntarily adopt, immediate or gradual abolishment of slavery within their respective limits; and that the effort to colonize persons of African descent with their consent upon this continent or elsewhere, with the previously obtained consent of the governments existing there elsewhere, will be continued.[502]

What is Lincoln referring to here? What does he mean when he says he wants to free and then deport all Africans out of the U.S.? In order to answer these questions we need to take an honest look at the institution of slavery.

---

502. Nicolay and Hay, ALCW, Vol. 2, p. 237.

SECTION TWO

SLAVERY, PROPAGANDA, & RACISM

The President, his advisers, his commanding generals . . . whose shaping hands have had so much to do with the conduct of the war, must all of them be weighed in the balance by the people and the generations to come. 'The great soul of the world is just,' and sooner or later all disguises will be thrown off, and every historical character will stand forth as he is, in the light of his deeds and deserts. . . . Justice will be done; but that justice may brand as a crime the blunders proceeding from a feeble, timid, ambidextrous policy, resulting in great sacrifices of life and treasure, and periling the priceless interests at stake.

George W. Julian (1817-1899)
Indiana Congressman under Lincoln

UNCLE TOM & THE WHIP

IT WILL COME AS A shock to some to learn that slavery was not practiced in the South.[503] What Northerners have long misleadingly called "slavery" was actually a mild form of servitude: a mutually beneficial relationship similar to that between a lord and a peasant, or a master and an apprentice.[504] The difference is enormous and worth examining.[505]

While in both institutions an individual is owned by another, under slavery an individual has no rights and is not paid; he or she is, in fact, defined as a "thing."[506] Under servitude, however, an individual possesses civil and legal rights and is financially compensated,[507] and is defined as a human being. In the South, black bondsmen and bondswomen were protected by numerous laws and received an income (either in cash,[508] or in the form of "free" food, clothing, housing, and health care).[509]

Therefore, "Southern slavery" was in fact involuntary servitude, and so-called "Southern slaves" were actually Southern servants.[510] This fact was noted as early as 1784, when Virginian Thomas Jefferson wrote a resolution ordering a ban on "involuntary servitude" in the Western Territories.

---

503. See Seabrook, TAHSR, pp. 613-614, 621.
504. David, p. 395.
505. For a full and objective study of American slavery, see Seabrook, EYWTAASIW, passim.
506. Hendelson, s.v. "slavery."
507. Stampp, p. 192.
508. M. M. Smith, pp. 184-185; Fogel and Engerman, p. 241.
509. Fogel and Engerman, pp. 151-152.
510. Grissom, p. 128.

The fact that the South practiced servitude not slavery was acknowledged even by the U.S. government: when the Thirteenth Amendment was ratified on December 6, 1865, and the institution was finally abolished in every state, South *and* North,[511] the writers, knowing that it was servitude, not slavery, that was practiced in the South, used both the term slavery, to appease uninformed biased Northerners, and the term involuntary servitude, for technical accuracy:

> Neither slavery nor involuntary servitude . . . shall exist within the United States, or any place subject to their jurisdiction.[512]

Another piece of evidence supporting this fact is that the freedom of slaves cannot be bought. However, the freedom of servants can, and even the most virulent South-hating crusader can recall hearing or reading about slaves who purchased their freedom in the Old South.[513]

The truth is that tens of thousands of bonded Southern blacks were purchased and freed by fellow blacks or sympathetic whites, or they purchased their own liberty—as well as the liberty of family members and friends. In fact, by the late antebellum period (1850-1860), nearly all manumissions were the result of free blacks buying their relatives, then freeing them.[514]

As servants, Southern blacks were permitted a lifestyle that set them completely apart from what was experienced by those living under authentic slavery. Almost all of the South's "slaves" earned a wage (just as ancient Greek slaves did),[515] married, had children, owned their own property, homes, clothing, livestock, transportation, and tools, and worked their own farms and plots of land (called "provision grounds")[516] from which they sold their products for extra income.[517] By both Southern custom and law they could also hire themselves out to other farms, demand religious instruction, and bring suit and give evidence in court.[518] It is because of such facts that the South's black bondsmen would

---

511. Fogel, p. 207.
512. Bliss, p. 40.
513. Seabrook, EYWTACWW, pp. 79-81.
514. Fogel, p. 194.
515. McKay, Hill, and Buckler, Vol. 1, p. 90.
516. Fogel, pp. 187-188.
517. See M. M. Smith, pp. 175-182, 184-185, 188-197; Fogel, pp. 189-193; Wiley, SN, pp. 137-138.
518. Hendelson, s.v. "slavery."

be much more accurately described as "proto-peasants" rather than slaves or even servants.[519]

Black servant artisans and other types of bonded craftsmen (such as blacksmiths, carpenters, engineers, brickmakers, landscapers, masons, weavers, millers, coopers, and shoemakers) even owned their own businesses, or hired themselves out,[520] often generating large profits for themselves and their families.[521] Black servant carpenters and masons literally built the South, constructing beautiful antebellum homes across Dixie, many which stand in splendid glory to this day. The interiors of these stately manors were filled with delicately carved woodwork and fine furniture, designed and created by extraordinarily talented black servant craftsmen and artisans, many who earned exorbitant incomes and whose work was much in demand across the South.[522]

Many, in particular those with highly specialized skills, such as black architects, earned far higher wages than many whites (at times a cause of racial friction), and a servant was always allowed to keep the money he or she earned in their spare time.[523]

In short, a nationwide "slave economy" thrived across the U.S., one created by the slaves themselves—providing extra income that became the means by which they often purchased freedom for themselves and their families. Among the more famous of those "slaves" who bought their liberty were Northern slave Frederick Douglass,[524] black racist-militant Denmark Vesey,[525] travel adventurer Gustavus Vassa,[526] and Lincoln's own modiste, Elizabeth Keckley, who purchased her freedom with money she made hiring herself out as a dressmaker.[527] If these four individuals had lived under authentic slavery they would have never been able to buy their independence. Instead, they would have remained enslaved for life.

Additionally, Southern servants were given Sundays, evenings,

---

519. Fogel, p. 190.
520. See Stampp, pp. 58-59, 72.
521. Fogel and Engerman, p. 56.
522. Fogel, p. 157.
523. Stampp, pp. 164-165.
524. Nye, pp. 146-147.
525. Garraty and McCaughey, p. 159; Rosenbaum, s.v. "Vesey, Denmark"; J. S. Bowman, CWDD, s.v. "May 1822."
526. K. C. Davis, p. 23.
527. C. Johnson, pp. 131, 188-189; Quarles, p. 128.

and holidays off (often they had the entire week free between Christmas and New Year's Day),[528] and extracurricular free time was always set aside for birthday celebrations, barbeques, weddings, fishing and hunting jaunts, parties, balls, prayer meetings, square dancing, and funerals, among numerous other activities.[529]

Many masters and mistresses allowed their servants to travel without passes, buy alcoholic beverages, attend "illegal" assemblies, carry guns, hunt and fish (for food), and trade without an official permit, while others taught, or at least encouraged, their bondsmen to read and write (unlawful in some states). There were also those owners who gave their servants near complete freedom, allowing them to live and work independently, coming and going as they pleased.[530] No true slave in the world has ever been given these types of liberties.

Finally, nothing (not even local laws) could prevent an owner from freeing his servants whenever he or she pleased, and "private emancipations" were common.[531] Such was the so-called "harsh" treatment of the so-called "slaves" of the Old South. At the time, living free was much harder for most blacks, which is why, when given a choice, many chose bondage over liberty.[532]

It was because servitude, not slavery, was practiced in the South that Thomas Jefferson often spoke of the "mild treatment our slaves experience."[533] And it was because of this fact that Southerners in general widely regarded their form of bondage as "altogether, one of the mildest and most beneficent systems of servitude in the world," as Edward A. Pollard called it in 1866.[534] Woodrow Wilson was of the same mind. In his book, *Division and Reunion: 1829-1889*, America's twenty-eighth president writes:

> Domestic slaves were almost uniformly dealt with indulgently and even affectionately by their masters. Among those masters who had the sensibility and breeding of gentlemen, the dignity and

---

528. Stampp, p. 169.
529. Quarles, p. 45; Wiley, SN, pp. 41-43.
530. Stampp, pp 228-229.
531. There were never any laws in the South against taking a servant to a slave-free state and emancipating him or her, and this is exactly what many Southerners did. Stampp, pp. 232-236.
532. Gates, p. 375.
533. Foley, p. 815.
534. Pollard, SHW, Vol. 2, p. 562.

responsibility of ownership were apt to produce a noble and gracious type of manhood, and relationships really patriarchal. 'On principle, in habit, and even on grounds of self interest, the greater part of the slave-owners were humane in the treatment of their slaves,—kind, indulgent, not over exacting, and sincerely interested in the physical well-being of their dependents,'—is the judgment of an eminently competent northern observer who visited the South in 1844. 'Field hands' on the ordinary plantation came constantly under their master's eye, were comfortably quartered, and were kept from overwork both by their own laziness and by the slack discipline to which they were subjected. They were often commanded in brutal language, but they were not often compelled to obey by brutal treatment.[535]

Well-fed, well-housed, and well-paid,[536] Southern slaves, in fact, lived almost identically to lower-, and in some cases, middle-class free whites and blacks.[537] Not only did they often dress better,[538] but many ate exactly what their white owners ate, received unlimited firewood, possessed an over abundance of clothing, and even had access to the best doctors around. Most plantations had their own live-in physicians, trained medical practitioners who treated both young and old slaves (many from the latter category who were deemed "worthless" by surprised Northerners who came upon them).[539]

"As a general rule," wrote anti-South, antislavery advocate Hinton Rowan Helper, in the South "poor white persons are regarded with less esteem and attention than negroes," with the condition of "vast numbers" of whites being "infinitely worse off."[540] This truth was so obvious that many 19th-Century Northerners were forced to admit that Southern slavery was far from the miserable institution that radical Yankee abolitionists tried to portray. Union officer Charles Francis Adams Jr. (great-grandson of famed U.S. Founder, President John Adams), wrote the following to his father Charles Francis Adams Sr.,[541] Lincoln's

---

535. W. Wilson, DR, pp. 125-126.
536. L. Johnson, p. 3.
537. C. Johnson, pp. 129-133.
538. Wiley, SN, p. 32.
539. See Stampp, pp. 280-281, 311-312.
540. Helper, ICS, p. 42.
541. As a Yankee diplomat in England, Charles Francis Adams Sr. created numerous problems for the Confederacy. One of his most monstrous actions was issuing Lincoln's order to threaten Great Britain with war should she aid the American South in any way. Such tactics were, of course, hypocritical since the U.S.

ambassador to Great Britain:

> I'm gradually getting to have very decided opinions on the negro question; they're growing up in me as inborn convictions and are not the result of reflection. I note what you say of the African race and 'the absence of all appearance of self reliance in their own power' during this struggle. From this, greatly as it has disappointed me, I very unwillingly draw different conclusions from your own. The conviction is forcing itself upon me that African slavery, as it existed in our slave states [the South], was indeed a patriarchal institution, under which the slaves were not, as a whole, unhappy, cruelly treated or overworked. I am forced to this conclusion.[542]

On November 9, 1862, the young Confederate diarist Sarah Morgan wrote sarcastically of Lincoln and the North's erroneous views of "Southern slavery." Sarah mingled, laughed, played, and worked with her family's black servants and knew the truth that the Yankee president dare not admit:

> If Lincoln could spend the grinding season on a plantation, he would recall his proclamation.[543] As it is, he has only proved himself a fool, without injuring us. Why last evening I took old [slave] Wilson's place at the baggasse chute, and kept the rollers free from cane until I had thrown down enough to fill several carts, and had my hands as black as his. What cruelty to slaves! And black Frank thinks me cruel, too, when he meets me with a patronising grin, and shows me the nicest vats of candy, and peels cane for me. Oh! very cruel![544]

One night Sarah sat in the lap of one of her servants, as a few dozen others gathered round a roaring fire and sang songs. Of the incident the nineteen year old Louisianian wrote:

---

herself had aided and supported "belligerent" nations in the past. For more on Adams and this topic, see Owsley, pp. 401-412.
542. W. C. Ford, Vol. 2, p. 215.
543. Sarah is referring here to Lincoln's Preliminary Emancipation Proclamation. Calling for abolition then black deportation, it was issued on September 22, 1862. Modern pro-North proponents, liberal educators, and fawning Lincolnites have tried to suppress this document, for obvious reasons. The entire document, with my commentary, can be found in my book *Lincolnology: The Real Abraham Lincoln Revealed In His Own Words*.
544. Dawson, pp. 277-278.

> Poor oppressed devils! Why did you not chunk us [whites] with the burning logs instead of looking happy, and laughing like fools? Really, some good old Abolitionist is needed here, to tell them how miserable they are. Can't Mass' Abe spare a few to enlighten his brethren?[545]

Fashionably and expensively dressed black servants "promenading" through town on Sundays almost always appalled Northern visitors to the South, for this image was the opposite of what they had been taught.[546] After fighting for some time in Virginia, one of Lincoln's soldiers, a private from New Hampshire, wrote: after now having seen Southern slavery for myself, I firmly believe that we Yanks have been fooled. It is nothing like we were taught. Why just the other day I saw slaves going to church who were as happy and cheerful as can be.[547]

When Northern landscape architect Frederick Law Olmsted traveled through Virginia in the early 1800s,[548] he was stunned by the incongruity of what he had believed about Southern "slavery" and the reality of Southern servitude: the slaves he witnessed working in the fields were either whistling or singing.[549] During his travels to America's Southland, English novelist William M. Thackeray (1811-1863) had a similar experience, as he discusses in his work, *Roundabout Papers*:

> How they sang; how they laughed and grinned; how they scraped, bowed, and complimented you and each other, those negroes of the cities of the Southern parts of the then United States! My business kept me in the towns; I was but in one negro-plantation village, and there were only women and little children, the men being out a-field. But there was plenty of cheerfulness in the huts, under the great trees—I speak of what I saw—and amidst the dusky bondsmen of the cities. I witnessed a curious gaiety; heard amongst the black folk endless singing, shouting, and laughter; and saw on holidays black gentlemen and ladies arrayed in such splendor and comfort as freeborn workmen in our towns seldom

---

545. Dawson, p. 278.
546. Stampp, p. 289.
547. Wiley, LBY, p. 43.
548. Olmsted, an anti-South author of numerous books, including, *A Journey in the Seaboard Slave States* (1856), is best known for being the designer of New York City's Central Park.
549. Stampp, p. 164.

exhibit.[550]

The anti-South community has tried long and hard to suppress and even destroy such descriptions of the Old South. But the Truth, Southern Truth, cannot be killed off. Despite the best efforts of South-loathing writers and educators, it lives on, for it is immortal.

We can never condone either slavery or servitude, for all forms of bondage violate the natural rights of humanity, and are thus immoral, unchristian, and undemocratic.[551] But resisting the urge to engage in presentism, we must face the facts, and the facts are that because of the South's equitable treatment of her black servants, their quality of life was, as studies show, superior to that of free blacks in almost every area,[552] including diet, health, housing, medical care, finances, clothing, death rates, life span, and childbearing.[553]

This was, in great part, because, like children, Southern servants were the legal charges of their masters and mistresses, and as such, by law, could not be fired, made homeless, or be allowed to starve.[554] To the contrary the owner was legally responsible for his or her servants' every need, from food, clothing, and shelter, to income, security, and health care.[555] But unlike actual children (who are considered adults at age eighteen), there was no time limit on this relationship. It lasted from birth to death.[556]

In 1857, Virginia planter George Fitzhugh wrote:

> The negro slaves of the South are the happiest, and, in some sense, the freest people in the world. The children and the aged and infirm work not at all, and yet have all the comforts and necessaries of life provided for them. They enjoy liberty, because they are oppressed neither by care nor labor. The women do little hard work, and are protected from the despotism of their husbands by their masters. The negro men and stout boys work, on the average, in good weather, not more than nine hours a day. The balance of their time is spent in perfect abandon. Besides, they

---

550. Thackeray, p. 127.
551. Nye, pp. 42-43.
552. Barrow, Segars, and Rosenburg, BC, pp. 153-154.
553. See Fogel and Engerman, pp. 84, 109-123, 124-125, 241, 261.
554. Hendelson, s.v. "slavery."
555. See Stampp, pp. 147, 279, 406-407.
556. Fogel, p. 191.

have their Sabbaths and holidays. White men, with so much of
license and liberty, would die of ennui; but negroes luxuriate in
corporeal and mental repose. With their faces upturned to the sun,
they can sleep at any hour; and quiet sleep is the greatest of human
enjoyments. 'Blessed be the man who invented sleep.' 'Tis
happiness in itself—and results from contentment with the present,
and confident assurance of the future. We do not know whether
free laborers ever sleep. They are fools to do so; for, whilst they
sleep, the wily and watchful capitalist is devising means to ensnare
and exploitate [exploit] them. The free laborer must work or
starve. He is more of a slave than the negro, because he works
longer and harder for less allowance than the slave, and has no
holiday, because the cares of life with him begin when its labors
end. . . . Free laborers have not a thousandth part of the rights and
liberties of negro slaves. Indeed, they have not a single right or a
single liberty, unless it be the right or liberty to die.[557]

Fitzhugh also commented on the unique relationship between the Southern slaveholder and the Southern servant:

The negro slave is free . . . when the labors of the day are over, and
free in mind as well as body; for the master provides food, raiment,
house, fuel, and every thing else necessary to the physical well-
being of himself and his family. The master's labors commence
when the slave's end. No wonder white slaveholders should prefer
the slavery of white men and capital to negro slavery, since the
white slave holding is more profitable, and is free from all the cares
and labors of black slave-holding.[558] . . . the master works nearly
as hard for the negro, as he for the master.[559]

Yes, free blacks were indeed free. But they were also free to be fired, free to go bankrupt, free to become homeless, free to suffer (even die) from untreated illnesses, and free to end up in the streets and starve. This was particularly true in the North where, as we will see, white racism was at its most severe and deeply ingrained.

Thus, despite their bondage, the "mildness" and humanity most Southern servants experienced must be taken into consideration. How else to explain the complete lack of slave revolts, riots, and insurrections

---

557. Stedman and Hutchinson, Vol. 6, pp. 324-325.
558. Mackay, p. 253.
559. Hacker, p. 543.

during Lincoln's War? While there were various reasons for this, one of them was certainly the humane treatment that most Southern black servants received from the owners.[560]

While we denounce servitude and slavery in all their varied forms, at the same time it must be acknowledged that Southern slavery offered other advantages to those in bondage. In the mid 1800s, for instance, Southern servants worked a mere 58 hours a week compared to between 60 and 72 hours for free workers in the American North and in England.[561] Black Southern slaves also consumed greater quantities of food than free blacks, and in height (considered an index of nutritional status) they were taller than most 19th-Century European workers, an indication that they were much better fed.[562]

It was for these very reasons, and others, that after Lincoln's "emancipation," the quality of life (including diet, death rates, health, skills, and wage gap) for newly freed Southern blacks immediately plummeted,[563] not recovering to the level it had been under servitude, so-called "Southern slavery," until 1939, at the start of World War II, nearly a century later.[564]

Adeline Grey, a black South Carolina servant, later noted that though a girl when "liberation" came, she could still vividly remember it, while slavery was but a dim memory. Why? Because life was much more difficult after emancipation than before.[565] Thus, just prior to Lincoln's War, Southerner James H. Hammond could write:

> I believe that our slaves are the happiest three millions of human beings on whom the sun shines. Into their Eden is coming Satan in the guise of an abolitionist.[566]

While today we cannot agree with Hammond that the Old South's system of servitude was an "Eden" for all blacks, we can certainly say that the institution as practiced in Dixie was nothing like Harriet

---

560. Ashe, p. 36.
561. Fogel, p. 28. See also p. 78.
562. See Fogel, pp. 137, 138-140.
563. L. Johnson, p. 190; Cooper, JDA, p. 690; see Bruce, passim.
564. Fogel and Engerman, p. 261.
565. Hurmence, p. 102.
566. Harper, Hammond, Simms, and Dew, p. 133.

Beecher Stowe and other Northern propagandists have painted it. In fact, for many of both races, life in the Old South was exactly as Margaret Mitchell depicted it in her classic Southern novel, *Gone With the Wind*. What Northerners and New South scallywags disparagingly call her "make-believe world," did exist after all,[567] and those who read her book will see the Old South as it really was, without the distortions, lies, and South-hating propaganda of Yankee folklore.[568]

With all its dangers and uncertainties, would "enslaved" blacks have traded servitude for freedom? Of course, and some did. But, weighing things in the balance, many more—95 percent of all Southern black servants—did not.[569] Instead, this group chose to remain in their homeland after "emancipation," on their masters' plantations, where safety and certainty reigned.[570] Though the Underground Railroad functioned throughout most of the War, only about 2,000 slaves (just 500 Southern servants a year) out of 3.5 million availed themselves of it—a mere 0.05 percent of the total.[571] The rest voluntarily stayed at home, defending both their owners' farms, and the owners themselves, from marauding Yanks.[572]

What occurred at the Confederate home of Sarah Morgan's parents was the norm, not the exception, as Northern myth insists. On the day of Jubilee (emancipation) in New Orleans, Louisiana, her family's slaves were (illegally) "set free" by arrogant Yankee officers, who ordered the servants to leave with them. All refused, however. One servant named Margret, snapped back at the Union soldiers: "I don't want to be any free-er than I is now—I'll stay with my mistress." Another of the Morgan's servants, a black man, was tossed a musket and commanded to join the Federal army, to which he replied: "I am only a slave, but I am a secesh nigger, and won't fight in such a damned crew!"[573]

---

567. M. M. Smith, p. 33.
568. C. Johnson, pp. 14-15. In a 1977 interview for *Newsweek* magazine (November 28), President Jimmy Carter said that his favorite film was *Gone With the Wind*. His, however, was a "different version" from the one normally seen. In Carter's rendition his favorite scenes were "the burning of Schenectady, New York, and President Grant surrendering to Robert E. Lee." Website: http://muendy.tripod.com/quotes.html.
569. Gragg, p. 88.
570. Current, LNK, p. 228.
571. Shenkman, p. 124. One other overly generous estimate puts the number of slaves aided by the Underground Railroad at an unlikely 4,000 individuals—even if accurate, still a fraction of the total. See Rosenbaum and Brinkley, s.v. "Underground Railroad."
572. Gragg, pp. 191-192.
573. Dawson, pp. 211-212.

It was this same loyal, stay-at-home group—representing 95 percent of all Southern blacks (a group even recognized by Lincoln)[574]—that eventually inspired the concept of sharecropping: as nearly all slaves refused to leave their plantations after emancipation, owners simply subdivided their land into small plots and turned them over to their new freedmen and freedwomen. This saved blacks from having to seek employment elsewhere (or worse, try and raise money to buy their own land), while it saved plantation owners the trouble of trying to find new employees.[575]

There was something far deeper going on here than just mere practicality, however.

Former slaves quite rightly considered themselves true Americans and true Southerners. After all, by 1860, 99 percent of all blacks were native-born Americans, a larger percentage than for whites.[576] Educator and former Southern servant Booker T. Washington eloquently spoke for the 95 percent of Southern blacks who remained in Dixie after Lincoln's emancipation, when he wrote:

> I was born in the South, I have lived and labored in the South, and I expect to die and be buried in the South.[577]

On September 29, 1865, just five months after Lincoln's War came to an end at Appomattox, North Carolina blacks held a "Negro Convention" that issued the following declaration:

> Born upon the same soil and brought up in an intimacy of relationship unknown in any other state of society, we have formed attachments for the white race which must be as enduring as life, and we can conceive of no reason that our God-bestowed freedom should now sever the kindly ties which have so long united us. . .
>
> We acknowledge with gratitude that there are those among former slave masters who have promptly conceded our freedom and have manifested a just and humane disposition

---

574. See e.g., Nicolay and Hay, ALCW, Vol. 2, pp. 473-474.
575. White, Foscue, and McKnight, p. 212. It should be pointed out that there were also white sharecroppers. Wilson and Ferris, s.v. "Plantations."
576. Fogel and Engerman, pp. 23-24.
577. Scott and Stowe, p. 321. Dr. Washington's expectation was fulfilled. He was buried in Tuskegee, Alabama, on November 17, 1915.

towards their former slaves. . .

> Though associated with many memories of suffering, as well as of enjoyment, we have always loved our homes, and dreaded, as the worst of evils, a forcible separation from them. Now that freedom and a new career are before us, we love this land and people more than ever before. Here we have toiled and suffered; our parents, wives, and children are buried here; and in this land we will remain, unless forcibly driven away.[578]

So strong was their attachment to Dixie that as late as the 1880s, a generation after the "Civil War," 90 percent of all Southern blacks still lived in the plantation belts of the Deep South.[579]

Naturally the North conveniently glosses over these facts, and instead focuses on anti-South Yankee myths. None are more popular, absurd, and misunderstood than those dealing with the whipping post and the separation of slave families on the auction block.

The person most responsible for these offensive and false stereotypes was Yankee author, Harriet Beecher Stowe, whose anti-South fiction, *Uncle Tom's Cabin*, made her a household name. Unfortunately for those who have embraced her fantasies about the South, Stowe—a resident of Cincinnati, Ohio[580]—never stepped foot in Dixie,[581] never saw a real working Southern plantation,[582] had no idea how Southern servitude actually worked, ignored the reality of both black and Native-American slave owners, and knew next to nothing about African-American culture itself.

Just as problematic, her book was "inspired" by *Truth Is Stranger Than Fiction*, the autobiography of Josiah Henson (1789-1883), a Northern slave who had no knowledge of the realities of Southern servitude.[583]

Much of the rest of Stowe's book was written entirely from information gathered secondhand,[584] usually from vitriolic, anti-South abolitionist tracts, whose wild tales were filled with two-dimensional,

---

[578]. S. Andrews, pp. 128-129, 130.
[579]. Cooper, JDA, p. 690.
[580]. Cartmell, p. 135.
[581]. C. Johnson, pp. 142-143.
[582]. Garraty and McCaughey, p. 230.
[583]. Stowe admitted as much, which is why Henson later republished his autobiography under the title: *The Memoirs of Uncle Tom*.
[584]. Rosenbaum and Brinkley, s.v. "Uncle Tom's Cabin."

cartoon-like characters that never existed in Dixie.[585] Even William Lloyd Garrison, the renowned Yankee abolitionist, admitted that *Uncle Tom's Cabin* could only be read as a novel, not as a true story.[586] Johnny Reb simply referred to the book as "that damn Yankee lie."[587]

Further proof that Stowe's book was pure fantasy is the fact that the violent horrors she depicted between black slaves and their white masters and mistresses were illegal, punishable by strict law, and denounced by all good Southern people.[588]

Her portrait of "Southern plantation life" was, in the end, full of inaccuracies[589] and gross generalizations and contradictions;[590] highly distorted and irrational, her black characters were atypical.[591] All this without a word of "how the North [too] is implicated in the guilt of slavery," as Southern abolitionist Angelina Grimké phrased it in 1837.[592] *Uncle Tom's Cabin* was considered so pernicious by Tennesseans that petitions were sent to local theater managers to ban theatrical performances of the book. Southern parents denounced the play as highly "exaggerated," correctly complaining that it would have "a very bad effect on the children who might see the drama."[593]

Uncle Tom's Cabin was a work of Yankee propaganda pure and simple, a political fable filled with both misinformation and disinformation meant to rouse Northern passions against the institution of slavery, a common ploy of Northern abolitionists. While even blacks, both then and today, have complained that she made her black hero Tom "too good to be true," Stowe herself, finally bowing to criticism and pressure, eventually admitted that her book was a far cry from reality.[594]

As it was all fakery, where then did Stowe come up with her illusionary ideas, exaggerated characters, and outlandish yarns? As mentioned, it is well-known that she took much of the material for her tall

---

585. Civil War Society, ECW, s.v. "Stowe, Harriet Beecher."
586. Nye, p. 161.
587. Wiley, LJR, p. 162.
588. Fox-Genovese, p. 360. Sadistic and abusive Southern white slave owners were routinely reported to authorities, not by their black servants, but by their white neighbors.
589. Boatner, s.v. *"Uncle Tom's Cabin."*
590. Hedrick, p. 9.
591. Garraty and McCaughey, p. 230.
592. Hacker, p. 558.
593. S. K. Taylor, p. 65.
594. Hedrick, pp. 9, 10.

tales from abolitionary tracts, South-hating leaflets put out by Northern antislavery societies.[595] The rest came from her own overwrought imagination, one that Southerner Mary Chesnut referred to as execrable, repugnant, damnable, and obscene.[596] It was, in fact, nothing more than an overly sentimentalized and fictional "pamphlet against the Fugitive Slave Law" written "under the disguise of a novel."[597]

Despite her ignorance and misrepresentations, however, Stowe succeeded in her own personal goal: to raise awareness about black servitude and the methods by which to rid the nation of it. For she, like her heroes Lincoln and Greeley (and, at one time, Garrison),[598] was an ardent colonizationist who looked forward to the day when all blacks would be shipped out of America.[599]

Unfortunately, Stowe's book, by coalescing antislavery sentiment, was also instrumental in aiding and abetting one of the most useless, illicit, and costly conflicts in world history: Lincoln's War. So powerful was her influence on Northern public opinion that Lincoln himself once called her "the little woman who made this great war."[600]

While this is an outright lie (Lincoln never once took responsibility for any of his own criminal actions), Stowe's real contribution was nearly as evil: *Uncle Tom's Cabin* helped prolong the conflict that Lincoln started by at least two years. During that period of time (January 1, 1863 to April 9, 1865), hundreds of thousands of Southerners *and* Northerners died, while slavery dragged on, all unnecessarily. And for this Stowe has been apotheosized and extolled by the North and the New South!

Stowe's book created other problems as well. Her fallacious perception of the South was taken as genuine fact by Victorian Yankees, which has unfairly damaged the South's image and reputation right into the present day. *Uncle Tom's Cabin* also helped whip up Northern support for the abolition movement, which anti-abolitionist Lincoln later cunningly used to his advantage against the Confederacy, as we will discuss shortly.

The truths that Stowe ignored were legion. The facts are that

---

595. Civil War Society, ECW, s.v. "Stowe, Harriet Beecher."
596. Chesnut, MCCW, p. 583.
597. Encyc. Brit., s.v. "slavery."
598. Fogel, p. 254.
599. Burlingame, p. 50.
600. Fields, p. 269.

black servant families were rarely separated; slaves were almost never sold after purchase; whites did not buy slaves to elevate their social status; there was no such thing as "slave breeding" (to the contrary, owners encouraged traditional marriage and family life);[601] and, as we have seen, slaves were not poorly fed, poorly housed, poorly clothed, or poorly cared for (enslaved blacks actually had larger houses, as well as better clothes, diets, and medical care than free blacks, and even many free whites). Lastly, the death and suicide rates among slaves were lower than those for whites, while slaves' life spans were longer; and we have the statistical studies of slavery scholars to prove it.[602]

Common sense alone obliterates Northern mythology regarding so-called Southern "slaves." The fact is that what was in the slave's best interest was also usually in the owner's best interest, and vice versa. For the cold but universal business maxim is that contented workers always produce more profit than discontented ones. As such, in some Southern states, Louisiana, for example, it was illegal to divide up slave families. But even where it was lawful, the practice was so heavily frowned upon by most Southerners that it rarely occurred.[603] Furthermore, the few restrictive laws that did exist, were unevenly or rarely enforced. The result? Most Southern servants lived a life of considerable freedom, personal independence, and self-reliance, one far from the nasty, brutish existence portrayed by anti-South writers like Harriet Beecher Stowe.[604]

Let us now look at the myth of the whipping post. This form of severe discipline was inhumane and thus was always bad for morale—for both servants *and* owners. Additionally, a servant with whip marks (a potential sign of disciplinary problems) was not worth as much as one without. Again, slave owners approached their occupation as a business, and even used professionally authored manuals to run their plantations and manage their servants (*all* early plantation manuals strongly advised against whipping and dividing families).

On the plantation, as in all forms of business, the bottom line was to keep the cost of labor low, production and profits high. Southern planters were, after all, competitive capitalists just like their industrial

---

601. See e.g., Seabrook, TAHSR, pp. 12-13.
602. See Fogel and Engerman, pp. 49-54, 70, 79-84, 109-126, 128.
603. U. B. Phillips, p. 493.
604. Brinkley, p. 323.

counterparts to the North.⁶⁰⁵ Separating families and whipping would have been counterproductive since these would have increased costs while decreasing profits. And in fact, it was for these very reasons that punishments for black Southern servants were by necessity much lighter than for free Southern whites for the same crimes.⁶⁰⁶

While we are on the topic of the South's so-called "lords of the lash and loom," it should be noted that the truth about the whip, slaves, and plantation discipline has been so thoroughly distorted by South-hating advocates, authors, and scholars over the years that it is scarcely recognizable now.⁶⁰⁷ Let us reestablish the facts then.

When a Southern slave owner was put in a position where force was needed (such as with a violent servant)—which for the average slaver was seldom if at all (many owners permanently banned the whip from their farms and plantations)⁶⁰⁸—it was not motivated by "the innate cruelty" or "sadistic tendencies of Southern whites," as Yankee myth ridiculously promotes. It was motivated by the same thing that motivates modern, free labor bosses: the desire for maximum profits. Jefferson Davis told the truth, one that no anti-South proponent wants to hear, when he commented on the alleged "cruelty" of servant owners. On Southern plantations, the Confederate president affirmed, inhumane treatment "probably exists to a smaller extent than in any other relation of labor to capital" in the world.⁶⁰⁹

Indeed, Southerners hated unmerciful slave owners and the use of the whip was widely regarded as completely unneeded and indefensible.⁶¹⁰ What is more, the violence, unethical treatment, and immorality portrayed between black slaves and their masters and mistresses in books like *Uncle Tom's Cabin*, was not only rare, but was, as mentioned, a punishable crime in the South.⁶¹¹ In fact, by the early 1800s, *all* Southern states had passed anti-cruelty laws that provided fines, imprisonment, and even execution for those who mistreated their servants, and more than one sadistic slaver died at the wrong end of a

---

605. Brinkley, p. 318.
606. Coit, p. 288.
607. Stonebraker, p. 50.
608. Fogel and Engerman, p. 146.
609. *Appendix to the Congressional Globe*, 31ˢᵗ Congress, 1ˢᵗ Session, 1850, Vol. 23, Part 1, p. 150.
610. Stampp, pp. 178, 179.
611. Fox-Genovese, p. 360; Hendelson, s.v. "slavery."

lawman's bullet.[612]

While today's supervisors use the threat of demotion and termination for inferior work or bad behavior, Victorian slavers used the threat of force, for this was then the accepted approach to discipline. One of the instruments of force sometimes resorted to, of course, was the infamous whip.

But whipping was not a corrective tool created especially for the institution of Southern slavery, as the North and New South teaches. Actually, from the 1600s to the 1800s it was the standard form of punishment in the U.S. for misdemeanors; and it was applied to lawbreakers of every kind, whether male or female, whether black, white, brown, or red.[613] As such, there can little doubt that far more American whites were whipped by the local sheriff than American blacks.[614]

The custom of whipping was a gift of the English, who left us records of "rogues" being "graciously whipped" from as early as the late 1500s. The practice was then brought to America with the very first wave of Anglo immigrants.[615]

As early as 1698, for example, Pennsylvanian Gabriel Thomas was writing that:

> Thieves of all sorts, are oblig'd to restore four fold after they have been Whipt and Imprison'd, according to the Nature of their Crime; and if they be not of Ability to restore four fold, they must be in Servitude till 'tis satisfied.[616]

Here we see that at the time criminals were not only whipped for their misdeeds, but were also sentenced to a form of bondage known as servitude, the exact same type that millions of black "slaves" would later serve under in the American South.

The truth, contrary to Northern, anti-South folklore, is that from New England to the Deep South, the whipping post was the centerpiece of the village green in hundreds of towns and cities across early America. The standard punishment for horse thieves, for example, nearly all who

---

612. Stampp, pp. 219-222.
613. Fogel and Engerman, p. 146.
614. Ashe, p. 64.
615. Hacker, pp. 29, 35.
616. G. Thomas, p. 47.

were white, was "three good whippings," each one consisting of thirty-nine lashes.[617]

Whipping was the standard military punishment at the time as well. During the Revolutionary War, while the "father of the nation," George Washington, served as General of the Continental Army, he had his white soldiers regularly whipped for a host of offences ranging from drunkenness to desertion.[618] His whippings were so terrible and extreme that Congress had to intervene and place a limit on the number of lashes that could be doled out to an individual.[619]

In 1812, an enlightened and more humane Congress made courts-martial whippings entirely unlawful (in one of the more notorious cases a white soldier had been branded, had his head shaved, and was given fifty lashes). Military officers objected, saying that it was the only sure means of enforcing discipline. Congress then later lifted the ban and whipping was reinstated in 1833.[620] On navy ships whipping was so common as a form of punishment that even abolitionists stepped in to protest on humanitarian terms.[621]

Before the start of Lincoln's War the custom of whipping was outlawed again—and ignored again. So widely accepted was it that both the Union and the Confederate Congresses felt the need to enact new, stronger prohibition laws. Passed in August 1861 (by the North), and in April 1862 (by the South), these acts too were completely disregarded, and whipping continued on as if it were perfectly legal. Men were not the only ones to ply the lash. In one case, Confederate Congressman George G. Vest of Mississippi was whipped by a woman.[622]

As the "Civil War" progressed, white farmers in the South risked being whipped by Confederate authorities for violating the government's ban on growing cotton instead of food.[623] Yankee troops whipped Southern noncombatants as readily as they whipped Rebel soldiers. In Screven County, Georgia, for instance, a white citizen who was found

---

617. Coit, pp. 37, 48.
618. Collier and Collier, p. 51.
619. Jensen, NN, p. 33.
620. Alotta, p. 3.
621. Stampp, p. 410.
622. W. B. Garrison, ACW, pp. 11-12.
623. Channing, p. 29; Wiley, SN, p. 45.

armed was given 200 lashes by a Union officer.[624]

It is well-known that both white and black Yankee soldiers used the whip on "stubborn" captured Southern blacks between 1861 and 1865.[625] "Insubordinate" black Yankee soldiers were sometimes whipped by their white superiors as well.[626] Black Union soldiers were known to whip white civilians during the War.[627]

An incident involving Yankee General Jefferson C. Davis (no relation to Confederate President Jefferson Davis) is instructive. In February 1863, several Union soldiers were caught molesting a young Confederate girl in Tennessee. As punishment Federal authorities had their heads shaved then tied them to cannon wheels. After receiving fifty lashes with a rawhide whip on their bare backs, they were thrown out of camp. (They were lucky Confederate General Nathan Bedford Forrest and his men had not gotten to them first.) One of the criminals turned "informer" and was spared the whip. However, in return he was forced to mete out the whippings on the others. A witness later wrote that one screamed and prayed passionately, another was completely silent, while a third whimpered profusely.[628]

It is true that aboard Yankee slave ships, unruly black slaves on their way from Africa to the Americas were sometimes whipped during the infamous Middle Passage. But what Northern mythology always leaves out is the fact that on these same slave runs, unruly white sailors were whipped as well. In fact, eyewitnesses described the practice as "constant flogging," with men dying from their wounds on a daily basis, both black *and* white.[629]

During Lincoln's War, Southern cotton plantations were "taken over" (i.e., stolen) from their owners and white Yankee officers and Northern businessmen were put in charge. Freed blacks were then transferred to these farms to labor at the same menial jobs they had performed while slaves. Worse, their white Yankee overseers were often permitted to use the whip. At times the use of the lash became so frequent that it had to be disallowed, but the practice continued behind

---

624. Harwell, p. 339.
625. Wiley, SN, pp. 213, 244, 245.
626. See Quarles, pp. 208-209; Wiley, SN, pp. 316-317.
627. Henry, ATSF, p. 246.
628. Wiley, LBY, p. 208.
629. Blassingame, p. 15.

closed doors.⁶³⁰ For, as Union General Thomas West Sherman reported to his superiors in Washington,

> the [freed] Negroes are disinclined to labor and will evidently not work to our satisfaction without . . . the driver and the lash.⁶³¹

It was this attitude that has caused objective modern historians to admit that freed blacks were better off working on plantations run by the far more lenient Southerner than his racist counterpart from the North.⁶³² Of this practice the black editors of the New Orleans newspaper, the *Tribune*, angrily noted that the South's plantations were rented out to greedy Northerners, whose only goal was to use and exploit freedmen for the sake of the almighty dollar. The former slaves were thus re-enslaved and "chained to the soil." This is what the 19th-Century Yankee called "freedom for the black man."⁶³³

Even after Lincoln's War was over, Yankees continued to use the whip as a method of punishment across the South during so-called "Reconstruction."⁶³⁴ Native-Americans too relied on the lash during this period: when freed blacks were caught coming into Indian territory, they were soundly flogged.⁶³⁵ And in the North, postwar whites in Massachusetts routinely whipped blacks who overstayed their welcome (the limit a nonresident black could remain in the "abolitionist" Bay State was two months).⁶³⁶

The whip then was the normal American penalty for unwanted behavior. Thus it was only natural that it was also used to enforce authority on plantations. In fact, black slaves themselves, such as those who worked in positions of power (e.g., mammies, overseers, and drivers), regularly used the whip on other black slaves when the situation warranted it.⁶³⁷ And we will note that *black* slave owners—of which there were tens of thousands across the South—occasionally used it on their

---

630. See e.g., Wiley, SN, pp. 213, 214, 244, 245.
631. *ORA*, Ser. 1, Vol. 6, p. 204.
632. Wiley, SN, p. 248.
633. J. M. McPherson, NCW, p. 295.
634. See e.g., J. Davis, RFCG, Vol. 2, p. 626.
635. Grissom, p. 183.
636. McManus, BBN, p. 183.
637. See Fogel, p. 26; Genovese, pp. 356, 368, 371, 374, 378-380, 385, 386, 542.

black servants as well.[638]

Such intimidation was not imposed to produce submissive and docile slaves, as Northern mythologists have long claimed. Rather it was used to create the largest and best product at the lowest cost in the most efficient manner.

While today even shoving a person can result in arrest for "assault and battery," in the 1800s brutal physical punishments of all kinds were regarded as the norm. As late as the mid-1800s, the English were still whipping child factory workers (all of them white) who underperformed. In America, black slave parents often brutally whipped their disobedient offspring (with switches), while black male slaves were known to whip their wives when they felt it was "necessary."[639] In most Western nations this approach to discipline lasted well into the 20th Century, and there are, no doubt, people reading this book who will recall being "whipped" with a belt or spanked with a paddle as a youngster. It is well-known, for example, that President Jimmy Carter was whipped as a child.[640]

In 18th-Century America then, the whipping of a slave was considered no more exceptional or barbaric than the whipping of an obstreperous child by its parents.[641] Lincoln's wife Mary Todd Lincoln, for example, often whipped their children, as the Yankee president unabashedly acknowledged in a letter dated October 22, 1846.[642] General Nathan Bedford Forrest, like most Victorian Southern children, was routinely whipped for poor behavior as a schoolboy,[643] so it was only natural that later in life, as a slave trader and slave owner, he occasionally used the whip on his black servants.

Does this shock and repulse us today? Of course. But perhaps not quite as much when we learn that as a military officer in the Confederate army, Forrest also whipped his white soldiers for a variety of infractions.[644]

It is important to remember that the U.S. judicial system expected slave owners (Northern and Southern) to attend to disciplinary matters themselves, so as not to clog up the courts with petty grievances

---

638. Drescher and Engerman, pp. 214, 215.
639. See Genovese, pp. 470, 482, 504, 508-511.
640. DeGregorio, s.v. "Jimmy Carter" (p. 619).
641. Horn, IE, p. 68.
642. Nicolay and Hay, ALCW, Vol. 1, p. 89.
643. Lytle, p. 14; Parks, p. 82.
644. Morton, pp. 148-149; Wyeth, p. 302.

concerning disobedient slaves.[645] Additionally, as there were far worse penalties (such as being branded with a hot iron or shot before a firing squad), use of the whip was an accepted and recognized form of penalizing not only black servants, but criminals of all colors and social statuses.

The truth is that only sadists, and those with other psychopathological forms of mental illness, engage in abuse. As psychopaths are rare, instances of extreme physical discipline on Southern plantations were also rare. When they were used, it was about pure economics. For too much force would have increased rather than decreased the cost of labor.

This is just one of the many reasons why African-American, Native-American, and European-American slave owners did not use physical coercion on their human chattel unless absolutely necessary.[646] Even in the most severe cases, owners were much more likely to rely on traditional methods of punishment, such as withdrawal of privileges, being assigned unpleasant tasks, or temporary confinement.[647]

In the end, actual use of the whip was indeed often unnecessary, for it was mainly seen across early America as a symbol of law and order. Knowing it existed, and that it *might* be used, was usually enough to keep even the most incorrigible citizens, free or enslaved, white or black, in line.

With such knowledge at hand, can we still believe that whipping was a purely Southern custom used only by sadistic whites only on black "slaves"?

In summary, it is a Northern myth that "slavery was universally cruel and barbaric," and that "it was practiced widely across the South." In truth, all "barbarities" against slaves, such as mutilation, branding, chaining, and of course, murder, were heavily regulated and banned by law in the South.[648]

Actually, the correct term for the Southern form of so-called "slavery" is servitude, which is why Victorian Southerners did not refer to their African bondsmen as slaves. Instead, like South Carolina belle Mary Chesnut and thousands of other Southerners, they correctly referred to

---

645. Horn, IE, p. 68.
646. See Fogel and Engerman, pp. 232, 238-239.
647. Drescher and Engerman, p. 207.
648. Hendelson, s.v. "slavery."

them as "servants," "domestics," "maids," "butlers," "menservants," "womenservants," "hands," "operatives," "tenants," and "peasants," almost anything but "slaves."

Was there cruelty on Southern farms and plantations? Absolutely. But, unlike what Northern myth would have us believe, it was infrequent and altogether uncommon. The normal dynamic between whites and blacks ranged from one of outright love and affection to one consisting of a formal and mutually respectful business relationship.

Little wonder then that as many as 80 percent of the black "slaves" who chronicled their lives in the "Slave Narratives" had only positive words when it came to assessing their relationships with their owners.[649] In 1868, for example, former servant Elizabeth Keckley wrote a book entitled *Behind the Scenes*. In it she assailed neither slavery or whites. Instead, Keckley recounts the positive experiences she had, including a joyous reunion with her former owners.[650]

Other Southern black servants concurred. One wrote: "I have no desire to represent the life of slavery as an experience of nothing but misery." Instead, he recalled

> jolly Christmas times, dances before old massa's door for the first drink of egg-nog, extra meat at holiday times, midnight visits to apple orchards, broiling stray chickens, and first-rate tricks to dodge work. The God who makes the pup gambol, and the kitten play, and the bird sing, and the fish leap, was the author in me of many a light-hearted hour.[651]

Many free American blacks and whites never experienced anything remotely similar.

---

649. Kennedy, p. 91.
650. Keckley, pp. 238-266.
651. Henson, p. 20.

African Slavery, Yankee Slave Trade

IF THE SOUTH DID NOT practice slavery, where then did the term "Southern slavery" come from?

This phrase is a piece of revisionist history invented by the North and imposed on the South to tarnish her honor and reputation. Like Stowe's polemic work of fiction, it too succeeded, and even now, in the 21st Century, it is the South that is still unjustly associated with slavery, along with all of its attendant evils, both real and imaginary.[652]

In 1886 Pollard wrote:

> . . . we [Southerners] use the term '*slavery*' . . . under strong protest. For there is no such thing in the South; it is a term fastened upon us by the exaggeration and conceit of Northern literature, and most improperly acquiesced in by Southern writers. There is a system of African *servitude* in the South; in which the negro, so far from being under the absolute dominion of his master (which is the true meaning of the vile word 'slavery'), has, by *law* of the land, his personal rights recognized and protected, and his comfort and 'right' of 'happiness' consulted, and by the *practice* of the system, has a sum of individual indulgences, which makes him altogether the most striking type in the world of cheerfulness and contentment.[653]

As mentioned, I am not defending either servitude or slavery. All

---

652. See Seabrook, EYWTAASIW, passim; Seabrook, S101, passim
653. Pollard, SHW, Vol. 2, p. 202.

rational people today abhor both as violations of natural, human, and civil rights. It is merely to reevaluate Northern mythology so that we may clarify and establish the truth about what was and what was not practiced in the Old South before and during Lincoln's reign.

Contrary to Yankee folklore, Lincoln's Emancipation Proclamation did not completely end "slavery" in the U.S. or anywhere else. For one thing, slavery continues to thrive around the globe today, with some 200 million people worldwide suffering under some type of bondage[654] (in contrast, the South never possessed more than 3.5 million servants;[655] in 1860, 86 percent which were American born).[656] As for the U.S. itself, according to a recent CIA study, 50,000 people (mostly women and children) of all colors and races are enslaved in the U.S. each year.[657] Theoretically then, the number of slaves in modern-day America must number in the many hundreds of thousands.

This is minor in comparison to modern day Africa, where millions now live under the harshest forms of slavery. This is no recent development. In what is known as the "Oriental Slave Trade" (as opposed to the "Occidental Slave Trade" of Europeans),[658] Africans have been enslaving each other for thousands of years, dating back to at least 2,200 years ago. It is at this time, during the continent's Iron Age, that we begin to see definitive evidence of African slavery, an institution already in progress over 1,600 years before the arrival of the first Arabic,[659] and later European and Yankee, slave ships.[660]

The victims of the pre-conquest African slave trade were captured inland or in East Africa, then exported to Persia, Arabia, India, and China.[661] Thus the first European slavers to venture to Africa (the Portuguese arrived in 1441)[662] only interrupted the booming slave trade that had already been going on there for centuries—after which they helped stimulate it.[663]

---

654. Website: www.pbs.org/newshour/bb/law/jan-june01/slavery_3-8.html.
655. Cooper, JDA, p. 378; Quarles, p. xiii.
656. Garraty and McCaughey, p. 214. See also Fogel and Engerman, pp. 23-24.
657. Website: www.pbs.org/newshour/bb/law/jan-june01/slavery_3-8.html.
658. Craig, Graham, Kagan, Ozment, and Turner, p. 571.
659. See Moore and Dunbar, pp. 112-116.
660. Davidson, TAST, p. 30.
661. Craig, Graham, Kagan, Ozment, and Turner, p. 252.
662. Penrose, p. 49; Willis, pp. 687-688; J. H. Parry, p. 27; Herring, p. 104.
663. Moore and Dunbar, pp. 103, 106; Durant, pp. 31-32.

Along with slavery, servitude, vassalage, and serfdom were also practiced among pre-European Africans, whose kingdoms routinely engaged in the mass subjugation of neighboring tribes.[664] The kingdom of Dahomey, for example, instigated an annual "war" every year for the sole purpose of acquiring slaves.[665] Some Africans were enslaved for nothing more than breaking African laws,[666] such as not paying off a financial obligation. If the individual was not able to discharge the debt he or she became a "lifetime slave."[667]

Native African rulers even went as far as enslaving their own subjects, often setting fire to villages at night in order to seize the terror stricken inhabitants as they fled.[668] After capture they were locked in wretched "slave prisons" (known as barracoons), sometimes for months at a time, after which they were summarily sold off to the highest bidder.[669] As enslaving POWs was also an innate part of the African slaving system, this was considered a "normal proceeding."[670] It is said that at one time large regions of Africa were completely depopulated by "barbarous" African kings in order to furnish slaves to Arabic countries.[671]

Besides the Dahomeans, other early African peoples who practiced indigenous slavery included the Swahili,[672] the Hausas, the Mandingos, the Ibos, the Efiks, the Krus, the Fantins, the Binis, the Sengalese,[673] the Malians,[674] the Gambians,[675] the Kenyans,[676] Mozambicans,[677] inhabitants of the Loango kingdom[678] and the Benin kingdom,[679] the Yoruba of western Nigeria, the Fon of Dahomey, and the

---

664. Dormon and Jones, pp. 62-63.
665. Herskovits, p. 35.
666. Bennett, BTM, p. 47.
667. Dormon and Jones, p. 63.
668. Encyc. Brit., "slavery."
669. Davidson, TBMB, p. 21.
670. J. H. Parry, p. 150.
671. Encyc. Brit., "slavery"; J. H. Parry, pp. 64-65, 150.
672. Dowley, p. 563.
673. Bennett, BTM, pp. 46-47.
674. Cappelluti and Grossman, p. 161.
675. Carruth, p. 1518.
676. Carruth, p. 1531.
677. Carruth, p. 1544.
678. Carruth, p. 1517.
679. V. M. Dean, p. 163.

Ashanti (or Asante) of Ghana.[680] Entire African civilizations were built on and maintained by slavery, using some of the world's most extreme, dehumanizing, exploitive, cruel, and savage forms of bondage known.[681]

Like the slavery-practicing Bornu people of Nigeria, the Ashanti divided their slaves into castes: 1) *Akyere*: a slave who was to be executed for a crime. 2) *Odonko*: a foreign-born slave. 3) *Awowa*: a creditor's pawn. 4) *Akoa pa*: a pawn who was to become a slave.[682]

Since numerous African slaving peoples, such as the Yoruba and the Ashanti, were known to ritually sacrifice human beings,[683] we should not be surprised at the barbaric treatment of their slaves.[684] On one occasion, for example, the Ashanti slaughtered some 2,600 African slaves at a single public sacrifice. In 1873, when the British seized Kumasi, a city in southern central Ghana, they discovered a huge brass bowl five feet in diameter: in it the Ashanti had collected the blood of countless thousands of sacrificed African slaves and used it to wash the footstools of deceased African kings.[685] Did anything in the American South ever compare to such horrendous savagery?

Indigenous slavery was so commonplace to the continent that "all peoples" of Central Africa later played a role in supporting the European slave trade.[686] Indeed, of the four classes of slavery identified by slavery scholars, 1) captives of war; 2) debtors and criminals; 3) individuals who have sold themselves or were sold as children into slavery; and 4) children of slaves, "Negro Africa" is one of the few regions on earth that possesses all four.[687] Famed Scottish missionary David Livingstone spent thirty years on the continent[688] trying to drain what he called the "open sore of Africa," the African slave trade—in this case, with Arabia.[689]

Although countless African regions exported African slaves, the chief six were Senegambia, Sierra Leone, Gold Coast, Bight of Benin,

---

680. Moore and Dunbar, pp. 86-87; Carruth, pp. 1519, 1585; Cappelluti and Grossman, p. 159; Craig, Graham, Kagan, Ozment, and Turner, pp. 556-557.
681. See Davidson, TAST, pp. 120-121, 123-124, 229, 242, 251; Stavrianos, p. 570.
682. Dormon and Jones, p. 93.
683. Dormon and Jones, p. 64.
684. Mbiti, p. 60.
685. Moore and Dunbar, p. 129.
686. Herskovits, p. 42.
687. Doubleday's Encyc., s.v. "slavery."
688. Haines and Walsh, p. 875.
689. Dowley, pp. 564-565.

Bight of Biafra, and West Central Africa, the last being responsible for some 45 percent of the total trade. Some historians describe these areas as existing in a constant state of warfare for the main purpose of slave raiding—all this despite the fact that the Afro-European slave trade was harmful to Africa in a myriad of ways.[690] And it remains harmful to her to this day.

Though African countries like Sierra Leone finally freed their *African* slaves in 1927,[691] many parts of the continent continue to engage in both the institution and the trade right into the present, primarily in Central and West Africa, where it has been reported that some 200,000 children alone are sold into slavery each year. While 19th-Century Americans paid an average of $1,500 for an African servant (the current equivalent of $50,000),[692] today's Africans sell one another for as little as $15 a person; and they are treated, not as servants, as in the Old South, but as true slaves: shackled and held at bayonet point, many slaves in modern Africa exist without an income, without civil rights, without proper diet or medical care, and without means or authority to buy their freedom.[693] This is *true* slavery, quite unlike what was practiced in 19th-Century Dixie.

While on the topic of slavery, let us address three other Northern myths, as all are directly or indirectly related to Lincoln: 1) "the South is responsible for American slavery"; 2) "the South got her slaves by sending ships to Africa"; and 3) "Lincoln's War was fought over slavery."

Concerning the first myth, that "the South is responsible for American slavery," let us establish the truth once and for all. American slavery got its start in the North, not in the South. It was not Mississippi, but Massachusetts that, in 1641, was the first state to legalize it,[694] and in 1700, the Bay State also became the first state to prohibit marriage

---

690. J. Thornton, pp. 304, 306. The loss of adult males, for example, probably had a negative impact on African sex ratios, the sexual division of labor, and dependency rates, as well as intensifying warfare and overall social inequality. This does not mean, however, as some scholars have suggested, that Africa was forced against her will to participate in the slave trade with Arabia, Europe, and later America. For, as I show here, Africa was engaged in indigenous slavery for millennia prior to the Afro-European trade. In fact, the Atlantic slave trade was merely a natural outgrowth of domestic African slavery. See J. Thornton, pp. 72-74.
691. Doubleday's Encyc., s.v. "slavery."
692. Seabrook, L, p. 349.
693. Website: www.infoplease.com/spot/slavery1.html.
694. G. H. Moore, pp. 5, 11, 17-19.

between whites and blacks.[695]

Far earlier, in the 1620s, the state's first slaves were white, fellow colonists who were sold into slavery as punishment for committing crimes. By the 1630s, Massachusetts Puritans were capturing, branding, and enslaving Native-Americans, which they either kept as personal servants or sold for profit to West Indian merchants.[696]

Boston began importing African slaves in 1638,[697] when Captain William Pierce brought New England's first shipload of Africans from the West Indies aboard the Salem vessel *Desire*.[698] By 1676, Boston slavers were routinely coming home with shiploads of human cargo from East Africa and Madagascar.[699] By the 1700s, Massachusetts had 5,000 black slaves and 30,000 bondservants.[700]

By 1639, Connecticut had slaves, and by 1645 New Hampshire had them as well. The largest slave concentrations in New England were in Rockingham County, New Hampshire; Essex, Suffolk, Bristol, and Plymouth Counties, Massachusetts; New London, Hartford, and Fairfield Counties, Connecticut; and Newport and Washington Counties, Rhode Island. There were so many slaves in Rhode Island's Narragansett region that they made up half the population.[701] At one time the state's slave traders owned and operated nearly 90 percent of America's slave trade.[702] By 1756 slaves made up at least 16 percent of Newport's population,[703] and as late as 1770 Rhode Island alone possessed some 150 slave ships.[704] As noted writer H. G. Wells once said, "Negro slavery is as old as New England."[705]

The slavers of Rhode Island and those of Massachusetts combined to make New England the leading slave-trading center in America and slavery "the hub of New England's economy." Two-thirds of Rhode

---

695. K. C. Davis, p. 9; Wilson and Ferris, s.v. "Miscegenation."
696. Norwood, pp. 27-30.
697. Bennett, BTM, p. 38.
698. Meltzer, Vol. 2, p. 139. Also see Cartmell, p. 26. The 120-ton *Desire* was built at Marblehead, Massachusetts, in 1636. Norwood, p. 31.
699. McManus, BBN, pp. 9, 10, 11.
700. Bowen, p. 217.
701. McManus, BBN, pp. 6-7.
702. For more on the topic of slavery in Rhode Island, as well as in other New England states, see Website: www.boston.com/bostonglobe/ideas/articles/2010/09/26/new_englands_hidden_history/?page=1.
703. David, p. 135.
704. Pendleton, p. 56.
705. Wells, Vol. 2, p. 705.

Island's fleets and sailors alone were devoted to the trade. Even the states' governors participated in it, such as Jonathan Belcher (of Massachusetts) and Joseph Wanton (of Rhode Island). So integral was slavery to New England that without it she would have collapsed into financial ruin.[706]

Many notable New England families owe their present-day wealth and celebrity to slavery.[707] Among them: the Cabots (ancestors of Massachusetts Senators Henry Cabot Lodge Sr. and Jr.), the Belchers, the Waldos (ancestors of Ralph Waldo Emerson), the Faneuils (after whom Faneuil Hall is named), the Saffins,[708] the Royalls, the Pepperells (after whom the town of Pepperell, Massachusetts, is named), the de Wolfs (or Dewolfs)—the largest slave-trading family in Rhode Island, the Champlains (after whom Lake Champlain is named), the Ellerys, the Gardners (after whom Boston's Isabella Stewart Gardner Museum is named), the Malbones, the Robinsons, the Crowninshields (after whom Crowninshield Island, Massachusetts, is named), and the Browns (after whom Brown University is named).[709]

The slave trading Royall family, who made millions from their slave plantations in Antigua, donated money and land to what would become the Harvard Law School. The educational center still uses a seal from the Royall family crest.[710] At least one half of the land in Brookline, Massachusetts, was once in the possession of slave owners, while in the town of Concord, Massachusetts, 50 percent of its government seats were occupied by slave owners.[711] In this quaint New England borough, where slavery continued well into the 1830s (decades after the official "abolition" of slavery there), those blacks fortunate enough to be freed were then, unfortunately, exiled to the woods surrounding Walden Pond, where they struggled for survival in fetid squatter camps.[712]

It was also in Massachusetts that the now wholly disgraced and defunct field of "race science"—or "niggerology," as many Yankees referred to it—got its start, at Harvard University in Cambridge, to be

---

706. McManus, BBN, pp. 6-7.
707. K. C. Davis, pp. 20, 23.
708. David, p. 135.
709. Meltzer, Vol. 2, pp. 145, 148; C. Johnson, pp. 125-126.
710. The Royall's original home and slave quarters have been turned into a museum located in Medford, MA. See Website: www.royallhouse.org.
711. For more on the topic of slavery in Concord and Brookline, MA, see Website: www.boston.com/bostonglobe/ideas/articles/2010/09/26/new_englands_hidden_history/?page=1.
712. Lemire, passim.

exact. It was this very pseudoscience, one which claimed that "blacks are inferior subhumans," that for hundreds of years allowed white Northerners to rationalize the exploitation of people of African descent.[713]

Little wonder that when William Lloyd Garrison went to Boston in 1830 to dig up support for the launch of his new antislavery newspaper, *The Liberator*, he was turned down by some of the city's most notable men, including William Ellery Channing, Daniel Webster, Jeremiah Evarts, and Jeremiah Mason. His plea was even rejected by Lyman Beecher, the town's most influential Christian leader and the father of abolitionist Harriet Beecher Stowe, the infamous author of *Uncle Tom's Cabin*. Garrison should not have been surprised: not only were many of Massachusetts' schools and churches segregated, nearly every one of Boston's clergymen—like the leaders of every major protestant denomination in the U.S.[714]—was a member of the American Colonization Society, a Yankee-founded organization devoted to deporting all blacks out of the country[715] (one of its future members and leaders is the focus of this book, Abraham Lincoln).[716] Boston itself was once a major center of these black colonization efforts,[717] whose main mission was "to return Negroes to Africa."[718]

In 1788, the state of Massachusetts forbade the emigration of free blacks from outside its boundaries,[719] and well into the early 1800s restrictive Black Codes across New England prohibited African-Americans from voting, testifying in court, intermarrying with whites,[720] or gaining access to jobs, housing, and education. Banned from most restaurants and hotels, New England blacks were also subject to segregation on public transportation, and in theaters, churches, and hospitals.[721] In the late 1830s, the famous black civil rights leader Frederick Douglass, now a freedman, could not get a job as a caulker in New Bedford, Massachusetts, because of the color of his skin (white Yankee caulkers refused to work

---

713. Farrow, Lang, and Frank, pp. 179-191.
714. Dowley, p. 547.
715. Nye, pp. 30, 49.
716. W. B. Garrison, LNOK, p. 186.
717. J. M. McPherson, NCW, pp. 78-79.
718. H. U. Faulkner, p. 318.
719. Smelser, DR, p. 44.
720. McManus, BBN, p. 183.
721. Garraty and McCaughey, p. 146.

alongside him).[722] This type of Northern white racism worked to both justify and expedite Yankee slavery for centuries.

Newport, Rhode Island, was one of the more profitable centers of the New England slave trade:[723] the city—which was literally constructed over the graves of thousands of Africans[724]—was built from the ground up using money entirely derived from the slave trade.[725] By 1790, when Liverpool had become England's primary slave port, her only serious competition was from the Yankee slave ship owners of Bristol and Newport, Rhode Island.[726] Rhode Island's state flag still bears a ship's anchor, an apt reminder of her days as the nation's largest slave trader, one that imported 100,000 African slaves—20 percent of all those brought into the U.S.[727]

It was not just slave trading that Rhode Island was involved in. It also possessed thousands of crop and cattle plantations, particularly in the fertile southern part of the state,[728] whose landed businessmen depended almost exclusively on slave labor.[729] In fact, due to the number of plantations that once dotted the Renaissance City, to this day the official name of the state of Rhode Island is "Rhode Island and Providence Plantations," a carryover from the 1600s when it was first named.[730]

Even after slavery was abolished in the North, both Rhode Island and Massachusetts continued to amass huge profits from the slave trade,[731] the same profits that would later help Lincoln fund his "Civil War" on the South.[732]

As for the capital of the American slave trade, it was not New

---

722. Douglass, NLFD, p. 116.
723. K. C. Davis, p. 7.
724. M. M. Smith, p. 25.
725. Kishlansky, Geary, and O'Brien, p. 531.
726. Garraty, p. 77.
727. C. Johnson, p. 125.
728. David, p. 135.
729. Hacker, pp. 19, 25.
730. October 25, 2010, "America Live," FOX News. For early evidence of Rhode Island's official full name, "Rhode Island and Providence Plantations," see Article 1 of *The Treaty With Great Britain*, the famous secession contract between England's King George III and America's original thirteen colonies, signed at Paris, France, November 30, 1782. J. Williams, p. 365; Rouse, pp. 78-79. Rhode Island's true official name was also mentioned in the first draft of the Preamble to the U.S. Constitution, written about August 1787. J. B. Scott, pp. 84-85. See also pp. 86-87.
731. Rosenbaum and Brinkley, s.v. "Slavery."
732. Spooner, NT, No. 6, p. 54.

Orleans, but New York City.[733] In fact slavery would not begin in the South for another 100 years: in 1749, Georgia, the last of the thirteen original colonies, became the first Southern state to use slaves.[734] By 1756, New York state possessed some 13,000 adult black slaves, giving it the dubious distinction of having the largest slave force of any Northern colony at the time. That same year, slaves accounted for 25 percent of the population in Kings, Queens, Richmond, New York City, and Westchester, making this area the primary bastion of American slavery throughout the rest of the colonial period.[735] Yankees moving south to Westchester and Long Island were eager slave purchasers, and by 1750 at least one-tenth of the province of New York's householders were slave owners.[736] At New York City's peak, at least one-fifth of the town's population were slaves.[737]

As in Boston and Newport, vast fortunes were accrued by New Yorkers who were associated with slavery.[738] Many of the most famous New York names—names such as the Lehman Brothers, John Jacob Astor, Junius and Pierpont Morgan, Charles Tiffany, Archibald Gracie, and many others—are only known today because of the tremendous riches they made from the town's "peculiar institution."[739] New York City, the center of America's cotton trade as early as 1815, was so deeply connected to the Yankee slave trade and to Southern slavery that it opposed all early attempts at abolition within its borders,[740] and, along with New Jersey, was the last Northern state to resist the passage of emancipation laws.[741]

Later, in December 1860, when the Southern states began seceding, New York City's mayor, Fernando Wood, advocated that the city secede as well, for its close relationship with King Cotton insured its economic stability.[742] When Lincoln's War finally erupted in April 1861, New York was one of the last states to recruit African-Americans: the state's governor, Horatio Seymour, refused to enlist them until he was

---

733. Seabrook, EYWTACWW, p. 76.
734. McKissack and McKissack, p. 3.
735. McManus, BBN, pp. 16, 17.
736. David, p. 135.
737. Countryman, p. 11.
738. Nevins and Commager, p. 39.
739. Farrow, Lang, and Frank, pp. 4-5.
740. Hacker, p. 525.
741. Ellis, FB, p. 103.
742. Farrow, Lang, and Frank, p. xxvii.

forced to by the U.S. War Department.[743] This occurred on December 23, 1863, a year after the Emancipation Proclamation was issued and nearly three years after the War began.[744]

In fact, there is only one reason that New York City is today America's largest and wealthiest municipality: for centuries it served as the literal heart of North America's slaving industry.[745] As a result, according to the U.S. Census, to this day the Big Apple still possesses by far the largest population of blacks of any American city (twice as many as Chicago, the city in second place).[746] It was because of New York City's massive slaving business that it was also the center of many of America's earliest and most violent slave uprisings.[747]

Baltimore, Maryland, and Philadelphia, Pennsylvania, were also great slave ports.[748] Baltimore in particular was one of the nation's most important slave trade centers: her slave ships were said to be packed "like livestock" with black human cargo, with mortality rates reaching as high as 25 percent.[749] Another Maryland city, Annapolis, also became one of America's most prosperous towns due to its thriving slave trade. It was a Northern slave ship that brought Kunta Kinte, the lead character in Alex Haley's saga *Roots*, to Annapolis from West Africa in 1767.[750] The city still goes by the nickname the "sailing capital of the world."

In the 1860s, under Lincoln, Northern slavery continued unabated in America's Yankee capital city, Washington, D.C., until the middle of his administration. Up until that time, Lincoln turned down numerous opportunities to abolish the institution here.

The District—where blacks were once fined ($25), given twenty-five lashes (with a bull whip), jailed (for thirty days), then returned to slavery, just for receiving Garrison's abolitionist newspaper *The Liberator*;[751] where hospitals were strictly segregated so that blood plasma

---

743. Buckley, p. 103.
744. February 4, 2011, *Who Do You Think You Are?*, NBC.
745. Farrow, Lang, and Frank, pp. 82-90.
746. Website: http://afgen.com/popula.html.
747. K. C. Davis, p. 24.
748. Lott, pp. 6-7.
749. Nye, p. 27.
750. For an illuminating African-American view of Alex Haley's *Roots*, see the following two Websites:
1) www.jewishworldreview.com/cols/crouch020602.asp.
2) www.jewishworldreview.com/cols/crouch011802.asp.
751. Adams and Sanders, p. 144; Nye, p. 54; Buckley, p. 61.

would not be used for both whites and blacks; and where even the White House press and photographers' pool was segregated (until the 1950s)[752]—had long been a major center for slave sales and boasted the nation's largest slave mart,[753] one located in full view of Northern members of Congress,[754] as Lincoln himself noted.[755] Numerous slave pens, located right across the street from the new Smithsonian building, overflowed with the human chattel of Yankee slave traders who lived and worked in the town. Northern politicians and statesmen alike passed by them on a daily basis without so much as a comment, criticism, or protest.[756]

It was these slaves, the *Northern* slaves from these *Northern* markets and pens, brought to America on *Northern* slave ships owned by *Northern* businessmen, who built the White House, the U.S. Capitol, and numerous other Federal buildings in the city, along with many of her city streets.[757]

Apparently the sight of slave pens, slave jails, auction blocks, thousands of African slaves laboring throughout the city,[758] and Yankee slave boats plying up and down the Potomac River,[759] bothered neither Lincoln or the U.S. Congress, for the town's citizens were allowed to own and trade in slaves right up through the first year of the "Civil War."

Whites who lived in the capital were greatly interested in keeping down the number of blacks in their city, which, in 1850, stood at 26 percent of the total population. In contrast, blacks in slave-owning St. Louis, Missouri, represented only 5.4 percent. Cincinnati, Ohio, was only 2.8 percent black. To maintain, or even decrease, the local black populace, Washington whites widely approved of the new Fugitive Slave Law. Why? Under it, runaway slaves had to be returned to their owners. Those who escaped, however, would blend back into the city's free black population, thereby swelling African-American numbers.[760]

To counter this trend, numerous anti-black laws were revisited in order to make them more stringent. New amendments required black

---

752. Adams and Sanders, pp. 272, 281.
753. De Angelis, p. 49.
754. W. Wilson, DR, p. 125.
755. Nicolay and Hay, ALCW, Vol. 1, p. 185.
756. C. M. Green, W, p. 180.
757. De Angelis, pp. 12-18; Lott, p. 65; J. J. Holland, passim.
758. De Angelis, p. 49.
759. Lott, pp. 61, 64.
760. C. M. Green, W, pp. 180-181.

emigrants to Washington, D.C. to "apply for residence" within five days of their arrival, or face a fine, a sentence in the workhouse, and banishment from town. "Secret meetings" by blacks were prohibited and anyone of African descent had to obtain the permission of the mayor to gather in public.[761]

In a city where already severe black codes were rigidly enforced and where blacks merely suspected of petty crimes were often savagely beaten by Washington's police force, even law-abiding, hard-working blacks lived in constant fear, mainly of white gangs.[762] Without a "certificate of freedom," no free black in the city was safe from harassment and arrest by the police—who devoted the majority of their time to tracking down and capturing African-Americans. The "Negro business" was so profitable in the District that slave catchers were attracted to the town from far and wide.[763]

Throughout the 1850s, white Washingtonians continued to reinforce slavery by endorsing the kidnaping of free blacks (to be sold into slavery) and engaging in the slave trade, even though it had been outlawed in 1850. And while blacks were three times as likely to be arrested as whites, black testimonies in court were regarded as both invalid and illegal, and overly harsh sentences were routinely handed out to black criminals.[764] Sometimes they were punished not so much for major crimes as for minor offenses, such as lighting off firecrackers, flying a kite in the wrong area, or swimming in the canal. The punishment? A "good whipping" with a Yankee lash.[765]

It was not just the 1,800 black slaves in the District that caused Northern whites so much distress. It was also the 9,000 free blacks who lived and worked in the city, all of whom were habitually treated with "fear and hatred." The depth of this loathing can be seen in the name of an area of the Third Ward, known by Northern whites as "Nigger Hill."[766]

It was into the white racist world of Washington, D.C., that white racist Lincoln walked in the spring of 1861. If he was truly the

---

761. C. M. Green, W, p. 181.
762. C. M. Green, W, p. 182.
763. Leech, p. 291.
764. C. M. Green, W, p. 186.
765. Leech, p. 292.
766. Leech, p. 292. Many other Northern cities have had areas called "Nigger Hill" as well, such as Boston, Massachusetts. See e.g., Bartlett, WP, p. 8; Furnas, p. 515.

"Great Emancipator," as Northern myth asserts, one would think that the first item on his agenda as president would have been to abolish slavery in the capital city. Instead, he stalled and deferred month after month, until over a year passed—infuriating the Radicals (socialists and communists) in his party.[767] As he himself had said just a few months prior to his inauguration:

> I have no thought of recommending the abolition of slavery in the District of Columbia, nor the slave-trade among the slave States.[768]

Lincoln's delay tactics in ridding Washington of slavery earned him yet another one of his many nicknames: "America's biggest slave owner." As an angry Charles Sumner put it:

> Do you know who, at this moment, is the largest slaveholder in this country? It is Abraham Lincoln; for he holds all of the three thousand slaves of the District, which is more than any other person in the country holds.[769]

On April 14, 1862, while Lincoln was still refusing to free Washington's slaves, noted black bishop, Daniel A. Payne, head of the African Methodist Episcopal Church, decided to pay him a visit. "Do you intend to sign a bill of emancipation or not?" he asked the president impatiently. Lincoln obfuscated, told stories and jokes. Forty-five minutes later, he still had not answered Payne's question, and the frustrated clergyman politely got up and left.[770]

Political expediency and constant pressure over the past year, including his meeting with Bishop Payne, finally forced Lincoln's hand, and two days later, on April 16, 1862, the country witnessed the passage of the District of Columbia Emancipation Act. Because of the president,

---

767. Hendelson, s.v. "Lincoln, Abraham."
768. Nicolay and Hay, ALCW, Vol. 1, p. 659. Lincoln made this statement in a "strictly confidential" letter to North Carolinian John A. Gilmer, on December 15, 1860. The president-elect was interested in appointing Gilmer secretary of the treasury. Desperate to have a Southerner in his cabinet, in his letter Lincoln laid out his position on slavery, hoping to allay any fears Gilmer might have about the future of the institution. Gilmer saw through it and the ploy failed. New Englander Salmon P. Chase became Lincoln's first secretary of the treasury.
769. Shotwell, p. 436.
770. Cromwell, pp. 121-122.

it had not come easily.[771] In fact, the entire process, from bondage to emancipation, had taken hundreds of years! But finally, to the great relief of the North's handful of vociferous abolitionists, slavery had at last been banned in Washington, D.C.[772]

This "humanitarian" act was tainted, however, by several things. One was the fact that Lincoln's emancipation proclamation in Washington, D.C. turned out to be for the benefit of colonizationists like himself, not for the benefit of the slaves. For he had included a clause in the bill insinuating a call for their immediate deportation upon liberation.[773] The day the bill was signed into law, April 16, 1862, the president even wrote a letter to the House and Senate applauding them for recognizing his call for the deportation of the city's newly freed blacks and for setting aside funds for their colonization.[774]

There was also the anger of the city's whites, most who had no taste for abolition to begin with.[775] At the same time, antislavery advocates fumed over Lincoln's concomitant demand of Congress that it appropriate funding to deport, to Liberia and Haiti, the very blacks he had just freed. (Though the crafty president finally liberated the city's slaves, cleverly he had never promised that he would not attempt to colonize them outside the U.S.)[776]

Lincoln's half-hearted attempt at ending slavery in the nation's capital, of course, had little effect on the endemic Yankee trade there. In 1864, some two years after the District of Columbia Emancipation Act had been issued, former Northern slave Sojourner Truth discovered, to her horror, that whites near Washington, D.C. were kidnaping the black children of freed Southern servants and forcing them back into Northern slavery. The small community the freed blacks lived in, ironically called "Freedman's Village," had been set up by the U.S. army to help newly

---

771. Though earlier in his presidency Lincoln had promised that he would never interfere with slavery in Washington, D.C., as usual, when it benefitted him he changed his mind. In this case, he needed the abolitionist vote for his upcoming bid for reelection. Additionally, freeing Washington's slaves allowed him to press Congress harder for black deportation and colonization.
772. J. C. Perry, p. 191. This did not end segregation, of course. If anything it exasperated the problem of Northern white racism. Indeed, total integration was not achieved in Washington, D.C. until 1956. See Weintraub, p. 147.
773. *The National Almanac* (1863), p. 250.
774. Nicolay and Hay, ALCW, Vol. 2, p. 144.
775. Lincoln and the abolitionists, Caucasian Washingtonians declared, were determined to make the city "a hell on earth for the white man." Leech, pp. 295, 298.
776. Buckley, p. 86; Leech, p. 298.

emancipated African-Americans adjust to living in free white society. Truth used the court system to have the children released and returned to their parents; but not before her own life was threatened by the violent and unrepentant Yankee slavers.

Lincoln, whose offices were not far away, must have been aware of these crimes, yet he did nothing. It was Lincoln's overt complicity in the institution of slavery that often prompted Truth to refer to the U.S. flag, not as the "Stars and Stripes," but as the "Scars and Stripes."[777]

America's capital city was so central to slavery that she probably would have become the nation's slave trading capital instead of New York City. The only reason Washington, D.C. did not was due to geography: at the time she was only a mere sixty-eight square miles, with no room to expand.[778] Nonetheless, a vestige of Washington's original function as a leading slave market is its black population, which peaked at 71 percent in 1970, one of the highest of any city in the U.S.[779]

As the founder of both the American slave trade and American slavery, and with her long history of deep economic ties to the slave industry, it should come as no surprise to learn that the top five American cities with the largest black populations today are all in the North and West (by rank they are New York City, New York; Chicago, Illinois; Detroit, Michigan; Philadelphia, Pennsylvania; and Los Angeles, California). Even the city with the highest percentage of blacks is in the North: Detroit.[780]

Let us now examine the second Northern myth pertaining to slavery, that "the South got her slaves by sending ships to Africa." America's African slaves arrived here, not aboard Southern ships, but aboard Northern ones. For the only slave ships to ever sail from the U.S. left from Northern ports, and all were commanded by Northern captains and funded by Northern businessmen, and all operated under the auspices of the U.S. flag,[781] the Stars and Stripes,[782] as even foreigners like the

---

777. Truth, p. 254. See also McKissack and McKissack, pp. 142, 143, 144.
778. Lott, p. 64.
779. Website: www.usatoday.com/news/washington/2007-09-01-dcdemographics_N.htm.
780. Website: http://afgen.com/popula.html. Some of these blacks, of course, came north to look for jobs during World War II. Nonetheless, a large number of them descend from Northern, not Southern, slaves.
781. Lott, pp. 35-60.
782. J. C. Miller, p. 146.

British understood.[783]

The South, on the other hand, did not own slave ships, was not involved in the industry, and had no interest in it; thus no Africans were ever removed from their native land under the Confederate flag, the Stars and Bars.[784] This is why, when the Southern states formed the Confederacy, February 4-9, 1861,[785] one of the first clauses they put into their Constitution was a prohibition against foreign slave trading.[786] Here, from the C.S. Constitution, Article 1, Section 9, Clause 1, is the exact wording:

> The importation of negroes of the African race, from any foreign country, other than the slaveholding States or Territories of the United States of America, is hereby forbidden; and Congress is required to pass such laws as shall effectually prevent the same.[787]

This was five years before the U.S. banned the foreign slave trade. Indeed the original U.S. Constitution, also Article 1, Section 9, Clause 1, allowed the

> . . . importation of such Persons as any of the States now existing shall think proper to admit . . .[788]

Those referred to here as "such Persons" were, of course, slaves.

If slavery was maintained in, fueled by, and run from the North, where then did the South get her "slaves"? Every one of the South's 3.5 million black servants was purchased, either directly or indirectly, from a Northern slave trader or Northern slave company. Thus, as pro-South historian Frank Lawrence Owsley writes, those truly responsible for Southern slavery are those who forced it on the South to begin with.[789]

As proof that those who forced slavery on the South were Yankees, consider the following. First, the only person ever tried, convicted, and executed for slaving was a Northerner: Captain Nathaniel

---

783. Pollard, LC, p. 126.
784. Ashe, p. 10.
785. Denney, p. 25.
786. Stonebraker, p. 46.
787. F. Moore, Vol. 2, p. 323.
788. E. McPherson, PHUSAGR, p. 93.
789. Simpson, p. 78.

Gordon, of New York, was put to death on February 21, 1862, by Lincoln's personal order,[790] as his February 4, 1862, letter reveals:

> Respite For Nathaniel Gordon.
> Abraham Lincoln, President Of The United States Of America, To all to whom these presents shall come, greeting:
>
> Whereas it appears that at a term of the Circuit Court of the United States of America for the southern district of New York, held in the month of November, A. D. 1861, Nathaniel Gordon was indicted and convicted for being engaged in the slave-trade, and was by the said court sentenced to be put to death by hanging by the neck on Friday the 7th day of February, A. D. 1862;
>
> And whereas a large number of respectable citizens have earnestly besought me to commute the said sentence of the said Nathaniel Gordon to a term of imprisonment for life, which application I have felt it to be my duty to refuse;
>
> And whereas it has seemed to me probable that the unsuccessful application made for the commutation of his sentence may have prevented the said Nathaniel Gordon from making the necessary preparation for the awful change which awaits him:
>
> Now, therefore, be it known that I, Abraham Lincoln, President of the United States of America, have granted and do hereby grant unto him, the said Nathaniel Gordon, a respite of the above-recited sentence until Friday, the 21st day of February, A. D. 1862, between the hours of twelve o'clock at noon and three o'clock in the afternoon of the said day, when the said sentence shall be executed.
>
> In granting this respite it becomes my painful duty to admonish the prisoner that, relinquishing all expectation of pardon by human authority, he refer himself alone to the mercy of the common God and Father of all men.
>
> In testimony whereof I have hereunto signed my name and caused the seal of the United States to be affixed.[791]

Second, the last American slave ship to be captured by the U.S. government was a Northern one: the *Nightingale*, also from New York, confiscated on April 21, 1861. At the time of its seizure, this vessel, from the so-called "abolitionist North," had nearly 1,000 manacled Africans on

---

790. Foote, Vol. 1, p. 537.
791. Nicolay and Hay, ALCW, Vol. 2, pp. 121-122.

board.[792] It was doing "business as usual" up until the first few weeks of Lincoln's War.[793]

In fact, it was the North's heavy dependence on the Yankee slave trade and on selling slaves to the South, that helped precipitate the War: when the Confederacy banned all slave trading with foreign nations, which included the U.S., the North panicked, deciding it was better to beat the South into submission than allow her to cut off one of the Yankees' primary streams of wealth.[794]

How can these things be true if they are not in our history books? Let us examine the facts.

Though Southerner George Mason tried, unsuccessfully, to prohibit the U.S. slave trade as early as 1787[795] (he referred to it as a "wicked, cruel, and unnatural trade"),[796] and though Southern President Thomas Jefferson finally permanently banned it in 1808,[797] the law (as even Lincoln observed)[798] was routinely ignored by Northerners (mainly from New England and New York),[799] who vigorously continued to illegally traffic in human chattel,[800] even during and after Lincoln's War.[801] Not a single slaving captain or trader was punished by the U.S. until Gordon in 1862,[802] and for good reason: the federal government was completely controlled by slave interests.[803] Indeed, this is how Lincoln funded his war: chiefly with the profits from Northern slavery and the Yankee slave trade.[804]

Now to the third popular Northern slavery myth, that "Lincoln's War was fought over slavery." As is now obvious, Northerners themselves knew that the War and slavery were not connected—and they would have

---

792. Farrow, Lang, and Frank, pp. 131-132.
793. Kennedy, pp. 104-105.
794. Stonebraker, p. 81.
795. C. Johnson, p. 107.
796. Rutland, p. 35.
797. DeGregorio, s.v. "Thomas Jefferson" (p. 50).
798. Nicolay and Hay, ALCW, Vol. 2, p. 6.
799. Morison and Commager, Vol. 1, p. 245.
800. Faust, s.v. "slavery."
801. See Stampp, p. 271; Meltzer, Vol. 2, pp. 247-248; C. Johnson, pp. 126-128; Rosenbaum and Brinkley, s.v. "Slave Trade"; Durden, p. 288.
802. In 1862, an old law, the 1842 Treaty of Washington, was revived and strengthened, requiring U.S. and British ships to search and detain any vessel suspected of trading in slaves. This and only this finally put an effective end to Yankee slave trading. J. C. Miller, pp. 146-147.
803. Meltzer, Vol. 2, p. 247.
804. See Spooner, NT, No. 6, p. 54; Pollard, LC, p. 154.

been extremely unhappy if it were otherwise. Yankee General Ulysses S. Grant, an Ohio slave owner[805] and colonizationist[806] who owned slaves before,[807] during, and after the War,[808] spoke for nearly all Federal soldiers when he said:

> The sole object of this war is to restore the union. Should I be convinced it has any other object, or that the government designs using its soldiers to execute the wishes of the Abolitionists, I pledge to you my honor as a man and a soldier. I would resign my commission and carry my sword to the other side.[809]

Most Northern newspapers too understood the true foundations of the conflict. On October 8, 1861, Washington, D.C.'s *National Intelligencer* wrote:

> The existing war has no direct relation to slavery. It is a war for the restoration of the Union under the existing Constitution.[810]

Confederate soldiers were of the exact same mind. After the War, Rebel Moses Jacob Ezekiel, one of 12,000 Jews who fought for the Confederacy[811] against anti-Semites Lincoln and Grant,[812] spoke on behalf of every Southern military man, saying: we did not fight to maintain slavery. We fought for states' rights, free trade, and in defense of our families, homes, and land.[813] Confederate Colonel Joseph F. Burke declared similarly:

> It has often been said that we were fighting for the perpetuation of

---

805. Hinkle, p. 125.
806. Adams and Sanders, pp. 215-216.
807. R. P. Jordan, p. 12.
808. Grant did not free his slaves until he was forced to by the ratification of the Thirteenth Amendment on December 6, 1865, eight months after Lincoln's War ended. Rutherford, FA, p. 38; Wallechinsky, Wallace, and Wallace, p. 11; Woods, p. 67. Other famous Northerners who were associated with slavery, either through actual ownership or through marriage, were: General Winfield Scott, Admiral David G. Farragut, General George H. Thomas, and Lincoln's wife, Mary Todd. McElroy, p. 357. Lincoln himself made reference to a slave-owning Yankee, the Honorable George Robertson, in a November 26, 1862, letter. See Nicolay and Hay, ALCW, Vol. 2, p. 259.
809. Meriwether, p. 219; Stonebraker, p. 70.
810. Rhodes, Vol. 3, p. 476.
811. Rosen, p. 161.
812. Simmons, s.v. "General Order, Number Eleven"; Horwitz, p. 204.
813. Ferris and Greenberg, p. 114.

slavery. This was not so. We were simply fighting for our right to keep slaves if we wanted to. We were fighting for State rights—rights to be allowed to make our laws for our particular States.[814]

In 1863, in her wonderful pro-South work *My Imprisonment and the First Year of Abolition Rule at Washington*, famed Confederate female spy Rose O'Neal Greenhow wrote:

> It is not my purpose to elucidate the causes which have brought about the downfall of the American Republic. I do not pretend to the character of a publicist, or that of a philosophical historian. But as an attentive, and, I trust, impartial observer, I think I can correct some grave misconceptions of the events which have gained credence.
>
> In the first place, slavery, although the occasion, was not the producing cause of the dissolution. The cord which bound the sections together was strained beyond its strength, and, of course, snapped at the point where the fretting of the strands was greatest.
>
> The contest on the part of the North was for supreme control, especially in relation to the fiscal action of the Government. This object could not be fully attained by a mere numerical majority. A majority of States was also necessary. To secure this majority, and thus complete the political ascendency of the North, the policy of 'no more Slave States' was formally set forth.
>
> A political party was formed, whose sole principle was the exclusion of slavery from the territories. There was no moral sentiment involved in this. It did not alter the status of slavery. It made not a human being free; nor did it propose to do so. 'Sir,' said Mr. [Daniel] Webster in the Senate, 'this is not a moral question: it is a question of political power.' Lord [John] Russell has more recently corroborated this bold assertion, by saying, that 'this was a struggle on one side for supremacy, and on the other for independence.'
>
> On the other hand, the Southern States, struggling for equality, and seeking to maintain the equilibrium of the Government, insisted upon the rights of their citizens to enter and live in the new territories upon terms of equality with the men north of Mason and Dixon's line. They contended for the right of extending their social institutions, not to propagate slavery—not

---

814. Parker, p. 343.

to make a single human being a slave that would otherwise be free—but simply to preserve the equilibrium of power between the two sections.

It is true that the anti-slavery fanaticism was brought to bear; and it is also true that there followed a rancorous agitation which divided churches, rent asunder political parties, diminished and embittered the intercourse of society, and unfitted Congress for the performance of its constitutional duties, and resulted in the estrangement of the Southern people from their Northern connection. But this estrangement was not an active or stimulating motive, and manifested itself rather in the want of any general anxiety to restrain the movement for disunion.[815]

The U.S. Congress generally agreed with Greenhow, Burke, and Ezekiel as to the purpose of Lincoln's War. Shortly after the start of the conflict, on July 22, 1861, it released a declaration stating that the Union's intention for going to war with the South was not for the

purpose of overthrowing or interfering with the rights or established institutions [i.e., slavery] of those States; but to defend and maintain the supremacy of the Constitution and to preserve the Union with all the dignity, equality, and rights of the several States unimpaired; that as soon as these objects are accomplished, the war ought to cease.[816]

Foreigners too were acutely aware that slavery had nothing to do with Lincoln's War. In their opinion it was about money. German progressive and socialist Karl Marx, no friend of the conservative, anti-socialist South (but a true friend of liberal Lincoln),[817] elucidated the sentiments of much of Europe, and certainly of London, England, where he wrote the following on October 20, 1861: "The American Civil War has nothing to do with slavery; only the tariff and the Yankee's lust for

---

815. Greenhow, pp. 324-326.
816. E. McPherson, PHUSAPR, p. 16.
817. In late November 1864, Marx wrote Lincoln a letter congratulating him on his "re-election by a large majority." The missive included Marx's sincere hope that Lincoln would "lead his country through the matchless struggle for the rescue of an enchained race and the reconstruction of a social world." The two socialistic men had much in common, far more than most modern day Lincoln apologists are prepared to admit. For the full text of Marx's letter, see pp. 575-580. Marx was so enamored with Lincoln that he and fellow socialist Friedrich Engels later wrote a glowing biographical book on the big government Yankee liberal entitled: *Abraham Lincoln und der Amerikanische Bürgerkrieg* ("Abraham Lincoln and the American Civil War").

power and dominance."[818]

As early as 1833, Virginian John Tyler, soon to become America's tenth president, gave the Southern people's viewpoint of the Yankee tariff:

> In plain terms . . . [it is] an unwarranted extension of the powers of the government and an appeal to the numerical majority of the North to grow rich at the expense of their section.[819]

Far earlier, in the 1820s, Calhoun wrote that when it came to South-North tensions, the Northern tariff was always "the great central interest, around which all the others revolved."[820] No less than Woodrow Wilson, America's twenty-eighth president, would later concur with these comments. For it was very evident, he wrote in 1892, that because of the North's increasing tariff pressures on the South,

> that she was to suffer almost in direct proportion as other sections of the country gained advantage from such legislation.[821]

Lincoln himself admitted that, at its foundation, his War was about the almighty dollar. Just prior to the conflict, several Southern peace commissioners had an interview with the newly sworn in president, an attempt to avoid the coming bloodbath. At the meeting, one of the commissioners, Alexander H. Stuart, pleaded for time and further discussions, to which Lincoln replied anxiously:

> If I do that (recognize the Southern Confederacy), what will become of my revenue? I might as well shut up housekeeping at once.[822]

Yes, from the Northern point of view at least, Lincoln was correct: the "Civil War" was very much about his "revenue." But if that is all it had been about, the proud and honorable people of Dixie would never have gone to war with him.

For them the conflict between the two regions involved a number

---

818. Thornton and Ekelund, p. 103; C. Adams, p. 79. My paraphrasal.
819. Tyler, LTT, Vol. 3, p. 28.
820. Anonymous, p. 32.
821. W. Wilson, DR, p. 50.
822. Christian, p. 14.

of other long-simmering issues, as history has attested. In essence it was a battle between Southern agrarianism and Northern industrialism;[823] between the farming and commerce capitalism of the South and the finance and industry capitalism of the North;[824] between Southern free trade and Northern protective tariffs;[825] between Southern traditionalism and Northern progressivism; between the South's desire to maintain Jefferson's Confederate Republic and the North's desire to change it into Hamilton's federate democracy.

Since these issues long preceded sectional debates over slavery, and in fact were at their bitterest level in 1860, and since they continued "long after slavery was abolished"—as Britain's representative in Washington, D.C., Minister Augustus J. Foster, pointed out—it is obvious that slavery was not the cause of the "Civil War." Indeed, in the 1820s, decades before Southern slavery was even considered a "problem," anti-South Yankee Daniel Webster noted that plans for a Southern Confederacy were already well under way.[826]

A Northerner, Gunning Bedford of Delaware, predicted a "civil war" as early as 1787. On June 30 he stood before the Constitutional Convention and said:

> . . . the larger states proceed as if our eyes were already perfectly blinded. Impartiality, with them, is already out of the question; the reported plan is their political creed and they support it, right or wrong. Even the diminutive state of Georgia has an eye to her future wealth and greatness. South Carolina, puffed up with the possession of her wealth and negroes, and North Carolina, are all, from different views, united with the great states. And these latter, although it is said they can never, from interested views, form a coalition, we find closely united in one scheme of interest and ambition, (notwithstanding they endeavor to amuse us with the purity of their principle and the rectitude of their intentions,) in asserting that the general government must be drawn from an equal representation of the people. Pretences to support ambition are never wanting. Their cry is, Where is the danger? and they insist that although the powers of the general government will be increased, yet it will be for the good of the whole; and although the

---

823. Simpson, pp. 69, 74.
824. Coit, pp. 170, 175.
825. Rozwenc, p. 50.
826. Coit, pp. 170-171, 186.

three great states form nearly a majority of the people of America, they never will hurt or injure the lesser states. *I do not gentlemen trust you.* If you possess the power, the abuse of it could not be checked; and what then would prevent you from exercising it to our destruction? . . . . The small states never can agree to the Virginia plan; and why then is it still urged? . . . Is it come to this, then, that the sword must decide this controversy, and that the horrors of war must be added to the rest of our misfortunes? . . . The states will never again be entrapped into a measure like this. The people will say, The *small* states would confederate, and grant further powers to Congress; but you, the *large* states, would not. Then the fault would be yours, and all the nations of the earth will justify us. But what is to become of our public debts, if we dissolve the Union? Where is your plighted faith? Will you crush the smaller states, or must they be left unmolested? Sooner than be ruined, there are *foreign powers who will take us by the hand*.[827]

Though South Carolina's "negroes" are mentioned, Bedford was not discussing slavery here. This was a debate between himself and Southerner James Madison over proportional representation in the Senate.[828]

Even when Southern secession came, the word slavery was scarcely mentioned in the secession documents of the eleven states who broke away from the Union.[829] What *was* mentioned were the topics of self-determination, personal liberty, states' rights, and the Union's "frequent violations" of the Constitution.[830] As Confederate General John B. Gordon declared to the women of York, Pennsylvania, during the War:

> Our Southern homes have been pillaged, sacked and burned; our mothers, wives and little ones driven forth amid the brutal insults of your soldiers. Is it any wonder that we fight with desperation? A natural revenge would prompt us to retaliate in kind, but we scorn to war on women and children. We are fighting for the God-given rights of liberty and independence as handed down to us in the Constitution by our fathers. So fear not: if a torch is applied to a single dwelling, or an insult to a female of your town by a soldier of this command, point me out the man and you shall have his

---

827. Elliot, Vol. 1, pp. 472-473.
828. Collier and Collier, pp. 167-168.
829. C. Johnson, p. 140.
830. See E. M. Thomas, pp. 307-322.

life.[831]

If there are any final doubts as to whether or not "Lincoln's War was fought over slavery," let us look at the words of the man who started the conflict.

In the summer of 1861, after angrily revoking an attempt by one of his officers to emancipate slaves in Missouri, Lincoln had a conversation with abolitionist Reverend Charles Edward Lester. The president expressed his impatience with Lester and other Northern abolitionists who were pushing for emancipation:

> I think [Massachusetts Senator Charles] Sumner, and the rest of you, would upset our apple-cart altogether, if you had your way. . . . We didn't go into the war to put down Slavery, but to put the flag back, and to act differently at this moment, would, I have no doubt, not only weaken our cause, but smack of bad faith; for I never should have had votes enough to send me here, if the people had supposed I should try to use my power to upset Slavery. Why, the first thing you'd see, would be a mutiny in the army. No! We must wait until every other means has been exhausted. This thunderbolt will keep.[832]

Note that in addition to acknowledging that "we didn't go into the war to put down Slavery," Lincoln also admits that the Northern people would never have elected him and that Northern soldiers would have mutinied if he had tried to "use his power to upset Slavery." How revealing this statement is of the true temperament of the Northern populace at the time!

On August 15, 1864, only eight months before the end of his War, Lincoln gave what is without question the most definitive and explicit statement regarding its cause. Once again, according to our sixteenth chief executive, it was not slavery:

> "My enemies pretend I am now carrying on this war for the sole purpose of abolition. So long as I am President, it shall be carried on for the sole purpose of restoring the Union. . . . Let my enemies prove to the country that the destruction of slavery is not necessary

---

831. Oglesby, p. 42.
832. Lester, pp. 359-360.

to a restoration of the Union. I will abide the issue."[833]

In 1870, Northern abolitionist Lysander Spooner put Lincoln, his "Wall Street Boys," and their War, in their proper perspective:

> The pretence that the 'abolition of slavery' was either a motive or justification for the war, is a fraud of the same character with that of 'maintaining the national honor.' Who, but such usurpers, robbers, and murderers as they, ever established slavery? Or what government, except one resting upon the sword, like the one we now have [war criminal and former slave owner Ulysses S. Grant was then president of the U.S.], was ever capable of maintaining slavery? And why did these men abolish slavery? Not from any love of liberty in general—not as an act of justice to the black man himself, but only 'as a war measure,' and because they wanted his assistance, and that of his friends, in carrying on the [Civil] war they had undertaken for maintaining and intensifying that political, commercial, and industrial slavery, to which they have subjected the great body of the people, both white and black. And yet these imposters now cry out that they have abolished the chattel slavery of the black man—although that was not the motive of the war—as if they thought they could thereby conceal, atone for, or justify that other slavery which they were fighting to perpetuate, and to render more rigorous and inexorable than it ever was before. There was no difference of principle—but only of degree—between the slavery they boast they have abolished, and the slavery they were fighting to preserve; for all restraints upon men's natural liberty, not necessary for the simple maintenance of justice, are of the nature of slavery, and differ from each other only in degree.[834]

Up to his final days Lincoln maintained that the War was not about slavery, but about "preserving the Union." In his last public address, given at the White House, he mentions slavery only once, but goes into great detail about the rebellion and secession. In fact, he states, *again* quite clearly, that the "sole object" of the entire conflict was bringing the Confederate states back into the United States:

> We all agree that the seceded States, so called, are out of their proper practical relation with the Union, and that the sole object

---

833. Seabrook, TUAL, p. 40.
834. Spooner, NT, No. 6, pp. 56-57.

of the government, civil and military, in regard to those States is to again get them into that proper practical relation.[835]

Lincoln uttered these words on April 11, 1865, just three days before he was shot down by a disgruntled Copperhead.[836]

The president of the Confederacy, Jefferson Davis, was also adamant about the real cause of the War—and it was not slavery:

> The truth remains intact and incontrovertible, that the existence of African servitude was in no wise the cause of the conflict, but only an incident. In the later controversies that arose, however, its effect in operating as a lever upon the passions, prejudices, or sympathies of mankind, was so potent that it has been spread like a thick cloud over the whole horizon of historic truth.[837]

Since the presidents, the congresses, and the military officers of both the C.S.A. and the U.S.A. agreed that the War was not over slavery, indeed, asserted that it was not in any way connected to slavery, we can now lay this Yankee fiction to rest once and for all.

---

835. Nicolay and Hay, ALCW, Vol. 2, p. 674.
836. Lincoln was assassinated on April 14, 1865. But it was not until the following day, April 15, that he perished from the mortal wound at the back of his head.
837. J. Davis, RFCG, Vol. 1, p. 80.

SOUTHERN ABOLITION, NORTHERN RACISM

PART ONE

ONE PARTICULARLY ODIOUS LINCOLNIAN MYTH is that "slavery would not have been abolished had the South won the War." The opposite is true. It was Lincoln and his nemesis, the abolitionists, socialists, and communists in his party—the notorious Radical Republicans,[838] or Black Republicans, as they were also called[839]—who delayed abolition by attacking Southern slave owners as "evil monsters," by agitating for emancipation without a definitive plan,[840] and by promising the South that when their black servants were freed they would rise up in a great insurrection and murder their former masters and mistresses.[841]

Lincoln and his minions badly miscalculated Southern blacks on this point. For had Dixie's African-Americans wished to arm themselves and fight, they could have easily overthrown and killed their owners, wrecked Southern plantations, burned Southern cities to the ground, and emancipated themselves. And yet, there were virtually no major, and scarcely any minor, slave insurrections in any Southern city at any time between 1619 and 1865,[842] this despite the North's numerous attempts to

---

838. See Seabrook, LW, passim.
839. W. B. Garrison, CWTFB, p. 134.
840. Henry, SC, p. 14.
841. Hacker, p. 582.
842. Wiley, SN, pp. 82-83.

incite such revolts.[843] In short, the "Black Terror," as it was known, never came.[844]

In particular it is most revealing that none occurred during Lincoln's War.[845] In fact, over a period of hundreds of years, only three so-called "slave revolts" were significant enough to have been given the names of their instigators:

1. The Gabriel Prosser Rebellion of 1800
2. The Denmark Vesey Rebellion of 1822
3. The Nat Turner Rebellion of 1831

The so-called "John Brown Rebellion" at Harper's Ferry, Virginia, might be mentioned as well. But New Englander Brown can hardly be placed in the same category with Prosser, Vesey, and Turner. For one thing, Brown was a white man; for another, not a single Southern slave left his or her home to follow him,[846] as even Lincoln himself noted.[847] Even black leader Frederick Douglass turned down Brown's offer to join him, calling the plan a suicide mission from which there would be no escape and only hell to pay.[848]

Despite the unanimous support, blasphemous apotheosization, and vulgar worship of John Brown by New England whites[849] (Yankees Henry David Thoreau, for example, likened him to the crucified Christ, and Emerson called him a "saint," while Louisa May Alcott referred to him

---

843. M. M. Smith, p. 37.
844. Nye, p. 18; E. M. Thomas, p. 237.
845. C. Johnson, p. 239.
846. Rozwenc, p. 29; Rosenbaum and Brinkley, s.v. "Slave Revolts."
847. Of John Brown and his "slave revolt," Lincoln said: "John Brown's effort was peculiar. It was not a slave insurrection. It was an attempt by white men to get up a revolt among slaves, in which the slaves refused to participate. In fact, it was so absurd that the slaves, with all their ignorance, saw plainly enough it could not succeed." From Lincoln's Cooper Union speech, February 27, 1860. Nicolay and Hay, ALCW, Vol. 1, p. 609.
848. J. M. McPherson, BCF, p. 205.
849. Brown's primary financial backers were all Northerners, men completely ignorant of both Southern culture and Southern slavery. Known as the Secret Six, their names are listed here in infamy, so that they will never be forgotten: Gerrit Smith, Thomas Wentworth Higginson, Theodore Parker, Samuel Gridley Howe, George L. Stearns, and Franklin B. Sanborn. It was the money from these six Northerners that helped fund Brown's insane murder spree across the country, which in turn fanned the flames that led to the War for Southern Independence. Not the flames of the South's small proslavery movement, as Yankee myth teaches, but the flames of the South's massive states' rights movement.

as "St. John the Just"),[850] the misguided psychopath eventually hung on the gallows for his murder of dozens of innocent Southerners, most who did not even own slaves and, like a majority of white Virginians, were abolitionists.[851]

In short, all four of the above "slave revolts" ended with the capture, imprisonment, or death of their leaders. The reasons that all of these "rebellions" ended in failure were the same reasons Lincoln's attempt at inciting a slave insurrection in the South ended in failure.

Long before the rise of Emperor Lincoln, during Jefferson's day, most of America's abolitionist organizations were in the South, not in the North.[852] For as Owsley notes, nearly the entire South was abolitionist in the late 1700s and early 1800s.[853] Indeed, of the 130 abolition societies established before 1827 by Northern abolitionist Benjamin Lundy, over 100, comprising four-fifths of the total membership, were in the South, many with foundations dating back to the early 1700s.[854]

The breakdown went like this: in the year 1827 the South possessed 106 abolition societies with 5,150 members, while the North had a mere twenty-four abolition societies with only 1,475 members;[855] this despite the fact that there were more Northern states (fourteen) than Southern states (ten) that year.

After Lincoln's dire 1861-prediction of Negro insurrections, anarchy, and widespread white deaths, however, Southern antislavery sentiment began to rapidly disappear, and the South, out of legitimate fear—as well as Southern pride and honor—understandably began to resist the idea of abolition.[856] For in the end, it was not the destruction of slavery that the South was against. She was against the premature, forced destruction of slavery, and that by a foreign power (the Northern states of

---

850. Not all New Englanders sided with John Brown. Of him the sagacious Nathaniel Hawthorne said: "Nobody was ever more justly hanged." Woods, p. 59.
851. Brown's first victim was not a white slave owner, but rather a free black man named Heyward Shepherd. Shepherd refused to join Brown's mob of madmen, and so Brown murdered him. Ashe, p. 39. Seventy-five years later, on October 10, 1931, the United Daughters of the Confederacy erected a monument at Harper's Ferry. It was dedicated to Shepherd and the millions of other blacks who remained loyal to the South during Lincoln's War. Grissom, p. 129. God bless them one and all.
852. Shenkman, p. 121.
853. Simpson, pp. 77-78, 85.
854. Cash, p. 63.
855. Fogel, p. 253.
856. White, Foscue, and McKnight, p. 211; Coit, pp. 298-299.

the U.S.) that had been unmercifully dominating her for decades.[857]

Why is this not more generally known? Because like most facts about the South and the War, the North has thoroughly suppressed it: nearly all school textbooks and history books are written by Northern authors and printed by Northern publishers, many with a barely disguised hatred of the South and her people, and literally no authentic knowledge of either.[858]

The same holds true of the hundreds of thousands of books written on the "Civil War": 99.99 percent have been written by Northerners, non-Southerners, anti-South partisans, or New South scallywags, skewing the facts toward the North's distorted, self-aggrandizing, one-sided version. Is it any wonder that the South is still so misunderstood and that her history, culture, and people continue to be scorned and ridiculed by the world?

The truth that you will not find in any of these works is that *the American abolition movement started in the South*, not the North. Originally Southerners detested slavery and did everything in their power to rid the country of it,[859] and in fact, up until at least 1830, Southerners were the country's leading abolitionists.[860] This is why the first American colony to outlaw slavery was in the South: in 1735, in an attempt to halt the development of slavery, Georgia's trustees banned the importation of blacks into the colony—the only one to ever pass such a law.[861]

Virginians in particular deplored slavery so much that their state became not only the first one in America to try and ban it, but the first to actually abolish the slave trade. This occurred in 1778, in a bill introduced by Virginian Patrick Henry.[862] Abolition fever took hold across the state, leading to the country's earliest and most successful emancipation program: between 1782 and 1790 alone, some 10,000 slaves were liberated in the Old Dominion.[863] Not surprising in a state (colony) where the first known voluntary emancipation in America took place in 1655.[864]

---

857. Coit, p. 306.
858. Grissom, pp. iv-v.
859. Kennedy, p. 91.
860. R. P. Jordan, p. 11.
861. Shenkman, p. 118.
862. C. Adams, p. 92.
863. Garraty and McCaughey, p. 81.
864. Seabrook, EYWTAASIW, p. 549.

George Washington and James Madison, both Virginians, were just a few of the more illustrious Southerners who came out against slavery in the opening years of the young nation.[865] Washington, who promised never to purchase another slave, and whose will contained provisions for the freeing of all his slaves upon his wife's death,[866] stated that it was his most ardent desire

> to see some plan adopted, by which slavery in this country may be abolished by slow, sure, and imperceptible degrees.[867]

Madison, who campaigned to emancipate the slaves and enlist them in the Colonial army,[868] considered slavery to be a form of "deep-rooted abuse," a "moral and political evil." Thus anyone who

> brings forward in the respective states, some general, rational and liberal plan, for the gradual emancipation of slaves, will deserve well of his country . . .[869]

In a January 18, 1773, letter to Robert Pleasants, Virginian Patrick Henry wrote:

> I believe a time will come when an opportunity will be offered to abolish this lamentable evil. Every thing we can do, is to improve it, if it happens in our day; if not, let us transmit to our descendants, together with our slaves, a pity for their unhappy lot, and an abhorrence of slavery.[870]

Then there was Thomas Jefferson, also from Virginia, no doubt the most vehement abolitionist in North America at the time;[871] a Southerner who, in 1787, said of the African slave trade:

> This abomination must have an end. And there is a superior bench

---

865. Smelser, DR, p. 42; Buckley, p. 37.
866. Ellis, FB, pp. 113, 158.
867. L. B. Evans, p. 525.
868. Brodie, pp. 168-169.
869. Ellis, FB, pp. 113, 114.
870. Vaux, p. 69.
871. Cousins, p. 147.

reserved in heaven for those who hasten it.[872]

As early as 1769, Jefferson was one of the chief leaders of the Southern abolition movement. In 1776, referring to slavery as a "wickedness," he tried to eliminate the trade altogether by adding a condemnation of England (for forcing slavery on the original thirteen colonies) to his rough draft of the Declaration of Independence. It read:

> [King George III] . . . has waged cruel war against human nature itself, violating its most sacred rights of life and liberty in the persons of a distant [African] people who never offended him, captivating and carrying them to slavery in another hemisphere, or to incur miserable death in their transportations thither. This piratical warfare, the opprobrium of INFIDEL powers, is the warfare of the CHRISTIAN king of Great Britain. Determined to keep open a market where MEN should be bought and sold, he has prostituted his negative [i.e., he withheld his power of veto for financial gain] for suppressing every legislative attempt to prohibit or to restrain this execrable commerce, and that this assemblage of horrors might want no fact of distinguished dye, he is now exciting those very people to rise in arms against us, and to purchase that liberty of which he has deprived them, by murdering the people upon whom he also obtruded them; thus paying off former crimes committed against the LIBERTIES of one people, with crimes which he urges them to commit against the lives of another.[873]

Why are these powerful antislavery words (Clause 20 in Jefferson's draft)—that were written by a Southerner—not in the Declaration of Independence as we know it today? According to an extremely irritated Jefferson, his denunciation of slavery was removed from the final draft, in part, because it would have angered not only Northern slave traders,[874] but also Northern businessmen,[875] nearly all who were deeply involved in the slave industry,[876] the same Yankee

---

872. Foley, p. 812.
873. Foley, p. 970.
874. Bowen, pp. 600-601.
875. Foley, p. 246.
876. K. C. Davis, pp. 10, 30. John Adams' favorite part of Jefferson's draft of the Declaration of Independence was his attack on King George for foisting slavery on the American colonies. J. C. Miller, p. 8. Primarily opposites on the political spectrum, Southerner Jefferson and Northerner Adams at least had abolition in common.

industry, as we have seen, whose profits were later used by Lincoln to fund his "Civil War."[877]

Later, in 1808, after years of struggle, Jefferson got a national law passed banning the importation of slaves (the ban was completely ignored by Yankee slave traders).[878] Finally, in 1826, when he drew up his will, like Washington, Jefferson provided for the emancipation of a number of his slaves, something nearly unheard of among Northern slave owners at the time.[879]

Thirty-six years earlier, other Virginians were also pushing for abolition. In 1790, Fernando Fairfax drafted his "Plan for Liberating the Negroes within the United States," while six years later, in 1796, St. George Tucker drew up another even more elaborate emancipation system.[880]

Twenty years before that, the Virginia Declaration of Rights, first drafted in 1776 by native son and antislavery advocate George Mason, included the phrase that all men are "born equally free and independent," and are possessed of certain "natural, essential, and unalienable rights."[881] Even Lincoln acknowledged that

> the plain, unmistakable spirit of that age toward slavery was hostility to the principle and toleration only by necessity.[882]

The ideas of abolition and equality were thus very much alive in the South, dating back to even before the founding of the U.S. During this same period, the Northern states were busy shipping thousands of Africans to the Americas, while passing laws making slavery legal and black freedom illegal.

Before Northern mythologists suppressed Southern Truth, knowledge of the universal Southern abolition movement was widely

---

877. See Spooner, NT, No. 6, p. 54.
878. Thousands upon thousands of Africans continued to be shipped from Africa to the U.S. by Yankee slave traders even after President Jefferson's prohibition of the trade in 1808. As we have seen, Northern slavers, in fact, openly continued the practice until at least 1862 (J. C. Miller, pp. 145-147), as President Lincoln himself noted. Nicolay and Hay, ALCW, Vol. 2, p. 6. After that, the Yankee slave trade seems to have gone underground until the passage of the Thirteenth Amendment in December 1865.
879. Ellis, AS, pp. 344-345.
880. Ellis, FB, p. 105.
881. McCullough, p. 221.
882. Nicolay and Hay, ALCW, Vol. 1, p. 203.

known in both regions. Early North Carolina, for example, had a number of celebrated "forceful" antislavery leaders, such as Benjamin Sherwood Hedrick and Daniel Reaves Goodlow,[883] and in South Carolina the famed Quaker sisters, Sarah and Angelina Grimké, were just a few of the hundreds of thousands of Southerners fighting for the cause of abolition.[884]

Among Tennessee's better known abolitionists were Jesse Willis, John Underhill, Marius Robinson, and Charles Osborne, all who pushed for emancipation as early as 1815. In Virginia, George Bourne was advocating black liberty in 1816, while James Duncan and John Rankin of Kentucky promoted the cause of abolition in 1824. James Thome was another antislavery advocate from the Bluegrass State.[885] In 1833, Virginian John Randolph voluntarily freed 400 of his slaves.[886]

North Carolinians were so against the institution that not one notable proslavery advocate was ever known there. Instead, a "vast network" of manumission societies and emancipation organizations exploded across the state. The North Carolina Manumission Society, founded in 1816, organized nearly 100 branches in central North Carolina alone.[887]

When Yankee Frederick Law Olmsted visited the Tar Heel state in 1854, he met a man living in a mountain home who turned his preconceived ideas about the "slave-ridden South" upside down. Wrote Olmsted:

> After a conversation about his agriculture, I remarked that there were but few slaves in this part of the country. He wished that there were fewer. They were profitable property here, I presumed. They were not, he said, except to raise for sale; but there were a good many people here who would not have them if they were profitable, and yet who were abundantly able to buy them. . . . he would not take one to keep if it should be given to him. 'T would be a great deal better for the country, he believed, if there was not a slave in it.
>
> . . . 'I see you have *Uncle Tom's Cabin* here,' said I; 'have you read it?'

---

883. H. C. Bailey, p. 197.
884. Oates, AL, p. 29.
885. Nye, pp. 25, 62.
886. Brinkley, p. 311.
887. Butler and Watson, pp. 195, 198.

'Oh, yes.'
'And what do you think of it?'
'Think of it? I think well of it.'
'Do most of the people here in the mountains think as you do about slavery?'
'Well, there's some thinks one way and some another, but there's hardly any one here that don't think slavery's a curse to our country, or who wouldn't be glad to get rid of it.'[888]

Yankee historians refuse to include such facts in their literary works, but the reality is that most of the rest of the South felt exactly the same way.

Pulitzer Prize-winning John C. Calhoun biographer, Margaret L. Coit, notes that during the late 1700s and early 1800s, while slavery was still both condoned and practiced in the North, there were countless abolition and antislavery societies busy pushing for emancipation throughout the Southern states.[889] Later, during Lincoln's War, men like Jefferson Davis, Robert E. Lee, Stonewall Jackson, and Albert Sydney Johnston, were just a few of the South's more famous abolitionists and emancipationists.[890]

Most 19th-Century Americans, South and North, knew servitude was coming to an end, dying a natural death all on its own. It need not be forced.[891] This view was so widely acknowledged and accepted that at one time even Lincoln embraced it—just one of the many reasons he promised not to interfere with slavery in his Inaugural Address,[892] and why, later, he had to be forced into issuing the Emancipation Proclamation (as even the most extreme Lincoln apologists have had to admit).[893] At a speech he gave on July 10, 1858, in Chicago, Lincoln said of the institution:

> I always believed . . . that it was in course of ultimate extinction.[894]

Naturally, Southerners, who had been unwillingly saddled with

---

[888]. Olmsted, JBC, pp. 263, 264.
[889]. Coit, p. 170.
[890]. McElroy, pp. 215-216, 357. General Lee's first cousin, Richard Henry Lee, was also an outspoken critic of both slavery and the slave trade. Countryman, pp. 34-35.
[891]. Smelser, ACRH, p. 188.
[892]. Seabrook, L, p. 198.
[893]. See e.g., Dumond, p. 113.
[894]. Nicolay and Hay, ALCW, Vol. 1, p. 252.

slavery to begin with,[895] were more aware that servitude was "in an expiring condition in the South"[896] than Northerners, and most were exceedingly pleased about it.[897] In fact, the vast majority of white Southerners, whether they owned slaves or not, did not believe in it or support it. Indeed, even before Lincoln's War was over, a number of Southern states, most notably Louisiana and Missouri, had already voted to abolish slavery.[898]

Some Southerners, like John Singleton Mosby (who upon catching the enemy would yell, "surrender you Yankee son-of-a-bitch!"),[899] believed that slavery only lasted as long as it did in the South because education (which would have exposed Southern children to ideas like natural rights) was not more widely available. Had the South had free schools (i.e., a year-round educational system that was available to all children), Mosby maintained, Lincoln's War would not have occurred and the Southern people would have abolished slavery before 1860 on their own.[900]

The "problem of slavery" had begun long before 19th-Century Southerners were even born, and its beginnings were rather innocent.

The South began as an agrarian society. In the 1600s and early 1700s, prior to the Industrial Revolution, there were no machines, and not enough people, to harvest crops like cotton and tobacco on large farms. So Southern planters bought blacks from Yankee slave traders to serve as agricultural laborers.[901]

The institution then, as it manifested in the South of the 1860s, had been inherited from previous Southern ancestors;[902] before that, from the North;[903] and finally, before that, from England.[904] The conundrum for Victorian Southerners was how to rid their region of an "inheritance" they now neither wanted or needed, one they actually detested. There was no simple easy solution.

---

895. Adams and Sanders, p. 137.
896. Pollard, LJD, p. 449.
897. Hacker, p. 579.
898. Wiley, SN, p. 197.
899. E. M. Thomas, p. 249.
900. Siepel, pp. 281-282.
901. Shorto, p. 38.
902. Stampp, p. 411.
903. Rosenbaum and Brinkley, s.v. "Slavery"; Chesnut, MCCW, p. 196.
904. P. L. Ford, Vol. 2, pp. 63-64; Vol. 9, p. 479.

In many Southern states, black slaves outnumbered whites. What would become of an orderly nation if millions of bonded blacks were suddenly freed? Pushy Northern abolitionists seemed oblivious to the fact that the emancipation model they used to abolish slavery in their region would not work in the South, yet it was this very one they expected Southerners to use. The slave population of the Northern states never exceeded 10 percent, while in some Southern states the slave population was greater than the white population.[905] In 1860, in South Carolina and Mississippi, for example, blacks made up over 50 percent of the total population.[906]

Even if the South could manage to free all its slaves, what was to prevent them from rising up in a great insurrection and violently overwhelming white society? The slave revolution in Haiti (then known as Santo Domingo), which lasted from 1791 to 1804, was still fresh in the minds of Victorian Southern whites. Crazed Haitian blacks had raped, tortured, and murdered some 80,000 innocent Caucasians across the island,[907] then torched their homes, shops, and farms to the ground (during the first month of fighting alone some 200 sugar estates were burned and 1,000 whites were captured and killed).[908] Eyewitnesses were so appalled by the horrific scenes they saw (in essence the Haitian Revolution was the modern world's first ethnic cleansing), they were at a loss for words to describe them.[909]

We must also consider that, at the time, there was not a single egalitarian, non-racist, co-racial society on earth that early Southerners could have used as a model. That is, as of the mid 1800s, there had never been a single known instance of a purely non-racist society in all of recorded history.[910] In every nation on earth, one race, whether it was black, red, yellow, brown, or white, dominated all others, often in what we would now think of as an inhumane and racist manner. Southerners had no equalitarian paradigm to work from, to build the future of the South upon. Thus, when it came to antebellum slavery, they were truly

---

905. Ellis, FB, p. 104.
906. In other Southern states, like Alabama, Florida, Georgia, Louisiana, and Virginia, the total populations were over 40 percent black in 1860. Rosenbaum and Brinkley, s.v. "Slavery."
907. Crocker, p. 23.
908. Curtin, RFPC, p. 165.
909. C. Adams, pp. 129-130.
910. Ellis, FB, p. 107.

caught between a rock and a hard place.

In 1820 Jefferson brilliantly captured the slavery situation in America's Southland:

> We have the wolf by the ears, and we can neither hold him, nor safely let him go.[911]

But not knowing how or when to free the slaves did not mean that Southerners found slavery good or even acceptable. To the contrary, as we have seen, throughout the early decades of the U.S., much of the South's time and energy was directed almost solely on how to deal with "the wolf." After all, freeing millions of servants all at once would have only substituted one problem for another.[912]

Most servant owners not only hated seeing blacks enslaved, they themselves felt enslaved by the slavery system. The weight of the responsibility for caring for slaves was such that it became a universal joke in the South: it was not the slaves one need fear would run away, but their employers.

Thackeray characterized slave ownership as being similar to owning an elephant when all that is needed is a horse.[913] Chesnut wrote that nearly all Southerners considered slaves "a nuisance that did not pay." It is far cheaper, she noted, to simply hire someone, than to own a man whose father, mother, wife, and numerous children had to be fed, clothed, housed, nursed, and have their taxes and doctor's bills paid, throughout their entire lives, from cradle to coffin.[914]

Most Southern slave owners agreed. One of these was fire-eating, die-hard Confederate Rebel, Edmund Ruffin.[915] Ruffin, like thousands of his comrades, eventually auctioned off his black servants. Not because they were poor producers. But because they were excellent consumers,

---

911. Foley, pp. 811-812.
912. Morison and Commager, Vol. 1, p. 245.
913. Thackeray, p. 127.
914. Chesnut, DD, p. 387.
915. Ruffin, a professional agriculturist who pioneered crop rotation and who is said to have been the person who fired the opening shot of Lincoln's War (at the Battle of Fort Sumter), committed suicide after Lee's surrender rather than live in ignoble humiliation under Yankee dictatorship. To this day Ruffin is honored as an archetypal, unreconstructed Confederate hero among traditional Southerners, one typifying Dixie's age-old love of personal liberty, states' rights, self-government, Constitutionalism, and political independence.

making the expense of maintaining them nearly impossible.[916] The cost of owning slaves only increased as Lincoln's War progressed and massive inflation (6,000 percent)[917] spread across the South,[918] leading many Southerners to declare that it was not they who owned slaves, it was the slaves who owned them.[919]

The truth that has been suppressed by Northern myth is that antislavery sentiment was nearly universal throughout Dixie,[920] dating back, as mentioned, to at least the time of Thomas Jefferson (1743-1826),[921] just one of millions of Southerners and slave owners who loathed the institution with every fiber of their being. In his famous work, *Notes on the State of Virginia*, penned in 1781 and 1782, our third president writes:

> I think a change already perceptible, since the origin of the present revolution. The spirit of the master is abating, that of the slave rising from the dust, his condition mollifying, the way I hope preparing, under the auspices of heaven, for a total emancipation . . .[922]

Mississippian Jefferson Davis had believed since the very formation of the Confederacy that the end of slavery was inevitable, whether the South won the War or not.[923] This is one reason he pushed for the governmental purchase of slaves, their enlistment, and their emancipation as a reward for military service, in November 1864. Robert E. Lee also recommended enlistment and liberty for Southern slaves.[924] On March 13, 1865, Davis and Lee got their wish when the Confederate Congress authorized the "Negro Soldier Law,"[925] which allowed for the enrollment of as many as one-fourth of all Southern male slaves between

---

916. Channing, p. 128.
917. W. B. Garrison, CWTFB, p. 164. By January 1, 1864, a gold dollar in the South was worth $20 in Confederate notes. E. M. Thomas, p. 197.
918. Wiley, SN, pp. 94-96.
919. Stampp, p. 314.
920. Weintraub, p. 54.
921. Ellis, AS, p. 102.
922. Jefferson, NSV, p. 171.
923. Crocker, p. 10.
924. Wiley, SN, p. 121.
925. Lanning, p. 55.

the ages of 18 and 45.[926]

With the South so obviously antislavery and pro-abolition, why do Northern history books continue to tell us that Southerners were proslavery and anti-abolition? Because the truth would expose Lincoln for what he really was: a despot and a war criminal who waged an illegal and needless military campaign against the Southern Confederacy, a Constitutionally formed sovereign nation.

However, in honor of all those who perished under Lincoln's autocratic rule (South and North, white and black, soldier and civilian), and in an effort to preserve authentic American history, we owe the world this much: to reveal the truth that Northern myth has for so long kept concealed. So reveal it we will.

Traditional Southern families supported the idea of self-government, asserting that the Federal government did not possess the right to appropriate their rights, their property, or their servants, by any means, especially by force. For Southerners, these were local state issues, not national ones. Thus, they only asked that they be left alone to manage their own personal and local affairs, a sentiment clearly articulated by all of the great Southern leaders, from John C. Calhoun to Jefferson Davis.[927]

Had Lincoln done just that, the South's slave owners would have eventually ended the institution in their own time and manner,[928] gradually, legally, and without violence—"by slow, sure, and imperceptible degrees," as Southerner President George Washington suggested decades earlier[929]—just as the North had allowed itself the privilege to do between the late 1700s and early 1800s.

Indeed, as early as 1787, at the Constitutional Convention in Philadelphia, Charles Pinckney of South Carolina maintained that if left to decide for themselves, the citizens of his state would eventually prohibit the slave trade—just as Virginia had already done. At the same assembly his compatriot, Virginian George Mason, said that slavery need not be interfered with in the South, for it was going extinct all on its own anyway.[930]

---

926. L. Johnson, pp. 178-179.
927. Coit, p. 452.
928. Crocker, p. 333.
929. Ellis, FB, p. 113.
930. Collier and Collier, p. 231.

In 1866, Yankee President James Buchanan, Lincoln's far more level-headed and intelligent predecessor, said of slavery:

> If left to the wise ordinance of a superintending Providence, which never acts rashly, it would have been gradually extinguished in our country, peacefully and without bloodshed, as has already been done throughout nearly the whole of Christendom. . . . If we would preserve the peace of the world and avoid much greater evils that we desire to destroy, we must act upon the wise principles of international law, and leave each people to decide domestic questions for themselves. Their sins are not our sins.[931]

In fact, Lincoln's War only postponed the inevitable destruction of slavery, which would have come much sooner had the nosey, arrogant, and self-righteous president simply left the South alone. As Captain Samuel A. Ashe correctly observed in 1911:

> . . . an independent South would have conformed to the ideas of the world at large. Slavery would have been abolished in a manner less hurtful to the South, naturally and peacefully, and in the meantime the South would have advanced in all the elements of prosperity.[932]

Indeed, by mid-1863, the South had already nearly reached the point of total emancipation.[933] Why not let her complete the process on her own? Why spend billions of dollars and kill untold thousands to accomplish what was already occurring naturally? And why push something on the South that the North had given itself the luxury to occur naturally in its own region, the very section of the country where slavery got its start?

At first the North acknowledged that it had instigated both slavery and the slave trade. And it fully accepted this fact as well—at least up until 1831, the year the loud, meddlesome, Radical Yankee abolitionist, William Lloyd Garrison, launched his antislavery gazette, *The Liberator*. Though, like Harriet Beecher Stowe, Garrison knew absolutely nothing about either the South or black servitude, he published articles in his paper

---

931. J. Buchanan, Vol. 12, pp. 51, 52.
932. Ashe, p. 58.
933. E. M. Thomas, p. 242.

condemning Southern slavery as a "crime" and Southern slave owners as "criminals." His columns brimmed with misinformation, disinformation, errors, and outright lies regarding the institution, all carefully calculated to whip the North into an anti-South frenzy.[934] It did cause agitation. But not the kind that would weaken Southern slavery. Instead, Garrison and his paper helped strengthen it, becoming one of the many embers that helped light the "Civil War."[935] How?

Though *The Liberator* was not widely influential (subscriptions never exceeded 3,000), many Southerners blamed Garrison for the Nat Turner Rebellion of 1831,[936] for his paper was read almost solely by radicalized free blacks. Though most were from the North (mainly from Boston, New York, and Philadelphia),[937] the paper found its way into the hands of a few Southern blacks. One of these was Turner.

On the evening of August 21, the Virginia slave led a gang of black thugs on a murderous rampage to "kill all whites." Before it was over some sixty European-Americans were dead.[938] Entire families were massacred that night, from newborn infants to senior citizens, their heads cut off while they slept.[939] Most of the decapitated victims were not only non-slave owners, they were ardent abolitionists, for Virginia had long been the center of Southern antislavery sentiment. Indeed, as we have noted, the American abolition movement got its start in Virginia.[940]

An unremorseful Turner and his racist madmen were all caught within a few weeks. Many of the mob, including their psychopathic leader, swung from the hangman's rope.[941] But the bloody mayhem was all for naught. In fact, if Turner was trying to end slavery, he had done the worst thing possible: his "rebellion" not only did not advance the cause of blacks, it actually reversed it. For in its aftermath at least 100 blacks were

---

934. Simpson, pp. 79-80.
935. Ironically, though he was partly responsible for inflaming already existing sectional animosities, Garrison himself believed that allowing the South to secede peacefully was preferable to war between the two regions. W. B. Garrison, LNOK, p. 144.
936. Garrison was already detested by Southerners for having publicly burned a copy of the Constitution on the Fourth of July. Not only that, he had called the beloved document an "agreement with Hell" (because it protected slavery). Buckley, p. 61; Grissom, p. 127; Woods, p. 44; Nivola and Rosenbloom, p. 510.
937. Furnas, p. 408; Nye, pp. 49, 52, 134; Rosenbaum and Brinkley, s.v. "Liberator, The." Garrison's paper had only fifty white readers, most of them from Boston, almost all of them personal friends. Nye, p. 55.
938. Stampp, pp. 132-134.
939. Blassingame, pp. 129-131.
940. Kennedy, p. 91.
941. For the complete *true* story of the Nat Turner Rebellion, see T. R. Gray, passim.

killed,[942] whites passed new, exceptionally harsh slave codes, and abolitionist sentiment, once strong across the entire South, was considerably dampened for decades.[943]

This was a revolutionary change in attitude for white Southerners, who had for so long viewed their black servants as "family" and free blacks as fellow citizens of Dixie. Thus, while nearly every Southerner had once been an abolitionist,[944] now the idea of emancipation was considered "too dangerous," and blacks everywhere, bonded and free, were viewed with suspicion.[945] Between Garrison's increasingly vociferous attacks on Dixie and Turner's bloody killing spree, white Southerners had had enough. Now, instead of discussing abolition, they dug in their heels and built up a defensive wall of resentment and fear. No one, especially Yankees, would tell them what to do, not when they and their family's lives were at stake.[946]

How would the South end slavery? This was her decision. *When* would the South end slavery? It was her right to decide this for herself, as the Constitution clearly affirmed.[947]

In an 1847 speech, the president of Washington College, Dr. Henry Ruffner of Virginia, spoke for the whole of the South when he commented on Dixie's defensive reaction to Northern attacks on the institution of slavery:

> . . . this unfavorable change of sentiment is due chiefly to the fanatical violence of those Northern antislavery men usually called Abolitionists. . . . They have not, by honourable means, liberated a single slave, and they never will by such a course of procedure as they have pursued. On the contrary they have created new difficulties in the way of all judicious schemes of emancipation by prejudicing the minds of slaveholders, and by compelling us to combat their false principles and rash schemes in our rear; whilst we are facing the opposition of men and the natural difficulties of the case in our front.[948]

---

942. J. S. Bowman, CWDD, s.v. "August 1831."
943. Rosenbaum and Brinkley, s.v. "Slave Revolts."
944. Simpson, p. 85.
945. Stonebraker, p. 250.
946. Garraty, p. 302.
947. Simpson, pp. 80-81.
948. Munford, pp. 52-53.

The situation was so obvious that even some Yankees understood. One of them, William Ellery Channing, wrote the following in 1835:

> The adoption of the common system of agitation by the Abolitionists has not been justified by success. From the beginning it created alarm in the considerate and strengthened the sympathies of the free states with the slaveholder. It made converts of a few individuals but alienated multitudes.
>
> Its influence at the South has been almost wholly evil. It has stirred up bitter passions and a fierce fanaticism which have shut every ear and every heart against its arguments and persuasions.[949]

Southern defensiveness was indeed the only natural reaction to Northern pushiness when it came to slavery, as even many Northerners, like Channing, acknowledged. President Francis Wayland, of Rhode Island's Brown University (named after the New England slave trading Brown family),[950] once told Garrison that his abolitionist newspaper, *The Liberator*, would only produce rebellion in the South. "It's attitude," Wayland protested,

> to slave-owners is menacing and vindictive. The tendency of your remarks is to prejudice their minds against a cool discussion of the subject.[951]

No truer words have ever been uttered, as Lincoln would discover years later.

The real question was this: why was the North striving to impose racial egalitarianism on the South when this was something that she herself would not even entertain?

On December 1, 1864, the Richmond *Sentinel* pointed out the rank hypocrisy of the Yankee. The North hates the negro, it declared, and does all it can to prevent the two races from associating. Yet, Yankees insist that Southerners treat blacks with complete equality. Thus the North does not practice what it preaches, but instead seeks to force upon Dixie that which she herself refuses to abide by. Furthermore, the South

---

949. Munford, p. 53.
950. C. Johnson, pp. 125-126; Meltzer, Vol. 2, pp. 145, 148.
951. Garrison and Garrison, Vol. 1, p. 243.

does not hate the negro, she loves the negro. No wonder the two sections came to detest one another!, the *Sentinel* concluded.[952]

Besides their constitutional rights, Southern slave owners had another dilemma to deal with: when it came to slavery, they were far more concerned about preserving their financial investment than preserving the institution. Slaves represented enormous private capital, each one being worth a small fortune (from between $25,000 and $50,000 each in today's currency). How would owners get the money back on their investment if their servants were simply freed? At about $1,500 a piece, the South's 3,500,000 slaves[953] were worth $14 billion (in 1860) converted into today's money. Where was this massive compensation to come from? In 1865 Lincoln only offered the Southern states the modern equivalent of about $7 billion, some $7 billion short,[954] and even this pitiful offer was later withdrawn.

These were serious questions about a serious issue, questions that needed time and careful deliberation. And it was this very problem that primarily stalled abolition in the South, not racism or a perverse obsession with slavery. And it is why Southerners wanted to be allowed to decide for themselves when and how to emancipate their servants. This was all they asked of the North.[955]

When it was to his advantage, however, Northerner Lincoln twisted these facts, turning the South's financial conservatism and her love of independence and self-government into the lie that Dixie wanted to "preserve slavery" above all else. It is this outrageous falsehood concerning Southern slavery—one that Southerners rightfully consider ignorant, hypocritical, uninvited, and disrespectful[956]—that continues to be promoted in anti-South books and on anti-South Websites.

As is nearly always the case when it comes to Yankee mythology, the truth is the complete opposite.

When slavery was deemed inefficient, economically unimportant, and finally unprofitable in the North by about 1800,[957] Yankees knew the

---

952. Durden, pp. 123-124.
953. Cooper, JDA, p. 378; Quarles, p. xiii.
954. Nicolay and Hay, ALCW, Vol. 2, pp. 635-636.
955. Hacker, p. 19.
956. Rosenbaum and Brinkley, s.v. "Civil War."
957. P. M. Roberts, p. 198; Garraty and McCaughey, p. 81; Morison and Commager, Vol. 1, p. 245; Rosenbaum and Brinkley, s.v. "Slavery"; "Slave States."

institution there had come to its natural conclusion.[958] And yet, despite the fact they felt "financially overburdened" by their slaves,[959] Northerners did not want to permanently end slavery across the U.S., for they were still capitalizing on it. After all, as future U.S. President John Quincy Adams of Massachusetts said in 1804, while slavery is immoral and evil, it still has vital functions when linked with commerce.[960]

One wealthy New York businessman, speaking to abolitionist Samuel J. May in the 1830s, put it this way:

> Mr. May, we are not such fools as not to know that slavery is a great evil, a great wrong. But it was consented to by the founders of our Republic. It was provided for in the Constitution of our Union. A great portion of the property of the Southerners is invested under its sanction; and the business of the North as well as the South has become adjusted to it. There are millions upon millions of dollars due from Southerners to the merchants and mechanics of New York alone, the payment of which would be jeopardized by any rupture between the North and the South. We cannot afford, sir, to let you and your associates succeed in your endeavor to overthrow slavery. It is not a matter of principle with us; it is a matter of business necessity. We cannot afford to let you succeed; and I have called you out to let you know, and to let your fellow-laborers know, that we do not mean to allow you to succeed. We mean, sir, . . . to put you Abolitionists down—by fair means if we can, by foul means if we must.[961]

As Yankee slavery was purely a "business necessity," Northerners faced a difficult problem: how to rid themselves of black slavery without injuring it, destroying it, or losing money. The solution was obvious.

Northern merchants and bankers simply transferred the institution southward, where the growing season was much longer and where the nutrient-rich, silty soil and broad expansive land were more conducive to large scale farming and the growing of lucrative crops like cotton.[962]

On September 19, 1861, South Carolinian Mary Chesnut commented on this topic in her diary. Northerners, who initiated slavery

---

958. K. C. Davis, p. 14.
959. Carman and Syrett, p. 40.
960. Fogel, p. 290.
961. O. Johnson, pp. 184-185.
962. Rosenbaum and Brinkley, s.v. "Slavery."

to begin with, she writes, pushed it on the South after it was no longer advantageous to them, then blamed Dixie for its existence:

> It is a crowning misdemeanor for us to hold still in slavery those Africans whom they [Yankees] brought here from Africa, or sold to us when they found it did not pay to own them themselves. Gradually, they slid or sold them off down here; or freed them prospectively, giving themselves years in which to get rid of them in a remunerative way. We want to spread them over other lands, too—West and South, or Northwest, where the climate would free them or kill them, or improve them out of the world, as our friends up North do [to] the Indians. If they had been forced to keep the negroes in New England, I dare say the negroes might have shared the Indians' fate . . .[963]

Eli Whitney's invention of the cotton gin in 1793 only made the Yankees' approach to ridding themselves of slavery all the more logical and practical, for it was in the South where cotton grew best and where all of the large cotton farms and plantations were already located.[964]

As we have discussed, far earlier Southerners too had pushed hard for abolition and emancipation. After "the late unpleasantness" of Lincoln's War, Confederate General Robert E. Lee, a rabid opponent of slavery,[965] wrote:

> The best men of the South have long desired to do away with the institution, and were quite willing to see it abolished.[966]

In 1856, five years before Lincoln's War, Lee, himself one of "the best men of the South," said:

> In this enlightened age there are few, I believe, but will acknowledge that slavery as an institution is a moral and political evil. It is useless to expatiate on its disadvantages. I think it is a greater evil to the white than to the colored race.[967]

---

963. Chesnut, DD, pp. 129-130.
964. C. M. Green, EW, pp. 61-62; Lerner, Meacham, and Burns, p. 732.
965. Warner, GG, s.v. "Robert Edward Lee."
966. Page, p. 38.
967. McGuire and Christian, p. 21.

Lee knew that servitude was doomed.[968] How? Because in 1861 he was one of 96.73 percent of small landholders (known as yeoman farmers) in the South who operated without labor assistance (other than their wives and children),[969] and who thus never owned slaves,[970] abhorred the institution, and wanted to see it eradicated. Lee was, in other words, a typical Southerner: one of the "plain folk,"[971] a small non-slave owning farmer.[972]

Slavery truly was expendable and not at all necessary to the life of the South, a fact proven near the end of the War: when the Confederacy was finally faced with the choice of emancipation in order to enlist blacks or the destruction of the South by Lincoln, she chose to enlist blacks.[973]

What about the other 3.27 percent of Southerners? Contrary to "Northern history," which maintains that most or even *all* Southerners owned black chattel, this tiny group, just fifty out of 1,000 people, made up the entire slave owning population of Dixie.[974] Even slavery's most fierce opponents had to acknowledge that Southern slaveholders comprised "an insignificant fraction of the population."[975]

To put this number in perspective, the South's 300,000 white slave owners made up only 1 percent of the total U.S. white population of 30,000,000 people in 1861, and only 3 percent of the South's 9,150,000 whites.[976] If America's 4,000,000 black slaves (North and South) are added to this figure, the South's white slave owners comprised only 0.8 percent of the total white and black population of America in 1861.[977]

---

968. Crocker, p. 98.
969. Stampp, p. 29.
970. White, Foscue, and McKnight, p. 209.
971. Brinkley, p. 319.
972. Stampp, p. 30.
973. Barrow, Segars, and Rosenburg, BC, p. 26.
974. To arrive at these numbers I used Hacker's figure of 9,150,000 Southern whites in 1861 (Hacker, p. 581) and the Kennedy brothers' figure of 300,000 Southern white slave owners in 1860 (Kennedy and Kennedy, SWR, p. 83).
975. Hacker, p. 542.
976. See Foner, FSFLFM, pp. 87-88.
977. In 1861 there were 20,750,000 million whites in the North, and 9,150,000 whites in the South (Hacker, p. 581), making the total American white population 29,900,000; or rounded off, 30,000,000. In 1861, there were 3,500,000 black slaves in the South (Quarles, p. xiii; Weintraub, p. 70; Cooper, JDA, p. 378; Rosenbaum and Brinkley, s.v. "Civil War"), and 500,000 black slaves in the North. Eaton, HSC, p. 93), making a total of 4,000,000 slaves nationwide. (Some estimates indicate that there were as many as 1,000,000 slaves in the North in the 1860s. See Hinkle, p. 125.) We will note here that these figures do

The reality is that land and black servants were extraordinarily costly in the 1800s, so invariably slavery was a rich man's business. Yet nearly all 19th-Century Southerners were poor farmers. This fact alone proves that in actuality very few Southerners owned black servants, and thus it was not, and could not have been, the "cornerstone of the Confederacy," as so many have claimed.[978]

There was no "slave owning majority," as Northern myth consistently maintains. Quite the opposite. The large slaveholding families of the South numbered only about 10,000, this out of literally millions of Southern families.[979] This was only 0.6 percent of the 1.5 million families who lived across the South in 1860.[980] They were so rare that most Southerners, being poor rural farmers, probably did not even personally know a slave owning family.

Indeed, according to the U.S. Census, in 1860 only 4.8 percent (or 385,000) of all Southerners owned slaves, the other 95.2 percent did not.[981] Of those that did, most owned less than five.[982] Correcting for the mistakes of Census takers—which would include counting slave-hirers as slave owners and counting more than once those thousands of slave owners who annually moved the same slaves back and forth across multiple states—this figure, 4.8 percent, is no doubt much smaller. Either way, Southerners themselves believed that only 5 percent of their number owned slaves, which is slightly high, but roughly accurate.[983]

---

not include the millions of Native-Americans (many who were also slave owners) who inhabited vast areas of North America, as well as other ethnic groups, such as Asian-Americans and Hispanic-Americans.
978. Stampp, pp. 402-403.
979. Long and Long, p. 702.
980. E. M. Thomas, p. 6.
981. M. M. Smith, pp. 4-5.
982. Gragg, p. 84; DiLorenzo, LU, p. 174.
983. Parker, p. 343. Important note: in an attempt to tarnish the South, anti-South proponents like to artificially inflate the numbers of white Southern slave owners (they completely ignore black and red slave owners) by calculating using the number of *households* ("families") instead of the *total number of white Southerners*. Using the lower number of households as opposed to the higher number of total whites, of course, gives a higher number of slave owners, which is why they use this method: it puts the South in the worst light possible, and gives further justification for Lincoln's unjustifiable War. For example, the socialist, anti-South, Yankee historian, Kenneth M. Stampp, who Northerners and scallywags consider the "authority" on slavery figures, states that in 1860, there were 385,000 Southern slave owners, about 1,500,000 free Southern families, and a total of 8,000,000 whites. Stampp, pp. 29-30. All of this is true, up to this point. Enemies of the South, however, compute the number of Southern slave owners by calculating what percentage 385,000 (the number of Southern slave owners) is of 1,500,000 (the number of Southern households). This gives a result of about 25 percent, the pro-North claim being then that "25 percent of all Southern whites were slave owners in 1860." This, indeed, is the exact figure and calculation formula

Going back in time, the number of Southern slave owners decreases precipitously. In 1850, for example, of the 8,039,000 whites living in the Southern states, only 186,551 were slave owners, a mere 2.3 percent of the total white population. Thus, 97.7 percent of Southern whites that year were non-slave owners.[984] Of these same whites, only 46,274 owned twenty or more servants (0.5 percent), only 2,500 owned thirty or more (0.03 percent), and a mere handful (0.02 percent) owned 100 or more.[985]

This last group, the so-called "Aristocratic Planters" (hated by Northerners more than they hated slavery),[986] eventually numbered about 150,000,[987] but still comprised only 1.6 percent of the total number of white Southerners (9,000,000) in the 1860s. In fact, the extremely wealthy planters, and thus those who owned the most servants, made up only one-half of 1 percent of the total population of the South.[988] According to the 1860 Census, only fifteen slave owners across the entire South owned more than 500 slaves.[989] In 1859 Lincoln himself acknowledged that

> in all our slave States except South Carolina, a majority of the

---

Stampp and his ilk use (see e.g., Stampp, p. 30). Unfortunately, as "households," women, and children did not (and could not) own slaves, this formula is not only disingenuous and misleading, it is mathematically incorrect. The correct calculation, the one I and other traditional Southern folks use, is to compute the number of Southern slave owners by calculating what percentage 385,000 is of 8,000,000 (the total number of Southern whites). This gives a result of 4.8 percent. When we correct for enumeration errors (see the following footnote), this number comes down to about 4 percent or less. Hence, we can safely *and* accurately say that only about 4 percent of Southern whites were slave owners in 1860. The other 96 percent were not. Be aware of this cowardly and treacherous pro-North trick, one found in nearly every anti-South book.

984. For the number of Southern whites in 1850, see Wilson and Ferris, s.v. "Plantations"; Bradley, p. 33. For the number of slave owners in 1850, see Helper, ICS, p. 148. How the total number of slave owners was arrived at: while "official" records state that there were 347,525 slave owners in the South in 1850, this is a gross error. Professor James D. B. DeBow, famed publisher and statistician, and Superintendent of the Census at the time, stated that this number wrongly includes slave hirers, a profession entirely different than that of a slave owner. Additionally, when slaveholders owned slaves in different states, or moved the same ones from state to state, they were erroneously counted more than once. Adjusting for these mistakes, we find the following: from 347,525 we must subtract 158,974 (the number of Southern slave-hirers) and 2,000 (the number of slave owners who were entered more than once). Thus the total number of slave owners in the South in 1850 was 186,551. See Helper, ICS, pp. 146-148.
985. Wilson and Ferris, s.v. "Plantations"; Bradley, p. 33.
986. Foner, FSFLFM, p. 68; Furnas, p. 514.
987. Kennedy and Kennedy, SWR, p. 83.
988. Channing, p. 8; Grissom, p. 131.
989. J. C. Perry, p. 99.

whole people of all colors are neither slaves nor masters.[990]

Let us compare these statistics with those for Northern slave owners. In the early 1700s, 42 percent of New York households owned slaves, and the share of slaves in both New York and New Jersey was larger than that of North Carolina.[991] By 1690, in Perth Amboy, New Jersey, as just one example, nearly every white inhabitant owned one or more black slaves.[992] Based on mathematics alone, it is clear that Yankees were far more enthusiastic slavers than Southerners.

There were so few Southern slave owners that the minority proslavery leaders were at a loss as to how to promote their cause. After trying everything from offering financial inducements to racist scare tactics, they eventually gave up.[993] The American abolition movement had got its start in the South and Southern antislavery sentiment was by now several centuries old.

Also contrary to Northern myth, that all U.S. slaves lived on massive plantations, the vast majority lived on modest, or even small farms. In 1850, for instance, there were only 125 plantations in the entire U.S. (including the North) with 250 or more slaves on them. These particular individuals represented a mere 2 percent of all U.S. slaves.[994]

Such facts destroy two Yankee myths at once: 1) that "all Southerners practiced slavery," and 2) that "the South's economy was based on slavery."

As for the latter view, the South's economy was clearly based on agriculture, not servitude, for her agrarian system did not require slavery to function.[995] As proof consider the fact that nearly 97 percent of all Southern farms were planted, cultivated, and harvested by the owners themselves. Besides, in 1861, if the South had truly wanted to continue slavery, all it had to do was *not* secede, and instead remain where it had always been: in the U.S., a nation in which slavery was still

---

990. Nicolay and Hay, ALCW, Vol. 1, p. 581.
991. Fogel, pp. 203-204.
992. McManus, BBN, p. 5.
993. Stampp, pp. 425-426.
994. Fogel, p. 185.
995. Simpson, p. 73.

constitutionally protected and legal[996]—and where it remained constitutionally protected and legal even after Lincoln's unlawful Final Emancipation Proclamation was issued on January 1, 1863.[997]

We have firmly established now, from these few facts alone, that the South would not have gone, and did not go, to war over "slavery." Neither did the North, as her own slogans, speeches, and rallying cries attest: nearly all referred to "preserving the Union"—not abolition.[998]

Further evidence comes from the records of Southerners and Northerners, both before and during the War. Almost to a man, every Rebel and Yankee soldier asserted in the strongest possible language that he would never risk his life, or that of his family, to either abolish or secure slavery.[999] Southern cemeteries from Virginia to Texas are filled with the bodies of brave Confederate soldiers. But most of them never owned a slave and had no intention of doing so in the future. Yes, they made the ultimate sacrifice. But it was not for abolition.[1000]

---

996. The antebellum U.S. Constitution protected slavery in five clauses: Article 1, Section 2; twice in Article 1, Section 9; Article 4, Section 2; and Article 5. These were nullified on December 6, 1865, by the ratification of the Thirteenth Amendment. K. L. Hall, s.v. "Slavery."
997. Horwitz, pp. 290-291; Kennedy, p. 229. Lincoln's Final Emancipation Proclamation did not end slavery in the North, nor was it intended to, as the document itself states. This is why Yankees like General Ulysses S. Grant were able to keep their slaves until almost three years after the Emancipation Proclamation was issued. Rutherford, FA, p. 38; Wallechinsky, Wallace, and Wallace, p. 11; Woods, p. 67.
998. Leech, p. 290.
999. For more on this topic, see Seabrook, CFF, passim.
1000. Rutland, p. 225.

SOUTHERN ABOLITION, NORTHERN RACISM

PART TWO

AS FOR NORTHERN SOLDIERS, MOST had never even heard of Harriet Beecher Stowe's world famous, highly fictitious antislavery book, *Uncle Tom's Cabin*.[1001] Even if they had, what would have prompted them to become soldiers in order to free a race that they abhorred, a people that, as freedmen, they believed would compete with them for jobs?[1002]

In February 1861, just two months before Lincoln's War, South Carolina fire-eater Robert Barnwell Rhett visited Washington, D.C. There he noted a glaring lack of enthusiasm among Northerners to don blue uniforms over slavery—or anything else. Observed Rhett: those who are friends with Yankee soldiers tell me that they would much rather that any violent conflict with the South be avoided. In fact, the overwhelming majority of Northern soldiers say that if war comes, they will refuse to fight against their Southern brethren. Instead, they will resign, or simply desert.[1003]

The idea of a war over slavery was indeed literally unthinkable to the majority of Americans, and for good reason: most white Southerners had no association with it, and in fact, wanted to be rid of the institution.

1001. Wiley, LBY, p. 40.
1002. Quarles, p. 238. See also Zinn, p. 184.
1003. From the Charleston *Mercury*, February 26, 1861. (See Mitgang, p. 239.)

Most white Northerners were afraid that Southern emancipation would send millions of African-Americans northward to intermix with their children, dilute and corrupt the white race, endanger racial purity, threaten prosperity, lower moral standards, scare off visitors and tourists, discourage new business, spread diseases, drive down property values, instigate a massive crime wave, thwart colonization, promote abolitionist doctrines, "Africanize" the white North, and worst of all, take away jobs from whites.[1004]

Famed inventor, statesman, Founding Father, slave owner, and white supremacist Benjamin Franklin[1005] could have been speaking for most Yankees and Northerners when he voted to prohibit slavery while at the same time complaining about the problem of disappearing whites in the face of an ever increasing black population.[1006] Slaves, Franklin wrote, have

> blackened half [of] America. . . why should we . . . [continue to] darken its people? Why increase the sons of Africa by planting them in America, where we have so fair an opportunity, by excluding all blacks and tawneys [pure Africans and mulattoes], of increasing the lovely white . . . ? I am partial to the complexion of my country . . .[1007]

The widely respected New Englander[1008] summed up the essential problem as he saw it: Black slaves depreciate the white families who own them.[1009]

Yes, Negrophobia was alive and well across Yankeedom from America's earliest days to the "Civil War" and beyond.[1010]

Like Franklin, Lincoln too was obsessed with the idea that freed Southern slaves would overrun the North. After all, like other Northerners, he had grown accustomed to living in a largely black-free region—and he wanted to keep it that way.

For Northerners, keeping slavery in the South was an ideal form

---

1004. Litwack, NS, pp. 113-152; Quarles, pp. 235-238; Garraty and McCaughey, p. 254.
1005. See Adams and Sanders, pp. 25-29.
1006. See Goodman, pp. 332, 333, 334, 336.
1007. B. Franklin, Vol. 2, p. 234.
1008. Franklin was born in Boston, Massachusetts, in 1706.
1009. Hacker, p. 112.
1010. L. Johnson, p. 129.

of race control: not only did it prevent blacks from emigrating northward, but with African-Americans far removed from Yankee society, the question of racial equality need never be confronted. Thus, the North's Free-Soil party was not about free land, as Yankee myth teaches.[1011] It was about keeping Northern and Western soil free of blacks.[1012] As Lincoln himself said in 1858, when the Republican senatorial candidate's party was accused of favoring racial equality (taboo in the North at the time): "[you] know that we advocate no such doctrines as those."[1013]

On September 16, 1859, in a speech at Columbus, Ohio, Lincoln voiced his specific concerns on this subject. For, if slavery is allowed to spread across the U.S., he said fearfully:

> They will be ready for Jeff Davis and [Alexander H.] Stephens and other leaders of that company, to sound the bugle for the revival of the slave-trade, for the second Dred Scott decision, for the flood of slavery to be poured over the Free States, while we shall be here tied down and helpless, and run over like sheep.[1014]

Earlier, in 1838, Lincoln's favorite politician, slave owner Henry Clay,[1015] articulated his dread of the situation as well:

> I am no friend of slavery. The Searcher of all hearts knows that every pulsation of mine beats high and strong in the cause of civil liberty. Wherever it is safe and practicable, I desire to see every portion of the human family in the enjoyment of it. But I prefer the liberty of my own country to that of any other people, and the liberty of my own race to that of any other race. The liberty of the descendants of Africa in the United States is incompatible with the liberty and safety of the European descendants. Their slavery forms an exception—an exception resulting from a stern and inexorable necessity—to the general liberty in the United States. We did not originate, nor are we responsible for, this necessity. Their liberty, if it were possible, could only be established by violating the incontestable powers of the states and subverting the Union; and beneath the ruins of the Union would be buried, sooner or later,

---

1011. Ransom, p. 173.
1012. DiLorenzo, LU, p. 101.
1013. Nicolay and Hay, CWAL, Vol. 3, p. 354.
1014. Nicolay and Hay, ALCW, Vol. 1, p. 556.
1015. Nicolay and Hay, ALCW, Vol. 1, p. 299.

the liberty of both races.[1016]

The Boston *Post* joined in the antiblack paranoia. If you liberate the slaves, it declared, the North's poorhouses will soon overflow with them.[1017]

As such, Yankees were reluctant to extend civil rights to blacks: any improvement in their condition in the North, so they believed, would surely lead to an unwanted massive migration of Southern blacks into their region. Thus, even after Lincoln's War, many Northern and Western states were still turning down constitutional amendments that would have authorized black suffrage. Such states included Connecticut, Michigan, Kansas, Wisconsin, Ohio, and Missouri. As late as 1868, black men were still refused the vote in nearly every Northern state.[1018]

Some from Lincoln's party, trying to stem the panic and reassure fearful Northern whites, turned the situation around, claiming hopefully that a Southern emancipation would actually create a "mass migration" of Northern blacks *southward* into Dixie. No one believed this, of course, and the North-wide scare continued. After issuing his Emancipation Proclamation Lincoln then tried following a "containment" policy, a method by which he could keep freed slaves "hemmed in," as Stephen A. Douglas put it, across the South.[1019] But this, like his emancipation itself, turned out to be nothing more than a transparent political maneuver meant to garner support and votes for his reelection.[1020]

As we will see, the racist dread Lincoln and his Northern constituents felt concerning a "great horde of blacks swarming Northward" was imaginary. Southern black people were mainly poor rural farmers, with no love of big city lights and industry, and no money to move long distances. More importantly, they adored their homeland Dixie, with its soothing weather, friendly people, spacious crop lands, and its bountiful mountains, rivers, and forests. Yankee soldiers stationed in the South admitted as much. One of them, Charles Nordhoff, noted sourly in March 1863, that despite the fact that, if they desired, *all* Southern blacks were allowed official passes to move North, less than twelve applications had

---

1016. Schurz, Vol. 2, pp. 166-167.
1017. Quarles, p. 235.
1018. Bailyn, Dallek, Davis, Donald, Thomas, and Wood, p. 29. Another minority, American women, black and white, would not be allowed to vote until 1920, thanks in great part to Lincoln.
1019. Nicolay and Hay, ALCW, Vol. 1, p. 241.
1020. Garraty and McCaughey, p. 254.

been submitted to his office since the start of the War. This was over a span of two years.[1021]

Southern blacks who had either been forcibly taken North or who had gone North voluntarily during the War usually regretted the move. Even free Northern blacks felt an affinity with the South that they never had for their own region. Thus, when they worked, especially on steamers that journeyed South, they could often be heard singing the classic Southern tune, *Dixie*:[1022]

> O, I wish I was in the land of cotton
> Old times there are not forgotten
> Look away! Look away!
> Look away! Dixie Land
>
> In Dixie Land where I was born in
> Early on one frosty mornin'
> Look away! Look away!
> Look away! Dixie Land
>
> O, I wish I was in Dixie!
> Hooray! Hooray!
> In Dixie Land I'll take my stand
> To live and die in Dixie
> Away, away,
> Away down south in Dixie![1023]

Confederate firebrand, Henry Hotze, wrote of the song that it

> expressed the negro's preference for his more genial and sunny native clime, the land which is the negro's true home, and the only land where he is happy and contented, despite the morbid imaginings of ill-informed or misguided philanthropists.[1024]

Why would free Northern blacks, many who had never been to

1021. Quarles, p. 235.
1022. Harwell, pp. 27-28.
1023. Lincoln could not always ignore, or hide, his Southern blood. When the song *Dixie* was first played for him he said: "Now that is one of the best tunes I have ever heard." C. Johnson, p. 53.
1024. Harwell, p. 29. While today Hotze's statement would be considered politically incorrect, at the time there was a kernel of truth to it, for the vast majority of American blacks in the 1860s had been born and raised in Dixie. This would have included Northern blacks, nearly all who, by then, were either born in the South or were descendants of Southern African-American families.

Dixie, want so desperately to voyage there, and even move there permanently? Was this not the white racist land of "cruel slavers and the whip"?

Here we touch on yet another Yankee myth, that "racism toward blacks was purely a Southern problem." Since Lincolnian mythology is deeply intertwined with this belief, let us investigate it for a moment.

Tocqueville was not the first, but only one of many, who noted that in early America racism was far worse in the North than in the South. During his tour of the states in 1831, the French aristocrat summed up his impressions this way:

> Whosoever has inhabited the United States must have perceived that in those parts of the Union in which the negroes are no longer slaves, they have in nowise drawn nearer to the whites. On the contrary, the prejudice of the race appears to be stronger in the States which have abolished slavery than in those where it still exists; and nowhere is it so intolerant as in those States where servitude never has been known.
>
> It is true that in the North of the Union marriages may be legally contracted between negroes and whites; but public opinion would stigmatize a man who should connect himself with a negress as infamous, and it would be difficult to meet with a single instance of such a union. The electoral franchise has been conferred upon the negroes in almost all the States in which slavery has been abolished; but if they come forward to vote, their lives are in danger. If oppressed, they may bring an action at law, but they will find none but whites among their judges; and although they may legally serve as jurors, prejudice repulses them from that office. The same schools do not receive the child of the black and of the European. In the theatres, gold can not procure a seat for the servile race beside their former masters; in the hospitals they lie apart; and although they are allowed to invoke the same Divinity as the whites, it must be at a different altar, and in their own churches with their own clergy. The gates of Heaven are not closed against these unhappy beings; but their inferiority is continued to the very confines of the other world; when the negro is defunct, his bones are cast aside, and the distinction of condition prevails even in the equality of death. The [Northern] negro is free, but he can share neither the rights, nor the pleasures, nor the labour, nor the afflictions, nor the tomb of him whose equal he has been declared to be; and he can not meet him upon fair terms in life or in death.
>
> In the South, where slavery still exists, the negroes are less carefully kept apart; they sometimes share the labour and the

recreations of the whites; the whites consent to intermix with them to a certain extent, and although the legislation treats them more harshly, the habits of the [Southern] people are more tolerant and compassionate. In the South the master is not afraid to raise his slave to his own standing, because he knows that he can in a moment reduce him to the dust at pleasure. In the North the white no longer distinctly perceives the barrier which separates him from the degraded race, and he shuns the negro with the more pertinacity, since he fears lest they should some day be confounded together.

Among the Americans of the South, Nature sometimes reasserts her rights, and restores a transient equality between the blacks and the whites; but in the North pride restrains the most imperious of human passions. The American of the Northern States would perhaps allow the negress to share his licentious pleasures if the laws of his country did not declare that she may aspire to be the legitimate partner of his bed; but he recoils with horror from her who might become his wife.

Thus it is, in the United States, that the prejudice which repels the negroes seems to increase in proportion as they are emancipated, and inequality is sanctioned by the manners while it is effaced from the laws of the country. But if the relative position of the two races which inhabit the United States is such as I have described, it may be asked why the Americans have abolished slavery in the North of the Union, why they maintain it in the South, and why they aggravate its hardships there? The answer is easily given. It is not for the good of the negroes, but for that of the whites, that measures are taken to abolish slavery in the United States.[1025]

In the 1840s, English writer James Silk Buckingham (1786-1855) wrote that "the prejudice of colour is not nearly so strong in the South as in the North."[1026] Here is how Robert Young Hayne, a South Carolina senator, described the treatment of those few Southern blacks who fled to the North:

> . . . there does not exist on the face of the whole earth, a population so poor, so wretched, so vile, so loathsome, so utterly destitute of all the comforts, conveniences, and decencies of life, as the unfortunate blacks of Philadelphia, and New York and Boston.

1025. Tocqueville, Vol. 1, pp. 383-385.
1026. Buckingham, Vol. 2, p. 112.

> Liberty has been to them the greatest of calamities, the heaviest of curses. Sir, I have had some opportunities of making comparison between the condition of the free negroes of the North, and the slaves of the South, and the comparison has left not only an indelible impression of the superior advantages of the latter, but has gone far to reconcile me to slavery itself. Never have I felt so forcibly that touching description, 'the foxes have holes, and the birds of the air have nests, but the Son of Man hath not where to lay his head,' as when I have seen this unhappy race, naked and houseless, almost starving in the streets, and abandoned by all the world. Sir, I have seen, in the neighborhood of one of the most moral, religious and refined cities of the North, a family of free blacks driven to the caves of the rocks, and there obtaining a precarious subsistence from charity and plunder.[1027]

Only a few years later, in 1835, Virginian James Madison met with English author Harriet Martineau and regaled her with stories about how the Northern states erected numerous barriers in an attempt to thwart Negro emigration.[1028] During the conversation our fourth president

> mentioned the astonishment of some strangers, who had an idea that slaves were always whipped all day long, at seeing his negroes go to church one Sunday. They were gayly dressed, the women in brightly-coloured calicoes; and, when a sprinkling of rain came, up went a dozen umbrellas. The astonished strangers veered round to the conclusion that slaves were very happy . . .[1029]

In 1841, after traveling through Philadelphia, an English Quaker, Joseph Sturge, met with former Illinois Governor Edward Coles. Writes Sturge:

> In the course of conversation, the Governor spoke of the prejudice against colour prevailing here as much stronger than in the slave States [the South]. I may add, from my own observation, and much

---

1027. Hawthorne, Vol. 2, pp. 109-110.
1028. M. D. Peterson, JM, p. 377.
1029. Martineau, Vol. 2, pp. 7-8.

concurring testimony, that Philadelphia appears to be the metropolis of this odious prejudice, and that there is probably no city in the known world, where dislike, amounting to hatred of the coloured population, prevails more than in the city of brotherly love![1030]

After a visit to New York City, English writer Edward Dicey recorded his observations concerning Yankee racism and Northern blacks. In the North, Dicey noted:

> Everywhere and at all seasons the coloured people form a separate community. In the public streets you hardly ever see a coloured person in company with a white, except in the capacity of servant. . . . On board the river steamboats, the commonest and homeliest of working [white] men has a right to dine, and does dine, at the public meals; but, for coloured passengers, there is always a separate table. At the great [Northern] hotels there is, as with us [in England], a servants' table, but the coloured servants are not allowed to dine in common with the white. At the inns, in the barbers' shops, on board the steamers, and in most hotels, the servants are more often than not coloured people. . . . White [Northern] servants will not associate with black on terms of equality. . . . I hardly ever remember seeing a black employed as shopman, or placed in any post of responsibility. As a rule, the blacks you meet in the Free [i.e., Northern] States are shabbily, if not squalidly dressed; and, as far as I could learn, the instances of black men having made money by trade in the North, are very few in number.[1031]

On August 15, 1862, a black Massachusetts justice of the peace, John S. Rock, made the following remarks about white racism there. According to Rock, the Bay State did not compare favorably with Southern states, such as South Carolina:

> The masses seem to think that we [blacks] are oppressed only in the South. This is a mistake; we are oppressed everywhere in this slavery-cursed land. Massachusetts has a great name, and deserves much credit for what she has done, but the position of the colored people in Massachusetts is far from being an enviable one. While

---

1030. Sturge, p. 40.
1031. Dicey, Vol. 1, pp. 70-72.

colored men have many rights, they have few privileges here. . . . The educated colored man meets, on the one hand, the embittered prejudices of the whites. And on the other the jealousies of his own race. . . . You can hardly imagine the humiliation and contempt a colored lad must feel by graduating the first in his class, and then being rejected everywhere else because of his color.

No where in the United States is the colored man of talent appreciated. Even in Boston, which has a great reputation for being anti-slavery, he has no field for his talent. Some persons think that, because we have the right of suffrage [in Massachusetts] . . . there is less prejudice here than there is farther South. In some respects this is true, and in others it is not true. We are colonized in Boston. It is five times as difficult to get a house in a good location in Boston as it is in Philadelphia, and it is ten times more difficult for a colored mechanic to get employment than in Charleston [South Carolina]. . . . if we don't like that state of things, there is an appropriation to colonize us.[1032]

Sadly for Northern blacks, white Northern abolitionists were often among the most racist of an already overwhelmingly racist population. White antislavery advocates, for example, often told former slave, black civil rights leader, and lecturer, Frederick Douglass, that he should try and not appear overly intellectual before his white audiences. "People won't believe that you ever were a slave, Frederick, if you keep on this way," said one. "Better have a little of the plantation speech than not; it is not best that you seem too learned," said another abolitionist.[1033] All this despite the fact that Douglass was half-white,[1034] and that he was then a well respected educator whose second wife was a white woman.[1035]

Many Northern white abolitionists liked to refer to blacks, as Lincoln often did, as "niggers," and comments about their "niggerly odour"[1036] and "woolly heads" were not uncommon at antislavery meetings.[1037] Such attitudes led one black teacher to remark that there are numerous Yankees ready and eager to take up the cross of abolition, but few who are able to bear it.[1038] The constitution of the American Anti-

---

1032. *The Liberator*, August 15, 1862.
1033. Douglass, LTFD, p.186.
1034. Website: www.nps.gov/archive/frdo/fdlife.htm.
1035. Douglass, NLFD, p. xiv; K. C. Davis, p. 439.
1036. Litwack, NS, p. 226.
1037. Garrison and Garrison, Vol. 1, p. 327.
1038. Barnes and Dumond, p. 380.

Slavery Society, a group founded in Philadelphia in 1833, did not even mention social equality as its goal.[1039]

During the "Civil War," Northern racism was at an all-time high, just one of the reasons white supremacist Lincoln waited several years before issuing his Emancipation Proclamation. In early 1862, for example, thousands of complaints were made against the U.S. government for "fraud, abuse, and suffering" toward newly freed blacks. Especially problematic was the fact that Lincoln's emancipated black workers were not being paid their promised wage. The money was being skimmed and pocketed by crafty white agents and officers. General order after general order was issued from Washington, with no compliance, no changes. The outrages, and the misery and complaints, continued. In a number of cases, freedmen worked for months without pay, "receiving only subsistence and shelter for their services." In other cases, their food rations were stolen and sold for profit by unscrupulous whites.[1040] Unfortunately, things only got worse.

Soon, in Virginia alone, Yankee soldiers began casting thousands of freedmen into squalid camps—"labor colonies," as they were termed by their Northern inventors—at Alexandria and Fort Monroe. Here, filthy, exhausted, starving, neglected, penniless, homeless, and cold, Lincoln's newly liberated blacks died by the hundreds. To relieve the horrific situation, Yankee Superintendent C. B. Wilder asked Massachusetts Governor John A. Andrew if some of them could be transported to his state. So vehement was Andrew's rejection that the entire proposal was scraped soon after, and the suffering and death at the wretched Union labor colonies went on unimpeded.[1041]

This same scenario played out all over the South: wherever Yanks occupied the land, the lives of once healthy, thriving blacks were reduced to below-poverty levels.[1042] General Nathaniel P. Banks visited one of these "contraband camps" and wrote to William Lloyd Garrison of the experience. According to Banks, the condition of those condemned to these places was one of "abject misery," with hundreds of blacks, young and old, crammed into small, smoke-filled tents. A chimney-less fire

---

1039. Litwack, NS, p. 227.
1040. Wiley, SN, pp. 201-202.
1041. *ORA*, Ser. 1, Vol. 18, p. 461.
1042. See e.g., Wiley, SN, pp. 212-213.

burned in the center of each one, around which all crowded, the sleeping, the sick, and the dying. "I saw this same scene played out at every single Union military post," Banks complained.[1043]

Lincoln's malodorous contraband camps were not even fit for livestock, let alone human beings. Thanks to the pitiless Yankee, here, unhygienic sanitation, exposure, malnutrition, and all manner of disease combined to sharply increase the South's black death toll.[1044]

In an effort to remedy the problem, Banks was appointed commander of the U.S. Department of the Gulf in December 1862. His solution was to force blacks back to work on their original plantations, where they were underpaid (when paid at all), abused, robbed, and even whipped by their new white Yankee bosses.[1045] The system was lambasted and Banks was repeatedly denounced for forcing the freedmen "back into slavery."[1046] Lincoln, of course, considered the enterprise a success! From his viewpoint, by transferring thousands of freedmen from the labor colonies and contraband camps back to the plantations, the government was relieved of the "burden" of caring for them.[1047]

Even after the War, most Northerners who moved South during "Reconstruction" (carpetbaggers) still could not hide their repugnance of the black race. While supporting abolition across the South, they had no desire to "Africanize" white Southerners by establishing integration or social equality between the races.[1048] Their real purpose was to "Northernize" Dixie in order to humiliate and punish her for seceding. More importantly, carpetbaggers wanted to nationalize America's industry for financial gain, which they could not do without industrializing the prostrate South.[1049]

In 1871, B. H. True, a liberal New Yorker who moved to Georgia after the War, spoke for the majority of Northerners when he made the following comments:

1043. Letter dated January 30, 1865; printed in the New Orleans *Daily True Delta*, March 19, 1865.
1044. J. M. McPherson, BCF, p. 709.
1045. A freedman could expect to earn as little as $3 a month (ten cents a day, or about one penny an hour) working under General Banks' labor system. Wiley, SN, p. 213; *ORA*, Ser. 3, Vol. 5, p. 633. This is the equivalent of about $66 a month today.
1046. See Wiley, SN, pp. 211-213, 216.
1047. Eaton and Mason, p. 127. See also pp. 142-166.
1048. Norton, Katzman, Escott, Chudacoff, Paterson, and Tuttle, Vol. 2, p. 435.
1049. J. H. Franklin, p. 176.

> . . . let me state here now, I do not care how friendly I might be toward the negro, I find that there is a natural antagonism against the race. I know it is so with myself, although I was brought up in New York. I probably feel as friendly toward them as anybody can, but there is an antagonism which we all have against the race; that I cannot get rid of; I do not believe any man can.[1050]

What True meant to say was, "I do not believe any *Northerner* can." For, as we have seen, most Southern whites did not hold this view.

Lincoln's "Reconstruction" soldiers were no better. Postwar Yankee troops stationed in South Carolina, for instance, had no problems with local whites. But they were well-known for tormenting, harassing, and molesting the local black population.[1051]

Not surprisingly, not even black Yankee soldiers were safe from the depredations of their fellow white comrades. One particularly racist Yankee officer, Augustus C. Benedict, a white lieutenant colonel in command of black troops, was known to regularly assault his men for minor infractions, such as forgetting to polish their buttons. For the crime of stealing food, Benedict had those caught staked spread-eagle on the ground and then had molasses smeared on their bare faces, feet, and hands. African-Americans unfortunate enough to be subjected to this form of Yankee torture were left all day to the mercies of the weather, insects, wild animals, and anything else that happened by. Getting hit in the face with the broad side of a sword, or even a severe whipping, were also not uncommon under Benedict's command.[1052]

It was because of this nearly ubiquitous white Yankee racism that Southern Congressmen enjoyed comparing

> the happy, well-fed, healthy, and moral condition of the southern slaves, with the condition of the miserable, vicious, and degraded free blacks of the North.[1053]

Such are the facts of what Northern mythologists and South-haters still deceptively refer to as the "abolitionist North."

1050. *Testimony Taken By the Joint Select Committee*, Vol. 2, p. 717.
1051. J. H. Franklin, p. 119.
1052. *ORA*, Ser. 1, Vol. 26, Pt. 1, pp. 456-479.
1053. *The Congressional Globe*, Vol. 13, p. 239.

This is the same region that barred blacks from voting, jury duty, holding political office, interracial marriage, hotels, restaurants, theaters, stagecoaches, trains, schools, steamboats, churches, lecture halls, hospitals, and even cemeteries, right up to and beyond Lincoln's War.[1054] Even African-Americans who risked their lives for the Union, such as black Yankee officers, were repeatedly denied first-class railroad accommodations across the North.[1055]

Why was the white North so much more racist than the white South? It was due, in great part, to a lack of familiarity with blacks.

In the South, whites intermingled with both free and servile blacks on a daily basis, developing strong, lasting, and affectionate bonds,[1056] especially with their own personal African servants.[1057] This intimate association helped banish both white and black racism while nurturing relationships that often endured from crib to grave.[1058] There was indeed a human dimension to Southern slavery that was lacking in both Northern slavery and Northern free labor (the latter in which employees could be fired and made penniless and homeless at a moment's notice).[1059]

While the average upperclass Northern white child could expect to have little or no contact with blacks, the average upperclass Southern white child was typically breast-fed and raised into adulthood by his black foster mother,[1060] the mammy, whom he often knew better than his own biological mother (when necessary, white mistresses, in turn, also often nursed the infants of their black female servants).[1061] Along with child-rearing, white mistresses and their black house servants worked closely together to organize and maintain the various duties of cleaning, washing, gardening, cooking, and food service around the home. In this way, servants often came to be considered integral members of their white families.

A well-known example of this type of relationship is Maria

1054. See J. M. McPherson, NCW, pp. 245-270; Litwack, NS, pp. 104-112.
1055. Greenberg and Waugh, p. 152.
1056. Wiley, SN, pp. 64-66.
1057. Barrow, Segars, and Rosenburg, BC, p. 4.
1058. Wiley, LJR, p. 328.
1059. Barrow, Segars, and Rosenburg, BC, pp. 155-156.
1060. Cash, p. 51.
1061. Blassingame, pp. 167-168; M. M. Smith, p. 263.

Reddick, a black servant girl born in Mississippi in 1832. For decades she worked at Carnton Plantation, a Franklin, Tennessee, farm owned by the McGavocks, an Irish-American family originally from Wythe County, Virginia.[1062] While at Carnton, Maria married a fellow servant, bore eight children, raised three generations of white children, and then, like most Southern blacks, fled further South (not North) during the War to escape the depredations of Lincoln's invading forces and the racist violence toward blacks—for which they were well-known.[1063] (The practice of sending black servants further southward to protect them from invading Yankee soldiers during Lincoln's War was known as refugeeing, or "running the Negroes."[1064] Refugeeing was often a hardship for both owner and servant, but it succeeded in saving the lives of thousands of blacks.)

After the War, now a free woman, Reddick voluntarily returned to Carnton Plantation to work as a paid employee. So loved was she by her white family that she was asked to give the eulogy at her mistress' funeral in 1909. So loved were the McGavocks by Maria that she gladly accepted. Even after the plantation was sold in 1911, she stayed on with her white employers—until the year 1919.

Maria, who finally passed away in 1922, had worked for the same European-American family for seventy-one years, longer than most of its own members had lived. I know of this remarkable African-American woman because I am related to the McGavocks, the white Tennessee family who she devoted her life to. The fact is that Maria Reddick's case was the norm in the South, not the exception, as Northern mythology would have us believe.[1065]

Unlike in the Old North, where segregation was "almost universal" before 1860,[1066] there was literally no segregation in the Old South.[1067] Instead, Southern black servants and their white owners

---

1062. For an in-depth history (and a complete family tree) of this fascinating Confederate clan, see my book, *The McGavocks of Carnton Plantation: A Southern History*.
1063. Greenberg and Waugh, p. 375; Gragg, p. 84. Yankee crimes against Southern blacks included harassment, theft, torture, rape, and murder. See e.g., Gragg, pp. 192-196; Wiley, SN, p. 235; Grissom, pp. 115-116.
1064. Quarles, pp. 46-47.
1065. Seabrook, CPGS, pp. 78-80.
1066. Rosenbaum and Brinkley, s.v. "Jim Crow Laws."
1067. C. Johnson, pp. 206-207.

routinely worked side by side in the cotton field.[1068] Then, when Lincoln's War came, they fought side by side on the battlefield.[1069]

Both Southern whites and Southern blacks prided themselves in having two families: a white one and a black one, which is why, during the War, European-American and African-American soldiers wrote home to inquire lovingly of both: their immediate family and their "extended family."[1070]

Southerners of every color were quite familiar with what author Robert F. Durden refers to as the copious supply of kindness and generosity that existed between the various races of Dixie.[1071] South Carolina planter Louis Manigault, like thousands of other white Southerners, spoke of the warm and tender feelings that passed back and forth between master and slave prior to Lincoln's illegal and unnecessary interference in 1861.[1072]

For the rest of his life, famed Rebel guerilla John Singleton Mosby of Virginia, felt an overwhelming tenderness toward the blacks who raised and nurtured him as a youngster. As the tough partisan ranger later noted in his memoirs:

> My father was a slaveholder and I still cherish a strong affection for the slaves who nursed me and played with me in my childhood. That was the prevailing sentiment in the South—not one peculiar to myself—but one prevailing in all the South . . .[1073]

Nearly fifty years after Lincoln's War, Mosby was still helping to support his former black body servant Aaron, who had faithfully attended him during the conflict.[1074]

The words inscribed on a Southern slave's gravestone, erected by his owners, reveals volumes about the relationship between Southern whites and blacks in the antebellum period. It reads:

1068. Garraty and McCaughey, p. 27; Stampp, p. 35; Rosenbaum and Brinkley, s.v. "Slavery"; Wiley, SN, p. 65.
1069. Barrow, Segars, and Rosenburg, BC, passim.
1070. Fox-Genovese, pp. 133-134.
1071. Durden, p. viii.
1072. Golay, p. 25.
1073. Russell, p. 5.
1074. Siepel, p. 24.

> John: A Faithful Servant and True Friend
> Kindly, and Considerate
> Loyal, and Affectionate
> The Family He Served Honours him in Death
> But in Life, They Gave Him Love
> For He Was One of Them[1075]

In his book *The Cotton Kingdom*, famed Connecticut landscape architect and white Yankee racist, Frederick Law Olmsted,[1076] wrote of a "scandalous" experience he had during a train ride through Virginia:

> I am struck with the close cohabitation and association of black and white—negro women are carrying black and white babies together in their arms; black and white children are playing together . . .; black and white faces are constantly thrust together out of the doors, to see the train go by. . . . A fine-looking, well-dressed, and well-behaved coloured young man sat, together with a white man, on a seat in the cars. I suppose the man was his master; but he was much the less like a gentleman of the two. The railroad company advertise to take coloured people only in second-class trains; but servants seem to go with their masters everywhere. Once, to-day, seeing a [white] lady entering the car at a way-station, with a family behind her, and that she was looking about to find a place where they could be seated together, I rose, and offered her my seat, which had several vacancies round it. She accepted it, without thanking me, and immediately installed in it a stout negro woman; took the adjoining seat herself, and seated the rest of her party before her. It consisted of a white girl, probably her daughter, and a bright and very pretty mulatto girl. They all talked and laughed together; and the girls munched confectionary out of the same paper, with a familiarity and closeness of intimacy that would have been noticed with astonishment, if not with manifest displeasure, in almost any chance company at the North.[1077]

This scene, however, would have "astonished" or "displeased" very few white Southerners, nearly all who were accustomed to, and even enjoyed, the company of blacks, as this incident clearly shows.

In 1842, after visiting America, English abolitionist and author

---

1075. J. C. Perry, p. 148.
1076. See Fogel and Engerman, pp. 179-180.
1077. Olmsted, CK, Vol. 1, p. 39.

James S. Buckingham noted that:

> This is only one among the many proofs I had witnessed of the fact, that the prejudice of colour is not nearly so strong in the South as in the North. [In the South] it is not at all uncommon to see the black slaves of both sexes, shake hands with white people when they meet, and interchange friendly personal inquiries; but at the North I do not remember to have witnessed this once; and neither in Boston, New York, or Philadelphia would white persons generally like to be seen shaking hands and talking familiarly with blacks in the streets.[1078]

Mary Chesnut wrote of an incident that too reveals the true state of race relations in the South. One hot August day during the War, she found herself traveling on a river boat in Alabama, one overseen, not by a white deck hand, but by a black one:

> Montgomery, July 30th, 1863: Coming on here from Portland there was no stateroom for me. My mother alone had one. My aunt and I sat nodding in armchairs, for the floors and sofas were covered with sleepers, too. On the floor that night, so hot that even a little covering of clothes could not be borne, lay a motley crew. Black, white, and yellow disported themselves in promiscuous array. Children and their nurses, bared to the view, were wrapped in the profoundest slumber. No caste prejudices were here. Neither [abolitionists] Garrison, John Brown, nor Gerrit Smith ever dreamed of equality more untrammeled.[1079]

Naturally, scenes such as this, interracial scenes of "familiarity and closeness of intimacy," as Olmsted called them, contradict Yankee myth, so they are almost wholly ignored by Northern and New South writers and historians.

Thankfully, famed Southern author William Faulkner preserved the Southern Truth of white and black "Civil War" relations in his literary works. In his novel *The Unvanquished*, for instance, a young Confederate boy named Bayard Sartoris describes his relationship with a slave friend, a black boy named Ringo, this way: they had been born in the same

---

1078. Buckingham, Vol. 2, p. 112.
1079. Chesnut, DD, p. 226.

month. They had nursed at the breast of the same woman. They had grown up together, spent so much time together, that Ringo referred to Bayard's grandmother as "Granny," just as Bayard did. At some point, Ringo was no longer black to Bayard, and Bayard was no longer white to Ringo. So tight was the bond between them that they did not even seem like human beings anymore, as Faulkner poetically phrased it.[1080]

Thomas Jefferson too, just as most other white Southerners did, referred to his black servants as members of "my family,"[1081] freeing, as we have seen, a number of his favorites in his will a generation before Lincoln's War.[1082] Blacks who were not part of his "extended family" were still respectfully referred to by Jefferson as "our black brethren."[1083]

Southern blacks almost always returned the favor. In 1901, African-American leader and former Virginia slave, Booker T. Washington, wrote:

> As a rule, not only did the members of my race entertain no feelings of bitterness against . . . [Southern] whites before and during the war, but there are many instances of Negroes tenderly caring for their former masters and mistresses who for some reason have become poor and dependent since the war. I know of instances where the former masters of slaves have for years been supplied with money by their former slaves to keep them from suffering. I have known of still other cases in which the former slaves have assisted in the education of the descendants of their former owners. I know of a case on a large plantation in the South in which a young white man, the son of the former owner of the estate, has become so reduced in purse and self control by reason of drink that he is a pitiable creature; and yet, notwithstanding the poverty of the coloured people themselves on this plantation, they have for years supplied this young white man with the necessities of life. One sends him a little coffee or sugar, another a little meat, and so on. Nothing that the coloured people possess is too good for the son of 'old Mars Tom,' who will perhaps never be permitted to suffer while any remain on the place who knew directly or indirectly of 'old Mars Tom.'[1084]

1080. W. Faulkner, pp. 7-8.
1081. Jefferson, TJFB, p. 18.
1082. Ellis, AS, pp. 175, 344-345.
1083. Foley, p. 624.
1084. B. T. Washington, pp. 13-14.

Such sentiments continued among the Southern black community long after the War ended.

While most Southern blacks were happy that slavery had been abolished, this did not mean that they turned on their former owners. In nearly every case during the Reconstruction period, freed blacks had the opposite reaction, as Booker T. Washington notes above.

An early black political convention in Alabama, for example, called for a policy of peace and friendship toward all people, in particular the white race. Likewise, in numerous states African-Americans were the first to try and repeal laws that hurt, penalized, or disenfranchised former Confederates, or prevented them from holding office.[1085]

These were not isolated acts. Most Southern blacks had a similar attitude toward whites, such as the former Missouri slave who had nothing but fond memories of her owners and numerous other whites she once knew.[1086] During Reconstruction, Beverly Nash, a former male slave, stood before the South Carolina Convention and declared that the white man was the "true friend of the black man." Above him hung a banner with the words "United we stand, divided we fall." Looking up at it, Nash said: the type of relationship we want with whites is one in which our arms are locked together in union and friendship.[1087]

None of this surprised Southern whites, of course. On thousands of Southern farms and plantations, whites and blacks lived within shouting distance, or even within sight, of each other. Skin color meant little or next to nothing to most folks. As they saw it, they were all part of the same familial unit.[1088]

At church on Sundays it was not uncommon to hear a black man pray, not only for his own biological family, but for his white family as well. In particular were the prayers blacks sent up for those loved ones who were off fighting Lincoln, both Confederate blacks and Confederate whites. An English tourist visiting the South in 1862 attended an all-black church, where he heard one of the members pray for the defeat of the Union. Marse Lord, the supplicant implored earnestly, only you can help

---

1085. Bailyn, Dallek, Davis, Donald, Thomas, and Wood, p. 7.
1086. Stampp, p. 379.
1087. *Negro Digest*, November 1961, p. 66.
1088. M. M. Smith, pp. 194, 250; Barrow, Segars, and Rosenburg, BC, p. 13.

our Rebel sons beat them evil Yanks.[1089]

Close quarters meant close association. Naturally, love and romance (both licit and illicit) between whites and blacks also flourished throughout the South, while in the North such relationships were frowned upon, and even illegal (as noted, Massachusetts was the first state to ban interracial marriage).[1090] Thus while Yankee lawyer-politicians like Lincoln were busy either supporting existing laws, or passing new ones, that prohibited the two races from marrying,[1091] in the far more lenient South, particularly in the cities, many whites and blacks ignored skin pigmentation and simply followed their hearts.

After the Emancipation Proclamation (in 1863), for example, the result was a higher percentage of mulattos in Dixie than in the North. In fact, the percentage of Northern mulattos went down during the same period.[1092] Three years earlier, in 1860, the Census reveals that mulattos already made up some 39 percent of the freedmen in Southern cities,[1093] and that at least 12 percent (about 500,000) of all Southern blacks were by then of mixed racial heritage.[1094]

Racial tolerance followed Southerners into the Afterlife. Southern whites and blacks often chose to be buried next to one another, and to this day one can still see 19th-Century white cemeteries and black cemeteries intimately adjoined on the bluegrass meadows of what was once the Old South.

On his deathbed, U.S. President Andrew Jackson—born in the Carolinas in 1767—was asked if he had a dying wish. His reply was

---

1089. Wiley, SN, p. 106.
1090. Wilson and Ferris, s.v. "Miscegenation"; K. C. Davis, p. 9.
1091. See e.g., Lincoln and Douglas, pp. 164, 206, 228, 239, 284; Stern, pp. 468, 492-493; Basler, ALSW, p. 450.
1092. Reuter, p. 120. In 1918, Edward Byron Reuter wrote: "While there has thus been a general and a decided increase [of mulattos] in all sections of the country since the emancipation of the slaves, the actual increase, of course, has been greatest in the former slave states [the South]. The percentage of mulattoes to blacks has also increased more rapidly in the Southern states. Many of the Northern states show a decrease in the mulatto percentages during the half century of freedom. . . . Where the proportion of whites in the total population is highest, the mulatto population, as a rule, is highest; and where the proportion of Negroes in the general population is highest, there as a rule, the percentage of mulattoes is lowest." Reuter, pp. 120, 122. See also p. 121.
1093. Fogel and Engerman, p. 132. It is important to note that the figure of 39 percent does not indicate wild promiscuity among 19th-Century Southern whites and blacks. In fact, when all the statistics are carefully analyzed (including both urban and rural populations), results show that only 1 to 2 percent of black plantation children were the product of a white and a black parent. In 1860, just 10.4 percent of Southern black servants were mulattos. See Fogel and Engerman, pp. 130-136.
1094. Stampp, p. 351.

typically Southern. He hoped that one day he would once again meet up with his friends in Heaven, "both white *and* black," he stressed emphatically.[1095] This was surely a sentiment nearly all Southerners could understand, slave owners and non-slave owners, free and enslaved.

To this day, despite Lincoln's fiendish attempt to poison race relations in the South, the bonds of friendship between Southern blacks and whites continues to improve,[1096] and still—as they did in the antebellum period—appear to be far healthier than those in North.[1097]

Love and affection between whites and blacks was indeed not commonly known in the North, where the topography was not conducive to large-scale farming,[1098] and where, when it finally became unprofitable,[1099] due in great part to Yankee racism,[1100] what little slavery existed had gradually diminished far earlier. Here, as a result, there were far less blacks. With less contact between the races in the North, racial prejudice took root and spread (particularly among Yankee abolitionists),[1101] initiating the infamous Northern "Black Codes," laws severely limiting the movements, freedoms, and rights of blacks.[1102]

These types of statutes, which included vagrancy laws, restrictions on voting rights, and anti-interracial marriage laws,[1103] were far more harsh in the racist North than in the more tolerant South[1104]—which is precisely why these types of regulations continued to multiply across Yankeedom right up to the time of Lincoln's War.[1105]

Among those who sponsored the North's infamous Black Codes was the individual who is the focus of our book, the infamous Mr. Lincoln;[1106] the same man who, during the 1860 election, was reported (by his own party's newspapers) to detest Thomas Jefferson for having had

---

1095. DeGregorio, s.v. "Andrew Jackson" (p. 117).
1096. Bultman, p. 285.
1097. C. Johnson, pp. 37-38.
1098. Meltzer, Vol. 2, pp. 141-142.
1099. P. M. Roberts, p. 198; Carman and Syrett, p. 40; Garraty and McCaughey, p. 81; Morison and Commager, Vol. 1, p. 245; The World Book Encyc., "slavery."
1100. Litwack, NS, pp. 4, 6.
1101. Fogel and Engerman, p. 136.
1102. Kennedy, p. 219.
1103. J. H. Franklin, pp. 50, 62.
1104. C. Adams, p. 132.
1105. Wilson and Ferris, s.v. "Miscegenation."
1106. See DiLorenzo, RL, pp. 257-258; DiLorenzo, LU, pp. 27-28.

a black mistress (allegedly Sally Hemings).[1107]

And here is yet another reason we know that the War was not fought over slavery.

"The Land of Lincoln," Illinois, Lincoln's adopted home state, was one of the most anti-black, Jim Crow states in America at the time,[1108] in large part because of Lincoln's work to restrict black civil rights there. White Illinoisans, for instance, arguably among the most racist Northerners in the 1850s and 60s, threatened to "commence a war of extermination" if blacks were given equal rights in their state.[1109] It was said that Illinois' Black Codes were so stringent that the civil rights of African-Americans there were "virtually nonexistent."[1110]

Lincoln himself even once admitted that his state was more racist than some of the Southern states. On November 14, 1864, for example, he said:

> A very fair proportion of the people of Louisiana, have inaugurated a new state government, making an excellent new constitution—better for the poor black man than we have in Illinois.[1111]

In 1857 Lincoln aided in the white supremacist movement there by asking the Illinois legislature to appropriate funds for the deportation of all blacks out of the state. Why? To help prevent one of his greatest fears: the dilution of the white race through interracial breeding.[1112]

Whites from central Illinois in particular had little use for blacks, considering them, not human beings, but lowly creatures, little more than barnyard animals "with wool on their heads."[1113] Wrote one newspaper editor from the area, who could not abide the idea of free blacks moving to Illinois: We don't want any Negroes around here. Send them all to the Northeast![1114]

An Illinois senator, Joseph Kitchell, was of the same mind as the

---
1107. J. C. Miller, p. 172.
1108. See e.g., Litwack, NS, pp. 70-72.
1109. Woodard, p. 15.
1110. Nye, p. 49.
1111. Nicolay and Hay, ALCW, Vol. 2, p. 597.
1112. Berwanger, pp. 4-5.
1113. DeCaro, p. 17.
1114. Berwanger, p. 30.

rest of the whites in his state, including Lincoln. The residence of Negroes among us, he announced,

> even as servants . . . is productive of moral and political evil. . . . The natural difference between them and ourselves forbids the idea that they should ever be permitted to participate with us in the political affairs of our government.[1115]

Illinoisans passed countless anti-integration and anti-immigration laws to prevent blacks from settling in or even traveling through their state, with punishments ranging from whipping to being sold back into slavery at public auction.[1116] In 1862, Illinois voters adopted a constitutional provision that barred the further admission of blacks into their state,[1117] a Black Code that Lincoln allowed to remain on the books until 1865, the year his War finally came to an end.[1118] In 1863, for example, eight blacks were arrested and convicted for entering Illinois unlawfully. Of these, seven were sold back into slavery (temporarily) to pay off their fines[1119]—all under Lincoln's watch.

Black Illinois residents complained bitterly of their treatment. One of these, John Jones, a wealthy African-American living in Chicago, sent the following to Governor Richard Yates. We, the colored people of Illinois, it began, are highly displeased with the degradation we are suffering under in our State. Though we were born here, we are viewed as strangers. A black man cannot even buy a burial plot in Chicago for himself. The hatred toward us all comes from the anti-Negro laws passed by the whites of Illinois.[1120]

Lincoln ignored Jones' complaint. Why?

Though it is a little known fact, it remains true that Lincoln publicly detested the presence of blacks in America, thought nothing of referring to them using the "n" word,[1121] and held that they should not be allowed to vote, sit on juries, hold political office, or intermarry with

---

1115. N. D. Harris, pp. 233-234.
1116. Litwack, NS, p. 70.
1117. W. B. Garrison, CWTFB, p. 179.
1118. Litwack, NS, p. 71.
1119. J. M. McPherson, NCW, p. 252.
1120. *Anglo-African*, January 14, 1865.
1121. See Nicolay and Hay, CWAL, Vol. 11, pp. 105-106; Nicolay and Hay, ALCW, Vol. 1, pp. 292, 298; Holzer, pp. 22-23, 67, 318, 361.

whites.[1122] "We cannot make them equals," he consistently maintained both privately and publicly.[1123]

Diametrically opposed to black civil rights, in September 1859, just a year before he was elected president, Lincoln said:

> Negro equality! Fudge!! How long, in the Government of a God great enough to make and maintain this universe, shall there continue [to be] knaves to vend and fools to gulp, so low a piece of demagoguism as this?[1124]

During his August 21, 1858, debate with Stephen A. Douglas at Ottawa, Illinois, Lincoln not only agreed with his opponent's call for continued white supremacy, he also complained that he had been misrepresented as having promoted interracial marriage. In response, he angrily denied the charge, saying that he had never intended to "set the niggers and white people to marry together."[1125] As if to try and put a permanent period on this sentiment, at the same debate Lincoln said:

> . . . this is the true complexion of all I have ever said in regard to the institution of slavery and the black race. This is the whole of it, and anything that argues me into this idea of perfect, social, and political equality with the negro, is but a specious and fantastic arrangement of words, by which a man can prove a horse chestnut to be a chestnut horse.[1126]

At the same debate, he answered Douglas' charge that he was trying to establish racial equality with this remark:

> I had no thought in the world that I was doing anything to bring about a political and social equality of the black and white races.[1127]

On October 18, 1858, from Springfield, Illinois, Lincoln wrote a letter to one J. N. Brown. Impatient with those who continually questioned and misunderstood him, the exasperated president again

---

1122. L. Johnson, p. 54.
1123. Nicolay and Hay, ALCW, Vol. 1, p. 288.
1124. Benson and Kennedy, p. 261; Basler, TCWOAL, Vol. 3, p. 399.
1125. Nicolay and Hay, ALCW, Vol. 1, p. 292.
1126. Bryan, p. 291.
1127. Lincoln and Douglas, p. 95.

expanded on his racial feelings:

> I do not perceive how I can express myself, more plainly, than I have done . . . I have expressly disclaimed all intention to bring about social and political equality between the white and black races . . . I say . . . that Congress, which lays the foundations of society, should . . . be strongly opposed to the incorporation of slavery among its elements. But it does not follow that social and political equality between whites and blacks, must be incorporated . . .[1128]

Like the majority of Northerners in his day, Lincoln's main interest was in preventing the expansion of slavery rather than ending it, and not for the reasons one might think. At his seventh and final debate with Douglas on October 15, 1858, at Alton, Illinois, Lincoln proclaimed:

> It is nothing but a miserable perversion of what I have said, to assume that I have declared Missouri, or any other Slave State, shall emancipate her slaves; I have proposed no such thing.[1129]

Lincoln's apathy toward black civil rights was rooted in his deeply held racist beliefs, which is why, when he began to consider emancipation, it was not for the benefit of blacks. It was for the benefit of Northern and Western whites, nearly all who, like himself, saw black servitude as something that degraded whites and their culture. Whether it degraded blacks or not was another matter entirely, one that held little concern for Lincoln, or for most other Yankees.

Why did Lincoln feel this way?

Our sixteenth president had a multitude of reasons, as we will see in our next chapter.

1128. Nicolay and Hay, ALCW, Vol. 5, pp. 87, 89.
1129. Lincoln and Douglas, p. 268.

LINCOLN, WHITE SEPARATISM, & BLACK DEPORTATION

IN 1846, NORTHERN REPRESENTATIVE DAVID Wilmot introduced his Wilmot Proviso to try and prevent the spread of slavery into Western lands acquired by the U.S. from Mexico during the Mexican-American War (1846-1848).[1130] His proposition was not for the sake of blacks, however. It was solely for whites.[1131]

In the winter of 1847, the Pennsylvania politician articulated the motivations behind his notorious document this way:

> I have no squeamish sensitiveness upon the subject of slavery, no morbid sympathy for the slave. I plead the cause and the rights of white freemen. I would preserve to free white labor a fair country, a rich inheritance, where the sons of toil, of my own race and own color, can live without the disgrace which association with negro slavery brings upon free labor. I stand for the inviolability of free territory. It shall remain free, so far as my voice or vote can aid in the preservation of its free character. . . . The white laborer of the North claims your service; he demands that you stand firm to his interests and his rights, that you preserve the future homes of his children, on the distant shores of the Pacific, from the degradation and dishonor of negro servitude. Where the negro slave labors, the free white man cannot labor by his side without sharing in his degradation and disgrace.[1132]

1130. Rosenbaum and Brinkley, s.v. "Wilmot Proviso."
1131. Weintraub, p. 64.
1132. *Appendix to the Congressional Globe*, 29th Congress, 2nd Session, February 8, 1847, p. 317.

Wilmot, who once commented that he had spent much of his adult life fighting against Northern Abolitionists,[1133] later remarked to a colleague:

> By God, sir, men born and nursed of white women are not going to be ruled by men who were brought up on the milk of some damn Negro wench![1134]

In 1860, the man who was to become Lincoln's secretary of state, New Yorker William H. Seward, described the African race as a

> foreign and feeble element, like the Indians, incapable of assimilation . . . it is a pitiful exotic unwisely and unnecessarily transplanted to our fields . . .[1135]

Lincoln could not have agreed more with Seward and Wilmot, and in fact, according to his own statement, he voted for the anti-black, pro-white Wilmot Proviso "as good as forty times."[1136]

On October 16, 1854, during a speech at Peoria, Illinois, the true white supremacist was revealed, along with the one of the real reasons he was against slavery (and its extension). Said Lincoln:

> Whether slavery shall go into Nebraska, or other new Territories, is not a matter of exclusive concern to the people who may go there. The whole nation is interested that the best use shall be made of the Territories. We want them for homes of free white people. This cannot be, to any considerable extent, if slavery shall be planted within them.[1137]

It is here that we finally uncover the reason Lincoln himself was not a slave owner like Grant and many other Yankees. It is here that we come to the very foundation of his antislavery views and of his Emancipation Proclamation: it was not so much slavery itself that bothered him. It was that the institution brought whites and blacks into close

---

1133. Ransom, p. 97.
1134. Klinkner and Smith, p. 42.
1135. Baker, Vol. 4, p. 317.
1136. Nicolay and Hay, ALCW, Vol. 1, p. 218.
1137. Nicolay and Hay, ALCW, Vol. 1, p. 197.

proximity with one another, the latter "degrading" the former. Thus to keep America white (one of Lincoln's stated lifelong goals), slavery would first have to be abolished (emancipation), then blacks would have to be deported to a foreign land (colonization).[1138] Lincoln, like the black racists, black separatists, and black colonizationists who came before and after him,[1139] felt a deep repugnance toward those of other races. Speaking from his own Caucasian point of view, he summed up his feelings on the matter:

> There is a natural disgust in the minds of nearly all white people, at the idea of an indiscriminate amalgamation of the white and black races . . .[1140]

Based on Lincoln's own words and actions, it is obvious that he included himself in the category of "nearly all white people." (That most Southern whites did *not* feel this way, I have already proven.)[1141]

Later, others in his party would concur: America's Western Territories (soon to become the Western states) should remain as white

---

1138. Catton, Vol. 1, p. 86.

1139. America's history of black racism and black racial separatism is nearly as long as that of whites. Former Northern slave, Frederick Douglass, for example, once said "I saw in every white man an enemy . . ." Douglass, NLFD, p. 109. Black racism toward Caucasians was particularly strong during the 1800s: many African-Americans at this time were revolted by the sight of white skin, a vestige of the native African belief that "only black skin is beautiful." Blassingame, p. 25. Early American black nationalism, some of which grew out of a revulsion toward white racism, was expedited by a black Massachusetts Quaker named Paul Cuffe, who financed the emigration of nearly forty other blacks to Sierra Leone in 1815. Garry and McCaughey, p. 145. In 1877, a number of blacks actually sought out the American Colonization Society (a Northern white supremacist organization to which Lincoln belonged), asking for help in resettling them in Liberia. Adams and Sanders, p. 228. In the 1920s, a black-sponsored "Back to Africa" movement emerged. Its founder, Jamaican-born black nationalist Marcus Garvey, promoted the ideas of black pride, economic independence from whites, and the establishment of a black-only state in Africa. Unfortunately for supporters of the Back to Africa movement, Garvey was later convicted of fraud, imprisoned, and eventually deported. Rosenbaum, s.v. "Garvey, Marcus Moziah." Even earlier, in the 19th Century, African-American abolitionist Martin Delany advocated a separation of the races, with an emphasis on black separatism specifically. Rosenbaum, s.v. "Delaney, Martin Robinson." Delany and Garvey were not the first, nor the last, American blacks to push for black separatism. The idea continues today among numerous African-American groups, many with extreme racist ideologies. Rosenbaum and Brinkley, s.v. "Back to Africa"; "Colonization." Like Lincoln and most other 19th-Century white Northerners, the majority of today's black racists are against interracial marriage and for racial separation. Needless to say, white separatist Lincoln, a lifelong champion of the idea of American apartheid and a former chapter leader of the American Colonization Society in Illinois, would have fully supported the Back to Africa movement. See Seabrook, L, pp. 584-633.

1140. Nicolay and Hay, ALCW, Vol. 1, p. 231.

1141. Lincoln was referring to "nearly all *Northern* white people." He repeatedly demonstrated that he knew almost nothing about how Southern whites felt toward blacks.

as New England.[1142] One of these members, Senator Lyman Trumbull, was certainly speaking for his good friend and neighbor Lincoln when he said publicly:

> I, for one, am very much disposed to favor the colonization of such free negroes as are willing to go in Central America. I want to have nothing to do either with the free negro or the slave negro. We, the Republican party [Lincoln's party], are the white man's party. [Great applause] We are for free white men, and for making white labor respectable and honorable, which it never can be when negro slave labor is brought into competition with it. [Great applause]
>
> We wish to settle the Territories with free white men, and we are willing that this negro race should go anywhere that it can to better its condition, wishing them God speed wherever they go. We believe it is better for us that they should not be among us. I believe it will be better for them to go elsewhere.[1143] . . . When we say that all men are created equal, we do not mean that every man in organized society has the same rights. We do not tolerate that in Illinois.[1144]

Trumbull made great efforts to reassure the public that neither he, Lincoln, or their party advocated the idea of Negro equality. As he said at a political debate:

> I by no means assent to the doctrine that negroes are required by the Constitution of the United States to be placed on an equal footing in the States with white citizens.[1145]

Both being from ultra Negrophobic Illinois, Trumbull and Lincoln had strong feelings about blocking the spread of slavery, not only from their state, but also from the Western Territories, for Illinois itself was considered a Western state at the time.[1146] On October 16, 1854, during a speech at Peoria, Illinois, for example, Lincoln could not have been more explicit:

1142. See DiLorenzo, LU, p. 101.
1143. Trumbull, p. 13.
1144. *The Congressional Globe*, 36th Congress, 1st Session, p. 58; Carey, p. 181.
1145. F. L. Riley, PMHS, Vol. 6, p. 233.
1146. Lincoln himself was often referred to, not as a Southerner or a Northerner, but as a "Westerner."

> Let it not be said I am contending for the establishment of political and social equality between the whites and blacks. I have already said the contrary. . . I am . . . arguing against the extension of a bad thing, which where it already exists, we must of necessity, manage as best we can.[1147]

This is precisely why liberal Lincoln had been against the Mexican-American War:[1148] unable to see it for what it actually was (a land war to expand U.S. territory; i.e., an aspect of Manifest Destiny),[1149] he viewed it as an intentional ploy by conservatives to spread slavery westward.[1150] He was dead wrong of course. But this did not stop him from pushing his white supremacist views, views he hoped to impose upon the entire North American continent.[1151]

Just a few years later, Trumbull, and by extension his boss, Lincoln, noted that

> There is a very great aversion in the West—I know it to be so in my State [of Illinois]—against having free Negroes come among us. Our people want nothing to do with the Negro.[1152]

Then, with the approach of the 1860 election, Trumbull, in an attempt to mollify the fears of the South, asserted that if given a chance Lincoln and his party would clearly demonstrate that they did not favor "negro equality or amalgamation."[1153] While his assurances had no effect on the South (which, by November, was already heading toward becoming a separate sovereign nation), they did succeed in the North, where some 60 percent of those who voted were completely indifferent toward the institution of slavery.[1154]

1147. Nicolay and Hay, ALCW, Vol. 1, p. 196.
1148. Basler, ALSW, pp. 382-383.
1149. Rosenbaum, s.v. "Mexican War." See also Buckley, p. 67.
1150. DeGregorio, s.v. "James K. Polk" (p. 170).
1151. The idea of white American, even world, domination (Manifest Destiny) was nothing new to Lincoln, the racist dictator who used violence to control the Northern states and force a sovereign nation (the Confederacy) into a Union which by then it had come to abhor. No doubt he would have agreed with William H. Seward, his secretary of state who, in 1867, said: "Give me fifty, forty, thirty more years of life, and I will engage to give you the possession of the American continent and the control of the world." Farrar, p. 113.
1152. *The American Annual Cyclopedia*, 1862, Vol. 2, p. 351.
1153. Current, LNK, p. 86.
1154. Cooper, JDA, p. 705.

Lincoln, the man who desperately wanted to be all things to all people, purposefully introduced the idea of white supremacy into his party's platform that year in the hope of getting the votes of the Negrophobes and the anti-abolitionists, two groups to which he belonged and which formed the majority of the Northern population. It was widely known at the time that he had no emotional feelings concerning slavery whatsoever.[1155]

Just two years earlier, in 1858, David Davis, a friend of Lincoln's, a fellow party member, and one of his political advisers, suggested to other Republican candidates that they

> emphatically disavow negro suffrage, negroes holding office, serving on the juries and the like.[1156]

As we will see, Lincoln agreed wholeheartedly with these sentiments and eventually acted on Davis' suggestion.

At national conventions Lincoln's party leaders revealed the real reason they were against slavery and its extension. It was not to liberate the slaves, or grant political or social equality to free blacks in the North.[1157] In Lincoln's words, it was to maintain "the superior position assigned to the white race."[1158] Speaking for Lincoln, one of his party executives went before a large and approving white Yankee audience and declared: it is not for negro civil liberties that we gather here today. It is to guard the civil liberties of working whites.[1159]

Lincoln's party newspapers spread the same gospel, with even more conviction. The reason we are against the extension of slavery, they stated, is because we prefer whites to blacks, and because the Caucasian is superior to the African. Containing slavery in the South is the only method of protecting the North and the Western Territories from the degrading presence of the Negro, they maintained.[1160]

No wonder so many blacks, such as civil rights leader Frederick

---

1155. Hacker, p. 580.
1156. N. A. Hamilton, p. 113; Foner, FSFLFM, p. 265.
1157. Fogel, pp. 386-387.
1158. Nicolay and Hay, ALCW, Vol. 1, p. 539.
1159. Mandel, p. 149.
1160. Berwanger, p. 135.

Douglass, refused to support Lincoln in the 1860 presidential election.[1161] By the middle of 1862, it was painfully clear to all enemies of slavery that one of the strongest barriers to black social progress was the Yankee's rank intolerance and bigotry,[1162] and that the institution would have ended much sooner had Lincoln, the rail-splitter from Illinois, not become president.[1163]

In both Lincoln's and Trumbull's opinion, black colonization (the deportation of all blacks out of the U.S.) was the only answer to what they viewed as "America's racial problem." In reality, this "problem" stemmed primarily from the prejudices of Northern white racists like Lincoln and Trumbull, a prejudice that was on public display for all to see.[1164]

On the issue of black colonization, Lincoln had the full backing of the rest of his cabinet, as well as the majority of his Northern constituents. Indeed, most Northerners were repulsed by the idea of racial integration, and instead pushed for colonization and forced expulsion, or at the very least, social proscription.[1165] Thus for Lincoln, emancipation, colonization, and white supremacy (or rather black insubordination), became the only logical solutions to the nation's racial woes.[1166] This is why, in the summer of 1861, when runaway Southern slaves started to appear in Yankee military camps, citizens all across the North began pushing harder than ever for the deportation of blacks.[1167]

Lincoln himself once summed up the quintessential "problem" of slavery and emancipation like this:

> I think no wise man has perceived . . . how it could be at once eradicated without producing a greater evil even to the cause of

---

1161. Barney, p. 124. Instead, Douglass and many other Northern blacks supported Gerrit Smith that year, the presidential candidate of the Radical abolitionist party.
1162. J. M. McPherson, NCW, p. 69.
1163. Quarles, p. 130.
1164. In fairness to Lincoln, we acknowledge here that racism, in all its ugly forms—white, black, red, yellow, and brown—was endemic to 19th-Century America. As we discuss throughout this book, even most of the so-called white Northern "abolitionists" pushed for emancipation, not to free blacks, give them civil rights, or integrate them into American society as equals. Rather it was primarily to rid the nation of the African race, which they viewed as a social, cultural, and economic threat to European-American hegemony. The focus of this book is on exploding the many Northern and New South myths that surround Lincoln—for example, that he was the "friend of the Negro"—rather than simply condemning him for adhering to the beliefs that nearly all other 19th-Century white Northerners embraced.
1165. Litwack, NS, p. 64.
1166. Rosenbaum and Brinkley, s.v. "Lincoln and Douglas."
1167. J. M. McPherson, NCW, p. 77.

human liberty itself.[1168]

According to Lincoln, for whites like himself, abolition was worse than slavery.

The famed abolitionist-racist, Hinton Rowan Helper, one of Lincoln's most passionate supporters, put the matter this way:

> [America will only have peace after the] country shall have been thoroughly cleansed of the vulgar and disgusting negroes and their next of kin . . .[1169]

Helper's anti-black book, *The Impending Crisis of the South*—which contained statements such as "we do not believe in the unity of the races"[1170]—was heartily endorsed by Lincoln[1171] (who even mentioned Helper and his book in his speeches),[1172] and in 1860 it was used as a campaign document by his party.[1173] Concerning blacks, a people that Helper described as a "God-forsaken race" and Lincoln called an "inferior race," the two men agreed on numerous points. These included white separatism, along with prohibitions against voting, sitting on juries, and interracial marriage.[1174] For his efforts on Lincoln's behalf, Helper was rewarded with a South American consulate.[1175]

We will note here that while liberal Northerner Lincoln was reading and avidly promoting Helper's white supremacist book, conservative Southerners were not only burning it,[1176] but also punishing whites who circulated it, owned it, or read it.[1177] Indeed, after pouring over its pages, Lincoln's only major criticisms of *The Impending Crisis of the South* were that it called for *immediate* emancipation and that it referred to proslavery slaveholders as "criminals."[1178] Lincoln was vehemently against both of these ideas.

1168. Nicolay and Hay, ALCW, Vol. 1, p. 174.
1169. Helper, NQC, p. 281.
1170. Helper, ICS, p. 184.
1171. H. C. Bailey, p. 195; Ashe, p. 59.
1172. See e.g., Nicolay and Hay, ALCW, Vol. 1, p. 609.
1173. Ashe, p. 15.
1174. H. C. Bailey, pp. 139, 141.
1175. Hacker, p. 542.
1176. Katcher, BA, p. 24.
1177. W. S. Powell, p. 128.
1178. H. C. Bailey, p. 59.

Lincoln's postmaster general, lawyer Montgomery Blair, agreed with Lincoln and Helper, insisting that the forced deportation of Negroes was vital, for after emancipation:

> It would be necessary to rid the country of its black population, and some place must be found for them.[1179]

Lincoln's secretary of state, William H. Seward, too had a copy of Helper's book. Of it he said:

> I have read the *Impending Crisis of the South* with great attention. It seems to me a work of great merit; rich yet accurate in statistical information, and logical in analysis.[1180]

In case his own views on race, white labor, and colonization were not clear to everyone, Lincoln continued to emphasize them time and time again: he was thoroughly committed to white supremacy,[1181] even if it meant allowing slavery to continue. One of his most notable declarations in this regard occurred in New York on February 27, 1860, during his renowned Cooper Union Speech, where he stated that he held the view of slavery of Thomas Jefferson and the other Founding Fathers. Said Lincoln:

> This is all Republicans ask—all Republicans desire—in relation to slavery. As those fathers marked it, so let it be again marked, as an evil not to be extended, but to be tolerated and protected only because of and so far as its actual presence among us makes that toleration and protection a necessity. Let all the guaranties those fathers gave it be not grudgingly, but fully and fairly, maintained.[1182]

Lincoln then quoted Jefferson himself, stressing his personal beliefs pertaining to white supremacy:[1183]

1179. Welles, Vol. 1, p. 152.
1180. W. C. Fowler, p. 205.
1181. L. Johnson, p. 54; DeGregorio, s.v. "Abraham Lincoln" (pp. 231-232).
1182. Nicolay and Hay, ALCW, Vol. 1, p. 605.
1183. C. Adams, p. 159.

> 'It is still in our power to direct the process of emancipation and deportation peaceably, and in such slow degrees, as that the evil will wear off sensibly; and their places be . . . filled up by free white laborers. If, on the contrary, it is left to force itself on, human nature must shudder at the prospect held up.'[1184]

Lincoln, a dyed-in-the-wool white separatist, was literally obsessed with the idea of apartheid (the geographical segregation of the races), which is one reason why, when he was a member of the Illinois legislature, he asked for funds to expel all free blacks from the state. This was also the reason he became a manager of the Illinois chapter of the American Colonization Society (ACS)—eventually headed by his *"beau ideal,"* slaver Henry Clay.[1185] Moreover, just two years before he was elected president of the U.S., he was publicly supporting the idea of corralling all African-Americans in their own all-black state if mass deportation proved unworkable.[1186]

Lincoln's favorite organization, the ACS, was founded in 1816 in Washington, D.C., by a Northerner, New Jerseyan Reverend Robert Finley.[1187] Among its early leaders, officers, and supporters were such famed Yankees as New England statesman Daniel Webster (after whom the town of Webster, Massachusetts, was named), New Yorker William H. Seward (Lincoln's secretary of state), and Marylander Francis Scott Key (author of the U.S. National Anthem, *The Star-Spangled Banner*).[1188] The nation's largest and most enthusiastic chapter was in Boston, Massachusetts, where both antislavery and anti-black sentiment was high (as we have seen, the two were not mutually exclusive in New England).[1189]

The stated mission of the ACS was the preservation of white culture through the deportation of all American blacks, both free and emancipated, out of the U.S., which some modern blacks have labeled, appropriately enough, "Abraham Lincoln's white dream."[1190] The African

---

1184. Nicolay and Hay, ALCW, Vol. 1, p. 608. Jefferson's words are from his autobiography, written in 1821, when he was seventy-seven years old. See Foley, p. 816.
1185. W. B. Garrison, LNOK, p. 186; DiLorenzo, LU, p. 28.
1186. Seabrook, TUAL, p. 81.
1187. Fogel, p. 252.
1188. Website: www.slavenorth.com/colonize.htm.
1189. Nye, p. 20.
1190. See Bennett, FIG, passim. See also DiLorenzo, LU, pp. 28, 49.

colony of Liberia was created by the ACS in 1822 for this very purpose: to "liberate" America from blacks, hence its name.[1191]

On June 26, 1857, at Springfield, Illinois, Lincoln lectured his Northern audience on the many benefits of "a separation of the races":

> Judge [Stephen] Douglas is especially horrified at the thought of the mixing of blood by the white and black races: agreed for once—a thousand times agreed. There are white men enough to marry all the white women, and black men enough to marry all the black women; and so let them be married. . . . A separation of the races is the only perfect preventive of amalgamation; but as an immediate separation is impossible the next best thing is to keep them apart where they are not already together. If white and black people never get together in Kansas, they will never mix blood in Kansas. That is at least one self-evident truth. A few free colored persons may get into the free States, in any event; but their number is too insignificant to amount to much in the way of mixing blood. . . . In 1850 there were in the United States 405,751 mulattoes. Very few of these are the offspring of whites and *free* blacks; nearly all have sprung from the black *slaves* and white masters. These statistics show that slavery is the greatest source of amalgamation.[1192]

By "amalgamation," Lincoln was referring to one of white Northerners' most monumental fears: miscegenation (interracial mixing, cohabitation, or marriage), something fairly common and much more widely accepted in the South. Indeed, the word miscegenation was coined by Northerners. Why? Anti-Lincoln Yankees wanted to play up on the Northern dread of "race-mixing," which they believed would be the certain result of Lincoln's Emancipation Proclamation.[1193]

But Lincoln loved the word, adopted it, and used it almost

1191. Some 12,000 to 15,000 American blacks were eventually deported to Liberia, many of them under Lincoln. But their "liberation" was short-lived: conditions were so despicable that hundreds died before they could find a way back to the U.S. To this day, the descendants of these 19th-Century inhabitants are still called "Americo-Liberians," and make up 10 percent of the nation's population. This group is to be contrasted with the other 90 percent, the native indigenous population of Africans, with whom they share ongoing rivalries and disputes in this, Africa's oldest black republic. Rosenbaum, s.v. "Liberia"; Nye, p. 17; Brunner, s.v. "Liberia;" Carruth, p. 1535.
1192. Nicolay and Hay, ALCW, Vol. 1, p. 234. Actually, Lincoln was wrong: later scientific studies, such as those done by Edward Byron Reuter, revealed that the percentage of mulattos went up only *after* slavery ended. Reuter, pp. 120-122. Thus there was almost no connection between slavery and "amalgamation" (race mixing), as Lincoln derogatorily referred to it. See Fogel and Engerman, pp. 130-136.
1193. Wilson and Ferris, s.v. "Miscegenation."

constantly thereafter. Indeed, even in his July 6, 1852, eulogy to his lifelong icon Henry Clay, Lincoln managed to bring up the topics of miscegenation and colonization, noting that the former could be allayed, even prevented, in the North by the latter. Sending blacks back to Africa would have an added benefit he noted: that of disseminating Christianity and civilization, with God's blessing, among a primitive and barbaric people. Quoting slave owner Clay, Lincoln said:

> 'There is a moral fitness in the idea of returning to Africa her children, whose ancestors have been torn from her by the ruthless hand of fraud and violence. Transplanted in a foreign land, they will carry back to their native soil the rich fruits of religion, civilization, law, and liberty. May it not be one of the great designs of the Ruler of the universe . . . thus to transform an original crime into a signal blessing to that most unfortunate portion of the globe?'[1194]

Lincoln himself then added that Clay's

> suggestion of the possible ultimate redemption of the African race and African continent, was made twenty-five years ago. Every succeeding year has added strength to the hope of its realization. May it indeed be realized.[1195]

Finally, Lincoln, one of the "friends of colonization," declares his true feelings on the matter:

> If, as the friends of colonization hope, the present and coming generations of our countrymen shall by any means succeed in freeing our land from the dangerous presence of slavery, and at the same time in restoring a captive people to their long-lost fatherland with bright prospects for the future, and this too so gradually, that neither races nor individuals shall have suffered by the change, it will indeed be a glorious consummation. And if to such a consummation the efforts of Mr. Clay shall have contributed, it will be what he most ardently wished, and none of his labors will have been more valuable to his country and his kind.[1196]

1194. Nicolay and Hay, ALCW, Vol. 1, p. 175.
1195. Nicolay and Hay, ALCW, Vol. 1, pp. 175-176.
1196. Nicolay and Hay, ALCW, Vol. 1, p. 176.

Six years later Lincoln came out publicly for mass black deportation once again, this time during a speech he gave on July 17, 1858, before an audience at Springfield, Illinois. According to the black colonizationist's own words:

> What I would most desire would be the separation of the white and black races.[1197]

Amazingly, the man who uttered these words is still referred to as "the great friend of the black man" by the very people who should know better: scholars, professors, teachers, educators, librarians, writers, museum managers, school administrators, and researchers.

Nine years on, now president of the United States, Lincoln was just as zealous about black colonization. In his Annual Message to Congress on December 3, 1861, he once again took the opportunity to promote the idea of deporting blacks, in this case, free blacks:

> It might be well to consider, too, whether the free colored people already in the United States could not, so far as individuals may desire, be included in such colonization.[1198]

As a result of this speech, in 1861 and 1862, the U.S. Congress had $600,000 (about $15,000,000 in today's currency) set aside to aid in Lincoln's colonization plan to send as many blacks as possible out of the country.[1199]

A year later, in his Second Annual Message to Congress on December 1, 1862, he reemphasized his position on the issue:

> I cannot make it better known than it already is, that I strongly favor colonization.[1200]

In this same speech Lincoln asks Congress to set aside funding for black deportation, and even suggests an amendment to the Constitution to

---

1197. Seabrook, TUAL, p. 91.
1198. E. McPherson, PHUSAGR, 134.
1199. Nicolay and Hay, ALAH, Vol. 6, p. 356. See also pp. 357-358.
1200. Nicolay and Hay, ALCW, Vol. 2, p. 274.

expedite it.[1201] It reads:

> Congress may appropriate money and otherwise provide for colonizing free colored persons, with their own consent, at any place or places without the United States.[1202]

Lincoln was so adamant about expatriating American blacks that he was willing to settle them almost anyplace—as long as it was, as he said, "without the United States." This included Europe, Latin America, or the Caribbean, or anywhere else they would be accepted. As such, he funded experimental colonies in what are now Panama and Belize, as well as in Haiti.[1203] But, being a manager in the American Colonization Society—the white founders of Liberia, he seemed to have a special interest in this particular African colony.

In his public debate with Douglas on August 21, 1858, at Ottawa, Illinois, Lincoln told a supportive Yankee crowd that his remedy for America's "racial problem" would be to first emancipate all enslaved blacks, then "send them to Liberia—to their own native land."[1204] This is a revealing statement, for his opponent had not asked Lincoln what he would do with blacks after they were freed. Only what he intended to do about slavery.[1205] Consumed with the idea of colonization, he himself added the comment about deporting them to Liberia.

Besides working hand-in-hand with the Yankee-founded ACS, white separatist Lincoln labored for years on his own personal emancipation-colonization plan, one that contained five clauses. The fifth stated that all emancipated blacks were to be shipped out of the U.S. and settled on foreign soil. For a variety of reasons, noted below, neither Congress, the border states, or most African-Americans themselves, ever showed any interest in his black deportation plan.[1206]

Nonetheless, Lincoln went on promoting it and, as we have seen, even included it in his Preliminary Emancipation Proclamation. In honor

---

1201. Cornish, p. 95.
1202. Nicolay and Hay, ALCW, Vol. 2, p. 271.
1203. Lincoln's colonization experiments in Panama, Belize, and Haiti all failed miserably, with death rates of over 50 percent in some cases. C. Johnson, p. 182.
1204. Nicolay and Hay, ALCW, Vol. 1, p. 288.
1205. See Holzer, p. 49.
1206. Current, LNK, pp. 221-222.

of his nearly nonstop efforts to rid the nation of African-Americans, one of Lincoln's senators, Samuel Pomeroy, came up with the idea of naming a black colony in Latin America, "Linconia."[1207]

Was this authentic abolitionism? Certainly not, and Lincoln knew it. Still, for him there was no shame in it, which is why he never tried to hide it. Most of his military officers were not true abolitionists either. Some, like Lincoln's favorite commander, Ulysses S. Grant, went so far as to say that: "I never was an abolitionist, not even what could be called anti-slavery."[1208] Hence, after the issuance of Lincoln's Emancipation Proclamation, Grant could happily write that white Americans were still "just as free to avoid the social intimacy with the blacks as ever they were . . ."[1209]

None of this should shock us. While Grant and his wife, Julia Boggs Dent, were ardent slave owners before, during, and after the War,[1210] Lincoln's days as a lawyer included defending not slaves, but slave owners.[1211] He even participated in a case that involved the selling of black slaves, a case for which he was well paid.[1212]

Lincoln was no radical. He was in the mainstream of American thought. Modern Americans who believe that their early leaders intended the nation to be a "Melting Pot," a rainbow of various races, colors, and cultures, are of course grossly mistaken. Lincoln is the most obvious example of just one of millions of Northerners who devoted their entire lives to creating what Southern President Woodrow Wilson saw, in reality, as the "Unmelted Pot,"[1213] a nation of geographically separated races—created in part by Lincoln. The fictions that the "Great Emancipator" was a civil rights activist, and that he inaugurated his War to end slavery in order to merge blacks into mainstream American society, can now also finally be laid to rest.

While strangely, today's anti-South, pro-Lincoln crowd refuses to acknowledge any of these well established facts, they have an even more difficult time accepting that our sixteenth president's unrelenting lobbying

---

1207. DiLorenzo, RL, p. 18.
1208. Foote, Vol. 2, p. 638. Grant uttered this remark in a letter to Elihu B. Washburne, August 30, 1863.
1209. U. S. Grant, Vol. 1, p. 215.
1210. Rutherford, FA, p. 38; Wallechinsky, Wallace, and Wallace, p. 11; Woods, p. 67.
1211. DiLorenzo, RL, pp. 15-16.
1212. Manning, p. 26.
1213. Wade, p. 148.

for colonization continued up until the very last day of his life. Actually, he never stopped thinking or talking about this subject.[1214] Indeed, there is no record of him ever renouncing his obsession with it.[1215]

To the contrary, according to the memoirs of Union General Benjamin "the Beast" Butler (like Lincoln also despised in the South for war crimes against humanity), in early April 1865, the president invited him to the White House to discuss his latest deportation plans to ship all blacks out of the country.[1216] This was just days before Lincoln was killed by John Wilkes Booth, a disillusioned Confederate supporter from Maryland who we will be coming back to shortly.

Of his last meeting with Lincoln in April, Butler writes:

> A conversation was held between us after the negotiations had failed at Hampton Roads [February 3, 1865], and in the course of the conversation he said to me: —
> 'But what shall we do with the negroes after they are free? I can hardly believe that the South and North can live in peace, unless we can get rid of the negroes. Certainly they cannot if we don't get rid of the negroes whom we have armed and disciplined and who have fought with us, to the amount, I believe of some one hundred and fifty thousand men. I believe that it would be better to export them all to some fertile country with a good climate, which they could have to themselves.
> 'You have been a staunch friend of the race from the time you first advised me to enlist them at New Orleans. You have had a good deal of experience in moving bodies of men by water,—your movement up the James was a magnificent one. Now we shall have no use for our very large navy; what, then, are our difficulties in sending all the blacks away?'[1217]

Butler responded by discussing his own idea of how to "send all the blacks away." The solution was simple: settle a colony for them in the Isthmus of Darien (modern Panama). To this Lincoln agreed, replying: "There is meat in that, General Butler; there is meat in that."[1218]

1214. W. P. Pickett, p. 317.
1215. C. Johnson, p.182.
1216. B. F. Butler, p. 903. See also W. P. Pickett, p. 326; M. Davis, pp. 147-148; Adams and Sanders, p. 192.
1217. B. F. Butler, p. 903. See also W. P. Pickett, pp. 326-327.
1218. B. F. Butler, p. 907.

Butler and Lincoln's Panama plan, like all the others, of course, was not meant to be. For as long and as hard as Lincoln pitched his colonization program, it never officially made it past his Preliminary Emancipation Proclamation: his cabinet removed all references to black deportation before he issued his final draft (on January 1, 1863)—the version best known to the public—because they feared it would alienate Republican radicals: the party's abolitionists, socialists, and communists.

Emancipation first. Colonization second. This was Lincoln's plan for blacks. Had he lived, there is no question that he would have done everything in his power to fulfill the second phase. Thus it was, in great part, John Wilkes Booth who truly and finally freed American blacks, not Abraham Lincoln. For the stark reality is that African-Americans would have never been completely free while Lincoln was alive.[1219]

His entire mad colonization scheme was eventually tossed out after his death, due mainly to the enormous costs and logistical complications that would have been involved. Nearly everyone seemed to be aware of these obstacles except Lincoln. Just as bizarre, while he was alive he seemed completely oblivious of the bold fact that whites and blacks could indeed live together, peacefully, harmoniously, even affectionately. One hundred largely quiet years of Southern slavery, whatever one thought of it at the time, had proven this for all who had eyes to see.[1220] But Lincoln did not view blacks and whites as equals, therefore he could not perceive what was obvious to nearly everyone else, particularly Southerners.

There was something else that Lincoln and other Northern supporters of colonization completely ignored: the feelings of blacks themselves. Most, who now rightly considered themselves Americans, not Africans, refused to leave the only homeland they had ever known.[1221] Why, many blacks must have wondered, was the President of the United States, the veritable "Great Emancipator," pushing for colonization when

---

1219. W. P. Pickett, pp. 328, 330. Lincoln's death in April 1865, at Booth's hands, allowed the Radicals (abolitionists, socialists, and communists) in his party to take over the government, after which they pushed through the Thirteenth Amendment in December 1865. It was this bill, not Lincoln's Emancipation Proclamation, that finally ended slavery across the entire U.S. In this sense then, Booth was the "Great Emancipator," not Lincoln.
1220. M. Perry, p. 49.
1221. Many white Northern abolitionists and colonizationists only finally abandoned their belief in black colonization when they realized that 99 percent of all African-Americans were not interested in it. Rosenbaum and Brinkley, s.v. "Colonization."

all this did was reinforce slavery?[1222] Why indeed.

Today we know the answer to this question because we have access to many of Lincoln's documents, letters, and assorted papers, items that were not readily available to the public in the 1860s. All clearly show that Lincoln was a white supremacist who cared little about black civil rights and was against any mixing of the two races.[1223]

Compare America's sixteenth president to one of the Confederacy's greatest officers, General Thomas "Stonewall" Jackson, who founded and oversaw an all-black Sunday school class, then donated $50 (today's equivalent of about $1,300) to the group to buy books.[1224]

Or consider the Confederacy's first and only president, Jefferson Davis: while Lincoln was plotting the exile of all blacks from America's shores, Davis and his wife Varina (Howell) adopted a young black boy, Jim Limber, who they raised as their own in the Confederate White House.[1225] During the War they always treated their black servants equitably and with the greatest respect, as part of their family in fact. After Lee's surrender, during the Davis family's escape southward, their coachman was a "faithful" free black.[1226]   Later, after the War, the one-time Rebel president and his wife sold their plantation, Brierfield, to a former slave.[1227] Davis even spoke once of a time when he led "negroes against a lawless body of armed white men . . .,"[1228] something we can be sure that white separatist Lincoln never did—or would have even considered.

Who then, we must now ask, was the authentic "Great Emancipator"? It is true that Lincoln wanted to end slavery. But this was primarily so he could deport all blacks out of the country. Davis too wanted to abolish the institution. However, he was against colonization. Instead, Davis wanted freed blacks to remain in the South, where they would continue to help build and maintain the region, just as they had

---

1222. Rosenbaum and Brinkley, s.v. "Colonization."
1223. L. Johnson, p. 54.
1224. Seabrook, TQSJ, pp. 17, 88, 137; Gragg, pp. 218-220.
1225. After the War, as the Davises were fleeing, Union troops caught up with them in Georgia and tore the screaming, sobbing boy away from his adoptive mother Varina. The Davis family was never able to find out what became of little Jim Limber, the beloved son who they had raised and educated as their own. Even after his death, Lincoln's devotees, propagandists, and mythographers continued to suppress the truth about the South, for had the public known about Jefferson Davis' black son, Lincoln's assault on Dixie would not have seemed so righteous. See C. Johnson, pp. 187-188.
1226. J. Davis, RFCG, Vol. 2, p. 701.
1227. Shenkman and Reiger, p. 124.
1228. J. Davis, RFCG, Vol. 1, p. 518.

since the late 1500s.

What Lincoln never understood, and what is completely unknown to the average American today, is that the apartheid he so desperately craved is actually another form of slavery (in this case one known as collective slavery), which is exactly how apartheid is defined by Anti-Slavery International, the world's oldest international human rights organization.[1229] Thus, it must go down as one of American history's greatest ironies that Lincoln is credited with ending chattel slavery, yet he actually spent his entire adult life promoting another form of the institution, collective slavery, one just as potentially onerous, degrading, and exploitative.

In great contrast to Lincoln were white Southerners, who, like Jefferson Davis, overwhelmingly preferred that blacks remain in America. Why?

Not only did they consider black Southerners their friends and "family members" in many cases, but many Southern whites also believed that blacks were better workers than whites, and they wanted to be able to hire their trusted laborers back after emancipation.

After the War, one of these, Southern hero and Confederate General Nathan Bedford Forrest (the only man in either the Confederate or Union army to rise from private to lieutenant general),[1230] even lobbied to repopulate and resettle the South, not only with freed blacks, but also with new African immigrants.[1231] Of his Southern black brothers and sisters, Forrest said:

> They are the best laborers we have ever had in the South. . . . there is no need for a war of the races. I want to see the whole country prosper.[1232]

One would have to search long and hard to find an example of a Yankee officer, or any Northerner for that matter, expressing similar sentiments. Lincoln's postbellum plan to deport all blacks out of the U.S., and Dixie's desire to import additional blacks into the U.S., were just two more of the many differences between South and North.

1229. Drescher and Engerman, p. 165.
1230. Strain, p. 52.
1231. Hurst, p. 330.
1232. Seabrook, NBF, p. 67.

SECTION THREE

ELECTIONS, WAR CRIMES, & EMANCIPATION

Lincoln is, to the extent of his limited ability and narrow intelligence, the [socialists'] willing instrument for all the woe which [has] thus far been brought upon the Country and for all the degradation, all the atrocity, all the desolation and ruin.

Franklin Pierce (1804-1869)
U.S. President

10

Lincoln's War Against the North

THOUGH LINCOLN PERIODICALLY TRIED TO appease the North's handful of boisterous, widely detested abolitionists, he himself was certainly not one of them,[1233] and he said so.[1234] He often made public comments on how he loathed and distrusted the group and considered its members a nuisance.[1235]

That Lincoln did not consider himself an abolitionist, that he in fact intentionally separated himself from them, is clearly evidenced by a statement he made during a speech at Chicago, Illinois, on July 10, 1858: "I have always hated slavery, I think, as much as any Abolitionist." Ten years earlier, in a March 22, 1848, letter to Usher F. Linder, Lincoln answered the question as to whether or not the Liberal Party (at the time the Republicans) had ever benefitted from associating with abolitionists. Absolutely. They helped us get the Whig candidate William Henry Harrison elected president, he replied. But, Lincoln added, we were careful not to embrace abolitionist doctrines, only the individual whose prestige induced the abolitionists to help us vote him into office.[1236]

Such words were guaranteed to anger abolitionists, which is why, of course, anti-slavery men like Massachusetts-born Lysander Spooner[1237]

1233. Quarles, p. 68.
1234. Hacker, p. 580.
1235. Nicolay and Hay, ALCW, Vol. 3, p. 33.
1236. Hertz, ALNP, Vol. 1, p. 29.
1237. DiLorenzo, LU, pp. 52-61.

disliked (and distrusted) him in return.[1238] Richard H. Dana typified the strong antislavery, anti-Lincoln sentiment within the president's own party. On February 23, 1863, abolitionist Dana wrote:

> . . . the lack of respect for the President in all parties is unconcealed. The most striking thing is the absence of personal loyalty to the President. It does not exist. He has no admirers. If a convention were held tomorrow he would not get the vote of a single State. He does not act or talk or feel like the ruler of an empire. He seems to be fonder of details than of principles, fonder of personal questions than of weightier matters of empire. He likes rather to talk and tell stories with all sorts of people who come to him for all sorts of purposes, than to give his mind to the many duties of his great post. This is the feeling of his Cabinet. He has a kind of shrewd common sense, slip-shod, low-leveled honesty that made him a good Western lawyer, but he is an unutterable calamity to us where he is.[1239]

Many fellow Yankees agreed with Dana, among them: Benjamin F. Wade, Thaddeus Stevens, John C. Frémont, David Hunter, John W. Phelps, Horace Greeley, Theodore Tilton, Wendell Phillips, Frederick Douglass, George B. Cheever, and Henry Ward Beecher. Other Northern detractors included William H. Seward, Edwin M. Stanton, Salmon P. Chase, Hannibal Hamlin, Charles Sumner, Lyman Trumbull, and Henry Winter Davis.[1240]

Lincoln considered most of these men his friends. Yet all turned out to be some of his worst and most vociferous critics; all denounced him at every opportunity;[1241] all made life very arduous for the anti-abolitionist president they frequently referred to as "the slow coach at Washington,"[1242] "the baboon at the other end of the avenue," and "that damned idiot in the White House."[1243]

Of Lincoln's laconic ineptness concerning all things political,

---

1238. W. B. Garrison, CWC, p. 97.
1239. Meriwether, p. 13.
1240. Christian, p. 11.
1241. Lincoln's "friends" made him so miserable that he once told his associate Ward Hill Lamon: "I wish I had never been born! I would rather be dead than as President thus abused in the house of my friends." Meriwether, p. 9.
1242. Quarles, pp. 132-133.
1243. Meriwether, p. 9.

Wendell Phillips once said: if Lincoln grows at all "it is because we have watered him."[1244] Fortunately for "Honest Abe," and contrary to Yankee mythology, genuine abolitionists[1245] never made up more than an extremely small percentage of the Northern populace.[1246] Which is why few Yankees ever gave slavery a second thought—until it became an issue during the 1860 election.[1247] If it had been otherwise, life would have been even more difficult and painful for him.

The rancorous relationships Lincoln had with his fellow Republicans once prompted someone to ask him how he felt about having abolitionists in his party. That's not a problem, he replied, "as long as I'm not tarred with the abolitionist brush."[1248] Again, anti-abolitionist Lincoln was among the majority on this issue.

White Northern feelings concerning both blacks and abolition were perfectly summarized by English *Times* correspondent Charles Mackay, who visited America in 1857 and wrote:

> The North, which will not tolerate slavery, shows its participation in this aristocratic notion by refusing to tolerate the social equality of the 'nigger.' [They say:] 'We shall not make the black man a slave; we shall not buy him or sell him; but we shall not associate with him. He shall be free to live, and to thrive if he can, and to pay taxes and perform duties; but he shall not be free to dine and drink at our board—to share with us the deliberations of the jury box—to sit upon the seat of judgment, however capable he may be—to plead in our courts—to represent us in the Legislature—to attend us at the bed of sickness and pain—to mingle with us in the concert-room, the lecture-room, the theatre, or the church, or to

---

1244. Hofstadter, TAPT, p. 129.
1245. I define a "genuine abolitionist" as one who desired abolition, complete civil rights for blacks, and the full integration of blacks into American society. The number of Northerners who actually fell into this category was minuscule. While many called themselves abolitionists, for instance, and truly wanted to see the institution of slavery destroyed, most were like Lincoln: they cared little if anything about black equality and wanted to see the entire race deported after emancipation. Abolitionists William Lloyd Garrison (the leader of the entire Northern abolition movement), Horace Greeley (owner of the liberal New York *Tribune*), and Harriet Beecher Stowe (author of the bestselling antislavery book *Uncle Tom's Cabin*), as just three examples, all at one time promoted black colonization. Fogel, p. 254; Burlingame, p. 50. Even some blacks supported it, and several thousand actually allowed Lincoln to deport them (with the inevitable horrible results months later). A rare example of a true lifelong abolitionist was the brilliant black civil rights leader, Frederick Douglass.
1246. Adams and Sanders, p. 144.
1247. Varhola, p. 201.
1248. C. Adams, p. 135; DiLorenzo, GC, p. 255; Johannsen, p. 55.

marry with our daughters. We are of another race, and he is inferior. Let him know his place, and keep it.' This is the prevalent feeling, if not the language of the free North.[1249]

You will find this quote in very few Northern or New South books on Lincoln or the "Civil War."

If "the abolitionist North was the true friend of the Negro" and "the slave-ridden South was the true enemy of the Negro," as Northern historians assert, even in the face of a mountain of evidence to the contrary, one must wonder why there was such a tremendous outpouring of rage and violence by white Northerners on their African neighbors in the mid 1800s.

Between July 12 and July 16, 1863, for example, 50,000 whites rioted in New York against Lincoln's military draft (New York's Governor Horatio Seymour had begged Lincoln to suspend the draft in his state, but the president refused).[1250] Tellingly, the mobs did not vent their anger on Lincoln or the government. They targeted blacks, who they harassed, beat, and even lynched, in great numbers over those four terrible days in what Northern authors still deceitfully call the "New York Draft Riots."[1251]

In fact, these were largely Northern anti-Negro riots, using Lincoln's new conscription policy as an excuse to intimidate Northern blacks.[1252] Even black women and children were murdered by white Yankee mobs, after which their corpses were set on fire in the streets. For those who believe that these particular blacks just happened to be in the wrong place at the wrong time, there is the fact that white abolitionists were also tracked down, viciously attacked, and had their property looted and torched.[1253] A little black girl, who was found hiding under a bed (she was being cared for by Catholic priests at the time), was summarily dragged out and killed.[1254]

Before it was all over, as many as 500 people, mostly blacks, lay dead.[1255] Even the Colored Orphan Asylum was targeted, pillaged, and

---

1249. Mackay, p. 240.
1250. See Nicolay and Hay, ALCW, Vol. 2, pp. 381-382.
1251. DiLorenzo, RL, pp. 43-45; K. C. Davis, pp. 315-316.
1252. Crocker, p. 62.
1253. Simmons, p. 75.
1254. Buckley, p. 102.
1255. Hacker, p. 586.

then torched.[1256] Days later the bodies of African-Americans could still be seen hanging from lampposts and trees, all the work of white New Yorkers.[1257] If this violence was truly about Lincoln's draft, as Northern historians maintain, why were blacks specifically selected as the focus of white rage?

A Northern newspaper, the *Christian Recorder*, raised the same issue:

> These rioters of New York could not be satisfied with their resistance of the draft and doing all the damage they could against the government and those of the white citizens who are friends to the administration, but must wheel upon the colored people, killing and beating every one whom they could see and catch, and destroying their property. . . . A gloom of infamy and shame will hang over New York for centuries.[1258]

Typically, white supremacist Lincoln refused to either set up a committee to investigate the horrendous cold-blooded murder of hundreds of blacks by Northern whites, or even comment on it.[1259]

Even before this incident, in February of 1863, white Yankee soldiers rioted in the nation's capital; not over the draft, but over the Final Emancipation Proclamation, which Lincoln had issued just a month earlier. Blacks were hunted down and stoned indiscriminately. Not even black Yankee soldiers were safe. In some areas white Union soldiers beat up every black person they came across, simply because they were of African descent.[1260] Many more such accounts could be given.

As even Lincoln admitted,[1261] the truth is that abolitionists and their "accursed doctrines"—as most Northerners referred to them,[1262] were so detested in the North that they were constantly harassed and

---

1256. Buckley, p. 102.
1257. Quarles, p. 239.
1258. *Christian Recorder*, July 18, 1863. The "gloom of infamy and shame" from this incident did not "hang over New York for centuries," as this writer predicted. Most New Yorkers are still completely unaware of the fact that their town was the center of the early American slave trade, and that it is today the nation's largest, wealthiest, and most powerful city mainly because of slavery. Even fewer seem to know about the so-called "New York Draft Riots" of 1863, and the terrible racial slaughter that took place.
1259. Gilmore, pp. 196-199.
1260. Leech, p. 310.
1261. For example, in a May 30, 1864, letter Lincoln referred to the "unpopularity" of abolitionist principles. See Nicolay and Hay, ALCW, Vol. 2, p. 527.
1262. Litwack, NS, p. 85.

threatened, both in the press and in the street. Attempts were made on their lives as well, with some success.

In Boston, Massachusetts, where American slavery got its start and where wealthy slave owner Peter Faneuil[1263] used some of the profits from slaving to bestow Faneuil Hall on the city in 1742,[1264] fiery Northern abolitionist, William Lloyd Garrison, was attacked by a lynch mob on October 21, 1835, (possibly incited by members of the Yankee version of the Ku Klux Klan).[1265] Dragged through the streets by a rope, he barely escaped with his life.[1266] In order to protect him, the city had him arrested and driven off to jail in a carriage surrounded by armed guards. A few years earlier, in 1830, when Garrison spoke out against Francis Todd, a Yankee slave trader from Newburyport, Massachusetts, the outspoken abolitionist was sued, found guilty, and spent forty-nine days in prison.[1267] His judge and jurors, of course, were not Southerners. They were fellow Northerners.

Bostonians were so upset with Garrison that in 1835, some 1,500 of them signed a petition to hold a public convention to discuss what to do about him, along with other antislavery advocates. On August 21, during the meeting at Faneuil Hall, Boston residents rightfully accused local abolitionists of trying to "scatter among our Southern friends firebrands, arrows, and death."[1268] Garrison fired back, declaring that the title of Faneuil Hall should be changed from "the Cradle of Liberty" to "the Refuge of Slavery."[1269] New Yorkers hated Garrison with the same passion New Englanders did, demanding that he and his "band of nigger minstrels"

1263. Hinkle, p. 111.
1264. Meltzer, Vol. 2, p. 147; Farrow, Lang, and Frank, p. 54.
1265. New England's version of the KKK was founded in the early 1800s, decades before the original Southern KKK was formed in 1865. Melish, p. 165. One of its later secret splinter groups, The Order of the Star Spangled Banner, was founded in Boston, Massachusetts, in 1849, sixteen years before the rise of the original Southern KKK. The Southern KKK adopted numerous "traditions" from the New England "KKK", including many of its secret codes, rituals, signals, identification methods, and handclasps. The Order of the Star Spangled Banner, an anti-immigrant, anti-Catholic political group, eventually evolved into the Know-Nothings, or American Party, as it was also known. Wade p. 39. The organization, which was most popular in New England, eventually dissolved, and in 1860 a majority of its members joined the political party they were most comfortable with, a party of intolerance and bigotry. The man this party nominated for president of the United States that year campaigned on a platform of white supremacy and non-interference with slavery. His name was Abraham Lincoln.
1266. Fogel, pp. 271-272; Farrow, Lang, and Frank, p. 32.
1267. Nye, pp. 27-29, 86-87.
1268. Oates, AF, p. 39.
1269. Hawthorne, Schouler, and Andrews, Vol. 5, p. 217.

be banned from the city.[1270]

In 1834, deeply entrenched Northern racism was the reason New Englanders forced the closure of Prudence Crandall's "High School for young colored Ladies and Misses" in Canterbury, Connecticut. For trying to offer blacks a free education in New England, Crandall, a Yankee Quaker and abolitionist, was harassed, arrested (three times), and imprisoned, while Northern white mobs attacked and stoned her school.[1271] To try and drive her out, local shopkeepers refused to sell food to her, and her Yankee neighbors smashed her windows out and filled the school's drinking well with cow dung.[1272]

When none of these attacks succeeded, they tried to burn Crandall's school to the ground. With the promise of nothing but more threats and violence in her future, she finally abandoned her dream of tutoring blacks, and moved out of state.[1273] "That nigger school shall never be allowed in Canterbury, nor in any other town in this State," she had been told repeatedly by her anti-abolition neighbors in Connecticut.[1274] Yankee politicians agreed. "Once open this door, and New England will become the Liberia of America," the town's elected officials bitterly proclaimed.[1275]

While as late as the 1860s, blacks could not safely walk the streets of Boston, Detroit, Albany, Chicago, and Cleveland after dark,[1276] Northern whites who supported black equality continued to be hounded, hunted down, and even killed by other Northerners. In 1837, Maine abolitionist-publisher Elijah Lovejoy was shot to death by an anti-abolition gang in Illinois, Lincoln's (adopted) home state.[1277] Lovejoy had been trying to protect his fourth printing press (his Yankee neighbors had already destroyed the three previous ones).[1278] Even earlier, in 1834, a New York gang attacked and gutted the home of Yankee abolitionist Lewis Tappan, and in 1835 Connecticut abolitionist Theodore Weld was stoned

---

1270. Wilder, p. 85.
1271. C. Adams, pp. 130-131.
1272. Nye, p. 63.
1273. Buckley, p. 62.
1274. G. W. Williams, HNRA, Vol. 2, p. 151.
1275. Garrison and Garrison, Vol. 1, p. 323.
1276. Quarles, pp. 237-238.
1277. Furnas, pp. 521-522.
1278. Buckley, p. 62.

by angry crowds in Ohio.[1279]

No doubt anti-abolitionist Lincoln felt some empathy for these Northern mobs. Not for their murderous ways, but because he had little use for or feeling toward blacks as anything but pawns in his political games. Thus in his 1860 autobiography,[1280] the "Great Emancipator" mentions nothing about abolition or even slavery,[1281] though he does describe an incident in which he and a white companion were viciously attacked by seven blacks in New Orleans, who intended to rob and murder them. He and his friend "were hurt in the melee," Lincoln wrote sourly, "but succeeded in driving the Negroes from the boat."[1282] That same year he ran for president on a party platform that called for upholding slavery in the South. His nomination in 1860 by fellow party members was, after all, due to the fact that as a white supremacist he was considered a "safe" candidate.[1283]

Lincoln was so far from being an abolitionist that he actually held that while slavery was wrong, in his words, "the promulgation of abolition doctrines tends rather to increase than to abate its evils."[1284] Little wonder that Garrison angrily denounced the sixteenth president as having "not a drop of antislavery blood in his veins,"[1285] and as being "nothing better than a wet rag."[1286] Even less surprising, Lincoln—"who had no toleration for the Abolitionists"[1287]—has become a hero to many modern-day white supremacists and white supremacy groups.[1288]

What about Lincoln's popularity? If he was truly a racial bigot and, as we will show, a morally bankrupt politician, an anarchical dictator, and a ruthless war criminal, how is it that he was elected twice to America's highest office?

1279. Fogel, p. 271.
1280. Lincoln's "memoirs," entitled *The Autobiography of Abraham Lincoln*, were nothing more than carefully cherry-picked materials taken from John G. Nicolay and John Hay's mammoth twelve-volume compendium, *Complete Works of Abraham Lincoln*. The purpose of the autobiography was for use as a "popular campaign biography," to be handed out to potential political supporters for the 1860 presidential election.
1281. Current, LNK, p. 217.
1282. Lincoln, p. 11.
1283. Litwack, NS, p. 276.
1284. Current, LNK, p. 218.
1285. Garrison and Garrison, Vol. 4, p. 33.
1286. Randall, pp. 65, 222, 225; Klingaman, p. 153; Nye, p. 175; Segal, p. 180; J. M. McPherson, BCF, p. 505; Fehrenbacher, LTC, p. 201.
1287. Encyc. Brit., s.v. "Lincoln, Abraham."
1288. M. Davis, pp. 149-151; Current, LNK, p. 231.

In his first election in 1860, Lincoln lost the popular vote by a large margin. In fact, he received only 39.8 percent (1,866,452 votes out of 4,680,193) of the ballots cast that year, while his Democratic opponents, Stephen A. Douglas, John C. Breckinridge, and John Bell, received 60.2 percent (2,813,741 votes). In other words, Lincoln received nearly one million votes less than his opponents combined,[1289] making him a minority president.[1290] Most shocking is the fact that out of the total population of the U.S. that November, only one out of every seventeen eligible whites voted for him.[1291]

How could he have possibly won then? Via the Electoral College. But this too was by a narrow margin: of the 303 electoral votes available, Lincoln received 180—all from non-Southern states—a mere 28 votes above the 152 needed to win. With the Democrats (Victorian conservatives) in disarray,[1292] Lincoln then was only able to claim the 1860 election because of a four-way split.[1293]

The division came, in great part, when Democrat William Lowndes Yancey, and most of the delegates from the other Southern states, walked out of the 1860 Democratic Convention in Charleston. This seemingly insignificant act caused a rift in the Democratic party that scattered the vote, opening the door for Lincoln's election.[1294] Without this "little miracle," Lincoln would have had no chance of winning at all that year.

In the 1864 election, helped along considerably by Confederate General John Bell Hood's disastrous loss at the Battle of Atlanta (July 22, 1864),[1295] Lincoln pulled out all the stops in an effort to get reelected, lowering himself to criminal behavior unheard of by any American president before or since. Unfortunately for Dixie, his reelection

---

1289. Hacker, p. 580.
1290. Garraty and McCaughey, p. 241; H. U. Faulkner, p. 374.
1291. W. B. Garrison, CWTFB, p. 145.
1292. The Standard American Encyc., s.v. "Lincoln, Abraham."
1293. Hacker, p. 580.
1294. E. M. Thomas, p. 49.
1295. See Woodworth, p. 290; Lytle, pp. 271-272; N. Bradford, p. 490; Sword, CLH, pp. 33-35; Groom, pp. 49-54; J. M. McPherson, NCW, pp. 305-306; Warner, GG, s.v. "John Bell Hood." In Margaret Mitchell's powerful and factual Confederate epic, *Gone With the Wind*, Southern belle Scarlett O'Hara says of Hood: "He left the damn Yankees to go through us with nothing but schoolboys and convicts and Home Guards to protect us." Mitchell, p. 475. Hood's incompetence at Atlanta that July boasted Lincoln's sagging ratings, helping to assure the unscrupulous president of a second victory at the polls in November.

illegalities succeeded and he was handed a second term.[1296]

Though Lincoln won both the popular and the electoral votes in 1864, this, his second victory, was nothing to brag about. Not only did he use countless tricks and crimes to insure the outcome, but none of the Southern states voted in the U.S. elections that year (for Lincoln a loss of 80 potential electoral votes). They were now part of a separate, sovereign, and foreign nation: the Confederate States of America.

Of the Northerners and Westerners who voted in the 1864 U.S. election, only 55 percent (2,218,388 individuals of 4,031,887) thought Lincoln deserved a second chance. A full 45 percent (1,813,499 individuals), nearly half, voted for Lincoln's main opposition, George B. McClellan, whose party platform and vice presidential running mate, George Hunt Pendleton, were antiwar and openly condemned Lincoln for flagrantly curbing civil liberties. Lincoln won then by a mere 400,000 votes,[1297] and many of these were illicitly obtained, as we will see.

In 1864, as in 1860, all of Lincoln's electoral votes came from non-Southern states (except for West Virginia, which Lincoln had illegally created for this very purpose).[1298] Yet, if only 38,111 people, a mere 1 percent of Northerners and Westerners, had changed their votes in specific regions, Lincoln would have forfeited even the electoral vote, and McClellan's peace party would have won.[1299] If the South had also voted, it is, of course, a dead certainty that Lincoln would have lost that year.[1300]

Looking at both the 1860 and 1864 elections, it is apparent that Lincoln did not have the mandate of the American people. How then did he manage to win the Electoral College two times in a row?

In the first presidential election on November 6, 1860, though the Confederacy had not yet been formed, ten of the Southern states did not even bother putting Lincoln on their ballots, considering him too perfidious to run the nation. In fact, that year all of his popular votes and all of his electoral ones, came from Northern or Western states: he did not

---

1296. Had Hood won Atlanta, Lincoln would have lost in 1864 to his rivals the Democrats (then the Conservatives), whose platform denounced the War as a "failure" and advocated an immediate end to hostilities. Some 120 million Southerners would today be living in peace, prosperity, safety, and happiness under the Confederate Flag. See Hendelson, s.v. "Lincoln, Abraham."
1297. Hacker, p. 589.
1298. C. Adams, p. 58; W. B. Garrison, LNOK, pp. 193-197.
1299. L. Johnson, p. 127.
1300. Donald, LR, p. 65.

receive a single popular vote in the South.[1301] Thus the only people who voted in his first election were those most likely to cast their ballot for Lincoln to begin with. And *all* of these were white, taxpaying males (non-taxpaying males, women, free blacks, black slaves, and Native-Americans were not allowed to vote).[1302]

Those white taxpaying Northern males who did vote in 1860 sided in great numbers with Lincoln. The most important segment of this group was his Wall Street Boys: Yankee financiers, merchants, and industrialists,[1303] all keen to put anyone into the Oval Office who would maintain the lucrative Northern slave trade. The candidate who promised to do just this was Abraham Lincoln.[1304] Later, these same backers rewarded him by donating millions of dollars from their slave profits to fund his war against the South.[1305]

Furthermore, there can be little question that bribery, lying, horse-trading, and cheating took place on Lincoln's behalf during the 1860 election, and that prime administrative positions and other political favors were swapped for votes. In May, at the national Republican convention, Lincoln's campaign manager, David Davis, interfered with the printing presses so that a ballot could not be taken, had fake tickets made in order to fill seats, then pledged other nominees their choice of governmental posts if they would support Lincoln.[1306]

Lincoln's secretary of war, Simon Cameron, only endorsed "Honest Abe" because he was pledged a cabinet position (Cameron would go on to allow administration-wide corruption regarding the approval of military contracts).[1307] Then there was Lincoln's secretary of the interior, Caleb B. Smith, also promised a post; this time in exchange for delivering the Indiana delegation.[1308] Lincoln also appointed countless numbers of political backers to high-ranking military posts, many of them, to the chagrin of Yankee soldiers, who had no military experience.[1309] The list goes on and on.

1301. Hacker, p. 580.
1302. W. B. Garrison, CWTFB, p. 145.
1303. Burns, Peltason, Cronin, Magleby, and O'Brien, p. 151.
1304. Nicolay and Hay, ALCW, Vol. 2, p. 1.
1305. See Spooner, NT, No. 6, p. 54.
1306. W. B. Garrison, ACW, pp. 194-195.
1307. DeGregorio, s.v. "Abraham Lincoln" (p. 237).
1308. Donald, L, p. 249; DeGregorio, s.v. "Abraham Lincoln" (p. 238).
1309. Wood, pp. 47, 237.

This all occurred, no doubt, under Lincoln's supervision,[1310] for his convention managers later admitted that they had promised "anything and everything" to anyone who would vote for him.[1311] (Lincoln would pay for this double-dealing: his sordid campaign promises necessitated appointing a myriad of individuals with opposing viewpoints, a split cabinet that he was forced to do battle with throughout his entire first term.)[1312]

Of the 1860 presidential election, Judge George L. Christian of Richmond, Virginia, writes that Lincoln

> was only nominated by means of a corrupt bargain entered into between his representatives and those of Simon Cameron, of Pennsylvania, and Caleb B. Smith, of Indiana, by which Cabinet positions were pledged both to Cameron and to Smith in consideration for the votes controlled by them, in the [1860 Chicago] convention, and which pledges Lincoln fulfilled, and, in that way made himself a party to these corrupt bargains.
>
> He was nominated purely as the sectional candidate of a sectional party, and not only received no votes in several of the Southern States, but he failed to get a popular majority of the section which nominated and elected him, and received nearly one million votes less than a popular majority of the vote of the country.[1313]

During his first term in office, Lincoln had more on his mind than just destroying states' rights in Dixie and then Northernizing her. He was desperate to get reelected. Thus between 1861 and 1864, he took time away from his War to make sure his political opponents did not gain an edge over him.

One of the first things he did was issue the Emancipation Proclamation, certainly the most overtly cynical campaign strategy ever devised by a U.S. government official. Maddening to Southerners and Northern abolitionists alike was the fact that even after emancipation, Lincoln favored forcing the South to give blacks the vote while he and the

---

1310. Current, LNK, p. 200.
1311. W. B. Garrison, LNOK, p. 75.
1312. Simmons, s.v. "Lincoln, Abraham."
1313. Christian, p. 25.

Northern states refused to offer them the same privilege.[1314]

This was just the beginning of his hypocrisy and felonious behavior. In an attempt to maintain power and insure his reelection, Lincoln became the greatest political criminal in U.S. history: a mob boss lording over an amoral thugocracy, the likes of which America had not seen before, has not seen since, and hopefully will not see again.[1315]

To begin with, using private vigilante gangs,[1316] Lincoln arbitrarily arrested (without warrants) and imprisoned (without charges) 38,000 Northerners (without trial)[1317] for speaking out against him[1318] (some for as long as four years)[1319]—sending many of them to his "government gulag," Fort Lafayette in New York Harbor;[1320] he illegally suspended *habeas corpus* for the first time in American history[1321]—and all across the U.S.;[1322] imposed martial law,[1323] under whose military courts those arrested for "treason" (i.e., for advocating peace and recognition of the Confederacy),[1324] were illegally tried;[1325] introduced forced conscription;[1326] expanded the army; ordered emergency spending;[1327] violated the concept of the separation of powers; gave away 270 million acres of public lands (under the 1862 Homestead Act);[1328] and spent $2 million ($50 million in today's currency), *all* without constitutional authority or congressional approval.

In order to silence his critics and prevent the truth about his lies and crimes from coming out, Lincoln, in fact, shut down entire Northern states. One of these was Maryland. President Jefferson Davis describes the outrageous crime:

1314. Nye, p. 185.
1315. See Seabrook, TGI, passim.
1316. L. Johnson, p. 124.
1317. Grissom, p. 155.
1318. Rutland, p. 226.
1319. Neely, pp. 113-116.
1320. Dilorenzo, LU, p. 168.
1321. Burns and Peltason, p. 192.
1322. Nicolay and Hay, ALCW, Vol. 2, pp. 541-542.
1323. L. Johnson, pp. 124-125.
1324. See e.g., Nicolay and Hay, ALCW, Vol. 2, p. 521.
1325. Hacker, p. 586.
1326. Mirabello, p. 164.
1327. A. Cooke, ACA, p. 216.
1328. Napolitano, p. 75.

A military force, under the authority of the Government of the United States, occupied the city of Baltimore at a time when no invasion of the State was threatened, and when there had been no application of the Legislature, or of the Executive, for protection against domestic violence, which circumstances alone could give a constitutional authority for this organized military force to occupy the state. The commanding [Union] general, [Robert C.] Schenck, soon issued an order, of which the following is an extract:

> Martial law is declared and hereby established in the city and county of Baltimore, and in all the counties of the Western Shore of Maryland. The commanding General gives assurance that this suspension of civil government within the limits defined shall not extend beyond the necessities of the occasion. All the civil courts, tribunals, and political functionaries of State, county, or city authority, are to continue in the discharge of their duties as in times of peace, only in no way interfering with the exercise of the predominant power assumed and asserted by the military authority.

It will be noticed that this military force of the Government of the United States had no constitutional permission to come into Maryland and exercise authority; that the commanding General says that the civil government of the State is suspended within certain limits; that this suspension will be continued according to the necessities of the occasion; that the courts and political functionaries may discharge their duties, only in no way interfering with the exercise of the predominant military power. Now, where were the 'just powers' of the State government at this time? They were suspended in a part of the State, says the commanding General, and for so long a time as the military authority may judge the necessities of the occasion to require, and that the courts and political functionaries may discharge their duties while recognizing the supremacy of the military power. Thus was the State government subjugated.

A further subversion of the [Maryland] State government was now commenced by an invasion and denial of some of the unalienable rights of the citizens, for the security of which that government was instituted. The Constitution of the United States says:

> No person shall be deprived of life, liberty, or property, without due process of law.
>
> The right of the people to be secure in their persons, houses, papers, and effects, against unreasonable searches and seizures, shall not be violated.
>
> Excessive bail shall not be required, nor excessive fines imposed, nor cruel and unusual punishments inflicted.
>
> Congress shall make no law abridging the freedom of speech or of the press.

The Declaration of Independence says:

> That they are endowed by their Creator with certain unalienable rights; that among these are life, liberty, and the pursuit of happiness; that, to secure these rights, governments are instituted among men.

Immediately upon the issue of the order of the commanding General, the arrests of [Maryland's] citizens commenced by provost marshals. The family residence of a lady was forced open; she was seized, put on board of a steamer, and sent to the Confederate States. A man was arrested for being 'disloyal' to the United States Government, and held for examination. Another was charged with interfering with the enrollment; he was held for further examination. Another, charged with being 'disloyal' to the United States Government, took the oath of allegiance, and was released. A woman charged with the attempt to resist the enrollment, was arrested and subsequently released. A man, on a charge of 'disloyalty,' took the oath, and was released. Another, charged with having given improper information to enrolling officers, was released on furnishing the information. Another, charged with having [gun] powder in his possession, was released on taking the oath of allegiance. Two others, charged with abuse of the negroes laboring on the fortifications, were held for examination. Another, charged with rendering assistance to wounded Confederate soldiers, and expressing treasonable sentiments, took the oath of allegiance and was released. Another, charged with being a soldier in the Confederate army and paroled, was ordered to be sent across the lines. A man, charged with treasonable language, was ordered to be sent across the lines. Two others, charged with aiding

Confederate soldiers, took the oath of allegiance and were discharged. Another, charged with receiving letters from Confederates for the purpose of delivery, took the oath of allegiance and was discharged. Another, charged with expressing treasonable sentiments, was held for examination. Two charged with cheering for Jefferson Davis, took the oath and were released.

One case more must be stated. On May 25, 1861, John Merryman, a most respectable citizen of the State, residing in Baltimore County, was seized in his bed by an armed force and imprisoned in Fort McHenry. He petitioned the Chief Justice of the United States [Roger B. Taney] that a writ of *habeas corpus* might be issued, which was granted. The officer upon whom it was served [Ward Hill Lamon] declined to obey the writ. An attachment was issued against the officer. The marshal was refused admittance to the fort to serve it.

... During the month of July arrests were made of 361 persons, on charges like the above mentioned by the military authority. Of this number, 317 took the oath of allegiance to the Government of the United States and were released; 5 were sent to Fort McHenry, 3 to Washington for the action of the authorities there, 11 to the North, 6 across the lines, and 19 were held for further examination.

On September 11, 1863, one of the city newspapers published the poem entitled 'The Southern Cross.' The publishers and editor were immediately arrested, not allowed communication with any person whatever, and on the same day sent across the lines, with the understanding that they should not return during the war. On July 2d an order was issued which forbade the citizens of Baltimore City and County to keep arms unless they were enrolled as volunteer companies. The Fifty-first Regiment of Massachusetts Volunteers was placed at the disposal of General Erastus B. Tyler, assisted by the provost marshal and the chief of police. The soldiers, in concert with the police, formed into parties of three or four, and were soon diligently engaged in searching houses. Large wagons were provided, and muskets, carbines, rifles, revolvers of all kinds, sabers, bayonets, swords, and bird and ducking guns in considerable quantities were gathered. The Constitution of the United States says:

> The right of the people to keep and bear arms shall not be infringed.

A further subversion of the State government of Maryland was next made by a direct interference with the elections. An election was to be held in the State for members of the Legislature and members of Congress on November 3, 1863. The commanding General, on October 27th issued an order to all marshals and military officers to cause their direct interference with the voters. The Governor [Augustus] (Bradford) applied to the President of the United States to have the order revoked, and protested against any person who offered to vote being put to any test not found in the laws of Maryland. President Lincoln declined to interfere with the order, except in one less important point. The Governor issued a proclamation on the day preceding the election, which the military commander endeavored to suppress, and issued an order charging that the tendency of the proclamation was to invite and suggest disturbance. One or more regiments of soldiers were sent out and distributed among several of the counties to attend the places of election, in defiance of the known laws of the State prohibiting their presence. Military officers and provost marshals were ordered to arrest voters guilty, in their opinion, of certain offenses, and to menace judges of election with the power of the army in case this order was not respected. But perhaps the forcible language of the Governor to the Legislature will furnish the most undeniable statement of the facts. He says:

> ... These abuses present a humiliating record, such as I had never supposed we should be called upon to read in any State, still less in a loyal one like this. Unless it be, indeed, a fallacy to suppose that any rights whatever remain to such a State, or that any line whatever marks the limit of Federal power, a bolder stride across that line that power never made, even in a rebel State, than it did in Maryland on the 3d of last November. A part of the army, which a generous people had supplied for a very different purpose, was on that day engaged in stifling the freedom of election in a faithful State, intimidating its sworn officers, violating the constitutional rights of its loyal citizens, and obstructing the usual channels of communication between them and their Executive.

The result was the election of a majority of members of the Legislature in favor of a State Constitutional Convention. The acts necessary for this object were passed. At the election of delegates the military authority again interfered in order to secure a majority in favor of immediate and unconditional emancipation.

The so-called Convention assembled and drafted a so-called Constitution, in which the twenty-third article of the Bill of Rights prohibited the existence of slavery in the State, and said, 'All persons held to service or labor as slaves are hereby declared free.'

. . . Thus was the State government [of Maryland] subjugated and made an instrument of destruction to the people; thus were their rights ruthlessly violated, and property millions of dollars in value annihilated.[1329]

Famed Southern General Robert E. Lee was so upset by Lincoln's persecution, oppression, and overthrow of the citizens of Maryland that he personally offered his services and those of his army in an effort to free them. On September 8, 1862, he dispatched a letter "to the people of Maryland" that read:

It is right that you should know the purpose that brought the army under my command within the limits of your State, so far as that purpose concerns yourselves. The people of the Confederate States have long watched with the deepest sympathy the wrongs and outrages that have been inflicted upon the citizens of a commonwealth allied to the States of the South by the strongest social, political, and commercial ties. They have seen with profound indignation their sister State deprived of every right and reduced to the condition of a conquered province. Under the pretense of supporting the Constitution, but in violation of its most valuable provisions, your citizens have been arrested and imprisoned upon no charge and contrary to all forms of law. The faithful and manly protest against this outrage made by the venerable and illustrious Marylander, to whom in better days no citizen appealed for right in vain, was treated with scorn and contempt; the government of your chief city has been usurped by armed strangers; your legislature has been dissolved by the unlawful arrest of its members; freedom of the press and of speech has been suppressed; words have been declared offenses by an arbitrary decree of the Federal Executive, and citizens ordered to be tried by a military commission for what they may dare to speak. Believing that the people of Maryland possessed a spirit too lofty to submit to such a government, the people of the South have long wished to aid you in throwing off this foreign yoke, to enable you again to enjoy the inalienable rights of freemen, and restore

---

1329. J. Davis, RFCG, Vol. 2, pp. 460-468. For more on Lincoln's illegal subjugation of Maryland, see Pollard, LC, pp. 123-125.

independence and sovereignty to your State. In obedience to this wish, our army has come among you, and is prepared to assist you with the power of its arms in regaining the rights of which you have been despoiled.

This, citizens of Maryland, is our mission, so far as you are concerned. No constraint upon your free will is intended; no intimidation will be allowed within the limits of this army, at least. Marylanders shall once more enjoy their ancient freedom of thought and speech. We know no enemies among you, and will protect all, of every opinion. It is for you to decide your destiny freely and without constraint. This army will respect your choice, whatever it may be; and while the Southern people will rejoice to welcome you to your natural position among them, they will only welcome you when you come of your own free will.[1330]

Even as Maryland was being put under military bondage, a host of other Northern states were falling prey to what Confederate Vice President Alexander H. Stephens called Lincoln's "reign of terror,"[1331] including one of his greatest supporters: New York.[1332]

Of Lincoln's usurious behavior toward his own people, Richmond's newspaper, *The Southern Illustrated News*, wrote that Lincoln would not permit any opposition toward himself or his War. Those who engaged in such anti-Union activity would be considered traitors and thrown in prison. The original U.S. Constitution, the editor noted, had been trampled into the mud, with the United States herself becoming a "military despotism" as horrible as anything seen, even in Russia.[1333]

Lincoln admitted, in so many words, that his "measures" were unlawful; but then defended them in his typically obscure way, as he did July 4, 1861, in a message to Congress:

> These measures, whether strictly legal or not, were ventured upon, under what appeared to be a popular demand and a public necessity; trusting then, as now, that Congress would readily ratify them.[1334]

1330. *ORA*, Ser. 1, Vol. 19, Pt. 2, pp. 601-602.
1331. Seabrook, TAHSR, pp. 871, 910, 955.
1332. For a description of some of Lincoln's crimes against the state of New York and her citizens, see J. Davis, RFCG, Vol. 2, pp. 477-495.
1333. Harwell, p. 137; Commager and Bruun, p. 581.
1334. Nicolay and Hay, ALCW, Vol. 2, p. 59.

There was no "popular demand" or "public necessity," of course, for the president to break the law and void the Constitution. These were "demands" and "necessities" he fabricated, then placed upon himself. And Congress had no choice but to ratify them, for as Lincoln had repeatedly demonstrated, those who stood in his way would be swiftly arrested and imprisoned—or worse.[1335]

Naturally, part of the financial burden for Lincoln's War fell on the backs of the long-suffering Northern people. Toiling under Lincoln's increased tariffs and taxes, and a new personal income tax (the first),[1336] Northerners saw prices increase nearly 120 percent between 1860 and 1865. Meanwhile, during the same period, money wages only increased 50 percent, while the real wages of Northern workers actually declined a staggering 30 percent. It was not until 1878, thirteen years after Lincoln's death, that the economy began to return to normal.[1337]

As his first term progressed, crime boss Lincoln showed an almost unlimited capacity for committing outrages against the American people and their Constitution. The criminal-minded president, who William H. Herndon (Lincoln's law partner and biographer) once described as a man who "cared little for simple facts, rules and methods,"[1338] went on to invade sitting courts, disrupt their proceedings, and threaten, intimidate, and even arrest judges.[1339] He also aggressively recruited thousands of foreigners into the U.S. army (of questionable legality); deported Northern politicians, such as Ohio Congressman, Clement Laird Vallandigham, for advocating peace;[1340] and curbed the press, closing down over 300 Northern newspapers for printing antiwar articles.[1341] Under Lincoln's direct orders, some printing presses were actually confiscated or destroyed and the papers' editors were jailed.[1342]

The following is a partial list of the hundreds of papers Lincoln

---

1335. Donald, WNWCW, p. 87.
1336. Lincoln imposed the nation's first income tax under the Revenue Act of 1861, lessening the distance the Founders had purposefully created between the central government and the American people. Napolitano, p. 74. Now, every April 15, Americans can thank Lincoln for creating the department that would become the IRS.
1337. Hacker, p. 585.
1338. Rubenzer and Faschingbauer, p. 224.
1339. L. Johnson, p. 125.
1340. Napolitano, p. 69.
1341. L. Johnson, p. 125.
1342. Donald, WNWCW, p. 87.

suppressed and shut down:

The *Chicago Daily Times* (Illinois)
The *Christian Observer* (Pennsylvania)
The *Day-Book* (New York)
The *Democrat* (New Hampshire)
The *Farmer* (Maine)
The *Freeman's Journal* (New York)
The *Herald* (Missouri)
The *Journal* (Missouri)
The *Journal of Commerce* (New York)
The *Missourian* (Missouri)
The *Morning News* (New York)
The *New York World* (New York)
The *Philadelphia Evening Journal* (Pennsylvania)
The *Republican Watchman* (Pennsylvania)
The *Sentinel* (Connecticut)[1343]

As always, the owners of these newspapers were imprisoned without legal representation or trial, a gross violation of both constitutional law and American civil rights.

It bears repeating that every one of the victims of these crimes, those he illegally harassed, arrested, and jailed, were Northerners, Lincoln's own constituents; and all this against the advice and counsel of many of his top administrators, well respected Yankees like Salmon P. Chase, David Davis, and Stephen J. Field. We can hardly be surprised then at how Lincoln treated Southerners during this same period.

The case of Vallandigham, in particular, reveals the depth of Lincoln's madness, as well as the lengths he was willing to go in order to silence his critics. What was it that the Ohio politician, head of the peace party and the Order of the Sons of Liberty, said that upset Lincoln so greatly?

The following excerpt from a speech given by Vallandigham on July 10, 1861, in the U.S. House of Representatives, provides the answer. The Northern Congressman targeted President Lincoln's "usurpations and

---

1343. C. Adams, p. 43.

infractions" regarding the Constitution and the War:

> Sir, however much necessity—the tyrant's plea—may be urged in extenuation of the usurpations and infractions of the President in regard to public liberty, there can be no such apology or defence for his invasions of private right. What overruling necessity required the violation of the sanctity of private property and private confidence? What great public danger demanded the arrest and imprisonment, without trial by common law, of one single private citizen, for an act done weeks before, openly, and by authority of his State? If guilty of treason, was not the judicial power ample enough and strong enough for his conviction and punishment? What, then, was needed in his case, but the precedent under which other men, in other places, might become the victims of executive suspicion and displeasure?
>
> As to the pretence, sir, that the President has the Constitutional right to suspend the writ of *habeas corpus*, I will not waste time in arguing it. The case is as plain as words can make it. It is a legislative power; it is found only in the legislative article; it belongs to Congress only to do it. Subordinate officers have disobeyed it: General [James] Wilkinson disobeyed it, but he sent his prisoners on for judicial trial; General [Andrew] Jackson disobeyed it, and was reprimanded by James Madison; but no President, nobody but Congress, ever before assumed the right to suspend it. And, sir, that other pretence of necessity, I repeat, cannot be allowed. It had no existence in fact. The Constitution cannot be preserved by violating it. It is an offence to the intelligence of this House, and of the country, to pretend that all this, and the other gross and multiplied infractions of the Constitution and usurpations of power were done by the President and his advisers out of pure love and devotion to the Constitution. But if so, sir, then they have but one step further to take, and declare, in the language of Sir Boyle Roche, in the Irish House of Commons, that such is the depth of their attachment to it, that they are prepared to give up, not merely a part, but the whole of the Constitution, *to preserve the remainder.* And yet, if indeed this pretext of necessity be well founded, then let me say, that a cause which demands the sacrifice of the Constitution and of the dearest securities of property, liberty, and life, cannot be just; certainly it is not worth the sacrifice.
>
> Sir, I am obliged to pass by, for want of time, other grave and dangerous infractions and usurpations of the President since the 4th of March. I only allude casually to the quartering of soldiers in private houses without the consent of the owners, and without any

manner having been prescribed by law; to the subversion in a part, at least, of Maryland of her own State Government and of the authorities under it; to the censorship over the telegraph, and the infringement, repeatedly, in one or more of the States, of the right of the people to keep and to bear arms for their defence. But if all these things, I ask, have been done in the first two months after the commencement of this war, and by men not military chieftains, and unused to arbitrary power, what may we not expect to see in three years, and by the successful heroes of the fight? Sir, the power and rights of the States and the people, and of their Representatives, have been usurped; the sanctity of the private house and of private property has been invaded; and the liberty of the person wantonly and wickedly stricken down; free speech, too, has been repeatedly denied; and all this under the plea of necessity. Sir, the right of petition will follow next—nay, it has already been shaken; the freedom of the press will soon fall after it; and let me whisper in your ear, that there will be few to mourn over its loss, unless, indeed, its ancient high and honorable character shall be rescued and redeemed from its present reckless mendacity and degradation. Freedom of religion will yield too, at last, amid the exultant shouts of millions, who have seen its holy temples defiled, and its white robes of a former innocency trampled now under the polluting hoofs of an ambitious and faithless or fanatical clergy. Meantime national banks, bankrupt laws, a vast and permanent public debt, high tariffs, heavy direct taxation, enormous expenditure, gigantic and stupendous peculation, anarchy first, and a strong government afterwards—no more State lines, no more State governments, but a consolidated monarchy or vast centralized military despotism must all follow in the history of the future, as in the history of the past they have, centuries ago, been written. Sir, I have said nothing, and have time to say nothing now, of the immense indebtedness and the vast expenditures which have already accrued, nor of the folly and mismanagement of the war so far, nor of the atrocious and shameless peculations and frauds which have disgraced it in the State governments and the Federal Government from the beginning. The avenging hour for all these will come hereafter . . .[1344]

It was for publicly stating such sentiments that Lincoln had Vallandigham, a Copperhead, arrested in the early morning hours by nearly seventy armed Yankee soldiers and tossed into a military prison.

1344. Vallandigham, pp. 320-322.

He was convicted and tried (without legal representation) by a military court comprised of a panel of eight army officers,[1345] then exiled out of the country.[1346] As usual, all of this was unconstitutional and illegal. But Lincoln had no compunctions about such acts, as long as he was reelected and won his War.[1347]

Had he listened to Vallandigham instead of deporting him, the disaster that became the "Civil War," the War for Southern Independence, could have been avoided, or at least shortened, and thousands of lives saved.

The Ohio attorney had summed up the essential belief of lovers of liberty everywhere, South and North: "The Constitution as it is, the Union as it was."[1348] This statement, the height of rationality, was in full accordance with Jeffersonianism, and Southerners admired Vallandigham for expressing it. Sadly for America, rationality was not among the attributes possessed by Lincoln, one of the most virulent anti-Jeffersonian liberals to have ever graced the halls of the U.S. government.

By such tactics as the military subjugation of Northern states and the arrest and deportation of Northern citizens who disagreed with him, America's sixteenth president virtually assured himself a win in the 1864 election, for not only could he now count on 180,000 extra votes from the free and freed blacks he had grudgingly allowed to enlist (nonmilitary blacks were still not allowed to vote and no blacks had full civil rights yet),[1349] but he ordered all Union soldiers to be furloughed at election time (late October to early November 1864), with the unwritten directive—verbally handed down by his officers in the field—that they were to vote for him. This admonition was aided along by an army slogan that was soon making the rounds among Yankee troops: *Soldiers, you fight for the Union. Now vote for the Union!*[1350] It was obvious to everyone, particularly Lincoln himself, that without the soldiers' vote he would not have won the 1864 election.[1351]

To help guarantee that the soldiers would return home in time to

---

1345. Grissom, p. 154.
1346. Shenkman and Reiger, pp. 129-130; DiLorenzo, LU, p. 163.
1347. K. L. Hall, s.v. "Lincoln, Abraham."
1348. Curti, Thorpe, and Baker, p. 553.
1349. Nye, p. 184.
1350. Daugherty, p. 214.
1351. Hesseltine, pp. 381, 382, 384. See also Donald, LR, p. 80; Simmons, s.v. "Lincoln, Abraham."

vote for him, Lincoln stooped to an all-time low, establishing what we now call "Thanksgiving Day."

While today we think of this holiday as one connected to the Pilgrims' peaceful, autumnal thanksgiving meal with Native-Americans in 1621, its inventor had no such quaint, romantic notions. For politically-minded Lincoln, it was to be a day of holy gratitude for the North's most recent military triumphs, or as he styled them, the "Almighty God's signal and effective victories" over the South.[1352]

As such, his first "Proclamation of Thanksgiving," issued on July 15, 1863, declared that the holiday would be observed on August 6. The document states, in part:

> It has pleased Almighty God to hearken to the supplications and prayers of an afflicted people, and to vouchsafe to the army and the navy of the United States, victories on land and on the sea, so signal and so effective as to furnish reasonable grounds for augmented confidence that the Union of these States will be maintained, their constitution preserved, and their peace and prosperity permanently restored. But these victories have been accorded not without sacrifices of life, limb, health and liberty incurred by brave, loyal and patriotic citizens. Domestic affliction in every part of the country follows in the train of these fearful bereavements. It is meet and right to recognize and confess the presence of the Almighty Father and the power of His Hand equally in these triumphs and in these sorrows . . .[1353]

Lincoln's mid-War motivation here was apparently to appear religious, patriotic, and compassionate, a naked attempt to shore up support from an increasingly despondent, hostile, and apathetic Northern populace. No doubt many lukewarm, antiwar proponents were persuaded to side with him after hearing this, his latest political and military ploy.

However, as the 1864 election loomed ever closer, Lincoln conjured up a new and even more self-serving purpose for observing a day of thanksgiving.

On October 3, 1863, and again on October 20, 1864—this time only a few weeks before election day—Lincoln issued new, updated

---
1352. Nicolay and Hay, ALCW, Vol. 2, p. 370.
1353. Arnold, p. 421.

proclamations announcing that subsequently Thanksgiving Day would be observed on the last Thursday of each November.[1354] Why the change of day and month?

This so-called act of "thanksgiving and praise to our beneficent Father" gave the Union military an excuse to send its soldiers "home for the holidays" in late October and early November, just in time for the November elections (for in most Northern states it was illegal, according to Lincoln himself, for soldiers "to vote away from their homes").[1355] Naturally, grateful Yankee soldiers went to the polls in huge numbers to vote overwhelmingly for the man who had granted them this holiday respite, this unexpected opportunity to get away from the cold, hunger, filth, dangers, and general horror of the battlefield.[1356]

Lincoln helped along his guileful plot by writing the following to Yankee General William T. Sherman in September 1864:

> Any thing you can safely do to let your soldiers, or any part of them, go home to vote at the State election, will be greatly in point.[1357]

Sherman got the "point," and complied, of course, as did numerous other Union officers.

In the fall of 1864, for example, Grant furloughed 15,000 of his troops just in time to return home and vote.[1358] But only those who supported liberal Lincoln. Those who did not were mysteriously "unable" to secure furloughs. Still, conservative-minded Yankee soldiers had ample opportunity to change their minds: as most Union troops were permitted to vote in the field, Lincoln sent party canvassers right to the front of the lines, persuading many a fence-sitter to vote for "Honest Abe."[1359]

In the majority of cases, however, soldiers were simply not allowed to vote against him. As the South had already painfully learned, when all else failed, Lincoln never hesitated to fall back on his favorite

---

1354. Donald, L, p. 471.
1355. Nicolay and Hay, ALCW, Vol. 2, p. 614.
1356. W. B. Garrison, LNOK, p. 214.
1357. McClure, AL, p. 83.
1358. *ORA*, Ser. 1, Vol. 45, Pt. 1, p. 1034.
1359. Donald, WNWCW, pp. 87, 89-90.

methods of governing: intimidation, threats, and even violent coercion.[1360]

While Lincoln's Republican (liberal) agents were assisting in gathering votes in the field, Democratic (conservative) agents who did the same were discouraged, and sometimes even arrested and imprisoned. More sinister still was Lincoln's practice of throwing out the votes of Democratic soldiers as "defective." At other times he replaced such ballots with Republican ones. On numerous other occasions, he refused to count Democratic votes at all.[1361]

Though today we celebrate Thanksgiving Day to give thanks for "divine goodness," we still observe it on the last Thursday of November, betraying its authentic roots in the political shenanigans of America's most exploitive, crafty, and politically astute president.

Lincoln's militarily controlled clamp down on civil rights insured a victory in the 1864 election in various other ways as well. He illegally banned the eleven states of the Confederacy from participating that year,[1362] allegedly because they were now an independent nation. This was illegal because, according to Lincoln himself, the Confederacy was not a legitimate foreign country, it was still part of the Union.

Indeed, for the rest of his life he never publicly recognized the Confederacy as anything other than eleven states "in rebellion" against the U.S.A.—even though, as Jefferson Davis pointed out privately, Lincoln was obviously fully aware that the C.S.A. was a separate nation, otherwise he would not have called up troops, enacted the Anaconda Plan, and blockaded the South (all which would have been unlawful otherwise).[1363] Yet Lincoln must have desperately wanted Dixie's 80 electoral votes. Why then did he block the Southern states from the 1864 U.S. election?

For the same reason he did everything: political expediency. Why risk the embarrassment of allowing states to participate in the North's political process that he knew would never vote for him? The overt hypocrisy of his position never seemed to bother him.

Lincoln need not have taken time to bar the South from the 1864 U.S. election, however. She would not have accepted an invitation from

---

1360. Ashe, p. 60.
1361. L. Johnson, p. 126.
1362. W. B. Garrison, LNOK, p. 215.
1363. Hansen, pp. 58-59; K. L. Hall, s.v. "Lincoln, Abraham." Lincoln's unlawful acts stirred up a number of court cases. See K. L. Hall, s.v. "Prize Cases."

him anyway. For since February 8, 1861, the eleven states of the Confederacy (and provisional Confederate governments in Missouri and Kentucky) had been operating as a legitimate, independent country, one preoccupied with setting up her own government.[1364]

We have now looked at just some of the crimes Lincoln committed in order to secure the *popular* votes he needed to get reelected. His attempts to specifically insure extra *electoral* votes for the '64 election were no less underhanded.

On June 20, 1863, for example, he generated five additional electoral votes for himself by illegally creating the thirty-fifth state, West Virginia[1365] (a clear violation of the U.S. Constitution's Article 4, Section 3, Clause 1).[1366] This he did by pushing the region that would become West Virginia, to secede from Virginia at a time when he had pronounced the secession of the Southern states unlawful.[1367] Again, his double standard did not concern him.[1368]

Shortly thereafter, Lincoln insidiously admitted the thirty-sixth state, Nevada, on October 31, a mere week before election day, November 8, 1864. Like West Virginia, a "Union" state, the hurried, last minute admission of Nevada raised Lincoln's electoral votes even higher, in this case by two (it would have been three, but one Nevada elector did not vote). While this latter action was not unlawful, it was not exactly proper,[1369] for he and his party had tampered with the government's Electoral College. We will note here that along with West Virginia and Nevada, the state of Kansas had been created under Lincoln's auspices for the same reason as well.[1370]

In light of such facts, could any sane person consider either Lincoln's 1860 or his 1864 victories fair and ethical?

Newspapers of the day spoke out against Lincoln's deviltries. He

---

1364. Denney, p. 25.
1365. W. C. Davis, HD, pp. 79-80.
1366. It is illegal for a section of a state to secede from the parent state without the parent's state's approval. Virginia never authorized the secession of West Virginia. Seabrook, L, pp. 763, 877.
1367. W. B. Garrison, LNOK, pp. 193-197.
1368. Lincoln knew this particular action was unconstitutional, which is why he brought the issue up with his cabinet members on December 23, 1862. Nicolay and Hay, ALCW, Vol. 2, p. 283. See also Nicolay and Hay, ALCW, Vol. 2, pp. 285-287, where Lincoln resorts to his usual tortured logic to justify his action regarding the secession of West Virginia.
1369. Donald, LR, p. 79.
1370. Napolitano, pp. 69-70.

had defrauded the American public in the most heinous ways, they cried, particularly in his use of armed Federal soldiers, who he posted ominously at polling stations to intimidate voters. In 1920, an angry Judge George L. Christian wrote of Lincoln's

> standing with the Northern people at the election in November, 1864, when nearly one-half of these people voted against him, and when, but for the improper use of the army in controlling the election, it is believed he would have been defeated by McClellan, since in many of the States carried by Lincoln the popular vote was very close.[1371]

Even before the 1864 votes were cast, dire predictions were made as to how "the Ape," as he was politely called across the South, would guarantee his victory. On November 7, for example, one day before the election, the *Richmond Dispatch* warned that Lincoln would use any means in his power, including his cabinet, his military officers, his spies, and fraud and bribery, to insure his election over McClellan. Lincoln's craftiness and guile were on display for all to see, with dishonesty and "the foulest corruptions" obvious at every level of his party. This is the most glorious prank ever committed by "the Ape," the paper bellowed.[1372]

The day after his reelection the *Richmond Dispatch* was, if anything, even more biting in its criticisms of Lincoln. On November 9, 1864, it ran another piece about "the vulgar tyrant" and "low buffoon," a despicable animal who had already wasted millions of lives without the slightest remorse, and who continued to demand more blood and more money in order to fulfill his direful schemes. After having stripped the North of her liberties by stationing soldiers at the polls, throwing out her legislatures, illegally arresting Yankee politicians, silencing his critics through false arrest and imprisonment, and cunningly forcing his armies to vote for him, it is clear that Lincoln has only one agenda, the newspaper reported bitterly: to crush and defeat all opponents in an attempt to rule the entire nation from Washington.[1373]

The *Richmond Dispatch* was far from being alone. At one time or another, hundreds of newspapers came out against Lincoln, many from the

---

1371. Christian, p. 26.
1372. Mitgang, p. 402.
1373. Mitgang, pp. 403, 404.

North, some from Europe, a few even from his own home state. Among them were:

Baltimore *American* (Maryland)
Charleston *Mercury* (South Carolina)
Chicago *Times* (Illinois)[1374]
Courier des États-Unis (France)
Daily Express (Virginia)
Daily Picayune (Louisiana)
Dallas *Herald* (Texas)
Illinois State Register (Illinois)
La Patrie (France)
London *Standard* (England)
London *Times* (England)
Louisville *Journal* (Kentucky)
New York *Daily News* (New York)
New York *Herald* (New York)
New York World (New York)
New York *Evening Day-Book* (New York)
Punch (England)
Richmond *Whig* (Virginia)
Richmond *Sentinel* (Virginia)
Richmond *Enquirer* (Virginia)
Southern Illustrated News (Virginia)
The Crisis (Ohio)
The Democrat (Maine)
The South (Maryland)
Tri-Weekly Telegraph (Texas)

1374. Lincoln mentions his "suspension" of the *Times* on June 4, 1863, in a letter to Secretary of War Stanton. Nicolay and Hay, ALCW, Vol. 2, p. 343.

11

LINCOLN: WAR CRIMINAL

AS THE *RICHMOND DISPATCH* NOTED, Lincoln's crimes seemed to know no bounds. Incredibly, it was also under his direct orders that the largest execution of Americans in our history took place.

On December 26, 1862, he personally authorized the hanging of thirty-nine Sioux Indians (one was later pardoned) for warring with the U.S. over broken treaties.[1375] Lincoln, who falsely claimed that the Indians had "manifested a spirit of insubordination,"[1376] had wanted to execute all 303 of the Native-Americans who had originally been condemned. But he changed his mind at the last moment for fear of tilting the support of humanitarian Europe toward the Confederacy.[1377] As mentioned earlier, it was just this type of cold brutality which later drew compliments from Lincoln's admirers, men like Adolf Hitler, who praised the skillfulness with which the U.S. exterminated its native peoples.[1378]

Actually, Lincoln had nothing to worry about regarding Europe. Though the region leaned strongly toward the South during the War for Southern Independence (and even smuggled arms and constructed warships for her),[1379] Europe dared not openly side with the Confederacy. Why?

In great part because through Lincoln's secretary of state, William H. Seward, Lincoln had privately threatened war on any nation that

---

1375. W. B. Garrison, CWTFB, p. 62; C. Adams, p. 210.
1376. Nicolay and Hay, ALCW, Vol. 2, p. 267.
1377. Donald, L, 392-395; DiLorenzo, RL, pp. 157-158.
1378. Toland, p. 506.
1379. P. M. Roberts, p. 221.

interfered with his invasion of the South,[1380] in particular England and France,[1381] where sympathy for the Confederacy was the strongest.[1382] England's and France's ruling classes, for example, were always highly interested in and supportive of the Confederate Cause,[1383] while the English population as a whole expressed "widespread sentiment" in favor of recognizing the Confederacy as a sovereign nation.[1384]

It was Lincoln's menacing warning, in place throughout the duration of the conflict, that prevented neutral Europe from publicly supporting "belligerent" Dixie, and which in turn prolonged the War, caused thousands of unnecessary deaths, and aided in the South's eventual downfall.[1385]

As usual, Lincoln was a hypocrite and his threat of violence was an outrageous political fraud, for the U.S. herself had long insisted on the right to assist "belligerent" nations, for example, in 1793, 1841, and 1855. As recently as the 1860s, Lincoln's secretary of state Seward, had declared that the U.S. be allowed to sell arms to Mexico, then at war with France. Such facts, however, did not suit Lincoln's purposes, so he chose not to remind the world of them.[1386]

On the surface, the president's lie about "abolishing slavery," along with his many other deceptions and violations (such as calling the legal formation of the Confederate States of America a mere "rebellion"), made the North appear to be the one taking the moral high road. And so Europe tried to remain neutral, though she was not always at peace with this decision, and on a number of occasions nearly went over to the South. For most Europeans were, like most Southerners, anti-totalitarian and pro-freedom while, as Lincoln himself would repeatedly demonstrate, he was pro-totalitarian and anti-freedom.

Lincoln tried to use and manipulate Europe in another way as well. He had naively believed that his Emancipation Proclamation would

---

1380. P. J. Buchanan, p. 131.
1381. L. Johnson, p. 150.
1382. Donald, WNWCW, pp. 59-62.
1383. Palmer and Colton, p. 543; Owsley, pp. 63-64; Hacker, p. 582.
1384. DeGregorio, s.v. "John Quincy Adams" (p. 91). See also Vanauken, passim.
1385. For examples of Lincoln's various dire warnings, threats, and promises to wage war on any European nation that impeded his assault on the South, see Owsley, pp. 309, 315, 331, 350, 359, 399, 401, 402, 408, 411, 423, 425, 436, 440, 446, 453, 464, 507, 510, 516-517, 524, 539-540, 544.
1386. Owsley, p. 405. See also, pp. 401-412.

win him favor across Europe,[1387] particularly since he had been spreading the lie throughout the continent and Great Britain that "slavery is the basis of the war."[1388] On September 13, 1862, still undecided as to whether to try and free the slaves in the South (he never mentioned anything about freeing the North's 500,000 to 1,000,000 slaves),[1389] he told a committee of pro-emancipation clergymen:

> I will also concede that emancipation would help us in Europe, and convince them that we are incited by something more than ambition.[1390]

After issuing his proclamation a few months later, he must have thought that Europe's pledge to mind its own business ("neutrality") meant that he had succeeded. If so, he was wrong.

When Confederate commissioners offered the possibility of abolition in exchange for recognition, both Britain and France said "no thank you," stating emphatically that Southern slavery, either its continuance or its destruction, had nothing to do with their decision to remain neutral.[1391] Both nations knew full well that slavery was still legal across the North, that blacks were still "cordially hated" in that region, that Lincoln's Emancipation Proclamation was a sham, and that the War was not being fought over slavery.[1392] Had not Lincoln himself promised not to disturb slavery in his First Inaugural Address?[1393] Millions of Europeans had read and even memorized this speech, and they were not going to be fooled by lame attempts to believe otherwise.

When the prospect of Southern abolition was proposed to France's Emperor Napoleon III, for example, he stated to the Confederate commissioner to France, John Slidell, that "he had never taken that [idea] into consideration; that it had not, and could not have, any influence on his action . . ." England's Prime Minister Lord Palmerston told Confederate diplomat to Britain, James M. Mason, that there were no

---

1387. P. M. Roberts, p. 211.
1388. Nicolay and Hay, ALCW, Vol. 2, p. 302.
1389. C. Eaton, HSC, p. 93; Hinkle, p. 125.
1390. Nicolay and Hay, ALCW, Vol. 2, p. 235.
1391. Cooper, JDA, p. 553.
1392. Hacker, p. 665; E. M. Thomas, p. 294.
1393. Nicolay and Hay, ALCW, Vol. 2, p. 1.

other obstacles to recognition than the South's inability to demonstrate that it could maintain its independence, and "that the objections entertained by his Government were those which had been avowed, and that there was nothing . . . underlying them."[1394]

Just as he had with blacks and the Emancipation Proclamation, Lincoln sorely misjudged Europe in this regard, and his lies, illegalities, and rank hypocrisy (which disgusted all thinking Europeans) did not help his situation. It was patently obvious to them, as it was to American Southerners (and even many Northerners), that the War was a "power struggle" between Northern industrialism and Southern agrarianism, and that Lincoln had altered the character of the conflict from a secular one to a holy one[1395] for the sole purpose of winning the support of the unenlightened masses for his "sinister undertaking."[1396] Ever since that time, the South has rightly claimed that in losing the "Civil War" to Lincoln, it had been cheated, not conquered.[1397] In the words of Jefferson Davis (quoting Seneca), under Lincoln, *"prosperum et felix scelus virtus vocatur."*[1398]

A man capable of this type of international intrigue was certainly capable of anything, as Lincoln proved himself to be.

One of his more monstrous but seldom discussed criminalities was his involvement in military executions, most of questionable legality: under his auspices at least 267 known Union soldiers were swiftly

---

1394. Richardson, Vol. 2, pp. 709, 713. For more on this subject see Owsley, pp. 538-541; Durden, pp. 149-150.
1395. Mitgang, p. 413.
1396. Simpson, pp. 73-74. Lincoln picked up on this ridiculous idea from the South-hating, English liberal John Stuart Mill. In an 1862 article (reprinted in the U.S. a few months later), the British philosopher proffered the notion that slavery was the sole reason for America's "Civil War." This gave the conflict the "noble cause" that Northerners had long been searching for. Not surprisingly, the absurd fallacy appeared just a few months later in Lincoln's Emancipation Proclamation. C. Adams, pp. 93-94. Obviously, Mill knew nothing about the South or even American history up to that point: both the president of the Confederacy (Jefferson Davis) *and* the president of the Union (Lincoln) had repeatedly stated, most emphatically, that the War was not over slavery. Furthermore, while the former was considering complete abolition, the latter was promising not to interfere with slavery, making Davis the true Great Emancipator, not Lincoln. Not only this, the Confederacy had banned the foreign slave trade a year earlier, while her greatest general, Robert E. Lee, was a non-slave owner who abhorred the institution, and throughout the War had pushed for both emancipation and black enlistment. See Seabrook, TQREL, passim; Seabrook, TOR, passim. Still, Mill's great lie about the "noble cause" took root in the North, finally becoming, among the ignorant and uninformed, the sole justification for Lincoln's unjustifiable War. Until the day he died, however, Lincoln himself held that the conflict was solely to "preserve the Union." While this too was a lie, it at least has the benefit of exposing Mill's ludicrous fabrication.
1397. Cooper, JDA, p. 648.
1398. "A prosperous and successful crime is called virtue." Burton, Vol. 1, p. 65.

arrested, hurriedly court-martialed, and quickly put to death for crimes ranging from robbery, assault, and rape, to disobedience, desertion, and murder. As Civil War record-keeping was haphazard at best, this number is probably woefully inaccurate, and Southern military historians conjecture that many more Yankee soldiers were literally murdered by Lincoln—many, no doubt, innocent—than will ever be known. And since due process takes time, there will always be the question of whether his ultra efficient military executions were truly just or not.[1399]

Lincoln's numerous other war crimes are well-known. Nonetheless, we will itemize some of them here for posterity's sake. They include: sanctioning the arrest and torture of his Northern critics,[1400] the taking of noncombatants as military hostages, and the arrest, trial, imprisonment (often sentenced to hard labor), deportation, and even murder of innocent Southern civilians (mainly women, children, and seniors). All this while Generals Philip H. Sheridan, Sherman (the "Nero of the 19th Century"), and other Yankee fiends burned and bombed their way across the South, robbing, beating, and killing whites and blacks indiscriminately.[1401] The exact number of Southern noncombatant deaths is of course unknown, for Lincoln's soldiers, like General Edward Hatch, intentionally burned down Southern courthouses where many civil records were kept.[1402]

As a result, some Southern historians reckon the number of Southern civilian deaths to be as high as two million, nearly 16 percent of the total population of 12,650,000 (free whites and enslaved blacks) in 1861.[1403] In the process, Lincoln recklessly disregarded both civil law and the Constitution, while violating many of the precepts of the Geneva

---

1399. Alotta, pp. 186-187.
1400. Neely, pp. 109-112.
1401. See Gragg, pp. 171-196.
1402. See e.g., Henry, ATSF, p. 188.
1403. Timothy D. Manning Sr., personal correspondence. Some Southern historians, like Manning and myself, estimate that Lincoln's War took the lives of as many as 1 million Northerners and 2 million Southerners. These figures include all races and both noncombatants and black slaves, men, women, and children. Additionally, it is important to note that nearly *all* civilian deaths occurred in the South. While the exact Southern death toll is not known, and will never be known, Jefferson Davis estimated that Lincoln killed at least half of the South's Negro population, or about 1,750,000 black men, women, and children, free and bonded. See F. Moore, pp. 278-279.

Conventions (the first which was formulated during the War, in 1863).[1404] In a sordid attempt to hide its atrocities, Lincoln's government, the U.S. government, censored photos of the War's battle dead for some eighty years afterward.[1405]

In 1920, Lyon Gardiner Tyler described Lincoln's crimes this way:

> By an act of Congress, approved July 17, 1862, and published with an approving proclamation by Lincoln, death, imprisonment or confiscation of property were denounced on five million white people in the South and all their abettors and aiders in the North. To reduce the South into submission Lincoln instituted on his own motion a blockade, a means of war so extreme that . . . it evoked from the Germans the most savage retaliation when applied to them. He threatened with hanging as pirates Southern privateersmen and as guerillas regularly commissioned partisans. He suspended the cartel of exchange, and when the Federal prisoners necessarily fared badly for lack of food on account of the blockade and the universal devastation, he retorted their sufferings upon the Confederate prisoners—thousands of whom perished of cold and starvation in the midst of plenty. Indeed, he refused to see or hear a committee of Federal prisoners permitted by Mr. Davis to visit Washington in the interest of the suffering [Yankee] prisoners at [the Confederacy's] Andersonville [prison].
>
> Medicines were made contraband, and to justify the seizure of neutral goods at sea a great enlargement of the principle of the 'ultimate destination' was introduced into the International Law. The property of non-combatants was seized everywhere without compensation, and within the areas embraced by the Union lines, the oath of allegiance was required of both sexes above sixteen years of age under penalty of being driven from their homes. Houses, barns, villages and towns were destroyed in the South, and in the North by the authority of the President thirty-eight thousand persons are said to have been arrested and confined as prisoners without trial or formal charge. Even the acts for which

---

1404. The Geneva Convention of 1863 did not create any new laws pertaining to the military. It codified earlier, well respected, well established international laws, some many centuries old. Among them it was decreed that: 1) Attacking defenseless cities and towns is a war crime; 2) Plundering and wantonly destroying civilian property is a war crime; 3) Only necessities can be taken from a civilian population, and then only if they are paid for. Many of Lincoln's officers, in particular Sherman and Sheridan, repeatedly broke all three of these laws. As the one who sanctioned these crimes, Lincoln, of course, was the "ringleader" and must be held accountable. See C. Adams, pp. 117-118.

1405. Horwitz, p. 227.

Lincoln has been most applauded in recent days—his emancipation proclamation—stands on no really humanitarian ground.
    He declared to a committee of clergymen from Chicago that in issuing his emancipation proclamation he would look only to its effect as a war measure, independent of its 'legal' or 'constitutional' character or of its 'moral nature in view of the possible consequences of insurrection or massacre in the Southern States.' This declaration, which involved directly the admission that, if he were once convinced that emancipation would contribute to ending the war, he would proclaim it regardless of massacre, is not exactly such as would recommend him as a champion of humanity to the Southern people. Massacre of women and children is a dreadful thing.[1406]

    Lincoln's behavior is not so shocking if we consider that he had quite consciously assumed the role of a consolidating dictator, the head of Clay's American System. This was, after all, part of the president's dream from the very beginning: just as liberals do today, Lincoln rejected both the natural rights principles of the Declaration of Independence and the idea of state sovereignty found in the U.S. Constitution. Believing instead in the supremacy of an all-powerful central government, he sought to totally control the economic and human resources of the American people, along with the nation's banking system and military establishment.[1407] Because of this, despots, totalitarians, and dictators, whose chief aim is the total control of nations, came to idolize the socialistic president.
    One of these, arch socialist Adolf Hitler, was fond of citing Lincoln as a shining example of how to destroy states' rights. In his book *Mein Kampf* ("My Struggle"), Hitler not only denies that originally the U.S.A. was a confederacy, he also repeats Lincoln's fantasy that a union always precedes (and thus creates) its states, and that therefore there is no such thing as state sovereignty.
    In 1926, here is how the Führer presented Lincoln's theory: the question is, should Germany be turned into a Confederacy or a Union, and just what is a Confederacy? It is a voluntary union of free and independent states. By this definition, today there are no true confederacies anywhere

---

1406. Tyler, PH, pp. 13-14.
1407. For more on the tyranny of Liberalism, see Levin, pp. 2-6, passim.

in the world, Hitler asserted. The least like a confederacy is the United States of America, for her individual states do not have, could not have, and never had, any sovereignty. Why? Because, as he concluded, it was the Union which created the individual states, not vice versa.[1408]

In short, Hitler was saying, the idea of "sovereign states" has never existed in America.

From this example alone there can be little question that Hitler used Lincoln's unhistorical, inaccurate, and self-serving ideas to justify demolishing states' rights as he rampaged his way across Europe,[1409] which is exactly what he did on January 30, 1934. Purposefully copying Lincoln's unconstitutional actions, it was on this day that Hitler had the sovereign powers and legislative functions of the individual German states completely abolished, and all political authority centralized in the Reich government.[1410]

Tragically, when "Führer" Lincoln set out to demolish states' rights across America, he did not heed the words of Founding Father and Southerner Jefferson. According to our third president:

> . . . the mass of citizens is the safest depository of their own rights . . .;[1411] it is a happy truth that man is capable of self-government, and only rendered otherwise by the moral degradation designedly superinduced on him by the wicked acts of tyrants.[1412]

One of the American tyrant's more overt legacies came from this same period of intense criminal activity.

By 1864, after overthrowing the confederate government of delegated and limited powers created by the Southern Founders, Lincoln replaced it with an oversized, overly powerful, centralized, military despotism, one that today has come to dictate the rights of both states and individuals. Lincoln even levied the first personal income tax, creating what would later become the IRS, a liberal boondoggle that all Americans continue to pay mightily for.[1413] The conservative Southern Founders

---

1408. See Hitler, Vol. 2, pp. 830-831.
1409. See DiLorenzo, LU, pp. 81-84.
1410. Benns and Seldon, p. 259.
1411. Beard and Schultz, p. 345.
1412. Foley, p. 798.
1413. Hacker, p. 584.

would have been horrified. Thankfully for them, most had passed away by the time Lincoln "took the throne."

Harnessing Americans to an income tax, rigging the 1860 and 1864 elections, torturing and imprisoning Northern antiwar advocates, subverting the Constitution, and overturning America's original Confederacy, however, were mere child's play to Lincoln. Arguably, his greatest crimes were starting a war and spending $2,000,000 without congressional approval;[1414] calling up troops without congressional approval; seizing rail and telegraph lines leading to the capital;[1415] issuing paper money (imaginary tender, or what Jefferson called "fictitious capital");[1416] defying the Supreme Court; intimidating Congress; delaying calling Congress into session for four months,[1417] despite the "extraordinary occasion" of the War;[1418] "checking" (i.e., arresting) clergymen who "become dangerous to the public interest" (i.e., who contradicted Lincoln);[1419] declaring all medicines contraband of war while refusing to exchange prisoners with the C.S.A. (both resulted in thousands of needless deaths, including Yankee prisoners at Andersonville prison *and* Southern noncombatants as well);[1420] forcing foreigners (i.e., citizens of the Confederate States of America) to take an oath of allegiance to the United States of America, or face arrest and imprisonment;[1421] arresting members of Northern state legislatures; creating heretofore unknown offices, such as "military governor," in conquered Southern states; instituting the first military draft in U.S. history; imposing so-called "Reconstruction" governments in Southern states;[1422] completely removing every inhabitant living in certain counties, "*en masse*," as Lincoln put it, in the Southern states;[1423] nationalizing the railroads; forcing all federal employees to contribute 5 percent of their annual income to his reelection

---

1414. Ingersoll and O'Connor, p. 22; C. Adams, p. 41.
1415. Tatalovich and Daynes, p. 322.
1416. Foley, pp. 76, 78.
1417. Burns and Peltason, p. 437.
1418. C. Adams, pp. 36, 39.
1419. Nicolay and Hay, ALCW, Vol. 2, p. 464.
1420. Grissom, pp. 126-127; C. Adams, p. 57.
1421. Nicolay and Hay, ALCW, Vol. 2, pp. 442-444.
1422. In the end, Lincoln's "Reconstruction" policies failed, and he only managed to install illegal Yankee governments in four Southern states: Arkansas, Louisiana, Tennessee, and Virginia. J. H. Franklin, p. 26. All of these were overturned when "Reconstruction" ended in 1877, after which they were replaced with Southern governments.
1423. Nicolay and Hay, ALCW, Vol. 2, p. 416.

campaign;[1424] censoring telegraph communications; declaring and executing Reconstruction policies (the Constitution gives the president no such power); countermanding the emancipation of slaves by his cabinet members and military officers, such as Simon Cameron,[1425] John W. Phelps,[1426] John C. Frémont,[1427] Jim Lane,[1428] and David Hunter[1429] (which proves once and for all, if nothing else does, that Lincoln did not wage war against the South over slavery.)[1430]

In addition, Lincoln is guilty of unlawfully ordering a naval blockade of Southern ports and 3,549 miles of Southern coastline (war had not yet been declared[1431]—yet this was an "act of war," one that required Congressional approval;[1432] also the blockade was never 100 percent effective; all of this made Lincoln's blockade illegal according to every known international law);[1433] upsetting world commerce with his naval blockade (which, for example, caused massive deprivations in England); confiscating private property (a violation of the Second Amendment); destroying private property; encouraging slave revolts; disrupting commerce with the Southern states; establishing martial law and provisional courts in vanquished Southern states (since Southern civilian courts were still open, this was unconstitutional);[1434] and proclaiming Confederate privateersmen "insurgents"[1435] and "pirates," subject to the death penalty.[1436]

1424. W. B. Garrison, LNOK, p. 281.
1425. Donald, L, p. 363; Leech, p. 155.
1426. Quarles, pp. 115-116.
1427. Leech, p. 151; Black, p. 165. Lincoln later stripped Frémont of his command for freeing slaves in his assigned military area. Why? It was not a "military necessity" yet, Lincoln said. Seabrook, L, pp. 318-320.
1428. Quarles, pp. 113-114.
1429. Black, p. 165; Wiley, SN, pp. 296-298; Leech, pp. 305-306.
1430. Lincoln admitted that he nullified the emancipation proclamations of his officers because, as he put it, there was no "indispensable necessity." Nicolay and Hay, ALCW, Vol. 2, p. 508. The nation's 4,000,000 slaves (North and South) must have wondered what he meant by this.
1431. W. B. Garrison, CWC, p. 13.
1432. Findlay and Findlay, pp. 84-85; C. Adams, p. 39.
1433. See Owsley, pp. 79-80, 229-267; K. L. Hall, s.v. "Lincoln, Abraham"; "Civil War." Lincoln's illegal blockade of Southern ports, from Virginia to Texas, was designed to split the Confederacy in two. Pritchard, pp. 104-105. Part of General Winfield Scott's Anaconda Plan (named after the snake), it was undoubtedly the most important element in the Yankee win over the Confederacy. W. B. Garrison, CWTFB, p. 266; Faust, s.v. "blockade." Thus, not only was Lincoln's War unlawful, but his victory was as well.
1434. Rosenbaum and Brinkley, s.v. "McCardle, Ex Parte"; C. Adams, p. 59; Ashe, p. 58.
1435. Nicolay and Hay, ALCW, Vol. 2, p. 146.
1436. Gragg, p. 73. Lincoln apparently did not understand (or did understand but pretended not to) the vast difference between a privateer and a pirate. The former is a crew member of "an armed private ship commissioned to cruise against the commerce of or warships of an enemy." Mish, s.v. "privateer." The latter

Contrary to popular opinion, Lincoln's outrages were not committed solely against the South. In fact, as we have seen, he made life almost as difficult and painful for his own Northern constituents as he did for those in Dixie. His crimes against his fellow Yankees include: preventing governmental debate over secession; nullifying the acts of state legislatures; imprisoning volunteer soldiers; the arrest, imprisonment, and murder of peaceful, unarmed citizens; invading Northern states without permission or authority for the purpose of subverting their governments and overthrowing the sovereignty of the people; the expulsion of state authorities; "removing" all of the inhabitants of certain counties in the Southern states; using state conventions to assume unlawful powers; the election and introduction of persons to offices still occupied; the abandonment of protection of the unalienable rights of the Northern people; declaring martial law throughout the North (and later the South) without authority; and emancipating Northern slaves in violation of local, state, and constitutional law.[1437]

All of these actions were patently illegal, not to mention immoral and grossly offensive to all law-abiding people. Furthermore, as noted, many were unconstitutional. But overstepping the presidential boundaries as laid down in the Constitution did not matter to Lincoln. So trample over them he did—despite his solemn pledge not to.

To fully appreciate how "Honest Abe" operated, consider the following. If I, the author, had lived in the North between 1861 and 1865, the book you now hold in your hand could not have been published. Lincoln would not have allowed it. Even if I had managed to get it out into the public, it would have been quickly banned; all known copies would have been confiscated and burned; and the publisher would have been arrested, his printing presses seized, and his offices shut down. I myself would have been arrested, tried, convicted, imprisoned, and sentenced to hard labor. That is, if I was lucky. It is just as likely that I would have been tortured and executed, the same fate that befell many Northerners who displeased our sixteenth president.[1438]

You, the reader, would have not been safe from Lincoln either.

---

is one who commits "robbery on the high seas." Mish, s.v. "pirate"; s.v. "piracy." The Confederacy's loyal privateers were in no way even remotely similar to pirates.
1437. J. Davis, RFCG, Vol. 2, pp. 473-476.
1438. Neely, pp. 109-112; Simmons, s.v. "Civil rights in the Confederacy."

The very act of owning and reading this book would have labeled you a felon, permitting his vigilante gangs, his spies, his henchmen, his detectives, or his soldiers, to bash down your door and drag you from your bed in the middle of the night without a warrant, arrest you without charge, imprison you without cause, and try you illegally in a military court without due process.

Like any one of the 38,000 Northerners and untold thousands of Southerners Lincoln unlawfully arrested during his War, you would have rotted in a cold, dank prison cell, without legal representation, proper food, clothing, or medical care, until at least April 1865. In the meantime, if you were not maimed and tortured, or even murdered, you would have been among the lucky ones.

Though all of this sounds like Nazi Germany, this was exactly how the United States judicial system operated during most of Lincoln's nearly five-year reign. No wonder Hitler felt such an affinity for the American Führer, the U.S. president who so willingly crushed human rights and overturned the Constitution in the name of the Liberals' imaginary, arbitrary, and highly subjective concept: "Higher Law" (that is, "justice").[1439]

Some of Lincoln's crimes teetered on the edge of illegality, such as when he falsely awarded medals to his soldiers. Near the end of June 1863, for example, he bribed the men of the 27th Maine Regiment, promising them that they would all receive the Medal of Honor if they reenlisted. Some 864 did reenlist, and all were duly given the esteemed award. But by reenlisting, had these men gone "above and beyond the call of duty," the requirement for receiving the Medal of Honor? A 1917 committee, the Adverse Action Medal of Honor Board, did not think so. As a result, all 864 men were disqualified and their medals were rescinded.[1440]

Also not quite illegal, but plain injudicious, Lincoln was the first president to "pack" the Supreme Court by personally choosing five justices, all who just happened to be staunch liberals and Lincoln

---

[1439]. Seabrook, CFF, pp. 23-24, 278-280, 282-284, 303. The belief that there is a "Higher Law" than the Constitution continues to be one of the American Left's favorite weapons against conservatism. The Constitution, however, was created in great part to combat exactly this type of liberalist fiction.
[1440]. Shenkman and Reiger, p. 112.

supporters.[1441] He is still known as the president who dismissed and replaced the most appointees in American history. During his first year in office alone, Lincoln threw out 1,457 men (leaving a mere 200 from former administrations), replacing them with his own hand-selected appointees.[1442] In fact, only two men served in Lincoln's cabinet through both his entire terms: William H. Seward and Gideon Welles.[1443]

Lincoln committed so many unconstitutional acts so quickly during his first year in office, that Congress did not have time to process and legalize them all. This was intentional, of course, as was his ploy of delaying calling Congress into session (for four months)[1444] so that there would be no debate over his illegalities.[1445] When Congress finally convened in July 1861, the hurried process of legitimatizing Lincoln's lawless offences still took weeks, sometimes months, to complete. By then, he had already committed a litany of new crimes.[1446] In most cases the Northern courts ignored what Lincoln was doing, or simply supported his actions in order to avoid scandal or trouble, for as we have seen, Lincoln had a nasty habit of arresting and imprisoning people who stood in his way.[1447]

Meanwhile, he continued to expand presidential power beyond anything ever seen in Washington, and certainly far beyond anything specified in the Constitution.[1448] Even some pro-Lincoln historians refer to his two terms in office as a "presidential quasi-dictatorship."[1449]

An example of Lincoln's complete disregard for local, state, and constitutional law, not to mention his brutality and inhumanity, can be seen in a sinister system of governing he set up in Washington. Cunningly designed to expedite the process of lawbreaking, it was nothing less than a breathtaking attempt to maintain absolute power over his Northern constituents. In his great work *The Rise and Fall of the Confederate Government*, President Jefferson Davis describes one aspect of Lincoln's system in all its repugnant detail:

1441. W. B. Garrison, CWC, pp. 12-13.
1442. Shenkman and Reiger, p. 103.
1443. K. C. Davis, p. 448.
1444. Burns and Peltason, p. 437.
1445. Christian, p. 14; Hacker, p. 581.
1446. Hacker, p. 581.
1447. C. Adams, pp. 39, 41.
1448. Ingersoll and O'Connor, pp. 22, 23.
1449. Burns and Peltason, p. 437.

The Secretary of State at Washington, William H. Seward, a favored son of the State of New York, would 'ring a little bell,' which brought to him a messenger, to whom was given a secret order to arrest and confine in Fort Lafayette [New York] a person designated. This order was sent by telegraph to the United States Marshal of the district in which would be found the person who was to be arrested. The arrest being forcibly made by the marshal with armed attendants without even the form of a warrant, the prisoner without the knowledge of any charge against him was conveyed to Fort Hamilton [New York] and turned over to the commandant. An aid with a guard of soldiers then conveyed him in a boat to Fort Lafayette and delivered him to the keeper in charge, who gave a receipt for the prisoner. He was then divested of any weapons, money, valuables, or papers in his possession. His baggage was opened and searched. A soldier then took him in charge to the designated quarter, which was a portion of one of the casemates for guns, lighted only from the port hole, and occupied by seven or eight other prisoners. All were subjected to prison fare. Some were citizens of New York, and the others of different States. This manner of imprisonment was subsequently put under the direction of the Secretary of War, and continued at intervals until the close of the war.

In the brief period between July 1 and October 19, 1861, the Secretary of State, William H. Seward, made such diligent use of his 'little bell' that one hundred and seventy-five of the most respectable citizens of the country were consigned to imprisonment in this Fort Lafayette, a strong fortress in the lower part of the harbor of New York. A decent regard for the memory of the friend of [George] Washington, and for the services rendered to the colonies in their struggle for independence, might have led Mr. Seward to select for such base uses some other place than that which bore the honored name of Lafayette.[1450]

Many Yankees also decried Seward's idea of law. Serving as both U.S. attorney general and secretary of state under President Buchanan, and U.S. Supreme Court Reporter under Lincoln, the celebrated Pennsylvanian Jeremiah S. Black wrote:

> When Mr. Seward went into the State Department he took a Little Bell to his office in place of the statute-book, and this piece of sounding brass came to be a symbol of the Higher Law. When he

---

1450. J. Davis, RFCG, Vol. 2, pp. 478-479.

desired to kidnap a free citizen, to banish him, to despoil him of his property, or to kill him after the mockery of a military trial, he rang his Little Bell, and the deed was done.[1451]

In his 1900 biography on Seward, author Frederic Bancroft wrote of how the secretary of state himself felt about his power:

> There was current a story that Seward boasted to Lord Lyons that he could ring a little bell and cause the arrest of a citizen of Ohio or order the imprisonment of a citizen of New York, and that no one on earth except the President could release the prisoner. If he made the remark, it is of no special importance. It was a fact that he was almost as free from restraint as a dictator or a sultan, and he was charged with acting accordingly.[1452]

Who was it that "charged" Seward with the authority to act like a dictator? Only one individual on earth had this power, and that was his employer Mr. Lincoln, someone who had personal experience in the art of dictatorship.

One man who experienced the horrors of Seward's "little bell" firsthand was Northerner Pierce Butler. Butler was arrested—without justification or due process of law—by order of Lincoln's secretary of war, Simon Cameron, in Philadelphia, on August 19, 1861. After his release five weeks later (again, no reason was given), Butler sued Cameron and had him arrested for "assault and battery and false imprisonment." After hearing of Cameron's arrest, however, Lincoln immediately tossed Butler's lawsuit out.[1453] Why? As Seward explained in a letter to Butler, dated April 18, 1862:

> The communication has been submitted to the President, and I am directed by him to say in reply that he avows the proceeding of Mr. Cameron referred to as one taken by him when Secretary of War, under the President's directions, and deemed necessary for the prompt suppression of the existing rebellion.[1454]

1451. C. F. Black, p. 153. See also Chesnut, DD, p. 206. To his credit Black also voted against Reconstruction.
1452. Bancroft, Vol. 2, p. 280.
1453. The self-inflicted drama was mentioned by Lincoln on April 18, 1862, in a "Message to Congress." Nicolay and Hay, ALCW, Vol. 2, p. 145.
1454. J. Davis, RFCG, Vol. 2, p. 481.

"Under the President's directions." In one of the few moments of true honesty in his life, Lincoln owned up to his complicity in the matter, even taking full responsibility for it. But despite this momentary lapse, shortly afterward he continued his flagitious plot to destroy states' rights and install big government by making it illegal for those he had unlawfully imprisoned to sue him or the U.S. government![1455]

America's sixteenth president engaged in countless other scandals and legal transgressions too numerous to list here. But one other in particular stands out for its heinousness.

In June 1861, Lincoln signed an arrest warrant for his own chief justice of the Supreme Court, Roger B. Taney. Why? Because Taney had rightly advised him that it was illegal for a U.S. president to suspend the right of *habeas corpus*. Lincoln's actions were unconstitutional, Taney asserted, because, according to the Constitution itself (Article 1), only Congress has the authority to suspend the writ. The president, the chief justice correctly charged, was merely an administrative officer whose primary responsibility was to faithfully enforce the laws, not break them.[1456]

Fortunately for Taney he was never taken into custody for, as we have seen, the arresting officer, federal marshal Ward Hill Lamon (one of Lincoln's close friends and a former law partner),[1457] gallantly refused the order.[1458] But this did not stop Lincoln, a man who could not bear to be questioned or challenged. Ignoring Taney's warning,[1459] he overturned the former attorney general's opinion and went on to imprison tens of thousands of people without due process.[1460]

Legal scholars are still discussing this astonishing breach of law. Why would a U.S. president seek to have his own chief justice handcuffed, booked, and jailed for trying to uphold constitutional law? By now, the answer is patently obvious.

The Yankee myth that the North's main concern in 1861 was to "maintain the nation's civil rights as laid out in the Constitution" can now be exposed for what it is: an abject falsehood. For Lincoln's

---

1455. J. Davis, RFCG, Vol. 2, pp. 484-485.
1456. K. L. Hall, s.v. "Civil War."
1457. Christian, pp. 4-5.
1458. See C. Adams, pp. 48-49.
1459. Rosenbaum and Brinkley, s.v. "Merryman, Ex Parte."
1460. DiLorenzo, LU, pp. 92-96.

unprecedented crackdown on civil rights, his imposition of dictatorial powers, and his total disregard for the Constitution (the very document he had sworn to uphold), not only helped him stay in power through two elections, but also greatly assisted him in winning his War.

We can now also do away with the associated Yankee myth that in the South there was no concern for civil rights at the time. In point of fact, it was Jefferson Davis' recognition of these birthrights that largely cost the South the War. Where Lincoln clamped down on antiwar sentiment, Davis permitted it. Where Lincoln blocked free speech, Davis sanctioned it. Where Lincoln prohibited freedom of the press, Davis encouraged it.[1461] Where Lincoln arrested, imprisoned, tortured, and even deported peace advocates, Davis granted them full freedom of expression and movement.[1462] Where Lincoln closed down hundreds of newspapers, Davis closed not a single one. Where Lincoln himself personally suspended *habeas corpus*,[1463] Davis correctly left this power to the Confederate Congress (which, unlike Lincoln, suspended it reluctantly and only for short periods of time).[1464]

The results?

In the liberal North, Lincoln's lawless strangulation of civil rights enabled him to conceal his true goals, and the nefarious means by which he intended to achieve them. In the libertarian South, however, Davis' insistence on maintaining full civil rights for all citizens, nurtured the growth of numerous peace societies, antiwar, even anti-Confederate, groups in states like Arkansas, Georgia, Alabama, Mississippi, Tennessee, and Florida. These organizations promoted desertion among Rebel troops by advising family members and loved ones to urge their sons, husbands, and fathers who were out on the battlefield to abandon the war effort and return home.

In this way, Dixie "peace societies" wreaked havoc on Rebel morale, and were the main cause of the skyrocketing desertion rates during the last two years of the War. And it was, in large part, because of the actions of these Southern antiwar societies that by the time of Lee's surrender on April 9, 1865, the Confederacy's armies were mere

---

1461. Donald, WNWCW, pp. 84-88.
1462. Simmons, s.v. "Civil rights in the Confederacy."
1463. See e.g., Nicolay and Hay, ALCW, Vol. 2, pp. 45-46.
1464. L. Johnson, p. 176.

skeletons of what had once been large, robust military forces.

Lincoln, on the other hand, prevented the burgeoning of a comprehensive antiwar movement and avoided Davis' massive desertion problem with a single act: the illegal, rigid abridgement of civil rights all across the North. Yet today, it is the South that is castigated for civil rights abuses in the mid-19th Century.[1465] To a great extent it is true, as a Lincoln scholar once observed, that the Confederacy perished because of democracy.[1466] But in the South this is not taken as a dishonor. It is an honor.[1467]

One of Lincoln's most serious offenses, of course, was issuing the Emancipation Proclamation. The *Richmond Examiner* referred to it as it the most shocking crime perpetuated by a politician in the history of the U.S.,[1468] and for good reason: it was unconstitutional, and therefore unlawful.[1469] A joke, circulated in the South at the time, illustrates the insanity of the edict: in retaliation for Lincoln's Emancipation Proclamation, Jefferson Davis would now issue an "Enslavement Proclamation" that would declare all blacks in the North slaves on January 1, 1864.[1470]

Lincoln was fully aware of the illegality of his proclamation because, as noted, two years earlier in his First Inaugural Address, March 4, 1861, he admitted as much:

> I have no purpose, directly or indirectly, to interfere with the institution of slavery in the States where it exists. I believe I have no lawful right to do so . . .[1471]

Yet just a few years later, he issued his emancipation decree anyway, another example of Lincoln's stunning political duplicity. Strangely, he never tried to conceal this.

In early 1864, a year after his final proclamation was published, he wrote of the actual motivation behind it:

1465. Simmons, s.v. "Peace societies"; "Peace and Constitutional Society"; "Peace Society, The."
1466. L. Johnson, p. 176.
1467. For more on this topic, see Pollard, LC, p. 178.
1468. Current, TC, s.v. "African-Americans in the Confederacy."
1469. H. U. Faulkner, p. 374.
1470. Wiley, SN, p. 39.
1471. Nicolay and Hay, ALCW, Vol. 2, p. 1.

> Things had gone from bad to worse until I felt that we had reached the end of our rope on the plan of operations we had been pursuing [that is, to quickly and efficiently crush the South]—that we had played our last card and must change our tactics, or lose the game. I determined on the Emancipation Proclamation, and . . . called a Cabinet meeting upon the subject.[1472]

Lincoln makes no mention here of black civil rights; there are no humanitarian gestures, no great sweeping oratory on the evils of slavery. Just talk of military "tactics" and a political "game" he was determined to win.

Is it really possible that the Emancipation Proclamation had nothing to do with black civil rights? Absolutely, and we have Lincoln's own thoughts and words to prove it.

On March 26, 1864, Lincoln explained to a group of Kentuckians why he issued his most famous document. Here he reveals the practical thinking and illegal maneuvering that went on behind the scenes, none of it having anything to do with black civil rights:

> I felt that measures, otherwise unconstitutional might become lawful by becoming indispensable to the preservation of the Constitution through the preservation of the nation. Right or wrong, I assumed this ground, and now avow it. I could not feel that, to the best of my ability, I had even tried to preserve the Constitution, if, to preserve slavery, or any minor matter, I should permit the wreck of government, country, and Constitution altogether. When, early in the war, General Frémont attempted military emancipation, I forbade it, because I did not then think it an indispensable necessity. When, a little later, General Cameron, then Secretary of War, suggested the arming of the blacks, I objected, because I did not yet think it an indispensable necessity. When, still later, General Hunter attempted military emancipation, I again forbade it, because I did not yet think the indispensable necessity had come. When, in March and May and July, 1862, I made earnest and successive appeals to the border States to favor compensated emancipation, I believed the indispensable necessity for military emancipation and arming the blacks would come, unless averted by that measure. They declined the proposition; and I was, in my best judgment, driven to the

---

1472. Coffin, pp. 330-331.

alternative of either surrendering the Union, and with it the Constitution, or of laying strong hand upon the colored element. I chose the latter. In choosing it, I hoped for greater gain than loss; but of this, I was not entirely confident. More than a year of trial now shows no loss by it in our foreign relations, none in our home popular sentiment, none in our white military force,—no loss by it anyhow or anywhere. On the contrary, it shows a gain of quite a hundred and thirty thousand soldiers, seamen, and laborers. These are palpable facts, about which, as facts, there can be no caviling. We have the men and we could not have had them without the measure.[1473]

Once when asked to defend his plan to free black slaves and enlist them, Lincoln replied:

... no human power can subdue this rebellion without the use of the emancipation policy and every other policy calculated to weaken the moral and physical forces of the rebellion.[1474]

As Lincoln clearly states over and over again, the Union needed more soldiers, and his Emancipation Proclamation provided them—end of story.

For those who still question the facts, Lincoln's words and actions beg an important question: if he had truly been interested in granting civil rights to blacks, why did he not also push for civil rights for women and other minorities?

The women's rights issue, for example, was on the front line of American politics at the time.[1475] The nation's first female rights assembly, the Seneca Falls Woman's Rights Convention (organized by Lucretia Mott and Elizabeth Cady Stanton), was held in 1848, while Lincoln was a U.S. Representative. Beginning in 1850, the first National Women's Rights Convention (at Worcester, Massachusetts), was held annually (except for 1857) right up to 1860, the year Lincoln was elected. And just seven years after Lincoln's death, on May 10, 1872, the first woman presidential candidate, Victoria Claflin Woodhull, was nominated

---

1473. Nicolay and Hay, ALCW, Vol. 2, pp. 508-509.
1474. Nicolay and Hay, ALCW, Vol. 2, p. 562.
1475. Weintraub, pp. 57-58.

by the Equal Rights Party.[1476]

During Lincoln's presidency women were clamoring ever more vigorously for equal rights. He could have easily resolved the entire issue with the stroke of a pen. But he never did, a fact made even more singular by white and black civil rights leaders, like William Lloyd Garrison,[1477] Wendell Phillips, Parker Pillsbury, Sojourner Truth,[1478] sisters Angelina and Sarah Grimké,[1479] and Frederick Douglass (a personal friend of Lincoln),[1480] all who were enthusiastic and vocal advocates of both abolition and women's suffrage.[1481] Not even the Thirteenth Amendment—first introduced via resolution by Yankee racist and black colonizationist, Illinois Senator Lyman Trumbull,[1482] and one of Lincoln's pet civil rights projects—included anything about women's rights, much to the bitter disappointment of American females everywhere.

Subsequently, women did not get the vote until 1920 (with the passage of the Nineteenth Amendment),[1483] and true equality did not come until 1972 (with the passage of the Equal Rights Amendment), 107 years after Lincoln's death.

Lincoln could have helped Native-Americans as well, but he refused. In great part, as a result, Indians—whom the Lincoln administration referred to as "savages"[1484]—were not allowed to become U.S. citizens until 1924.

Black civil rights fared little better under Lincoln. Right up to the last days of his life, he was against giving African-Americans the power to vote. In his last public address on April 11, 1865, just four days before he was shot, he admitted in his typical understated style that

---

1476. Kane, p. 209.
1477. K. C. Davis, p. 440. Unlike Lincoln, Garrison, like most other abolitionists, was also an advocate of Native-American rights. J. S. Bowman, ECW, s.v. "Garrison, William Lloyd."
1478. McKissack and McKissack, pp. 97, 105.
1479. Hacker, pp. 554-559.
1480. Simmons, s.v. "Douglass, Frederick."
1481. The motto of Douglass' newspaper *The North Star* was: "Right is of no sex, truth is of no color—we are the equal children of a common Father, and all men are brothers." *Testimony Taken Before the Committee on Immigration*, 57th Congress, 1st Session, Report 776, Pt. 2, Washington, D.C., 1902, p. 75. If Lincoln ever read a copy of *The North Star*, he did not comment on its motto, nor did he need to. By his actions and words the atheist president had made it quite clear throughout his political career that he did not agree with it.
1482. Neilson, s.v. "Trumbull, Benjamin."
1483. Weintraub, p. 97.
1484. *ORA*, Ser. 3, Vol. 1, p. 184.

> it is . . . unsatisfactory to some that the elective franchise is not [yet] given to the colored man.[1485]

But he offered no explanation as to why he had personally blocked the franchise for the entire time he occupied the White House; nor did he ever offer any solution, reasonable or even unreasonable, to the problem. He simply ignored it, as he did all issues that he did not truly care about.

In truth, it was largely because of Lincoln that blacks were not officially allowed to vote until 1870 with the passage of the last of the three "Civil War amendments," the Fifteenth Amendment.[1486] This was five years after Lincoln died. But blacks would have to wait another 100 years for complete equal rights when, in 1965, Congress passed the Voting Rights Act.[1487]

The record clearly shows that Lincoln did nothing during his life to further the cause of civil rights for either blacks or women, or for any other minority group for that matter. It was perfectly legal, for instance, to hire young children to work in American factories well into the 20th Century, until 1938 in fact, when the passage of the Fair Labor Standards Act prohibited child labor under sixteen years of age.[1488] (Appallingly, Lincoln, himself a father, apparently did not believe that children possessed any "inalienable rights.")

With these facts at hand it is hardly accurate then to call Lincoln a "great civil rights leader" or "the friend of blacks." Indeed, it was for these very reasons that Southerners considered him the enemy of whites and blacks alike.[1489] And he was obviously no champion of women or children—or any other minority for that matter.

Why was Lincoln so removed from these issues? Because his primary interest was never civil rights. It was big government.

In short, he did not "free the slaves" to make African-Americans equal citizens, as Northern myth falsely teaches.[1490]

1485. Nicolay and Hay, ALCW, Vol. 2, p. 674.
1486. The three Civil War amendments are the Thirteenth, Fourteenth, and the Fifteenth. They are so called because each was a direct result of Lincoln's War. All three greatly enlarged the powers of the central government, one of liberal Lincoln's primary goals. Kelly, Harbison, and Belz, Vol. 2, pp. xxiii, 326. All three, particularly the Fourteenth, possessed anti-South elements.
1487. Rosenbaum and Brinkley, s.v. "Fifteenth Amendment."
1488. Weintraub, p. 119.
1489. M. Davis, p. 83.
1490. Napolitano, pp. 75-76.

Unfortunately for the Kentuckian-turned-Illinoisan, two of the goals of what he called his "last card," his trump card, his Final Emancipation Proclamation, utterly failed: it did not free any slaves,[1491] and neither was there a great slave revolt across the South. Why?

Lawyer Lincoln had carefully worded his emancipation so that it was active only in the Confederacy, the Southern states, where he had no legal power, for it was a sovereign, foreign nation at the time. Here, from the proclamation, is his exact wording concerning *where* slavery was to be outlawed:

> Now, therefore I, Abraham Lincoln President of the United States, by virtue of the power in me vested as Commander-in-Chief, of the Army and Navy of the United States in time of actual armed rebellion against the authority and government of the United States, and as a fit and necessary war measure for suppressing said rebellion, do on this first day of January, in the year of our Lord one thousand eight hundred and sixty-three, and in accordance with my purpose so to do publicly proclaimed for the full period of one hundred days, from the day first above mentioned, order and designate as the States and parts of States wherein the people thereof, respectively, are this day in rebellion against the United States, the following, to wit: Arkansas, Texas, Louisiana (except the parishes of St. Bernard, Plaquemines, Jefferson, St. John, St. Charles, St. James, Ascension, Assumption, Terrebonne, Lafourche, St. Mary, St. Martin, and Orleans, including the City of New Orleans), Mississippi, Alabama, Florida, Georgia, South Carolina, North Carolina, and Virginia (except the forty-eight counties designated as West Virginia, and also the counties of Berkeley, Accomac, Northampton, Elizabeth City, York, Princess Ann, and Norfolk, including the cities of Norfolk and Portsmouth); and which excepted parts are for the present left precisely as if this proclamation were not issued.[1492]

A studious reading reveals something quite stunning about this document, one that is widely held to have "ended slavery across America": it says nothing about freeing slaves in either the North[1493] or in Southern areas occupied by Northern troops, such as several Louisiana parishes,

---

1491. Kane, p. 179.
1492. Nicolay and Hay, ALCW, Vol. 2, pp. 287-288.
1493. Denney, p. 251.

where servitude was still legal and practiced.[1494] It does not even mention Tennessee, though it was a loyal member state of the Confederacy at the time. The reason?

Tennessee was largely under Yankee domination by January 1863 (the state's capital city, Nashville, had been captured a year earlier on February 23, 1862),[1495] and was well on her way to being forced back into the Union.[1496] Indeed, the last state to secede (on June 8, 1861),[1497] after the War the Volunteer State would be the first Confederate state to be reunionized (on July 24, 1866).[1498]

Was all of this a simple mistake, an error of judgment, a memory lapse, or lack of knowledge of geography on Lincoln's part? Hardly. In Missouri he did the same thing: after illegally invading the state and illegally putting it under martial law, he issued an illegal emancipation proclamation to illegally free Missouri's slaves. But not all of them. Only those belonging to supporters of the Confederacy. Those slaves who belonged to supporters of the Union were allowed to remain in perpetual servitude.[1499]

And herein lies a vital clue as to Lincoln's true motivations.

It is apparent by omitting the Confederate state of Tennessee from his Emancipation Proclamation, along with all other Northern-held Southern regions, that he overtly and purposefully intended to allow slavery to continue in these areas. Why else would he activate the illegal decree *only* in those regions engaged in hostile acts against the United States?[1500]

Even more astonishing, as we have discussed, Lincoln does not say anything about freeing the 500,000 to 1,000,000 slaves who still lived and worked in the "abolitionist North" itself,[1501] the United States of America.[1502] Instead, he quite clearly states that this particular region will

---

1494. R. S. Phillips, s.v. "Emancipation Proclamation."
1495. R. L. Mode, p. 31.
1496. According to a September 11, 1863, letter from Lincoln to Tennessee Governor Andrew Johnson: "All of Tennessee is now clear of armed insurrectionists." Nicolay and Hay, ALCW, Vol. 2, p. 405.
1497. Cromie, p. 248.
1498. It was Tennessean Andrew Johnson, acting as military governor of that state from 1862 to 1864, who persuaded Lincoln to leave Tennessee out of the Final Emancipation Proclamation, which essentially allowed slavery to continue in the state unhindered. DeGregorio, s.v. "Andrew Johnson" (p. 251).
1499. J. Davis, RFCG, Vol. 2, pp. 475-476.
1500. Palmer and Colton, p. 543.
1501. C. Eaton, HSC, p. 93; Hinkle, p. 125.
1502. Neilson, s.v. "Lincoln, Abraham."

be "left precisely as if this proclamation were not issued." Thus, since his "emancipation" was only operative in those areas of the South where he had no authority, and since it was completely inoperative in the North where he had full authority, not a single slave was freed.[1503]

All of this was deliberately and meticulously crafted, for Lincoln hoped that issuing the emancipation would silence his abolitionist critics, while its ineffectualness would generate support from the rest of Northern whites, most who, like Lincoln, were Negrophobes, racial bigots who were horrified at the thought of "hordes" of freed Southern blacks "swarming northward" and, as white racist Lincoln himself put it, being "run over like sheep."[1504]

We should not be shocked by now to learn that even the timing of the Emancipation Proclamation was skillfully premeditated. For Lincoln, America's most calculating president, was not one to leave anything to chance.

To make sure newly freed, enlisted blacks (as well as whites) voted, and voted for him specifically, he cunningly waited to issue his proclamation until the U.S. army achieved a momentous victory. This was all urged on by Seward, who whined that if not, it will perceived as an acknowledgment of military failure, like "the last shriek on our retreat."[1505]

If the plot worked, it would renew public support and revitalize his image among both black and white troops, helping him in his bid for reelection in 1864.[1506] So while four million blacks (in the South and the North) remained enslaved, Lincoln waited patiently for the right political opportunity to launch his next self-serving scam on the American people.

He did not have to wait long. In Maryland, on September 17, 1862, the devastating Battle of Sharpsburg (Antietam to Yanks) was fought, marking the bloodiest day in the War up until that time.[1507] Though according to official military standards the conflict was a no-win draw,[1508] Lincoln observed that Confederate General Robert E. Lee had

---

1503. Garraty and McCaughey, p. 253; Hacker, p. 584; Grissom, p. 127.
1504. Nicolay and Hay, ALCW, Vol. 1, p. 556.
1505. J. M. Burns, p. 625; Current, LNK, p. 224.
1506. W. B. Garrison, LNOK, p. 169.
1507. Long and Long, p. 267.
1508. W. B. Garrison, LNOK, p. 169.

retreated the next day.[1509] In the president's eyes this seemed to be "at least a substitute for victory."[1510]

Though completely nonreligious and anti-Christian, atheist Lincoln then declared that the "South's defeat" at Sharpsburg was an omen, an expression of "Divine will," a veritable message from God that it was time to issue his Preliminary Emancipation Proclamation.[1511] Thus, on September 22, 1862, Lincoln made public his plans for liberating then deporting all freed blacks out of the country.

Here we have an example of some of the most brazen political scheming in the history of the presidency, a plot involving not the protection of African-Americans, but one involving first their exploitation, then their removal. For all of Jefferson Davis' faults and sins, he never began to approach the level of guileful criminality achieved by Lincoln in the years between 1861 and 1865.

Despite his long public record on the matter of race, many people are still perplexed as to why Lincoln never mentioned slavery in his famous Gettysburg Address, the one whose first sentence ends with the words "all men are created equal."[1512] Actually, what he meant was "all *white* men are created equal." For a Northern white separatist speaking before a crowd of Northern white racists and white supremacists, however, this would have been vastly overstating the obvious, a trait completely and utterly lacking in "Honest Abe."

1509. Civil War Society, CWB, s.v. "Antietam, Campaign and Battle of"; Simmons, s.v. "Antietam."
1510. Current, LNK, p. 224.
1511. Donald, L, p. 374.
1512. Nicolay and Hay, ALCW, Vol. 2, p. 439.

12

BLACKS IN LINCOLN'S ARMY

PART ONE

THOUGH TODAY MOST AMERICANS BELIEVE that Lincoln's Emancipation Proclamation was well received throughout the North, and that it "freed all the slaves," the majority of 19th-Century Americans knew that it did neither. In fact, the document was an outrageous lie and a reckless and arrogant political ploy.[1513] For one thing, Lincoln's armies were already "freeing" Southern servants wherever they went, so the decree had no immediate effect on the War whatsoever—except to stir up more animosity.[1514] In any case, abolitionists hated it, white Northern racists detested it, white Southerners loathed it, and Southern blacks despised it.

It was abhorred over much of Europe as well. London's newspaper, the *Spectator*, called the proclamation "a very sad document," and "a hypocritical sham,"[1515] one the London *Standard* said was meant to intentionally "deceive England and Europe." The London *Times* denounced it as "the wretched makeshift of a pettifogging lawyer," one who was doing his best to "excite a servile war in the States he cannot occupy with his armies."[1516]

An Irish newspaper, *The Belfast News*, called the edict "the latest and foulest crime perpetuated by the Lincoln administration." Lincoln's

---

1513. Grissom, p. 127.
1514. Harwell, p. 137.
1515. W. B. Garrison, CWTFB, p. 93.
1516. Foster, pp. 392-393.

Emancipation Proclamation, the Irish editor wrote, was nothing more than a permit to murder men and rape women. The cruel and contemptible "outburst" was the greatest example of vindictiveness ever seen from a so-called "Christian" dictator. For the sake of posterity, the Hibernian paper noted, all of Europe should rise up in protest and do all that is necessary to try and stop the blood bath that was sure to follow.[1517]

At home in the U.S., while the Northern public was now condemning Lincoln for going too far (by turning the conflict into a "nigger war"),[1518] Yankee abolitionists complained that he had not gone far enough. One of these, Lysander Spooner, publicly excoriated Lincoln, writing that the president and his party did not abolish slavery as

> an act of justice to the black man himself, but only 'as a war measure,' and because they wanted his assistance, and that of his friends, in carrying on the war they had undertaken for maintaining and intensifying that political, commercial, and industrial slavery, to which they have subjected the great body of the people, both black and white.[1519]

Spooner's comment on "political, commercial, and industrial slavery" was in no way a reference to black slavery. He was speaking of what he felt was the literal enslavement of all free American citizens, who were now forced to toil under the heels of dictator Lincoln and his empire-building thugs. Few Southerners could have expressed this view with more clarity and gumption, and we applaud libertarian Spooner for doing so.

Like Southerners, Europeans also understood that there was little difference between plantation slavery (forced labor with rights) and wage slavery (forced labor without rights).[1520] As such, a South Carolina newspaper could assert that:

1517. Harwell, p. 218.
1518. McMaster, p. 259.
1519. Spooner, NT, No. 6, p. 57.
1520. Stampp, p. 401; Hacker, p. 544. Let us note here that there is no such thing as "unforced labor." All labor is "forced" in the sense that everyone must work for a living in one way or another. Indeed, slavery scholars consider unforced labor, however one defines it, as the vast exception in a world where forced labor has been the near universal rule since the dawn of humanity. The Bible itself supports this view (see e.g., Genesis 3:19). See Drescher and Engerman, p. 204.

> Slavery is the natural and normal condition of the laboring man, whether black or white.[1521]

Of America's "Civil War," 19th-Century Scottish essayist and historian Thomas Carlyle wrote:

> There they are cutting each other's throats, because one half of them prefer hiring their servants for life, and the other by the hour.[1522]

As obvious as this fact was to all Southerners and most Europeans, and even to many Northerners, Lincoln did not care about the similarities between wage slavery and plantation slavery. His guileful agenda now called for emancipation, and so emancipation it was.

The issuance of Lincoln's several emancipations—the first, a draft submitted privately to his cabinet on July 22, 1862;[1523] the second, the Preliminary one released publicly on September 22, 1862;[1524] the third, a draft of the Final proclamation submitted to his cabinet on December 30, 1862;[1525] and the fourth, the Final version issued on January 1, 1863[1526]—truly took the world by surprise. Reactions ranged from stupefaction and outrage, to embarrassment and revulsion.

Little wonder. All four documents, though titled "Emancipation Proclamation," lacked any reference to black civil rights. Instead, each one restated Lincoln's position that the "object" of the War was to "restore" the Union, and then referred to the liberation of blacks as merely "a fit and necessary military measure."

Furthermore, the Preliminary (second) version called for the deportation of all "persons of African descent . . . upon this continent or elsewhere."[1527] Worse, the Final (fourth) version not only implied the need for a massive slave insurrection across the South (to include the overthrow and murder of white slave owners and their families), but it also revealed the authentic motivation behind Lincoln's emancipation plan:

1521. Carlton, p. 147.
1522. Duff, Vol. 1, pp. 203-204.
1523. Nicolay and Hay, ALCW, Vol. 2, p. 213.
1524. Nicolay and Hay, ALCW, Vol. 2, pp. 237-238.
1525. Nicolay and Hay, ALCW, Vol. 2, p. 285.
1526. Nicolay and Hay, ALCW, Vol. 2, pp. 287-288.
1527. Nicolay and Hay, ALCW, Vol. 2, p. 237.

his official approval, for the first time, of black enlistment.[1528] This is why, after all, on March 26, 1864, he referred to the edict accurately and truthfully as a "military emancipation."[1529]

Strangest of all, as discussed, Lincoln's document only freed slaves in the South, and then only in areas of the South not occupied by Yankee troops.[1530] All other slaves, including the North's 500,000 to 1,000,000 slaves,[1531] were to remain in bondage![1532]

Southerners, like Kate Stone of Louisiana, of course, were indignant at this flagrant and illegal abuse of power. After hearing of the issuance of Lincoln's Preliminary Emancipation Proclamation, she predicted that the president was going straight to Hell when he died.[1533]

Southerners were not alone. Even Lincoln's own cabinet members were shocked and confused. One of them, Lincoln's secretary of state, William H. Seward, wrote of his boss' liberation order:

> We show our sympathy with slavery by emancipating slaves where we cannot reach them, and holding them in bondage where we can set them free.[1534]

Other Northerners were quick to see through the charade that Lincoln wanted all to believe was an "abolitionary" document. The *New York World* reported that the president had intentionally written his proclamation so that it would be "inoperative" wherever slaves were accessible, and operative where they were not, and where he had absolutely no authority. "Futile and ridiculous," the irritated Yankee editors called it.[1535]

Europe certainly noticed what Lincoln seemed completely oblivious of. The president's way of thinking, the London *Spectator* rightly declared,

> is not that a human being cannot justly own another, but that he

---

1528. Nicolay and Hay, ALCW, Vol. 2, pp. 287-288.
1529. Seabrook, TUAL, pp. 110-111.
1530. T. A. Bailey, p. 341.
1531. C. Eaton, HSC, p. 93; Hinkle, p. 125.
1532. Nicolay and Hay, ALCW, Vol. 2, p. 288.
1533. Anderson, pp. 145-146; Waugh, p. 179; McAfee, p. xix.
1534. Piatt, p. 150.
1535. *New York World*, January 7, 1863.

cannot own him unless he is loyal to the United States.[1536]

Many in Lincoln's own state were infuriated. On January 7, 1863, a week after he issued his proclamation, Illinois issued its own. It read:

> That the emancipation proclamation of the president is as unwarrantable in military as in civil law, a gigantic usurpation, at once converting the war, professedly commenced by the administration for the vindication of the authority of the constitution, into the crusade for the sudden, unconditional, and violent liberation of 3,000,000 of negro slaves; a result which would not only be a total subversion of the federal Union, but a revolution in the social organization of the Southern States. The proclamation invites servile insurrection as an element in this emancipation crusade, a means of warfare, the inhumanity and diabolism of which are without example in civilized warfare, and which we denounce, and which the civilized world will denounce, as an ineffaceable disgrace to the American name.[1537]

This resolution was carried unanimously by Illinoisans.

As always, Lincoln pretended to try and please everyone, and ended up pleasing no one. Little wonder: his edict was illegal, and he was the first Yankee official to publicly say so.[1538] As he wrote in a letter to Secretary of the Treasury Salmon P. Chase, dated September 2, 1863: "The original proclamation has no constitutional or legal justification . . ."[1539] A year earlier, on September 22, 1862, he told a group of abolitionist ministers that it was pointless to issue a proclamation of emancipation, for it would "necessarily be inoperative, like the Pope's bull against the comet."[1540]

Why was the Emancipation Proclamation unlawful?

Lincoln claimed that because of the "rebellion" he was permitted a type of imaginary but extraordinary "war power." However, as noted famed Yankee historian James Ford Rhodes writes:

1536. Bancroft, LWHS, Vol. 2, p. 339.
1537. Moses, p. 669.
1538. W. B. Garrison, CWTFB, p. 117.
1539. Nicolay and Hay, ALCW, Vol. 2, pp. 402-403.
1540. Nicolay and Hay, ALCW, Vol. 2, p. 234.

There was, as every one knows, no authority for the proclamation in the letter of the Constitution, nor was there any statue that warranted it.[1541]

Indeed, on March 4, 1861, Lincoln took an oath swearing to "preserve, protect, and defend the Constitution of the United States." Article 4, Section 2, of that document reads, in part:

> No person held to service or labor in one state, under the laws thereof, escaping into another state, shall, in consequence of any law or regulation therein, be discharged from such service or labor, but such persons shall be delivered up on claim of the party to whom such service or labor may be due.[1542]

The words "in consequence of any law or regulation therein," void and nullify Lincoln's proclamation, making it completely ineffective, unlawful, and unconstitutional.[1543]

Virginia judge, George L. Christian, writes:

> . . . the issuing of that [emancipation] proclamation . . . was a palpable violation of the Constitution and of Mr. Lincoln's oath of office; and the only plea on which the friends of Mr. Lincoln can justify his conduct is the plea of 'necessity,' the last refuge of every tyrant.[1544]

Tyrant Lincoln's edict also makes the bold promise that he will not return any slave to his or her owner who is set free by the Emancipation Proclamation. But the Constitution states that "such persons shall be delivered up on claim of the party to whom such service or labor may be due."

Who had the ultimate power, Lincoln or the Constitution? The Constitution itself answers this question in Article 6:

> This Constitution, and the laws of the United States which shall be

---

1541. Rhodes, Vol. 4, p. 213.
1542. Benton, Vol. 2, p. 776. This Clause, which concerned runaway slaves, was made obsolete by the Thirteenth Amendment, ratified December 6, 1865. Findlay and Findlay, p. 164. But it was still active during Lincoln's presidency.
1543. J. Davis, RFCG, Vol. 2, p. 621.
1544. Christian, p. 13.

made in pursuance thereof . . . shall be the supreme law of the land.[1545]

Jefferson Davis correctly observed that by issuing the Emancipation Proclamation, Lincoln did not obey the Constitution, the supreme law of the land. Rather, like the true dictator he was, he disobeyed it, disregarded it, subverted it, and finally overturned it;[1546] this despite his inaugural pledge to "preserve, protect, and defend the Constitution of the United States."[1547]

On November 9, 1864, the day after his reelection to a second term, Lincoln had the nerve to, as he put it,

> give thanks to the Almighty for this evidence of the people's resolution to stand by free government and the rights of humanity.[1548]

Here we have a statement that is a perfect example of political hubris, treachery, sanctimoniousness, and incongruity, at their worst. First, Lincoln was an atheist.[1549] Second, he rigged the 1864 election.[1550] Third, as a monarchical oriented "king," he was solidly opposed to "free government." And fourth, he had absolutely no regard for "the rights of humanity," as his thousands of criminal actions proved.

Of course, Lincoln's larger crime here was that he issued the Emancipation Proclamation in the Confederacy, a separate, constitutionally formed, sovereign nation. Though as a self-created dictator he *could* do this, as a publicly elected U.S. official he had no legal authority whatsoever to do this, making his decree meaningless, unlawful, inoperative, and powerless. Then again, he dared not recognize the Confederacy as a sovereign nation. Why? Because it would have exposed his many illegalities, from establishing a naval blockade without declaring war to waging war without congressional approval.[1551]

1545. E. McPherson, PHUSAGR, p. 95.
1546. Only a dictator can issue laws overturning constitutional rights. Crocker, p. 59.
1547. J. Davis, RFCG, Vol. 2, pp. 621, 622.
1548. Nicolay and Hay, ALCW, Vol. 2, p. 595.
1549. See e.g., *Southern Review*, January 1873, Vol. 12, No. 25, p. 364; Current, LNK, pp. 58, 61; Oates, AL, pp. 5, 40, 53; Lamon, LAL, p. 488; W. B. Garrison, LNOK, p. 265; Kane, p. 163.
1550. DiLorenzo, LU, p. 52.
1551. See K. L. Hall, s.v. "Prize Cases."

In his own self-serving, sinister way, however, Lincoln knew exactly what he was doing. After all, his Emancipation Proclamation was eventually successful in at least seven ways:

1) In the North, the "subhuman" label had been politically removed from free blacks (though it remained socially) so that he could enroll them in his military apparatus.[1552]

2) In turn, freed blacks were no longer regarded as personal property, making them eligible for deportation (part of his black colonization program).[1553]

3) Freeing Southern blacks would siphon off the South's labor supply, so Lincoln believed,[1554] thereby weakening the enemy.[1555]

4) Issued not only as a temporary "war measure"[1556] but also as a "civil necessity," his emancipation helped prevent the Radicals (socialists and communists) in his party from challenging his leadership[1557] and "openly embarrassing the government," as he put it.[1558] (Seward stated the truth that Lincoln often concealed: throughout the War, *all* measures taken by Lincoln to end slavery had been *war measures*—without exception.[1559] Lincoln's more faithful military officers, like Grant, agreed.)[1560] Prior to releasing his Emancipation Proclamation, Lincoln himself spoke candidly of the issue, saying:

> I view this matter as a practical war measure, to be decided on according to the advantages or disadvantages it may offer to the suppression of the rebellion.[1561]

1552. L. Johnson, p. 133.
1553. L. Johnson, pp. 130-134.
1554. Garraty and McCaughey, p. 253.
1555. Nicolay and Hay, ALCW, Vol. 2, p. 235.
1556. See Greenberg and Waugh, p. 355.
1557. Hendelson, s.v. "Lincoln, Abraham."
1558. Rice, RAL, p. 533.
1559. L. Johnson, pp. 140-141.
1560. Leech, p. 319.
1561. Nicolay and Hay, ALCW, Vol. 2, p. 235.

5) The escalating death rate of white Yankee soldiers made it imperative that a "more expendable" substitute be found. Northern white racists, like Lincoln, found blacks to be the ideal replacements: as something that Northerners considered to be only half human, they were considered "less valuable." In this way white bigotry in the North fueled support for black enlistment in Lincoln's military.[1562]

6) The U.S. enrollment act of March 3, 1863, allowed drafted soldiers to "purchase" a substitute to serve in their stead. With blacks now in the service, this proved to be a great, though short-lived, boon for white soldiers seeking to escape a tour of duty. Whites were now able to purchase blacks as "cheap replacements." Blacks, being "less valuable," cost less than whites. This in turn allowed substitute brokers, "professional recruiters," to buy up "ignorant and needy Negroes" at low rates for use as substitutes. White draftees benefitted, as did the recruiters, who accrued massive profits in the bargain. (The practice soon became so corrupt that in July 1863, the War Department issued an order that blacks could only substitute for other blacks.)[1563]

7) As Lincoln correctly predicted, the numerical advantage of his newly added 180,000 black soldiers would eventually prove vital in the North's victory over the South.[1564] On June 6, 1863 (six months after the Emancipation Proclamation was issued), Gideon Welles, Lincoln's Secretary of the Navy, admitted that "all of our increased military strength now comes from Negroes."[1565] In a letter to Lincoln, General Grant wrote:

> I have given the subject of arming the negro my hearty support. This, with the emancipation of the negro, is the heaviest blow yet given the Confederacy. . . . by arming the negro we have added a powerful ally. They will make good soldiers and taking them from the enemy weakens him in the same proportion they strengthen us. I am therefore most decidedly in favor of pushing this policy to the enlistment of a force sufficient to hold all the South falling into our

---

1562. See Jimerson, p. 96.
1563. *ORA*, Ser. 3, Vol. 5, pp. 632-633.
1564. Mullen, p. 22.
1565. Klinkner and Smith, p. 55; Jimerson, p. 97.

hands and to aid in capturing more.[1566]

From the North's perspective, all seven of these points were indeed "successful" to one extent or another.

But Lincoln's proclamation failed in a number of ways as well, as he noted dejectedly in a September 28, 1862, letter to Vice President Hamlin:

> My Dear Sir: Your kind letter of the 25th is just received. It is known to some that while I hope something from the proclamation, my expectations are not as sanguine [i.e., optimistic] as are those of some friends. The time for its effect southward has not come; but northward the effect should be instantaneous.
>
> It is six days old, and while commendation in newspapers and by distinguished individuals is all that a vain man could wish, the stocks have declined, and troops come forward more slowly than ever. This, looked soberly in the face, is not very satisfactory. We have fewer troops in the field at the end of six days than we had at the beginning—the attrition among the old outnumbering the addition by the new. The North responds to the proclamation sufficiently in breath; but breath alone kills no rebels.
>
> I wish I could write more cheerfully; nor do I thank you the less for the kindness of your letter. Yours very truly, A. Lincoln.[1567]

Lincoln had good reason for being depressed, disappointed, perplexed, and upset.

Far from starting a mass slave revolt and exodus in the South on January 1, 1863, as he had hoped, as many as 300,000 loyal Southern blacks (nearly 200,000 free and 100,000 bonded)[1568] simply picked up arms and instead fought against him,[1569] 33 percent more than the nearly

---

1566. Nicolay and Hay, ALAH, Vol. 6, p. 466. Nothing here by slave owner Grant about black civil rights.
1567. Nicolay and Hay, ALCW, Vol. 2, pp. 242-243. Lincoln's letter to Hamlin concerned the Preliminary Emancipation Proclamation issued on September 22, 1862. The Final Emancipation Proclamation, issued on January 1, 1863, had much the same effect: nothing happened.
1568. There were some 182,000 free blacks in the eleven states of the Confederacy (Quarles, p. 35), nearly all who sided with Dixie. In addition, most traditional Southern historians believe that between 100,000 and 300,000 Southern slaves fought for Dixie. See following footnote.
1569. Barrow, Segars, and Rosenburg, BC, p. 97; *The United Daughters of the Confederacy Magazine*, Vols. 54-55, 1991, p. 32. Though the exact number is not known, estimates of the number of Southern blacks who fought for the Confederacy range from 30,000 to 93,000, from 100,000 to 300,000. See e.g., Hinkle, p. 106; R. M. Brown, p. xiv; Shenkman and Reiger, p. 106. I have chosen to go with the largest figure for

200,000 that fought for Lincoln.[1570] At least 3,000 Louisiana blacks alone officially served under the Confederate flag.[1571] A full 25 percent of the Confederacy's Ordnance Department was black.[1572] These numbers are more impressive when we consider that Southern blacks were exempt from the draft: though thousands were impressed into service, many times that volunteered.[1573]

Few of these brave black men will be found in the official muster rolls of the Confederate record, of course. We know of them mainly through photographs, county histories, obituaries, grave markers and memorials, period newspapers, genealogical histories,[1574] personal letters, logbooks, diaries, journals, plantation books, postwar reunion notes, and most importantly, pension applications.[1575]

On February 3, 1865, by Lincoln's own overly generous estimate, a mere 200,000 of the South's 3,500,000 black servants were eventually "freed" under his emancipation, after which they went North.[1576] Only about 100,000 of those, according to Lincoln, joined the Union army[1577]—most, we will note, to their great regret. The other 3,300,000, however, remained with their black and white families across the South, protecting them, growing foods and providing supplies for the Confederate army,[1578] working in factories and mines, taking over plantations, and assuming numerous positions of authority in order to maintain social stability.[1579] So immensely beneficial was the Southern black contribution during the War, that their impact on Dixie was greater in those four years than during the entire antebellum period.[1580]

Thus, of the South's 3,500,000 black servants, only one in

---

reasons that will be discussed shortly. Skewing the already confusing figures were the thousands of blacks who posed as whites (presumably the lighter skinned blacks), eager to join the Confederate army or navy. See e.g., E. L. Jordan, p. 217. Since these particular men were never counted, the number 300,000 must be considered quite conservative—as I will show shortly.
1570. Interestingly, 300,000 is the same number of blacks authorized for enlistment by the Confederate Congress' General Ordinance No. 14, issued in March, 1865. Greenberg and Waugh, p. 395.
1571. Greenberg and Waugh, pp. 362, 385.
1572. Barrow, Segars, and Rosenburg, BC, p. 7.
1573. E. M. Thomas, p. 236.
1574. Segars and Barrow, BSCA, p. ii.
1575. Barrow, Segars, and Rosenburg, BC, p. 111.
1576. Stephens, CV, Vol. 2, p. 611.
1577. Nicolay and Hay, ALCW, Vol. 2, p. 454.
1578. J. H. Franklin, p. 179.
1579. Quarles, p. xiii.
1580. E. M. Thomas, p. 236.

twenty, or just 5 percent, joined the Yanks. The other 95 percent maintained their loyalty to Dixie.[1581] Those thousands who marched off to war against Lincoln proudly wore Confederate gray, with placards on their hats reading: "We will die by the South."[1582]

Though, thanks to the burning of Southern courthouses by Lincoln's troops, official record of the black Confederate soldier is scarce, we have overwhelming evidence that black patriotism for the South was deep, widespread, and implacable.[1583]

Among the known loyal Southern African-Americans who fought for the Confederacy and states' rights were Jacques Esclavon, Gabriel Grappe, Charles Lutz, Jean Baptiste Pierre-August, Levin Graham, Peter Vertrees, and Lufray Pierre-August,[1584] Henry Love, Hiram Kendael, Joe Warren, Dan Humphreys, George Briggs, Hardin Blackwell, Lewis McConnell, Daniel Robinson, and Fielding Rennolds,[1585] just a few of untold thousands. Most are unnamed and so are destined to be forever unknown. At least 30,000 alone served as faithful body servants to their white Confederate masters.[1586] Many of these men, though merely servants, carried their own weapons, firing whenever possible on the invading Yankees.

All told, the numbers of Confederate blacks were overwhelming. Even anti-South historians have been forced to admit that a "puzzling" number of Southern blacks were ready and willing to fight against Lincoln, the North, and the "damned buckram abolitionists,"[1587] many blacks even going so far as to buy Confederate bonds,[1588] donate money, food, and livestock, sew uniforms, sponsor auctions and bake sales, hold balls, fairs, and parties, and sell off property and anything else that might help advance the Confederate Cause.[1589]

In the summer of 1861, Thomas "Blind Tom" Wiggins, a popular and talented black musician from Georgia, gave free concerts for the Confederate ill and injured. One Memphis black who volunteered to fight

---

1581. Current, LNK, p. 228; Gragg, p. 88. See also Barney, p. 141.
1582. Barrow, Segars, and Rosenburg, BC, pp. 8, 25.
1583. Wiley, SN, pp. 139-145.
1584. *Civil War Book of Lists*, pp. 169-170.
1585. Segars and Barrow, BSCA, pp. 48, 99, 142, 200, 221.
1586. Barrow, Segars, and Rosenburg, BC, p. 71.
1587. Helper, NQC, p. 206.
1588. L. Johnson, p. 180.
1589. Quarles, p. 37; Greenberg and Waugh, pp. 372-373.

Lincoln offered to outfit himself at his own expense. His only stipulation was that his family and home be protected while he was away. Just weeks after Sumter, sixty blacks in Richmond, Virginia, showed up carrying a Confederate flag, requesting to be enlisted. In Nashville, a group of blacks formed a well-trained company, then offered their services to the Confederate government. Though they had no weapons or uniforms, two all-black companies drilled at Fort Smith, Arkansas, in preparation for being called up.[1590]

Some of the largest groups of Southern blacks who wished to serve their country came from New Orleans. Voicing their eagerness "to take arms at a moment's notice and fight shoulder to shoulder with other citizens," thousands of coloreds, mulattos, and Creoles formed themselves into well drilled, well dressed regiments known as the famous "Native Guards." One spoke for all when he told a white officer:

> General, we come of a fighting race. Our fathers were brought here [as] slaves because they were captured in war, and in hand to hand fights, too. We are willing to fight. Pardon me, General, but the only cowardly blood we have got in our veins is the white blood.[1591]

From every corner of the new Confederacy were heard accounts of both free and enslaved blacks who were anxious to contribute in some way to the new nation.[1592] One impromptu poll found that 60 out of 72 Southern slaves (nearly 84 percent) were ready and willing to take up arms in defense of the homes of both their own families and those of their owners, to fight until their last breath against the Yankee foe.[1593]

Known for their Yankee-centric view of the world, most white Northerners, of course, never understood this type of sentiment, not even when it was a Northern black who evinced sympathy for the South. In October 1861, John Jones, a black New Yorker, stood before a huge crowd and gave a speech in which he articulated his undying support for the Confederacy. He was promptly arrested and silenced, and from that

---

1590. Quarles, pp. 37-38.
1591. B. F. Butler, p. 498.
1592. W. C. Davis, LA, p. 142.
1593. L. Johnson, p. 181.

moment on was labeled mad, fit only for the lunatic asylum.[1594]

British soldier Colonel Arthur J. Fremantle, a member of Her Majesty's Coldstream Guards, happened to be in Pennsylvania in the summer of 1863, when he made note of the following incident shortly after the Battle of Gettysburg:

> I saw a most laughable spectacle this afternoon—viz., a [Southern] negro dressed in full Yankee uniform, with a rifle at full cock, leading along a barefooted white man, with whom he had evidently changed clothes. [Confederate] General [James] Longstreet stopped the pair, and asked the black man what it meant. He replied, 'The two [Rebel] soldiers in charge of this here Yank have got drunk, so for fear he should escape I have took care of him, and brought him through that little town.' The consequential manner of the negro, and the supreme contempt with which he spoke to his prisoner, were most amusing. This little episode of a Southern slave leading a white Yankee soldier through a Northern village, *alone and of his own accord*, would not have been gratifying to an abolitionist.[1595]

Patriotism, having no color barrier, was the primary motivation behind the thousands of Southern blacks who "joined up" to go off and fight for "Jeff Davis." They could hate slavery, but still love the South and their white "families."[1596] Lincoln himself was not even intellectually capable of making this distinction.

In May 1861 several blacks were seen marching stoically along with a Confederate military company in Virginia. One of them stopped to tell a white onlooker that if "ole Lincoln" tries to send his boys into "Varginny," he would raise a regiment of Negroes as fast as greased lightnin', for it's the South, not the North, who is the true friend of the black man.[1597]

On February 4, 1862, the Virginia legislature passed a bill to enroll all of the state's free Negroes for service in the Confederate army. Earlier, on November 23, 1861, a seven-mile long line of Confederate soldiers was marched through the streets of New Orleans. Among them

---

1594. E. L. Jordan, p. 372.
1595. Fremantle, p. 281.
1596. Quarles, pp. 39, 50.
1597. E. L. Jordan, p. 216.

was a regiment of 1,400 free black volunteers.[1598]

In 1905, Walter Lynwood Fleming wrote:

> The free negro population [of Alabama], though less than 3000 in number, were devoted supporters of the Confederacy, and nearly all free black men were engaged in some way in the Confederate service. Some entered the service as substitutes, others as cooks, teamsters, and musicians. In Mobile they asked to be enlisted as soldiers under white officers. The skillful artisans usually stayed at home at the urgent request of the whites, who needed their work, but, nevertheless, they contributed. All accounts agree that they never avoided payment of the tax-in-kind, and other contributions.[1599]

When Rebel General Richard Taylor, the son of former U.S. President Zachary Taylor, met up with some black Confederate troops in Mobile, Alabama, in late 1864, he found them hard at work on fortifications. When the conversation turned to the African-American war effort, one of the black soldiers told Taylor:

> If you will give us guns we will fight for these works, too. We would rather fight for our own white folks than for strangers.[1600]

When James Chesnut Jr. spoke to his black servants about enlisting in the Confederate military, his wife Mary noted that nearly all were keen to enlist and fight.[1601] They were happy, the famed diarist said, to serve in the Confederate army if Mr. Chesnut would only give them arms and in return grant them land and their freedom.[1602]

Confederate Secretary of State Judah Benjamin had a similar experience. One day during the War his slaves came to him and said:

> Master, set us free, and we will fight for you. We had rather fight for you than for the Yankees.[1603]

1598. Greeley, AC, Vol. 2, p. 522.
1599. Fleming, p. 208.
1600. R. Taylor, p. 210.
1601. Foote, Vol. 3, p. 755.
1602. Chesnut, DD, p. 147.
1603. Lubbock, p. 561.

On July 4, 1861, one of the many thousands of Southern "slaves" who joined the Confederate army, Thomas A. Phelps, wrote home to his mother from Virginia, saying:

> I take this opportunity of writing to you to let you know that I am well and doing well, and I hope that this letter will find you as well as I am now in Yorktown. I will leave at 4 o'clock p. m. today for a scout about the woods for the Yankees. . . . We are looking out for a fight on the 5th of July by the 5th Regiment Louisiana volunteers. Give my love to Mistress and Master Jim Phelps, and to all of them in New Orleans. You must excuse this bad writing. I am writing in a hurry; have not time to write. I am about to leave for the Mill. So good by all. No more at present.
> Your devoted son, THOMAS A PHELPS
> P. S. — Good by to the white folks until I kill a Yankee.[1604]

On December 22, 1861, New York troops were attacked near Newmarket Bridge, Virginia, by a Confederate force of 700 armed blacks. Six of the African-American Rebels were killed, but, it was said, these could easily be replaced from an endless supply of highly zealous blacks.[1605]

Eventually there were so many black Confederates on the battlefield that Northern soldiers, most who were overtly racist, were completely dumbstruck at the sight. General Stonewall Jackson's army alone contained some 3,000 black soldiers, an image that froze Yankees in their tracks in fear and revulsion.[1606]

On September 10, 1862, a Union doctor caught sight of Jackson's troops and recorded the following entry in his diary:

> At four o'clock this morning the Rebel army began to move from our town, Jackson's force taking the advance. The movement continued until eight o'clock P.M., occupying sixteen hours. The most liberal calculation could not give them more than 64,000 men. Over 3,000 Negroes must be included in the number. These were clad in all kinds of uniforms, not only in cast-off or captured United States uniforms, but in coats with Southern buttons, State buttons, etc. These were shabby, but not shabbier or seedier than those worn by white men in the rebel ranks. Most of the negroes

---

1604. Wallcut, p. 20.
1605. E. L. Jordan, p. 222.
1606. Hinkle, p. 106.

had arms, rifles, muskets, sabres, bowie-knives, dirks, etc. They were supplied, in many instances, with knapsacks, haversacks, canteens, etc., and they were manifestly an integral portion of the Southern Confederacy Army. They were seen riding on horses and mules, driving wagons, riding on caissons, in ambulances, with the staff of generals and promiscuously mixed up with all the rebel horde.[1607]

The free blacks of Mobile, Alabama, were mostly slave owners who, one white citizen said, "are as true to the South as the pure white race."[1608] In 1861, none of them had done service in the Confederate army yet, but all were "anxious to do so." By 1862, they had organized and were helping to defend their city against Lincoln's invaders.[1609]

When raw percentages are taken into account, far more blacks fought for the Confederacy than for the Union: the Union possessed about three million soldiers. Of these about 200,000 were black, 6 percent of the total. The Confederacy had about one million soldiers.[1610] Of these an estimated 300,000 were black,[1611] 30 percent of the total—24 percent more than fought for Lincoln.

And these numbers are conservative if we use the definition of a "private soldier" as determined by German-American Union General, August Valentine Kautz, in 1864:

> In the fullest sense, any man in the military service who receives pay, whether sworn in or not, is a soldier, because he is subject to military law. Under this general head, laborers, teamsters, sutlers, chaplains, etc., are soldiers.[1612]

As most of the 3,500,000 black servants living in the South at the time of Lincoln's War remained loyal to Confederacy, and as at least 500,000 to

---

1607. L. H. Steiner, pp. 19-20.
1608. ORA, Ser. 4, Vol. 1, p. 1088.
1609. Greenberg and Waugh, p. 394.
1610. The exact number of Yanks and Rebels, by some estimates, was 2,898,304 of the former, 1,234,000 of the latter. Livermore, p. 63. Also see Katcher, CWSB, p. 46.
1611. Barrow, Segars, and Rosenburg, BC, p. 97; *The United Daughters of the Confederacy Magazine*, Vols. 54-55, 1991, p. 32.
1612. Kautz, p. 11. Using Kautz's definition of a "private soldier," some 2 million Southerners fought in the Confederacy: 1 million whites and perhaps as many as 1 million blacks. (These numbers do not include the other three "races," yellow, brown, and red, that sided with and fought for the Confederacy. See C. Johnson, pp. 169-197.)

1 million of these either worked in or fought in the Rebel army and navy in some capacity, Kautz's definition raises the percentage of Southern blacks who defended the Confederacy as literal soldiers to as many as 50 percent of the total Confederate soldier population![1613] If accurate, five times or 500 percent more blacks fought for the Confederacy than for the Union.[1614]

While Northerners pride themselves in erecting monuments to white racists, black colonizationists, and anti-Semites like Lincoln, Grant, and Sherman (the latter who founded the theory of "modern warfare"),[1615] in the South you are more likely to see monuments like the one in Fort Mill, South Carolina, whose inscription reads:

> Dedicated to the faithful Slaves, who, loyal to a sacred trust, toiled for the support of our army with matchless devotion and sterling fidelity, guarding our defenseless homes, women and children during the struggle for the principles of our Confederate States of America.[1616]

Sadly, and strangely, many African-Americans today, ignorant of their own deep Southern heritage, have tried to prevent the construction of monuments honoring faithful black Confederates. One of these, the National Association for the Advancement of Colored People (NAACP)—which, in 1991, ratified a resolution to prohibit and censor anything connected with the Southern Confederacy[1617]—publicly opposed just such a monument in Nottoway County, Virginia, in 1993.[1618]

The NAACP's stated mission, however, is to "eliminate racial hatred and racial discrimination." (As racism is found among all races, allegedly their mission would include eliminating hatred of and discrimination toward whites, reds, browns, and yellows, as well.) Just how prohibiting the commemoration of the millions of blacks who

---

1613. Using Kautz's definition and these numbers, 200,000 blacks fought for the Union, 1,000,000 blacks for the Confederacy. Thus, 80 percent more blacks wore Rebel gray than wore Yankee blue.
1614. Seabrook, CFF, p. 195.
1615. Sherman's theory of modern warfare included waging "total destruction" upon the civilian population, as thousands of innocent Southern men, women, and children were to discover. Warner, GB, s.v. "William Tecumseh 'Cump' Sherman."
1616. C. A. Evans, Vol. 5, p. 911.
1617. Seabrook, CFF, p. 300.
1618. E. L. Jordan, p. 373.

supported the South against white supremacist Lincoln helps accomplish this goal, or aids in the "advancement of colored people," has never been fully explained.[1619]

Not only were blacks in the South from its very inception (as early as 1526, they first appeared in what would later be Virginia[1620]—not, we will note, as slaves, but like most whites, as indentured servants),[1621] but in a number of Southern regions blacks eventually came to far outnumber whites, enabling them to wield enormous influence over the development of Southern society and culture (by 1776, for example nearly half of Virginia's population was black).[1622]

Thus it is well-known throughout Dixie that blacks helped establish, and profoundly shape, the American South and her four year old Confederacy. Though the anti-South movement tries to ignore this fact, neither the "Civil War" or American history can be properly understood without the knowledge of African-American Confederates and their many wonderful contributions to the South, and her wartime cause.[1623]

It remains a mystery why anyone would want to prevent this knowledge from being disseminated. It is healing knowledge, desperately needed in a nation still trying to recover from the social, cultural, political, economic, and racial wounds left by Lincoln and his illicit War.

Fortunately, the construction of one of America's most famous Rebel memorials, the Confederate Monument at Arlington National Cemetery, Arlington, Virginia, was authorized in 1906, three years before the formation of the NAACP (in 1909)[1624]—otherwise it might not have

---

1619. See the NAACP's Website: www.naacp.org. It is for just such actions that even many blacks today, such as Reverend Jesse Lee Peterson, have denounced the NAACP as an intolerant "hate group." See Peterson's Brotherhood Organization of a New Destiny (BOND) Website: www.bondinfo.org.
1620. Meltzer, Vol. 2, p. 127.
1621. Ransom, p. 41.
1622. Hey, p. 76.
1623. See E. L. Jordan, p. 1.
1624. What is now Arlington National Cemetery was originally the antebellum home of Southern hero General Robert E. Lee. Known then as Arlington House, during the War for Southern Independence it was stolen and ruthlessly plundered by the Yanks. A. Cooke, ACA, p. 214. Cruelly, Union soldiers were intentionally buried throughout the yard, right up to the house, to prevent Lee and his family from ever returning to reclaim their property. Grissom, p. 206. Then, on June 15, 1864, Lincoln's secretary of war, Edwin M. Stanton, designated it a military cemetery, the beginning of what was to become one of America's most hallowed pieces of ground. See Website: www.arlingtoncemetery.org. After the War, though hundreds of Confederate soldiers had been buried there as well, it was still insensitively referred to as a "Union cemetery." The North was using Arlington to continue its campaign of shaming and punishing the South. According to the Cemetery's official Website: "Family members of Confederate soldiers were denied permission to decorate their loved ones' graves and in extreme cases were even denied entrance to the

seen the light of day.[1625] A sculpture at the site includes a scene of a number of Confederate soldiers tramping off to battle. Close inspection of this wonderful piece of art reveals what many Northerners and New South scallywags consider a scandalous revelation: one of the men portrayed is a black man. Not merely a black slave, a "lowly" body servant, or even a teamster, but a real, armed, uniformed, black Confederate soldier, marching proudly side by side with his white Confederate brothers.

The memorial was designed by Moses Jacob Ezekiel, one of 12,000 Jewish Confederate military men[1626] who routinely witnessed thousands of blacks in the Rebel armed forces firsthand. Ezekiel only portrayed what he saw, was familiar with, and knew to be true.

About the time this monument was constructed in the early 1900s, the North began suppressing the truth about the reality of black Confederate soldiers. Why? Because it exposed the lie about Lincoln's War; namely, that it had been fought to "free the slaves." Silently and stubbornly defying this contrived Yankee nonsense is Ezekiel's Confederate Monument at Arlington National Cemetery. May it stand long and proud.

If more proof of the reality of the black Confederate soldier is needed, we have numerous more examples to choose from. On February 27, 1865, for instance, Grant sent a field dispatch to Union General Edward R. S. Canby, which concluded with the following words:

> It is also important to prevent, as far as possible, the planting of a crop this year and to destroy their railroads, machine-shops, &c. It is also important to get all the negro men we can before the enemy put them in their ranks.[1627]

---

cemetery." The bitter sectional feelings only began to fade with the Spanish-American War (in 1898), when former Rebels and Yanks joined forces against a common enemy. For more on this topic, see Website: www.arlingtoncemetery.org/Visitor_information/Confederate_Memorial.html. Tragically, the idea to establish a Yankee cemetery on Lee's confiscated property came from Southern turncoat, Yankee General Montgomery C. Meigs of Georgia, who believed that Lee was a "traitor." Highsmith and Landphair, p. 104. Thus, one of America's greatest and most beloved cemeteries was founded by Northerners on personal vindictiveness and sectional animosity toward the South.

1625. The Confederate Monument at Arlington was unveiled on June 4, 1914, the 106th anniversary of the birthday of President Jefferson Davis. Appropriately, Southerner President Woodrow Wilson gave the address. Website: www.arlingtoncemetery.org/Visitor_information/Confederate_Memorial.html.

1626. Rosen, p. 161.

1627. *ORA*, Ser. 1, Vol. 49, Pt. 1, p. 781.

There is also the famous letter written by former Northern slave Frederick Douglass to Lincoln in 1862. In it, the black civil rights leader used the example of the overwhelming number of blacks in the Confederate army to urge the president to allow blacks to officially enlist in the Union army (Lincoln had steadfastly refused up until this time). Wrote Douglass to the reluctant leader, now widely known as the "tortoise President" for hindering abolition:[1628]

> There are at the present moment, many colored men in the Confederate Army doing duty not only as cooks, servants and laborers, but as real soldiers, having muskets on their shoulders and bullets in their pockets, ready to shoot down loyal [Yankee] troops, and do all that soldiers may do to destroy the Federal [U.S.] government and build up that of the traitors and rebels. There were such soldiers at Manassas, and they are probably there still. There is a negro in the [Confederate] army as well as in the fence, and our Government is likely to find it out before the war comes to an end. That the negroes are numerous in the rebel army, and do for that army it heaviest work, is beyond question.[1629]

Douglass was highly desirous of a military commission himself, in this case as an assistant adjutant to Yankee General Lorenzo Thomas. But he was ignored, and the invitation he "fondly hoped" for (to become a member of Lincoln's armed forces) never came.[1630] Douglass, a "friend" of Lincoln's, rightly accused the president of fighting with his "white hand" while keeping his "black hand" tied and bound.[1631]

Revealingly, much of the Northern white press agreed with Douglass. In its pages the Chicago *Tribune* asked Lincoln the following: What is the reason for not allowing captured Southern blacks to fight for the United States? Many thousands now serve in the Confederate armies. "Why not let 'nigger' fight 'nigger'?," it urged.[1632]

Northern black owned newspapers wondered the same thing. The *Rochester Negro Leader* reported that the South was using African-Americans, not just as laborers, but as combatants in countless units it

---

1628. W. Phillips, p. 456.
1629. *Douglass' Monthly*, September, 1861, Vol. 4, p. 516.
1630. Douglass, LTFD, p. 805.
1631. Buckley, p. 89.
1632. The Leavenworth, Kansas, *Daily Conservative*, September 13, 1861.

called "Colored Brigades"; authentic soldiers, well drilled, well armed, well prepared to do battle with Union soldiers.[1633]

When it came to the Northern armies, black civil rights leaders, like Sojourner Truth, complained endlessly to Lincoln about his pitiful treatment of blacks, but to no avail.[1634] Douglass rightly asked the president: if blacks were good enough to serve under General George Washington, why are they not now good enough to serve under General George McClellan?[1635]

However, most black men probably did not want to serve under McClellan. Like many other Northern officers, McClellan spent much of his time enforcing the Fugitive Slave Law of 1850, returning runaway servants to their owners. This was the same law that Lincoln promised to strengthen in his First Inaugural Address,[1636] despite the fact that overturning it, or even ignoring it, would have helped bring slavery to an end much sooner.[1637]

The North likes to brag about being the first to enroll blacks during Lincoln's War, claiming that the idea was received with "universal enthusiasm." However, this is a deliberate falsehood that has misled generations.

Actually, the South was the first to enroll blacks, an act that was favored by both "nearly all" Southern white soldiers *and* the "great mass" of the Southern citizenry.[1638] In early 1865, Confederate Representative Ethelbert Barksdale stood before the House and went even further, saying that *all* military men wanted black enlistment, from the lowly private to the Rebels' General-in-Chief Robert E. Lee himself.[1639]

So strongly "favored" was Southern black enlistment that it came even before the War's first major conflict, the Battle of First Manassas (First Bull Run to Yanks) on July 18, 1861.[1640] In June 1861, one year and three months before the Union officially sanctioned the recruitment of blacks in August 1862,[1641] and almost two years before Lincoln began

---

1633. Cornish, pp. 4-5, 62.
1634. McKissack and McKissack, pp. 138-139.
1635. N. A. Hamilton, p. 120; Förster and Nagler, p. 207; Masur, p. 110; J. M. McPherson, NCW, p. 163.
1636. Nicolay and Hay, ALCW, Vol. 2, p. 1.
1637. DiLorenzo, RL, p. 21.
1638. Durden, pp. 160, 209.
1639. Durden, p. 245. See also J. B. Jones, Vol. 2, pp. 432-433.
1640. Cornish, p. 15.
1641. E. L. Jordan, pp. 218, 266.

arming blacks in March 1863, the Tennessee legislature passed a statute allowing Governor Isham G. Harris to receive into military service "all male free persons of color, between the ages of 15 and 50 . . ."[1642] Tennessee's black soldiers, unlike Lincoln's, were paid, treated, clothed, and fed on an equal basis with Tennessee's white soldiers.[1643] Just months later, in October 1861, the Leavenworth, Kansas, *Daily Conservative* observed: it is widely known that both Indians and Negroes have been enrolled in the Confederate military, and that more are expected.[1644]

Another piece of Northern evidence for black Confederates comes from the hand of Yankee abolitionist Horace Greeley who, in 1867, wrote:

> For more than two years, negroes had been extensively employed in belligerent operations by the Confederacy. They had been embodied and drilled Rebel soldiers, and had paraded with White troops at a time when this would not have been tolerated in the armies of the Union.[1645]

Indeed, from the very first day of hostilities, the Confederate military impressed blacks both young and old, male and female, for a vast array of occupations, from teamsters and nurses, to orderlies and waiters—and nearly all were happy to comply.[1646] Southern black impressment actually took place even before the Confederate government began drafting white

---

1642. *ORA*, Ser. 4, Vol. 1, p. 409.
1643. E. L. Jordan, pp. 218-219.
1644. Buckley, p. 83.
1645. Greeley, AC, Vol. 2, p. 524. Technically speaking, the South began officially enrolling blacks a century and a half earlier. On December 23, 1703, South Carolina passed an act allowing for the arming and training of slaves for the military. Slaves who captured or killed one of the enemy were automatically emancipated. It was only Nat Turner's psychopathic killing spree in 1831 (inspired by meddling Yankee abolitionist William Lloyd Garrison) that made white Southerners reluctant to enlist blacks from then on. Though they had been *unofficially* armed since the beginning of Lincoln's War (even before, as early as January 1861, Southerners were advocating arming and drilling blacks), it was not until March 1865 that President Jefferson Davis, America's true "Great Emancipator," officially sanctioned the return of the black Confederate. This was nine months before the U.S. ratified the Thirteenth Amendment, freeing all American slaves. Sadly for the South, by then Davis' act was too late to have any great impact. Appomattox was only weeks away. See Wiley, SN, pp. 146-149, 156-159. We will note here that the Confederacy would have begun official enlistment of blacks at the very start of Lincoln's War, but for two reasons: 1) there were already more than enough white soldiers at the time, and even these could not all be armed due to lack of weapons; 2) during the first few years of the conflict, Southern blacks were needed more as laborers than as soldiers. See Quarles, pp. 39-40.
1646. Quarles, pp. xiii, 48.

soldiers.[1647]

Why the widespread near universal black support for the South and the Confederacy?

African-Americans were attached to the Southern Cause for a variety of reasons. For one thing, Southern blacks did not hate whites (as the North and New South falsely teach). They hated slavery.[1648] Thus the sooner they could help their white Southern brothers bring the War to an end, the sooner they knew they would gain their freedom.[1649]

Just as importantly, blacks donned Confederate gray and butternut[1650] over personal concern for friends and immediate family, affection for their white families (owners), and love for their Southern homeland. Other factors included negative experiences with Northerners (most, who they had learned, were rabid racists), strong social and cultural ties to their area, and, as mentioned, the certain knowledge that slavery was coming to end.[1651] In short, they understood that their fortunes were irrevocably linked to those of the South, not the North.[1652]

The most obvious reason that most Southern blacks sided with the South, however, was the knowledge that it was the North which first sent ships to Africa in search of slaves; that it was the North which first bought their ancestors from African slavers; that it was the North which first stole their ancestors away from their African homeland; that it was the North which first implemented slavery in what was to become the United States; that it was the North which first forced their ancestors to work in American factories and on American farms; and finally that it was the North which first sold their ancestors to the South to be enslaved all over again.[1653] With such a history no reasonable person can possibly wonder why 19th-Century Southern blacks felt so attached to Dixie, or why they were so willing to take up arms against the Yankee and die in their thousands.

1647. McPherson, BCF, p. 354; Buckley, p. 81.
1648. Durden, pp. 27-28.
1649. L. Johnson, p. 181.
1650. As official Confederate gray uniforms were scarce, homemade outfits were commonly worn by Johnny Reb. These were sometimes dyed using the yellowish skins of the butternut (*Juglans cinerea*), a species of American walnut, turning the clothing a soft tan-brown; hence the term "butternut" for both the garments and for Confederate soldiers themselves. Watts, s.v. "butternuts."
1651. Greenberg and Waugh, p. 374
1652. Barrow, Segars, and Rosenburg, BC, p. 4.
1653. Hinkle, p. 108.

This powerful connection between Southern blacks and the South, not to mention that between black servants and their masters and mistresses, has been remarked on by many historians, including Comer Vann Woodward. Concerning the degree which Southern-Americans and African-Americans had in shaping each other's destinies, Woodward noted that they eventually came to share and mold a common culture, one so intertwined that today one cannot conceive of either one in isolation.[1654] True Southerners, both white and black, both red and brown, both yellow and colored, are today proud of their multiracial heritage, not ashamed of it. It is only the uneducated and the ignorant, permeated with Yankee mythology, who continue to believe that "the South is racist." It never was—and still is not—as bigoted as the white North, for numerous reasons that we have discussed in detail.

During the 19th Century, the close-knit bond between Europeans and Africans in America's Southland was only startling to Northerners. Southerners took it for granted. In May 1865, in her diary, Mary Chesnut noted the words of a freed black slave to his former white owner after the War:

> When you all had de power you was good to me, and I'll protect you now. No niggers nor Yankees shall tech [touch] you. If you want anything call for Sambo. I mean, call for Mr. Samuel; dat my name now.[1655]

Literally millions of other Southern freedmen held the same sentiment toward their white families.

Most Southern blacks who went to war for the Confederacy were particularly happy with their lot. While many went as body servants for their masters or as cooks, laborers, shoemen, stewards, farriers, drivers, firemen, barbers, bodyguards, buglers, musicians, fifers, drummers, and teamsters, untold thousands served in far more important roles, such as Confederate spies, ammunition runners, artillerymen, infantrymen, cavalrymen, nurses, and sharpshooters. The following gives an idea of the important role they played: the first Northerner killed in the entire "Civil War," U.S. Major Theodore Winthrop, was brought down by a highly

---

1654. Greenberg and Waugh, p. 369.
1655. Chesnut, DD, p. 389.

skilled, unknown black Confederate sharpshooter at the Battle of Bethel Church, Virginia, June 10, 1861.[1656] The last gun fired at the Battle of Yorktown, Virginia (April 5 to May 4, 1862) was by a black Confederate soldier.[1657]

We even know of black female Rebel soldiers,[1658] some, like "Confederate Mary," who served as spies; some, like Hattie Carter, who served as ammunition runners; others who disguised themselves as males in order to get a shot at Lincoln's men and proudly defend Dixie, their beloved homeland. As part of their training, many all-black Confederate military units set up a dummy of Lincoln and practiced running it through with swords. The brag among black Confederate soldiers was: a Southern Negro can whip any Northern Negro—and the white Yankee to boot.[1659]

Countless numbers of Southern blacks voluntarily enlisted in the Confederate army and the Confederate navy, many in brigades that had their own voluntarily all-black musical bands.[1660] Thousands more ran away from their plantations, not to join the Yankees and kill Rebels, but to join the Rebels and kill Yankees. In Charleston, it was noted that there were thousands of blacks building fortifications for the Confederacy. Their main interest was not insurrection and flight northward, but the chance to take up arms and shoot some Yanks.[1661] In Memphis, Tennessee, hundreds of free blacks marched in a soldierly parade. As the *Memphis Avalanche* "joyously proclaimed":[1662]

> "A procession of several hundred stout Negro men, members of the 'domestic institution,' marched through our streets yesterday in military order, under command of Confederate officers. They were all armed and equipped with shovels, axes, blankets, etc. A merrier set were never seen. They were brimful of patriotism, shouting for Jeff. Davis and singing war songs." And four days later it again said: "Upward of one thousand Negroes, armed with spades and pickaxes, have passed through the city within the past few days. Their destination is unknown; but it is supposed that they are on their way to the other side of Jordan." The drafting of colored

---

1656. Barrow, Segars, and Rosenburg, BC, p. 19; Greenberg and Waugh, p. 385.
1657. Quarles, p. 266.
1658. Barrow, Segars, and Rosenburg, BC, p. 95.
1659. Greenberg and Waugh, pp. 373, 382, 387, 393.
1660. See e.g., Salley, Vol. 1, pp. 218-219.
1661. Rogers, AGA, p. 151.
1662. See the *Memphis Avalanche*, September 3, 1861.

men, and especially of slaves, by thousands to work on Confederate fortifications, was, in general, rather ostentatiously paraded through the earlier stages of the war. A paper published at Lynchburg, Virginia, had as early as April, chronicled the volunteered enrollment of seventy of the free Negroes of that place to fight in defense of their State; closing with, "Three cheers for the patriotic free Negroes of Lynchburg."[1663]

Granted pensions by the Confederate government during the War, afterwards thousands of former black Rebel soldiers attended Confederate reunions, where they were repeatedly recognized by their white comrades.[1664] What Rebel General John C. Breckinridge said of Tom Ferguson, one of the blacks who served under him, could have been said for nearly all: in every instance of danger and difficulty, Tom proved himself to be brave, honorable, and loyal.[1665]

Sixty-five blacks served with General Nathan Bedford Forrest, a half dozen acting as his personal armed guard.[1666] Of them all the gallant Rebel officer later proudly said:

> These boys stayed with me, drove my teams, and better Confederates did not live.[1667]

Distinguished African-American historian Benjamin Quarles maintains that the Southern black's contributions to the Confederate Cause were beyond counting,[1668] and for good reason. The support of countless Southern slaves (and also free Southern blacks) who served in the Confederate Army as teamsters, construction workers, drivers, cooks, nurses, body servants, and orderlies,[1669] not to mention the hundreds of thousands who served as soldiers,[1670] helped prolong the South's military efforts against Lincoln and his Northern invasion of Dixie.[1671]

1663. Alexander, p. 338.
1664. Historical note: the last reunion of the United Confederate Veterans took place in 1951. Three elderly Rebel soldiers attended. W. B. Garrison, CWTFB, p. 151.
1665. Quarles, p. 267.
1666. Ashdown and Caudill, pp. 184-185.
1667. Cincinnati *Commercial*, August 28, 1868.
1668. Quarles, p. 273.
1669. E. M. Thomas, p. 236.
1670. Barrow, Segars, and Rosenburg, BC and FC, passim. See also Segars and Barrow, BSCA, passim.
1671. Kennedy and Kennedy, SWR, p. 89.

Even prior to Lincoln's War, Southern blacks were eager to join the fight and defend the Confederate Cause. Free blacks in Charleston and Columbia, South Carolina, for example, sent a letter to Governor Francis W. Pickens that stated:

> We are by birth citizens of South Carolina. In our veins flows the blood of the white race—in some, half, in others, much more than half, white blood. Our attachments are with you; our hopes of safety and protection from you; our allegiance is due to South Carolina, and in her defense, we are willing to offer up our lives, and all that is dear to us. . . . We are willing to be assigned to any service where we can be most useful; and in tendering ourselves through you . . . we only ask that we be disposed of under your approval, and if ordered off [to battle], that our wives and children be taken care of and provided for.[1672]

In a letter home, here is what one black South Carolina servant had to say about being a Confederate soldier: "I've been havin' a great

time; seen plenty of beautiful sights and winsome gals; been on the battlefield too and heard the bullets whiz by my head. When the Yanks run off, they leave behind loads of supplies, more than I can tote. I've got it made since I joined up, and I'm ready to reenlist all over again. Anytime I gun down a Yankee the day is a success, and I usually get a watch and a pair of boots too. How other Negroes stay home while we're out here havin' fun, fightin' for the South, is impossible for me to comprehend!"[1673]

1672. E. Collins, p. 88.
1673. This letter appeared in the Charleston *Daily Courier*, May 29, 1863. My paraphrasal.

13

BLACKS IN LINCOLN'S ARMY

PART TWO

SADLY FOR THOSE AFRICAN-AMERICANS who joined Lincoln's army and navy, the times were not nearly as good. For one thing, at first, believing that blacks were too "lazy and stupid" to make good soldiers,[1674] Lincoln refused to let them serve as active combatants.[1675] For another, the fierce, haughty racism, and lack of humanity toward blacks, for which the North was justly famous, continued unabated. As such, many of the new black recruits were used as Union shock troops: sent into battle first, they spared white lives by absorbing the brunt of the attack.[1676]

The result? With 38,000 killed,[1677] the mortality rate among Lincoln's black soldiers was 40 percent higher than for white soldiers.[1678] But this was just how Lincoln planned it. As he himself once said:

> I thought that whatever negroes can be got to do as soldiers, leaves just so much less for white soldiers to do in saving the Union.[1679]

This included, of course, taking cold Confederate steel.

Others in Lincoln's party put it more bluntly. Samuel J.

1674. Wiley, SN, p. 301.
1675. Hacker, p. 584.
1676. Cornish, pp. 87, 269.
1677. Garraty and McCaughey, p. 254.
1678. Current, TC, s.v. "African-Americans in the Confederacy."
1679. Nicolay and Hay, ALCW, Vol. 2, p. 398.

Kirkwood, Iowa's governor, said that he would rather sacrifice the lives of "niggers" than the lives of the nation's white sons.[1680] Another man from Lincoln's party, Illinois Senator John A. "Black Jack" Logan, a Yankee general in the War, stated publicly that he would rather that "six niggers" be killed than a single white man.[1681] In the winter of 1864, the London *Telegraph* stated what the North has still yet to find the courage and honesty to acknowledge: not once did Lincoln ever consider arming Negroes on his own. It was only when he could not afford to lose anymore white soldiers that the decision came.[1682]

Lincoln later admitted that he relied much more heavily on his nearly 200,000 black soldiers than his 2,700,000 white soldiers. Why? Because, as he himself flatly stated, without our black soldiers the War would have stripped the North of much of its white population.[1683] Since his first priority was the preservation of the white race, white culture, and white jobs, he could simply not allow this to occur; thus the need for the Emancipation Proclamation and black enlistment.

Preferring to stand by the Confederacy and its cause (self-determination), the vast majority (95 percent) of Southern slaves had no use for a racist army like Lincoln's. Yet, he had decided he needed soldiers, warm bodies on the battlefield—whatever their color.

To this end, beginning in the summer of 1864, Lincoln sent 1,045 agents into occupied areas of Dixie to "round up" black recruits. Using barbaric methods nearly identical to those of bounty hunters and slave catchers,[1684] only 5,052 Southern blacks were enrolled in this manner,[1685] a failure of such magnitude that the original act that had authorized the procedure was repealed after only eight months. An embarrassed Yankee provost marshal general later drily remarked in his report:

> No material advantage to the service resulted from this undertaking. All, or nearly all, of the [Negro] recruits to be had in the rebel States were being obtained through the proper military officers and agents of the War Department. Without increasing the

---

1680. Voegeli, p. 102; L. Johnson, p. 134; Jimerson, p. 96.
1681. L. Johnson, p. 134.
1682. Durden, p. 133.
1683. Durden, pp. 76, 83-84.
1684. Cornish, p. 318.
1685. Quarles, p. 193.

number of men enlisted, the law enabled States in the North to lay claim to credits for the men enlisted in the South, and thus reduce their quota for draft. To obtain these credits local bounties were lavishly provided. They were unnecessary, and did not have the effect of increasing the number of [Negro] recruits obtained, but in many instances [they] enriched bounty brokers and corrupted military officers.[1686]

But black Southern resistance was no impediment to Lincoln. In fact, it only seemed to rouse the dictator in him. Those blacks who refused to enroll voluntarily were taken, at gunpoint, from the peace and safety of their farms and plantations, to the filth, hardships, and dangers of life on the battlefield.[1687] As a result, at least 50 percent of these reluctant soldiers died alone in muddy ditches fighting for the Yanks against their own native homeland: the South.[1688]

Those who resisted "involuntary enlistment" were usually shot or bayoneted on the spot, without trial. When blacks rebelled against the abuse of white Yankee soldiers, they were whipped.[1689] Those who deserted were mercilessly tracked through the wilderness by Northern bounty hunters and their hound dogs.[1690] Both white and black Union soldiers mistreated Southern slaves who remained loyal to Dixie, entering their homes, shooting bullets through their walls, overturning furniture, and stealing various personal items.[1691] A Northerner visiting South Carolina told how Southern blacks were "hunted like wild beasts and ruthlessly dragged from their families" by Yankee recruiters.[1692]

The Yankees' own *Official Records* reveal what most Northerners and scallywags will still not admit. In December 1864, a disgusted Yankee General Rufus Saxton reported on Lincoln's racist and often violent "recruiting tactics." Southern blacks, Saxton said,

> were hunted to their hiding places by armed parties of their own people, and, if found, compelled to enlist. This conscription order is still in force. Men have been seized and forced to enlist who had

---

1686. *ORA*, Ser. 3, Vol. 5, p. 662.
1687. L. Johnson, p. 134.
1688. Pollard, SHW, Vol. 2, pp. 196-198.
1689. Wiley, SN, pp. 241, 309-310, 317.
1690. L. Johnson, p. 134.
1691. Henry, ATSF, p. 248.
1692. L. Johnson, p. 134.

large families of young children dependent upon them for support and fine crops of cotton and corn nearly ready for harvest, without an opportunity of making provision for the one or securing the other.

Three [black] boys, one only fourteen years of age, were seized in a field where they were at work and sent to a regiment serving in a distant part of the department without the knowledge or consent of their parents.

A [black] man on his way to enlist as a volunteer was stopped by a recruiting party. He told them where he was going and was passing on when he was again ordered to halt. He did not stop and was shot dead, and was left where he fell. It is supposed the [Union] soldiers desired to bring him in and get the bounty offered for bringing in recruits.

Another [black] man who had a wife and family was shot as he was entering a boat to fish, on the pretense that he was a deserter. He fell in the water and was left. His wound, though very severe, was not mortal. An employee [black] in the [U.S.] Quartermasters Department was taken, and without being allowed to communicate with the quartermaster or settle his accounts or provide for his family, was taken to Hilton Head and enrolled, although he had a certificate of exemption from the military service from a medical officer.

I protested against the order of the major-general commanding (General Foster) and sent him reports of these proceedings, but had no power to prevent them. The order has never to my knowledge been revoked.[1693]

Of Lincoln's "shot-gun policy" of coercive black enlistment, it was said that it always succeeded in getting his conscript.[1694] What the president did not seem to grasp, however, was that the very definition of recruitment insinuates *voluntary* enlistment. Thus, many of Lincoln's black "recruits" were actually more akin to prisoners of war than enlisted soldiers. Yet, he still counted them as legitimate servicemen, which, of course, greatly over exaggerated the number of "black Union soldiers."

Speaking before the Confederate Congress on December 7, 1863, President Jefferson Davis commented on the Yankees' conduct toward Southern blacks; or as he put it, the "unrelenting warfare [that has] been waged by these pretended friends of human rights and liberties against the

---

1693. *ORA*, Ser. 3, Vol. 4, p. 1029.
1694. J. M. McPherson, NCW, p. 170.

unfortunate negroes":

> Wherever the enemy have been able to gain access, they have forced into the ranks of their army every able-bodied [black] man that they could seize, and have either left the aged, the women, and the children to perish by starvation, or have gathered them into camps, where they have been wasted by a frightful mortality. Without clothing or shelter, often without food, incapable, without supervision, of taking the most ordinary precaution against disease, these helpless dependents, accustomed to have their wants supplied by the foresight of their masters, are being rapidly exterminated wherever brought in contact with the [Yankee] invaders. By the Northern man, on whose deep rooted prejudices no kindly restraining influence is exercised, they are treated with aversion and neglect. There is little hazard in predicting that, in all localities where the enemy have gained a temporary foothold, the negroes, who under our care increased six fold in number since their importation into the [Yankee] colonies of Great Britain, will have been reduced by mortality during the war to not more than one half their previous number.
>
> Information on this subject is derived not only from our own observation and from the reports of the negroes who succeeded in escaping from the enemy, but full confirmation is afforded by statements published in the Northern journals, humane persons engaged in making appeals to the charitable for aid in preventing the ravages of disease, exposure, and starvation among the negro women and children who are crowded into [Union] encampments.[1695]

After their violent forced enlistment, most Southern blacks fled from Lincoln's armies at their first opportunity,[1696] back to the comfort, warmth, security, and domesticity of their homes in the South.[1697] The Yankee top brass was not amused. While stationed at Camden, South Carolina, one of Sherman's officers, Lieutenant Thomas J. Myers, wrote to his wife on February 26, 1865:

> The damned [Southern] niggers, as a general rule, preferred to stay at home, particularly when they found out that we [Yanks] only

---
1695. F. Moore, pp. 278-279.
1696. Wiley, SN, pp. 12-14.
1697. Gragg, p. 85.

wanted the able bodied men (and to tell you the truth the youngest and best looking women).[1698]

Northern newspapers too were confused by the homesick Southern black's propensity for fleeing back to Dixie whenever the chance arose. In the summer of 1862, Rhode Island's *Providence Post* wrote that most Southern blacks evinced no friendliness toward the Yankees whatsoever. And neither had they attempted to flee north out of Dixie, or attack and overwhelm their white owners. In fact, the few who had crossed over into Union lines showed no urge to work or fight; only a desire to live off Northern whites, for their hearts were with the Southern Confederacy.[1699]

Elizabeth Keckley, a *Northern* slave who worked for the Lincolns at the White House after she purchased her freedom, explained the Southern black attachment to Dixie:

> Well, the emancipated [Southern] slaves, in coming North, left old associations behind them, and the love for the past was so strong that they could not find much beauty in the new life so suddenly opened to them. Thousands of the disappointed, huddled together in camps, fretted and pined like children for the 'good old times.' In visiting them in the interests of the Relief Society of which I was president, they would crowd around me with pitiful stories of distress. Often I heard them declare that they would rather go back to slavery in the South, and be with their old masters, than to enjoy the freedom of the North. I believe they were sincere in these declarations . . .[1700]

Blacks who survived the Yankees' brutal "enlistment" process and could not escape back South, did not have it easy. Even after they were allowed to become combatants and carry weapons, they were still prohibited from serving as officers. Instead, Lincoln put them to work as garrison troops, tedious guard duty watching over Union forts, stations, and prisons, just as he had promised to do in his Final Emancipation Proclamation.[1701]

1698. H. C. Dean, p. 83.
1699. Barrow, Segars, and Rosenburg, BC, p. 15.
1700. Keckley, p. 140.
1701. Nicolay and Hay, ALCW, Vol. 2, p. 288.

The reason? Neither he nor his officers felt that blacks were intelligent or trustworthy enough to hold important positions, nor did they have any confidence that blacks could lead assaults.[1702] (Compare this to the Confederacy where, at the very beginning of the War, in April 1861, blacks were appointed commissioned officers in Louisiana.)[1703]

Black soldiers, Lincoln believed, would not be much of a bother after emancipation and enlistment,[1704] except that they might lose their weapons, by then a rare and valuable item.[1705] As a hesitant Lincoln put it to a group of abolitionist clergyman on September 13, 1862, a few days prior to issuing his Preliminary Emancipation Proclamation:

> . . . I am not so sure we could do much with the blacks. If we were to arm them, I fear that in a few weeks the arms would be in the hands of the rebels; and, indeed, thus far we have not had arms enough to equip our white troops.[1706]

The thousands of blacks Lincoln refused to arm after emancipation were herded like cattle onto "government plantations," Southern farms whose peaceful and harmless white owners had been driven off or killed,[1707] and whose land and wealth the socialistic president then redistributed to affluent Yankee businessmen.[1708] Here so-called "freed" black men, women, and children, were put to work doing ordinary labor, the same drudgery they had performed previously as slaves (mainly laundry, cooking, and cleaning), and from which Lincoln was allegedly trying to free them. A ten-hour work day, twenty-six days a month, was mandatory. The pay was $10 a month ($0.26 a day, or 2.6 cents an hour). "Insubordination" was punishable by "imprisonment in darkness on bread and water."[1709] This was Lincoln's idea of "emancipation."

Many "freed" blacks were simply returned to the status of

1702. Cartmell, p. 141.
1703. Shenkman and Reiger, p. 105.
1704. Leech, p. 310.
1705. L. Johnson, p. 131.
1706. Nicolay and Hay, ALCW, Vol. 2, p. 235.
1707. Pollard, SHW, Vol. 2, p. 198; L. Johnson, p. 135. For official reference to Lincoln's "government plantations," see, for example, ORA, Ser. 1, Vol. 26, Pt. 1, p. 764. See also Nicolay and Hay, ALCW, Vol. 2, pp. 471-472.
1708. Seabrook, CFF, p. 288.
1709. ORA, Ser. 1, Vol. 15, p. 595. See also pp. 593-594.

domestics and body servants,[1710] the latter being slave-like personal attendants whose only job was to wait on Yankee officers.[1711] Grant, who, like Lincoln, was not fond of African-Americans (once, after having excluded them from his picket lines, Grant was harshly reprimanded by Halleck),[1712] was known for intentionally keeping his black soldiers "in the rear, guarding his wagon trains."[1713] Most other blacks in this particular group drove supply wagons, cooked for white soldiers, or worked on fortifications.[1714] This is not what they had signed up for.

This slave-like treatment of newly freed blacks was no accident. As mentioned, Lincoln had carefully worded his Emancipation Proclamation so that black soldiers would remain subservient to white soldiers. Rather than warmly welcoming blacks into the Union military as legitimate armed combatants, Lincoln's edict states that

> . . . such [black] persons of suitable condition, will be received into the armed service of the United States to garrison forts, positions, stations, and other places, and to man vessels of all sorts in said service.[1715]

This, in essence, confined most black soldiers to "post and garrison duty," if they were lucky.[1716]

The rest could expect to work as common laborers, digging ditches, constructing bridges, filling sandbags, unloading ships, and draining swamps.[1717] Others would end up working as laundresses, longshoremen, commissary workers, medical assistants, masons, carpenters, blacksmiths, orderlies, pioneers, or spies, almost anything except armed soldiers. This was, after all, as both Lincoln and the U.S. Congress maintained, a "white man's war."[1718] A newly "freed" black servant once complained to Mary Chesnut about the treatment he and other freedmen were receiving from Lincoln and his Yankee officers: they

---

1710. Quarles, p. 94.
1711. Wiley, SN, pp. 200-201.
1712. See *ORA*, Ser. 1, Vol. 24, Pt. 3, pp. 156-157.
1713. Woodward, p. 279.
1714. Cornish, p. xv.
1715. Nicolay and Hay, ALCW, Vol. 2, p. 288.
1716. Cornish, p. 240.
1717. Quarles, p. 205.
1718. Buckley, p. 82; Barney, p. 128.

have removed the chains from our feet, but left them on our wrists, he told her bitterly.[1719]

Despite black resistance to Lincoln's idea of "colored enlistment," he had the support of most of his party members. One Northern senator later put the matter this way:

> The shovel and the spade and the ax have ruined thousands of the young [white] men of the country, and sent hundreds of them to their graves.
> . . . we could have employed thousands of colored men at low rates of wages to do that ditching, and thus saved the health, the strength, and the lives of our brave [white] soldiers.[1720]

Lincoln could not have agreed more. But his prejudice did not stop there.

After exploiting "freed" African-Americans for little more than cannon fodder and servile labor, he ordered all black troops to be segregated[1721] and led by white officers[1722]—an order followed closely at conflicts like the Battle of Nashville.[1723] These were the fortunate ones.

As mentioned, Lincoln used most of the blacks in his military, not for soldiering, but as road and bridge builders, chefs, and as "officers' servants"—in the North a euphemism for "slaves."[1724] Some officers, such as General Benjamin F. Butler—who, like Lincoln, was at first against Negro enlistment in the Union military—openly used the Southern blacks they came across as a slave work force for their own army projects.[1725] These projects, of course, required heavy labor and other monotonous mundane duties, the exact type of work from which Lincoln wanted his

---

1719. See Chesnut, MCCW, p. 829.
1720. *The Congressional Globe*, 37th Congress, 2nd Session, p. 3203.
1721. Barrow, Segars, and Rosenburg, BC, p. 4; Mullen, p. 31.
1722. L. Johnson, p. 134.
1723. Horn, DBN, p. 74. Thanks, in great part to Lincoln, neither the U.S. military or the federal civil service were desegregated until 1948. It was President Harry Truman's Executive Order 9981 that finally put an official end to Lincoln's institutionalized white military racism. Adams and Sanders, p. 269. Sadly, Truman's integration policy was not implemented immediately: it was not until half way through the Korean War (1950-1953) that American forces became officially integrated for the first time since the Revolutionary War. Thus the Vietnam War (1959-1975) became the first conflict in which whites and blacks served as equals from beginning to end. Buckley, p. xx. This is the pitiful legacy of the so-called "Great Emancipator," a man who failed to do a single thing during his presidency to promote, create, or maintain racial equality within his military.
1724. Simmons, s.v. "Negro troops"; L. Johnson, p. 135.
1725. Hansen, p. 168.

white soldiers spared.[1726]

As black soldiers who were segregated from whites, Lincoln had them named the United States Colored Troops (USCT),[1727] a title never officially used by the Confederacy, whose military was fully integrated from day one. Thus, the 300,000 Southern blacks who eventually fought for the South[1728] joined seamlessly with the Confederate military's 1,000,000 European-Americans,[1729] 70,000 Native-Americans, 60,000 Latin-Americans,[1730] 50,000 foreigners,[1731] 12,000 Jewish-Americans,[1732] and 10,000 Asian-Americans.[1733] As in Southern society itself, there was no segregation among the South's military forces.[1734] For unlike in the North, Southern troops neither wanted it or needed it.

Appallingly—but perhaps not surprisingly with white supremacist Lincoln acting as commander-in-chief—white Yankee troops sometimes used the fog of war to kill their own fellow black soldiers.[1735] Apparently they saw this as an efficient and safe method of disposing of those whom Lincoln liked to refer to as an "inferior race."[1736]

One such incident occurred at the Battle of the Crater on July 30, 1864, at Petersburg, Virginia, a conflict that pitted Yankee General Ambrose E. Burnside[1737] against Rebel General Robert E. Lee.

Even before the fight began, many of Burnside's white soldiers had expressed the sentiment that they would not be "caught in the company of niggers." Thus, when in the heat of battle their black comrades were driven back into a thirty-foot deep bomb crater by the Confederates, they were met with a "fate worse than death": waiting white Yankee soldiers bayoneted them, then later bragged lustfully of the

---

1726. See Nicolay and Hay, ALCW, Vol. 2, p. 398.
1727. Faust, s.v. "black soldiers."
1728. Barrow, Segars, and Rosenburg, BC, p. 97; Hinkle, p. 106; *The United Daughters of the Confederacy Magazine*, Vols. 54-55, 1991, p. 32.
1729. C. Eaton, HSC, p. 93.
1730. Hinkle, p. 108. See also Quintero, Gonzales, and Velazquez, passim.
1731. Lonn, p. 218.
1732. Rosen, p. 161.
1733. Hinkle, 108; Blackerby, passim.
1734. C. Johnson, pp. 206-207.
1735. L. Johnson, p. 134.
1736. See Nicolay and Hay, ALCW, Vol. 1, p. 284; Basler, ALSW, pp. 400, 402, 403-404; Stern, pp. 492-493; Holzer, pp. 189, 251.
1737. Owing to his voluminous muttonchops, Burnside—who was relieved of his command after the disastrous Battle of the Crater—went on to give his name to the male facial hair style, sideburns.

murders.[1738]

Of this outrage Yankee General Benjamin F. Butler later lamented that "in the [Union] Army of the Potomac negro troops were thought of no value . . ."[1739] Indeed, some 1,327 black Yankee soldiers were killed at the Battle of the Crater, the largest single loss of African-Americans during the entire War—due, in part, to the racism of Lincoln's white soldiers. Yet despite their valor and the great sacrifice of life, white Northerners blamed Burnside's black soldiers for the Yankee defeat.[1740] Grant referred to the battle as the "saddest affair" of the entire War. Not because his white soldiers mercilessly slaughtered their black comrades, but because the Union lost a total of 4,000 men against the South's 1,500.[1741]

A war correspondent for the New York *Evening Post* described what he witnessed in the typical Yankee army camp: most of the white Yankee soldiers and their officers routinely approached black soldiers in the harshest, most vulgar, and most inhumane manner, only speaking to them with depraved curse words and vicious criticisms.[1742]

Lincoln's navy was no less difficult for African-Americans. Aboard the USS *Constellation*, for example, a white eyewitness reported that white Yankee sailors routinely referred to their fellow African soldiers as "God damn nigger," "bitch," and "black dog," and that they constantly shoved and "kicked them around." While this is not unexpected, considering what we know of white Northern racism at the time, what is unexpected is the fact that only three of the crew of thirty-six were white.[1743]

Yes, life was not easy for blacks in Lincoln's military forces, as another case, that of Alexander T. Augusta, illustrates. A highly trained physician from Virginia, he was one of only eight black doctors commissioned by the U.S. government during the entire War.[1744]

After receiving his commission in April 1863, Augusta was on his way to Baltimore, Maryland, to begin his service, when a group of

---

1738. Cornish, p. 276.
1739. B. F. Butler, p. 721.
1740. Buckley, pp. 105-106.
1741. Current, TC, s.v. "Petersburg Campaign."
1742. Channing, p. 129.
1743. E. L. Jordan, p. 142.
1744. G. W. Williams, HNTWR, p. 143.

Northern whites assaulted him on a train. After having his uniform defaced, he was able to escape to a nearby military post, where he reported the incident. He was then escorted back to the train under a heavily armed military squad and a detachment of detectives, who protected Augusta the rest of his journey with drawn pistols. This was only the beginning of the doctor's troubles, however.[1745]

In February 1864, now head surgeon at Camp Stanton, Maryland, Augusta was shocked to learn that his white assistants had written a private letter to Lincoln requesting that his position be terminated. Why? Because of the "unexpected, unusual, and most unpleasant relationship in which we have been placed." In other words, they did not want to serve under a black man. Lincoln, of course, obliged the whites, and Augusta was quickly expelled from Camp Stanton and put on "detached service."

The black physician was appalled once again when he discovered that he was to be paid the same amount as a lowly black private ($7 a month). Under Lincoln's racist, unequal pay system, this was $6 less than what even white privates were paid ($13 a month). After numerous letters of complaint, the U.S. government eventually agreed to pay Augusta according to his rank—one year later.[1746] If this is how Lincoln treated the highest ranking black officer in the Union military, it is not surprising that he treated all his other black soldiers so poorly.[1747]

After earlier promising equal pay,[1748] Lincoln's order (via the Militia Act of July 17, 1862)[1749] that black soldiers receive half the pay of white soldiers,[1750] infuriated both blacks and abolitionists.[1751] This was a "necessary concession" to white Northern racism,[1752] Lincoln explained to a stunned Frederick Douglass in the summer of 1863.[1753] Many of Lincoln's black soldiers were *never* paid. Former slave Susie King Taylor wrote:

> I was the wife of one of those men who did not get a penny for

---

1745. Sterling, pp. 333-334.
1746. Quarles, pp. 203-204.
1747. Buckley, p. 93.
1748. *ORA*, Ser. 3, Vol. 3, p. 252.
1749. Cornish, p. 46.
1750. Wiley, SN, pp. 322-323; Mullen, p. 25.
1751. See Cornish, pp. 181-196.
1752. Douglass, LTFD, p. 303.
1753. Barney, pp. 146-147.

eighteen months for their services, only their rations and clothing.[1754]

There was also the issue of white recruitment: Lincoln and his cabinet feared that granting equal pay to black soldiers would discourage Northern whites from enlisting,[1755] most who did not want to fight next to blacks anyway, however noble the Union cause.[1756]

Adding fuel to the fire, black Yankee officers, those rare few that existed,[1757] were paid the same as white Yankee privates.[1758] Yet when the Confederacy also finally officially enlisted blacks, March 23, 1863, they were immediately integrated and given equal pay and equal treatment with white soldiers.[1759]

Resistance by white Union soldiers to black officers was so severe that even Lincoln's 100 black commissioned officers,[1760] representing just 0.005 percent of the entire Union military of 2,000,000 men, were ultimately replaced by whites.[1761] General Nathaniel P. Banks discusses this topic in an official field report dated February 12, 1863. Speaking of the Union's all-black 1st, 2nd, and 3rd, Louisiana Native Guards (infantry), Banks writes:

> The three regiments first named have ten companies each; their field and staff officers are white men, but they have negro company officers, whom I am replacing, as vacancies occur, by white ones, being entirely satisfied that the appointment of colored officers is detrimental to the service.
>
> It converts what, with judicious management and good officers, is capable of much usefulness into a source of constant embarrassment and annoyance. It demoralizes both the white troops and the negroes. The officers of the Fourth Regiment will

---

1754. S. K. Taylor, p. 51.
1755. Quarles, pp. 200-201.
1756. Page Smith, p. 308.
1757. Though 5,000 white Union officers eventually commanded all-black troops, only "about one hundred" blacks ever held Union officer commissions during Lincoln's War, and this despite the apathy, protests, and even outright opposition of Lincoln and his War Department. Cornish, pp. 214-215.
1758. Alotta, p. 27. Lincoln paid his black soldiers $7 a month; he paid his white soldiers $13 a month. Quarles, p. 200.
1759. E. M. Thomas, p. 297.
1760. Cornish, p. 214.
1761. Wiley, LBY, p. 313; J. M. McPherson, NCW, pp. 238-239.

be white men.[1762]

Though blacks seem to have been more readily accepted into Lincoln's navy than in his army, as noted, they were still confronted by rank bigotry from all sides. At the start of Yankee black enlistment, for instance, African-American sailors were not allowed to rise above the lowest rank, known as "Boy."[1763]

When Governor John A. Andrew of Massachusetts went to Lincoln to ask that he be allowed to grant qualified blacks military commissions, the president said absolutely not. As usual, the reason he gave for this decision was that the racist Northern public would not accept them.[1764] However, this was only partially true, for Lincoln himself would also not accept black officers.

Let us note here that unlike Lincoln's black soldiers—most who were violently forced into service, Southern blacks were only recruited voluntarily, "with their own consent."[1765] And while Lincoln's black soldiers served as *freed*men, Confederate black soldiers served as *free*men, an enormous difference to all concerned.[1766] All except for Lincoln, that is.

Though he made many promises to his black soldiers regarding the inequality of their pay, Lincoln did little or nothing to fulfill them, and full and equal pay was not granted to black Yankee soldiers until *after* the War. The money involved was so small that there is only one way to explain the procrastination: Northern white racism.[1767] Just as a fish rots from the head down, that racism, of course, started at the top—with the president.

Lincoln was certainly his own worst enemy in this regard, for though he desperately needed blacks to join, most refused the "offer." Even Frederick Douglass, who constantly encouraged other blacks to become soldiers, had little success at this game. After he gave a recruitment speech before a black audience in New York City, for example, only one man came forward. Insulted, Douglass told the crowd that he felt sorry for them, insinuating that they were cowards. But it was

---

1762. *ORA*, Ser. 3, Vol. 3, p. 46.
1763. Buckley, p. 83.
1764. Pearson, Vol. 2, pp. 70-74.
1765. See W. C. Davis, JDMH, p. 599; Quarles, p. 279; Durden, pp. 203, 269, 272.
1766. E. M. Thomas, pp. 296-297.
1767. See Cornish, pp. 184, 192, 195.

not cowardice. It was Lincoln's racist military policies that made many blacks think twice about enlisting. A man named Robert Johnson stood up, faced Douglass, and said of "the Negroes of New York":

> If the [U.S.] government wanted their services, let it guarantee to them all the rights of citizens and soldiers, and, instead of one man, he would insure them 5,000 men in twenty days.[1768]

Johnson was entirely correct. But guaranteeing black soldiers full civil rights was something that neither Lincoln, his cabinet, nor most of his officers were prepared to do, which is precisely why most African-Americans had to be physically forced into Yankee military service.

Douglass himself eventually conceded that the trouble lay not with blacks or cowardice, but with Lincoln and his racism. Why should Negroes enlist when the U.S. military is so prejudiced against them?, he asked the president rhetorically.[1769]

In October 1862, a Northern reporter for the New York *Tribune* visited Union troops in North Carolina and wrote the following report on the condition of black Yankee soldiers. The situation of the miserable lowly Negroes, he said,

> is such as should excite the sympathy of every Christian man. I am sorry to say that they are treated with great sternness and severity amounting to positive cruelty, by our own soldiers who seem to regard them as hardly better than beasts. Not a few of our [Union] officers conduct themselves in the most unfeeling manner toward these unfortunate creatures . . .[1770]

Naturally, Lincoln's black soldiers were extremely displeased with the entire situation, and many protested. At least eighteen of those who did were charged with "mutiny," and executed by hanging or firing squad. Amazingly, these executions went on even after Lincoln's death and the War had ended. As late as December 1, 1865, for example, six black privates accused of mutiny (i.e., for objecting to Lincoln's racist pay scale) were rounded up and killed by musketry at Fernandina, Florida.

1768. *The Liberator*, May 22, 1863.
1769. *Douglass' Monthly*, March 1863, Vol. 5, p. 802.
1770. *Charlotte Daily Bulletin*, November 13, 1862.

This was a full year-and-a-half after the U.S. Congress authorized retroactive equal pay for black soldiers in June 1864.[1771]

A final indignity: under Lincoln, the "great friend of the black man," African-American soldiers were also denied the bounties,[1772] pensions, bonuses, and support for dependents accorded to whites.[1773] They were also given inferior or obsolete weapons, some completely unworkable.[1774]

Lincoln's black soldiers were even refused equal medical care. According to the president's rules, medical supplies and medical attention were to go first to injured European-American soldiers. As a result, of the 178,975 black soldiers in Lincoln's three million-man army, 35,130 died of sickness and disease alone, a staggeringly high percentage (20 percent). As if this type of Northern prejudice was not enough, Lincoln made sure that most black units were stationed in out-of-the-way sectors, and that their white officers were those judged unfit for service in more vital departments.[1775] One wonders how many black Yankee soldiers finally realized that it was Lincoln who was their enemy, not the South.

Throughout the War, despite the "elevated" standing that Lincoln's all-black Yankee troops had acquired over their former status as "subhumans," they continued to suffer racial discrimination, humiliation, abuse, and harassment at the hands of fellow whites,[1776] for few Northerners liked the idea of working alongside the common former slave.[1777] Racial tension in Lincoln's armies would only deteriorate from this point on.

Halfway through the conflict, in a publicly acknowledged attempt to procure more soldiers, Lincoln, as we have seen, added insult to injury by issuing his Final Emancipation Proclamation. After being told of the edict, along with Lincoln's new black enrollment policies, the great majority of his white soldiers, who vociferously described themselves as "anti-abolitionist," hissed and booed, and officers reported widespread

---

1771. Alotta, pp. 26-28.
1772. Leech, p. 312.
1773. Current, TC, s.v. "African Americans in the Confederacy."
1774. Quarles, pp. 204-205.
1775. Cartmell, pp. 144, 145.
1776. Faust, s.v. "black soldiers."
1777. Simmons, s.v. "Negro troops"; Quarles, p. 64.

"demoralization" among their men.[1778]

One of the most demoralized of Lincoln's commanders was Yankee General Joseph "Fighting Joe" Hooker,[1779] who sent the president a scathing letter about his Emancipation Proclamation, reporting that much of the Union army was solidly against it. Wrote Hooker:

> At that time . . . a majority of the officers, especially those high in rank, were hostile to the policy of the Government in the conduct of the war. The emancipation proclamation had been published a short time before, and a large element of the army had taken sides antagonistic to it, declaring that they would never have embarked in the war had they anticipated the action of the Government.[1780]

Even in those troops where abolition sentiment was deepest, the average Yankee soldier was hesitant to interfere with slavery, an institution that he was used to and which he knew to be legal under the Constitution. So accepted was slavery among most Union officers that they nearly always allowed Southern slaveholders into their lines to search for runaway slaves.[1781]

Another disgruntled Yankee general, the infamous Fitz John Porter,[1782] wrote that Lincoln's Emancipation Proclamation was widely jeered throughout the Union army, inducing disgust, dissatisfaction, and words of infidelity toward the U.S. president that were very close to treasonous.[1783]

Shortly after the Battle of Sharpsburg, one of the president's Yankee soldiers wrote that Lincoln's proclamation was denounced by most men of the Northern army, for none wanted to fight for the black man, but only to preserve the Union. Subdue the Rebs first, talk about the civil rights of the "nigger" afterward, they fumed.[1784]

In July 1862, a Yankee soldier from New York remarked that just

---

1778. Page Smith, p. 308.
1779. C. Adams, p. 134.
1780. Henderson, Vol. 2, p. 411.
1781. Leech, p. 291.
1782. Lincoln formally dismissed Porter from military service in January 1863, over problems at the Battle of Second Manassas, on August 29, 1862. As usual, Lincoln acted incorrectly. In 1879, fourteen years after his death, more intelligent individuals prevailed: Porter's dismissal was revoked and he was reinstated in the Federal army. J. S. Bowman, CWDD, s.v. "10 January 1863"; "21 January 1863."
1783. Donald, L, p. 385.
1784. B. Thornton, p.176.

about everyone in the U.S. army was infuriated with Lincoln and the Negro issue, and that most wanted nothing more than to put a noose around the neck of Northern abolitionist Horace Greeley.[1785] Another Union soldier said I really don't care what happens to the "Niggar," and I'm certainly not going to risk my life for him. I'd rather fight him than Johnny Reb. Yet another U.S. serviceman wrote: no doubt the ideal way to solve the dilemma of the black man would be to shoot all of them.[1786] One of the many thousands of Yankees who defected over to the Confederate side announced: I'd just as soon live with Satan in Hell than lift a finger to free the slaves.[1787]

In early 1863, not long after Lincoln issued his Emancipation Proclamation, a Yankee soldier from his home state, Illinois, expressed the following sentiment: I have suffered long and hard through this war, all for the "poor nigger." Yet I see no evidence that my suffering has helped him in anyway.[1788] Not atypical was the comment of a New England soldier. In 1863, while stationed in New Orleans, he wrote to his brother: I was out walking today and came upon a small black baby crawling along. My first instinct was to crush the horrid thing to death, there and then.[1789]

In the summer of 1862, some of McClellan's staff "seriously discussed" marching to Washington to "intimidate the president," in the hopes that he would refrain from interfering with slavery and simply bring the War to a quick and peaceful close. Union General John Pope noted that among the Army of the Potomac there were frequent comments made about Lincoln's flaws and the possibility of replacing him with someone more able.[1790]

The president's military men were not the only ones disappointed with his new focus on abolishing slavery for the sole purpose of enlisting blacks. Northern Catholics—who had once said that abolitionist Garrison was a "hoary hypocrite" who should be immediately sent to Africa where he could live in "love and harmony with the wild negroes"[1791]—were highly displeased as well. New York's Archbishop John Hughes declared

---

1785. Murphy, p. 86.
1786. Barrow, Segars, and Rosenburg, BC, p. 45.
1787. E. L. Jordan, p. 141.
1788. Wiley, LBY, p. 281.
1789. Barrow, Segars, and Rosenburg, BC, p. 45.
1790. Donald, L, p. 385.
1791. Nye, p. 140.

that he and his flock, along with the overwhelming majority of Union troops, had no intention of fighting a bloody and costly war just to satisfy a group of rabid Yankee abolitionists.[1792]

White racism among Lincoln's soldiers got so out of hand that eventually Lincoln had to legally ban the use of the "n" word in the military, the "demeaning punishment" of blacks, and any and all "insulting language" directed toward black soldiers.[1793] Yankee General Lorenzo Thomas, for example, promised white soldiers a quick dismissal from the army if they persisted in abusing and tormenting black soldiers. The threat had little impact and Thomas ended up removing a number of white Union officers who refused to treat blacks equitably.[1794]

Yankee slave owner General Ulysses S. Grant, no friend of the black man, faced a similar problem in his ranks. It became so serious that on April 22, 1863, just four months after the emancipation was issued, he had to send out a general order demanding

> that all commanders will especially exert themselves in carrying out the policy of the Administration, not only in organizing colored regiments and rendering them efficient, but also in removing prejudice against them.[1795]

Lincoln still had a long way to go to get white Northerners used to the idea of fighting with black soldiers.

None understood this more perfectly than Southern blacks themselves, particularly those who Lincoln had violently dragooned into his military.

James Ward, a former black servant from Virginia, risked his life fleeing back home through Yankee lines in order to warn other slaves about the racist horrors of life as a black Union soldier in Lincoln's army. Among these he related how he and other blacks were continually forced to the front lines in the heat of battle, while whites who had been ahead of them were allowed to fall back. I'd rather be owned by the cruelest slaver in the South, Ward attested, than live free in the North. They call

---

1792. Foote, Vol. 1, p. 538.
1793. Page Smith, p. 309.
1794. Cornish, pp. 118-119.
1795. *ORA*, Ser. 1, Vol. 24, Pt. 3, p. 220.

this freedom, but if it is, I'd prefer slavery any day, thank you.[1796]

While Lincoln was busy instituting new martial laws to protect his black soldiers from racial abuse, Northern white soldiers, appalled and nauseated by his emancipation, began deserting in great numbers. At the same time, white Yankee officers began resigning their commands, complaining that leading black troops was less prestigious than leading white ones (white officers of white troops in particular looked down their noses at white officers of black troops).[1797]

One of the inevitable results of Lincoln's racist military policies was that many black Union regiments eventually came to be led by white privates, for few white officers could be found who were willing to command them.[1798] Those privates who signed up usually did so, not out of sympathy for the black man, but because an automatic promotion came with the position.[1799] As Greeley noted:

> There were few, if any, instances of a White sergeant or corporal whose dignity or whose nose revolted at the proximity of Blacks as private soldiers, if he might secure a lieutenancy by deeming them not unsavory, or not quite intolerably so; while there is no case on record where a soldier deemed fit for a captaincy in a colored regiment rejected it and clung to the ranks, in deference to his invincible antipathy to 'niggers.'[1800]

A typical example was the case of white New Yorker Daniel Ullmann. In January 1863, the non-racist Ullmann was appointed brigadier general and ordered to raise an all-black Louisiana volunteer infantry for the Union. After acquiring the proper number of black soldiers, he set out to find officers for the unit, who, by Lincoln's order, had to be white. Ullmann found it to be an impossible task and his quest nearly failed for lack of interest. Outraged, he later wrote that many Yankee officers and volunteers absolutely refused to have anything to do with the "Negro service," even if it meant a promotion.[1801]

On December 4, 1863, from Port Hudson, Louisiana, General

1796. Charlottesville, Virginia, *Daily Chronicle*, March 30, 1864.
1797. J. M. McPherson, NCW, p. 195.
1798. Simmons, s.v. "Negro troops."
1799. W. B. Garrison, CWC, p. 105; Quarles, p. 197.
1800. Greeley, AC, Vol. 2, p. 527.
1801. Cornish, p. 101.

Ullmann wrote to Senator Henry Wilson concerning the difficulties he was having due to the overt Yankee racism coming from Washington:

> I have long had it in view to write to you, as the head of the Military Committee of the Senate, on a subject of grave importance, namely, the organization of colored troops.
>
> You are well acquainted with my status in the premises. I have had every opportunity during the last seven months to examine this policy in all its bearings.
>
> The first point to settle is whether it be intended to make these men soldiers or mere laborers; if the latter, the mode pursued is the right one, and I have nothing more to say. If the former, then there are some vital changes to be made. I fear that many high officials outside of Washington have no other intention than that these men shall be used as diggers and drudges. Now, I am well satisfied from my seven months intercourse with them that with just treatment they can be made soldiers of as high an average as any in the world. Their qualifications in most respects are equal to any and in one superior, to wit, their habit of subordination. All that is necessary is to give them a fair chance, which has not been done. Since I have been in command such has been the amount of fatigue work thrust upon the organization that it has been with the utmost difficulty that any time could be set aside for drill. Months have passed at times without the possibility of any drill at all. The amount of actual labor performed by these men has been enormous. Much of it was done by them in the trenches during the siege of this place, whilst more exposed to the severe fire of the enemy than any other of our troops. They discharged their duties with cheerfulness, alacrity, and marked courage.
>
> Then, again, I have been forced to put in their hands arms almost entirely unserviceable, and in other respects their equipments have been of the poorest kind. But there is another injustice done to these men, which they appreciate as well and feel as keenly as anybody. It is a mistake to think that these poor fellows do not understand these matters just as well as we do. They are all the constant subject of conversation among them. The point is this: While other soldiers are fed, clothed, have superior arms, and are paid $13 per month, and the non-commissioned officers receive, respectively, $17 and $20, they are fed, have unserviceable arms, and receive $10 per month, from which is deducted $3 for clothing, and no addition whatever for non-commissioned officers, and have no clothing allowance.
>
> Now, general, I assure you that these poor fellows, with all their warm, enthusiastic patriotism—and it is even greater than

that of most other troops—are deeply sensible to this gross injustice. It breaks down their 'morale,' and to an extent which I, who command and come into constant contact with them, daily deplore. . . .

There is one other notion that must be eradicated, i.e., that anybody can command negro troops. So far from this, they require a superior grade of officers, though I well know that those prophets who declare that negroes never will make soldiers are striving to force their prophecies to work out their own fulfillment by appointing ignoramuses and boors to be officers over men who are as keensighted as any to notice the shortcomings of those placed over them. Men have been made field officers in this section who are not fit to be non-commissioned officers—men so ignorant that they cannot write three consecutive sentences without violating orthography and syntax.

My own judgment is, that in the great future before us we shall have to draw largely from this element for soldiers, and the sooner we set about it in earnest the better. This will be best accomplished by establishing the better regiments on the same footing and permanence as the Regular Army, if not actually a part of it. . . .

Notwithstanding the persistent hostility, open and covert, which strove to defeat my mission here as a pioneer, the progress made in the right direction is eminently encouraging, and I feel strong to carry it out to a successful issue if the right help shall come from Washington. I shall be glad if you will submit this letter to the Honorable the Secretary of War [Edwin M. Stanton]. I am, my dear general, your very faithful friend and obedient servant, Daniel Ullmann, Brigadier-General, Commanding.[1802]

With a bigoted president in the White House and little interest from other white officers (despite the offer of a promotion), Ullmann faced a long and uphill battle, as his own letter intimated.

But those few Yankees, like Ullmann, who strove for equal rights in Lincoln's armies, had another problem as well: most white Northern soldiers, as well as civilians, were against both the Emancipation Proclamation and black enlistment. Nowhere was this more true than in Lincoln's hometown, Springfield, Illinois. In August 1863, in an attempt to get an explanation from him, his Springfield constituents, including old friend James C. Conkling, invited Lincoln to speak on the topic of black

---

1802. *ORA*, Ser. 3, Vol. 3, pp. 1126-1128.

enlistment. The president could not make it, and instead sent a letter to Conkling to be read aloud before the audience.

Bristling with defensiveness, in the letter we find Lincoln commenting on a variety of issues, including the Northern public's "dissatisfaction about the negro," its "dislike of both the emancipation proclamation" and its "unconstitutionality," and the fact that Northern whites, by and large, "will not fight to free negroes. . . ."[1803] Lincoln's missive is enlightening, for it demonstrates not only the depth of Northern racism at the time, but also the near total lack of support he had from other Yankees pertaining to emancipation and black soldiers.

The very fact that Lincoln and his officers accepted and used the absurd racist term "contraband"[1804] (probably coined by Yankee General Benjamin "the Beast" Butler) for all captured Southern blacks,[1805] reveals that the North still regarded blacks as inferior to whites[1806] (the "superior race," as Lincoln referred to them),[1807] and as the legitimate property of whites, even after emancipation.[1808] Likewise, Lincoln and his cohorts never referred to liberated blacks as "freemen." Instead they called them "freedmen": one who had been emancipated but who was still tainted with the odium of being both black and a former slave.

A man from Massachusetts wrote of the effect of Lincoln's emancipation decree on the North and her soldiers: it has divided both. Lincoln's soldiers in particular hate to think that the War has anything to do with liberating the Negro, he stated.[1809]

Those Northerners who contested Lincoln over his desire to abolish slavery, then aid "the poor Negro" by enrolling him in the armed services, had it all wrong, however.

Lincoln never claimed the Emancipation Proclamation was for the benefit of blacks, that it was a civil rights measure meant to forward their position in American society. In fact, as we have seen, he quite clearly pronounced it "a fit and necessary *war measure*,"[1810] one whose sole aim was

---

1803. Nicolay and Hay, ALCW, Vol. 2, pp. 396-399.
1804. See e.g., Nicolay and Hay, ALCW, Vol. 2, p. 126.
1805. Leech, p. 293.
1806. Quarles, p. 60.
1807. Nicolay and Hay, ALCW, Vol. 1, p. 539.
1808. Wiley, SN, p. 175.
1809. K. C. Davis, p. 276.
1810. Nicolay and Hay, ALCW, Vol. 2, p. 287.

to deprive the South of her black military personnel (which numbered in the hundreds of thousands), then enlist them in the Union armies to fight against their own homeland, the Confederacy. Lincoln even emphasized that his proclamation was meant to be temporary; that slavery could be reestablished once the War had ended.[1811] Why?

1811. Weintraub, p. 73.

14

LINCOLN'S VIEWS ON BLACKS, SLAVERY, & EMANCIPATION

PART ONE

LINCOLN HAD NO INTENTION OF making black emancipation permanent because he had no authentic interest in black civil rights. While this is the opposite of what Northern "history" books have taught us, it is true nonetheless, and we will prove it.

Lincoln said repeatedly that his main concern was "preserving the Union," and that he would go to any lengths to achieve this. One of these "lengths" was allowing the South to continue practicing slavery after it rejoined the U.S. When he was attacked for forcing the War to drag on by once absent-mindedly calling for *complete* emancipation in all the Southern states, he quickly sent out a notice on July 18, 1864, rescinding the demand. It read:

> Any proposition which embraces the restoration of peace, the integrity of the whole Union, and the abandonment of slavery . . . will be received and considered . . . and will be met by liberal terms on other substantial and collateral points . . .[1812]

What were these "substantial and collateral points" that he was so willing to "receive and consider"?

[1812]. *ORA*, Ser. 3, Vol. 4, pp. 503-504. See also E. McPherson, PHUSAGR, p. 301.

At least one of them, according to Lincoln himself, included the possibility of ending the War without total and permanent emancipation. His response to the attacks on his emancipation plan is revealing. On August 17, 1864, he wrote:

> To me it seems plain that saying reunion and abandonment of slavery would be considered, if offered, is not saying that nothing *else* or *less* would be considered, if offered. . . . If [Confederate President] Jefferson Davis wishes, for himself, or for the benefit of his friends at the North, to know what I would do if he were to offer peace and reunion, saying nothing about slavery, let him try me.[1813]

At the Hampton Roads Conference Lincoln clarified his position on the matter for his Confederate guests. According to those present, Lincoln's

> . . . own opinion was, that as the Proclamation was a *war measure*, and would have effect only from its being an exercise of the war power, as soon as the war ceased, it would be inoperative for the future. It would be held to apply only to such slaves as had come under its operation while it was in active exercise. This was his individual opinion . . .[1814]

Another individual at Hampton Roads remembers Lincoln saying to Confederate Vice President Alexander H. Stephens:

> Let me write 'Union' at the top of this page, and you may then write any other terms of settlement you may deem proper.[1815]

What does all of this mean in plain English?

Lincoln did not want to interfere with Southern slavery (a position he had held for decades), and had only issued the Emancipation Proclamation because he needed soldiers. Thus, when peace was reestablished and the Southern states were brought back into the Union, the proclamation would cease, slaves would no longer be freed, and the

---

1813. Nicolay and Hay, ALAH, Vol. 9, pp. 215, 217.
1814. Nicolay and Hay, ALAH, Vol. 10, p. 123.
1815. Christian, p. 22.

institution of slavery itself would be allowed to continue indefinitely, in both the North and the South.[1816] Those slaves who managed to attain freedom would have to do it on their own: through escape.[1817]

At this same four-hour meeting, Lincoln's right-hand man, William H. Seward, even cheerfully suggested that the South could defeat the Thirteenth Amendment (which had passed Congress only days earlier) by voting against it as a group. This would deprive the three-fourths majority necessary for ratification, Seward said.[1818] All of this occurred on February 3, 1865, just two months before the War ended.

Lincoln had held such views even prior to the War, almost two years before issuing the Emancipation Proclamation. Back on February 1, 1861, a month before he had even been inaugurated, he shared his thoughts regarding assuaging the South's fears with Seward:

> As to fugitive slaves, . . . slave-trade among the slave States, and whatever springs of necessity from the fact that the institution is amongst us, I care but little . . .[1819]

Four weeks later, on February 27, 1861, President-Elect Lincoln met with a Southern peace delegation in Washington, D.C. that included Charles S. Morehead and William C. Rives. In their attempt to avert war with the U.S., the Confederate envoy pleaded with Lincoln to withdraw his troops from Fort Sumter and promise the border states that they would be safe within the Union. Lincoln replied that he would not yield on blocking the expansion of slavery into the Western Territories (as this was always his primary goal regarding the institution). But, he added, he would most certainly be willing to approve a constitutional amendment allowing slavery to continue indefinitely where it already existed. And he wasted no time in standing behind his promise.[1820]

Lincoln's proposed amendment, known as the Corwin Amendment (because it was introduced by Ohio Representative Thomas

---

1816. For more on the Hampton Roads Conference, see Seabrook, TAHSR, pp. 966-1001; Stephens, CV, Vol. 2, pp. 599-619; Kirkland, pp. 206-258; J. Davis, RFCG, Vol. 2, pp. 617-620.
1817. Quarles, p. 259.
1818. Stephens, CV, Vol. 2, pp. 611-612.
1819. Nicolay and Hay, ALCW, Vol. 1, p. 669.
1820. M. Davis, p. 49.

Corwin),[1821] allowed slavery to continue in perpetuity (without any interference from the U.S. government). It was passed by the U.S. House of Representatives the very next day (February 28, 1861), and by the U.S. Senate on March 2, 1861, two days before his presidential inauguration.[1822] By this time, three states had actually ratified the amendment, and certainly the rest would have as well, if given the chance. However, the act was dropped with the start of the Battle of Fort Sumter, on April 12, 1861. Had hostilities not exploded between the South and the North that spring day, what can only be called Lincoln's "proslavery amendment" would have been signed into law, and American slavery would have continued indefinitely.[1823]

Thus, while Lincoln preached against slavery in public, behind closed doors he was trying to use the Constitution to make slavery "irrevocable"—permitting it, in fact, to persist as long as the Southern states returned to the Union, remained,[1824] and paid their taxes.[1825]

Two days later, in his First Inaugural Address, March 4, 1861, Lincoln reiterated his views on the subject. As he often did, he opens with an outrageous lie, in this case pretending to know nothing about his own amendment. However, he ends by emphatically stating that he supports it:

> I understand a proposed amendment [the Corwin Amendment] to the Constitution—which amendment, however, I have not seen—has passed Congress, to the effect that the Federal Government shall never interfere with the domestic institutions of the States, including that of persons held to service [i.e., slavery]. To avoid misconstruction of what I have said, I depart from my purpose not to speak of particular amendments so far as to say that, holding such a provision to now be implied constitutional law, I have no objection to its being made express and irrevocable.[1826]

In plain English Lincoln says here that he supports the idea of an amendment that would forever prohibit the U.S. government from

---

1821. Seabrook, EYWTAASIW, pp. 706-707.
1822. DiLorenzo, LU, pp. 24, 25.
1823. Beard and Beard, Vol. 2, p. 65.
1824. Nicolay and Hay, ALCW, Vol. 2, p. 296.
1825. Nicolay and Hay, ALAH, Vol. 10, p. 123. See also, DiLorenzo, LU, pp. 24, 25.
1826. Nicolay and Hay, ALCW, Vol. 2, p. 6.

interfering with slavery.

A few months later, on August 17, 1864, though he never finished it or mailed it, Lincoln wrote a revealing letter that is germane to our discussion. Addressed to Charles D. Robinson, Lincoln states that he would have preferred that blacks had been left in slavery,[1827] but because of the dwindling number of white soldiers, he had no choice but to emancipate, then enlist, Southern African-Americans. If I were to break my promise to free the slaves, Lincoln begins:

> All recruiting of colored men would instantly cease, and all colored men now in our service, would instantly desert us. And rightfully too. . . . The party who could elect a President on a War and Slavery Restoration platform would, of necessity, lose the colored force; and that force being lost, would be as powerless to save the Union as to do any other impossible thing.
>
> It is not a question of sentiment or taste, but one of physical force, which may be measured and estimated, as horse-power and steam-power are measured and estimated. And, by measurement, it is more than we can lose and live. Nor can we, by discarding it, get a white force in place of it.[1828]

From Lincoln's own pen here we are told that his Emancipation Proclamation was not a matter of "sentiment or taste," but rather one of "physical force," sheer numbers of black men who were needed to replace whites on the battlefield. If this need had not existed emancipation would not have taken place. After all, for Lincoln the main point of the Emancipation Proclamation was its effect on the final outcome of the War.[1829] As he himself said:

> The colored population is the great available and yet unavailed of force for restoring the Union. The bare sight of fifty thousand armed and drilled black soldiers upon the banks of the Mississippi would end the rebellion at once; and who doubts that we can present that sight if we but take hold in earnest?[1830]

Again, as always, Lincoln mentions nothing about black civil rights. Only

---

1827. L. Johnson, p. 140.
1828. Nicolay and Hay, ALCW, Vol. 2, pp. 564-565.
1829. Ransom, p. 174.
1830. Nicolay and Hay, ALCW, Vol. 2, p. 318.

"restoring the Union" and winning the War.

We will note here that Lincoln was not alone in this view. Most of his officers agreed with him, even those most concerned with racial equality. Men like Yankee Colonel Thomas Wentworth Higginson, for instance. An ardent abolitionist from Massachusetts who officered an all-black troop, he had to admit that black enlistment, not black civil rights, was the most important outcome of emancipation. Said Higginson:

> No officer in this regiment now doubts that the key to the successful prosecution of this war lies in the unlimited employment of black troops.[1831]

This was the president's point exactly.

Further evidence of Lincoln's true agenda is supplied by his "Ten Percent Plan," issued on December 8, 1863.[1832] Here, a Confederate state could be "readmitted" to the Union if just 10 percent of its citizens took an oath of allegiance to the U.S. Afterward, that state could reestablish slavery if it so desired.[1833] In 1864, according to Confederate Secretary of State Judah Benjamin, far from demanding complete and immediate abolition, Lincoln let it be known that he was willing to let the issue be decided on by a general vote in both the South and the North.[1834]

It was just such duplicitous politics that prompted Spooner to rightly call Lincoln and his cabinet imposters and con-artists,[1835] "double-faced demagogues" who were trying to "ride into power on the two horses Liberty and Slavery."[1836]

Lincoln's efforts to allow slavery to continue indefinitely perturbed some of his military officers as well. One of them was Yankee General George B. McClellan, with whom Lincoln had a long and rancorous relationship. Not only would they run against each other in the 1864 presidential election, but at one point, in late 1862, there was so much animus between them that the two had spies sent out to investigate

---

1831. C. A. Evans, Vol. 6, p. 106.
1832. W. S. Powell, p. 144. See Nicolay and Hay, ALCW, Vol. 2, pp. 442-444.
1833. See Current, LNK, pp. 223, 239, 240, 241.
1834. Harwell, p. 307.
1835. DiLorenzo, LU, p. 55.
1836. Website: www.lysanderspooner.org/letters/SESP012260.htm.

one another.[1837]

Lincoln's major problem with McClellan was what he called "the slows";[1838] that is, McClellan's seeming reluctance to fight. In truth, however, it was not an unwillingness to wage combat on McClellan's part. It was that he and his men simply disagreed with Lincoln's charade to change the character of the War from one meant to preserve the Union (in the North) to one that would preserve slavery (in the South).[1839]

In the end, just as Lincoln never advocated either social or political equality for blacks,[1840] he never insisted on permanent emancipation. In fact, as we have just seen, he was even willing to terminate his proclamation as soon as the War ceased.[1841] Clearly, he was not only in no hurry to abolish slavery, he also had little concern about its continuance: in his own personal five-part emancipation plan he included a clause for allowing the Southern states nearly another fifty years, until the year 1900 specifically, to abolish the institution.[1842]

Many of our greatest and most objective historians, such as Louis M. Hacker, acknowledge that the real Lincoln was completely apathetic when it came to the topic of slavery, and that during the 1860 election his party was totally "silent on the issue." Indeed, Lincoln went out of his way to assure the American people, both North and South, that he had no intention of doing anything that might disturb the Union—including interfering with slavery[1843]—just as he did during his First Inaugural Address, March 4, 1861.[1844]

For delaying, even ignoring, emancipation, Lincoln was vigorously castigated by fellow Yanks. Indiana Representative George W. Julian, for example, a member of Lincoln's own party, offered the following review of the president's actions to a governmental committee on February 7, 1865:

> . . . it was that the President, instead of striking at slavery as a military necessity, and while rebuking that policy in his dealings

---

1837. Donald, L, p. 385.
1838. Current, LNK, p. 220.
1839. Leech, p. 249.
1840. Rosenbaum and Brinkley, s.v. "Lincoln and Douglas."
1841. Current, LNK, pp. 242-243.
1842. Nicolay and Hay, ALCW, Vol. 2, p. 270. See also Hacker, p. 583; Wiley, SN, p. 195.
1843. Hacker, p. 580.
1844. Nicolay and Hay, ALCW, Vol. 2, p. 1.

with Hunter and Frémont, was at the same time so earnestly espousing chimerical projects for the colonization [deportation] of negroes, coupled with the policy of gradual and compensated emancipation, which should take place some time before the year 1900, if the slaveholders should be willing. . . . Hence it was that for nearly two years of this war the government, while smiting the rebels with one hand, was with the other guarding the slave property and protecting the constitutional rights of the men who had renounced the Constitution . . . [Lincoln's] purpose to crush the rebellion and spare slavery was found to be utterly suicidal to our cause.[1845]

Those who are still having difficulty abandoning the belief that Lincoln started the War for the welfare of blacks and the abolition of slavery, will be interested in his public reply to Yankee abolitionist Horace Greeley.

On August 19, 1862, Greeley published an open letter to Lincoln in his New York newspaper, the *Tribune*, assaulting the president's abysmal civil rights record and accusing of him of prolonging the war by refusing to abolish slavery. Those who voted for you, Greeley, began,

are sorely disappointed and deeply pained by the policy you seem to be pursuing with regard to the slaves of the rebels. . . We think you are strangely and disastrously remiss in the discharge of your official and imperative duty with regard to the emancipating provisions of the new Confiscation Act. . . . Had you, sir, in your Inaugural Address, unmistakably given notice that . . . you would recognize no loyal person as rightfully held in slavery by a traitor, we believe the rebellion would therein have received a staggering, if not fatal blow.[1846]

Four days later, on August 22, 1862, a haughty Lincoln responded to the withering public attack with his own. Dear Mr. Greeley, he wrote to the celebrated antislavery advocate:

If there be those who would not save the Union unless they could at the same time save slavery, I do not agree with them. If there be those who would not save the Union unless they could at the same

---

1845. Julian, p. 234.
1846. Brockett, pp. 308, 309, 311.

time destroy slavery, I do not agree with them. *My paramount object in this struggle is to save the Union, and is not either to save or destroy slavery. . . . If I could save the Union without freeing any slave, I would do it . . . What I do about slavery and the colored race, I do because I believe it helps save the Union . . .*[1847]

This letter was written exactly one month before he issued his Preliminary Emancipation Proclamation (in which he calls for deporting all blacks out of the U.S.) and just four months before issuing his Final Emancipation Proclamation (in which he refers to his edict, not as a civil rights measure, but as a temporary "war measure").

Despite antiblack statements like the ones he made to Greeley, oddly Lincoln continues to be known globally as the "Great Emancipator." Yet the perceptive and enlightened perceive him more correctly as the most cunning, shrewd, tricky, secretive, and racist politician in American history.[1848]

On those rare occasions when Lincoln did speak out against slavery, his venom was always directed, of course, at *white* slave owners. Like modern enemies of the South (in particular, reparationists), Lincoln conveniently disregarded the reality of America's tens of thousands of *black* slave owners.[1849]

Indeed, one of the first slave owners in the American colonies was a black servant by the name of Anthony Johnson. After his arrival in 1621, he quickly worked off his term of indenture and began purchasing human chattel.[1850] The Virginia slaver from Angola (Africa), who owned both black *and* white slaves, actually helped launch the American slave trade by forcing authorities to legally define the meaning of "slave ownership."[1851] In 1652 his son John Johnson imported and bought eleven white servants, who worked under him at his plantation, located on the banks of the Pungoteague River.[1852]

Johnson and his family were just the first of countless thousands of American black slave owners and traders.[1853]

1847. Nicolay and Hay, ALCW, Vol. 2, pp. 227-228. Emphasis added.
1848. See Christian, passim.
1849. Grissom, p. 131; Stonebraker, p. 46.
1850. Bennett, BTM, p. 37.
1851. C. Johnson, pp. 81-84.
1852. Bennett, BTM, pp. 37-38.
1853. J. C. Perry, p. 174.

In 1830, in the Deep South alone, nearly 8,000 slaves were owned by some 1,500 black slave owners (about five slaves apiece). In Charleston, South Carolina, as another example, between 1820 and 1840, 75 percent of the city's free blacks owned slaves. Furthermore, a stunning 25 percent of all free American blacks owned slaves, South and North.[1854] We will recall that in 1861, the South's 300,000 white slave owners made up only 1 percent of the total U.S. white population of 30,000,000 people.[1855] Thus, while only one Southern white out of every 300,000 owned slaves (1 percent), one black out of every four blacks owned slaves (25 percent). In other words, far more blacks owned black (and sometimes white) slaves than whites did.

Due to poor census taking, we can be sure that there were thousands of additional black slave owners who were never counted, making the figure of 25 percent a gross underestimate. As an example, one calculation concludes that at least 50 percent of the black slave owners of Charleston, South Carolina, were left out of the 1860 Census.[1856]

Most black slave owners were not only proslavery, they were also pro-South, supporting the Confederate Cause as fervently as any white Southerner did. At church each Sunday, thousands of blacks would pray for those blacks, both their slaves and their free friends, who wore the Rebel uniform. Their supplications were simple: they asked God to help all African-American Confederates kill as many Yankees as possible, then return home safely.[1857]

Wealthy blacks bought, sold, and exploited black slaves for profit, just as white slave owners did. Some, like the African-American Metoyers, an anti-abolition family from Louisiana, owned 400 black slaves.[1858] At $1,500 a piece,[1859] they were worth a total of $600,000, or $20,000,000 in today's currency.[1860] This made the Metoyers among the wealthiest people in the U.S., black or white, then or now. Louisiana's all-black Confederate army unit, the Augustin Guards, was named after

---

1854. Greenberg and Waugh, p. 376.
1855. See Foner, FSFLFM, pp. 87-88. See also Hacker, p. 581; Quarles, p. xiii; Weintraub, p. 70; Cooper, JDA, p. 378; Rosenbaum and Brinkley, s.v. "Civil War"; C. Eaton, HSC, p. 93; Hinkle, p. 125.
1856. J. C. Perry, p. 175.
1857. Wiley, SN, pp. 106, 148.
1858. Greenberg and Waugh, pp. 392-393.
1859. M. M. Smith, p. 205.
1860. In the 1850s, prime field slaves cost as much as $1,800, about $51,000 apiece in today's money. Garraty and McCaughey, p. 214.

the family patriarch, Augustin Metoyer.[1861]

The third largest slaveholder in South Carolina was William Ellison, a former black slave who owned ninety-seven African servants, worth a total of about $4,000,000 today.[1862] One of the richest men in the state, he was wealthier than 90 percent of his white neighbors.[1863] The Ellison family became the social core of Charleston's many black slave owners and was a staunch supporter of the Southern Cause.[1864] Of the clan it was written: they were the epitome of loyal Rebels.[1865]

One of Ellison's fellow South Carolinians, John Stanley, was a black man who owned 163 black slaves, worth about $6,300,000 today. In 1860, the African-American women of Charleston, who owned 70 percent of the town's black-owned slaves, used the wealth they accumulated from the so-called "peculiar institution" to start up their own prosperous businesses.[1866]

Born into slavery, black man Horace King of Russell County, Alabama, was later freed, after which he founded a highly lucrative bridge-building company using black slave labor. King, a generous Confederate benefactor, donated money and purchased uniforms for Rebel soldiers throughout the War.[1867] In 1905 it was noted that he had been

> a constant and liberal contributor to the support of the Confederacy. He also furnished clothes and money to the sons of his former master who were in the army, and erected a monument over the grave of their father.[1868]

Andrew Durnford of Louisiana was a free black millionaire who owned seventy-five black slaves. Durnford complained about both the price of his slaves and their poor work ethic, calling them "rascally negroes." Unlike George Washington, Thomas Jefferson, Nathan Bedford Forrest, and thousands of other white Southern slave owners, Durnford never freed any of his slaves (except one body servant who he favored).

1861. Greenberg and Waugh, p. 393.
1862. Greenberg and Waugh, p. 376.
1863. C. Johnson, pp. 133-134.
1864. Greenberg and Waugh, pp. 386-387.
1865. Johnson and Roark, p. 208.
1866. Greenberg and Waugh, p. 376.
1867. Greenberg and Waugh, p. 377.
1868. Fleming, p. 208.

Indeed, he never expressed any misgivings about the institution at all.[1869]

Countless other examples of black slavers abound, such as the Virginia black who owned seventy-one slaves; the Louisiana black who owned seventy-five; and two in South Carolina who each owned eighty-four slaves.[1870] All were black planters of great wealth and influence in their communities. Then there was William Johnson of Natchez, Mississippi. A free African-American, Johnson saved up his money, purchased a plantation, and bought fifteen black slaves. His famous farm, called "Hardscrabble," is today part of the Natchez National Historical Park.[1871]

It was not just blacks who traded in and owned other blacks. There were thousands of Native-American slave owners as well,[1872] particularly in the lower South.[1873] Despite Lincoln's early racist military ban on Indian and black enlistment,[1874] some of these tribes, along with their black slaves, eventually fought in the Western Territories for the Union throughout the entire war.[1875]

Many more Native-American slave owners supported and fought for Davis and the Confederacy, however, among them the Five Civilized Tribes, as they were known.[1876] Some of the more famous examples from among this group were followers of Cherokee chief Stand Watie,[1877] the last Confederate officer to surrender to Lincoln (on June 23, 1865). Watie's strongest allies were the southeastern Indian slave owners who had been relocated to the West by a callous Union army.[1878]

1869. J. C. Perry, p. 178.
1870. Stampp, p. 194.
1871. J. C. Perry, p. 173. For more on the Natchez National Historical Park, see Website: www.nps.gov/natc/index.htm. For more on black slave owners, see Koger, passim; Johnson and Roark, passim.
1872. Rosenbaum and Brinkley, s.v. "Five Civilized Tribes."
1873. M. Perry, p. 183.
1874. *ORA*, Ser. 3, Vol. 1, p. 184.
1875. Grissom, p. 182.
1876. The Five Civilized Tribes were the Cherokee, Seminole, Choctaw, Creek, and Chickasaw. Quite unlike Lincoln and the North, Davis and the South enlisted Native-Americans almost from the beginning of the War. Also unlike Lincoln, Confederate Indians were treated as equals, not as an "inferior race," as Lincoln called them. Davis even signed a treaty with the Five Civilized Tribes promising not to "trouble or molest" them from that day forward. E. M. Thomas, p. 188. After the War, however, the U.S. military drove the Indians off their lands, nearly to extinction. Many of the U.S. officers involved were the same ones who had illegally invaded the Confederacy and had engaged in the cultural genocide of the Southern people.
1877. Warner, GG, s.v. "Stand Watie."
1878. Simmons, s.v. "Stand Watie."

The 1860 Census lists how many slaves were owned by the various Indians tribes, numbers that must be considered vastly undercounted due to the many inherent errors of the enumeration process:

Choctaw: 385 red slave owners, 2,297 black slaves
Cherokee: 384 red slave owners, 2,504 black slaves
Creek: 267 red slave owners, 1,651 black slaves
Chickasaw: 118 red slave owners, 917 black slaves[1879]

While the average white slave owner owned five or less slaves,[1880] the average Native-American slaveholder owned six. One Choctaw slaver owned 227.[1881] Again, it was non-white slave owners who individually owned the most slaves, not whites.

The full extent of Native-American slave ownership will never be known, but we do have proof that—besides the Choctaw, Chickasaw, Cherokee, and Creek—the Seminoles[1882] also possessed African-American slaves.[1883] Evidence for red slaveholders comes from the reports, journals, and diaries of the many whites who came in contact with them.[1884]

1879. J. C. Perry, p. 99.
1880. Gragg, p. 84; DiLorenzo, LU, p. 174.
1881. J. C. Perry, p. 101.
1882. Rosenbaum and Brinkley, s.v. "Five Civilized Tribes."
1883. Simmons, s.v. "Indians, in the War."
1884. See Jahoda, pp. 85, 148, 154, 225, 241, 246, 247, 249; J. C. Perry, pp. 96, 99, 101; Grissom, p. 182. Native-Americans also made captives (slaves) out of some of the earliest whites to land on North America's shores, European-Americans such as Virginia Dare, the first child born of English parents in America. Furnas, p. 28.

President Lincoln (center) with his official biographers: John George Nicolay (left) and John Hay (right).

15

A BRIEF STUDY OF THE TRUE ORIGINS OF SLAVERY

OF COURSE, IN THE BEGINNING, not only did slavery exist among Native-Americans—e.g., the Aztecs,[1885] Incas,[1886] and Mayans[1887]—long before the arrival of Christopher Columbus[1888] (the man responsible for starting the American slave trade),[1889] but Western slavery itself was purely a white man's occupation and had nothing to do with Indians, Africans, or any other people of color, or even racism.

Indeed, historically speaking, both the earliest known slave traders and the earliest known slaves were Caucasians: the Babylonians, Assyrians, Sumerians, Akkadians, Mesopotamians, Phoenicians, Egyptians, Mycenaeans, Arameans, East Indians, Chaldeans, Hittites, Scythians, Persians, Arabians, and Hebrews—at some point in their history—all either enslaved other whites or were themselves enslaved by other whites.[1890]

1885. See e.g., Meltzer, Vol. 2, pp. 60, 61, 62, 63, 64; Drescher and Engerman, p. 371; Vaillant, pp. 124, 126, 133, 200, 220, 221, 225-226, 255, 258; Johnson and Earle, p. 267.
1886. See e.g., Drescher and Engerman, p. 389; MacQuarrie, pp. 21-23, 31, 58, 201, 209-210, 229-230, 311, 353-356; Howells, p. 298.
1887. See e.g., Meltzer, Vol. 2, pp. 61, 62, 64; Drescher and Engerman, pp. 147-148; R. S. Phillips, s.v. "Slavery"; Hendelson, s.v. "slavery."
1888. Garraty and McCaughey, p. 7; Leonard, p. 102.
1889. Meltzer, Vol. 2, p. 4.
1890. Meltzer, Vol. 1, pp. 9-201; Nye, p. 46; McKenzie, s.v. "Slave, slavery"; Hartman and Saunders, pp. 54, 62, 70, 383, 446; Kramer, pp. 81-83; Westermann, p. 90; Breasted, AT, pp. 83, 153, 218, 220; Magoffin and Duncalf, pp. 76, 100, 112, 113; Becker and Duncalf, pp. 41-42, 50; McKay, Hill, and Buckler, Vol. 1, pp. 30, 44, 67; Swain, p. 47; Jones and Pennick, p. 184; Warnock and Anderson, p. 94; Wells, Vol. 1, p. 186; Childe, p. 163; Andrewes, p. 26; Hayes, Baldwin, and Cole, p. 15; Johnson and Earle, p. 248;

During slavery's peak in the region, nearly every household in Mesopotamia (ancient Iraq) possessed several white slaves, a country where parents thought little of selling their children into slavery—to other whites.[1891] If a Babylonian father got into debt, he would sell his entire family into slavery. Fortunately, the Law of Hammurabi stipulated that their bondage could last no more than three years.[1892] White female slaves in ancient Iraq suffered doubly: as their bodies belonged to their masters, they could be forced into prostitution.[1893] By 1300 BC, slavery had become "widespread" in ancient Egypt, with warrior-pharaohs bringing home thousands of Caucasian slaves from Palestine and Syria.[1894]

Like other early Caucasian peoples, the ancient Jews obtained their white slaves through warfare or purchase at the slave markets that dotted the Near and Middle East.[1895] Known among the Hebrews from the time of Moses (1391–1271 BC), white slavery was an ordinary aspect of their society, one that required the writers of the Torah (Old Testament) to record dozens of complex laws in order to govern it. For example, both adults and children could be enslaved,[1896] a man could sell himself into slavery,[1897] a man's creditors could enslave him for unpaid bills,[1898] thieves could be enslaved,[1899] the children of indebted parents could be put into bondage,[1900] the children of white slaves were themselves considered slaves,[1901] and Hebrew daughters could be sold into slavery by their fathers.[1902]

Many other peoples from the same period, such as Thracians,[1903] Greeks,[1904] and Romans, were slaves of white, Caucasian, or European

---

Breasted, TCOC, p. 75; Cappelluti and Grossman, pp. 94-96; Craig, Graham, Kagan, Ozment, and Turner, pp. 11-12.
1891. Kramer, p. 83.
1892. Westermann, p. 36.
1893. Willis, pp. 21, 115.
1894. McKay, Hill, and Buckler, Vol. 1, pp. 25-26.
1895. Riedel, Tracy, and Moskowitz, p. 298.
1896. 2 Samuel 8:2.
1897. Exodus 21:2.
1898. Leviticus 25:39.
1899. Exodus 22:1-7.
1900. 2 Kings 4:1; Isaiah 50:1.
1901. Exodus 21:4.
1902. Exodus 21:7.
1903. Langer, p. 68.
1904. Breasted, TCOC, p. 312.

extraction, enslaved by other Europeans.[1905] Today modern people underestimate the popularity of white slavery in the ancient world. In 5th-Century Greece, for instance, fully one-third of the population of Attica was made up of white slaves, while half of the Greek city of Pergamum were bonded Caucasians. At one time the city of Rome may have had as many as 330,000 white slaves;[1906] though some estimates put the figure at 500,000, nearly half the population during the 1st Century.[1907] Some private Roman estates were maintained by as many as 20,000 white slaves.[1908] In short, an enormous proportion of the empire was made up of slaves.[1909]

Though the *Odyssey* and the *Iliad* portray kindly relationships between master and slaves,[1910] often such servants were treated with extreme cruelty, for they had no rights.[1911] Ancient Roman and Greek owners, for instance, could do anything they wanted to their white slaves, except murder them.[1912] Even then, a disgruntled Roman slaveholder could hire the municipal executioner to legally torture and kill an unruly white slave, usually by burning him or her alive.[1913] Sick, injured, and aged white slaves were dropped off on an island in the Tiber River, where they were left to die of starvation and exposure to the elements.[1914]

White slaves who were trained to become Roman gladiators were treated with unthinkable brutality in order to turn them into beasts.[1915] But even ordinary white slaves did not have it easy. Beatings, chaining, branding, and even torture were not uncommon,[1916] and the ill were left to die—doctoring costing more than a new slave.[1917] Ancient Greek families who fell behind on their rent were split up and sold into slavery, even the children.[1918] Greek field slaves lived wretched lives in large

---

1905. David, pp. 62-90; Craig, Graham, Kagan, Ozment, and Turner, pp. 92, 104.
1906. Becker and Duncalf, pp. 92, 174.
1907. Warnock and Anderson, p. 314.
1908. Myers, p. 408.
1909. Easton, p. 356.
1910. Westermann, p. 90.
1911. Westermann, p. 149; Becker and Duncalf, p. 175.
1912. McKay, Hill, and Buckler, Vol. 1, p. 91.
1913. Ariès and Duby, pp. 59, 65-67, 69.
1914. Myers, p. 524.
1915. Westermann, pp. 354-355.
1916. McKay, Hill, and Buckler, Vol. 1, p. 13; Breasted, TCOC, p. 562.
1917. Myers, pp. 408, 409.
1918. Becker and Duncalf, p. 83.

"cellar barracks," under constant watch by armed guards.[1919]

Cato the Elder wrote a book, *On Agriculture*, in which he outlines, in a harsh and inhumane manner, "how to get the best results from [white] slaves on the least money."[1920] According to the Roman statesman:

> Slave laborers should get thirty-two quarts of wheat each during the winter, thirty-six in the summer. The overseer, housekeeper, foreman, and chief shepherd are to receive twenty-four quarts each. Let the supply for the fettered slaves [chain-gangs] be four pounds of bread through the winter, five pounds when they have begun to dig the vineyard . . . then afterwards switch them back to four pounds again. After the vintage for three months let them drink the thin wine of the skin of the grapes . . . Let the shackled slave receive additional wine proportioned to the work accomplished. . . . [For a relish for the slaves' food] store up as many fallen olives as you can; afterwards [use only] the ripe olives from which you can make very little oil, but be sparing with them that they may last as long as possible. When the olives are eaten, give the slaves fish-pickle and sour wine. Give each slave eighteen ounces of olive oil per month. In a year to give each slave eight quarts of salt is enough. . . . [For clothing] each slave receives one tunic, three and a half feet in length, plus a coarse cloak every other year. As often as you give each a tunic or a cloak, first take the old one to make out of it rag-garments. You must give the slaves good wooden shoes on alternate years.[1921]

Caucasian slavery was well-known in the Medieval Middle East. Turkey, under the Ottomans, for instance, enslaved its own citizens: between the years 1280 and 1566, the ten sultans who reigned over the empire possessed an enormous number of officials from among the ruling class, or Ottomans, as they were known. All of these Caucasian administrators worked as slaves under their respective rulers.[1922] In an empire in which even ordinary citizens were virtual slaves, the sultan took 3,000 white children a year from conquered Christians in the Balkans. These boys were then brought up in Turkey as Muslims, to be trained in

---

1919. Willis, p. 185.
1920. Westermann, p. 333.
1921. Paraphrased from Oliver, pp. 91-92.
1922. Winks, Brinton, Christopher, and Wolff, Vol. 1, p. 242.

the arts of warfare and administration.[1923] The Ottomans also procured white slaves from Spain, Italy, Albania, Bosnia, Hungary, and Romania.[1924]

During the 9th Century Arabs purchased Turkish boys to serve as slaves to the Abbasids, Islam's second dynasty, whose capital was centered at Baghdad. Arabs used adult Turks captured in war as slaves for the caliphs, Islamic spiritual leaders. Though plantation slaves were rare in the early Middle East, household slaves were common enough, most who were taken from the Arabs' large pool of war captives and those children sold into slavery by their parents. While early Islam recognized slavery and issued no prohibitions against it,[1925] its prophet, Muhammad, ordered slave owners to treat their chattel humanely.[1926]

In the early years of the Roman Empire, three out of four residents of what we now call Italy were slaves, some 21 million in total. Though a tiny minority were black slaves from Nubia, in the main both the owners and their chattel were white,[1927] culled from places like Carthage, Spain, Gaul, Macedonia, Greece, and Asia Minor.[1928] (Contrast this number with the much smaller figure 3.5 million, the total number of black slaves in the American south in 1860,[1929] an area many times the size of Italy.)[1930] Rome acquired 150,000 white slaves from the Adriatic region alone.[1931]

Though some were the product of slave breeding,[1932] most were captured in war. Plutarch wrote that during the Gallic Wars (58-51 BC), Julius Caesar sacked at least 800 European towns and enslaved (or killed) some 3 million Caucasian men.[1933] In one campaign alone Caesar captured and sold 53,000 whites into bondage.[1934] Many of Rome's white slaves

---

1923. McKay, Hill, and Buckler, Vol. 1, p. 546.
1924. McKay, Hill, and Buckler, Vol. 2, p. 726.
1925. Hayes, Baldwin, and Cole, p. 130.
1926. Goldschmidt, pp. 79, 106; Hendelson, s.v. "slavery."
1927. Fogel, p. 17.
1928. Breasted, TCOC, p. 561.
1929. Cooper, JDA, p. 378.
1930. To put these numbers into perspective: Italy is 116,345 square miles. The Confederacy was 850,000 square miles. Thus, while the American South was 87 percent larger than Italy, ancient Italians owned 84 percent more slaves than Southerners.
1931. Breasted, AT, p. 642.
1932. Thompson and Johnson, p. 13.
1933. Herm, p. 189.
1934. Easton, p. 356.

ended up in the huge slave gangs that sustained the *latifundia*, or great landed estates of the wealthy and powerful.[1935] Such affluent Italian families kept white slaves "as a matter of course."[1936]

Those who managed to evade capture during warfare were hunted down by Rome's infamous professional slave catchers—white men pursuing white men. Sometimes fellow whites were caught by Roman pirates,[1937] who then sold them to wealthy landowners to be used as cheap labor.[1938] These Roman buccaneers often engaged in "wholesale kidnaping" of other whites as the sailed throughout the Aegean and eastern Mediterranean Seas.[1939]

After winning the Battle of Pydna (168 BC), Roman General Lucius Aemilius Paullus punished the people of Epirus (northwestern Greece) by selling 150,000 of their white inhabitants into slavery.[1940] According to evidence found in early literature, the ancient Italians also captured and enslaved Gauls, or Celts.[1941] After the 2nd-Century Roman General Gaius Marius' victories over the invading Germanic tribes, some 150,000 Teutons and Cimbri were sold into slavery. After one particular battle, Julius Caesar placed 53,000 captured white soldiers into slavery.[1942]

Though we are speaking of white slavery here, race made little difference to the Romans. African black slaves, though extremely rare in places like ancient Greece,[1943] were considered just as good as Spanish ones, with blond Germans being favored above all others.[1944] So popular was white slavery in ancient Greece, that the number one type of financial speculation of the Middle Class was to invest in slaves, often using one's savings or an inheritance.[1945]

As in all parts of the ancient world, white slavery was found in Italy from the very beginning. Following the First Punic War (264-241 BC), for example, 75,000 whites from around the Mediterranean,

---

1935. Bark, pp. 118-120; Clough, p. 130.
1936. Heer, p. 80.
1937. Breasted, TCOC, p. 562.
1938. Swain, pp. 172, 211.
1939. Smith, Muzzey, and Lloyd, p. 103.
1940. Westermann, pp. 332-333.
1941. Boardman, Griffin, and Murray, p. 47.
1942. Becker and Duncalf, p. 174.
1943. Frost, p. 83.
1944. McKay, Hill, and Buckler, Vol. 1, p. 147.
1945. Frost, p. 76.

including Sardinia, were put in bondage and sold at market.[1946] The first slave rebellion ever recorded was by white slaves in Italy in the year 198 BC. Numerous other white slave uprisings took place in the following decades, "inflicting great damage upon Italy."[1947]

One rebel servant army in Sicily contained some 200,000 white slaves, a power so great that they were able to hold off the Roman government for three years while defeating four Roman armies. When they were finally captured, the Romans crucified 20,000 of them as punishment.[1948] The Helots of Greece were treated so inhumanely that it sparked a thirty year slave rebellion, from 650 to 620 BC. The white slave insurrection was only finally suppressed by the Spartans with great difficulty and viciousness.[1949]

Since ancient Romans considered slaves "overgrown children," such revolts were viewed as a form of parricide, punishable by death. Virgil said that any slave who participated in an insurrection would be abandoned in the lowest regions of Hell.[1950] Hades must be overflowing with white slaves then.

Such individuals would include the Roman slave Spartacus,[1951] well-known to this day: a white man from Thrace, the slave revolt he led in 73 BC has become legendary.[1952] After amassing an army of 120,000 white slaves, Spartacus was able to vanquish the Roman legions sent against him.[1953] However, he was eventually killed in battle, and 6,000 of his followers were crucified on the Appian Way between Rome and Capua, their mangled rotting bodies a gruesome warning to other white slaves who might be considering a rebellion.[1954]

In ancient Sicily, which was said to be "flooded with slaves," some 60,000 white bondsmen rebelled, murdering their owners and wreaking havoc in the area for years afterward.[1955] At the Battle of Carrhae (53 BC),

---

1946. Willis, p. 185.
1947. Swain, pp. 178-179.
1948. Myers, p. 409.
1949. Willis, p. 111.
1950. Ariès and Duby, p. 61.
1951. M. Grant, p. 27; Peters, p. 342.
1952. Neilson, s.v. "Spartacus"; Westermann, p. 355; Boardman, Griffin, and Murray, p. 436; Wells, Vol. 1, p. 371.
1953. Boren, p. 69.
1954. Willis, p. 189.
1955. Smith, Muzzey, and Lloyd, p. 103.

white Parthian soldiers conquered a Roman army four times the size of their own, then marched the 10,000 Italian survivors into Iran and sold them into slavery.[1956] Since most industry and agriculture was run by white Roman slaves, it is not surprising that many of the empire's more learned professions, such as doctors, tutors, clerks, managers, and farm bailiffs, were actually slaves working under the ownership of kings and ministers.[1957]

In a society like ancient Rome, where it was legal, and common, for slave owners to kill the unwanted infants of their white slaves,[1958] we should not be shocked by any of this. Consider the following 19th-Century description of the life of a typical white slave living under the auspices of the Roman Empire:

> When the slaves landed in Sicily, they were kept by the dealers in slave-pens, waiting for the purchasers. The wealthy capitalists would buy whole batches at once, brand or mark the slaves like cattle, and send them off to the country to work. The young and robust were employed as shepherds, and the others in agricultural and other labour. Some worked in fetters, to prevent them running away. All of them had hard service, and their masters supplied them scantily with food and clothing. They cared little about their slaves. They worked them while they were able to work, and the losses by death were replaced by fresh purchases. This want of humanity and prudence in the masters soon produced intolerable mischief. The slaves who were employed in looking after sheep and cattle of necessity had more freedom than those who were kept to cultivating the ground. Their masters saw little of them, and left them unprovided with food, supposing that they would be able to look after themselves and cost nothing. Many of these greedy slave-owners were Italians, some of whom probably did not reside in Sicily, but entrusted the management of their estates to overseers, and consumed the produce of their wool and the profits of their cattle either at Rome or in some of the Italian towns. These slave shepherds, an active and vigorous set of men, soon found out ways of helping themselves. They began by robbing and murdering, even in frequented places, travellers who were alone or only in small companies. They next attacked the huts of the poorer people, plundered them of their property, and, if

---

1956. Wells, Vol. 1, p. 372.
1957. Childe, pp. 266-267, 282.
1958. Ariès and Duby, p. 9.

resistance was made, murdered them. It became unsafe for travellers to move about by night, nor could people any longer safely live on their lands in the country. The shepherds got possession of huts which the occupants abandoned, and of arms of various kinds also, and thus they became bolder and more confident. They went about with clubs and spears, and the staves which were used by herdsmen, dressed in wolfskins or hogskins, and already began to make a formidable appearance. They had a great number of fierce dogs with them, and abundance of food from the milk and flesh of their beasts. The island was filled with roaming bands of plunderers, just as if the masters had allowed their slaves to do what they liked. . . . Though all the slave-owners would suffer from the depredations of these robbers, every man would be unwilling that his own slaves should be put to death when they were caught, and would claim them as fugitive labourers; and thus disputes might easily arise between the governors and the owners. The true state of the case is probably this. Slaves were bought cheap, and could be made profitable by working them hard; and thus the greediness of gain, the total want of any humane feeling in the masters, the neglect of proper discipline among the slaves, and the careless feeling of security produced by many years of prosperity, brought things gradually to such a state, that repression of the disorder was beyond the power of the masters or the governors; for the masters could not reduce such sturdy fellows to obedience on estates far removed from towns, and a Roman governor of Sicily had no army at his command.[1959]

Needless to say, the black slaves of the American South never experienced anything like this, and were treated like royalty in comparison.[1960]

White slavery was common enough in ancient Rome so that even the poorest families had at least one or more, and great white slave gangs (working the fields of massive estates) were a familiar sight throughout the region.[1961] The average affluent Roman owned between 400 and 500 white slaves.[1962] A historian living at the time wrote that when one particular Roman experienced a financial setback, leaving him nearly bankrupt, he was left with *only* 4,116 slaves—all white of course.[1963] By

---

1959. Philip Smith, Vol. 2, pp. 546-547.
1960. For an in-depth evaluation of so-called "slavery" in the Old South, see Seabrook, TMOCP, pp. 65-231.
1961. Swain, pp. 189-190, 211.
1962. Willis, p. 185.
1963. Celeste, pp. 141-142.

the 2nd Century AD, there were so many white slaves in Rome that they were outproducing free labor,[1964] creating embitterment and widespread unemployment,[1965] and ruining countless small farmers and small businessmen.[1966] Flooded with slaves, free labor all but vanished.[1967]

When the supply of white slaves from military raids and outright war ran low, Roman slave dealers turned to "wholesale kidnaping."[1968] White slavery remained "commonplace" throughout Italy and the entire eastern Mediterranean region well into the early Middle Ages.[1969] White slaves were considered so invaluable to the running of society, that the wealthiest slave owners were willing to pay up to $20,000 for a single servant, the modern equivalent of many millions of dollars.[1970]

Just as early Romans obtained some of their white gladiators and slaves from Greece (as spoils of war), the early Greeks secured many of their white slaves in the same manner from Italy and Sicily.[1971] In ancient Athens specifically—where the white slave population reached 400,000 individuals by the year 370 BC[1972]—white slaves were purchased in Thrace and the Black Sea region in exchange for olive oil, silver, marble, lead, and works of art.[1973]

In early Sparta, where white slaves existed in disproportionate numbers,[1974] the Helots worked the land as state slaves, kept in subjugation by the "harsh measures" of their overlords, the ruling class known as the Spartiates.[1975] There were so many Helots that they posed a danger to the Spartan aristocracy, which was constantly trying to think up new ways to rid itself of their numbers. As property of the state, the "lowly" Helots could not be disposed of by their masters. So Sparta's officials simply declared annual war on them, an efficient way to exterminate the "overly abundant" white slaves with a clear conscience.[1976]

1964. Bone, p. 161.
1965. Boren, p. 49.
1966. Winks, Brinton, Christopher, and Wolff, Vol. 1, p. 138; Myers, pp. 408, 409.
1967. Dimont, p. 92.
1968. Van Nostrand and Schaeffer, p. 137.
1969. Winks, Brinton, Christopher, and Wolff, Vol. 1, p. 138.
1970. Myers, p. 524.
1971. Van Nostrand and Schaeffer, pp. 131, 137.
1972. Dunner, p. 880.
1973. Wells, Vol. 1, p. 233.
1974. Clough, Garsoian, and Hicks, p. 64.
1975. Ferguson and Bruun, Vol. 1, pp. 37, 44.
1976. Andrewes, pp. 93, 139-140.

At Laurium, Greece, some 30,000 white slaves were employed in the town's silver mines.[1977] As Greek slaves had no legal or political rights,[1978] and since their masters held "life-and-death power" over them,[1979] untold thousands died while working miserable ten-hour shifts in the dark damp mine shafts.[1980] It is said that these manacled, overworked white laborers endured "almost every brutality."[1981]

At Athens if a white slave was asked to give testimony in court, Greek law required that it been done under torture.[1982] Indebted Attican[1983] and Athenian families who were unable to pay their loans were split up and sold into slavery,[1984] or they sold themselves.[1985] White Greek sharecroppers could be turned into slaves for underproduction.[1986] As in Rome, most of Greece's white slaves were procured through piracy, kidnaping, and war.[1987]

White slaves in ancient Greece "greatly outnumbered the free population." Since it was considered "a real hardship to function with less than half a dozen slaves," nearly every freeman was a white slave owner.[1988] In fact, all Athenian industry was built on white slavery. Thus the smallest farmer owned at least one or two bondsmen. Even Athens' policemen were slaves.[1989]

By the year 338 BC, there were some 150,000 white slaves working in the mines in Attica alone. Nicias, an Athenian politician and military officer, is said to have owned over 1,000 white slaves. Ancient Greeks held slavery to be just as necessary as oxygen. As an essential aspect of both Greek society and Greek civilization itself,[1990] it was a commonplace but important institution that was taken for

---

1977. Andrewes, pp. 136-137.
1978. McNeill, pp. 224-225; Cappelluti and Grossman, p. 178.
1979. Warnock and Anderson, p. 94.
1980. McKay, Hill, and Buckler, Vol. 1, p. 91.
1981. Brinton, Christopher, and Wolff, Vol. 1, p. 62.
1982. Burns, p. 245.
1983. Kagan, p. 256.
1984. McKay, Hill, and Buckler, Vol. 1, p. 78.
1985. Breasted, AT, p. 345.
1986. Willis, p. 115.
1987. McKay, Hill, and Buckler, Vol. 1, p. 114; Warnock and Anderson, p. 94.
1988. Myers, p. 335.
1989. Childe, p. 216.
1990. J. M. White, p. 61.

granted[1991]—like cooking utensils,[1992] just as it was among all ancient peoples.[1993] If slavery had been abolished at the height of Grecian civilization, and free labor put in its place, the leisure upper classes would have disappeared, completely dissolving Greek society as a whole.[1994]

This is why one cannot find a single anti-slavery statement in any of the literature of, for example, the ancient Near East.[1995] In fact, the only ancient Mediterranean people to discourage slavery were the Ptolemies, and this was purely for economic reasons: slavery would have competed with free labor.[1996]

Without the economic foundation of white slavery, neither Athenian culture or the Roman imperial system could have developed. Indeed, none of the world's ancient civilizations could have existed without the enslavement of whites,[1997] for it was the foundation of the economy and society of *all* early Western peoples dating back to prehistory.[1998] In 1904 Philip Van Ness Myers wrote:

> If ever slavery was justified by its fruits, it was in Greece. The brilliant civilization of the Greeks was its product, and could never have existed without it. As one truthfully says, 'Without the slaves the Attic democracy would have been an impossibility, for they alone enabled the poor, as well as the rich, to take a part in public affairs.' Relieving the citizen of all drudgery, the system created a class characterized by elegant leisure, refinement, and culture.[1999]

During the 10th Century, Verdun, France, was a major trading center of white slaves: imported from the Slavonic east, they were sold primarily to Spaniards to serve in the courts of the Caliphs.[2000] As late as the 1700s, the chamber of commerce at Nantes, France's main slave trading port, stated publicly that French colonial commerce would have

---

1991. Breasted, AT, p. 349.
1992. Myers, p. 335.
1993. Winks, Brinton, Christopher, and Wolff, Vol. 1, pp. 38-39, 48, 64; McKay, Hill, and Buckler, Vol. 1, p. 91.
1994. Andrewes, p. 133.
1995. McKenzie, s.v. "Slave, slavery."
1996. McKay, Hill, and Buckler, Vol. 1, p. 114.
1997. Doubleday's Encyc., s.v. "slavery."
1998. Hendelson, s.v. "slavery."
1999. Myers, p. 336.
2000. Heer, p. 74.

been unachievable without slavery.[2001]

Britons were enslaving each other as early as the 5th Century, and among the English (as with the Germans) there had been a white slave class from their earliest days as a separate and distinct people. White English slaves had no rights whatever and were viewed as simply a part of the livestock of their owner's estate.[2002] Bristol, England, was once a thriving slave port, where enslaved English men and women, known as "thralls," were sold to the Irish.[2003]

In the late 6th Century the future Roman pope, Saint Gregory the Great, was surprised to see fair-skinned slaves for sale at a slave market in Rome;[2004] stunned not because they were in bondage, but because of their "well formed features and beautiful blond hair." When he asked about them he was told that they were Angles (Anglo-Saxons), the people who gave their name to Angles' Land (England).[2005] In the 9th Century, when Bishop Wilfrid I of York, England, was granted land by King Ethelwulf, the cleric found he had also inherited 250 white male and female slaves attached to the property. He promptly baptized them and set them free.[2006]

Ancient Europe's casual and pragmatic view of white slavery was summed up by the slavery approving Aristotle in the 4th Century.[2007] According to the famed Greek philosopher, a certain percentage of society are born to be slaves, "animated instruments,"[2008] or "tools with voices," as he referred to them, natural-born servants who need to be enslaved for their own good.[2009] Besides, he went on, as most Greek slaves were non-Greek, and therefore inferior, it was only right that they were ruled by a superior people.[2010] Plato, who believed that slavery would continue indefinitely into the future,[2011] held that slavery was simply the inherent

---

2001. Chambers, Grew, Herlihy, Rabb, and Woloch, p. 662.
2002. J. R. Green, Vol. 1. pp. 17, 27-28.
2003. Hall, Albion, and Pope, p. 25.
2004. Hall, Albion, and Pope, p. 11.
2005. Saint Bede, pp. 99-100.
2006. Saint Bede, p. 229.
2007. Hale, p. 359; Wells, Vol. 1, p. 266.
2008. Muller, p. 121.
2009. Drescher and Engerman, pp. 195, 230.
2010. Greer, p. 17.
2011. Cornford, p. 54.

fate of certain individuals.[2012]

Roman diplomat Marcus Terentius Varro referred to slaves as "vocal agricultural instruments."[2013] The Greek historian Xenophon held that civilization itself could not exist without a privileged class freed by white slave labor, so that its members could use their leisure time to pursue the development of government, education, art, warfare, philosophy, and science.[2014]

Just like Western civilization, the institution of Western slavery has its roots in white bondage. This explains the etymology of the word slave itself: slave derives from the word "Slav," from the name of a European people, the Slavs,[2015] today the largest European ethnic and language group inhabiting central and eastern Europe, as well as Siberia. All 225 million speak one of the Slavonic languages.[2016]

The word Slav became synonymous with slavery due to the enslavement, by other Europeans (mainly Celts[2017] and Germans)[2018] of thousands of Slavic individuals during Europe's early history.[2019] Germans, for example captured Slavic men, women, and children during internecine conflicts, then traded them to Roman merchants for jewelry, farming equipment, wine, and household wares. The Slavic men seized in this manner were sold into slavery as gladiators, the women as domestic servants, and the children as field hands.[2020]

As their names indicate, the Slovenes (of *Slove*nia), the Slovaks (of *Slova*kia), and the Yugoslavians (of Yugo*slavia*), are the modern (white) descendants of the ancient Slavs, untold thousands who were sold in the slave markets across Europe by their brutal conquerors.[2021]

In Europe, where avaricious white slave dealers routinely enslaved white peasants for sale to Middle Eastern countries,[2022] white slavery was such a dominant aspect of the region that it eventually spilled over into

---

2012. Warnock and Anderson, p. 94.
2013. Myers, p. 524.
2014. Dunner, p. 880.
2015. Mish, s.v. "slave."
2016. Rosenbaum, s.v. "Slavs"; "Slavonic Languages."
2017. Gwatkin and Whitney, Vol. 2, pp. 421, 430.
2018. Encyc. Brit., "slavery."
2019. Meltzer, Vol. 1, p. 3.
2020. Simons, p. 18.
2021. Compton's Encyc., s.v. "Slavs"; McKay, Hill, and Buckler, Vol. 1, p. 280.
2022. Van Nostrand and Schaeffer, p. 281.

both Asia and the Arabic world. Throughout the 9th Century, for example, Swedish Vikings enslaved whites from the northern forests of Russia[2023] (once literally known as the "nation of slaves"),[2024] then traded them to Muslims for Oriental goods.[2025] It was not until the latter half of the 19th Century that Russia abolished its own "widespread" system of slavery, emancipating some 10,000 white slaves in Uzbekistan alone.[2026]

The Vikings, of course, were zealous practitioners of white slavery, which was a routine aspect of their culture for several centuries.[2027] During the Children's Crusade in 1212, countless numbers of French and German boys were kidnaped by white slave dealers and sold into captivity in Arabia.[2028] German royal Henry the Lion turned captured Danish Christians into slaves, and Bavarian nobleman Diepold von Vohburg sold Italians into slavery.[2029]

In Western Europe specifically, white slavery existed long before the Roman Empire, with peoples like the Venetians specializing in the import of white slaves right up into the Medieval Period.[2030] Between the years 1414 and 1423 some 10,000 white slaves were sold just in Venice.[2031] White slavery did not begin to disappear in Europe until the 12th Century,[2032] though it continued to flourish in places like Florence, Italy, where in 1363 the government sanctioned the unlimited importation of white slaves. White slavery persisted in Southern Italy, Spain, Crete, and Sicily well into 1500s. During the Renaissance Genoese slavers established white slaving stations in the Crimea and in the Black Sea region in order to fully exploit the lucrative business.[2033]

Despite increasing disapproval by the Church,[2034] English slaves (mainly criminals and political prisoners) were sent to plantations in the New World well into the 17th Century, and kidnaped English children

---

2023. Simons, p. 128.
2024. Radzinsky, p. 33.
2025. Boorstin, pp. 208-209.
2026. Stavrianos, p. 528.
2027. G. Jones, pp. 3, 23, 109, 119, 127, 131, 146-150, 164, 215-218, 256.
2028. Van Nostrand and Schaeffer, p. 307.
2029. Heer, p. 49.
2030. Hayes, Baldwin, and Cole, p. 182.
2031. McKay, Hill, and Buckler, Vol. 1, pp. 408-409, 494.
2032. Doubleday's Encyc., s.v. "slavery."
2033. McKay, Hill, and Buckler, Vol. 1, p. 494.
2034. Myers, p. 524; E. A. Livingstone, s.v. "Slavery."

were sold there as slaves as late as 1744.[2035] Many of the original 17th-Century American colonists were white slaves and white indentured servants from England, Ireland, and Scotland.[2036] Medieval European white slaves (serfs) were legally the lord's chattel and had few rights, could not own property, were viewed as human livestock, and were often sold for less than the cost of a horse.[2037] Parents from Thrace, what is now the southeastern Balkans, regularly sold their children into slavery to pay off their debts.[2038]

Mediterranean Europe only stopped trading in white slaves when it was forced to: in 1453, when the Ottoman Empire conquered Constantinople—cutting off the flow of white slaves from the Balkans and the area around the Black Sea—it had no choice but to turn to Africa as a source for slaves. By the late 1400s, black slaves were working in the vineyards and on the sugar plantations of Majorca and Sicily. Mediterranean Europeans had developed an "American" form of slavery even before Columbus sailed to the Americas.[2039]

White slavery was not just a phenomenon of the ancient world the Middle Ages, or even the 1700s. Soviet dictator Joseph Stalin, for example, enslaved an estimated 12 million[2040] to 18 million Caucasians during his reign of terror in the 1930s,[2041] as many as 14.5 million more white slaves than the American South's 3.5 million black slaves. "Harshly treated," and forced to live in labor camps that were located in the northern wilderness of Siberia, Stalin's white slaves were assigned spirit-breaking work in mines and forests.[2042]

Between 1941 and 1945, nearly 8 million Caucasians were enslaved across Europe under Nazi Germany, including children as young as six years of age. This means that the Nazis owned 4.5 million more white slaves than the American South owned black slaves. Under Nazi socialist leader Adolf Hitler, white European families were routinely separated and forced to work in factories, fields, and mines, where they

---

2035. Doubleday's Encyc., s.v. "slavery."
2036. A. O'Brien, p. 524.
2037. Thompson and Johnson, p. 329.
2038. Andrewes, p. 135.
2039. McKay, Hill, and Buckler, Vol. 1, p. 494.
2040. Rayfield, p. 180.
2041. Montefiore, p. 643.
2042. I. L. Gordon, p. 362.

were dehumanized, beaten, whipped, and starved by their German overlords.[2043]

By definition, *all* Nazi concentration camp prisoners were considered slaves, which is why Hitler's right-hand man Heinrich Himmler wanted the concentration camps themselves to be turned into modern factories—mainly for the production of German armaments. As sanitary conditions were poor, disease and mortality rates were "extraordinarily high."[2044]

Among the millions of whites who had been violently coerced into the Nazi Slave Labor Program were Jews, Poles, Russians, Slavs, and Italians. Many of Hitler's white slaves were housed five at a time in dog kennels only three feet high. Imprisonment could last for as long as six months in camps that lacked water and even rudimentary sanitation. Overworked and underfed, millions of European slaves died at the hands of fellow whites during this period.[2045]

White Nazi slavery was the largest revival of the institution in the 20th Century, and one of the fastest and most monumental expansions of slavery in world history.[2046] If the Nazis had been victorious, Hitler was planning to operate a massive "slave empire" that ran from Europe's Eastern coast on the Atlantic Ocean to the Ural Mountains in Western Russia.[2047] All of this occurred a mere sixty-four years ago.

Not all modern whites are enslaved by other whites, however. It was common among some Caucasian peoples, such as the Russians, to sell themselves into slavery during periods of economic duress.[2048]

The vast majority of white immigrants who came to America's original thirteen English colonies—at least two-thirds[2049]—came as white servants.[2050] In fact, white indentured servitude, being much preferred over African slavery (Africans were considered "alien" by early white colonialists),[2051] was the institution that paved the way for black slavery in

---

2043. Meltzer, Vol. 2, pp. 270-277.
2044. Speer, pp. 472-474.
2045. Shirer, pp. 946-951.
2046. Drescher and Engerman, p. 289.
2047. Shirer, pp. 946-951.
2048. Fogel, p. 454.
2049. Drescher and Engerman, p. 239.
2050. Stampp, p. 16.
2051. Garraty and McCaughey, p. 26.

America.[2052] Two of the signers of the Declaration of Independence arrived in the U.S. as indentured servants,[2053] and at least two future U.S. presidents began their adult life as white servants: Millard Fillmore and Andrew Johnson.[2054]

President Martin Van Buren's third great-grandfather, Cornelius Maesen Van Buren, emigrated from the Netherlands to New York as an indentured servant.[2055] Henry Wilson, President Ulysses S. Grant's second vice president and a cofounder of the Free-Soil party, worked as an indentured slave for eleven years, from age ten to twenty-one.[2056] Even one of Lincoln's ancestors, an early relation who was part of the Massachusetts Bay Colony, came to America as an indentured servant.[2057]

Life was not easy for America's early white slaves. In the colonies, for instance, white indentured servants, of both genders, were obliged to perform any labor asked of them. Their term lasted for up to five years, after which they were dismissed with nothing but the clothes on their backs—unless they were found guilty of misconduct, for which the length of their indenture could be extended. Maryland's white slaves were given a bonus: fifty acres of land on which to set up their own farms.[2058] Up until the end of the 17th Century, much of the American South's economy was based around, not African slavery, but European slavery; that is, indentured whites.[2059]

White slavery was also practiced in the U.S. under the headright system.[2060] To accrue property in the American British colonies, wealthy Europeans would pay for the oceanic passage of indentured white servants from England in exchange for land. John Maddison, an ancestor of America's fourth president, James Madison, did just this, acquiring some 2,000 acres of property by 1664.[2061]

2052. Wilson and Ferris, s.v. "Plantations." Many Northern whites, like Yankee judge Samuel Sewall, disliked blacks so much that they advocated using white slaves instead. See Sewall, Vol. 2, pp. 17-18.
2053. Smelser, ACRH, p. 58.
2054. Shenkman and Reiger, p. 96; DeGregorio, s.v. "Millard Fillmore" (pp. 188-189); DeGregorio, s.v. "Andrew Johnson" (pp. 248-249).
2055. DeGregorio, s.v. "Martin Van Buren" (pp. 123-124).
2056. DeGregorio, s.v. "Ulysses S. Grant" (pp. 268-269).
2057. Furnas, p. 108.
2058. Morison and Commager, Vol. 1, p. 51.
2059. Carman and Syrett, p. 39.
2060. Hacker, pp. 17-18.
2061. DeGregorio, s.v. "James Madison" (pp. 55-56).

As the earliest recorded slave societies were built on the white ownership of white slaves (e.g., ancient Mesopotamia, Babylon, Assyria, India, Phoenicia, Greece, Rome, and Judea),[2062] and as Africans were practicing slavery on one another thousands of years before the arrival of Arab, Portuguese[2063] (who were assisted by the Venetians, Genoese, Catalans, Flemings, and Florentines),[2064] Spanish, French, Dutch, Danish, Swedish, English,[2065] and finally, Yankee slave traders,[2066] it is obvious that the institution of slavery itself is not by definition a white and black racial issue. Indeed, throughout the Western world slaves were made up of every race, including the white race, until around 1450.[2067]

And it is certainly not accurate to refer to it as the "South's peculiar institution," for slavery was neither Southern in origin or peculiar. Rather, as we have seen, it was a worldwide custom,[2068] a "fact of life,"[2069] literally a basic, most would say essential, building block in the foundation of all known human societies.[2070] Some go as far to say that prehistoric and ancient slavery was a "normal condition."[2071]

The institution is so inherent to human society that many anthropologists consider slavery a sign of civilization rather than a sign of primitiveness,[2072] for during our species' hunting-gathering period enemies were simply killed rather than captured and put into bondage.[2073] (Being nomadic, prehistoric peoples had no use for slaves. Instead, captive men were sacrificed to Pagan gods and goddesses or slaughtered outright, while

---

2062. Meltzer, Vol. 1, pp. 9-201; Craig, Graham, Kagan, Ozment, and Turner, pp. 11-12; Magoffin and Duncalf, p. 76; Dunner, pp. 878-881; McKenzie, s.v. "Slave, slavery"; Hendelson, s.v. "slavery."
2063. Boorstin, pp. 166-167, 209; Encyc. Brit., s.v. "slavery"; Greer, p. 210; Carruth, p. 1502; V. M. Dean, p. 177.
2064. Van Nostrand and Schaeffer, p. 446.
2065. Trevelyan, pp. 113-114; Moore and Dunbar, p. 109; Goubert, pp. 237-238; Hendelson, s.v. "slavery."
2066. Shillington, pp. 174-176; A. C. Bailey, pp. 11-12; Meltzer, Vol. 2, p. 10.
2067. Winks, Brinton, Christopher, and Wolff, Vol. 1, p. 338; Dormon and Jones, p. 62.
2068. Van Loon, p. 350.
2069. McKay, Hill, and Buckler, Vol. 1, p. 12.
2070. For more on the important topic of white slavery, see Jordan and Walsh, passim; Hoffman, passim; Hildreth, passim; Ballagh, passim; Baepler, passim.
2071. Dormon and Jones, p. 62.
2072. The World Book Encyc., "slavery."
2073. Encyc. Brit., s.v. "slavery." As human society became more organized and agriculture was discovered, a system of division of labor was needed to increase food production and profitability. In this early period before the domestication of animals, people naturally turned to other humans for the needed labor, which they procured through war, kidnaping, exchange, barter, and outright purchase. In this way enslavement was eventually substituted for butchery. Dunner, pp. 877-878.

captive women and children were absorbed into the group.)[2074] Thus, for example, 6th-Century prisoners taken by the English in warfare welcomed slavery, since it saved them from torture and ultimately death.[2075]

According to Britain's Anti-Slavery Society, slavery is still found all over the world, even in the U.S., though it continues to flourish most consistently in Africa, the Middle East, the Far East, and parts of South America.[2076]

Not surprisingly then, throughout world history white slavery has been even more common than black slavery. Ancient Germans[2077] and ancient Celts, as just two more examples, were engaged in white slavery long before the start of the American-African slave trade.[2078] In early Ireland, where the white slave trade flourished for centuries, the aggressive, warring Iron Age Celtic people based their entire society on white slavery. When Saint Patrick (he himself a former white slave) arrived on the Emerald Isle in the 5th Century, he referred to the institution as a "horrible and unspeakable crime," then wept with dismay when he discovered that his Irish female converts had been abducted and enslaved by the British chieftain King Coroticus.[2079] Russia engaged in white slavery up until quite recently,[2080] and as late as the 1950s Caucasian slavery was still openly practiced in Turkey.[2081]

Africans themselves, as we have seen, were enslaving each other[2082] back to at least the African Iron Age, some 2,200 years ago,[2083] and it is well-known among slavery scholars that indigenous African slavery was "widespread." Not only that, it had its origins in ancient legal and well established African institutions,[2084] for it had existed among the peoples of preconquest Africa since time immemorial.[2085] Experts in the study of comparative slavery agree that in pre-colonial Africa slavery was

---

2074. Wells, Vol. 1, p. 185. Even after the Agricultural Revolution some 10,000 years ago, forms of this practice continued in Greece well into the 8th Century BC, the time of Homer. Andrewes, p. 46.
2075. J. R. Green, Vol. 1, p. 27.
2076. The World Book Encyc., "slavery."
2077. Van Nostrand and Schaeffer, p. 278; Hayes, Baldwin, and Cole, pp. 79-80.
2078. K. C. Davis, p. 5.
2079. Cahill, pp. 81, 110, 112, 134.
2080. Encyc. Brit., "slavery."
2081. Compton's Encyc., s.v. "slavery and serfdom."
2082. Davidson, TBMB, p. 21; Cappelluti and Grossman, p. 371.
2083. Davidson, TAST, pp. 30, 32.
2084. J. Thornton, p. 74.
2085. Rozwenc, p. 253.

prevalent and commonplace,[2086] and that it was so old there that it had "no distinct beginning."[2087]

This is how we know that none of the Africans taken by Europeans and Yankees started off as free men and women.[2088] Instead, they inevitably began as slaves in their own native land—having been subjugated and beaten (to break their will) by other members of their own race and nationality[2089]—after which they were brought to America already in bondage.[2090]

Contrary to Yankee myth, Africans were never actually hunted down and captured directly by the crews of visiting slave ships. Rather, they were captives who had already been taken during intertribal raids and then enslaved by enterprising African kings,[2091] who quite eagerly traded them to non-African slavers for rum, gunpowder, and textiles.[2092] Wars were often started on purpose by greedy Negro chiefs in order to obtain slaves, a practice that eventually became "endemic" across many parts of the continent.[2093] For making slaves of POWs was an everyday proceeding in early Africa,[2094] a continent where slavery has been an accepted institution since time immemorial.[2095]

Thus, as objective historians now admit, nearly every one of the Africans brought to America on Yankee slave ships had already been enslaved in their home country, after which they were sold to whites by fellow Africans[2096]—black middlemen who worked as agents of African chieftaincies and kingdoms.[2097] Indeed, so tyrannical were the dictatorial kings and queens of early Africa, that by the time the European and American slave trade routes opened up, many African slaves actually looked forward to being shipped off to America: having never experienced authentic freedom, they assumed that the move could only improve their

---

2086. Drescher and Engerman, p. 29.
2087. U. B. Phillips, p. 6.
2088. David, p. 395.
2089. K. C. Davis, p. 19.
2090. Lott, pp. 17, 19, 187.
2091. Strayer and Gatzke, p. 500.
2092. Furnas, p. 115.
2093. Blassingame, p. 14.
2094. J. H. Parry, p. 150.
2095. Stavrianos, p. 569.
2096. Garraty, p. 77.
2097. Craig, Graham, Kagan, Ozment, and Turner, p. 573.

miserable condition[2098]—and American slavery being extremely "mild" in comparison, it nearly always did.[2099]

Due to the rough topography, hostile native peoples,[2100] and numerous slave ports along Africa's coast, Europeans did not attempt to venture inland.[2101] Thus, whites played no role in the actual enslaving process that took place in the African interior, and had no idea what went on beyond the coastal areas.[2102] Even slavery-defending Lincoln once admitted as much, saying:

> ... the African slave trader ... does not catch free negroes and bring them here. He finds them already slaves in the hands of their black captors, and he honestly buys them at the rate of about a red cotton handkerchief a head. This is very cheap, and it is a great abridgement of the sacred right of self-government to hang men for engaging in this profitable trade![2103]

Likewise, in 1908 J. Clarence Stonebraker wrote:

> Slave dealers only obtained their slaves by one tribe conquering another and delivering same into the hands of the slave dealers, or by the consent of parents, getting up their children and selling them. The very false stories that a vessel's crew could go into the jungles and drive out as many negroes as they wished is grossly vile, and was hatched along with many others by the unconscionable and incorrigible prejudice of [Northern] partisans, and for an equally vile purpose. Such things are still being taught and believed to an extent in the frigid [Yankee] section of our country ...[2104]

Africa herself then, along with her many early despotic tribal chiefs and greedy black traders,[2105] must be held accountable for taking part in the enslavement and forced deportation of both 15 million of her

---

2098. David, p. 395.
2099. See e.g., Seabrook, TQJD, p. 65. See also Seabrook, TAHSR, pp. 261, 613, 621.
2100. Chambers, Grew, Herlihy, Rabb, and Woloch, p. 662.
2101. Stavrianos, p. 528.
2102. J. Thornton, p. 307.
2103. Nicolay and Hay, ALCW, Vol. 1, p. 197.
2104. Stonebraker, pp. 50-51.
2105. Stavrianos, p. 570.

own people during the Atlantic slave trade[2106] between the 16th and the 19th Centuries,[2107] and the deaths of some 9 million African slaves who perished from heat, cruel treatment, thirst, and starvation during their journey from Africa's heartland to the Americas.[2108]

In short, it was African chiefs who first enslaved other Africans,[2109] and it was African slave dealers who then carried them to the coast and sold them to Arabs, Europeans, and eventually Yankees.[2110] And it was on this walk to the coast, forced violently along by their African owners, that most African slaves died—not on the infamous Middle Passage to the Americas, as anti-South propagandists have long maintained.[2111]

Medieval Western slavery had Christian roots. As the Bible nowhere disapproves of slavery but instead actually condones and encourages it,[2112] the early Christian Church never came out completely against it.[2113] In fact, having incorporated Aristotle's pro-slavery sentiment into its sacred canon,[2114] Catholicism tolerated and supported the institution[2115] for 1,000 years after the decline of Rome,[2116] and even operated as a large scale and lucrative slaveholder during the early Middle Ages—which helps explain its resistance to abolition at the time.[2117]

The Medieval Papacy certainly had little to say on the matter; and in fact beginning in the 14th Century, the popes routinely threatened their critics and foes with slavery.[2118] One Church leader, Pope Sixtus IV, who possessed 250 personal "servants,"[2119] issued a decree ordering all wayward Florentines to be sold into slavery.[2120] Pope Clement V placed the citizens of Venice under slavery in 1309, and in the early 16th Century Pope Paul

---

2106. Moore and Dunbar, p. 109. Some estimate the total number of Africans removed from their native land during the Atlantic slave trade to be "30 or 40 million." V. M. Dean, p. 163.
2107. Blassingame, p. 3.
2108. K. Clark, p. 323.
2109. Hacker, p. 18.
2110. Shillington, pp. 174, 175.
2111. Drescher and Engerman, p. 34.
2112. Seabrook, TAHSR, pp. 158-162, 651-653.
2113. McKay, Hill, and Buckler, Vol. 1, p. 281.
2114. Childe, p. 232.
2115. Walker, s.v. "Slavery"; Muller, p. 154.
2116. Warnock and Anderson, p. 94.
2117. Winks, Brinton, Christopher, and Wolff, Vol. 1, p. 138.
2118. Heer, pp. 49-50.
2119. De Rosa, p. 170.
2120. Reyes, p. 120.

III condemned all of the English who supported Henry VIII to slavery.[2121]

During the 15th Century, while Christian Rome was serving as a major slave market, Ferdinand the Catholic of Aragon gave Pope Innocent VIII 100 Moorish slaves as a gift. The pontiff promptly divided them up and gave them to his cardinals as presents.[2122] In mid 16th-Century Brazil, Jesuit priests not only approved of slavery, but each had several of his own.[2123] During this same period, after enslavement by the Spanish and the Portuguese, Native-Americans were forced to convert to Catholicism as part of the Church's "official policy."[2124]

It was due to just such Church practices that canon law recognized slaves as one of the three basic social classes (along with the clergy and freemen), and it is why numerous clerics were themselves slave owners.[2125]

Many of the Church Fathers, such as Saint Gregory of Nazianzus and Saint Augustine, saw the institution as a consequence of Original Sin and the Fall of Man,[2126] one that helped maintain an orderly society.[2127] Bishop Ambrose defended slavery and argued that slaves had an advantage over free Christians: they could more readily practice the Christian virtues of humility, forgiveness, and patience.[2128] Saint Thomas Aquinas taught that slavery was Divine punishment,[2129] while Martin Luther believed that it was a social system ordained by God.[2130] Later, among the early American colonists of the 17th and 18th Centuries, Christians and Jews helped one another run the African slave trade[2131] out of the Northeast.[2132]

Though anti-slavery proponents have long tried, they can find no condemnation of the institution in the New Testament, for none exists.[2133] Jesus, Christianity's founder, and Paul, Christianity's greatest apostle, for example, mention servitude and slavery numerous times without ever

---

2121. Heer, p. 50.
2122. Thompson and Johnson, p. 873.
2123. Herring, p. 226.
2124. Hinnells, p. 188.
2125. Simons, p. 88.
2126. Dunner, p. 882.
2127. Boardman, Griffin, and Murray, p. 418.
2128. Muller, p. 186.
2129. Cross and Livingston, s.v. "Slavery."
2130. Dunner, pp. 883-884.
2131. Dimont, p. 359.
2132. Seabrook, EYWTACWW, pp. 69-98.
2133. E. A. Livingstone, s.v. "Slavery."

speaking out against them.[2134] In one incident, Paul returned a runaway (white) slave to his owner,[2135] then admonished slaves to "obey in all things your masters . . ."[2136] Paul refers to himself as "the slave of Christ,"[2137] and the Disciples are frequently called the "slaves of the Lord."[2138]

Far from objecting to slavery, Jesus told his Disciples that whoever wanted to be chief among them should be the "slave of all."[2139] And in one of his many parables Jesus mentions a slave owner who whipped his slave. Never once does Christ say anything against either slavery or even the brutal beating. The moral of the story is that much is asked of those to whom much is given.[2140]

Like the New Testament, the Old Testament is also completely silent on the evils of slavery. Instead it offers many examples of both the backhanded approval of slavery and its full sanction by God.[2141] The institution was openly practiced by the early Hebrews throughout their era,[2142] with one of the more famous of them, Joseph, shown being sold into slavery by his own brothers.[2143] Many of the Old Testament Patriarchs were slave owners, such as Jacob, Joseph, and Job. Abraham, the man to whom God gave the covenant that is "the cornerstone of the whole Christian system," was both a slave owner and a slaver dealer.[2144]

The Fourth and Tenth Commandments recognize slavery as "moral law,"[2145] and the book of Leviticus actually requires early Jews to buy and own slaves.[2146] Although details are lacking on ancient Jewish slavery, it was probably similar, if not identical, to the institution as it was practiced by surrounding early peoples.[2147] For under Hebrew law a slave was defined as "a possession," one that could be bought and sold like

---

2134. See e.g., Matthew 8:5-13; 10:24-25; Luke 12:47; Ephesians 6:5; I Timothy 6:1; Titus 2:9-10.
2135. Philemon 1:1-25.
2136. Colossians 3:22.
2137. Galatians 1:10.
2138. Acts 4:29; 16:17.
2139. Mark 10:44.
2140. Luke 12:42-48.
2141. See e.g., Exodus 21:26-27; Proverbs 29:19.
2142. Dunner, p. 879.
2143. Genesis 37:26-28.
2144. See Seabrook, TAHSR, pp. 158-162.
2145. Exodus 20: 10, 17.
2146. Leviticus 25:44-46. See also W. Smith, s.v. "slave."
2147. McKay, Hill, and Buckler, Vol. 1, p. 44.

livestock.[2148]

The Koran too recognizes slavery,[2149] and mentions it numerous times, enjoining slave owners to be merciful to their human chattel.[2150] In ancient times entire Islamic armies were made up of slaves. Some of these soldier-slaves rose up the ranks becoming officers themselves, or even governors. In some cases Muslim slaves attained their freedom, founded dynasties of their own, and became kings.[2151]

The list of slave owning societies is nearly endless.

Slavery is indeed a ubiquitous worldwide phenomenon, one that stubbornly persists into modern times, and which dates far back into the mists of prehistory on all continents, and among all races, ethnic groups, religions, societies, and peoples.[2152] All of us then, no matter what our race, color, or nationality, have ancestors who were once in bondage or who once held others in bondage. *We are all descendants of slaves and slave owners.*[2153]

2148. See Exodus 12:44; Leviticus 25:44-46; Ecclesiastes 2:7.
2149. Hayes, Baldwin, and Cole, p. 130.
2150. See e.g., Dawood, pp. 60, 63, 70, 89, 192, 241, 248-249, 297, 398, 406, 426.
2151. Zaehner, pp. 181-182.
2152. Meltzer, Vol. 1, pp. 1-6.
2153. For a comprehensive look into world and American slavery, see Seabrook, EYWTAASIW, passim.

16

LINCOLN'S VIEWS ON BLACKS, SLAVERY, & EMANCIPATION

PART TWO

THOUGH IT HAS BEEN FORGOTTEN, ignored, or suppressed today, the truth about the origins of American black slavery was once common knowledge, among both whites and blacks. Thus the 19th-Century black Yankee author and civil rights advocate, W. E. B. Du Bois, could write:

> I shall forgive the white South much in its final judgment day: I shall forgive its slavery, for slavery is a world-old habit . . .[2154]

Unlike many modern blacks, blacks from the Old South too were once well aware of the facts. This awareness was the reason they could not lay the blame for the institution solely on whites. Instead, they readily admitted that: "Our fathers were brought here as slaves because they were captured in war . . . [in Africa]."[2155]

Lincoln, of course, never mentioned such facts, or cared about them. His target was always *white* Southern slave owners (despite the widespread and obvious presence of tens of thousands of black and red slave owners). And it was not because they supported slavery, though he

---

2154. Du Bois, p. 172.
2155. B. F. Butler, p. 498.

pretended it was (in order to curry the abolitionist vote). It was because white Southern slave owners supported states' rights.

Still, it was no secret that Lincoln disliked the idea of his race having to share America with the black race. To his credit, he seldom tried to hide it. It has only been concealed from the general public by modern-day Lincolnian sycophants, Yankee apologists, and Northern folklorists, who portray Lincoln as they want him to be seen, not as he really was. This is why we must continually turn to Lincoln's own words, where the authentic man burns through the haze of idolatry and myth that has been built up around him.

While, as I have shown, Lincoln was ambiguous on many topics and issues, he left no doubt as to his position on race. In fact, he seemed desperate for the world to know where he stood on the matter, and he took great pains to make sure they did. During his Ottawa, Illinois, debate with Douglas in 1858, for instance, the gangly orator with the high pitched voice stood before his Northern audience and said:

> I have no purpose to introduce political and social equality between the white and black races. There is a physical difference between the two, which, in my judgement, will probably forever forbid their living together upon the footing of perfect equality, and, inasmuch as it becomes a necessity that there must be a difference, I . . . am in favor of the race to which I belong having the superior position. I have never said anything to the contrary . . .[2156]

Many other such examples abound, such as his October 16, 1854, speech at Peoria, Illinois, where he spoke of black colonization, Liberia, white superiority, and the difficulty of getting rid of both slavery and freed blacks. Here he also acknowledged the reality of near universal white racism in the North:

> If all earthly power were given me, I should not know what to do as to the existing institution. My first impulse would be to free all the slaves, and send them to Liberia [Africa]—to their own native land. But a moment's reflection would convince me, that whatever of high hope (as I think there is) there may be in this, in the long run, its sudden execution is impossible. If they were all landed

---

2156. Nicolay and Hay, ALCW, Vol. 1, p. 458.

there in a day, they would all perish in the next ten days; and there are not surplus shipping and surplus money enough in the world to carry them there in many times ten days. What then? Free them all, and keep them among us as underlings? Is it quite certain that this betters their condition? I think I would not hold one in slavery at any rate; yet the point is not clear enough to me to denounce people upon. What next? Free them, and make them politically and socially our equals? My own feelings will not admit of this; and if mine would, we well know that those of the great mass of white people will not.[2157]

On September 18, 1858, at Charleston, Illinois, the fourth debate between Lincoln and Douglas, Lincoln said:

> I will say, then, that I am not, nor have ever been, in favor of bringing about in any way the social and political equality of the black and white races—that I am not, nor ever have been, in favor of making voters or jurors of negroes, nor of qualifying them to hold office, nor to intermarry with white people; and I will say in addition to this, that there is a physical difference between the white and black races, which, I believe, will ever forbid the two races living together on terms of social and political equality. And inasmuch as they cannot so live, while they do remain together there must be the position of superior and inferior, and I, as much as any other man, am in favor of having the superior position assigned to the white race.
> . . . I will add to this, that I have never seen, to my knowledge, a man, woman, or child who was in favor of producing a perfect equality, social and political, between negroes and white men. . . . I will also add to the remarks I have made . . . that I have never had the least apprehension that I or my friends would marry negroes, if there was no law to keep them from it; but as Judge Douglas and his friends seem to be in great apprehension that they might, if there were no law to keep them from it, I give him the most solemn pledge that I will to the very last stand by the law of this State, which forbids the marrying of white people with negroes.[2158]

Lincoln got a good many laughs from his all-white Northern supporters with remarks like these, particularly his prediction that

---

2157. Nicolay and Hay, ALCW, Vol. 1, p. 288.
2158. Nicolay and Hay, ALCW, Vol. 1, pp. 539, 540.

European-Americans and African-Americans would never live in harmony together. But blacks found little humor in his racist comments, and civil rights leaders and abolitionists were absolutely scandalized.

Lincoln, however, did not see black civil rights or interracial marriage as serious social matters. Dismissing them as nothing more than "false issues,"[2159] the atheist took a typically analytical approach. On September 16, 1859, he wrote to David R. Locke:

> I shall never marry a negress, but I have no objection to anyone else doing so. If a white man wants to marry a negro woman, let him do it,—if the negro woman can stand it.[2160]

Lincoln loyalists like to pretend that his racism softened, and even disappeared, as time passed, particularly during his War. But this is not true.

On August 14, 1862, almost a year-and-a-half into the conflict, Lincoln requested that a group of blacks meet with him at the White House. They were the first free African-Americans to ever enter those hallowed halls. But the event was not something that many would want recorded in the pages of American history.[2161] The fact that the five black men were hand-picked by Reverend James Mitchell, Lincoln's commissioner of emigration, hints at the enormous social fiasco Lincoln was about to create, surely the worst to ever occur inside the White House.

None of the Negroes who were hurriedly ushered into the president's office that day were well-known. In fact, four of them were "lowly contrabands" (captured Southern slaves). The awe-struck, passive group had been selected purposefully to avoid a "scene." For as it turns out, Lincoln wanted a captive, uneducated audience who would sit and listen to a racist monologue on the advantages of black deportation (colonization), not engage him in an intellectual debate about slavery.[2162]

As the colored delegation sat in stunned silence, Lincoln removed a crumbled up piece of paper from inside his large stovepipe hat. On it was a speech, written in hastily scrawled words. In his thin alto voice,

---

2159. Nicolay and Hay, ALCW, Vol. 1, p. 508.
2160. W. E. Curtis, p. 320.
2161. Hacker, p. 584.
2162. Quarles, pp. 146-147.

Lincoln began to read aloud the following:

> . . . many men engaged on either side [of the Civil War] do not care for you one way or the other. . . . It is better for us both, therefore, to be separated. . . .
>
> There is an unwillingness on the part of our people, harsh as it may be, for you free colored people to remain with us. . . . The colony of Liberia has been in existence a long time. In a certain sense it is a success. . . . The question is, if the colored people are persuaded to go anywhere, why not there? . . .
>
> The place I am thinking about for a colony is in Central America. . . . The country is a very excellent one for any people . . . and especially because of the similarity of climate with your native soil, thus being suited to your physical condition. . . . this particular place has all the advantages for a colony. . . .
>
> The practical thing I want to ascertain is, whether I can get a number of able-bodied [black] men, with their wives and children, who are willing to go when I present evidence of encouragement and protection. . . . I want you to let me know whether this can be done or not.[2163]

Those blacks, if there were any, who wanted to help Lincoln with his insane plan, would not be allowed to think for themselves, however. Instead, as the president told the group:

> It is exceedingly important that we have [black] men at the beginning capable of thinking as white men . . .[2164]

As a final affront to common sense and social propriety, Lincoln added that any blacks who refused to leave the United States were taking "an extremely selfish view of the case."[2165] "For the sake of your race," he told the disquieted black committee in closing,

> you should sacrifice something of your present comfort for the purpose of being as grand in that respect as the white people.[2166]

2163. For the full text see Nicolay and Hay, ALCW, Vol. 2, pp. 222-225. See also W. P. Pickett, pp. 317-323.
2164. Nicolay and Hay, ALCW, Vol. 2, p. 223.
2165. Nicolay and Hay, ALCW, Vol. 2, p. 223.
2166. Nicolay and Hay, ALCW, Vol. 2, p. 224.

Lincoln waited, but did not receive an immediate answer to his question concerning how many African-Americans would allow themselves to be shipped to Central America, or "back to Africa." Unbeknownst to the "Great Emancipator," there was good reason for this: the five black delegates were in a state of humiliation, confusion, anger, and shock, and needed time to formulate a response.

A few days later, their reply arrived at the White House. The missive was brief and to the point. Furious, the black committee members scolded Lincoln for campaigning for the deportation of America's colored population, then asked him to please mind his own business.[2167]

Lincoln must have scratched his head in bewilderment. He never grasped what every black and nearly every white Southerner understood instinctively: if America was ever to rid herself of color prejudice, Lincoln's black colonization plans were certainly not the "solution." In fact, it was obvious to nearly everyone that the deportation of blacks would only aggravate the problem;[2168] obvious to everyone, that is, except Lincoln. But then again, he was never truly interested in working toward a racist-free society. For him it was either deportation or ongoing racism.

When educated black leaders heard about the White House conference they were enraged. Easily seeing through the charade, Frederick Douglass, the prominent abolitionist, former Northern slave, and Lincoln's confidant, publicly denounced the president for his white racial pride, disdain for blacks, and rank dishonesty.[2169] Furthermore, wrote a fuming Douglass in his newspaper:

> The tone of frankness and benevolence which Mr. Lincoln assumes in his speech to the colored committee is too thin a mask not to be seen through. The genuine spark of humanity is missing in it. It expresses merely the desire to get rid of them . . .[2170]

A New Jersey newspaper printed the response of an exasperated black citizen. In lambasting the "meddlesome, impudent" president, he asked Lincoln to remember that in God's eyes there is only one race on

---

2167. See R. L. Riley, p. 109.
2168. Quarles, p. 148.
2169. Oates, AL, p. 103. See also Janessa Hoyte, "Taking Another Look at Abraham Lincoln," *The Crisis*, November/December 2000, pp. 52-54.
2170. *Douglass' Monthly*, September 1862, Vol. 5, pp. 707-708.

earth: the human race.[2171] But being an anti-Christian "infidel," Lincoln never understood, or believed, this simple but powerful divine truth.

Black people across the country were indeed disgusted after learning what Lincoln had told the committee at the Executive Mansion, for by 1862 nearly all blacks in both the U.S. and the C.S. were native-born Americans. Most were fourth and fifth generation Americans[2172]—some were as much as sixth and seventh generation Americans, or more (we will recall that blacks were in the area now known as Virginia by 1526).[2173] A great many whites, however, were not more than first, second, or third generation Americans. In light of this, which race was more American, the white or the black one, blacks rightly asked? After all, by 1860, 99 percent of all blacks were native born Americans, a larger percentage than for whites.[2174]

We already know how Lincoln would have answered this question. The fact remained that the vast majority of African-Americans had no intention of taking the president up on his offer to be shipped to a foreign land, for it meant leaving behind their loved ones (both black and white), their homes and farms, and their family cemeteries, filled with ancestors dating back to the early 1600s, and in some cases, even beyond.

Angered about Lincoln's endless and insensitive promotion of colonization, blacks from Long Island, New York, put their foot down:

> This is our native country; we have as strong attachment naturally to our native hills, valleys, plains, luxuriant forests, flowing streams, mighty rivers and lofty mountains, as any other people.[2175]

Taking a spiritual approach, a group of black men from Pennsylvania wrote up "An Appeal From the Colored Men of Philadelphia to the President of the United States." It read:

2171. See the *National Anti-Slavery Standard*, September 6, 1862.
2172. Fogel, pp. 31-32.
2173. Meltzer, Vol. 2, p. 127.
2174. Fogel and Engerman, pp. 23-24. Contrary to Northern mythology, of the South's 3,500,000 black servants, only 14 percent (or about 500,000 individuals) were imported from Africa between the settling of Jamestown, Virginia, and 1861. The other 3,000,000 (86 percent), all American-born, were the result of natural reproduction. Garraty and McCaughey, p. 214.
2175. Blight, p. 141.

> We can find nothing in the religion of our Lord and Master teaching us that color is the standard by which He judges His creatures, either in this life or in the life to come.... We ask, that by the standard of justice and humanity we may be weighed, and that men shall not longer be measured by their stature or color.[2176]

On August 28, 1862, just two weeks after Lincoln's racial debacle at the White House, African-American Robert Purvis spoke for nearly all American blacks in an open letter to the president:

> The children of the black man have enriched the [American] soil by their tears, and sweat, and blood. Sir, we were born here, and here we choose to remain. For twenty years we were goaded and harassed by systematic efforts to make us colonize [abroad]. We were coaxed and mobbed, and mobbed and coaxed, but we refused to budge. We planted ourselves upon our inalienable rights, and were proof against all the efforts that were made to expatriate us. For the last fifteen years we have enjoyed comparative quiet. Now again the malign project is broached, and again, as before, in the name of humanity are we invited to leave.
>
> In God's name what good do you expect to accomplish by such a course? If you will not let our brethren in bonds go free, if you will not let us, as did our fathers, share in the privileges of the government, if you will not let us even help fight the battles of the country, in Heaven's name, at least, *let us alone*. Is that too great a boon to ask of your magnanimity?
>
> I elect to stay on the soil on which I was born, and on the plot of ground which I have fairly bought and honestly paid for. Don't advise me to leave, and don't add insult to injury by telling me it's for my own good; of that I am to be the judge. It is in vain that you talk to me about the 'two races,' and their 'mutual antagonism.' In the matter of rights there is but one race, and that is the *human* race. 'God has made of one blood all nations to dwell on all the face of the earth' [Acts 17:26]. And it is not true that there is a mutual antagonism between the white and colored people of this community. You may antagonize us, but we do not antagonize you. You may hate us, but we do not hate you.[2177]

All of these "appeals" were forwarded directly to the President.

2176. *An Appeal*, pp. 4, 7-8.
2177. W. W. Brown, pp. 258-259.

If he ever read any of them, no one would have known. For despite them, he continued to pursue his plan to deport all blacks out of the U.S. as vigorously as ever.

The five African-Americans Lincoln invited to the White House in order to ask them to leave the country were not the first to be disappointed in their visit with the bigoted president. Still they were fortunate to get in. During Lincoln's entire administration, right up until his final months of life, while black slaves worked on finishing the White House (its construction had not yet been completed when he took office), free blacks, like Frederick Douglass, were barred from the premises.[2178] Another famous example was abolitionist, former Northern slave, and black separatist, Sojourner Truth.

On February 25, 1862, a year into Lincoln's presidency, Truth was denied admission to the White House on account of her skin color. On other occasions she was able to make her way inside. But according to her own testimony, even then she was seldom made to feel welcome, had to wait longer than whites, and was never received with any "reverence." An eyewitness at one of the rare meetings between the two said that Lincoln kept referring to Truth pejoratively as "aunty," just "as he would his washerwoman."[2179]

Though calling black women "aunt" or "aunty" was considered a harmless pet-name by Lincoln and other racist white Yankees, most Northern African-Americans saw it for what it really was: a term of derision meant to "keep blacks in their place."[2180] Nonetheless, before she left, the always racially insensitive Lincoln autographed his black "friend's" scrapbook with the following words: "For Aunty Sojourner Truth, A. Lincoln, October 29, 1864."[2181]

Certainly blacks, like Miss Truth, who lived through Lincoln's War, would be aghast to hear him referred to today as the "Great Emancipator," for this is one of the North's more recent and most pernicious myths. As mentioned, not only did Lincoln never officially require permanent emancipation, his proclamation never freed a single

---

2178. Buckley, p. 65.
2179. See Greenberg and Waugh, pp. 351-358.
2180. See, e.g., Chesnut, MCCW, p. 435. We will note that in the South "aunty" (and "uncle" for men) was considered a term of endearment by both whites and blacks, particularly when applied to one's own servants.
2181. McKissack and McKissack, p. 146; Coffin, p. 457.

slave. In fact, servitude was only finally officially abolished and outlawed "forever" in all states across the entire U.S. on December 6, 1865, with the ratification of the Thirteenth Amendment—eight months *after* Lincoln died.[2182]

While today Lincoln masquerades as the liberator of the black people, many 19th-Century African-Americans saw him for what he really was: a white racist, a white supremacist, and a white separatist.[2183]

On April 14, 1876, Frederick Douglass, as just one example, gave a speech in Washington, D.C., known as the "Oration Delivered Upon the Occasion of the Unveiling of the Freedman's Monument in Memory of Abraham Lincoln." In it, Douglass made his largely white audience squirm by summarily dismissing the president's efforts on the behalf of blacks. Speaking directly to the African-Americans in the audience, he said:

> It must be admitted, truth compels me to admit, even here in the presence of the monument we have erected to his memory, Abraham Lincoln was not, in the fullest sense of the word, either our man or our model. In his interests, in his associations, in his habits of thought, and in his prejudices, he was a white man.
>
> He was preeminently the white man's President, entirely devoted to the welfare of white men. He was ready and willing at any time during the first years of his administration to deny, postpone, and sacrifice the rights of humanity in the coloured people to promote the welfare of the white people of this country. In all his education and feeling he was an American of the Americans. He came into the Presidential chair upon one principle alone, namely, opposition to the extension of slavery. His arguments in furtherance of this policy had then motive and mainspring in his patriotic devotion to the interests of his own race. To protect, defend, and perpetuate slavery in the States where it existed, Abraham Lincoln was not less ready than any other President to draw the sword of the nation. He was ready to execute all the supposed constitutional guarantees of the United States Constitution in favour of the slave system anywhere inside the slave States. He was willing to pursue, recapture, and send back the fugitive slave to his master, and to suppress a slave rising for liberty, though his guilty master were already in arms against the Government. The race to which we belong were not the

---

2182. Findlay and Findlay, p. 227; Fogel, p. 207.
2183. Garraty and McCaughey, p. 254.

special objects of his consideration.[2184]

Informed 20th- and 21st-Century blacks have agreed. Black activist Malcolm X thought that Lincoln did more to hurt and deceive blacks than anyone else, before or since,[2185] while Southern professor and author Julius Lester declared that blacks should feel anger not gratitude toward Lincoln.[2186]

One of the more recent and objective African-American examinations of Lincoln comes from the editor of *Ebony* magazine, Lerone Bennett Jr., who maintains that Lincoln was the very embodiment of the white supremacist, though one with good intentions. But, Bennett asserts, his good intentions only went so far: Lincoln was not opposed to slavery itself.[2187] As Douglass stated above, Lincoln was opposed to the *extension* and *spread* of slavery, a view substantiated by thousands of others, including, as we have seen, no less an authority than America's twenty-eighth president, Woodrow Wilson.[2188] In 1854, Lincoln himself said: "I now do no more than oppose the extension of slavery."[2189] This was to be done, according to a speech Lincoln gave on May 29, 1856, not by national abolition, but in this manner:

> Let us draw a cordon, so to speak, around the slave states, and the hateful institution, like a reptile poisoning itself, will perish by its own infamy.[2190]

Pro-North historians claim that Lincoln later changed his views from wanting to merely limit slavery to the South to wanting nationwide abolition. It is true that over time he altered his *public* statements to reflect sociopolitical trends (in an effort to procure votes and remain in power). *Privately*, however, he never wavered from the idea that whites must be accommodated by restricting slavery to where it already existed. Here is what the venerable *Encyclopedia Britannica* says on this topic:

2184. Douglass, LTFD, p. 872.
2185. Warren, p. 262.
2186. M. Davis, pp. 154-155.
2187. Bennett, FIG, passim.
2188. W. Wilson, DR, p. 125.
2189. Nicolay and Hay, ALCW, Vol. 1, p. 218.
2190. Tarbell, Vol. 4, p. 116.

[Checking the extension of slavery] was the key-note to his thought *ever after*, both in regard to the territories and in regard to the preservation of the Union. He admitted frankly that his overmastering concern was the welfare of the free poor people of the white races.[2191]

Let us let Lincoln speak for himself. On December 15, 1860, a little over a month after he had been elected president, he wrote a letter to North Carolinian John A. Gilmer, in which the uttered the following words:

Do the people of the South really entertain fears that a Republican administration would, directly or indirectly, interfere with the slaves, or with them about the slaves? If they do, I wish to assure you, as once a friend, and still, I hope, not an enemy, that there is no cause for such fears. The South would be in no more danger in this respect than it was in the days of [George] Washington. I suppose, however, this does not meet the case. *You think slavery is right and ought to be extended, while we think it is wrong and ought to be restricted. That, I suppose, is the rub. It certainly is the only substantial difference between us.*[2192]

This, of course, was merely a continuation of the views he had held all along, from the beginning of his political career. For example, just two years earlier, on October 15, 1858, Lincoln made this statement at Alton, Illinois, during his seventh and final joint debate with Judge Stephen A. Douglas:

Now, irrespective of the moral aspect of this question as to whether there is a right or wrong in enslaving a negro, I am still in favor of our new [Western] Territories being in such a condition that *white men* may find a home—may find some spot where they can better their condition—where they can settle upon new soil, and better their condition in life. I am in favor of this not merely (I must say it here as I have elsewhere) for our own people who are born amongst us, but as an outlet for *free white people* everywhere, the world over—in which Hans, and Baptiste, and Patrick, and all other men from all the world, may find new homes and better their condition in life.[2193]

2191. Encyc. Brit., s.v. "Lincoln, Abraham." Emphasis added.
2192. Seabrook, L, p. 406. Emphasis added.
2193. Seabrook, L, pp. 420-421. Emphasis added.

SECTION FOUR

INVASION, SUBJUGATION, & RECONSTRUCTION

[If the North] was the cause of brute force, blind passion, fanatical hate, lust of power, and the greed of gain, against the cause of constitutional law and human rights, then who was better fitted to represent it than the talented, but the low, ignorant and vulgar, rail-splitter of Illinois? Or if, as we also believe, it was the cause of infidelity and atheism, and against the principles and the spirit of the Christian religion, then who more worthy to muster its motley hosts, and let them slip with the fury of the pit than the lowbred infidel of Pigeon Creek, in whose eyes the Saviour of the world was "an illegitimate child," and the Holy Mother as base as his own?

Albert Taylor Bledsoe (1809-1877)
April 1873

17

SOUTH-HATING IN VICTORIAN AMERICA

WHY HAVE THE NORTH, THE politically correct, and New South scallywags—the latter a group that has turned against its own heritage—continued to promote anti-South, pro-Lincoln mythology for the last 150 years, most of it absurd, insulting, and degrading, and all of it untrue and unhistorical?

It is to justify an unjustifiable war, one both senseless and illegal. For if the world can be convinced that the South is a land of ignorance, vice, immorality, violence, stupidity, savagery, and sloth, one that once practiced a barbaric form of slavery—as the anti-South movement has long claimed, then Lincoln's War against her was excusable, and even warranted.

Many Yankees have attempted to do just that by preaching overt, hurtful, and hateful anti-South propaganda. This was, after all, the real reason most Northern abolitionists wanted to end slavery: not to free black Southern slaves, but to inflict pain on their white Southern masters.[2194] One at the forefront of this group was New Englander, abolitionist-racist, and liberal Transcendentalist Ralph Waldo Emerson.

Emerson—who once predicted that because blacks were inferior, they would eventually become as extinct as the Dodo bird,[2195] who worshiped and deified the South-loathing psychopath John Brown,[2196] and

---

2194. Garraty and McCaughey, p. 253.
2195. R. W. Emerson, JMNRWE, Vol. 13, p. 286.
2196. Ashe, p. 18. Brown's family was known to have a history of mental illness. Hinkle, p. 114.

who was against slavery, not because it exploited blacks, but because it threatened to undermine the moral fiber of white New England[2197]—regarded Dixie as a primitive, dark land, awash in cruelty and sin, populated by inbred hicks and savage rednecks. Here is how the famed Concord Brahmin described the men of Dixie:

> The young Southerner comes here [to New England] a spoiled child, with graceful manners, excellent self-command, very good to be spoiled more, but good for nothing else,—a mere parader. He has conversed so much with rifles, horses and dogs that he has become himself a rifle, a horse and a dog, and in civil, educated company, where anything human is going forward, he is dumb and unhappy, like an Indian in a church. Treat them with great deference, as we often do, and they accept it all as their due without misgiving. Give them an inch and they take a mile. They are mere bladders of conceit. Each snipper-snapper of them all undertakes to speak for the entire Southern States. . . . They are more civilized than the Seminoles, however, in my opinion; a little more. Their question respecting any man is like a Seminole's,—How can he fight? In this country [i.e., the North], we ask, What can he do? His pugnacity is all they prize in man, dog, or turkey. The proper way of treating them is not deference, but to say as Mr. Ripley does, 'Fiddle faddle,' in answer to each solemn remark about 'The South.'[2198]

An even more outspoken South-hater was New England Congressman Charles Sumner, after whom Boston's well-known Sumner Tunnel was named. Sumner, like many other Northerners, enjoyed emphasizing the differences between South and North, with the latter always in the superior position, the former in the inferior. On the one side there were the moral, diligent, Christian people of the North, while on the other, there were the perverted, beastly, illiterate, bullies of the South,[2199] "hirelings picked from the drunken spew and vomit of an uneasy civilization," as Sumner phrased it.[2200] (For his intolerance and hidebound South-hating views, Sumner was once caned—to the delight and approval of most Southerners—and crippled for several years, in the Senate

---

2197. Donald, LR, p. 31.
2198. R. W. Emerson, JRWE, Vol. 4, pp. 312-313.
2199. See L. Johnson, p. 34.
2200. Sumner, p. 30.

chamber by South Carolina Representative Preston S. Brooks.)[2201]

This old hatred, of course, was transferred into Lincoln's War, and remained very much alive even after the South surrendered. Not long after Lee stacked arms at Appomattox, T. R. Kennan, a Yank with the 17th Massachusetts Volunteers, wrote to his sister:

> If I should speak my real feelings, I should say that I am sorry the war is ended. Pray do not think me murderous. No; but all the punishment we could inflict on the rebels would not atone for one drop of the blood so cruelly spilled. I would exterminate them, root and branch. They have often said they preferred it before subjugation, and, with the good help of God, I would give it them. I am only saying what thousands [of other Yanks] say every day. Our army is sorry that they have done their work; they have a deep-seated love for Abraham Lincoln, and when they see no chance for further chastisement of our enemy, they give vent to their feelings in other ways. I do hope you won't think me violent. I cannot help it.[2202]

Yes, even after the War had supposedly "cleansed" the South of its "uppity attitude," the old Northern loathing continued. After Lincoln's forces had crushed much of Dixie into rubble and killed over a quarter of her people, Laura Towne, like hundreds other self-righteous Yanks, decided it was time to go down and educate "ignorant Southerners." In 1866, after spending four years in South Carolina, she had this to say about the beautiful people of Dixie: ". . . our ways are not their ways, and it is bothersome to know them."[2203]

To this day there is only one cultural group left in the U.S. for which it is still socially acceptable and politically permissible to ridicule, criticize, and condemn: Southerners. The South, one of the most unique and enchanting regions in all of America, and the only section of the U.S. ever invaded by another section,[2204] has had her heritage denigrated, her

---

2201. J. S. Bowman, CWDD, s.v. "May 1856." On May 20, 1856, Senator Sumner took the floor to denounce South Carolina Senator A. P. Butler, who wanted the Nebraska Territory to be able to join the Union as a slavery-optional state (a "slave state" to Yanks). Two days later, disgusted with Sumner's constant anti-South remarks, Representative Brooks went to Sumner's desk and said: "I have read your speech twice over carefully; it is a libel on South Carolina, and Mr. Butler, who is a relative of mine." Out came Brooks' cane, and the rest is history. Annunzio, p. 18. I am honored to be cousins with both Butler and Brooks.
2202. Post, p. 468.
2203. R. S. Holland, p. 252.
2204. Grissom, p. 226.

folkways mocked, her flags torn down and banned from public display, her songs barred from sports games, and the statues and monuments of her heroes desecrated. Her 120 million people, along with their speech, attire, foods, and lifestyles, are repeatedly made the butt of jokes on TV, and serve as idiotic and often negative stereotypes in film. All this despite the fact that today Dixie is one of the most desirable places to live in the Western hemisphere: the American South now has the highest quality of life and the lowest cost of living in the U.S.[2205]

Little wonder that many Southerners are again uniting to form organizations, like the League of the South, that are pushing for a second secession and the creation of a new independent Southern Confederacy.

The truth is that the South was, and is, none of the things that men like Emerson and Sumner claimed. No better, more faithful, hard-working, educated, decent, humane, civilized, and well-mannered people ever lived. All Southerners have ever wanted, as we have shown, is to be left alone. Left alone to live their lives as they see fit, without the interference of an increasingly progressive and invasive government. This Lincoln refused to do, even knowing that secession was a legal constitutional right, that slavery had gotten its start in the North, that abolition had begun in the South, and that Southern slavery was well on its way out by 1860.[2206]

Why should the South be blamed for her own climate, topography, and geography? After all, it was Nature who dealt the fateful hand by giving Dixie lush, sprawling, green fertile lands, long hot summers, and countless navigable rivers, perfect for the outdoor businesses of agriculture and commerce; while Nature gave to the North hilly terrain, rocky, sandy soil, and long cold winters, ideal for the indoor businesses of manufacturing and finance.[2207] As Lyon Gardiner Tyler points out, it was not slavery that created sectional tensions between South and North:

2205. See C. Johnson, pp. 1-29, 232. *Travel & Leisure* magazine, for example, called Nashville, Tennessee, one of "America's Friendliest Cities," while Relocate-America.com placed Brentwood and Nashville, Tennessee, on its "Top 100 Places to Live" list. *Tennessee Homes*, October/November, 2009, p. 6.

2206. Though slavery was more profitable than ever in 1860 (see Fogel and Engerman, pp. 158-257), by then, hundreds of years of Southern abolition had worked to finally turn nearly all of Dixie against what had started out as the North's "peculiar institution."

2207. P. M. Roberts, pp. 195-196.

... geography had marked out the character of the two sections of the United States before any white man came along.[2208]

During his seventh and final debate with Lincoln at Alton, Illinois, on October 15, 1858, Illinois Senator Stephen A. Douglas pointed out that the U.S. Constitution, along with the concept of states' rights, themselves had been constructed around the geography of North America:

> This government was made upon the great basis of the sovereignty of the States, the right of each State to regulate its own domestic institutions to suit itself, and that right was conferred with the understanding and expectation that inasmuch as each locality had separate interests, each locality must have different and distinct local and domestic institutions, corresponding to its wants and interests. Our [Founding] fathers knew, when they made the government, that the laws and institutions which were well adapted to the green mountains of Vermont were unsuited to the rice plantations of South Carolina. They knew then, as well as we know now, that the laws and institutions which would be well adapted to the beautiful prairies of Illinois would not be suited to the mining regions of California. They knew that in a republic as broad as this, having such a variety of soil, climate, and interest, there must necessarily be a corresponding variety of local laws—the policy and institutions of each State adapted to its condition and wants. For this reason this Union was established on the right of each State to do as it pleased on the question of slavery, and every other question, and the various States were not allowed to complain of, much less interfere with, the policy of their neighbors.[2209]

Thus, due to geography, Africans were eventually sent from Northern slave merchants southward to the great cotton plantations, against the will and interests of nearly 95 percent of the Southern people. This is why, in the early 1800s, Virginia's antislavery senator, John Randolph, could truthfully say that slavery was never something the South sought out. Rather, it was "imposed" upon her against her choosing.[2210]

Lincoln himself knew better than to attack a foreign nation, one

---

2208. *Tyler's Quarterly Historical and Genealogical Magazine*, 1929, Vol. 10, "General Lee's Birthday," p. 263.
2209. Nicolay and Hay, ALCW, Vol. 1, p. 487.
2210. Coit, p. 166.

made up primarily of poor farmers and soft-hearted, defenseless country folk. He knew full well that if the tables had been turned and it was the North that had been burdened with slavery, its citizens would have done exactly what the South's did: develop a "leave us alone" bunker mentality. During the August 21, 1858, Ottawa, Illinois, debate between himself and Douglas, Lincoln made this remarkable statement:

> ... I think I have no prejudice against the Southern people. They are just what we would be in their situation. If slavery did not now exist among them, they would not introduce it. If it did now exist among us, we should not instantly give it up. This I believe of the masses north and south. ...
>
> When southern people tell us they are no more responsible for the origin of slavery than we, I acknowledge the fact. ... I surely will not blame them for not doing what I should not know how to do myself.[2211]

Despite this seemingly tender sentiment, three years later Lincoln used what he ludicrously called his "better angel"[2212] to viciously and illegitimately invade the South, using a scorched earth policy of total war to destroy her infrastructure, and burn her homes, shops, towns, schools, churches, hospitals, libraries, courthouses, and universities to the ground, killing nearly two million (one million Southern whites and one million Southern blacks) of her people in the process. Horribly, most of these were non-combatants, as almost all civilian deaths during the War occurred in the South.[2213]

In my Tennessee hometown alone some 1,750 Confederate men and boys were slaughtered by Lincoln's invaders on a single afternoon in the Fall of 1864 in one of the goriest and most senseless battles of his War. Cut down like wheat before the scythe, as one eyewitness described the horrific scene,[2214] many a brave Southern soldier died within sight of his own home, as parents, wives, and children raged and sobbed in disbelief at Lincoln's bewildering aggression. Another 4,500 Rebels were wounded and maimed that day in one of the darkest and bloodiest chapters

---

2211. Nicolay and Hay, ALCW, Vol. 1, p. 288.
2212. That is, the good side of his nature, as opposed to the evil one. See Nicolay and Hay, ALCW, Vol. 2, p. 7.
2213. J. M. McPherson, ACW, p. 9.
2214. Logsdon, EBF, p. 36.

in American history: the Battle of Franklin II.[2215] Confederate soldier Sam Watkins, who was on the Franklin battlefield that day, called it "the blackest page" of the War, and "the finishing stroke to the independence of the Southern Confederacy."[2216]

In 1864 my own third great-grandfather, Confederate cavalryman Elias Jent Sr., who served in the 1st Regiment of the 13th Kentucky Cavalry (known as "Caudill's Army"), was unlawfully executed by Yankee soldiers while at home in Kentucky on furlough. Elias thus became one of the conservatively estimated 329,000 Confederate soldiers who died needlessly due to Lincoln's illegitimate war-mongering.

Tragically, Elias' wife, Rachel Cornett, my third great-grandmother, was also murdered. The unarmed, gentle farming couple had been visiting relatives in Perry County when they were discovered by marauding Union soldiers. Ignoring the heart-rending screams and futile entreaties of kin, the pitiless Yankee wretches dragged Elias and Rachel unceremoniously into the yard and, at gunpoint, hanged them side-by-side from a large tree in front of family, friends, and neighbors. No reason was given and no punishment was ever meted out. This was typical Lincolnian military procedure, and our family still holds "Honest Abe" directly responsible for Elias and Rachel's deaths.

In 1863 it was this very type of behavior that inspired Confederates, like Sergeant Edwin Fay, to avow: even if peace is ever made with the North, if I live another 100 years I will murder every single Yankee I come across. As long as I can kill him without much risk, I will.[2217]

Indeed, for their crimes, the name Lincoln, along with those of hundreds of other Yankee war criminals, among them Sherman, Sheridan, Butler, Hatch, Hunter,[2218] Pope, Grant (who Spooner called "the chief murderer of the war"),[2219] and Robert Huston Milroy, will never be

---

2215. McDonough and Connelly, p. 157. For a detailed account of Franklin II, see Seabrook, EOTBF.
2216. Watkins, p. 209.
2217. Fay, p. 12; C. Adams, p. 149.
2218. Hunter alone was responsible for destroying millions of dollars of Southern property in Virginia's beautiful Shenandoah Valley. His destruction included torching the town of Lexington, tearing up miles of railroad, razing factories, mills, and private residences, and burning down the Virginia Military Institute. What military advantage there was in leveling our schools is still a mystery here in the South. It was obviously just plain cruelty, both unnecessary and illegal. For more on Hunter's crimes see below, and also Gragg, pp. 88-89.
2219. DiLorenzo, LU, p. 58.

forgotten in Dixie.[2220] All bragged of the destruction they wreaked on the South.[2221] Entire Southern cities disappeared under the commands of these and other Northern officers. This Lincoln and his Yankee cohorts called "preserving the Union"!

At Roswell, Georgia, one of Lincoln's most ruthless henchmen, Sherman—who was deemed "unstable and mentally deranged" even by other Yankees[2222]—ordered his men to destroy every mill and factory in the area, arrest the employees (male and female) on charge of "treason," then murder the innocent owners.[2223] In another order he demanded of his troops that their "destruction be so thorough that not a rail or tie can be used again,"[2224] then boasted that many of the towns he and his army marched through would not be found on future maps. On March 7, 1864, he reported on one of these, Meridian, Mississippi, saying:

> For five days 10,000 men worked hard and with a will in that work of destruction, with axes, crowbars, sledges, clawbars, and with fire, and I have no hesitation in pronouncing the work as well done. Meridian, with its depots, store-houses, arsenal, hospitals, offices, hotels, and cantonments, no longer exists.[2225]

We will repeat here Sherman's arrogant pronouncement: "Meridian no longer exists."[2226]

The town was later rebuilt. But to this day, the only evidence that many of the places he obliterated were once thriving communities are small stone markers.

After leveling Meridian, Sherman robbed, burned, and bombed his way through the rest of the Magnolia state, cutting, as he bragged, "a swath of desolation fifty miles broad across the state of Mississippi, which the present generation will not forget."[2227] In Savannah, Georgia, he admitted that 80 percent of the devastation he had caused was "simple

---

2220. Many Southerners consider *all* Yankee officers to have been war criminals. See Christian, p. 15.
2221. Ashe, p. 57.
2222. Warner, GB, s.v. "William Tecumseh 'Cump' Sherman."
2223. D. Evans, pp. 13, 19-20, 51, 487.
2224. *ORA*, Ser. 1, Vol. 38, Pt. 5, p. 688.
2225. *ORA*, Ser. 1, Vol. 32, Pt. 1, p. 176.
2226. See Montgomery, TSAH, p. 490.
2227. *ORA*, Ser. 1, Vol. 32, Pt. 2, p. 498.

waste and destruction."[2228] In late December 1864, after subduing and occupying the city, a cocky Sherman sent a telegram to Lincoln, offering the defeated town to the president as a Christmas present.[2229] It read:

> SAVANNAH, GEORGIA, December 22, 1864.
> To His Excellency President Lincoln, Washington, D.C.:
> I beg to present you as a Christmas-gift the city of Savannah, with one hundred and fifty heavy guns and plenty of ammunition, also about twenty-five thousand bales of cotton.
> W. T. Sherman, Major-General.[2230]

Lincoln's reply to this missive deserves special mention since it reveals his complicity in Sherman's war crimes:

> My Dear General Sherman: Many, many thanks for your Christmas gift, the capture of Savannah.
> When you were about to leave Atlanta for the Atlantic coast, I was anxious, if not fearful; but feeling that you were the better judge, and remembering that 'nothing risked, nothing gained,' I did not interfere. Now, the undertaking being a success, the honor is all yours; for I believe that none of us went further than to acquiesce.
> And taking the work of General [George H.] Thomas into the count, as it should be taken, it is indeed a great success. Not only does it afford the obvious and immediate military advantages; but in showing to the world that your army could be divided, putting the stronger part to an important new service, and yet leaving enough to vanquish the old opposing forces of the whole,—Hood's army,—it brings those who sat in darkness to see a great light. But what next?
> I suppose it will be safe if I leave General Grant and yourself to decide.
> Please make my grateful acknowledgments to your whole army—officers and men.
> Yours very truly, A. Lincoln.[2231]

On rare occasions Lincoln's soldiers "kindly" first allowed

2228. *ORA*, Ser. 1, Vol. 44, p. 13.
2229. Civil War Society, *CWB*, s.v. "Sherman's March to the Sea."
2230. W. T. Sherman, Vol. 2, p. 231.
2231. Nicolay and Hay, *ALCW*, Vol. 2, p. 622.

Southern women and children to select a few important items to be saved and carried out into the street before attacking their home. Then as the horrified family looked on, their house was ransacked and pillaged, jewelry and other valuables pocketed, paintings sliced to ribbons with bayonets, pianos hammered to pieces, windows smashed out with rifle butts, doors violently ripped off their hinges, bookcases pulled down, beds overturned, and furniture broken apart.[2232] The dwelling was then set afire, instantly rendering the family homeless refugees.[2233]

What was the point of such actions? They were both illegal and cruel. Yet Sherman and his men laughed when the Southern women whose homes they were destroying would "cry aloud for mercy." Such scenes were never witnessed in any Northern towns or cities.[2234]

Admitting that he pilfered some $20 million from Southern banks and citizens, and bragging that he had destroyed $100 million worth of private property, Sherman then declared that the enormous number of Southerners he and his men had killed was "a beautiful sight," for the quicker more of them died, the sooner the War would end.[2235]

At Atlanta, Sherman illegally forced the deportation of thousands of citizens, then attempted to bomb the town into gravel. Razing most of the private homes there, by the time the heartless Yankee general departed, 90 percent of the city was literally nonexistent. Lincoln's troops robbed girls and women of their trinkets, and even vandalized Southern cemeteries, digging up corpses for their jewelry.[2236] So lightly did Sherman and his men take such crimes upon the Southern citizenry that they humorously referred to it as "treasure-seeking," enjoyable "excitements of the march."[2237]

Beloved family pets, mainly dogs and cats, were shot on the spot, along with any other type of animal, such as horses, pigs, hogs, geese, and

---

2232. Lincoln was aware of such acts. See e.g., Nicolay and Hay, ALCW, Vol. 2, pp. 471-472.
2233. See Gragg, pp. 90-93, 175-192.
2234. Critics here may point to Confederate General Jubal Early's burning of Chambersburg, Pennsylvania. See Warner, GG, s.v. "Jubal Anderson Early." But this was not wantonly savage in the manner of Northern soldiers. Early had merely requested a levy of $500,000 from the town's citizens for damages made against the South, particularly for the burning of thousands of homes and farms in the Shenandoah Valley. When this was refused, he understandably set fire to the city. Simmons, s.v. "Early, Jubal Anderson"; C. Johnson, p. 160; E. M. Thomas, p. 276.
2235. Napolitano, p. 73.
2236. Gragg, pp. 177-181.
2237. J. Davis, RFCG, Vol. 2, p. 634.

cattle, that could not be carried off.[2238] In one typical case, one of Lincoln's soldiers saw some Southern children playing with a frisky young greyhound. Walking over to the startled children, the insolent bluecoat grabbed the puppy and cruelly pummeled its brains out in front of them.[2239]

Those Atlantans who were not beaten, arrested, or killed, fled into the mountains. Those civilians unlucky enough to be left behind faced a demonic force of unparalleled evil. Writes Stonebraker:

> At one place Sherman took four hundred factory girls and sent them north of the Ohio River, away from home and friends. Such things are inhuman, and one's blood is made to boil to even relate them.
>
> All the white inhabitants were made to leave the city without regard to age or condition. All who would not take Lincoln's oath were sent South to famish.
>
> Such a stream of men, women and children with their all in their hands, could be seen wending their way from the desolated city. [Rebel General John Bell] Hood retorted against this cruelty, but Sherman said, 'War is cruelty! This year we will take your property, and next year your lives!'[2240]

In their wake, the Yanks often left nothing but thousands of solitary, charred chimney stacks, known as "Sherman's sentinels," and miles of grotesquely twisted railroad track, known as "Sherman's neckties," to indicate their wicked progress.[2241] Steel-toed boots aided the Yanks in their destruction, enabling them to kick down the strongest doors and break open the toughest locks.[2242]

Following in Sherman's path were the bummers: great mobs of criminals, felons, outlaws, refugees, prostitutes, and stevedores, picking through the spoils of devastation, preying on the Southern victims of the general's wrath.[2243] Finally, rounding up this motley menagerie, were trailing throngs of newly freed blacks, homeless, hungry, and confused. The South could not help them now, and Sherman, a lifelong racist, was

---

2238. Hurmence, pp. 99-102; J. Davis, RFCG, Vol. 2, p. 716.
2239. Gragg, pp. 182-183, 188.
2240. Stonebraker, pp. 170-171. See also *Confederate Veteran*, October 1896, Vol. 4, No. 10, p. 344.
2241. Gragg, pp. 169-175, 239.
2242. Gragg, p. 189.
2243. Wiley, LBY, p. 203.

certainly not going to.[2244]

As the North's soldiers moved across Dixie terrorizing her inhabitants and leveling her cities, untold thousands of defenseless girls and women, both white and black, free and bonded, were threatened, intimidated, beaten, maimed, wounded, tortured, raped, and killed.[2245] Age was no barrier to the battle-hardened Yankee interlopers. All were considered fair game, including innocent children and fragile seniors.[2246]

Confederate General Jubal Early followed Yankee General David Hunter through the Shenandoah Valley, the "Breadbasket of the Confederacy,"[2247] and so became just one of millions of eyewitnesses to the outrages perpetuated under the auspices of President Lincoln. In his book, *A Memoir of the Last Year of the War for Independence in the Confederate States of America*, Early describes what he saw:

> The scenes on Hunter's route from Lynchburg [Virginia] had been truly heart-rending. Houses had been burned, and helpless women and children left without shelter. The country had been stripped of provisions and many families left without a morsel to eat. Furniture and bedding had been cut to pieces, and old men and women and children robbed of all the clothing they had except that on their backs. Ladies trunks had been rifled and their dresses torn to pieces in mere wantonness. Even the negro girls had lost their little finery. We now had renewed evidences of the outrages committed by Hunter's orders in burning and plundering private houses. We saw the ruins of a number of houses to which the torch had been applied by his orders. At Lexington he had burned the Military Institute, with all of its contents, including its library and scientific apparatus; and Washington College had been plundered and the statue of Washington stolen. The residence of Ex-Governor [John] Letcher at that place had been burned by orders, and but a few minutes given Mrs. Letcher and her family to leave the house. In the same county a most excellent Christian gentleman, a Mr. Creigh, had been hung, because, on a former occasion he had killed a straggling and marauding Federal soldier while in the act of insulting and outraging the ladies of his family. These are but some of the outrages committed by Hunter or his

---

2244. M. Perry, p. 223.
2245. See e.g., J. Davis, RFCG, Vol. 2, pp. 632-633; C. Johnson, p. 157; Lott, pp. 158-159; L. Johnson, p. 188; Grissom, pp. 115-116; Christian, p. 15.
2246. Gragg, pp. 192-196.
2247. W. B. Garrison, CWTFB, p. 170.

orders, and I will not insult the memory of the ancient barbarians of the North by calling them "acts of Vandalism." If those old barbarians were savage and cruel, they at least had the manliness and daring of rude soldiers, with occasional traits of magnanimity. Hunter's deeds were those of a malignant and cowardly fanatic, who was better qualified to make war upon helpless women and children than upon armed soldiers.[2248]

Blacks, the very people Lincoln's troops were supposed to be invading the South to "liberate," were particularly targeted by white Union soldiers. The following field dispatch (dated December 30, 1864) from Union General Rufus Saxton to U.S. Secretary of War Edwin M. Stanton, offers a glimpse into the violent, sordid, crime-infested world created by "mob boss" Lincoln. Reporting from his post at Beaufort, South Carolina, the appalled Yankee Saxton writes:

> I found the prejudice of color and race here [in this U.S. camp] in full force, and the general feeling of the army of occupation was unfriendly to the blacks. It was manifested in various forms of personal insult and abuse, in depredations on their plantations, stealing and destroying their crops and domestic animals, and robbing them of their money.
>
> The [Negro] women were held as the legitimate prey of lust, and as they had been taught it was a crime to resist a white man they had not learned to dare to defend their chastity.
>
> Licentiousness was widespread . . . in the [Northern] army of occupation. Among our [Union] officers and soldiers there were many honorable exceptions to this, but the influence of too many was demoralizing to the negro, and has greatly hindered the efforts for their improvement and elevation. There was a general disposition among the [U.S.] soldiers and civilian speculators here to defraud the negroes in their private traffic, to take the commodities which they offered for sale by force, or to pay for them in worthless money.
>
> At one time these practices were so frequent and notorious that the negroes would not bring their produce to market for fear of being plundered. Other occurrences have tended to cool the enthusiastic joy with which the coming of the Yankees was welcomed.[2249]

2248. Early, p. 48.
2249. *ORA*, Ser. 3, Vol. 4, p. 1029.

Under such treatment, "freed" Southern blacks often had difficulty discerning the difference between "working for nothing as a slave and working for the same wages under the Yankee . . ."[2250]

In 1862 an eyewitness living on Hilton Head Island, South Carolina, reported that the occupying white Yankee soldiers there speak horribly to the blacks, using the most insulting words, while in Norfolk, Virginia, a freed black woman wrote of seeing other blacks being abused "in every possible way" by Union men. Yankee crimes in the Palmetto State included the destruction of property, pillage, assault and battery, and even rape, against innocent black females who had fled to them, believing them to be liberators. The woman forlornly penned: it looks like I'm Master Lincoln's slave from now on.[2251]

How could any of this be true? It is not in our history books.

We know about these crimes because both eyewitness accounts and Federal field orders instructing the purposeful harassment, arrest, imprisonment, and even killing of noncombatants still survive. Naturally, anti-South authors ignore or suppress these accounts. Yet they exist for all to see.

One of these is the North's own 158-volume work entitled, the *Official Records of the War of the Rebellion*, better known to historians and scholars as simply the *ORA*. On October 29, 1864, for example, at Rome, Georgia, the *ORA* tells us that Sherman sent out an order to a subordinate officer that read:

> Cannot you send over about Fairmount and Adairsville, burn ten or twelve houses of known secessionists, kill a few at random, and let them know that it will be repeated every time a train is fired on from Resaca to Kingston?[2252]

Note that besides ordering the killing of civilians (at the time an offence punishable by hanging), Sherman also ordered the destruction of private property, a war crime under the Geneva Convention of 1863.

During Sherman's twenty-six day "March to the Sea"[2253] as he and

---

2250. Knox, p. 317.
2251. Channing, p. 131; Jimerson, p. 81; J. D. Fowler, p. 317.
2252. *ORA*, Ser. 1, Vol. 39, Pt. 3, p. 494.
2253. Sherman's March to the Sea lasted from November 15 to December 10, 1864. W. B. Garrison, CWTFB, p. 248.

his men approached South Carolina (the first Southern state to proudly secede from the Union), the dastardly Northern officer revealed their real motivation, one that had nothing to do with Lincoln's fraudulent goal of "preserving the Union":

> The truth is, the whole army is burning with an insatiable desire to wreak vengeance upon South Carolina. I almost tremble at her fate, but feel that she deserves all that seems to be in store for her.[2254]

South Carolina's "fate" under Sherman's auspices was later described by Reverend Dr. John Bachman of Charleston:

> When Sherman's army came sweeping through Carolina, leaving a broad track of desolation for hundreds of miles, whose steps were accompanied with fire, and sword, and blood . . . I happened to be at Cash's Depot, six miles from Cheraw. The owner was a widow, Mrs. Ellerbe, seventy-one years of age. Her son, Colonel Cash, was absent. I witnessed the barbarities inflicted on the aged, the widow, and young and delicate females. [Yankee] [o]fficers, high in command, were engaged tearing from the ladies their watches, their ear and wedding rings, the daguerreotypes [a type of early photograph] of those they loved and cherished. A lady of delicacy and refinement, a personal friend, was compelled to strip before them, that they might find concealed watches and other valuables under her dress. A system of torture was practiced toward the weak, unarmed, and defenseless, which as far as I know and believe, was universal throughout the whole course of that invading army. Before they arrived at a plantation, they inquired the names of the most faithful and trustworthy family servants; these were immediately seized, pistols were presented at their heads; with the most terrific curses, they were threatened to be shot if they did not assist them in finding buried treasures. If this did not succeed, they were tied up and cruelly beaten. Several poor creatures died under the infliction. The last resort was that of hanging, and the officers and men of the triumphant army of General Sherman were engaged in erecting gallows and hanging up these faithful and devoted servants. They were strung up until life was nearly extinct, when they were let down, suffered to rest awhile, then threatened and hung up again. It is not surprising that some should have been left

---

2254. W. T. Sherman, Vol. 2, pp. 227-228.

hanging so long that they were taken down dead. Coolly and deliberately these hardened men proceeded on their way, as if they had perpetrated no crime, and as if the God of heaven would not pursue them with his vengeance. But it was not alone the poor blacks to whom they professed to come as liberators that were thus subjected to torture and death. Gentlemen of high character, pure and honorable and gray-headed, unconnected with the military, were dragged from their fields or their beds, and subjected to this process of threats, beating, and hanging. Along the whole track of Sherman's army, traces remain of the cruelty and inhumanity practiced on the aged and the defenseless. Some of those who were hung up died under the rope, while their cruel murderers have not only been left unreproached and unhung, but have been hailed as heroes and patriots. The list of those martyrs whom the cupidity of the officers and men of Sherman's army sacrificed to their thirst for gold and silver, is large and most revolting.[2255]

On March 5, 1865, Mary Chesnut recorded the following in her diary:

> Sherman's men had burned the convent. . . . Men were rolling tar barrels and lighting torches to fling on the house when the nuns came. Columbia is but dust and ashes, burned to the ground. Men, women, and children are left there, houseless, homeless, without a particle of food—reduced to picking up corn that was left by Sherman's horses on picket grounds and parching it to stay their hunger.[2256]

Even many Northerners were horrified by Sherman's actions. One of them happened to be a Yankee officer, General Don Carlos Buell.[2257] After resigning from the military over the issue, he said:

> I believe that the policy and means with which the war was being prosecuted were discreditable to the nation and a stain upon civilization.[2258]

A number of formally pro-Northern newspapers were equally

[2255]. Letter dated September 14, 1865. J. Davis, RFCG, Vol. 2, pp. 710-711.
[2256]. Chesnut, DD, p. 358.
[2257]. Warner, GB, s.v. "Don Carlos Buell."
[2258]. Grimsley, p. 182.

disturbed by the inhumane policies of Sherman and Sheridan (the Yankee demon who killed my cousin, Southern hero Jeb Stuart). In 1864, a Washington, D.C. paper asked the villainous pair the following question: what prompted you to drive children, women, and the aged from their burning homes, out into the streets to freeze, starve, and die? Was all the misery and suffering you heaped upon the Southern people merely to liberate Southern slaves, a race who was far more content before you arrived than after you left?[2259]

Yankee news reporter Sidney Andrews visited Dixie in the winter of 1865. In his book chronicling the journey, *The South Since the War*, Andrews wrote:

> The 'Shermanizing process,' as an ex Rebel colonel jocosely called it, has been complete everywhere. To simply say that the people hate that officer is to put a fact in very mild terms. [The highly detested General Benjamin 'the Beast'] Butler is, in their estimation an angel, when compared to Sherman. They charge the latter with the entire work and waste of the war so far as their State is concerned,— even claim that Columbia was burned by his express orders. They pronounce his spirit 'infernal,' 'atrocious,' 'cowardly,' 'devilish,' and would unquestionably use stronger terms if they were to be had. I have been told by dozens of men that he [Sherman] couldn't walk up the main street of Columbia in the daytime without being shot; and three different gentlemen, residing in different parts of the State, declare that Wade Hampton expresses a purpose to shoot him at sight whenever and wherever he meets him. Whatever else the South Carolina mothers forget, they do not seem likely in this generation to forget to teach their children to hate Sherman.[2260]

Another Yankee, General Carl Schurz, no friend of the South, also journeyed through Dixie in 1865, and recorded this observation:

> My travels in the interior took me to the track of Sherman's march, which, in South Carolina at least, looked for many miles like a broad black streak of ruin and desolation—the fences all gone; lonesome smoke stacks, surrounded by dark heaps of ashes and cinders, marking the spots where human habitations had stood; the

---

2259. C. Adams, p. 117.
2260. S. Andrews, p. 31.

fields along the road wildly overgrown by weeds, with here and there a sickly looking patch of cotton or corn cultivated by negro squatters. In the city of Columbia, the political capital of the State, I found a thin fringe of houses encircling a confused mass of charred ruins of dwellings and business buildings, which had been destroyed by a sweeping conflagration.[2261]

In all, Sherman's "March to the Sea" inflicted some $100,000,000 of damage on Georgia alone,[2262] almost two billion dollars in today's currency. It was for this remorseless devastation that Henry C. Work's ode to Sherman, "Marching Through Georgia," became the most detested song in Dixie,[2263] and Sherman himself became the most hated man across the South, for a time even more so than Lincoln.[2264]

Yankee war criminal General Philip H. Sheridan was no less barbaric and unfeeling.[2265] During the Union's Shenandoah Valley Campaign, Sheridan personally approved the torching of barns and crops,[2266] after which he and his men left the region a blackened wasteland, pillaging, burning, and murdering as they went. Sheridan then joked that "a crow could not fly over it without carrying his rations with him."[2267] Civilians who opposed him were hanged on the spot.[2268] In October 1864, Sheridan boasted to Grant:

> I have destroyed over 2,000 barns, filled with wheat, hay, and farming implements; over 70 mills, filled with flour and wheat; have driven in front of the army over 4,000 head of stock, and have killed and issued to the troops not less than 3,000 sheep. . . . all the houses within an area of five miles were burned.[2269]

Sheridan's soldiers bragged that "we stripped the Valley to the bare earth; when we got through there weren't enough crumbs left to feed

---

2261. Bancroft and Dunning, Vol. 3, p. 167.
2262. W. B. Garrison, CWTFB, p. 162.
2263. W. B. Garrison, CWTFB, p. 75.
2264. J. S. Bowman, ECW, s.v. "Sherman, William Tecumseh."
2265. Sheridan's restrictive, cruel, and overly severe policies continued even after the War. Finally, during "Reconstruction," President Andrew Johnson was forced to remove him from his post as commander of the Fifth Military District after only six months. Warner, GB, s.v. "Philip Henry Sheridan."
2266. J. C. Bradford, p. 90.
2267. C. T. Brady, p. 408.
2268. E. M. Thomas, p. 284.
2269. *ORA*, Ser. 1, Vol. 43, Pt. 2, p. 308.

a pigeon." Sheridan himself—a man who, for "some light entertainment," would often burn every fifth house[2270]—pronounced his "scorched earth" approach to warfare a "humanitarian" policy, since he believed that Southerners would give in rather than die of starvation.[2271]

He was wrong.

A Confederate officer who survived the Shenandoah Holocaust described the scene this way:

> I rode down the Valley with the advance after Sheridan's retreating cavalry beneath great columns of smoke which almost shut out the sun by day, and in the red glare of bonfires which, all across the Valley, poured out flames and sparks heavenward and crackled mockingly in the night air; and I saw mothers and maidens tearing their hair and shrieking to Heaven in their fright and despair, and little children, voiceless and tearless in their pitiable terror.[2272]

Grant, who was soon to become America's second worst president, was no better than Sheridan or Sherman. In several letters to Sheridan, dated August 16, 1864, he ordered the wanton destruction of private property (adding theft to the crime), the murder of Rebel soldiers "without trial," and the hostage taking, military arrest, and imprisonment of noncombatants (civilians), all illegal. One of these dispatches has been preserved in the *ORA*. Grant writes:

> The families of most of [Confederate Colonel John S.] Mosby's men are known, and can be collected. I think they should be taken and kept at Fort McHenry or some secure place, as hostages for the good conduct of Mosby and his men. Where any of Mosby's men are caught hang them without trial.
> . . . If you can possibly spare a division of cavalry, send them through Loudoun County [Virginia], to destroy and carry off the crops, animals, negroes, and all men under fifty years of age capable of bearing arms. In this way you will get many of Mosby's men. All male citizens under fifty can fairly be held as prisoners of war, and not as citizen prisoners.[2273]

2270. Grissom, p. 116.
2271. W. B. Garrison, CWTFB, p. 211.
2272. Douglas, p. 315; Catton, Vol. 3, p. 343.
2273. *ORA*, Ser. 1, Vol. 18, Pt. 1, p. 811.

Just weeks before, on August 5, 1864, Grant had written to General Hunter:

> In pushing up the Shenandoah Valley, where it is expected you will have to go first or last, it is desirable that nothing should be left to invite the enemy to return. Take all provisions, forage, and stock wanted for the use of your command; such as cannot be consumed destroy.[2274]

In an official report dated March 25, 1862, Union commander General Henry W. Halleck made this confession from his headquarters at St. Louis, Missouri, to Lincoln's Secretary of War Stanton:

> It cannot be denied that some of our volunteer regiments have behaved very badly, plundering to an enormous extent. I have done everything in my power to prevent this and to punish the guilty. Many of the regimental officers are very bad men and participate in this plunder.[2275]

As a direct result of Lincoln's "badly behaved" soldiers, by the end of the conflict some 500,000 Southern farms and plantations had gone bankrupt, become insolvent, or were ruined, real property value had plummeted 30 percent, and between 10 and 25 percent of the South's inhabitants were dead.[2276] Most of her cities were desolate, the total assessed property evaluation of the Southern states had decreased by 43 percent, and two-thirds of her railroads were gone. All of this was a direct result of Lincoln's order to invade the South. In Mississippi alone, one-third of the state's white men had been killed or were disabled.[2277]

Did Lincoln know about all of this and actually sanction it? Of course. Not only had he personally issued military orders that violated the Geneva Convention,[2278] but he also personally approved his officers' illegalities, such as, for example, Sherman's plan to level Georgia to the ground,[2279] as well as the red-head's total war and scorched earth

---

2274. *ORA*, Ser. 1, Vol. 34, Pt. 1, p. 26.
2275. *ORA*, Ser. 1, Vol. 8, p. 642.
2276. Cartmell, p. 16.
2277. Bailyn, Dallek, Davis, Donald, Thomas, and Wood, pp. 8, 15.
2278. Christian, p. 16.
2279. Civil War Society, CWB, s.v. "Sherman's March to the Sea."

policies.[2280] After all, General Lee took his orders directly from President Davis. It is obvious then that Sherman, Grant, Sheridan, and the rest took their orders directly from Lincoln.[2281]

Why else would "Honest Abe" repeatedly dine with,[2282] thank, reward, and promote men like Grant and Sherman?[2283] Indeed, not only had Lincoln been in constant telegraph contact with both officers throughout the War, but on March 28, 1865, he excitedly met with them at City Point, Virginia, to hear about their "achievements" and congratulate them on their work in person.[2284] Only a few months earlier he had sent a telegram to Grant in the field that read:

> Hold on with a bulldog grip, and chew and choke as much as possible.[2285]

What Lincoln meant by these words would have been clear to every Southerner. They were certainly well understood by Grant, for he acted on them to the letter.

One of those closest to Lincoln was his chief of staff at the time, General Halleck. It was Halleck who, in daily contact with the president, wrote the following to Sherman on December 18, 1864:

> Should you capture Charleston, I hope that by some accident the place may be destroyed, and if a little salt should be sown upon its site it may prevent the growth of future crops of nullification and secession.[2286]

The dispatch was from Halleck. But the "message" was from Lincoln.

The official public stamp of approval for committing war crimes came from the U.S. Congress, which gave Grant, Sheridan, and Sherman the "Thanks of Congress" for achieving "significant victories" during the War (Sherman received two).[2287] These "significant victories," of course,

---

2280. Oates, AL, p. 136.
2281. Christian, p. 18.
2282. See e.g., Nicolay and Hay, ALCW, Vol. 2, p. 494.
2283. See e.g., Nicolay and Hay, ALCW, Vol. 2, pp. 457, 461, 493, 533, 555, 572, 573.
2284. Denney, p. 551. See also Nicolay and Hay, ALCW, Vol. 2, p. 556.
2285. Nicolay and Hay, ALCW, Vol. 2, p. 563.
2286. *ORA*, Ser. 1, Vol. 44, p. 741.
2287. J. S. Bowman, ECW, s.v. "Thanks of Congress."

were often the result of scorched-earth, total war policies that included larceny, wide destruction of civilian property, rape, maiming, torture, and the mass murder of Southern noncombatants.

Of the war crimes of Lincoln's commanders, the Honorable Judge George L. Christian states,

> we know . . . that these officers would not have dared to thus violate [the rules of civilized warfare] . . . unless these violations had been known by them to be sanctioned by their official head, Mr. Lincoln, from whom they received their appointments and commissions, and whose duty it was to prevent such violations and outrages.
>
> . . . Who alone had any semblance of authority to give this permission to Sherman and who gave it? There can be but one answer—Abraham Lincoln, the then President of the United States. Will the people of the South lick the hand that thus smote their fathers, their mothers, their brethren and their sisters by now singing paeans of glory to his name and fame?
>
> . . . We charge, and without the fear of successful contradiction, that Mr. Lincoln, as the head of the Federal Government, and the Commander-in-Chief of its armies, was directly responsible for the outrages committed by his subordinates; and that the future and unprejudiced historian will so hold him responsible. We verily believe.
>
> But this is not all. Mr. Lincoln was [also] directly responsible for all the sorrows, sufferings and deaths of prisoners on both sides during the war.[2288]

While today many Northerners and New South scallywags continue to lamely deny Lincoln's role as a war criminal, 19th-Century Northerners had the gall to fabricate numerous horror stories about Southern soldiers: that they made goblets of Yankee skulls and ladies' necklaces from Yankee teeth (never happened);[2289] that they "took scalps for trophies" (never happened);[2290] that black Northern soldiers were routinely and intentionally beaten, shot, and burned, as was alleged to

---

2288. Christian, pp. 15, 17, 20.
2289. Bailyn, Dallek, Davis, Donald, Thomas, and Wood, p. 5.
2290. Christian, p. 30.

have occurred at the Battle of Fort Pillow (never happened);[2291] and that Union prisoners were purposefully "starved, frozen, and killed off" (most of the Yanks who perished in Southern prisons died because of Lincoln's war-long refusal to exchange prisoners,[2292] and also due to lack of food, medicines, and clothing caused by his illegal naval blockade).[2293]

In reality, it was Lincoln's troops who perpetrated the vast preponderance of war crimes. One of General Nathan Bedford Forrest's officers, Lieutenant Colonel W. M. Reed, wrote out the following report on March 21, 1864. It concerns various outrages committed by Yankee Colonel Fielding Hurst against both Rebel soldiers and innocent Southern civilians. Hurst had been sent by another Yankee war criminal, General William Sooy Smith, to "grub up" West Tennessee:

> [Confederate] Private Silas Hodges, a scout, acting under orders from Colonel Tansil, states that he saw the body of [Confederate] Lieutenant Dodds very soon after his murder, and that it was most horribly mutilated, the face having been skinned, the nose cut off, the under jaw disjointed, the privates cut off, and the body otherwise barbarously lacerated and most wantonly injured, and that his death was brought about by the most inhuman process of torture.
> . . . On or about the 5th February, 1864, Private Martin, Company—, Wilson's regiment Tennessee volunteers, was captured by [the] same command and was shot to death and the rights of sepulture forbidden while the command remained, some four days. Mr. Lee Doroughty, a citizen of McNairy County, Tenn, a youth about sixteen years of age, deformed and almost helpless, was arrested and wantonly murdered by [the] same command about 1st January, 1864.[2294]

A complete compilation of these types of Yankee atrocities would fill volumes. Lincoln was aware of nearly all of them and directly, or more often indirectly (to legally protect himself), sanctioned them.[2295]

2291. See my books: 1) *Nathan Bedford Forrest: Southern Hero, American Patriot*; 2) *A Rebel Born: A Defense of Nathan Bedford Forrest*; 3) *The Quotable Nathan Bedford Forrest*; 4) *Forrest! 99 Reasons to Love Nathan Bedford Forrest*; and 5) *Give 'Em Hell Boys! The Complete Military Correspondence of Nathan Bedford Forrest*.
2292. C. Adams, pp. 208-209.
2293. Bailyn, Dallek, Davis, Donald, Thomas, and Wood, p. 5.
2294. *ORA*, Ser. 1, Vol. 32, Pt. 1, pp. 118-119.
2295. Christian, pp. 15-20.

If there is any doubt as to Lincoln's knowledge and involvement, consider the case of one of Lincoln's generals, John B. Turchin. Turchin was rightfully ousted from the Yankee army by his superiors for burning down the town of Athens, Alabama, in 1862. However, Lincoln later reversed the order, restored Turchin to his command, and even gave him a promotion.[2296]

Why did Lincoln push his officers to win at any cost, even to the point of destroying entire cities and savagely murdering thousands of innocent Southern men, women, and children?

Politics, of course.

The upcoming 1864 election weighed heavily on Lincoln's mind throughout 1863 and early 1864. He felt that victories in the field would mean a victory at the polls. And he was correct. Sherman's and Sheridan's many successes during the period gave the president a 10 percent margin that November, all he needed to be reelected.[2297]

Long before this, on July 20, 1861, Jefferson Davis had spoken out against Lincoln's war crimes, condemning him for destroying "private residences in peaceful rural retreats," and for the "outrages [rapes] committed on defenseless [Southern] females by [Yankee] soldiers."[2298] In bringing nationwide attention to Lincoln's crimes, Davis made special note of the following:

> In this war, rapine is the rule; private houses, in beautiful rural retreats, are bombarded and burnt; grain crops in the field are consumed by the torch, and, when the torch is not convenient, careful labour is bestowed to render complete destruction of every article of use or ornament remaining in private dwellings, after their inhabitants have fled from the outrages of brute soldiery.[2299]

In essence, as Davis correctly observed years before Sherman's infamous and deliberate campaign of destruction—known innocuously by Northerners as his "March to the Sea"[2300]—Lincoln was already

---

2296. Grissom, pp. 117-118.
2297. Grissom, p. 117.
2298. Current, TC, s.v. "Lincoln, Abraham."
2299. Stephens, CV, Vol. 2, p. 466; McElroy, p. 319.
2300. Hacker, p. 588.

waging an indiscriminate war upon . . . all, with a savage ferocity unknown to modern civilization.[2301]

All of this so that Lincoln could inaugurate his vaunted American System, the exact type of government that President George Washington warned Americans about in his Farewell Address, issued on September 19, 1796. Stating that he wished to leave office by offering several "all-important" sentiments, the "disinterested warnings of a parting friend," the nation's first president declared:

> The unity of government, which constitutes you one people, is also now dear to you. It is justly so; for it is a main pillar in the edifice of your real independence—the support of your tranquility at home, your peace abroad, of your safety, of your prosperity, of that very liberty which you so highly prize. But as it is easy to foresee that, from different causes and from different quarters, much pains will be taken, many artifices employed, to weaken in your minds the conviction of this truth; as this is the point in your political fortress against which the batteries of internal and external enemies will be most constantly and actively (though often covertly and insidiously) directed,—it is of infinite moment that you should properly estimate the immense value of your national union to your collective and individual happiness; that you should cherish a cordial, habitual, and immovable attachment to it; accustoming yourselves to think and speak of it as of the palladium of your political safety and prosperity; watching for its preservation with jealous anxiety; discountenancing whatever may suggest even a suspicion that it can, in any event, be abandoned; and indignantly frowning upon the first dawning of every attempt to alienate any portion of our country from the rest, or to enfeeble the sacred ties which now link together the various parts.[2302]

Washington goes on to advise the citizens of the U.S. to avoid foreign alliances, becoming embroiled in wars, and

> over-grown military establishments, which, under any form of government, are inauspicious to liberty, and which are to be regarded as particularly hostile to republican liberty . . .[2303]

2301. Richardson, Vol. 1, p. 119.
2302. Hickey, pp. 217-218.
2303. Hickey, p. 219.

Governmental change is allowed, even encouraged, Washington writes in his Farewell Address. But only by way of Constitutional amendments supported by the people. For changes brought about by force would surely lead to the destruction of self-government:

> . . . let there be no change by usurpation; for though this, in one instance, may be the instrument of good, it is the customary weapon by which free governments are destroyed.[2304]

Sixty-five years later, Lincoln would conveniently ignore all of these stern admonitions and destroy the free government that Southerner President Washington had himself helped create.

In 1825, one year before his death, Thomas Jefferson too sounded the alarm bell, cautioning of the dangers of the centralization of governmental power. Liberal Northerners were continuing their efforts to strengthen and nationalize the central government and weaken the state governments in an attempt to turn the U.S. into a monarchical empire. That year, from Monticello, America's third president eerily predicted what few others could have seen thirty-six years in advance: the "consolidation" of the national government and the "usurpation" of states' rights by a monarchist named Abraham Lincoln:

> I see with the deepest affliction, the rapid strides with which the federal branch of our government is advancing towards the usurpation of all the rights reserved to the States, and the consolidation in itself of all powers, foreign and domestic; and that too, by constructions which, if legitimate, leave no limits to their power. . . .
>
> . . . this opens with a vast accession of strength from their [the Federalists] younger recruits, who, having nothing in them of the feelings or principles of '76, now look to a single and splendid government of an aristocracy, founded on banking institutions, and moneyed incorporations under the guise and cloak of their favored branches of manufactures, commerce and navigation, riding and ruling over the plundered ploughman and beggared yeomanry. This will be to them a next best blessing to the monarchy of their first aim, and perhaps the surest stepping-stone to it.[2305]

2304. Hickey, p. 224.
2305. Foley, pp. 132, 295.

Lincoln, one of the "younger recruits," a Federalist who had "nothing in him of the feelings or principles of 1776," could not have stated his own agenda any better.

18

DESTRUCTION OF THE UNION & UNPLANNED EMANCIPATION

AS PREVIOUSLY STATED, FORTUNATELY WASHINGTON, Jefferson, Madison, Pinckney, Mason, and the rest of the Southern Founding Fathers, did not live long enough to see the dictatorial, aristocrat Lincoln "riding and ruling" over a "plundered and beggared" American citizenry; nor were they forced to watch as his new monarchy, the American System, used a nationalized banking system and moneyed corporations to dissolve their beloved Confederacy and transform the U.S. government from a conservative republic into a liberal empire; or as the Charleston *Mercury* phrased it, from a "confederated republic to a national sectional despotism."[2306]

Lincoln had pledged to "preserve the Union." Instead he destroyed it,[2307] making his title, "the Savior of Our Country," darkly ironic indeed.[2308] For a union, by definition, is a *voluntary* association between groups, whether they are groups of people or groups of states.[2309]

In an 1870 essay, Yankee Lysander Spooner wrote of Lincoln's idea of "union," and how the president and his partners in crime, his Wall Street Boys, had perverted its authentic meaning:

> Their pretenses that they have 'Saved the Country,' and 'preserved

---

[2306]. T. D. Morris, p. 202.
[2307]. C. Adams, p. 49.
[2308]. W. B. Garrison, CWC, p. 220.
[2309]. J. Davis, RFCG, Vol. 1, p. 439.

the Glorious Union,' are frauds like all the rest of the pretenses. By them they mean simply that they have subjugated, and maintained their power over, an unwilling people. This they call 'Saving the Country'; as if an enslaved and subjugated people—or as if any people kept in subjugation by the sword (as it is intended that all of us shall be hereafter)—could be said to have any country. This, too, they call 'preserving our Glorious Union'; as if there could be said to be any Union, glorious or inglorious, that was not voluntary. Or as if there could be said to be any union between masters and slaves; between those who conquer, and those who are subjugated.[2310]

Spooner is correct. A "union" held together by force is *not* truly a union. It is a dictatorship, an empire. This is why Lincoln was, and still is, often rightly referred to in the South not only as the "American Caesar,"[2311] but as the Tyrant, Czar, King, Cambyses, Charles IX, Philip II, the Northern Nero, King John, George II, and the American Nebuchadnezzar.[2312] Jefferson Davis referred to Lincoln as "His Majesty Abraham the First."[2313]

In a January 26, 1863, letter to Yankee General Joseph "Fighting Joe" Hooker, Lincoln acknowledged that he was willing to assume the role of dictator if necessary:

> I have heard, in such way as to believe it, of your recently saying that both the army and the government needed a dictator. Of course it was not *for* this, but in spite of it, that I have given you the command. Only those generals who gain successes can set up dictators. What I now ask of you is military success, and I will risk the dictatorship.[2314]

Whether meant in jest or not, Southerners honestly believed that Lincoln, the American Caesar, had been a practicing dictator since the day he first stepped into the White House. Lincoln's own friend and biographer, John Hay, described the manner in which the president ruled over his cabinet

---

2310. Spooner, NT, No. 6, p. 55.
2311. See C. Adams, p. 36.
2312. M. Davis, p. 80.
2313. Cooper, JDA, p. 551.
2314. Nicolay and Hay, ALCW, Vol. 2, p. 307.

as "tyrannous."[2315]

President Andrew Johnson (who, as vice president, took over the Oval Office after Lincoln's death) realized too late what all traditional Southerners had been predicting for years: Lincoln's oppressive and violent four-year rule would shatter the Framers' Union, not maintain it. On December 3, 1867, in his third annual message to the Union, Johnson lamented:

> . . . candor compels me to declare that at this time there is no Union as our fathers understood the term, and as they meant it to be understood by us. The Union which they established can exist only where all the States are represented in both Houses of Congress—where one State is as free as another to regulate its internal concerns according to its own will, and where the laws of the central Government, strictly confined to matters of national jurisdiction, apply with equal force to all the people of every section. That such is not the present 'state of the Union' is a melancholy fact . . .[2316]

In 1833, long before "Emperor Lincoln" moved to hold the Union together by force, Southern political hero John C. Calhoun vocalized the South's feelings on the matter:

> We are told that the Union must be preserved. And how is it proposed to preserve the Union? By force? Does any man in his senses believe that this beautiful structure,—this harmonious aggregate of States, produced by the joint consent of all,—can be preserved by force? Its very introduction will be certain destruction to the Federal Union. No, no! You cannot keep the States united in their constitutional and federal bonds by force. Force may, indeed, hold the parts together; but such union would be the bond between the master and slave—a union of exaction on one side, and unqualified obedience on the other. It is madness to suppose that the Union can be preserved by force. Disguise it as you may, the contest is one between power and liberty.[2317]

A half century earlier, even Federalist Alexander Hamilton, one

---

2315. Encyc. Brit., s.v. "Lincoln, Abraham."
2316. *The American Annual Cyclopedia*, 1867, Vol. 7, p. 633.
2317. Chambers, Vol. 1, p. 451.

of Lincoln's political forerunners, revealed that he understood the essential meaning of states' rights when he said:

> . . . to coerce the States is one of the maddest projects that was ever devised. . . . What picture does this idea present to our view? A complying State at war with a non-complying State; Congress marching the troops of one State into the bosom of another; . . . Here is a nation at war with itself. Can any reasonable man be well disposed toward a government which makes war and carnage the only means of supporting itself—a government that can exist only by the sword? . . . But can we believe that one State will ever suffer itself to be used as an instrument of coercion? The thing is a dream; it is impossible.[2318]

Franklin Pierce—President Buchanan's predecessor, and a man who supported the right of self-government—made the following sagacious comment in a Fourth of July speech in 1863. Noting the unnecessary bloodshed that had just been spilled at Gettysburg, America's fourteenth president said: "How futile are all our efforts to maintain the Union by force of arms." Pierce was a Yankee from New Hampshire.[2319]

General Robert E. Lee (who Southerners are proud to say never took the Union's despised "Oath of Allegiance")[2320] was among the 96 percent of the South's non-slave owners, and was thus of the same mind as Pierce, his Northern counterpart. On January 23, 1861, on the eve of Lincoln's War, the Southern icon wrote to his son:

> . . . a Union that can only be maintained by swords and bayonets, and in which strife and civil war are to take the place of brotherly love and kindness, has no charm for me.[2321]

In 1881, sixteen years after Lincoln's War, Jefferson Davis elucidated what was already well-known by every Southern and nearly every Northerner—except Lincoln:

2318. Stephens, CV, Vol. 1, pp. 281-282.
2319. DeGregorio, s.v. "Franklin Pierce" (p. 206).
2320. As a result, he was not "pardoned" for "treason" against the U.S. until December 25, 1868. J. H. Franklin, p. 33.
2321. Seabrook, TQREL, p. 97.

> The invasions of the Southern States, for purposes of coercion, were in violation of the written Constitution, and the attempt to subjugate sovereign States, under the pretext of 'preserving the Union,' was alike offensive to law, to good morals, and the proper use of language. The Union was the voluntary junction of free and independent States; to subjugate any of them was to destroy constituent parts, and necessarily, therefore, must be the destruction of the Union itself.[2322]

On the eve of Lincoln's War, Davis' vice president, Alexander Hamilton Stephens,[2323] echoed these sentiments to Lincoln in an attempt to stave off the coming bloodshed:

> Under our system, as I view it, there is no rightful power in the General Government to coerce a State in case any one of them should throw herself upon her reserved rights, and resume the full exercise of her Sovereign Powers.[2324]

Lincoln never replied to Stephens' letter, for the Yankee president wanted war, and thus "the war came," as he himself obliquely put it.[2325]

What truly perplexed the world was that Lincoln said he had invaded the Southern Confederacy, a sovereign nation, to preserve liberty. He had even lied, promising that there would not be "any coercion, any conquest, or any subjugation."[2326] Yet violently coerce the South he did. Why? Is not coercion the exact opposite of liberty? The London *Times* put it this way:

> . . . a fight for nationality between men of the same nationality is to us, we candidly confess it, an inexplicable enigma; nor can we better understand a people, fighting to put down rebellion, to force their fellow citizens to remain in a Confederacy which they detest, and to submit to institutions which they repudiate, can be called the champions of liberty. If the South seriously threatened to conquer

---

2322. J. Davis, RFCG, Vol. 1, p. 439.
2323. Stephens was born Alexander Stephens. As a young man, while attending the Academy at Washington, Georgia, he fell under the tutelage of the esteemed cleric Reverend Alexander Hamilton Webster. So enamored was Stephens of Webster that he took his middle name, "Hamilton," as his own. Seabrook, TQAHS, p. 12.
2324. Seabrook, TAHSR, p. 778.
2325. Hunt, p. 330.
2326. Nicolay and Hay, ALCW, Vol. 2, p. 65.

the North, to put down trial by jury, freedom of the press, and representative government, the contest must be for liberty; but, as this is not so, the introduction of such topics is mere rhetorical amplification.[2327]

While the South was fighting for the venerable concept of self-government, the *Times* wrote further, Lincoln is fighting for something quite different: not satisfied to leave Dixie alone, he is fighting to coerce her.[2328] On November 7, 1861, the English paper put it bluntly:

> . . . the contest is really for empire on the side of the North, and for independence on that of the South, and in this respect we recognize an exact analogy between the North and the Government of [King] George III, and the South and the [original] Thirteen Revolted Provinces. These opinions . . . are the general opinions of the English nation.[2329]

In his 1888 book, *The American Commonwealth*, British author James Bryce rightly declared that "Lincoln exercised more authority than any Englishman since Cromwell."[2330] And indeed, Lincoln had much in common with Lord Oliver Cromwell, a 17th-Century British military leader during England's Civil War.[2331] The English tyrant committed countless appalling war crimes, was utterly ruthless on the battlefield, and illegally attempted to rule Great Britain through parliament.[2332] He even temporarily replaced the English monarchy with a full blown military dictatorship,[2333] the country's only experience with purely authoritarian rule.[2334] Thus it is highly appropriate that Cromwell was one of the many nicknames for Lincoln,[2335] the worst known war criminal of Victorian America; the man who subjugated the sovereign South, imposed a military dictatorship on the Unionized North, and robbed his nation of its political foundation: states' rights.

2327. F. Moore, pp. 341-342.
2328. Donald, WNWCW, p. 76.
2329. Rhodes, Vol. 3, p. 545.
2330. Neely, p. 114.
2331. See Rickard, pp. 105-110, 116-118.
2332. M. Parry, s.v. "Cromwell, Oliver"; Montgomery, TLFOEH, pp. 248-251.
2333. Burrell, p. 137.
2334. R. J. White, p. 104.
2335. M. Davis, p. 80.

Southern historian Robert Selph Henry said it best. With the death of the Confederacy and the close of the War for Southern Independence, the original Union itself perished, replaced by a nation whose states, both North and South, now lacked the sovereignty they enjoyed in 1787, and which have become "little more than convenient administrative subdivisions of government."[2336] The U.S. had become, as Florida's postwar governor, David S. Walker, succinctly phrased it, a "government of the bayonet."[2337]

Despite the obvious, in his Second Inaugural Address, on March 4, 1865, one month before the end of his War, atheist, war-hawk Lincoln had the nerve to portray himself as a religious peacemaker, saying:

> With malice toward none, with charity for all, with firmness in the right as God gives us to see the right, let us strive on to finish the work we are in, to bind up the nation's wounds.[2338]

The height of arrogance and hypocrisy, these words ring as untrue as any words ever spoken or written. For by his actions, words, and beliefs, it is clear that Lincoln detested his own homeland, the South, and for reasons still not completely understood, wished to crush her into dust. After raking up an unnecessary bill of $7 billion[2339] (nearly $180 billion in today's currency), destroying much of the South, nearly bankrupting the U.S. Treasury, and callously expending the lives of as many as three million of his own citizens, can we really believe that he had "malice toward none," and "charity for all"? Can we honestly accept his assertion that he was acting out of the "better angel" of his nature, as he expressed it in his First Inaugural Address,[2340] when he chose to illegally and violently invade Dixie just four weeks later?

No wonder Southerners long believed that one could not love both the South *and* Lincoln. As Berkeley Minor wrote in the *Baltimore Sun*, February 4, 1903, it is obvious that Jeff Davis was a patriot and that Lincoln was a dictator, for the facts are that Lincoln's War "cost the lives

---

2336. Henry, SC, p. 11.
2337. *The American Annual Cyclopedia,* 1866, Vol. 6, p. 326.
2338. Nicolay and Hay, ALCW, Vol. 2, p. 657.
2339. Lincoln's War cost every Northerner $150 ($2,045 in today's currency) and every Southerner $376 ($5,126 in today's currency). C. Johnson, p. 200.
2340. Nicolay and Hay, ALCW, Vol. 2, p. 7.

of two noble republics," the original U.S. Confederacy and the new Southern Confederacy.[2341]

Two noble republics indeed were toppled, and millions of lives were expended, by a lawyer-president who—irrationally and illicitly—decided to use the battlefield instead of the courtroom to decide sectional differences. Why?

Let us examine the facts. Unlike the leaders of nearly ever other civilized nation in the world, late in his War Lincoln attempted to end slavery in North America by physical force, using bayonets, swords, pistols, rifles, cannon, even warships. There was no logical reason to do so and every logical reason not to do so. He was an attorney, and an intelligent, successful, and wealthy one at that. Why turn to bloodshed as a means of social reform when the court system was available for that very purpose?

Additionally, many black abolitionists and former Northern slaves, such as Lincoln's friend and advisor, Sojourner Truth, were pacifists who were wholeheartedly against the use of violence.[2342] Why then did he not use legal procedure to eradicate slavery and manumit Southern slaves gradually, peacefully, and legally the way nearly every other Western nation had done?

Between 1700 and 1900 all of the following countries abolished slavery through the courts, most slowly, and many with compensation paid to former slave owners: Britain, France, Canada, Prussia, Spain, Portugal, the Netherlands, Scotland, Denmark, Sierra Leone, Madeira, Brazil, Russia, India, Cuba, Puerto Rico, Sweden, Argentina, Austria, Colombia, Ecuador, Bolivia, Mexico, Venezuela, Belgium, Chile, and Uruguay.[2343]

There is one nation missing from the above list, conspicuous by its absence: the United States of America. For unlike nearly every other country on earth, under Lincoln's auspices, American slavery was abolished suddenly and aggressively, and without compensation or regard for either slave or slave owner. In the process, a once great nation was split asunder, millions died, and her Constitution lay in ruins. As just one

---

2341. M. Davis, pp. 122-123.
2342. McKissack and McKissack, p. 117.
2343. Many of these countries, such as Great Britain, also offered compensation to slaveholders. Ferguson and Bruun, Vol. 2, p. 704.

example, Lincoln unconstitutionally used the legal power of the U.S. government to destroy individual property rights, something the Western world had never seen up until that time.[2344]

Here is what one Northern abolitionist, Lysander Spooner, thought about Lincoln's violent and unplanned emancipation. In an 1864 letter to Yankee "abolitionist" Charles Sumner, Spooner spoke eloquently of his empathy for the South's position, and of Northern hypocrisy and its relation to the Emancipation Proclamation and the U.S. Constitution:

> [Spooner begins by citing an essay he wrote in 1845] . . . slavery, from its first introduction into this country, to this time, has never had any legal or constitutional existence; but has been a mere abuse, tolerated by the strongest party, without any color of legality, except what was derived from false interpretations of the Constitution, and from practices, statutes, and adjudications, that were in plain conflict with the fundamental constitutional law. And these views have been virtually confessed to be true by John C. Calhoun, James M. Mason [grandson of Jeffersonian George Mason], Jefferson Davis, and many other Southern men; while such professed [Northern] advocates of liberty as Charles Sumner, Henry Wilson, William H. Seward, Salmon P. Chase, and the like, have been continually denying them.
>
> Had all those men at the North, who believed these ideas to be true, promulgated them, as was their plain and obvious duty to do, it is reasonable to suppose that we should long since have had freedom, without shedding one drop of blood; certainly without one tithe of the blood that has now been shed; for the slaveholders would never have dared, in the face of the world, to attempt to overthrow a government that gave freedom to all, for the sake of establishing in its place one that should make slaves of those who, by the existing constitution, were free. But so long as the North, and especially so long as the professed (though hypocritical) advocates of liberty, like those named, conceded the constitutional right of property in slaves, they gave the slaveholders the full benefit of the argument that they were insulted, disturbed, and endangered in the enjoyment of their acknowledged constitutional rights; and that it was therefore necessary to their honor, security, and happiness that they should have a separate government. And this argument, conceded to them by the North, has not only given them strength and union among themselves, but has given them

---

2344. Palmer and Colton, p. 543.

friends, both in the North and among foreign nations; and has cost the nation hundreds of thousands of lives, and thousands of millions of treasure. [End of Spooner's 1845 essay.]

[Spooner now addresses Sumner:] Upon yourself, and others like you, professed friends of freedom, who, instead of promulgating what you believed to be the truth, have, for selfish purposes, denied it, and thus conceded to the slaveholders the benefit of an argument to which they had no claim,—upon your heads, more even, if possible, than upon the slaveholders themselves, (who have acted only in accordance with their associations, interests, and avowed principles as slaveholders) rests the blood of this horrible, unnecessary, and therefore guilty, war.

Your concessions, as to the pro-slavery character of the Constitution, have been such as, if true, would prove the Constitution unworthy of having one drop of blood shed in its support. They have been such as to withhold from the North all the benefit of the argument, that a war for the Constitution was a war for liberty. You have thus, to the extent of your ability, placed the North wholly in the wrong, and the South wholly in the right. And the effect of these false positions in which the North and the South have respectively been placed, not only with your consent, but, in part, by your exertions, has been to fill the land with blood.

The South could, consistently with honor, and probably would, long before this time, and without a conflict, have surrendered their slavery to the demand of the Constitution, (if that had been pressed upon them,) and to the moral sentiment of the world; while they could not with honor, or at least certainly would not, surrender anything to a confessedly unconstitutional demand, especially when coining from mere demagogues, who were so openly unprincipled as to profess the greatest moral abhorrence of slavery, and at time same time, for the sake of office, swear to support it, by swearing to support a Constitution which they declared to be its bulwark.

You, and others like you have done more, according to your abilities, to prevent the peaceful abolition of slavery, than any other men in the nation; for while honest men were explaining the true character of the constitution, as an instrument giving freedom to all, you were continually denying it, and doing your utmost (and far more than any avowed pro slavery man could do) to defeat their efforts. And it now appears that all this was done by you in violation of your own conviction of truth.

In your pretended zeal for liberty, you have been urging on the nation to the most frightful destruction of human life; but your love of liberty has never yet induced you to declare publicly, but has permitted you constantly to deny, a truth that was sufficient for, and vital to, the speedy and peaceful accomplishment of freedom. You have, with deliberate purpose, and through a series of years, betrayed the very citadel of liberty, which you were under oath to defend. And there has been, in the country, no other treason at all comparable with this.[2345]

Here Spooner not only rightfully lambasts Sumner, Lincoln, Chase, and all of the other "hypocritical" Northerners for subverting the Constitution for selfish, political gain, but also for their double-dealing in regards to slavery.

Though Yankee abolitionist Spooner was keenly aware of it, Lincoln seems to have conveniently forgotten that slavery only takes root where there is a shortage of labor and where profits can be made,[2346] as was the exact situation in the colonial North in the 1600s and 1700s.[2347] Lincoln also failed to recall that it was for these very reasons that slavery and the cotton industry had once been hugely profitable in the North—the capital of not only the slave trade, but also the infamous Cotton Triangle and its notorious Middle Passage, both inventions of New Englanders.[2348]

Here Yankee slave ships sailed to Africa, where rum (made in Yankee distilleries)[2349] was traded for African slaves (always already enslaved by other Africans)—known as the "Outward Passage." These slaves were brought back to the Americas—the "Middle Passage," usually to the Southern states,[2350] where they were sold and used in the cotton growing industry on Dixie's expansive farms and plantations.[2351] The Yankee slave ships then journeyed back to their ports in the Northeast—the "Homeward Passage."[2352] The cotton harvested by

---

2345. Website: www.lysanderspooner.org/sumner.htm.
2346. See e.g., Diamond, pp. 279-280.
2347. McManus, BBN, p. 1; White, Foscue, and McKnight, p. 38.
2348. See Weintraub, p. 51; Meltzer, Vol. 2, p. 143; K. C. Davis, pp. 11-12; Rosenbaum and Brinkley, s.v. "Slave trade"; Garraty and McCaughey, p. 39; Foner, FSFLFM, p. 45.
2349. This rum was made from sugar grown in the West Indies by African slaves, which Yankee slavers had sold to the French sugar plantation owners (located there) to begin with. The Yankees would then return to New England with a shipload of sugar to make both rum and molasses, in preparation for another trip to Africa. Brinton, Christopher, and Wolff, Vol. 2, p. 41.
2350. As mentioned above, Yankee slave ships also brought African slaves to the West Indies (to work the sugar plantations), and to the Northeast (where they served on Northern plantations and in Northern homes) as well. See Seabrook, EYWTACWW, pp. 69-98.
2351. Garraty, p. 78.
2352. Moore and Dunbar, p. 110. English slave traders had their own Cotton Triangle. See Penrose, p. 225.

Southern slaves was sold to New England's textile mills, whose products were peddled worldwide at huge profits. These profits were then used to fund more Yankee slave expeditions to Africa, starting the Cotton Triangle all over again.[2353] So vital was the triangular Yankee slave trade to the Northeast, that without it the rum industry would have been seriously curtailed.[2354]

In 1839, Ohio Senator Thomas Morris lectured the Senate on this very topic. Stressing the importance of emancipation, he promised that from then on he would devote himself fully to fighting

> against the power of these two great interests—the slave power of the South, and [the] banking power of the North—which are now uniting to rule this country. The cotton bale and the bank note have formed an alliance; the credit system with slave labor.[2355]

The existence of the remunerative Cotton Triangle is why Yankees universally sanctioned, legalized, accepted, and financed slavery for nearly 200 years. It was only when it began to prove to be inefficient and hence unprofitable[2356] in the late 1700s and early 1800s[2357]—due to the North's short growing season, the development of the manufacturing industry (which required more highly skilled labor), rapidly increasing white birth rates,[2358] one-man farms, immigration, urbanization,[2359] and most importantly, rampant Yankee racism (which blacks responded to by being "lazy, idle, proud, vicious, and at length wholly useless to their [Northern] masters")[2360]—that the North began to gradually and peacefully emancipate her black chattel.[2361]

Thus in the North slavery went officially extinct *slowly*, a process that was spread out over many decades: in Vermont slavery officially ended in 1777; in New Hampshire and Pennsylvania in 1780; in

---

2353. Shillington, p. 173; Meltzer, Vol. 2, p. 43; Farrow, Lang, and Frank, pp. 48-49; Hacker, p. 18; P. M. Roberts, p. 49; McManus, BBN, p. 9.
2354. Carman and Syrett, p. 68.
2355. B. F. Morris, p. 119.
2356. The World Book Encyc., "slavery"; Carman and Syrett, p. 40; Morison and Commager, Vol. 1, p. 245.
2357. P. M. Roberts, p. 198; Garraty and McCaughey, p. 81.
2358. McManus, BBN, pp. 175-179.
2359. R. P. Jordan, p. 13.
2360. U. B. Phillips, pp. 119-120.
2361. Kennedy, p. 230.

Massachusetts in 1783; in Rhode Island in 1784; in Connecticut in 1784 and 1797; in New York in 1799 and 1817; in Ohio in 1802; in New Jersey in 1804; in Indiana in 1816; and in Illinois in 1818.[2362]

Though Lincoln knew better, having lived in a Northern state that gradually abolished slavery only when it became unprofitable, he never granted the same prerogative to the South. Instead, here he abolished it by force, and almost instantaneously. As Margaret L. Coit writes of this event, the fragile issues surrounding slavery, which could have only been sorted out by a deliberate and meticulous intellectual process, were instead resolved brutishly by the gun barrel.[2363]

At first, slavery was hugely profitable in the South as well, particularly from 1793 on, the year Yankee Eli Whitney invented the cotton gin.[2364] By providing a larger supply of cotton[2365] at a lower price,[2366] Whitney's gin greatly increased rather than decreased the need for manual labor,[2367] intensifying the need to find cheap and easy sources of slaves from Africa.[2368] Even Lincoln admitted as much on October 13, 1858:

> Mr. [Preston Smith] Brooks, of South Carolina, once said, and truly said, that when this government was established, no one expected the institution of slavery to last until this day; and that the men who formed this government were wiser and better than the men of these days; but the men of these days had experience which the fathers had not, and that experience had taught them the invention of the cotton-gin, and this had made the perpetuation of the institution of slavery a necessity in this country.[2369]

After that, as it spread from the Atlantic Coast west through the

---

2362. See Litwack, NS, p. 3; Fogel, p. 206. We will note that slavery, to one extent or another, continued in nearly all of the Northern states even after official abolition. Since it was "unofficial," however, it was usually ignored, especially if Yankee slave owners kept a low profile. One of these, as has been mentioned, was Northern General Ulysses S. Grant, who kept his slaves until December 1865, nearly three years after the Emancipation Proclamation was issued and eight months after Lincoln's War ended. Woods, p. 67; Wallechinsky, Wallace, and Wallace, p. 11; Rutherford, FA, p. 38.
2363. Coit, p. 229.
2364. Nevins and Commager, p. 160.
2365. Haines and Walsh, Vol. 2, p. 646.
2366. Lerner, Meacham, and Burns, p. 732.
2367. C. M. Green, EW, pp. 61-62; Simpson, p. 78; W. B. Garrison, CWTFB, p. 106.
2368. Lerner, p. 503.
2369. Nicolay and Hay, ALCW, Vol. 1, p. 480.

Deep South and across the Mississippi River into Texas, cotton did indeed become king in the South.[2370] But not because Southerners were enthusiastic cotton growers. It was, in great part, because Northern banks—most which were wholly dependent on Dixie's agricultural products—would only lend money to Southern farmers who agreed to grow cotton![2371]

In the end, however, this worked out well for servant-owning Southerners, because when it came to labor productivity, slavery was found to be a far more efficient method than free labor.[2372] Plantations that used slave labor, for example, were 50 percent more efficient than those that used free labor, giving the South an enormous advantage: her farms were 35 percent more productive than slave-free farms in the North.[2373] Indeed, Southern slavery became more productive, and thus more lucrative, right up to Lincoln's War.[2374]

But money was not everything to Southerners. By the mid 1800s, the reverberations of the Age of Enlightenment and the ever advancing technologies of the Industrial Revolution, had made servitude more unappealing to them than ever before. English philosopher John Locke, in particular, with his emphasis on natural law[2375] (also known as natural rights),[2376] had a profound impact on the South, and white, black, and Native-American slave owners began to reconsider the institution in light of his concepts. In *The Second Treatise of Government*, Locke wrote:

> Men being . . . all free, equal and independent, no one can be put out of this estate, and subjected to the political power of another, without his own consent.[2377]

The concept of natural rights was adopted by the Founding

2370. Weintraub, p. 55.
2371. Coit, p. 330.
2372. Stampp, pp. 408-418; E. M. Thomas, p. 15.
2373. Fogel, pp. 73-76. See also Fogel and Engerman, pp. 158-257. This explains other studies which show that after emancipation blacks produced 50 percent less than when they were slaves. Garraty and McCaughey, p. 268.
2374. See Fogel and Engerman, pp. 38-106.
2375. Napolitano, p. xvi.
2376. Locke's philosophy of natural rights is based on the belief that people, as "natural beings," have basic inalienable rights pertaining to "life, liberty, and property," that cannot be blocked, withheld, or renounced by society or government.
2377. Locke, p. 163.

Fathers. One of them was John Adams, America's second president. In 1765, Adams was speaking of the God-given freedoms of the people when he said:

> You have rights antecedent to all earthly governments; rights that cannot be repealed or restrained by human laws; rights derived from the Great Lawgiver of the Universe.[2378]

Who could justify slavery after hearing such words? Many tried, but such words rang out across the decades. They would not go away.

America's black slaves themselves, having observed freedom all around them for several centuries, now longed for liberty more desperately than ever before.[2379] The abolition train was in motion, and it could not be stopped.

By 1860, though it was still proving to be a very profitable institution[2380] (contrary to Yankee myth, from the 1840s onward, the American slave economy accelerated rapidly),[2381] socially, politically, and culturally slavery was no longer acceptable to an American populace that had, by now, embraced the European Enlightenment. Criminalized, as we have seen, by busybodies like Northerner William Lloyd Garrison,[2382] slavery had become, in a word, obsolete, as nearly all Americans, both South and North, knew. By 1860, and certainly by mid-1863, white Southerners were well on their way to complete emancipation.[2383]

Aware of this himself, why then did not Lincoln unconditionally offer Dixie the same option the North had given herself: gradual, compensated emancipation?

In January 1863, and again in December 1865, the U.S., under both Lincoln's Emancipation Proclamation and the Thirteenth Amendment respectively, abolished slavery suddenly, illegally, and violently.[2384] And he did all of this without restitution to owners, even though compensation (buying every Southern slave from their owners at

---

2378. McCabe, p. 138.
2379. C. Adams, p. 129; E. M. Thomas, p. 242.
2380. See Fogel and Engerman, pp. 38-106.
2381. Fogel, p. 412.
2382. Simpson, p. 79.
2383. E. M. Thomas, p. 242.
2384. Fogel, p. 207.

market value and then freeing them) would have cost the nation ten times less than what it cost to go to war.[2385]

In short, Lincoln had no organized plan to admit freed blacks into American society as equal citizens;[2386] nothing to help the elderly, the ill, or orphaned blacks who could not work and who had previously been under the lifelong care of their owners;[2387] no education, no loans or grants, no job training, no housing to ease freedmen and freedwomen into the world of capitalism, competition, and a free, highly skilled, and often hostile labor force. Lincoln did not even give them any legal protection.[2388] All were merely "liberated" to roam the streets and make their way as best they could; or as Lincoln flippantly styled it, to "root, pig, or perish."[2389]

It is true that Lincoln had promised freed Southern blacks "forty acres and a mule." But as with most of the North's other pledges to blacks, this one too turned out to be a lie:[2390] there were no mules,[2391] only deprivation, starvation, and vagrancy.[2392] And Lincoln's so-called "black land giveaways" were only meant to be temporary[2393]—and most of those that were issued ultimately went to rich white Northerners,[2394] railroads, land speculators, and lumber companies.[2395] After the reality sank in, all hope of free land for blacks evaporated.[2396] (Lincoln and the U.S. Congress did eventually create the Bureau of Refugees, Freedmen, and Abandoned Lands. But this was in March 1865,[2397] over two years after the Emancipation Proclamation—too late to mitigate the myriad of problems caused by sudden and violent abolition in January 1863.)

Black civil rights leader W. E. B. Du Bois summed up Lincoln's

---

2385. In other words, it cost Americans ten times more to fight and kill each other for four years than if they would have simply ended slavery. Rutland, p. 226. See also C. Johnson, p. 200. This is more definitive proof, if such is needed, that Lincoln's War was not over slavery.
2386. Rosenbaum and Brinkley, s.v. "Lincoln and Douglas."
2387. Thornton and Ekelund, p. 96.
2388. Haggard, p. 90.
2389. Stephens, RAHS, pp. 83, 137; Stephens, CV, Vol. 2, p. 615.
2390. Mullen, p. 33; Rosenbaum and Brinkley, s.v. "Forty Acres and a Mule."
2391. J. H. Franklin, p. 37.
2392. Grissom, p. 162.
2393. Foner, R, pp. 70-71.
2394. Thornton and Ekelund, p. 96.
2395. K. C. Davis, p. 427.
2396. Bailyn, Dallek, Davis, Donald, Thomas, and Wood, p. 16.
2397. K. C. Davis, p. 426.

emancipation "plan" this way: former slaves are now free to do whatever they want with the nothing they never had to begin with.²³⁹⁸ Thomas Hall, an ex-slave, held similar sentiments:

> Lincoln got the praise for freeing us, but did he do it? He give us freedom without giving us any chance to live to ourselves and we still had to depend on the Southern white man for work, food, and clothing, and he held us through our necessity and want in a state of servitude but little better than slavery. Lincoln done but little for the negro race and from a living standpoint nothing.²³⁹⁹

White Southerners too were appalled at Lincoln's inhumanity. An incredulous General Robert E. Lee posed a rhetorical query to the Yankee president:

> What will you do with the freed people? That is a serious question today. Unless some humane course, based on wisdom and Christian principles, is adopted, you do them a great injustice in setting them free.²⁴⁰⁰

Lee was correct, of course. Under Lincoln's "root, pig, or perish" emancipation plan, blacks who as servants had lived quality lives equal to and often superior to many whites and most free blacks, now found themselves living out in the open or in makeshift tents, begging for food and work. Disease, homelessness, starvation, beggary, poverty, prostitution, and thievery now became the lot of untold thousands of former black servants.

Lincoln's unplanned emancipation affected former white and black slave owners just as severely. Many, who had invested millions of dollars in their servants, found themselves bankrupt and without labor of any kind. Crops died in the ground, fields went fallow, farms were deserted, sold, or foreclosed. Besides his illegal naval blockade, the ruthless bombing of Southern cities, and the unprovoked murder of thousands of Southern civilians, Lincoln's "emancipation" must be counted among the most destructive of his assaults on the South.

2398. Buckley, p. 116.
2399. Website: www.archives.gov/nae/news/featured-programs/lincoln/080920Lincoln02Transcript.pdf.
2400. Page, p. 38.

The problem was not due to Southern slaves being liberated. It was that they were set free without any aid to either the slave or the slave owner. In this way, economically and racially, Lincoln's "emancipation" set the South back decades, making a mockery of his so-called "Reconstruction" program.[2401] In fact, many areas, especially those that lost schools, universities, and libraries due to Yankee atrocities, are still recovering in the 21st Century.[2402]

Is it any wonder that today's South, despite her many wonderful colleges and public and private schools, sometimes lags behind the rest of the nation in education? One-hundred-fifty years has not been enough time to rebuild all of the establishments of learning Lincoln and his soldiers turned to rubble during his criminal four-year raid on the South.[2403]

It will be a revelation to many Northerners and scallywags to learn that traditional Southerners still talk about these events on an almost daily basis, as if they occurred yesterday. Why?

Since Lincoln invaded the South, his War took place primarily in Dixie (the South never had any interest in invading or seizing the North), and thousands of historical markers, cemeteries, and monuments dot the landscape to prove it; cold, mute testimony to the ruthlessness of a Northern tyrant. These, along with regular battle reenactments and the proud display of a variety of Confederate flags, keep the memories very much alive in the South. Thus, even after a century and a half, the War is still fresh here.

In the North, however, where few battles were fought, where almost no civilians perished,[2404] where there are few Civil War cemeteries or monuments, and where no cities were bombed into oblivion, the War

---

2401. C. Adams, pp. 139-140.
2402. At Columbia, South Carolina, Sherman and his henchmen torched the once beautiful city, and along with it, "some of the finest private libraries in the South." S. Andrews, p. 35. One of the more conspicuous schools destroyed by Lincoln's soldiers was the University of Alabama, which Yankee troops mercilessly and needlessly burned to the ground on the eve of the end of the War in April 1865. Along with the destruction of the school was her enormous library, filled with rare one-of-a-kind books, now forever lost to history. See C. Johnson, p. 157.
2403. Despite Lincoln's heartless attempt to destroy the South's educational system, today Dixie possesses fourteen of the top fifty universities in the U.S. C. Johnson, pp. 50-56. CNNMoney.com recently named Nashville, Tennessee, one of the "Brainiest Cities in the United States." *Newsweek* ranked two Nashville area high schools twenty-third and twenty-fourth on the nation's best high schools list. And *U.S. News & World Report* rated Nashville's Vanderbilt University eighteenth on the list of America's top universities. *Tennessee Homes*, October/November, 2009, p. 6.
2404. See J. M. McPherson, ACW, p. 9.

is seldom discussed or even thought of. Yet another one of the many differences between South and North.

19

SOUTHERN & NORTHERN VIEWS OF LINCOLN

PART ONE

LINCOLN BELIEVED THAT THE SECESSION of the Southern states would "destroy the Union,"[2405] create anarchy,[2406] and cause representative government to "perish from the earth."[2407] But secession does not lead to destruction and anarchy. It leads to two smaller but stronger and healthier separate nations by acting as a decentralizing constraint against the abusive, corrupting, federating, and consolidating tendencies of the national government and its civil servants. This is one reason the Founding Fathers were so devoted to the right of secession. It was part of the "checks and balances" system they created to inhibit the monarchical and tyrannical proclivities of the central government and its officials.

Why did Lincoln ignore the wisdom of the Founders, trample on the Constitution, declare secession illegal, and set out to demolish states' rights? Why did he send hundreds of thousands of soldiers into a legally formed, independent nation with the express purpose of forcing it back into a voluntary union at the tip of a bayonet? Why did he not work out the disunion and reunion of the Southern states in a court of law?

Throughout history, hundreds, perhaps thousands, of regions have

---

2405. Nicolay and Hay, ALCW, Vol. 2, pp. 4, 62, 93.
2406. Nicolay and Hay, ALCW, Vol. 2, p. 5.
2407. Nicolay and Hay, ALCW, Vol. 2, p. 439.

separated peacefully and legally from their parent countries. In 1905, for example, Norway broke away from its union with Sweden. Today they possess two of the most robust economies and stable governments in the world.[2408]

Bosnia, Croatia, Herzegovina, and Slovenia recently seceded from Yugoslavia, and although there was bloodshed, Yugoslavia did not descend into anarchy and her government did not "perish from the earth," as Lincoln would have predicted. Latvia, Estonia, and Belarus all recently seceded from Russia, but Russia was not destroyed. With twice the land mass of the U.S., she remains one of the largest and most powerful countries on the planet.

Had they been allowed to part peacefully, the U.S. would not have dissolved with the secession of the Southern states either. In fact, disunion would have made the U.S. stronger by checking both Lincoln's dictatorial propensities and the imperialistic expansion of the central government under his rule. In time, the U.S. and the C.S. would have reopened trade with one another and learned to live in harmony as neighboring nations, perhaps even rejoining again at some point in the future. Lincoln interfered with the natural procession of these constitutional safeguards, purposefully put in place by the Founders, by initiating war on the South on April 12, 1861.

And so another Northern myth, William H. Seward's monstrous fable that the War was an "Irrepressible Conflict," must be struck down.[2409] The South wanted peace and, before the War, did everything in its power to maintain it. As threats of violence begin to come from Washington, D.C. in early 1861, she sent one peace committee after another to the White House in an attempt to prevent bloodshed. During the War, it did everything it could to draw the conflict to a close as soon as possible.

Lincoln, in contrast, actively sought war then created one illegally, all in pursuit of his agenda. Along the way, he spurned all attempts, both by his cabinet members and by his Northern constituents, to end the War and allow the South to go its own way in peace. Had

---

2408. DiLorenzo, RL, p. 117.
2409. The phrase "the irrepressible conflict" was coined by Lincoln's future secretary of state Seward in a speech he gave at Rochester, New York, on October 25, 1858. For the full speech, see Baker, Vol. 4, pp. 289-302.

differences been settled legally in court—or at least diplomatically, as they should have been, and as the South repeatedly tried to do, the War could have been prevented. It was not irresistible, inevitable, as Northerners saw it. This is only another Yankee folktale designed to justify Lincoln's terrible actions.

Lincoln's true character in this regard was recognized even by many Northerners. One of these was New Yorker and future American president, Theodore Roosevelt. On September 8, 1900, at Grand Rapids, Michigan, he admitted that during the War,

> on every hand Lincoln was denounced as a tyrant, a shedder of blood, a foe to liberty, a would be dictator, a founder of an empire—one orator saying, 'We also have our emperor, Lincoln, who can tell stale jokes while the land is running red with the blood of brothers.' Even after Lincoln's death the assault was kept up.[2410]

Lincoln is also called the "Great Emancipator." Yet as a lawyer he had at one time defended, not abolitionists, but slave owners,[2411] and later as U.S. president, he barred blacks from both the White House and the military; this while he delayed both black enlistment and the issuance of the Emancipation Proclamation for years—despite the desperate pleas of abolitionists, clergymen, and black leaders. In fact, he once intimated that he felt forced to free the slaves, and that he would not have done so had the South not "rebelled." In a conversation with black separatist Sojourner Truth,[2412] he told the former servant that it was only because Southerners had not "behaved themselves" that he had been "compelled" to issue his January 1, 1863, edict. Otherwise, according to Lincoln himself, there would have been no Emancipation Proclamation.[2413]

An interesting incident occurred midway through the War that sheds further light on this topic.

After North Carolina was captured by Union troops, Lincoln appointed the proslavery, states' rights Unionist, Edward Stanly, to act as military governor. The North Carolinian only agreed to accept the post

---

2410. Minor, p. 35. See also Ashe, p. 60.
2411. Current, LNK, pp. 218-219; W. B. Garrison, LNOK, pp. 35-37; Greenberg and Waugh, p. 355.
2412. K. C. Davis, p. 447.
2413. Greenberg and Waugh, p. 353. See also Coffin, p. 457; Current, LNK, p. 225.

because Lincoln had promised him that he would not interfere with slavery, just as he had pledged to the public in his First Inaugural Address.[2414]

After Lincoln issued the Emancipation Proclamation, however, a furious Stanly made a trip to the White House to resign from his appointment in person. But the resignation never came. Lincoln had several meetings with the disgruntled Southerner and assured him that the edict had nothing to do with blacks, abolition, or civil rights. According to James C. Welling, the editor of the Washington paper, the *National Intelligencer*, Stanly later told him that

> the President had stated to him that the proclamation had become a civil necessity to prevent the Radicals [socialists and communists] from openly embarrassing the government in the conduct of the war.[2415]

Then we have Lincoln's two Confiscation Acts. Though issued illegally in the summers of 1861 and 1862 respectively, the U.S. Congress passed both, the first which automatically freed Southern slaves who were serving in the Confederacy, the second which freed slaves whose owners were serving in the Confederacy. But Lincoln showed no enthusiasm for either law, never followed up on them, never made sure they were carried out or enforced,[2416] and almost vetoed the second, considering it unconstitutional.[2417] Little wonder. "I cannot learn that that law has caused a single slave to come over to us," Lincoln complained on September 13, 1862, to a group of abolitionist clergymen.[2418]

Lincoln's Yankee critics were quick to respond. Wendell Phillips called the president "a first-rate second-rate man,"[2419] while Garrison referred to his policies as "stumbling, halting, prevaricating, irresolute, weak, besotted."[2420]

Meanwhile, the U.S. Congress interpreted the second Confiscation Act as an act of emancipation, and it was. But it was not for

---

2414. Nicolay and Hay, ALCW, Vol. 6, p. 170.
2415. Haygood, p. 67; see also Hendelson, s.v. "Lincoln, Abraham."
2416. Zinn, p. 186.
2417. Current, LNK, p. 221.
2418. Nicolay and Hay, ALCW, Vol. 2, p. 234.
2419. W. Phillips, p. 457.
2420. Wilbur, p. 70.

the purpose of setting blacks free and giving them equal rights and American citizenship, something Lincoln had long been against.[2421] Its real purpose was to liberate Southern blacks so they could then be deported out of the country, and as far away as possible. As Lincoln worded the act, it would authorize him to provide for colonization "in some tropical country beyond the limits of the United States, of such persons of the African race, made free by the provisions of this act, as may be willing to emigrate."[2422] Lincoln's political idol, Henry Clay, who died in 1852 while serving as president of the American Colonization Society (in which Lincoln himself was a leader),[2423] would have wholeheartedly supported this action.[2424]

A few months later, on December 1, 1862, Lincoln gave his Second Annual Message to Congress. Though he had just issued his Preliminary Emancipation Proclamation (on September 22, 1862), and was only days from issuing his Final Emancipation Proclamation (on January 1, 1863), the president did not want to talk about abolition. He wanted to talk about black colonization: the deportation of all American blacks out of the U.S.

After asking Congress to "appropriate money and otherwise provide for colonizing free colored persons . . . at any place or places without the United States,"[2425] Lincoln drove his point home:

> I cannot make it better known than it already is, that I strongly favor colonization.[2426]

One of the reasons he gives for this sentiment is that the presence of blacks "would injure and displace white labor and white laborers."[2427] The only rational solution, according to the president, is deportation; that is, colonization. As he put it to his congressional peers:

> With deportation, even to a limited extent, enhanced wages to white labor is mathematically certain. Labor is like any other

---

2421. See e.g., Lincoln and Douglas, p. 187; Holzer, p. 226; Barney, p. 124; Napolitano, p. 64.
2422. Nicolay and Hay, ALAH, Vol. 6, pp. 356-357; Long and Long, p. 241.
2423. W. B. Garrison, LNOK, p. 186.
2424. W. P. Pickett, p. 310.
2425. Nicolay and Hay, ALCW, Vol. 2, p. 271.
2426. Nicolay and Hay, ALCW, Vol. 2, p. 274.
2427. Nicolay and Hay, ALCW, Vol. 2, p. 274.

> commodity in the market—increase the demand for it, and you increase the price of it. Reduce the supply of black labor by colonizing the black laborer out of the country, and by precisely so much you increase the demand for, and wages of, white labor.[2428]

Remove blacks from the U.S., problem solved—according to Lincoln.

The white separatist president had another fearful issue he felt compelled to address before Congress that December day: the white Yankee concern of a hoard of Africans flooding northward into their region from Dixie after emancipation. Lincoln was ready with an answer:

> But it is dreaded that the freed people will swarm forth and cover the whole land. Are they not already in the land? Will liberation make them any more numerous? Equally distributed among the whites of the whole country, and there would be but one colored to seven whites. Could the one in any way greatly disturb the seven? There are many communities now having more than one free colored person to seven whites, and this without any apparent consciousness of evil from it. The District of Columbia, and the States of Maryland and Delaware, are all in this condition. The District has more than one free colored to six whites; and yet in its frequent petitions to Congress I believe it has never presented the presence of free colored persons as one of its grievances. But why should emancipation south send the free people north? People of any color seldom run unless there be something to run from. Heretofore colored people, to some extent, have fled north from bondage; and now, perhaps, from both bondage and destitution. But if gradual emancipation and deportation be adopted, they will have neither to flee from. Their old masters will give them wages at least until new laborers can be procured; and the freedmen, in turn, will gladly give their labor for the wages till new homes can be found for them in congenial climes and with people of their own blood and race. This proposition can be trusted on the mutual interests involved. And, in any event, cannot the North decide for itself whether to receive them?[2429]

In short, Lincoln says here, Yankees need not fear the dreaded possibility of Southern blacks migrating North if colonization is implemented and new, stricter anti-black laws are put in place.

2428. Nicolay and Hay, ALCW, Vol. 2, p. 275.
2429. Nicolay and Hay, ALCW, Vol. 2, p. 275.

On December 31, 1862, just a few weeks later, Lincoln signed a contract with a group who promised to help him colonize free blacks in Haiti. Though the deal turned sour when the men were discovered to be swindlers, this did not slow the president down in his push to force colonization upon America's blacks.[2430] The very next day, January 1, 1863, he issued his Final Emancipation Proclamation, largely in the hope—as he had clearly stated in his Preliminary Emancipation Proclamation—that it would eventually help lead to the deportation of all Americans "of African descent."[2431]

Despite such words and actions, Lincoln is still remembered as the "Great Emancipator." Why?

As we have seen, he was no abolitionist, hated the entire movement, said abolition was worse than slavery, stalled the Emancipation Proclamation for several years, was a leader in the American Colonization Society, had slaves complete the construction of the White House, implemented extreme racist military policies, used profits from Northern slavery to fund his War, often referred to blacks as "niggers" (both privately and publicly), said he was willing to allow slavery to continue in perpetuity if the Southern states would come back into the Union, pushed nonstop for the deportation of blacks, defended slave owners in court, proposed the proslavery Corwin Amendment to the Constitution in 1861, and continually blocked black enlistment, black suffrage, and black citizenship. These represent but a fragment of his anti-black deeds.

Lincoln the "friend of the black man"? The "Great Emancipator"? The "unifier of a racially divided nation"? We think not!

Thus instead, let us remember America's true abolitionists.[2432] These would include the South's "Great Emancipators": Jefferson Davis, Robert E. Lee, and Patrick R. Cleburne. And in the North there was Elijah Lovejoy, Charles Sumner, and Benjamin F. Wade.[2433]

While we have been led to believe otherwise by dishonest historians and Yankee mythologists, the party platform of white racism, white supremacy, and white separatism was alive and well in the White

---

2430. J. M. McPherson, NCW, pp. 96-97.
2431. L. Johnson, p. 133.
2432. Leech, p. 307.
2433. Though Old South abolitionists rarely agreed with the ploys of Old North abolitionists like Lovejoy, Sumner, and Wade, they could at least respect them for being authentic fellow abolitionists—something Lincoln was not, and never pretended to be.

House throughout Lincoln's entire administration, due in great part to the president himself.

This should not surprise any of my readers by now. Lincoln's Negrophobia had deep roots dating back to his earliest days as a politician. In 1840, for example, the young Illinois Whig rebuked Martin Van Buren for voting in favor of black suffrage, and, in 1856, as noted, he came out against black citizenship[2434] shortly after the Dred Scott case was settled.[2435]

In 1858, during his debate with Douglas at Ottawa, Illinois, Lincoln said of the black man:

> . . . he is not my equal in many respects—certainly not in color, perhaps not in moral or intellectual endowments . . .[2436]

In 1864, Lincoln, the attorney who represented slaveholders in court,[2437] supported the Louisiana constitution, which prohibited blacks from voting.[2438]

Lincoln could have pushed through black suffrage any time he liked. Instead, he waffled. On April 11, 1865, only two days after his War ended and three days before he was shot by disgruntled Copperhead John Wilkes Booth, the president gave a public speech, his last in fact, at the White House. In it he deflected Yankee criticism that he still had not granted blacks total civil rights, obfuscating and wavering, finally acknowledging that he would now consider voting rights, if nothing else, for blacks. But *only* for "the very intelligent" and those who had served in the U.S. army. I know it is unsatisfactory to some, Lincoln told his audience,

> that the elective franchise is not [yet] given to the colored man. I would myself prefer that it were now conferred on the very intelligent, and on those who serve our cause as soldiers.[2439]

2434. Litwack, NS, p. 83.
2435. Nicolay and Hay, ALCW, Vol. 1, p. 407.
2436. Nicolay and Hay, ALCW, Vol. 1, pp. 458-459.
2437. Current, LNK, pp. 218-219; W. B. Garrison, LNOK, pp. 35-37; Greenberg and Waugh, p. 355.
2438. J. M. McPherson, NCW, p. 302.
2439. Nicolay and Hay, ALCW, Vol. 2, p. 674.

Bizarrely, pro-Lincoln historians and scholars consider this the first time a U.S. president "endorsed black suffrage."[2440] But was "conferring" it only on "very intelligent" blacks and black Union soldiers really an endorsement? Hardly. It was just more typical Lincolnian politics: muddling, trickery, delay tactics, and word twisting. What about the millions of African-Americans who did not fit into either of these categories? This question the strident black colonizationist left for future generations to grapple with.

It is patently clear that in the end it was not the South but Lincoln who stood in the way of the black vote and black citizenship. Indeed, both only came after his death: universal Negro citizenship was not instituted until 1868, and universal Negro suffrage did not come until 1870.[2441]

Lincoln has also been called "Honest Abe." This after unlawfully taking upon himself congressional war powers (unlawful, in part, because he refused to recognize the conflict as a war, merely a "rebellion"); after lying and rigging his way into the White House (not once, but twice); after committing innumerable heinous crimes during an illicit War he himself started, a war initiated against the advice of his own cabinet and against the wishes of both the Northern and Southern people.[2442]

Where did Lincoln get the idea that he had unlimited powers? From an imagined theory he called "military necessity."[2443] The Constitution, as we have discussed, gives the president no such power or authority, however; in fact quite the opposite.[2444] As Salmon P. Chase, Lincoln's chief justice of the United States, stated emphatically:

> Neither President, nor Congress, nor courts, possess any power not given by the Constitution.[2445]

In 1866 (in *Ex parte Milligan*), the Supreme Court itself specifically denounced Lincoln's theory of "necessity" as completely erroneous:

2440. Foner, R, p. 74.
2441. Kinder and Hilgemann, Vol. 2, p. 117.
2442. Meriwether, p. 157.
2443. Nicolay and Hay, ALCW, Vol. 2, p. 216.
2444. The Tenth Amendment is clear on this point: "The powers not delegated to the United States by the Constitution, nor prohibited by it to the States, are reserved to the States respectively, or to the people." Calvert, Vol. 8, p. 37.
2445. Christian, p. 13.

> The Constitution of the United States is a law for rulers and people, equally in war and in peace, and covers with the shield of its protection all classes of men, at all times, and under all circumstances. No doctrine involving more pernicious consequences was ever invented by the wit of man than that any of its provisions can be suspended during any of the great exigencies of government. Such a doctrine leads directly to anarchy or despotism, but the theory of necessity on which it is based is false; for the government, within the Constitution, has all the powers granted to it, which are necessary to preserve its existence; as has been happily proved by the result of the great effort to throw off its just authority.[2446]

And who was it who "threw off the Constitution's just authority" under the "false" theory of necessity? None other than Mr. Lincoln.

"Honest Abe"? Absolutely not.

From the beginning to the end of his political life, he used ambiguous speech, obfuscation, passivity, prevarication, stall tactics, secrecy, deception, pseudo-religiosity, opportunism, do-nothing policies, and political double-talk to convince a nation that he cared about the Constitution and black civil rights, when it was clear that he was in fact an autocrat, a rank political opportunist, an atheist, and a racial bigot.

How did he hide all of this from the public for so many years? His *modus operandi* was to simply say the least possible whenever possible. "My policy," the crafty bureaucrat often said to his friends, "is to have no policy."[2447]

While today he is called "the black man's greatest friend," during his political life he spent every spare minute plotting to deport all Americans of African descent out of the country. He never even commented on, let alone thanked, blacks for the many amazing architectural, linguistic, artistic, sartorial, choreographic, culinary, and musical contributions they had made to American culture up to that time.[2448] In the 1800s, for example, blacks comprised 80 percent of the South's artisan class,[2449] meaning that the vast majority of Dixie's buildings

---

2446. Christian, p. 13.
2447. Nicolay and Hay, ALAH, Vol. 4, p. 76.
2448. Faust, s.v. "slavery." For examples of black contributions to American culture, see Wilson and Ferris, s.v. "Black life." See also M. M. Smith, p. 30.
2449. Fogel, p. 157.

and her works of art were created by blacks. No notice was given of this amazing achievement by Lincoln, nor of the fact that, as we have seen, black slaves built most of the governmental buildings in Washington, D.C., including both the White House and the U.S. Capitol.[2450]

Moreover, tens of thousands of African-Americans were maimed and killed fighting for the Union, all without a single public word of praise or gratitude from Lincoln.[2451] Instead, he underpaid and exploited the 180,000 black soldiers in his armies, then allowed their wives and children to remain enslaved for nearly the entire duration of his War.[2452] Little wonder that some 14,887 black Yanks, or over 8 percent of their total number, "went over the hill" (i.e., deserted).[2453]

Lincoln did come close, on one occasion, to at least acknowledging black war service. But it was not self-motivated. He had to be pushed into it by blacks themselves. Even then, his acknowledgment was not specific. It was haphazardly mentioned in a personal letter pertaining to black suffrage.

In the winter of 1863 a group of New Orleans freemen asked Yankee General Nathaniel P. Banks for permission to vote. Banks rejected their request. They then went to Lincoln. He completely ignored them, of course. But on March 13, 1864, the day after meeting with two blacks (Arnold Bertonneau and Jean Baptiste Roudanez) who urged the president to sign legislation authorizing black suffrage,[2454] he sent a rather apathetic letter to Michael Hahn, the new governor of Louisiana:

> My dear Sir: I congratulate you on having fixed your name in history as the first free-State governor of Louisiana. Now you are about to have a convention, which, among other things, will probably define the elective franchise. I barely suggest for your private consideration, whether some of the colored people may not be let in—as for instance, the very intelligent, and especially those who have fought gallantly in our ranks. They would probably help, in some trying time to come, to keep the jewel of liberty within the

---

2450. De Angelis, pp. 12-18; Lott, p. 65.
2451. See e.g., Donald, L, p. 471.
2452. In Kentucky, for example, Lincoln did not free the wives and children of the state's 22,000 black Union soldiers until March 3, 1865, just one month before the War ended. J. Davis, RFCG, Vol. 2, pp. 472-473.
2453. Cornish, p. 289.
2454. Foner, R, p. 49.

family of freedom. But this is only a suggestion, not to the public, but to you alone.²⁴⁵⁵

This private missive was far from any kind of public declaration supporting black enfranchisement, and in fact he shows no interest at all in allowing *all* blacks to vote. Again, he prefers that only "the very intelligent" from among those who served in the Union military be given the right. Since he was no doubt referring to black officers, this would have been a small number indeed, for there were never more than 100 who held commissions in the entire Union army of 2,000,000 men.²⁴⁵⁶

There are two points to be made here: 1) just one year before his War ended, Lincoln had the opportunity to endorse *universal* black suffrage, or at least suggest it. He chose to do neither. 2) He steadfastly refused to publicly acknowledge the military service of his black soldiers.²⁴⁵⁷

On another occasion Lincoln mentions his "colored" soldiers in this fashion:

> . . . these people who have so heroically vindicated their manhood on the battle-field, where, in assisting to save the life of the Republic, they have demonstrated in blood their right to the ballot, which is but the humane protection of the flag they have so fearlessly defended. . . . The restoration of the Rebel States to the Union must rest upon the principle of civil and political equality of both races; and it must be sealed by general amnesty.²⁴⁵⁸

Once again, these sentiments were confined to a private letter, not meant for the public.²⁴⁵⁹ And once again no mention is made of universal black suffrage. The right to vote is only for those blacks who served in the military, Lincoln reasserts. Finally, he states here that restoring the Southern states to the Union will require "civil and political equality of both races," something he never established—and never

---

2455. Nicolay and Hay, ALCW, Vol. 2, p. 496.
2456. As we have seen, even these few black U.S. officers, just 0.005 percent of the total Union soldier population, were eventually replaced by whites under Lincoln's racist rules. Cornish, p. 214.
2457. See e.g., Donald, L, p. 471.
2458. Nicolay and Hay, ALCW, Vol. 11, pp. 130-131.
2459. The letter, probably written sometime between January and February 1864, was addressed to General James Wadsworth. Nicolay and Hay, Lincoln's official biographers, added a cryptic remark to it: "Given by F. B. Carpenter." Nicolay and Hay, ALCW, Vol. 11, p. 130.

showed any interest in establishing—in the North. Thanks in great part to Lincoln, "these people," as he referred to Northern blacks, would have to wait another 100 years for full civil rights.

Lincoln's racist policies continued to affect his black soldiers even after he was gone. In May 1865, for example, General Grant and his Northern compatriots planned to hold what they termed the "Grand Review," a gargantuan two-day victory celebration in Washington that included a parade down Pennsylvania Avenue. All of Lincoln's armies were invited, except one: the United States Colored Troops (USCT). Why?

The reason was simple enough: Grant and Sherman did not want black soldiers associated with their white soldiers.[2460] Sherman, who threatened to pull his troops from the parade if black soldiers were allowed to march, had once said:

> A nigger as such is a most excellent fellow, but he is not fit to marry, associate, or vote with me or mine.[2461]

Does this appall us? Not with what we know about Yankee racism.

But here is something that should: according to slavery studies, in the Americas at least 75 percent of the total value of American products traded in the Atlantic area during the 17th and 18th Centuries were produced by black slaves. Furthermore, the colonization of America itself was carried out largely by forced African labor.[2462] In other words, Lincoln was seeking to deport all those of African descent out of the very country their people had largely helped found and construct.

Thus while Davis and the South were improvising plans to integrate blacks into Southern society, Lincoln and the North were plotting their expatriation "back to Africa." The sociopolitical chasm between South and North was indeed truly deep and wide.

Lincoln, who is believed to have had the genetic disorder Marfan Syndrome,[2463] has also been deified as the epitome of the "great all-American," a god-king who has even been granted his own Pagan-styled

---

2460. C. Johnson, pp. 166-167.
2461. Flood, p. 400; Kennett, p. 107; C. Johnson, p. 167.
2462. Drescher and Engerman, p. 109.
2463. W. B. Garrison, CWC, p. 220.

temple (the Lincoln Memorial) and Zeus-like statue (the Lincoln Monument) in Washington, D.C.[2464] His marbleized visage graces the American penny, the five-dollar bill, and one of America's most hallowed commemorations, the National Memorial at Mount Rushmore.

Yet, here was a man, a Victorian, who in his day was widely considered to be:

• *Cruel and Bestial*: he had once ordered a cheerful minstrel tune to be played while he toured the bloody battlefield of Sharpsburg.[2465] Another example occurred on the evening of his assassination, as Meriwether describes: "'Shall the orchestra play Dixie?' he was asked as he sat in his box in Ford's theatre that fatal night. 'We have conquered the South,' returned Lincoln gleefully, 'we may as well take her music.'"[2466]

• *Unfeeling and Insensitive*: when it was reported to Lincoln that one of his officers, Edwin H. Stoughton, had been captured by the Rebels, the president said: "I don't mind so much the loss of a general—I can make another in five minutes. It's the horses I hate to lose."[2467]

• *Churlish, Selfish, and Curmudgeonly*: Lincoln observers often reported that he "had no heart," that he "seldom praised anybody," that "he did nothing out of mere gratitude," and that he "forgot the devotion of his warmest partisans as soon as the occasion for their services passed." He had not, it was written, a single "particle of sympathy with the great mass of his fellow-citizens who were engaged in similar scrambles for place."[2468]

• *Superficial and Materialistic*: while his War raged and thousands were dying, he spent much of his time indulging in pointless frivolities, such as discussing Shakespeare,[2469] and attending theater, balls,[2470] and parties.[2471]

2464. C. Adams, p. 225.
2465. M. Davis, p. 68. The song Lincoln requested was known as *Picayune Butler*. According to eyewitnesses, he also requested several other comical tunes while touring the Sharpsburg battlefield. Naturally the president later denied the allegations. However, he never issued a public statement to that effect, even though he could have, and even though he actually wrote one out (it was never used). Bowing to the obvious, the *New York World* later published the following rhyme: "Abe may crack his jolly jokes o'er bloody fields of stricken battle, while yet the ebbing life-tide smokes from men that die like butchered cattle, and even before the guns grow cold, to pimps and pets Abe cracks his jokes." Meriwether, p. 75.
2466. Meriwether, p. 162.
2467. Gragg, p. 211.
2468. Lamon, LAL, p. 481.
2469. Nicolay and Hay, ALCW, Vol. 2, pp. 392-393.
2470. See e.g., Nicolay and Hay, ALCW, Vol. 2, p. 658.
2471. M. Davis, p. 68.

• *Socially Inept*: Lincoln's bizarre even antisocial public behavior included various incidents that occurred during his journey from Illinois to Washington to assume the presidency in March 1861. As the trip progressed, he placated the crowds with pleasant but meaningless sophisms such as, "keep cool," for there is "nothing going wrong." At public receptions he would entertain himself by calling other tall men up to the stage to measure their height against his own. During his inauguration ceremony, he insisted on kissing all thirty-four girls (representing the thirty-four states then in the Union) in a parade, wasting valuable time and making both the young women and many onlookers uncomfortable. All of this with the country on the verge of war and in a fearful and deadly serious mood.[2472]

• *Bereft of a Sense of Propriety*: he unthinkingly dressed himself each morning in front of an uncurtained White House window.[2473]

• *Rude, Discourteous, and a Poor Communicator*: Lincoln, the president who seemed to prefer the taste of his own foot over anything else, was constantly apologizing for one gaffe or another; or more often, for one imagined or real insult or another.[2474]

• *Crude and Unrefined*: those individuals Lincoln seemed to be most drawn to, those he was most apt to make "boon companions," were the "coarsest men on the list of his acquaintances—low, vulgar, unfortunate creatures," whom, it was said, he used as mere "tools."[2475] As birds of a feather flock together, this is not surprising as Lincoln himself told ribald jokes and was known to be uncultivated, artless, and "undeniably awkward."[2476]

• *Unpleasant Company*: well-known as "morbid," "moody," "strange," "contradictory,"[2477] "unsocial," and "gloomy,"[2478] with a "streak of insanity,"[2479] Lincoln also suffered from severe depression (then called

---

2472. Pollard, LC, p. 102.
2473. M. Davis, p. 67.
2474. See e.g., Nicolay and Hay, ALCW, Vol. 2, pp. 162, 241-242, 250, 345, 424-425, 465-466, 504, 520, 540, 602-603.
2475. Lamon, LAL, pp. 482, 483.
2476. Encyc. Brit., s.v. "Lincoln, Abraham."
2477. Christian, pp. 4, 9.
2478. Lamon, LAL, p. 493.
2479. Encyc. Brit., s.v. "Lincoln, Abraham."

melancholia),[2480] "hypochondriasm,"[2481] and a host of other psychoneurotic complexes, such as a mother fixation, fear of his father, an overdeveloped super-ego, and narcissism.[2482] In the 1830s he even wrote a poem called "Suicide" that was published in Springfield, Illinois' *Sangamon Journal*,[2483] and in 1841 he called himself "the most miserable man living."[2484] On February 25, 1842, Lincoln began a letter to his friend Joshua F. Speed with these words: "How miserably things seem to be arranged in this world."[2485] Known for being intensely tightlipped, overly cautious, and unnecessarily inhospitable, it is little wonder that so many people shunned his companionship.[2486]

• *Guileful, Two-faced, and Untrustworthy*: even Lincoln's few close associates noted with disdain the president's air of cunning, secretiveness, and craftiness. This made him difficult to deal with and impossible to trust. Of him Herndon writes: "The first impression of a stranger, on seeing Mr. Lincoln walk, was that he was a tricky man."[2487] Stanton noted: "I met Lincoln at the bar and found him a low, cunning clown."[2488] It was this very mendacious reputation, which had been noted in Lincoln from his youth, that earned him the reverse nickname "Honest Abe"—just as a tall man named John might be nicknamed "Little John."[2489]

• *Demagogic*: Lincoln, often described as a man who presented to the world a host of bizarre and appalling "contrasts and contradictions of character," was the personification of a political chameleon.[2490] As such, he had no difficulty saying what people wanted to hear in different sections of the country (even though these statements often completely contradicted one another), while conspiring his own villainous schemes behind closed doors.

• *Bordering on Being Maritally Unfaithful*: in a July 11, 1848, letter,

---

2480. Current, LNK, p. 62.
2481. Simon, p. 238.
2482. Basler, ALSW, pp. 62-63, 114.
2483. W. B. Garrison, LNOK, p. 265.
2484. Encyc. Brit., s.v. "Lincoln, Abraham."
2485. Nicolay and Hay, ALCW, Vol. 1, p. 64.
2486. Lamon, LAL, pp. 482, 483. Once, when he was criticized for telling lewd jokes, Lincoln replied: "You cannot be more anxious than I have been constantly since the beginning of the war; and I say to you now, that were it not for this occasional vent I should die." Encyc. Brit., s.v. "Lincoln, Abraham."
2487. Christian, p. 10.
2488. Meriwether, p. 19.
2489. Seabrook, TGI, p. 36.
2490. Christian, p. 9.

Lincoln told his law partner and future biographer William H. Herndon that there was a pretty girl he wanted to kiss, but he knew she would not let him. Mr. Lincoln and his wife Mary Todd had been married six years at the time.[2491] While none of us are perfect, this certainly breaks Jesus' admonition that "whosoever looketh on a woman to lust after her hath committed adultery with her already in his heart."[2492] But as we will see shortly, Lincoln was not a Christian—or even a theist, so he would not have been troubled by this, or any other spiritual sin.

• *Coarse and Unsophisticated*: Lincoln was widely known for his off-color, offensive, even vulgar and inappropriate jokes and bawdy stories, which he loved to tell in front of both his more sophisticated cabinet members and, to the horror of Victorian society, women.[2493] George B. McClellan called the salty president "a teller of low stories,"[2494] while one of Mary Chesnut's friends termed him "the ugliest, most uncouth, the nastiest joker."[2495] Tyler, as many others did, made reference to Lincoln's "grotesque humor," "coarse suggestions," and "base insinuations."[2496]

It was thus that Yankee General Don Piatt took up his pen and wrote:

> The man who could open a Cabinet meeting called to discuss the Emancipation Proclamation by reading Artemus Ward,[2497] who called for a comic song on the bloody battle-field, was the same man who could guide with clear mind and iron hand the diplomacy that kept off the fatal interference of Europe, while conducting at home the most horrible of all civil wars that ever afflicted a people. He reached with ease the highest and the lowest level, and on the very field that he shamed with a ribald song he left a record of eloquence never reached by human lips before.[2498]

McClellan and Piatt were far from being the only influential Northerners who had criticisms of Lincoln. In 1863, before the U.S. Congress, Yankee Senator Willard Saulsbury of Delaware stood up and,

---

2491. Basler, ALSW, p. 232.
2492. Matthew 5:28.
2493. Faust, s.v. "Lincoln, Abraham"; Page Smith, p. 576.
2494. W. B. Garrison, CWTFB, p. 84.
2495. Grissom, p. 72.
2496. Tyler, PH, p. 11. For more on Lincoln's faults as viewed by Southerners, see Meriwether, pp. 42-43.
2497. The pseudonym of Charles Farrar Browne, a popular 19th-Century humorist and writer from Maine.
2498. Rice, RAL, p. 352.

insinuating that the president was an "enemy of the country," boldly asserted the following:

> Thus has it been with Mr. Lincoln—a weak and imbecile man; the weakest man that I ever knew in a high place; for I have seen him and conversed with him, and I say here, in my place in the Senate of the United States, that I never did see or converse with so weak and imbecile a man as Abraham Lincoln, President of the United States. . . . if I wanted to paint a tyrant, if I wanted to paint a despot, a man perfectly regardless of every constitutional right of the people, who's sworn servant, not ruler, he is, I would paint the hideous form of Abraham Lincoln.[2499]

Famed Yankee abolitionist William Lloyd Garrison said of him: he may be a giant in height, but he is a midget in intellect.[2500] A number of Lincoln's military officers were ill-disposed toward him, as well. McClellan had this to say about his commander-in-chief:

> The president is nothing more than a well meaning baboon. He is the original gorilla. What a specimen to be at the head of our affairs now![2501]

South-hating Bostonian Ralph Waldo Emerson called Lincoln "the clown,"[2502] while New Yorker and fellow party member George Templeton Strong said of the president:

> He is a barbarian, Scythian, Yahoo, or gorilla, in respect of outside polish . . .[2503]

If Lincoln's own Northern compatriots could express such views it is certainly no surprise that the crude, timid, indecisive, fatuous,[2504] sad-faced leader was known across Dixie as cunning, dangerous, shrewd,[2505]

2499. *The Congressional Globe*, 37th Congress, 3rd Session, pp. 549, 550.
2500. Guelzo, p. 90; Nye, p. 169.
2501. Minor, p. 49; DeGregorio, s.v. "Abraham Lincoln" (p. 243); Beschloss, p. 113; K. C. Davis, p. 219; Flood, p. 37; Donald, L, p. 319.
2502. Cmiel, p. 120.
2503. Website: www.mrlincolnandnewyork.org/inside.asp?ID=43&subjectID=3.
2504. Encyc. Brit., s.v. "Lincoln, Abraham."
2505. W. B. Garrison, CWC, p. 215.

primitive, deceitful, uncultivated, weak, contemptible, idiotic, demagogic, and heartless (that is, the very opposite of the archetypal Southern gentleman);[2506] or that he was widely referred to in Dixie as the "Illinois Ape"[2507] and as "a cross between a sandhill crane and an Andalusian jackass."[2508] Being from a more well mannered strata of Southern society, Jefferson Davis (who once turned down a request to write an article on Lincoln after his assassination),[2509] referred to him simply as "nothing."[2510]

Far less genteel comments were made in the Charleston *Mercury*, perfectly capturing the Southern view of Lincoln in 1860:

> A horrid looking wretch he is, sooty and scoundrelly in aspect, a cross between the nutmeg dealer, the horse swapper, and the night man, a creature 'fit evidently for petty treason, small strategems and all sorts of spoils.' He is a lank-sided Yankee of the uncomeliest visage, and of the dirtiest complexion. . . . It is humiliating, if not disgusting, to see a party in this country putting forward a man for the presidential chair, once occupied by Washington and Jefferson, whose only achievements have been that he split a few hundred rails in his early life, and at a later period vilified the armies of his country while fighting her battles on foreign soil.[2511]

Then there was the Savannah *Republican*, which referred to Lincoln as

> the imperial gorilla who, from his throne of human bones at Washington, rules, reigns and riots over the brutish and degraded north.[2512]

In 1864, a Yankee Catholic newspaper, the *New-York Freeman's Journal and Catholic Register*, called the president "Abraham Africanus the First," and suggested that he had a "taint of Negro blood," which is why, they pointed out, he possessed "obscene" and "brutal" habits.[2513]

2506. M. Davis, p. 63.
2507. Pollard, LC, p. 101.
2508. M. Davis, p. 67.
2509. Cooper, JDA, p. 691.
2510. Seabrook, TQJD, p. 70.
2511. Fite, PE, p. 210.
2512. J. T. Wilson, p. 154.
2513. Slotkin, p. 107; J. M. McPherson, BCF, p. 790.

In 1911, Confederate Captain Samuel A. Ashe denounced Lincoln as far too reckless to be running the United States of America:

> He had already declared that the Union could not exist half free and half slave, although slavery had existed in it from its formation . . . . He had no regard for the Constitution in his acts as President, and but little for his statement of facts. He proved to be a dangerous man and without regard to the happiness of the people North and South. Never was there such a horrible besom of destruction as Abraham Lincoln inaugurated in our Christian country.[2514]

And what about Lincoln's reputation for being a philanthropic lover of humanity? We will remember that Lincoln's own friend, black civil rights leader Frederick Douglass, felt strongly that the president was missing "the genuine spark of humanity."[2515] And we have examined, in detail, his attitude toward blacks, Latinos, women, and Native-Americans. But his intolerance extended to other minorities, ethnicities, and religious groups as well. One of these was the Jew.

Based on numerous complaints about "illicit trade" among Jews in the Western theater of operations, on December 17, 1862, General Grant issued his ill-famed General Order No. 11.[2516] It read:

> The Jews, as a class violating every regulation of trade established by the Treasury Department and also department orders, are hereby expelled from the department within twenty-four hours from the receipt of this order. Post commanders will see that all of this class of people be furnished passes and required to leave, and any one returning after such notification will be arrested and held in confinement until an opportunity occurs of sending them out as prisoners, unless furnished with permit from headquarters. No passes will be given these people to visit headquarters for the purpose of making personal application for trade permits. By order of Maj. Gen. U. S. Grant.[2517]

Bear in mind that this was no insignificant military edict. When Grant says, "All of this class of people," he meant exactly that. *All*

2514. Ashe, p. 44.
2515. *Douglass' Monthly*, September 1862, Vol. 5, pp. 707-708.
2516. Neely, p. 108.
2517. *ORA*, Ser. 1, Vol. 17, Pt. 2, p. 424.

Southern Jewish men, women, and children, were to vacate large areas of the South occupied at the time by Union soldiers—and within just one day. The heartless order applied not only to transient Jewish peddlers, but to everyday, law-abiding Confederate Jewish townspeople, living in homes they and their Southern ancestors had inhabited for generations.[2518] In essence, it turned every Southern Jew into a criminal.

Grant's order would be truly shocking were it not for the already well-known anti-Semitism of a great many of the Northern people.[2519] Indeed this is why, for the first year of the War, Lincoln (and the U.S. Congress) prohibited Jews from serving as army and navy chaplains;[2520] it is why August Belmont, the American agent for the British Rothschilds (a family of distinguished Jewish investors and bankers), was unfairly accused of aiding and abetting the Confederacy;[2521] it is why Grant referred to Jews as "an intolerable nuisance"; and it is why he once ordered Yankee railroad conductors to prevent Jews from traveling south of Jackson, Mississippi.[2522]

Though Grant's General Order No. 11 understandably offended thousands of Jewish soldiers and citizens across both the North and the South, the ban remained in effect until January 3, 1863, when Jewish Kentuckian, Caesar J. Kaskel, went directly to Lincoln to protest it. Halleck revoked Grant's order the next day, then, a few weeks later (on January 21),[2523] he sent Grant the following feeble note explaining Lincoln's actions:

> It may be proper to give you some explanation of the revocation of your order expelling all Jews from your department. The President has no objection to your expelling traitors and Jew peddlers, which, I suppose, was the object of your order; but, as it in terms proscribed an entire religious class, some of whom are fighting in our ranks, the President deemed it necessary to revoke

---

2518. Simmons, s.v. "General Order, Number Eleven;" Shenkman and Reiger, p. 84.
2519. Neely, p. 107.
2520. In 1861, for example, the 5th Pennsylvania Cavalry appointed a rabbi to be its chaplain. When Lincoln found out about it, the Jewish clergyman was forced to resign. At the time, under Lincoln's orders, only ordained Christian ministers were allowed to serve as chaplains. Katcher, CWSB, pp. 176-177. The law, passed by the U.S. Congress, stated that a chaplain in the Union army must be a "regularly ordained minister of a Christian denomination." Gamoran, p. 203.
2521. K. C. Davis, p. 273; Neely, p. 109.
2522. Horwitz, p. 204.
2523. J. S. Bowman, CWDD, s.v. "21 January 1863."

it.²⁵²⁴

Lincoln definitely had no love for "Jew peddlers."

One wonders how many displaced, innocent Jewish families lost everything in this forced expulsion from their homes, or how long Lincoln would have allowed Grant's ban to stand had Kaskel not paid a visit to the White House. The perceptive reader will have another question: why would Grant even think of issuing such a decree if he had not thought it acceptable to Lincoln? The answer is obvious.

It was for this same reason that the order raised no eyebrows among Lincoln's cabinet or party members. In fact, one of them, Congressman Elihu B. Washburne of Illinois, expressed approval of Grant's order to Lincoln in person. Afterward, he paid a visit to Halleck, who told Representative Washburne that if Grant had only inserted the word "peddler" after the word "Jew," it would have been "all right," and that "no exception would have been taken" by anyone.²⁵²⁵

2524. *ORA*, Ser. 1, Vol. 24, Pt. 1, p. 9.
2525. Neely, pp. 108-109.

SOUTHERN & NORTHERN VIEWS OF LINCOLN

PART TWO

NOW LET US CONSIDER LINCOLN'S "religious" persona. He liked to pass himself off as a "good Christian," yet he was actually a skeptic, a humanist, and an "infidel," one who opposed organized religion, told impious stories,[2526] mocked Christian revivals,[2527] never prayed, never attended church, never joined any religious faith or denomination,[2528] never opened a Bible, never mentioned Jesus, and was well-known for his lack of belief in the divinity of Christ, Christian salvation, the sanctity of the Bible, and even in God himself. Lincoln even once declared Jesus a "bastard" while asserting that the Bible's miracles went against the laws of Nature.[2529] In fact, our sixteenth president, who often criticized fellow politicians for mixing theology and politics, and who enjoyed arguing against the Bible in public,[2530] much preferred reading the works of atheists, like Thomas Paine, Count Volney (Constantin François de Chassebœuf), and Voltaire, over the works of religionists.[2531]

Lincoln himself authored an essay demonstrating that, far from

---

2526. Oates, AL, pp. 5, 40; Current, LNK, p. 60.
2527. Encyc. Brit., s.v. "Lincoln, Abraham."
2528. Kane, p. 163.
2529. *Southern Review*, January 1873, Vol. 12, No. 25, p. 364.
2530. Current, LNK, pp. 58, 61.
2531. Oates, AL, p. 53; Encyc. Brit., s.v. "Lincoln, Abraham."

being inspired, the Bible was actually "uninspired" and historically inaccurate,[2532] and in Illinois in the mid 1830s, he wrote "a little book on infidelity."[2533] Lincoln was saved from eternal disgrace by one Samuel Hill, his employer at the time, who—knowing it would certainly ruin the author's future—ripped the manuscript from young Abe's hands and hurled it into a burning stove.[2534] If this book had survived, we can be sure that Lincoln would not be worshiped as the Christ-like, canonized figure he is today!

Ward Hill Lamon writes of Lincoln's "burnt book," that the future president, being "thoroughly familiar" with atheistic thought,

> felt an itching to write [on the subject]. He did write, and the result was a 'little book.' It was probably merely an extended essay, but it was ambitiously spoken of as a 'book' by himself and by the persons who were made acquainted with its contents. In this book he intended to demonstrate: 'First, that the Bible was not God's revelation; and Secondly, that Jesus was not the Son of God.'[2535]

Lincoln's book, Lamon continues,

> was an attack upon the whole grounds of Christianity and especially was it an attack upon the idea that Jesus was the Christ the true and only begotten Son of God as the Christian world contends.[2536]

After a thorough study of Lincoln's writings, as well as the opinions of the president's family members, friends, and political associates, John E. Remsburg summed up Lincoln's views on religion this way:

> 1. In regard to a Supreme Being he entertained at times Agnostic and even Atheistic opinions. During the later years of his life, however, he professed a sort of Deistic belief, but he did not accept the Christian or anthropomorphic conception of a Deity.
> 2. So far as the doctrine of immortality is concerned, he

2532. Current, LNK, p. 58.
2533. Lamon, LAL, p. 488.
2534. W. B. Garrison, LNOK, p. 265.
2535. Barton, p. 146.
2536. Lamon, LAL, p. 493.

was an Agnostic.

3. He did not believe in the Christian doctrine of the inspiration of the Scriptures. He believed that [Robert] Burns and [Thomas] Paine were as much inspired as David and Paul.

4. He did not believe in the doctrine of Christ's divinity. He affirmed that Jesus was either the son of Joseph and Mary, or the illegitimate son of Mary.

5. He did not believe in the doctrine of a special creation.

6. He believed in the theory of Evolution, so far as this theory had been developed in his time.

7. He did not believe in miracles and special providences. He believed that all things are governed by immutable laws, and that miracles and special providences, in the evangelical sense of these terms, are impossible.

8. He rejected the doctrine of total, or inherent depravity.

9. He repudiated the doctrine of vicarious atonement.

10. He condemned the doctrine of forgiveness for sin.

11. He opposed the doctrine of future rewards and punishments.

12. He denied the doctrine of the freedom of the will.

13. He did not believe in the efficacy of prayer as understood by orthodox Christians.

14. He indorsed, for the most part, the criticisms of Thomas Paine on the Bible and Christianity, and accepted, to a great extent, the theological and humanitarian views of Theodore Parker.

15. He wrote a book (which was suppressed) against the Bible and Christianity.

16. His connection with public affairs prevented him from giving prominence to his religious opinions during the later years of his life, but his earlier views concerning the unsoundness of the Christian system of religion never underwent any material change, and he died, as he had lived, an unbeliever.[2537]

William H. Herndon, Lincoln's law partner, friend, and biographer, a man who knew the secretive president better than anyone, had this to say on the topic of Lincoln's "spiritual life":

> As to Mr. Lincoln's religious views he was, in short, an infidel, ... He did not believe that Jesus was God, nor the Son of

---

2537. Remsburg, pp. 17-18.

God,—[he] was a fatalist, denied the freedom of the will. Mr. Lincoln told me *a thousand times* that he did not believe the Bible was the revelation of God, as the Christian world contends. . . . *I assert this on my own knowledge and on my veracity.* Judge Logan, John T. Stuart, James H. Matheny, and others, will tell you the truth. I say they will confirm what I say, with this exception,—they all make it blacker than I remember it. Joshua F. Speed of Louisville, I think, will tell you the same thing.[2538]

In another source Herndon says:

> Lincoln was a deep-grounded infidel. He disliked and despised churches. He never entered a church except to scoff and ridicule. On coming from a church he would mimic the preacher. Before running for any office, he wrote a book against Christianity and the Bible. He showed it to some of his friends and read extracts. A man named [Samuel] Hill was greatly shocked and urged Lincoln not to publish it; urged it would kill him politically. Hill got this book in his hands, opened the stove door, and it went up in flames and ashes. After that Lincoln became more discreet, and when running for office often used words and phrases to make it appear that he was a Christian. He never changed on this subject; he lived and died a deep-grounded infidel.[2539]

In an 1870 letter to Lamon, Herndon stated the following:

> In New Salem [Illinois] Mr. Lincoln lived with a class of men, moved with them, had his being with them. They were scoffers of religion, made loud protests against the followers of Christianity. They declared that Jesus was an illegitimate child. On all occasions that offered they debated on the various forms of Christianity. They riddled old divines [clerics], and not infrequently made those very divines skeptics by their logic; made them disbelievers as bad as themselves. In 1835 Lincoln wrote a book on infidelity and intended to have it published. The book was an attack on the idea that Jesus was Christ. Lincoln read the book to his friend Hill. Hill tried to persuade him not to publish it. Lincoln said it should be published. Hill, believing that if the book was published it would kill Lincoln forever as a politician, seized it and thrust it in the stove. It went up in smoke and ashes before Lincoln could get it

---

2538. Lamon, LAL, p. 489.
2539. Christian, p. 7.

out. When Mr. Lincoln was candidate for the Legislature he was accused of being an infidel, and of having said that Jesus was an illegitimate child. He never denied it, never flinched from his views on religion. In 1854 he made me erase the name of God from a speech I was about to make. He [himself] did this to one of his friends in Washington City. In the year 1847 Mr. Lincoln ran for Congress against the Rev. Peter Cartright. He was accused of being an infidel; he never denied it. He knew it could and would be proved on him. I know when he left Springfield for Washington he had undergone no change in his opinion on religion. He held many of the Christian ideas in abhorrence. He held that God could not forgive sinners. The idea that Mr. Lincoln carried a Bible in his bosom or in his boots to draw on his opponent is ridiculous.[2540]

John T. Stuart, mentioned above by Herndon, wrote:

> I knew Mr. Lincoln when he first came here, and for years afterwards. He was an avowed and open infidel, sometimes bordered on atheism. I have often heard Lincoln and one W. D. Herndon, who was a freethinker, talk over this subject. Lincoln went further against Christian beliefs and doctrines and principles than any man I ever heard: he shocked me. I don't remember the exact line of his argument: suppose it was against the inherent defects, so called, of the Bible, and on grounds of reason. Lincoln always denied that Jesus was the Christ of God,—denied that Jesus was the Son of God, as understood and maintained by the Christian Church. The Rev. Dr. Smith, who wrote a letter, tried to convert Lincoln from infidelity so late as 1858, and couldn't do it.[2541]

In a letter to Herndon, James H. Matheny (also mentioned above) declared:

> I knew Mr. Lincoln as early as 1834-5; know he was an infidel. He and W. D. Herndon used to talk infidelity in the clerk's office in this city, about the years 1837-40. Lincoln attacked the Bible and the New Testament on two grounds: first, from the inherent or apparent contradictions under its lids; second, from the grounds of reason. Sometimes he ridiculed the Bible and New Testament, sometimes seemed to scoff it, though I shall not use that word in its

---

2540. Meriwether, pp. 54-55.
2541. Lamon, LAL, p. 488.

full and literal sense. I never heard that Lincoln changed his views, though [I was] his personal and political friend from 1834 to 1860. Sometimes Lincoln bordered on atheism. He went far that way, and often shocked me. I was then a young man, and believed what my good mother told me. Stuart & Lincoln's office was in what was called Hoffman's Row, on North Fifth Street, near the public square. It was in the same building as the clerk's office, and on the same floor. Lincoln would come into the clerk's office, where I and some young men—Evan Butler, Newton Francis, and others—were writing or staying, and would bring the Bible with him; would read a chapter; argue against it. Lincoln then had a smattering of geology, if I recollect it. Lincoln often, if not wholly, was an atheist; at least, bordered on it. Lincoln was enthusiastic in his infidelity. As he grew older, he grew more discreet, didn't talk much before strangers about his religion; but to friends, close and bosom ones, he was always open and avowed, fair and honest; but to strangers, he held them off from policy. Lincoln used to quote [Scottish poet Robert] Burns. Burns helped Lincoln to be an infidel, as I think; at least, he found in Burns a like thinker and feeler. Lincoln quoted *Tam O'Shanter*. 'What send one to heaven and ten to hell!' etc.

From what I know of Mr. Lincoln and his views of Christianity, and from what I know as honest and well-founded rumor; from what I have heard his best friends say and regret for years; from what he never denied when accused, and from what Lincoln has hinted and intimated, to say no more,—he did write a little book on infidelity at or near New Salem, in Menard County, [Illinois,] about the year 1834 or 1835. I have stated these things to you often. Judge Logan, John T. Stuart, yourself, know what I know, and some of you more.

Mr. Herndon, you insist on knowing something which you know I possess, and got as a secret, and that is about Lincoln's little book on infidelity. Mr. Lincoln *did* tell me that he *did write a little book on infidelity*. This statement I have avoided heretofore; but, as you strongly insist upon it,—probably to defend yourself against charges of misrepresentations,—I give it you as I got it from Lincoln's mouth.[2542]

Lincoln, the man who wanted to be all things to all people, did not like being accused of atheism, or "infidelity," as he called it, and he fought earnestly against the charge, particularly in the early part of his

---

2542. Lamon, LAL, pp. 487-488.

political career when it was most obvious and most well-known. When the accusation began appearing regularly in the newspapers, Lincoln exploded, firing off refutations, none of them convincing, like the letter to the editor of the Illinois *Gazette* on August 11, 1846, in which he admitted that he was not a member of any Christian Church.[2543] Wrote the cynical skeptic:

> I have never united myself to any church because I have found difficulty in giving my assent, without mental reservations, to the long complicated statements of Christian doctrine which characterize their Articles of Belief and Confessions of Faith.[2544]

As "a majority" of Lincoln's associates said they could prove he was an "infidel,"[2545] few believed such defenses, particularly when his own friends and admirers contradicted him on the issue. One of these was his close friend, Ward Hill Lamon, who wrote:

> Mr. Lincoln was never a member of any church, nor did he believe in the inspiration of the Scriptures in the sense understood by evangelical Christians. . . . Overwhelming testimony out of many mouths, and none stronger than out of his own, place these facts beyond controversy. . . . When he went to church at all, he went to mock, and came away to mimic.[2546]

Lincoln's own wife, Mary (Todd) Lincoln, who admitted that her husband had never committed himself to any conventional faith,[2547] said the following of his "religiosity":

> Mr. Lincoln had no hope and no faith in the usual acceptance of those words.[2548]

An interesting incident in Lincoln's life sheds light on his so-called "faith." One Sunday, while he was a candidate for Congress, he showed up in church, no doubt to poke fun and canvass for votes. At one point in

---

2543. Zall, p. 71.
2544. Encyc. Brit., s.v. "Lincoln, Abraham."
2545. Basler, ALSW, pp. 188-189.
2546. Lamon, LAL, pp. 486, 487.
2547. Current, LNK, p. 65.
2548. Lamon, LAL, p. 489.

his sermon the minister said to the congregation: "All who wish to go to Heaven, please stand up." Everyone in the chapel promptly got to their feet; all except one man: Abraham Lincoln. The surprised clergyman turned to the towering ill-dressed rustic and asked: "Mr. Lincoln, where do you wish to go?" "I wish to go to Congress," he replied snidely.[2549] Regular churchgoers were not amused. And neither was the local clergy. Twenty out of the twenty-three ministers, as well as "a very large majority" of the prominent members of the churches in his hometown of Springfield, Illinois, later opposed him for president.[2550] Why, if Lincoln was not an anti-Christian atheist?

Lincoln provided plenty of ammunition for his critics on this topic, such as the admission he made in a May 7, 1837, letter to Mary Owens in which he said:

> I've never been to church yet, nor probably shall not be soon. I stay away because I am conscious I should not know how to behave myself.[2551]

Lincoln was so hostile toward religion, and in particular Christianity, and so arrogantly intolerant of preachers, priests, and evangelists, that he did not trust himself to be in their presence for fear of making a public spectacle.

Lincoln's own remarks have condemned him for all time as an atheist, or at the very least, a non-believing skeptic and agnostic. "I am not a Christian," he once told Newton Bateman, the Superintendent of Public Instruction for the state of Illinois.[2552] On another occasion, when Lincoln was considering fighting a duel with James A. Shields, his friends intervened saying that such violence was against the Bible and the teachings of Jesus. Lincoln snapped back: "The Bible is not my book, nor Christianity my profession."[2553]

As late as 1862, despite his promise to be more discreet about his atheism, Lincoln was still denouncing religion, and in particular Christianity. That year Judge John A. Wakefield had written Lincoln,

---

2549. Ashe, p. 62.
2550. Minor, p. 25.
2551. Nicolay and Hay, ALCW, Vol. 1, p. 16.
2552. J. G. Holland, p. 236.
2553. Remsburg, p. 292.

inquiring as to whether he had finally accepted Christianity yet, to which the Yankee president replied:

> My earlier views of the unsoundness of the Christian scheme of salvation and the human origin of the scriptures have become clearer and stronger with advancing years and I see no reason for thinking I shall ever change them.[2554]

Around the same time, *Manford's Magazine* quoted Lincoln as saying:

> It will not do to investigate the subject of religion too closely, as it is apt to lead to Infidelity [i.e., atheism].[2555]

Religiosity has long been one of the major differences between South and North. Nowhere is this more apparent than in the political leaders of both sections. President Jefferson Davis, for example, proclaimed far more days of fasting and prayer than Lincoln,[2556] and while the U.S. Constitution is curiously lacking the word "God," the C.S. Constitution not only mentions him, but refers to him as "Almighty God."[2557]

Widely known as an "open scoffer of Christianity,"[2558] Lincoln—the man who bragged that he had once written "a little book on infidelity,"[2559] called Jesus a bastard,[2560] and belonged to no church[2561]—admitted that he embraced an atheistic concept called the "Doctrine of Necessity."[2562] According to this antireligious belief, said Lincoln,

> the human mind is impelled to action, or held at rest by some

---

2554. Remsburg, p. 292.
2555. Remsburg, p. 296.
2556. Wiley, LBY, p. 359.
2557. Lang, pp. 215, 216.
2558. DeGregorio, s.v. "Abraham Lincoln" (p. 228).
2559. Lamon, LAL, p. 488.
2560. *Southern Review*, January 1873, Vol. 12, No. 25, p. 364.
2561. Lamon, LAL, pp. 486, 487.
2562. The word similarity between this, Lincoln's "Doctrine of Necessity," and his political theory of "military necessity," is intriguing. Someday a psychological study might be performed to try and establish why Lincoln seemed so drawn to "necessity," an unusual word he sprinkled hundreds of times throughout his speeches and writings.

power, over which the mind itself has no control . . .[2563]

No definition of atheism has ever been more aptly or concisely expressed.

One of the few times he mentioned the Supreme Being is when his trick of faulting the South for "starting the War" was rejected by most Americans. To save face, Lincoln then tried to avoid taking the responsibility for both instigating it and maintaining it by blaming the entire fiasco on the Almighty.

In his Second Inaugural Address, on March 4, 1865, one month before Lee surrendered at Appomattox, Virginia, Lincoln said that God

> gives to both North and South this terrible war . . . Fondly do we hope—fervently do we pray—that this mighty scourge of war may speedily pass away. Yet, if God wills that it continue . . . so still it must be said, 'The judgments of the Lord are true and righteous altogether.'[2564]

Few agnostics or atheists have been able to combine politics and religion so advantageously—and so ominously. Entire books have been written on this topic.[2565]

An atheist, an anti-Semite, and a racist—and a heartless savage too. For Lincoln banned all medicines from the South, then denied President Jefferson Davis' request to buy medicines from the North; not just for Rebel soldiers, but also for Yankee soldiers held prisoner in Southern prisons. Incredibly, accusations were then hurled at the South for allowing Yankee prisoners to languish and die "unnecessarily," such as at Andersonville. However, despite the fact that Southern military prisons held 50,000 more inmates than Northern ones, many more Rebels died in Northern prisons than Yankees died in Southern ones.[2566]

Here is yet another crime that must be laid at the feet of the "Great Emancipator": it was Lincoln who refused to exchange prisoners with the South,[2567] and who ordered the rations of Confederate prisoners

---

2563. Donald, L, p. 49; Guelzo, p. 32; DeGregorio, s.v. "Abraham Lincoln" (p. 228).
2564. Nicolay and Hay, ALCW, Vol. 2, p. 657.
2565. See e.g., the works of J. Lewis, and in particular his volume, *Lincoln the Atheist*.
2566. The South's military prisons held 50,000 more inmates than the North's did. Yet, according to Edwin M. Stanton, Lincoln's own secretary of war, 26,246 Confederate prisoners died in the North against 22,576 Union prisoners who died in the South. Seabrook, TAHSR, pp. 317, 921-924.
2567. Seabrook, TQAHS, p. 17; C. Adams, pp. 57, 208-209; Grissom, pp. 126-127.

being held in Northern prisons cut by 20 percent.[2568]

After all is said and done, is this really the type of person we want representing the United States of America? Was he really "the archetypal American," as so many millions continue to claim? In the traditional South you will still receive a resounding "no!" to both of these questions. In 1909, Virginia judge George L. Christian wrote:

> In all our reading, we know of no man whose merits have been so exaggerated and whose demerits have been so minimized as have those of Abraham Lincoln.[2569]

Rebel Captain Samuel A. Ashe, summed up traditional Southern sentiment toward Lincoln and his illegal invasion this way:

> This unnecessary war was Lincoln's real gift to posterity, his contribution as a citizen—all else was accidental. So Mr. Lincoln stands in history as one who did more evil than any man known to the world.[2570]

No true lover of liberty and the Constitution could have put it better.

As we have seen, during Lincoln's two terms in office, he was extremely disliked in both the North and the South.[2571] Indeed, not only was Grant far more popular,[2572] but Americans considered Lincoln the worst president up to that time,[2573] some even referring to him as "America's most hated president."[2574] And yet today he is annually voted the number one "most popular" and "best" president in American history by uninformed citizens,[2575] some even going so far as to call him "a revered, almost saintly figure,"[2576] "the highest example of democracy," a "symbol of man's striving for freedom,"[2577] and "the greatest American in

---

2568. Ashe, p. 57.
2569. Christian, p. 4.
2570. Ashe, p. 64.
2571. A. Cooke, ACA, p. 216.
2572. January 10, 2011, *U.S. Grant: Warrior*, PBS.
2573. See e.g., Oates, AL, p. 17.
2574. See e.g., Tagg, passim.
2575. Ellis, AS, p. 5; DeGregorio, s.v. "Abraham Lincoln" (p. 241).
2576. Hendelson, s.v. "Lincoln, Abraham."
2577. The Collegiate Encyc., s.v. "Lincoln, Abraham."

history."[2578] Is it not time these individuals were informed?[2579]

How unfortunate that Northerners, and now many Southerners, have forgotten the crimes of America's most recreant, controversial, and sectional leader. Is it not time they were reminded?

How tragic that so many Americans are so completely unlearned when it comes to their sixteenth chief executive. Is it not time they were educated?

In the end, Lincoln did not preserve the Union and he freed no slaves,[2580] the very reasons he gave the American public for starting, waging, and prolonging his War.[2581] As U.S. president, his only primary functions were to support the Constitution and enforce federal laws,[2582] both jobs which he either flagrantly ignored or refused to do. Then, for political gain, he contaminated race relations in the South[2583] (by artificially and self-servingly pitting the two races against one another).[2584] Finally, he destroyed the concept of Union (a *voluntary* association of states) as laid down by the Founding generation.[2585]

Many in the South still consider America's deep-seated racism to be the greatest legacy of Lincoln's War.[2586] After all, the antebellum South, in comparison to the antebellum North, was relatively free of the type of racism found above the Mason-Dixon Line at the time.[2587] It was only *after* the conflict that race relations truly deteriorated in the South. As one Southerner observed in the postbellum period, the whites of Virginia were much more prejudiced against blacks after Lincoln's War than they had been before.[2588]

Thankfully, interracial relations have improved enormously since Lincoln's horrid Reconstruction programs ended and the last Yankee soldier was forced from the South in 1877. Left on their own, white and

---

2578. Faust, s.v. "Lincoln, Abraham."
2579. Incredibly, Lincoln's yearly top spot ranking places him above even the Founding Presidents: George Washington, the "Father of our nation"; Thomas Jefferson, the author of the Declaration of Independence; and James Madison, the "Father of the U.S. Constitution."
2580. Kane, p. 179.
2581. Hacker, p. 584.
2582. Napolitano, p. 235.
2583. J. S. Bowman, ECW, s.v. "Reconstruction."
2584. Garraty and McCaughey, p. 253.
2585. L. Johnson, pp. 181-182.
2586. See, e.g., K. C. Davis, p. xx.
2587. Tocqueville, Vol. 1, p. 383. See also Vol. 1, pp. 384-385.
2588. J. H. Franklin, p. 58.

black Southerners have naturally gravitated back toward the open and affectionate relationships they had before Lincoln invaded their homeland.[2589]

But Lincoln did accomplish what he actually truly set out to do in private: stamp out both states' rights and the secession movement while instituting a liberal, socialistic form of government—in reality, an empire—that has made political slaves of all Americans. In the process, he turned what U.S. Presidents George Washington, Thomas Jefferson, and Andrew Jackson all lovingly called a "Confederated Republic" (i.e., a "Confederacy")[2590] into a nation, something the Southern Founders certainly never intended or envisioned. As the Washington *Post* wrote on August 14, 1906:

> Let us be frank about it. The day the people of the North responded to Abraham Lincoln's call for troops to coerce sovereign States, the Republic died and the Nation was born.[2591]

As such, nation-building nationalist Lincoln must be considered nothing less than the "Great Federator": the creator of American big government for big business, with its big spending, Big Brother mindset.[2592] He is also either fully or partially responsible for the following: America's internal revenue program (the IRS), American protectionism, American imperialism, American expansionism, America's bloated military despotism, America's enormous standing army, America's central banking system, America's corporate welfare system (which Lincoln called "internal improvements"), America's nation-building agenda, and America's deeply entangled foreign alliances. (Lincoln apparently never read Jefferson's admonition that America's approach to foreign affairs should be: "Peace, commerce, and honest friendship with all nations, entangling alliances with none.")[2593]

Is it any wonder that President Lincoln surrounded himself with

---

2589. See C. Johnson, pp. 31, 37-39, 236.
2590. Seabrook, TAHSR, pp. 404, 479, 536, 571-572, 578.
2591. Christian, p. 3.
2592. For current news on the conservative fight against the big government that Lincoln helped install, see Website: www.breitbart.com.
2593. Foley, p. 684; Weintraub, p. 44.

Marxists;[2594] that he filled his administration and armies with socialists and communists, anti-American revolutionaries like Charles A. Dana, August Willich, Robert Rosa, Fritz Anneke, Max Weber, and Carl Schurz;[2595] that he was supported by a group of radical socialists called the "Forty-Eighters";[2596] that he is still idolized by socialists[2597] and communists[2598] alike; that the 1939 U.S. Communist Party Convention in Chicago, Illinois, affectionately displayed an enormous image of Lincoln over the center of its stage, flanked by pictures of Russian communist dictators Vladimir Lenin on one side and Joseph Stalin on the other;[2599] or that he has long been adored by nationalists, totalitarians, and bolsheviks from around the world,[2600] including socialists such as Francis Bellamy, author of America's *Pledge of Allegiance*?

Bellamy, who wrote the Pledge in 1892, asserts that the motivation behind it was to thoroughly inculcate Americans (particularly youngsters) with Lincoln's socialist views. These, as we have seen, called for the remaking of the U.S., from the decentralized Confederacy of the Founding Fathers into a socialist utopia with an all-powerful, Federate government, "one nation, indivisible, with liberty and justice for all," as Bellamy styled it.[2601] Imperialist Lincoln, who advocated blind obedience to the central government, would have been proud to be associated with such a man.[2602]

And here, politically at least, is Lincoln's greatest legacy, for big government opened the door to federal tyranny and its many dangers and horrors: the consolidation of governmental powers, the centralization of Executive power, unchecked presidential power, the growth of the nanny state, unlimited abuses and corruption, and the progressive, intrusive, oppressive, tax-and-spend government that American citizens now labor under, whether they are Lincolnian liberals themselves, independent, conservative, or libertarian. And all at the expense of individual civil

---

2594. See Benson and Kennedy, passim.
2595. Seabrook, ALWALJDWAC, passim; Seabrook, LW, passim.
2596. Seabrook, HJDA, p. 68.
2597. See McCarty, passim.
2598. See Browder, passim.
2599. Seabrook, TGYC, p. 60.
2600. See DiLorenzo, LU, pp. 149-155.
2601. Harrison, p. 158.
2602. See DiLorenzo, LU, pp. 156-160.

liberties and states' rights.[2603]

Victorian Southerners predicted, with unerring accuracy, the course the U.S. would take if Lincoln's liberal American System were adopted. In December 1866, not even two years after the War ended, Robert E. Lee wrote the following in a letter to Lord Acton:

> . . . I yet believe that the maintenance of the rights and authority reserved to the States and to the people, not only essential to the adjustment and balance of the general system, but the safeguard to the continuance of a free government. I consider it as the chief source of stability to our political system, whereas the consolidation of the States into one vast republic, sure to be aggressive abroad and despotic at home, will be the certain precursor of that ruin which has overwhelmed all those that have preceded it.[2604]

As Lee unerringly predicted, thanks in great part to Lincoln, the U.S. Federal government has continued to consolidate, growing more aggressive abroad and more despotic at home with each passing year.

Between the Depression years (1930s) and the World War II era (1940s), for example, tremendous governmental expansion occurred, particularly in the Executive Branch, with new committees, bureaus, agencies, boards, and administrations multiplying almost beyond imagination.[2605] Between 1998 and 2008 alone the U.S. government grew 71 percent, a trend that continues unabated with the election of the Lincoln-worshiping radical socialist and progressive liberal, Barack Hussein Obama, to the presidency in 2008 and 2012.[2606] During his first term alone he quadrupled the national debt. According to GOP.gov:

> Since President Obama took office the national debt has increased by $3.7 trillion. To put that in perspective, it took the U.S. 216 years, from 1776 until 1992, to accumulate the same amount of debt that Obama has borrowed in 2.5 years.
>
> It's higher than any time in American history, equaling more than 95% of our entire economy. We are currently borrowing roughly 40 cents of every dollar we spend and sending

---

2603. Napolitano, p. 76.
2604. Seabrook, TQREL, p. 217.
2605. Weintraub, p. 143.
2606. December 2, 2008, "Your World With Neil Cavuto," FOX News.

the bill to our children and grandchildren.[2607]

Following in the footsteps of big government liberal Lincoln, this is what today's progressives and socialists call "progress."

In 1980, Ronald Reagan spoke for traditional Southerners, as well as for lovers of liberty everywhere, when he stated that many Americans now feel similar to what their colonial ancestors felt two centuries ago: encumbered, smothered, and even subjugated by a government that has become too big, too complex, too controlling, too impersonal, and too inefficient to work for the benefit of the average person.[2608]

The outsized, gluttonous, power-hungry, political behemoth Reagan is referring to was the unrealized dream of nearly every Federalist, Whig, liberal, centralist, and consolidationist between 1776 and 1860. In 1865, at Appomattox, it was Abraham Lincoln who finally made that Federalist dream come true:[2609] on April 9 of that year, the doctrine of secession was finally suppressed, along with the constitutional view that the U.S. was a confederation of independent nation-states,[2610] that is, "distinct nations."[2611] Now, under Lincoln's anti-South program of invasion, emancipation, confiscation, conflagration, extermination, occupation, penalization, and humiliation,[2612] America's people were "irrevocably bound together,"[2613] the states lost their sovereignty, and the U.S. became a single federated nation operating under an all-powerful, centralized big government[2614]—more menacing and omnipotent than at any other time in American history up to that point.[2615] The Old South died and the so-called "New South" was born the day Lee stacked arms at Appomattox.

2607. Website: www.gop.gov/indepth/balancethebudget/charts.
2608. J. S. Brady, p. 53; H. Smith, p. 154.
2609. Ellis, AS, p. 352.
2610. Technically speaking the American "Civil War" did not end on April 9, 1865, with Lee's surrender. President Johnson attempted to *legally* terminate the conflict by issuing a Peace Proclamation on April 2, 1866. However, because the edict left out Texas, on August 20, 1866, he issued a second Peace Proclamation, this one that included the Lone Star State. It is this date that marks the official end to Lincoln's War. Benedict, pp. 44-45; Muzzey, Vol. 2, p. 3.
2611. Hamilton, Madison, and Jay, p. 21.
2612. This is a combination of my views and those found in Bailyn, Dallek, Davis, Donald, Thomas, and Wood, p. 6.
2613. Palmer and Colton, p. 543.
2614. Rosenbaum and Brinkley, s.v. "Civil War."
2615. Bailyn, Dallek, Davis, Donald, Thomas, and Wood, p. 4.

Sadly, as President Obama is now doing, American presidents (from both major parties) have been walking through the socialistic door Lincoln opened ever since, even committing many of the same crimes he did; but now without punishment or recrimination, often without notice or comment, and sometimes even with the blessings of a majority of the American people.[2616]

One of the U.S. presidents who patterned his social legislation after Lincoln was Franklin Delano Roosevelt,[2617] the man who launched the modern welfare state.[2618] As with his liberal "Civil War" predecessor, Roosevelt's "New Deal" programs and other policies led to growing concern over governmental centralization, American imperialism, interference with free enterprise, fears of socialism, and alarm that the U.S. was turning into an "international police power." Indeed, it was under Roosevelt, who was given dictatorial control over nearly all areas of human life (agriculture, industry, finance, and labor),[2619] that the federal government first truly exploded in size, with the creation of countless "committees, bureaus, agencies, administrations and boards." And even though the U.S. government itself acknowledges that the result has been "great waste, inefficiency and expense," new, unnecessary federal agencies continue to be created into the present day.[2620]

It is no surprise to learn then that the term "New Deal" was not an invention of the Roosevelt administration. Rather, it dates back to 1865, when it was coined to describe Lincoln's socialist domestic policies.[2621] A partial list of items from Lincoln's own New Deal program includes:

Morrill Tariff (1861)
First Income Tax (1861)
Expanded Postal Service (1861)
Homestead Act (1862)
Morrill Land-Grant College Act (1862)
Department of Agriculture (1862)

2616. See e.g., Napolitano, pp. 221-241.
2617. Napolitano, pp. 131-138.
2618. DeGregorio, s.v. "Franklin D. Roosevelt" (p. 498).
2619. Weintraub, p. 116.
2620. Weintraub, pp. 121, 123.
2621. Thornton and Ekelund, p. 99.

Bureau of Printing and Engraving (1862)
Transcontinental Railroad land grants (1862, 1863, 1864)
National Banking Acts (1862, 1863, 1864, 1865, 1866)
Comptroller of the Currency (1863)
National Academy of Science (1863)
Free Urban mail delivery (1863)
Yosemite nature reserve land grant (1864)
Contract Labor Act (1864)
Office of Immigration (1864)
Railway mail service (1864)
Money order system (1864)[2622]

How similar Lincoln and Roosevelt were! If the Lincoln years represent the Second American Revolution, then the Roosevelt years were truly the "Third American Revolution." For it was during this period that the concept of the national government underwent a complete transformation, from passive and aloof to aggressive and interventionist.[2623]

With the ongoing and unrelenting erosion of her Constitution and civil liberties, we have to wonder how much longer what was intended by the Founding Fathers to be the "States United"[2624] will remain the "United States." We began as a conservative country of enlightened laws and standards, built on what was originally a republic with a confederated government (the Confederacy), held in place by a confederate constitution (the Articles of Confederation). Our Constitution, in turn, was founded on the ideas of inalienable natural rights, states' rights, self-government, the right of secession, a system of checks and balances, and, the very heart of the document, the separation of powers.[2625] Without these, what will become of what was once the world's greatest confederacy, what Confederate Vice President Alexander H. Stephens rightly called "the best government the world ever saw"?[2626] Our leaders have forgotten Jefferson's sagacious statement that "the people . . . are the ultimate

---

2622. Thornton and Ekelund, p. 99.
2623. Hacker, pp. 1125-1126.
2624. Seabrook, TAHSR, pp. 378, 386, 415, 420.
2625. Collier and Collier, p. 245.
2626. Seabrook, TAHSR, pp. 329, 605, 619.

guardians of their own liberty."[2627]

More to the point, is the government we now "enjoy" the one the Southern Founders had in mind for 21st-Century America? Hardly. Throughout their lives, most, like Thomas Jefferson (author of the Declaration of Independence), James Madison (the "Father of the Constitution"), and George Mason (the inspiration behind the Bill of Rights), all ardently preached and warned against both the federating tendencies (empire building) of government and the very crimes and excesses that politicians like Lincoln repeatedly engaged in. Will the American people ever reclaim their Ninth and Tenth Amendment rights, rights they once held precious but which were ripped from their grasp in 1865 by "Honest Abe"?[2628]

It is for instituting big government, infringing on individual rights, and launching a needless and illegitimate War comprising some 10,455 bloody battles and skirmishes[2629]—one that (according to Northern statistics) killed at least 3,000 people a week for 208 weeks (note: 25 percent of all Southern white men of military age and one of every nineteen white Southerners died)[2630]—that Lincoln will always be remembered in the traditional, conservative, and libertarian South.

Amazingly, in the progressive, liberal, and socialist North, then as now, war criminal and political tyrant Lincoln is likened to such beloved biblical figures as Melchizedek,[2631] Abraham, Moses, and even "the Prince of Peace," Jesus of Nazareth. Lincoln's own mother, Nancy Hanks (a relative of actor Tom Hanks),[2632] has even been compared to the Virgin Mary.[2633] (Adding to the South's humiliation, Northerners accused Judah P. Benjamin—"the brains of the Confederacy" and one of Dixie's greatest statesmen—of taking part in Lincoln's murder, comparing him to Judas Iscariot.)[2634]

2627. Foley, p. 276.
2628. DiLorenzo, HC, p. 197.
2629. Gragg, p. 97.
2630. Cartmell, p. 16.
2631. Christian, p. 7.
2632. Davenport, p. 25.
2633. Lewis, p. 325. To this day, Lincoln's parentage, indeed much of his ancestry, is still in question. His father is certainly not known for sure. Some even believe Lincoln and Confederate President Jefferson Davis were brothers. Both were born in Kentucky within 100 miles of each other, and within one year of each other. They are also similar in height, body type, and overall appearance. For more on this topic, see e.g., W. B. Garrison, LNOK, pp. 5-13.
2634. Shenkman and Reiger, p. 105.

Absurdly, one writer called Lincoln the "one great man, and mystery and miracle of the nineteenth century." Another stretched truth to the breaking point when he referred to him as the "greatest, wisest and godliest man that has appeared on the earth since Christ."[2635] Still another Yankee, Reverend Charles Francis Potter of New York, characterized the president as the "future social Christ" of America, and predicted the coming of an "American Church" and an "American Bible" in which the masses "will find in parallel columns the stories of Christ and of Lincoln."[2636]

How contrary all of this is to the Southern view of Lincoln is very aptly summarized by Mississippian, Elizabeth Avery Meriwether, who shortly after the War, bristled at the apotheosization of America's sixteenth president:

> Is it insanity or pure mendacity to liken a man of this nature to the gentle and loving Nazarene? Who for an instant can imagine Jesus swinging a bottle of whiskey around his head, swearing to the rowdy crowd that he was the "big buck of the lick"? Or with a whip in his hand, lashing a faithful old slave at every round of her labor? Who can imagine Jesus sewing up hogs' eyes?[2637] What act of Lincoln's life betrays tender-heartedness? Was he tender-hearted when he made medicine contraband of war? When he punished women caught with a bottle of quinine going South? The laws of war of all civilized people exempt surgeons' and hospital supplies from capture or intent of harm. Not only did Lincoln prevent medicine from going South, but when the whole South was devastated, when she was unable, properly, to feed and medicine the Union soldiers in her prisons, the Southerners paroled a Federal prisoner and sent him with a message to Lincoln, informing him of the South's condition in that respect, and telling him if he would send his own surgeons with medical supplies they would be allowed to minister to the needs of the Union men in prison. Lincoln refused. Was this tender-hearted? When [Horace] Greeley implored Lincoln not to inaugurate war on the South, and told him if he "rushed on carnage" he would clearly put himself in the

---

2635. Christian, pp. 2, 7.
2636. Tyler, PH, p. 10.
2637. On page 48 of her wonderful book, *Facts and Falsehoods Concerning the War on the South, 1861-1865*, Meriwether describes an eyewitness account in which a sadistic Lincoln once sewed the eyes of several hogs shut so he could move the nervous animals over a plank onto a waiting boat. (The cruel strategy did not work, and Lincoln ended up carrying each one onto the vessel in his arms.)

wrong, was it tender-hearted to despise Greeley's prayer, rush on carnage, and for four years drench the whole Southland with human blood? And when Lincoln's legions were devastating the South, when with wanton cruelty, at the point of the bayonet, Sherman drove 15,000 women and children of Atlanta, Georgia, out of their homes, out of the city, to wander in the woods, shelterless, foodless, and then laid the whole city in ashes, did Lincoln give one thought to the sufferings of those innocent women and children? Did he once, during the four years of the cruel war, utter or write one kind word of the people on whom *he* had brought such unspeakable misery?[2638]

After calling the North's portrait of Lincoln a fable that "amounts to a patent perversion of the truth, and a positive fraud on the public,"[2639] disgusted postwar Southerners demanded that school textbooks be rewritten to reflect historical reality. One of these was Mildred Lewis Rutherford, the historian-general of the Confederate Southern Memorial Association. In the 1920s she aggressively campaigned to remove pro-North, anti-South history books from Southern schools so that Dixie's children could finally be taught the truth, Southern Truth.[2640]

Such books would have included the following Southern history lesson for elementary schoolers, from the marvelous 1863 textbook, *The Geographic Reader for the Dixie Children*. The United States, it reads,

> was once the most prosperous country in the world. Nearly a hundred years ago it belonged to England; but the English made such hard laws that the people said they would not obey them. After a long and bloody war of seven years they gained their independence; and for many years were prosperous and happy. In the mean time both English and American ships went to Africa and brought away many of these poor heathen negroes, and sold them for slaves. Some people said it was wrong, and asked the King of England to stop it. He replied that 'he knew it was wrong; but that the slave-trade brought much money into his treasury, and it should continue.' But both countries afterward did pass laws to stop this trade. In a few years the Northern States, finding the climate too cold for the negro to be profitable, sold them to the people living farther South.

2638. Meriwether, pp. 49-50.
2639. Christian, p. 4.
2640. Oates, AL, p. 19.

Then the Northern States passed laws to forbid any person owning slaves in their borders. Then the Northern people began to preach, to lecture, and to write about the sin of slavery. The money for which they sold their slaves was now partly spent in trying to persuade the Southern States to send their slaves back to Africa. And when the Territories were settled they were not willing for any of them to become slaveholding. This would soon have made the North stronger than the South; and many of the Northern men said they would vote for a law to free all the negroes in the country. The Southern men tried to show them how unfair this would be; but still they kept on [preaching and lecturing against the South].

In the year 1860 the Abolitionists became strong enough to elect one of their men for President [though Lincoln himself was not an abolitionist]. Abraham Lincoln was a weak man, and the South believed he would allow laws to be made which would deprive them of their rights. So the Southern States seceded, and elected Jefferson Davis to be their President. This so enraged President Lincoln that he declared war, and [he] has exhausted nearly all the strength of his nation in a vain attempt to whip the South back into the Union. Thousands of lives have been lost, and the earth has been drenched with blood; but still Abraham is unable to conquer the 'rebels,' as he calls the South. The South only asked to be let alone, and to divide the public property equally. It would have been wise in the North to have said to her Southern sisters, 'If you are not content to dwell with us longer, depart in peace. We will divide the inheritance with you, and may you be a great nation.'[2641]

Sadly, Rutherford's endeavor failed and such Southern pearls of wisdom have been relegated to history's scrapheap. Today, the oversized Yankee propaganda machine rolls on, completely ignoring genuine Southern history while smearing, smashing, and suppressing everything that does not reflect the North's version of the War.

During the conflict, Confederate hero General Patrick R. Cleburne had warned his compatriots that if the South lost, it would spell cultural disaster. Losing the fight against the Northern aggressors, he wrote,

means that the history of this heroic struggle will be written by the

---

2641. "A Dixian Geography," *Harper's New Monthly Magazine*, Vol. 33, June to November 1866, p. 111.

enemy; that our youth will be trained by Northern school teachers; will learn from Northern school books their version of the war; will be impressed by all the influences of history and education to regard our gallant dead as traitors, our maimed veterans as fit objects for derision.[2642]

How right Cleburne was. Long gone are the days when Southern school teachers, for example, taught their young pupils that the men to emulate are Lee, Jackson, and Davis, not Lincoln,[2643] and that:

A despotism is a tyrannical, oppressive government. The administration of Abraham Lincoln is a despotism.[2644]

Quite the opposite situation exists today. "Father Abraham," sainted, canonized, deified, and completely recast as a "sympathetic and charitable man of strict morality,"[2645] is now revered by millions of unenlightened devotees, North *and* South, as the savior of the Union—though he was actually its destroyer!

While our children's schools, teachers, and textbooks are now all skewed Northward, there is still hope for Southern Truth. Books, such as the work you now hold in your hand, as well as my children's book, *Honest Jeff and Dishonest Abe: A Southern Children's Guide to the Civil War*, will aid in disseminating a fuller, more realistic view of Abraham Lincoln as he is known and seen by traditional, conservative Southerners. Now, nearly 100 years later, we will continue where the brave and honorable Confederate woman, Mrs. Rutherford, left off. Only when the Southern perspective is provided to the public will Lincoln's War be set in its proper historical perspective. Only then will America be able to make any sense of its "Civil War," a conflict whose origins, meaning, and lessons most Americans still completely misunderstand—thanks in great part to Dishonest Abe himself.

During the War, a naive Northern populace, already indoctrinated with Lincoln's own personal anti-South biases and myths, eagerly gobbled up every Dixie-hating newspaper article that came along,

---

2642. *ORA*, Ser. 1, Vol. 52, Pt. 2, p. 587.
2643. M. Davis, p. 123.
2644. Rable, p. 183; Marten, p. 58; Browne and Kreiser, pp. 22-23.
2645. M. Parry, s.v. "Lincoln, Abraham."

trusting that their president and the Northern media would not lie to them. But lie they did, and repeatedly.

Behind all of this was, of course, the "Illinois Ape."[2646] At one time a newspaper agent and journalist (for the Springfield, Illinois, *Sangamon Journal*) and a newspaper owner (of the *Illinois Staats-Anzeiger*), Lincoln was highly aware of the power of the press in shaping public opinion. Little wonder then that newspaperman Lincoln often used and manipulated the media, not only to assist with his own political aspirations, but in aiding and abetting the creation of what is now a large corpus of spurious anti-South myths.[2647] As he himself said on August 21, 1858,

> . . . public sentiment is everything. With public sentiment, nothing can fail; without it, nothing can succeed. Consequently he who molds public sentiment goes deeper than he who enacts statutes or pronounces decisions. He makes statutes and decisions possible or impossible to be executed.[2648]

How much Lincoln's media blitz of disinformation contributed to the North's victory over the South is impossible to establish, but contribute it certainly did. Though nearly every word of it was false, the world still considers Lincoln's wartime propaganda to be "Gospel." Indeed, it is Lincoln's view of the "Civil War" that is still taught in every school, not only in America, but around the globe.

How different the outcome of the War would have been if, for instance, Lincoln had not used the press to spread lies throughout Europe about the South's "rebellion," declaring that she had split from the Union to "preserve slavery," that the Confederacy was "not a legitimate sovereign nation," and that secession was "illegal." Such fallacies delayed, and finally killed off, any hope of official European support for Dixie, in turn destroying one of the South's last great chances for victory.

However, for the man many Southerners still call "Stinkin' Lincoln," this was just "business as usual."

2646. Pollard, LC, p. 101.
2647. Mitgang, pp. 8-12, 205. The *Sangamon Journal* (later the *Illinois Journal*) is sometimes written *Sangamo Journal*. See Mitgang, p. 11. The two words are European-American translations of the Algonquian word *saginawa*, meaning "river's mouth." The *Sangamo*, or the *Sangamon*, later came to refer to Illinois' once vast prairie lands. Faragher, pp. 74-75.
2648. Nicolay and Hay, ALCW, Vol. 1, p. 298.

Reconstruction: Lincoln's Final Crime

Part One

OUR SIXTEENTH PRESIDENT DID NOT live long enough to see the long-term consequences of his invasion of the South. Thus, Lee's surrender to Grant at Appomattox, Virginia, on April 9, 1865, and Lincoln's death a few days later, on April 15, 1865, would seem to mark the end of our story. But as we have seen, the repercussions of Lincoln's actions and words persisted long after his demise, and in fact continue right into the present day.[2649]

Indeed, for Victorian Southerners, Lincoln's death only added more suffering to the four years of misery they had already experienced under his autocratic violent rule. As the postbellum period is deeply tied to Lincoln and his mythology, we will briefly examine it.

Though John Wilkes Booth was a Northern Confederate sympathizer—a "Copperhead" (snake) in Lincoln's anti-South parlance—he could not have done anything worse for the South than take Lincoln's life. For one thing, as severe as Lincoln's Northernization plans were for the postwar South, those of his successors were in many ways, as we will see, even more senseless and brutal.

Lincoln, for example, refused to sign the Radicals' Wade-Davis Bill (passed by the U.S. Congress on July 4, 1864),[2650] a Reconstruction

---

2649. For a more detailed discussion of Reconstruction, see Seabrook, NBFATKKK, passim.
2650. The Collegiate Encyc., s.v. "Lincoln, Abraham."

program that prescribed severe punishment for Confederate states.[2651] Massachusetts' Radical Senator Charles Sumner, who inspired the bill, believed that the seceded states had "committed suicide," were no longer states, and were thus obliged to be governed by Northern military rule.[2652] To his everlasting credit, Lincoln did not agree with this extremist view. However, his fellow Republicans made him pay for it.

For pocket vetoing the Wade-Davis bill, members of Lincoln's own party published a scathing public manifesto in the New York *Tribune*, criticizing him. "How little of the rights of war and the law of nations our President knows," cried ultra-liberal Yankee Thaddeus Stevens, a Radical progressive who believed that Lincoln was being far too soft on the South.[2653]

It was this very "softness" that has led many to believe, particularly in the South, that had Lincoln lived, Reconstruction would have been much milder. Even Jefferson Davis once opined that next to the destruction of the Confederacy itself, "the death of Abraham Lincoln was the darkest day the South has ever known."[2654] In *The Rise and Fall of the Confederate Government*, Davis writes:

> . . . but for the untimely death of Lincoln . . . the wounds inflicted on civil liberty by the 'reconstruction' measures might not have left their shameful scars on the United States.[2655]

However, like President Harry Truman, who once said: "If Lincoln had lived, he would have done no better than [Andrew] Johnson,"[2656] I am not a member of the Davis school of thought. For as much as we admire the Confederate president, there was something he did not consider before making this statement.

We have seen firsthand that one of Lincoln's chief attributes was demagoguism: his proclivity for instantly shifting stances to accord with the prevailing political winds. Just as he finally gave into the Radicals' demand to emancipate Southern black servants (and that without

---

2651. Simmons, s.v. "Wade-Davis Bill."
2652. Hacker, p. 589.
2653. Woodburn, p. 321.
2654. McClure, OP, p. 201.
2655. J. Davis, RFCG, Vol. 2, p. 686.
2656. N. Miller, p. 133.

compensation), as just one example, he no doubt would have eventually given into their unshakeable desire to impose severe Reconstruction policies on the South.

Thus as Truman, and even some historians have noted, it is highly doubtful that Lincoln could have succeeded where Johnson failed, particularly when pitted against the Radical abolitionists of his party. They were determined to stay in power by controlling the Southern congressional seats, and no one, especially demagogic Lincoln, would have dared try and stop them.[2657]

In short, at the time of his death the political winds in the Republican party were blowing far left, and this is where an already left-leaning Lincoln would have eventually drifted (either voluntarily or by coercion) had he lived.

We have a very good example of how he easily caved into political pressure.

On March 7, 1864, in a letter to John A. J. Creswell, Lincoln is seen giving up his much beloved plan to emancipate the slaves gradually for one to emancipate them immediately. Yet, he had been working on the idea of gradual emancipation for many years:

> I am very anxious for emancipation to be effected in Maryland in some substantial form. I think it probable that my expressions of a preference for gradual over immediate emancipation, are misunderstood. I had thought the gradual would produce less confusion and destitution, and therefore would be more satisfactory; but if those who are better acquainted with the subject, and are more deeply interested in it, prefer the immediate, most certainly I have no objection to their judgment prevailing. My wish is that all who are for emancipation in any form, shall cooperate, all treating all respectfully, and all adopting and acting upon the major opinion when fairly ascertained. What I have dreaded is the danger that by jealousies, rivalries, and consequent ill-blood—driving one another out of meetings and conventions—perchance from the polls—the friends of emancipation themselves may divide, and lose the measure altogether. I wish this letter to not be made public; but no man representing me as I herein represent myself will be in any danger

---

2657. Furnas, p. 751.

of contradiction by me. Yours truly, A. Lincoln.[2658]

We see here a wishy-washy man, one who would not have stood by his own convictions when it came to Reconstruction.

Years after the War, here is what George L. Christian had to say on this topic:

> We have reached the conclusion . . . that there is no good reason to believe, and certainly no satisfactory evidence on which to found the opinion, that had Mr. Lincoln survived the war he would have been either willing or able to withstand the oppressions of the malicious and revengeful men in his cabinet and in Congress in their determination to further punish the people of the already prostrate and bleeding South, to which condition of affairs he had done so much to contribute. . . . [Thus] we are constrained to say, if Mr. Lincoln was a true friend of the South, 'Good Lord, deliver us from our friends.'[2659]

Many of Lincoln's own relations would have agreed with this assessment. One of them was Confederate Captain Nathaniel Dawson.[2660] As the War dragged on, Dawson angrily wrote: Lincoln will never make peace with the South, for he is nothing more than a pawn of his party, one too cowardly to risk upsetting his fellow Republicans.[2661]

Second, Lincoln, despite his many misdeeds, had gotten one thing right: he had long campaigned for compensated emancipation; that is, for reimbursing Southern slave owners for the loss of their black labor forces. The plan, however, was consistently ignored or rejected by his associates during his presidency, and he himself eventually gave up on it.[2662] Then, after his death, Radicals in his party tossed the idea out the window completely, asserting that Dixie's slavers did not deserve to be repaid for anything, let alone for giving up their "black chattel"—this from the very people who sold the South these slaves to begin with!

Now some claim that because Yankee Radicals (extremists,

2658. Nicolay and Hay, ALCW, Vol. 2, p. 492.
2659. Christian, p. 24.
2660. Dawson was related to Lincoln through marriage: Dawson's wife, Elodie Todd, was the half-sister of Lincoln's wife Mary Todd, making Elodie Lincoln's sister-in-law. Dawson then, was Lincoln's brother-in-law.
2661. Sword, SI, p. 95.
2662. See e.g., E. L. Jordan, p. 295.

abolitionists, socialists, and communists) took over the Republican (then the Liberal) Party after he died, Lincoln was not responsible for Reconstruction. This is false. For one thing, Lincoln began implementing Reconstruction policies long prior to the War's end, several years before his death. Also, in early 1865, when Confederate President Davis asked Lincoln to put a halt to the conflict so that the Southern states could return to the Union, Lincoln said no.[2663] He would only accept "unconditional surrender," which the South would, of course, not accept.[2664] When the War finally terminated, Lincoln then launched full scale Reconstruction, making him, directly or indirectly, completely responsible for everything that occurred subsequently.[2665]

What occurred subsequently was that Lincoln, and later the Northern Radicals, forced thousands of Southern families (of all races) into bankruptcy, utterly destroying their lives and livelihoods in the process. For the love of power and money, the destruction of the South and her people was, after all, the North's true goal, one that might have been mitigated had Lincoln lived and his plan of compensated emancipation been instituted.

We will never know though, for one primary question remains: why did he not simply push his compensated emancipation plan through *during* the War, when his Reconstruction policies were being formulated? He forced many unpopular ideas and programs on his cabinet, his military, and his people, even violating the Constitution and breaking dozens of laws to do so.

We can only surmise that compensated emancipation was, in the end, not truly important to him, as the Creswell letter cited above explicitly indicates. Was pretending to favor compensated gradual emancipation just another Lincolnian political ploy to try and win public favor, flatter Europe, and curry votes? Lincoln took the answer to his grave. But I am willing to bet that it was.

Third, could we really expect someone who believed in and still fanatically supported American apartheid and black colonization even after Appomattox (April 9, 1865), to have a firm enough grasp on reality to

---

2663. J. S. Bowman, ECW, s.v. "Hampton Roads Peace Conference."
2664. Ashe, p. 63.
2665. Ashe, p. 56.

"bind up the nation's wounds" in postwar America?[2666]

Fourth, in the North at least, Lincoln's death on Good Friday made him a symbolic martyr, politically and religiously.[2667] Both his untimely demise (he died young, at age fifty-six) and the manner in which he was killed (shot from behind while sitting with his wife at the theater), made him, understandably to many, an immensely sympathetic figure, one directly associated with the crucifixion of Christ.[2668]

Because of this, while his death was widely celebrated in the South, while Rebel soldiers cheered in the streets,[2669] his canonization in the North meant that his many stupidities, crimes, atrocities, and sins would be quickly forgotten by most Yankees, swept away and buried by loyal Lincolnian apologists, rabid monarchists, big government businessmen, and Unionist fanatics.[2670]

Thus many of Lincoln's harshest Northern critics reversed their views of him after his passing, becoming, strangely, the most devout of Lincolnites. One of these, Henry Ward Beecher, brother of the anti-South propagandist Harriet Beecher Stowe, ridiculed and criticized Lincoln when alive, but after his death tenderly wrote: "And now the martyr is moving in triumphal march, mightier than when alive."[2671]

Though Horace Greeley was once furious with Lincoln for continually delaying emancipation and using it as a political tool, after his assassination the abolitionist-newspaperman referred to the late president as one "of our country's greatest men."[2672] Such was the power Lincoln's unseasonable end had over the minds and hearts of Americans, even those who had previously detested him. Lincoln's friend, Ward Hill Lamon, wrote:

> Discriminating observers and students of history have not failed to note the fact that the ceremony of Mr. Lincoln's apotheosis was not

---

2666. Furnas, pp. 750-751.
2667. Christian, p. 7.
2668. M. Davis, p. 3.
2669. J. Davis, RFCG, Vol. 2, p. 580. For the average Johnny Reb, Lincoln's death was a blessing. Confederate Private R. W. Waldrop, for instance, made the following observation in his diary on April 19, 1865: today everyone is mourning over Lincoln, a tyrant who should have been killed in 1861. Wiley, LJR, p. 312. A woman from Augusta, Georgia, wrote of Lincoln's demise: at least one positive thing has come from his death, and that is that he can't gloat over his evil victory. Foote, Vol. 3, p. 997.
2670. Garraty, p. 332.
2671. Deems, p. 478.
2672. Schauffler, p. 15.

only planned but executed by men who were unfriendly to him while he lived, and that the deification took place with showy magnificence some time after the great man's lips were sealed in death. Men who had exhausted the resources of their skill and ingenuity in venomous detraction of the living Lincoln, especially during the last years of his life, were the first when the assassin's bullet had closed the career of the great-hearted statesman, to undertake the self-imposed task of guarding his memory,—not as a human being endowed with a mighty intellect and extraordinary virtues, but as a god.[2673]

In essence, Lincoln's death made him "all things to all men," resulting in the curious modern-day phenomenon in which politicians from all parties claim him as their own. Observing white conservatives and black liberals, for example, both adoringly associating themselves with the racist left-wing Lincoln, illustrates the depth to which Lincolnian mythology has penetrated the American psyche, and masked, even obliterated, Lincoln's true persona.

After his demise Northern mythologists wasted no time in beginning their revision of Lincoln's life. Even as his body was being transferred to its final resting place at Oak Ridge Cemetery in Springfield, Illinois, the "Myth of Lincoln," the great president, the great all-American, the "Great Emancipator," was already being carefully, skillfully, and guilefully crafted. Eulogists, rhetoricians, writers, artists, composers, journalists, even poets, spun out a myriad of excessive, romantic images for public consumption, portraying the sixteenth president, not as he was, but as they wanted him to appear: a tender humanitarian, a civil rights leader from the benevolent North, who subdued the lazy, illiterate, savages of the godless, slave-ridden South.

One in the poet category was Long Islander Walt Whitman, whose brother George Whitman, was a Yankee officer. Walt, author of the controversial book of poems, *Leaves of Grass*—and who during his walks often saw the mysterious, sad-faced president riding with his cavalry escort to and from the Soldiers' Home in Washington, D.C.—was particularly drawn to Lincoln,[2674] even stating publicly that he "loved"

2673. Lamon, RAL, p. 169.
2674. W. B. Garrison, CWTFB, p. 76.

him.[2675] After the president's assassination, the bard, a long-standing member of the antislavery Free-Soil party, over-glorified Lincoln in flowery prose in his famous poems, "O Captain! My Captain!" and "When Lilacs Last in the Dooryard Bloom'd."[2676]

Empurpled literature such as Whitman's completely altered Lincoln from the man he actually was to a man who would have been almost completely unrecognizable to his contemporaries. After the president's death, for example, Yankee General Don Piatt noted:

> With us, when a leader dies, all good men go to lying about him. [Thus the real] Abraham Lincoln has almost disappeared from human knowledge. I hear of him, and I read of him in eulogies and biographies, but I fail to recognize the man I knew in life.[2677]

Southerner Lyon Gardiner Tyler wrote:

> ... the character of Lincoln is so represented by the Northern press that the true Lincoln in no longer recognizable. Everything in any way tending to lessen his importance is studiously kept in the background.[2678]

So thoroughly did mythographers rewrite Lincoln's life, so fantastic was his deification, so complete was the "false glamour" they constructed around him, that as George L. Christian said in 1909,

> the lapse of nearly half a century has failed to dispel the delusions manufactured at that time and amid these surroundings by these people.[2679]

Even before a single myth of Lincoln had been invented, even before his death, however, plans were already well underway to instigate his punitive Reconstruction program—one that had begun, in fact, on April 12, 1861,[2680] the day Dishonest Abe tricked the South into firing the

---

2675. Daugherty, p. 246. See also Oates, AL, pp. 8-9.
2676. See Whitman, LG, pp. 278, 286.
2677. Christian, p. 4.
2678. Tyler, PH, p. 10.
2679. Christian, p. 6.
2680. Bedford and Colbourn, p. 243.

first shot at Fort Sumter.[2681]

Four years later, on April 15, 1865, the day he died, his vice president, Andrew Johnson, became our seventeenth president, taking over the White House, and Lincoln's Reconstruction plan, to head what would turn out to be nothing more than a massive, vicious anti-South deception.[2682] Like nearly everything else Lincoln did in regard to the South, the very word "Reconstruction" was false, misleading, self-serving, and insulting to all Southerners.

There would be no true reconstructing—that is, no rebuilding of Dixie—as the word implies. The North's idea of reconstructing the South was to vengefully remake it in the North's image, in part by forcefully introducing Northern ways that were completely foreign to Southern mentality.[2683] Instead of mercy, there was to be humiliation;[2684] instead of conciliation, there was to be punishment—both via the enforcement of strict Northern policies.[2685] Ohio liberal John Sherman spoke for many Northerners when he viciously declared:

> We should not only brand the leading rebels with infamy, but the whole rebellion should wear the badge of the penitentiary, so that for this generation at least, no man who has taken part in it would dare to justify or palliate it.[2686]

In an August 26, 1862, letter, another Yank, Massachusetts politician Amos A. Lawrence, put it like this: we must "ruin them completely and settle their lands with Yankees."[2687]

The president of Harvard University, Thomas Hill, agreed, saying that it was now the North's solemn responsibility to "spread knowledge and culture over the regions that sat in darkness"; that is, to intellectually

---

2681. Seabrook, EYWTACWW, pp. 33-37.
2682. In the hope of winning Southern support and ridding the Republicans (the Liberals of the day) of the widespread public opinion that it was a "purely sectional party," in June 1864 Lincoln had chosen Johnson, a Democrat from Tennessee, to replace New Englander Hannibal Hamlin as his vice president. Muzzey, Vol. 2, p. 2. But the plan backfired: considered a traitor in the South, Johnson was repeatedly threatened with death and hung in effigy across his home state for siding with Lincoln and the North. DeGregorio, s.v. "Andrew Johnson" (pp. 251, 252).
2683. Norton, Katzman, Escott, Chudacoff, Paterson, and Tuttle, Vol. 2, p. 435.
2684. W. S. Powell, p. 144.
2685. J. S. Bowman, ECW, s.v. "Reconstruction."
2686. Rhodes, Vol. 5, pp. 172-173.
2687. Lawrence, p. 180.

Northernize the "ignorant" Southern mind.[2688] These arrogant and nefarious ideas were still current in 1865, when another misguided Yank said that the South needed to be "regenerated by Northern ideas and free institutions,"[2689]—as if the South did not have its own ideas and free institutions.

From the South's point of view, "Reconstruction" should have been more correctly called "Deconstruction," or even more accurately, "Northernization." For Lincoln and his cronies had every intention of eradicating all Southernness from the South and then turning it into a duplicate version of Yankeedom, the "hub of the solar system," as North-centric Bostonians still like to refer to their particular region.[2690] (Lincoln's devotees might have preferred to call the Northernized South, Lincolndom.) Outrageously, Lincoln and his accomplices even threatened to eliminate the South's current state lines and rearrange the former Confederate states to their liking if the South did not cooperate.[2691]

Whatever Northerners chose to name Reconstruction, the very idea of it could not have provoked and enraged Southerners more. And that was, after all, one of the very reasons Lincoln and his cabinet selected this particular word to begin with.

As usual, commerce, banking, and business came first with the Yankees. Thus, they did not even wait until the Southern battlefields were cleared of the dead before heading down to Dixie to begin Northernizing her. Yankees like journalist Sidney Andrews and newspaperman Whitelaw Reid aided in the diabolical process by encouraging Northern businessmen to resettle in the South as soon as possible. Thousands of the ambitious and greedy answered the call. Within a few months after the War, Yankees were buying up or investing in every business venture the South had to offer, from plantations and railroads, to turpentine and lumber businesses.[2692]

Seeing the so-called "underdeveloped South" as an "important new economic frontier" from which to derive vast wealth, by November 1865 New Englanders were already opening businesses in Charleston, South

---

2688. Simpson, p. 63.
2689. J. H. Franklin, p. 4.
2690. Smelser, DR, p. 39.
2691. W. S. Powell, p. 144.
2692. J. H. Franklin, p. 10.

Carolina, with some 50 percent of the shops now being run by Yankees. By the autumn of 1866, some 5,000 Yankee soldiers (carpetbaggers to Southerners) had moved to Louisiana alone.[2693] From the South's point of view at least, "Reconstruction" looked a lot more like a massive profit-making scheme than a helping hand from the North.

Behind so-called "Reconstruction" was a second motivation, one just as sinister and inhumane: as if four years of shooting, burning, bombing, pillaging, robbing, raping, torture, and murder across the South was not enough, Reconstruction was to be further punishment for Dixie's audacity to break from the Union. Yankee Radicals Thaddeus Stevens of Vermont and Charles Sumner of Massachusetts led the way in doling out vindictive, punitory justice against Dixie, all in an attempt to crush the South's political power and ensconce the North as sovereign ruler over the entire Union.[2694]

As part of their "punishment, repentance, and regeneration" program,[2695] Northern Radicals (mainly socialists and communists) intended to confiscate Southern plantations and estates, divide them up, and portion them out to landless blacks, mainly former servants (or what Yanks demeaningly called "slaves").[2696] Also, all Southern white males were to be involuntarily enrolled by Federal marshals, then forced to pledge their allegiance to the Union.[2697] One can only imagine the fear, horror, and disgust these types of Northern policies had on the white people of the South. Naturally, most Southern blacks were revolted by them as well.

The awful concept of "Reconstruction" inevitably later led, in 1886, to the creation of the phrase the "New South," coined by Georgia newspaperman Henry W. Grady.[2698] According to Grady and other scallywags, in opposition to the "bad" Old South, the "good" New South denoted a "reconciled" South, one made pliable by war and now ready for Northern settlement and investment; that is, for remodeling into a

---

2693. J. H. Franklin, pp. 92, 94.
2694. DeGregorio, s.v. "Andrew Johnson" (p. 253).
2695. L. Johnson, p. 191.
2696. Hacker, p. 583.
2697. Hacker, p. 589.
2698. A gifted speaker who was known as the "Spokesman for the New South," naturally, Grady was far more popular in the North than in the South. Rosenbaum and Brinkley, s.v. "New South."

political, social, and economic facsimile of the North.[2699]

The "harsh, cynical, vindictive septuagenarian," Yankee Radical Thaddeus Stevens, arrogantly called it the "Conquered Province" policy:[2700] the entire South was to be confiscated to pay for the costs of the War (that Lincoln started),[2701] and the Confederate states themselves would only be "readmitted" to the Union if they had been "redeemed";[2702] that is, thoroughly cleansed of their states' rights movements and "rebellious attitudes."[2703] Said Stevens in 1865 before the U.S. House of Representatives:

> The whole fabric of southern society must be changed and never can it be done if this opportunity is lost. . . . If the South is ever to be made a safe republic let her lands be cultivated by the toil of the owners or the free labor of intelligent citizens. This must be done even though it drive her nobility into exile. If they go, all the better.[2704]

Who but a 19th-Century Yankee could presume to say such things to a constitutionally formed foreign country? Particularly one that now lay prostrate and bleeding.

That the Conquered Province policy was much on Lincoln's mind during the War as well is evidenced by a brazen comment he made to Interior Department official T. J. Barnett in 1862: not only is the character of the war to be altered to one of "subjugation," Lincoln told the stunned civil servant, but "the South is to be destroyed and replaced with new propositions and ideas."[2705]

In 1863, South-hating Yankee Henry Ward Beecher declared that winning the War would allow the North to spread "New England ideas" across poor uncultured Dixie. Such ideas included abolitionism, Fourierism,[2706] free-loveism,[2707] "and the whole brood of Yankeeisms."

2699. Simpson, pp. 193-194.
2700. Muzzey, Vol. 2, p. 5.
2701. Chodes, p. 98; P. M. Roberts, p. 226.
2702. J. H. Franklin, p. 196.
2703. Hacker, p. 589.
2704. *"Reconstruction": Speech of the Hon. Thaddeus Stevens*, p. 7. Delivered at Lancaster, Pennsylvania, September 7, 1865.
2705. Seabrook, NBFATKKK, pp. 44, 108; Catton, Vol. 2, p. 443.
2706. A type of communism promoted by French socialist Charles Fourier.
2707. In essence, the belief in intimate relations without marriage.

According to Beecher, culturally Northernizing the South would secure a victory more complete than physical violence—the bloody path Lincoln had chosen.[2708]

The Radicals in Lincoln's party, formerly known simply as abolitionists,[2709] (but many who were actually socialists and communists) agreed, asserting that before there could be reconciliation between the two regions, the "misguided" Southern states "must first be drastically remade."[2710] The South would have no say in the matter of her future destiny, of course; not with interfering, prying, bossy, intolerant, bigoted, self-righteous Northerners at the helm.

To open up the path to "reconciliation," Yankee Reconstruction policy called for the establishment of martial law across the former Confederacy (which was unconstitutional since civil courts were still open in Dixie).[2711] In early 1867 a new Reconstruction Act, known to be "the most brutal proposition ever introduced into the Congress of the United States by a responsible committee,"[2712] divided the South's ten states (her eleventh, Tennessee, having been exempted from reconstruction several years earlier by Tennessean Andrew Johnson[2713]) were divided into five military districts, "conquered territories," each overseen by a Northern officer. The five districts and their commanding officers were:

1) Virginia: U.S. General John Schofield
2) North Carolina and South Carolina: U.S. General Daniel Sickles
3) Alabama, Florida, and Georgia: U.S. General John Pope
4) Arkansas and Mississippi: U.S. General Edward Ord
5) Louisiana and Texas: U.S. General Philip Sheridan[2714]

Each officer was in charge of "supervising elections," setting up new governments, and writing new state constitutions.[2715]

2708. Durden, p. 112.
2709. Hacker, p. 582.
2710. DiLorenzo, LU, p. 38; Current, LNK, p. 254; Handlin, p. 402; Brinton, Christopher, and Wolff, Vol. 2, p. 257.
2711. Rosenbaum and Brinkley, s.v. "McCardle, Ex Parte."
2712. Muzzey, Vol. 2, p. 13.
2713. DeGregorio, s.v. "Andrew Johnson" (p. 251).
2714. J. Davis, RFCG, Vol. 2, p. 732. As mentioned, some of these officers, such as the demonic Sheridan, were replaced before Reconstruction ended.
2715. J. H. Franklin, pp. 70-71.

In the typical style of the Northern oppressors, the five commanding officers were given unlimited powers with no time limit on military rule; nor did they need to answer to President Johnson: only to General Grant, a South-hating slave owner.[2716] In other words, Generals Schofield, Sickles, Pope, Ord, and Sheridan were given complete free reign in Northernizing their districts, the worst course of action possible for the independent-minded, individualistic South.[2717]

In each of the ten Southern states now under military rule, the constitutional right of secession was repealed and the emancipation of all slaves was recognized[2718] (even though slavery continued openly in some areas of the North). The ten Southern states were then further divided into subdistricts, each headed by Yankee "military commissioners" who were given police powers to "suppress disorder and violence."[2719] No public acts were allowed without their authorization. In support of the commissioners, provost marshals were stationed across each state whose job was to "regulate local affairs."[2720]

Command centers were set up across the five districts and the streets were patrolled by unruly, vengeful, often violent, armed Federal troops, many of them made up of angry blacks inculcated by Yanks to hate their former owners.[2721] On every corner was posted an armed Yankee guard, and governmental buildings in principle Southern cities were "completely surrounded by a cordon of sentinels." To top things off, the legislatures of the Southern states were either forcibly ejected or seized, then replaced by hand-picked Union men who were paid to implement the North's Radical Reconstruction agenda.[2722]

Former Confederate President Jefferson Davis described the insane, topsy-turvy world the Yankees created in the South this way:

> The uppermost then had come to be the undermost now, and that which was nothing then had grown to be over all now.[2723]

2716. J. Davis, RFCG, Vol. 2, p. 732.
2717. Chodes, p. 99.
2718. Kelly, Harbison, and Belz, Vol. 2, p. 325.
2719. This despite the fact that nearly all of the "disorder and violence" that occurred in the South was a direct result of the Yankees' presence!
2720. J. Davis, RFCG, Vol. 2, pp. 734, 735, 746.
2721. A. Cooke, ACA, p. 219.
2722. J. Davis, RFCG, Vol. 2, p. 762.
2723. J. Davis, RFCG, Vol. 2, p. 763.

The purpose of all this was to strike terror and fear into the hearts of Southerners, and humiliate and punish them. In truth, it merely created greater animus, only widening the original wound between South and North that Lincoln had first inflicted at Fort Sumter in the spring of 1861. For Southerners felt, and rightly so, that they "had nothing to repent of in their fight for independence."[2724]

None of this was necessary. Most of it was counterproductive. All of it was unlawful.

Even many Northerners, particularly Northern businessmen, understood that Reconstruction not only aggravated the already existing problems between the South and the North, but that it also stalled the reopening of business relations between the two regions, the one thing they were most interested in.[2725] Indeed, for a nation close to bankruptcy, and with inflation running rampant in the South, what could have been worse for the national economy than Lincoln's Reconstruction program?

But in this time of overheated emotions, rational thought meant little to the Northern Radicals. Acting as overly strict parents, they saw the South as a wayward child that needed to be admonished for "firing upon the United States flag" at Sumter,[2726] for leaving the Union, for "rebelling" against its "parent," the superior North. Dixie had, in short, destroyed herself, so the Yankees claimed, and would now need to be "reconstructed."[2727]

In order to subdue, punish, and "reconstruct" the South, Lincoln had long "defended the theory that the war powers of the president formed a virtual dictatorship . . ."[2728] As such, he had taken upon himself the extraordinary right of "extraordinary powers"[2729]—despite the fact that it was unconstitutional and therefore illegal.[2730] But even if it had been legal, what was the point? Much of Dixie's infrastructure may have been

---

2724. U.S. official Carl Schurz, working under President Johnson as his special envoy, traveled across the Deep South shortly after the War and reported, unsurprisingly, that there was "an utter absence of national feeling" among Southerners (i.e., a desire to reunite the South with the North). Muzzey, Vol. 2, p. 8.
2725. J. H. Franklin, p. 200.
2726. Nicolay and Hay, ALCW, Vol. 2, p. 346.
2727. A. Cooke, ACA, p. 219.
2728. Encyc. Brit., s.v. "Lincoln, Abraham."
2729. See Nicolay and Hay, ALCW, Vol. 2, pp. 60, 124. Lincoln believed, without proof, that during civil disruption the president possessed certain powers not available to him during times of peace. As he himself said: "*I think* the Constitution invests its Commander-in-Chief with the law of war in time of war." (Emphasis mine.) Nicolay and Hay, ALCW, Vol. 2, p. 397.
2730. Christian, p. 13.

bombed to smithereens, but what was left of her people and property was still safe, and her legal system was still functioning. In fact, it was Lincoln's postwar Reconstruction plan that brought crime and further destruction to the South.[2731]

Southerners who lived through Reconstruction described it as a terrifying period, one that for us today brings forth images of occupied Northern Ireland: hostile foreign soldiers standing on every street corner, guns at the ready, imposing their culture, by force, on a proud but angry, humiliated, and conquered people. (May Northern Ireland, along with Scotland and Wales, one day reestablish themselves as independent, sovereign nations, free of British tyranny.)

The inhumanity and savagery of Lincoln and the Radicals' Reconstruction policies on the South are almost completely unknown to most modern Americans. The main reason for this is that in the decades following World War II (1950s and 1960s), liberal, Marxist, and socialist revisionist historians, working through the lens of the civil rights movement, rewrote most of the true history of Reconstruction,[2732] diluting the horrors, suppressing the facts, altering the statistics, in order to portray the South as evil, the North as righteous.[2733] Still, what little truth has been retained from that period is illuminating. For it is all part of Lincoln's legacy.

After illegally dividing the South into five military districts, agents from the U.S. Treasury Department were sent into Dixie to seize "abandoned property" in the name of the Federal government. The word "abandoned," of course, was loosely defined, leading to countless outrages and crimes against Southern families. Worse still, Yankee agents were allowed to levy taxes on seized property, then skim 25 percent off the top for themselves. At other times the rightful owners of "abandoned property" were able to gain it back. But only after paying a "tribute" to corrupt agents.[2734]

Gangs of former slaves, brainwashed by U.S. government agencies, were led across the conquered South by secretly racist

---

2731. See Hacker, pp. 644-653.
2732. Butler and Watson, p. 286.
2733. L. Johnson, pp. 195-196.
2734. J. H. Franklin, p. 40.

carpetbaggers and scallywags,[2735] continuing the pillaging, plundering, and marauding that Lincoln's soldiers had been perpetrating over the past four years.[2736] As these misadvised black militia marched through Southern towns, whites were shoved off the sidewalks into the streets, pets and livestock were shot dead, and guns were fired off over homes and churches (some while in service) in order to terrorize the populace. Having been told that all Southern white men were now their enemies, many European-Americans died at the hands of these ruthless gangs. One was an innocent civilian named Matthew Stevens of Unionville, South Carolina: one day he was hauled from his horse and wagon by a black mob, taken to a nearby forest, and shot through the head, for no reason other than that he was white.[2737]

Northern salt continued to be rubbed into Southern wounds.

Land and plantations stolen from their owners were sold at auction to rich Northerners, while Southerners made poor by war were forced into Yankee armies in an attempt to "Unionize" them and finally break their "rebellious spirits."[2738]

Confederate uniforms were not allowed to be worn[2739] (some former Rebel officers were arrested for this "crime"), and even weddings were not permitted in many areas of the South unless the groom, the bride, and the minister had all taken the Yankee Oath of Allegiance.[2740]

Know-it-all, do-gooder dandies from Massachusetts and naive, freshly scrubbed ladies from Connecticut poured into the South to "improve" Dixie's "inferior educational system."[2741] From that moment forward, Southern school children read only Northern literature, learned only from Northern textbooks, were taught only Northern history. This, despite the protests of outraged Southern parents, Southern organizations, and Southern children themselves.[2742]

Northern educators in Dixie, in fact, now completely ignored the South. And when they did mention her, it was with disgust and revulsion.

2735. Norton, Katzman, Escott, Chudacoff, Paterson, and Tuttle, Vol. 2, p. 435.
2736. Horn, IE, pp. 287-288.
2737. Horn, IE, pp. 191, 219, 225.
2738. Simpson, pp. 62-63.
2739. Grissom, p. 180.
2740. L. Johnson, p. 191.
2741. J. H. Franklin, p. 52.
2742. Simpson, p. 65.

In classrooms from Richmond to Dallas, the South's institutions were criticized, her traditions condemned, her heroes debased, her way of life denounced as "old-fashioned" and "backward." Meanwhile, Yankee industry was commended, growth was approved, progress emphasized, and Lincoln was praised. In this way, nearly every Southern child since Lincoln's War has grown up with a tainted self-image, stigmatized by decades of Northern mythology, pronounced "guilty of treason" by 150 years of South-hating Northern propaganda.

As Southern historian Frank Lawrence Owsley put it, the North crushed the South in war, humiliated her in peace, and finally attempted to kill off every last vestige of Southernness through intellectual and spiritual conquest.[2743]

Yet this was only the beginning of "Reconstruction."

Uneducated former black slaves (individuals that Lincoln would not even allow to vote or become U.S. citizens) were now intentionally given the franchise and the right to hold political office.[2744] This despite the fact that at the time only six Northern states (Maine, New Hampshire, Vermont, Massachusetts, New York, and Rhode Island) had given blacks the suffrage![2745] In order to sway the vote, at the polls newly enfranchised blacks were given pre-marked, liberal Northern ballots.[2746]

At the same time, former Confederates, many of them now bankrupt from the War, were prohibited from these same rights,[2747] while exorbitant taxes were imposed on them[2748] (taxes in Louisiana, for instance, went up 400 percent in just four years).[2749] By the time registration was finished across the ten former Confederate states (as mentioned, Tennessee had earlier been exempted from Reconstruction), there were 703,400 eligible black voters and only 660,000 eligible white voters.[2750] During the previous election there had been no eligible black voters and millions of eligible white voters.

Now, not only were whites a minority at the polls, at least half of

---

2743. Simpson, pp. 65-66.
2744. Grissom, p. 171; Hofstadter, GIIAH, p. 6.
2745. Muzzey, Vol. 2, p. 15.
2746. Horn, IE, p. 217.
2747. Simpson, p. 62.
2748. J. H. Franklin, p. 144.
2749. Grissom, p. 172.
2750. J. H. Franklin, p. 80.

the blacks who filled the membership of the state legislatures were illiterate. In Alabama, for example, the governor was removed and all the government jobs formerly filled by Confederates were given to blacks. In the overall state legislature, blacks outranked whites three to one.[2751] Of this period one historian noted that "the combination of imported carpetbaggers, unprincipled scalawags, and gullible negroes" now in public office, completely overwhelmed the system, resulting in "an orgy of extravagance and fraud."[2752]

As one can imagine, these actions alone turned Southern society upside down, caused insufferable enmity, produced social chaos and political anarchy, and drove a wedge between the two races that had not existed previously.[2753]

The majority of Yanks supported these types of unforgiving and foolish Reconstruction policies, and certainly would have agreed with U.S. General John Pope, who said:

> [It is] surely better to have an incompetent but loyal man in office than to have a rebel of whatever ability.[2754]

It should be said that the rank hypocrisy of the North during this period was absolutely breathtaking, for there was almost no real support for black suffrage among Yankees. In fact, the idea remained as unpopular as ever across Yankeedom after the War. Why then had the Radicals in Lincoln's party pushed black suffrage through in the South? It was to insure, so they hoped, that the Northern values of centralization, industrialization, and commercialization would be permanently implemented across Dixie, in turn enabling the North to dominate the nation both politically and economically.[2755] Or as Thaddeus Stevens put it, it was the duty of the Northern liberals (then the Republicans) to "secure perpetual ascendancy to the party of the union."[2756]

Many other horrors followed, including the robbery, assault, and rape of Southerners by U.S. troops. As these vicious, lawless Northern

---

2751. A. Cooke, ACA, p. 219.
2752. Muzzey, Vol. 2, p. 16.
2753. Hacker, pp. 629-631.
2754. Muzzey, Vol. 2, p. 17.
2755. Unger, p. 436.
2756. Burgess, p. 54.

militia roamed the countryside of Dixie, they not only stole and destroyed private property, but they also tormented, abused, and even murdered men, women, and children. Some of the South's most harmless sons and daughters were put in racks and sadistically tortured with thumbscrews.[2757] Why? What possible purpose could there have been for such crimes against innocent, unarmed civilians?

Even anti-South Yankees were moved by the pitiful scene presented by the "prostrate South." One of these was the above mentioned Ohio journalist Whitelaw Reid, who worked for the *Cincinnati Gazette*. After the War he traveled down South to see the damage firsthand. At Hanover Junction, not far from Richmond, Virginia, Reid observed that the town

> presented little but standing chimneys and the debris of destroyed buildings. Along the [rail]road a pile of smoky brick and mortar seemed a regularly recognized sign of what had once been a depot . . . Not a platform or water-tank had been left.[2758]

Yankee soldiers too, such as economist and future President of Rhode Island's Brown University, Elisha Benjamin Andrews, evinced some sympathy for the South. Andrews described Reconstruction like this:

> The war left the South in indescribable desolation. Great numbers of Confederates came home to find their farms sold for unpaid taxes, perhaps mortgaged to ex-slaves. The best Southern land, after the war, was worth but a trifle of its old value. Their ruin rendered many insane; in multitudes more it broke down all energy. The braver spirits—men to whom till now all toil had been strange—set to work as clerks, depot-masters and agents of various business enterprises. High-born ladies, widowed by Northern bullets, became teachers or governesses. In the comparatively few cases where families retained their estates, their effort to keep up appearances was pathetic. One by one domestics were dismissed; dinner parties grew rare; stately coaches lost their paint and became rickety; carriage and saddle-horses were worn out at the plow and replaced by mules. At last the master learned to open his own gates, the mistress to do her own cooking.
> In a majority of the Southern cities owners of real estate

2757. Horn, IE, pp. 258-260.
2758. W. Reid, pp. 329-330.

found it for years after hostilities closed a source of poverty instead of profit. In the heart of Charleston charred ruins of huge blocks or stately churches long lingered as reminders of the horrid past. Many mansions were vacant, vainly flaunting each its placard "for rent." Most of the smaller towns, like Beaufort, threatened permanent decay, their streets silent and empty save for negro policemen here and there in shiny blue uniforms. The cotton plantations were at first largely abandoned owing to the severe foreign competition in cotton-growing occasioned by the war. It was difficult to get help on the plantation, so immersed in politics and so lazy had the field-hands become.

Causes were at work which soon lessened Sambo's respect for "Old Massa," and "Old Massa's" for Sambo. Republicans from the North flocked to the South, whom the [uneducated] blacks, viewing them as representing the emancipation party, naturally welcomed and followed. These "carpet-baggers," as they were called, were made up, in the main, of military officers still or formerly in service, Freedmen's Bureau agents, old Union soldiers who had bought Southern farms, and people who had settled at the South for purposes of trade.

There were, no doubt, many perfectly honest carpet-baggers, and the fullest justice should be done to such. They considered themselves as true missionaries *in partibus*, commissioned by the great Republican party to complete the régime of righteousness which the war and the emancipation proclamation had begun. A prominent [Southern] Democratic [then a conservative] politician, describing a reconstruction governor of his State, whom he had done his best to overthrow, said: "I regard him as a thoroughly honest man and opposed to corruption and extravagance in office. I think his desire was to make a good Executive and to administer the affairs of the State in the interest of the people, but the want of sympathy between him and the white people of the State, and his failure to appreciate the relations and prejudices of the two races, made it next to impossible for him to succeed." . . .

The good carpet-baggers and the bad alike somehow exerted an influence which had the effect of morbidly inflaming the negro's sense of independence and of engaging him in politics. His former wrongs were dwelt upon and the ballot held up as a providential means of righting them. The negro was too apt a pupil, not in the higher politics of principle, but in the politics of office and "swag." In 1872 the National Colored Republican Convention adopted a resolution "earnestly praying that the colored Republicans [then the liberals] of States where no Federal positions were given to colored men might no longer be ignored, but be stimulated by some recognition of Federal patronage." The average negro expressed his views on public affairs by the South Carolina catch: "De bottom rail am on de top, and we's gwineter keep it dar." "The reformers complain of taxes being too high," said Beverly Nash in 1874, after he had become State Senator; "I tell you that they are not high enough. I want them [white Southerners] taxed until they put those lands back where they belong, into the hands of those who worked for them. You [blacks] worked for them; you labored for them and were sold to pay for them, and you ought to have them."

The tendency of such exhortation was most vicious. In their days of serfdom the negroes' besetting sin had been thievery. Now that the opportunities for this were multiplied, the fear of punishment gone, and many a carpet-bagger at hand to encourage it, the prevalence of public and private stealing was not strange. Larceny was nearly universal, burglary painfully common. At night watch had to be kept over property with dogs and guns. It was part, or at least an effect, of the carpet-bag policy to aggravate race jealousies and sectional misunderstandings. The duello [a set of rules], still good form all over the South, induced disregard of law and of human life. "The readiness of white men to use the pistol kept the colored people respectful to some extent, though they fearfully avenged any grievances from whites by applying the torch to out-buildings, gin-houses, and often dwellings. To white children they were at times extremely insolent and threatening. White ladies had to be very prudent with their tongues, for colored domestics gave back word for word, and even followed up words with blows if reprimanded too cuttingly. It was also, after emancipation, notoriously unsafe for white ladies to venture from home without an escort. . . If a white man shot a colored man, an excited mob of blacks would try to lynch him. His friends rallied to the rescue, and a riot often resulted. The conditions were reversed if a white man was shot by a negro." Negro militia at the governors' beck and call alarmed the whites. White companies formed and offered themselves for service, swearing to keep the peace, but were made to disband. . . .

Colored men were quite too unintelligent to make laws or even to elect those who were to do so. At one time dozens of engrossed bills were passed back and forth between the two Houses of the Alabama Legislature that errors in them might be corrected. . . . One easily imagines how intolerable the doings of such public servants must have been. . . .

The colored legislators of South Carolina furnished the State House with gorgeous clocks at $480 each, mirrors at $750, and chandeliers at $650. Their own apartments were a barbaric display of gewgaws, carpets and upholstery. The minority of a congressional committee recited that "these ebony statesmen" purchased a lot of imported china cuspidors at $8 apiece, while Senators and Representatives "at the glorious capital of the nation" had to be "content with a plain earthenware article of domestic manufacture. . . ."

There were said to be in South Carolina alone, in November, 1874, two hundred negro trial justices who could neither read nor write, also negro school commissioners equally ignorant, receiving a thousand [dollars] a year each, while negro juries, deciding delicate points of legal evidence, settled questions involving lives and property. Property, which had to bear the burden of taxation, had no voice, for the colored man had no property. Taxes were levied ruinously, and money was appropriated with a lavish hand.[2759]

So it was that the South was "reconstructed" under a Yankee cloud of corruption, dishonesty, bribery, disorder, harassment, fraud, thievery, violence, rapine, torture, and murder. Is it any wonder that Confederate Vice President Alexander H. Stephens later referred to it all as a "reign of terror"?[2760]

In the midst of all this—as Yankees were initiating "the heaviest taxes ever levied in any civilized country of the world" (in order to pay off the enormous national debt accrued by Lincoln's War)[2761]—many Confederates came to regret their decision to capitulate to Lincoln and his Northern henchmen. One of the foremost of these was General Robert E. Lee, who always referred to Yankees with the impersonal phrase, "those people."[2762] In 1870, shortly before his death, Lee told Fletcher Stockdale, the former Confederate governor of Texas:

> Governor, if I had foreseen the use those people designed to make of their victory, there would have been no surrender at Appomattox Courthouse; no, sir, not by me. Had I foreseen these results of subjugation, I would have preferred to die at Appomattox with my brave men, my sword in this right hand.[2763]

2759. E. B. Andrews, pp. 113-117, 123-124.
2760. Seabrook, TAHSR, pp. 871, 910, 955.
2761. Muzzey, Vol. 2, p. 23.
2762. E. M. Thomas, p. 161.
2763. Seabrook, TQREL, p. 213.

The North innocently pretended that the atrocities it committed during Reconstruction were altruistic policies, meant to help rebuild the ravaged Southland. But the real motivation behind them was clear to every red-blooded Southerner: they were meant to keep Dixie in a state of pandemonium and disequilibrium long enough for the Yankees to overthrow the South's political power and finally dominate her from Washington.[2764]

There was a psychological message as well, one that was to be burned into the pages of American history for all time: the South's "Stainless Banner," the Confederacy's national flag, would, from then on, be sullied with shame, dishonor, and disgrace, and all future generations of Southerners would live in "everlasting repentance" for the "sin of slavery."[2765]

Much of so-called "Reconstruction" then was about vengeance and humiliation, pure and simple.

While Reconstruction started unofficially the day a Southern city was captured by the Yanks,[2766] its official beginning was in 1867 with the U.S. government's issuance of the unconstitutional Reconstruction Acts.[2767] To make matters worse for Dixie, the most radical, South-hating members of the late president's party decided to toughen Reconstruction policies after his death, making them even harsher than Lincoln himself had envisioned. Only hours after Lincoln passed into the better world, members from this group met secretly to discuss their new, unanticipated options, excitedly declaring that "his death is a godsend to our cause."[2768]

Southerner and now U.S. president, Andrew Johnson, eventually realizing his mistake in siding with Lincoln, now fought back as best he could, trying to soften the blow on his homeland by offering early amnesty, filling the judiciary with pardoned Confederates,[2769] and

---

2764. See L. Johnson, pp. 191-194; J. H. Franklin, p. 70.
2765. Simpson, p. 63.
2766. As such, Lincoln issued his first act in connection to Reconstruction on December 8, 1863. It was pompously entitled the "Proclamation of Amnesty and Reconstruction." Naturally, since it came from white supremacist Lincoln, it excluded blacks from the political process (oath-taking, voting, holding office, etc.). Unlike the Radicals of his party who came after him, Lincoln had no intention of letting anyone but whites run the new Reconstruction governments in the South. Nicolay and Hay, ALCW, Vol. 2, pp. 442-444.
2767. The North's four so-called "Reconstruction Acts" were issued on the following dates: March 2, 1867; March 23, 1867; July 19, 1867; and March 11, 1868. Rosenbaum and Brinkley, s.v. "Reconstruction."
2768. Donald, LR, p. 4.
2769. K. L. Hall, s.v. "Lincoln, Abraham."

restoring lands to reprieved Southerners.[2770] His pardons alone eventually totaled some 13,500.[2771] He even dismissed Lincoln's secretary of War, Edwin McMasters Stanton, one of the numerous Northern Radical liberals who wished for revenge on the South.

While many of Johnson's Reconstruction efforts were appreciated in the South, they had the opposite effect in the North. For being "too soft" on the "wayward states," in 1868, anti-South forces in Lincoln's party "waved the bloody shirt" and impeached the seventeenth president.[2772] Though the Radicals failed in their effort to get Johnson removed from office, the affair did not bode well for Dixie. The incumbent President Johnson was unable to win enough support to become the Democratic presidential nominee, and on November 3, 1868, one of the men most reviled by Southerners was elected into the nation's highest office.

2770. K. C. Davis, p. 427. One Rebel that Johnson appointed to office, for example, was Confederate Colonel M. F. Pleasants, who was made clerk of pardons.
2771. L. Johnson, p. 198.
2772. This phrase came about during Johnson's trial. Benjamin F. Butler—nicknamed "Spoons" for his propensity for stealing silverware from the homes of Southern civilians in which he headquartered—stood before the court and literally waved a shirt stained with the blood of a Yankee carpetbagger who had been roughed up by some Mississippians. Butler's shirt waving was meant to agitate anti-South sentiment toward President Johnson—and it did. From then on the term "waving the bloody shirt" came to indicate anything that "inflamed passions" about the War. W. B. Garrison, CWTFB, p. 128; Horn, IE, p. 151; Shenkman and Reiger, p. 84.

While Lincolnites have done their best to obscure the real man, as these two Lincoln-friendly books show, many have always been aware of his true nature. Top, the cover of Earl Browder's 1936 work, *Lincoln and the Communists*. Bottom, the cover of Burke McCarty's 1910 work, *Little Sermons in Socialism by Abraham Lincoln*. For an in-depth discussion on the socialist-communist foundation of the Lincoln administration and the 1860s Republican Party see my books, *Abraham Lincoln Was a Liberal, Jefferson Davis Was a Conservative: The Missing Key to Understanding the American Civil War*, and *Lincoln's War: The Real Cause, the Real Winner, the Real Loser*.

RECONSTRUCTION: LINCOLN'S FINAL CRIME

PART TWO

ULYSSES S. GRANT, AMERICA'S EIGHTEENTH president, led the country in one of the more corrupt administrations on record, not for one, but for two terms.[2773] Besides the usual Lincolnian policies of suspending *habeas corpus*[2774] and authorizing mass arrests[2775] (and even an economic debacle that led to a stock market crash),[2776] Grant's many outrages included the Tweed Ring in New York City, which used the town's treasury as its own personal bank account; the Credit Mobilier scandal, which involved Grant's vice president Schuyler Colfax, as well as members of Congress;[2777] the Whiskey Ring scandal, in which Grant's own private secretary and others, swindled the government out of millions of dollars;[2778] and the Belknap Bribery, in which Grant's secretary of war, William W. Belknap, was caught accepting yearly kickbacks from Indian traders.[2779] Grant's two diabolical terms in office gave us the modern noun Grantism, meaning "a corrupt and materialistic

---

2773. L. Johnson, pp. 255-264.
2774. Garraty and McCaughey, p. 248. See e.g., Nicolay and Hay, ALCW, Vol. 2, pp. 45-46.
2775. DeGregorio, s.v. "Ulysses S. Grant" (p. 272).
2776. K. C. Davis, p. 440. Lincoln's September 22, 1862, Preliminary Emancipation Proclamation—in which he asked Congress for money to deport blacks out of the country—had caused stocks to take a nosedive, as he himself acknowledged in a private letter to his vice president Hannibal Hamlin on September 28, 1862. See Nicolay and Hay, ALCW, Vol. 2, pp. 242-243.
2777. J. H. Franklin, p. 147.
2778. Weintraub, p. 76.
2779. DeGregorio, s.v. "Ulysses S. Grant" (p. 271).

presidential administration."[2780]

During his eight years in office, not only did Grant engage in the most heinous nepotism (e.g., he appointed thirteen members of his family to governmental positions),[2781] more importantly, he continued to occupy, wound, demoralize, and humiliate the South, aggressively supporting and maintaining Lincoln's and the Radicals' Reconstruction policies, using a brute military dictatorship to implement them.[2782]

Behind all of this was a stunning hypocrisy: Grant, a former slave owner, Negrophobe, and anti-Semite, had run for office in 1868 on a platform that called for forcing black suffrage on the South, but which allowed the Northern states to decide the issue for themselves.[2783] In his Second Inaugural Address on March 4, 1873, Grant boldly said:

> Social equality is not a subject to be legislated upon, nor shall I ask that anything be done to advance the social status of the colored man . . .[2784]

The image of the man who spoke these words today appears on America's fifty-dollar bill.

In the 1872 election, Grant ran against New Yorker Horace Greeley, prompting the following comment from Eugene H. Roseboom: "Never in American history have two more unfit men been offered to the country for the highest office."[2785] Other Yankees concurred.[2786] During Lincoln's War, Murat Halstead, the editor of the Cincinnati *Gazette*, had written:

> Our noble army of the Mississippi is being wasted by the foolish, drunken, stupid Grant. He can't organize or control or fight an

---

2780. L. Johnson, p. 264.
2781. Shenkman and Reiger, p. 85.
2782. Kinder and Hilgemann, Vol. 2, p. 117.
2783. DeGregorio, s.v. "Ulysses S. Grant" (p. 265).
2784. W. Livingstone, Vol. 1, p. 275.
2785. Cummins, p. 113; DeGregorio, s.v. "Ulysses S. Grant" (p. 267).
2786. Though a loud, raving, anti-South busybody, Greeley had at least one thing to be proud of: after the War, believing that Jefferson Davis' constitutional rights had been violated by his extensive imprisonment under U.S. authorities, Greeley was one of over a dozen men who signed the Confederate president's bail bond. K. C. Davis, p. 441. Greeley and two others, New York abolitionist Gerrit Smith and New York tycoon Cornelius Vanderbilt (after whom Nashville's Vanderbilt University is named), stood for $25,000 each (the equivalent of $375,000 in today's currency). Ten others each stood for $2,500. Cooper, JDA, p. 610. For this rare act of 19th-Century Yankee kindness, the South thanks them.

army. I have no personal feeling about it, but I know he is an ass.²⁷⁸⁷

The twenty-eighth man to occupy the White House, a Virginian, Woodrow Wilson, summed up the South's feelings about Grant this way: "He ought never to have been made president."²⁷⁸⁸

In 1868 the Northern barbarism of Grant and his administration was eased somewhat by the readmission of seven of the Southern states to the Union (Alabama, Arkansas, Florida, Georgia, Louisiana, North Carolina, and South Carolina).²⁷⁸⁹ But Southerners continued to live in constant fear of everything from simple harassment and detention to arrest and imprisonment without trial. Outrageously, at the end of the War, former Confederate officers had been charged with "treason" against the U.S. government and placed on parole. Most were completely stripped of their civil rights and not "pardoned" until nearly a decade later.

None of this was right, moral, or legal. But Southerners expected little else from a despotic region that had pitilessly invaded, brutalized, and pulverized their nation over the four previous years. Lincoln's criminal legacy of fabrication, abuse, physical force, violence, racism, and constitutional perversions indeed lived long after him in the Reconstruction policies that he himself had initiated years earlier.

Naturally, the South did not submit to all of this lying down. In response to the severities of Lincoln's so-called "rehabilitation" program, it formed a self-protective organization, one that functioned as both a police force and as a social aid society for the welfare of war widows and children. This secret group, created in Pulaski, Tennessee, on Christmas Eve, 1865, would come to be called the Ku Klux Klan.²⁷⁹⁰

According to Yankee mythology, the KKK was a purely Southern invention. However, this is incorrect. In fact, it borrowed heavily from numerous similar secret *Northern* organizations which preceded it.

One of these was the anti-Catholic, anti-immigrant group known as The Order of the Star Spangled Banner, founded in Boston, Massachusetts, in 1849. The original Southern KKK adopted many of The

---

2787. Edmonds, p. 169.
2788. W. Wilson, HAP, Vol. 9, p. 112.
2789. Tennessee had been "readmitted" in 1866, while Virginia, Mississippi, and Texas rejoined the U.S. in 1870.
2790. C. Adams, p. 151.

Order's traditions, such as its esoteric signals, handclasps, rituals, and codes, and later perhaps even some of it strong arm tactics, including nighttime terrorist attacks, and general deception, fraud, and hocus-pocus antics (known as "dark lantern tactics").[2791]

In 1854 The Order of the Star Spangled Banner evolved into the Know-Nothing or American Party, a rabid anti-immigration, anti-Catholic, anti-foreigner movement that got its start in New York.[2792] When this too dissolved in 1856, the organization's xenophobic, racially intolerant members cast about for a political group to join. By 1860 there was only one logical choice: the party of white supremacy, white racism, and white separatism, the party of Abraham Lincoln.[2793]

Also contrary to Northern folklore, the original Southern KKK was not an anti-black organization. It was an anti-carpetbag organization, one that quite correctly described itself as an institution of "chivalry, humanity, mercy, and patriotism."[2794] In fact, during the first two years of its existence, it was comprised of both thousands of white *and* black members,[2795] for its sole mission was to protect and care for the weak, the disenfranchised, and the innocent, whatever their race. And not only did thousands of blacks support and assist it,[2796] what I call the "Reconstruction KKK," there was even an all-black Ku Klux Klan chapter that operated for several years in the Nashville area.[2797]

The KKK's other primary goal was to help maintain law and order across the South. Though Lincoln's Reconstruction program had called for military rule, its implementation had the opposite effect. Lawlessness and vicious criminal behavior became commonplace, problems exacerbated by the appearance of soulless, greedy, racist carpetbaggers (Northerners) and treasonous, unscrupulous, opportunistic scallywags (Northernized Southerners), both groups which sought to prey on and

---

2791. Wade, p. 39.
2792. Weintraub, p. 89.
2793. Wade, p. 39.
2794. Fleming, p. 665.
2795. Hurst, p. 305; Lester and Wilson, p. 26; Rogers, KKS, p. 34.
2796. Seabrook, NBFATKKK, pp. 29, 104.
2797. Horn, IE, pp. 362-363. We will note that at one time (1920s-1930s) even the modern KKK—though it has no connection with the original KKK of the Reconstruction period—possessed African-American members, and treated both whites and blacks the same. Terkel, p. 239. In Indiana, for example, white Klansmen decided to broaden their racial base by organizing a "colored division" whose uniform was comprised of white capes, blue masks, and red robes. Blee, p. 169.

exploit the long-suffering Southern survivors of Lincoln's War.[2798]

In 1869 the social atmosphere in the South changed dramatically. By this time, the government-sponsored black Loyal Leagues and the Freedmen's Bureau had been formed, organizations meant to aid Southern blacks dispossessed by Lincoln's emancipation (note that no U.S. government leagues were ever formed to aid dispossessed Southern whites specifically). Instead, widespread corruption among the bureau's officials ensued.[2799] For example, carpetbagger and scallywag agents used the Leagues to inculcate freed slaves in Northern anti-South propaganda,[2800] training them to use weapons and military tactics to taunt, punish, and even murder their former owners.[2801]

As part of their counter-Reconstruction efforts, KKK members responded by carrying coffins through the streets with the names of prominent Bureau leaders on them. Underneath their names were the words: "Dead, Damned, and Delivered!"[2802]

The Bureau, as it turned out, was not only unnecessary, as Southerners had long maintained, but it was also an absolute hindrance to any kind of racial healing in the South. This is why former Confederates saw it as nothing less than the imposition of an alien government, reinforced by an occupying army.[2803]

The Bureau's overtly racist efforts (to make former slaves hate their former white owners) were intended to further divide the Southern people by breaking down their morale. Ultimately, to the great remorse

---

2798. The word scalawag or scallywag probably derives from a district in the Shetland Islands called Scalloway. Here, small stocky horses and cattle were bred, whose chief traits were an earthy smell and a coarse mangy appearance. Scalloway livestock were inevitably compared by Southerners to those fellow Southerners who had betrayed Dixie (by siding with the North). Thus the name scallywag. Few things were worse to traditional Southerners than the scallywag. Known widely across the South as "vile, vindictive, unprincipled," and "scaly, scabby runts in a herd of cattle" (J. H. Franklin, pp. 98, 101), Wade Hampton referred to them as "the mean, lousy and filthy kind that are not fit for butchers or dogs." Harrell, Gaustad, Boles, Griffith, Miller, and Woods, p. 525. Known by Southern conservatives as "the lepers of the community," scallywags were hated even more than carpetbaggers. A former governor of North Carolina said: We have no problem with Northerners per se, even those who fought us in Lincoln's War. What we can't and won't abide is one of our own here in the South turning against us. Such a man will never get respect and will never be trusted. Foner, R, p. 297. To this day, revulsion toward the scallywag is a sentiment still very much alive across the South.
2799. Bedford and Colbourn, p. 247.
2800. Horn, IE, pp. 124, 169, 264-265; Simpson, p. 62.
2801. C. Adams, p. 153; Weintraub, p. 75.
2802. *Index to Reports of the Committees of the House of Representatives for the Second Session of the Forty-Third Congress, 1874-1875*, p. 344.
2803. See J. H. Franklin, pp. 38-39.

of Northern Radicals, it did not work. But various white elements in the KKK began, understandably, to turn their attention, some of it violent, toward African-Americans, particularly those who were committing hate crimes against white families under the directives of the U.S. government's Black Leagues. Again, these particular white groups were acting out of self-preservation, not racism.[2804]

Proof of this is that when carpetbag rule ended that year, in 1869, this, the original KKK, immediately came to an end as well all across the "Invisible Empire" (i.e., the Southern states). For when Southerners were allowed to begin to take back political control of their own states, there was no longer any need for a self-protective organization like the KKK. This is why former Confederate officer and Southern hero General Nathan Bedford Forrest, the Klan's most famous and influential supporter, called in its members and shut the entire fraternity down in March of that year.[2805] By the end of 1871, the KKK had disappeared from most areas of the South.[2806]

Still, now inaccurately associated with bigotry, the damage had been done, and to this day the original Reconstruction KKK has been branded, unfairly and unhistorically, with the racist label.

We will note here for the record that the KKK of today (the "Knights of the Ku Klux Klan"), which emerged in 1915, is in no way similar or even connected to the original Reconstruction KKK, which lasted a mere three years and four months: December 1865 to March 1869.[2807] In fact, there are indications that the modern KKK is far more popular in the North and West than in the South, with flourishing clans in Indiana, New York, California, Oregon, and Connecticut, just to name a few.[2808] Illinois, Lincoln's adopted home state, has also seen a recent resurgence of Klan activity.[2809]

A year later, in 1870, the last of the remaining "Rebel" states were

---

2804. C. Adams, pp. 153-155.
2805. Lytle, p. 385; Morton, p. 345; Hurst, p. 327. It is nothing but a pernicious Yankee myth that Forrest was both the founder of the KKK and its first Grand Wizard (leader). See my books, *Nathan Bedford Forrest: Southern Hero, American Patriot*, *Give 'Em Hell Boys: The Complete Military Correspondence of Nathan Bedford Forrest*, *A Rebel Born: A Defense of Nathan Bedford Forrest*, *The Quotable Nathan Bedford Forrest*, and *Forrest! 99 Reasons to Love Nathan Bedford Forrest*.
2806. Butler and Watson, p. 293.
2807. Seabrook, NBFATKKK, pp. 14, 24, 40-41, 47-49, 113-114.
2808. See Wade, passim.
2809. December 17, 2000, "Sunday Morning News," CNN.

"readmitted" to the Union: Texas, Virginia, and Mississippi. Still, no aid was offered by the U.S. government to help Southern whites or to assist in rebuilding the South's economy, no doubt because the North had intentionally set out to liquidate both to begin with. Dixie had simply been bombed and subdued, then left to fend for herself. This was the North's idea of "reconstruction," and it would continue for another seven long years.

Lincoln's hellacious program to Northernize the South finally terminated with the election of Ohioan Rutherford Birchard Hayes to the presidency in 1876. In the spring of 1877, under the "Compromise of 1877," the sagacious Hayes mercifully put an end to the martial madness Lincoln had inaugurated almost two decades earlier.[2810] America's nineteenth president was certainly the answer to many a Southerner's prayers. But by this time even most white Northerners, as well as nearly all Southern freedmen, had come to believe that Reconstruction was wrong, that it was a failure, and that it was time to put a stop to it.[2811] And they were correct. Yankees were so war weary that they even gave up on racial reform that year.[2812]

Hayes also believed it was time to halt the Lincolnian insanity. In his First Inaugural Address, March 5, 1887, he said:

> Let me assure my countrymen of the Southern States that it is my earnest desire to regard and promote their truest interests, the interests of the white and of the colored people, both and equally, and to put forth my best efforts in behalf of a civil policy which will forever wipe out in our political affairs the color line, and the distinction between North and South, to the end that we may have, not merely a united North or a united South, but a united country.[2813]

Sticking to his pledge, on April 10, 1877, Hayes pulled all U.S. troops out of South Carolina.[2814] On April 24, 1877, he withdrew them from Louisiana, as well, sounding the death knell for the carpetbag

---

2810. P. M. Roberts, p. 229; L. Johnson, p. 267.
2811. Cooper, JDA, p. 676; Norton, Katzman, Escott, Chudacoff, Paterson, and Tuttle, Vol. 2, p. 437.
2812. Norton, Katzman, Escott, Chudacoff, Paterson, and Tuttle, Vol. 2, p. 421.
2813. C. R. Williams, Vol. 2, p. 13.
2814. J. H. Franklin, p. 216.

regime,²⁸¹⁵ along with Lincoln's ridiculous, illegal, and insulting plan to Northernize the South.²⁸¹⁶ Hayes then halted the enforcement of the much hated, anti-South Fourteenth²⁸¹⁷ and Fifteenth Amendments,²⁸¹⁸ and appointed ex-Confederates to various administrative posts.²⁸¹⁹

In September he toured Dixie, promising reconciliation, solidarity, and *genuine* reconstruction (as opposed to Lincoln's *fake* "reconstruction") through a policy of pacification. Finally, despite opposition within his own party, Hayes made government appointments based on merit rather than on party loyalty and political patronage.²⁸²⁰

All of this was refreshingly un-Lincoln-like; especially considering the fact that Hayes, as a Yankee officer under General John C. Frémont, had fought for Lincoln and the Union.²⁸²¹

One of Hayes' Supreme Court appointments, William B. Woods of Georgia (the first Southerner appointed to the Court since Lincoln's War), spoke for the majority by wisely calling for an end to government efforts to combat the South's social aid organization, the KKK.²⁸²²

After nearly sixteen years to the day (April 12, 1861 to April 10, 1877)—during which time the South was subjected to an illegal invasion and the massive social and political upheaval and unnecessary bloodshed that went along with it—Southerners instigated a counter-revolution,²⁸²³ and took back control of their region.²⁸²⁴ In the process, the last Northern

---

2815. Weintraub, p. 76.
2816. Kane, p.217.
2817. By declaring that "all persons born . . . in the United States . . . are citizens of the United States and of the State wherein they reside," the Fourteenth Amendment was, in essence, an attempt by Northern Liberals to supersede the Tenth Amendment, the part of the Bill of Rights that guarantees states' rights—which tacitly includes the right of both accession and secession. Spaeth and Smith, p. 211; Palmer and Colton, p. 543; W. S. Powell, p. 145. For more on why the Fourteenth Amendment was condemned across Dixie, see L. Johnson, pp. 241-242; Woods, pp. 86-90; Findlay and Findlay, pp. 228-235; Muzzey, Vol. 2, pp. 11-12; DiLorenzo, RL, pp. 207-208, 211. Note: Anti-South, pro-North proponents often use the Fourteenth Amendment to "prove" that secession is no longer legal. However, there is nothing in it *prohibiting* this important states' right, just as the original U.S. Constitution contained no such clause.
2818. Bradley, p. 138. At the time the Fifteenth Amendment was passed, Radical Yankee liberal Thaddeus Stevens said: "I shall vote for this not because of any constitutional right, but because we have the power." Stonebraker, p. 76.
2819. Rosenbaum, s.v. "Hayes, Rutherford Birchard."
2820. M. Parry, s.v. "Hayes, Rutherford B."
2821. J. S. Bowman, ECW, s.v. "Hayes, Rutherford Birchard."
2822. DeGregorio, s.v. "Rutherford B. Hayes" (pp. 286, 287).
2823. Palmer and Colton, p. 544.
2824. Southerners had not stood idly by while the North imposed "Reconstruction" upon them, of course. Besides forming the self-protective, social aid organization known as the KKK, during Johnson's short time in office alone the Confederacy's vice president (Alexander H. Stephens), four Confederate generals, five

liberal administrations in the South collapsed and disappeared. The carpetbaggers were ousted from power, home rule was restored to the Southern states, and the Southern men who reclaimed their governments were rightly hailed as "redeemers."[2825]

Jubilation was felt in every home across Dixie: while the crusading, intolerant North's campaign of imposing its will on the South would continue into the present day, Lincoln's "Reconstruction" program at least had utterly failed in its twelve-year attempt (1865-1877) to turn the agricultural South into an exact image of the industrial North.

In the end, trying to Northernize Dixie was "a fool's errand," as Ohio carpetbagger Albion W. Tourgee put it:

> The North and the South are simply convenient names for two distinct, hostile, and irreconcilable ideas,—two civilizations they are sometimes called, especially at the South. At the North there is somewhat more of intellectual arrogance; and we are apt to speak of the one as civilization, and of the other as a species of barbarism. These two must always be in conflict until the one prevails, and the other falls. To uproot the one, and plant the other in its stead, is not the work of a moment or a day. That was our mistake. We [Yankees] tried to superimpose the civilization, the idea of the North, upon the South at a moment's warning. We presumed, that, by the suppression of rebellion, the Southern white man had become identical with the Caucasian of the North in thought and sentiment; and that the slave, by emancipation, had become a saint and a Solomon at once. So we tried to build up communities there which should be identical in thought, sentiment, growth, and development, with those of the North. It was A FOOL'S ERRAND.[2826]

With his Reconstruction plan having gone down to an inglorious death, the absurd, unnecessary, wasteful, counterproductive, and unlawful conflict Lincoln had underhandedly initiated a decade and a half earlier at Fort Sumter was finally over.

Confederate colonels, six Confederate cabinet officers, and fifty-eight Confederate congressmen were sent to the Thirty-ninth Congress, elected by a loyal Southern populace. Former Confederates, most of them still "unpardoned," also took control of the state governments, even proudly wearing their Rebel uniforms to work (though it was against the law to do so), while Confederate flags were sold openly in the streets (also a crime under Yankee rules). See J. H. Franklin, pp. 43-44, 53.
2825. Dinnerstein and Jackson, p. 26.
2826. Tourgee, p. 300.

But the Union was not preserved because of the War, and slavery would have died out in the South without the War. So what was the point of the tremendous bloodshed, devastation, and nationwide suffering? Why did the man who was so vehemently against warring with Mexicans,[2827] a people he referred to as "mongrels" and "greasers," and whom he despised as an "inferior race,"[2828] believe that it was good and necessary to go to war with the American South, the land of his birth,[2829] and the home to a people he claimed to love?[2830] We will leave the answers to these questions to those who worship Lincoln.

Despite Hayes' good will, much of the Northern populace was not as forgiving: his decency toward the South lost him the support of his own party in the North.[2831] Not only that, the Confederate flags captured by Yanks during Lincoln's War were not returned to the South until the year 1905—due to Northern indignation.[2832] And it was not until a full 128 years later, in 1976, that a man from the deep South was again elected president of the United States, the first, in fact, since Zachary Taylor in 1848.

That man was Jimmy Carter. In 1978, the liberal American president from Plains, Georgia,[2833] courageously restored U.S. citizenship to the conservative Confederate President Jefferson Davis,[2834] a status that had been illegally stripped from the former Rebel leader by Lincoln himself.[2835]

The year 1877 thus marked the end of what I call the "Southern Holocaust," a sixteen-year period (four of it under war, twelve of it under "Reconstruction") in which the South had endured invasion, destruction,

---

2827. I am speaking here of the Mexican-American War, 1846-1848.
2828. Seabrook, L, pp. 581-582, 954.
2829. Lincoln was born on February 12, 1809, in Hardin (now Larue) Co., Kentucky.
2830. In his First Inaugural Address Lincoln lied to the South, saying: "We are not enemies, but friends." Nicolay and Hay, ALCW, Vol. 2, p. 7. However, in the same speech, in reference to Southern forts occupied by Yankee troops, he turned around and declared that: "The power confided to me will be used to hold, occupy, and possess the property and places belonging to the [U.S.] Government . . ." Pollard, LC, p. 104. As was so often the case, in the same breath Lincoln was both contradictory and hypocritical, pacific and aggressive.
2831. K. C. Davis, p. 441.
2832. W. B. Garrison, CWTFB, p. 123.
2833. Historical note: President Carter's great-grandfather, Littleberry Walker Carter, proudly fought for the Confederacy in the War for Southern Independence.
2834. K. C. Davis, p. 438.
2835. DeGregorio, s.v. "Abraham Lincoln" (p. 240).

degradation, and death at the hands of an aggressive and lawless Northern leader.

Conservatively counting Southern and Northern military deaths (650,000),[2836] Southern white civilian deaths (1 million), Southern black civilian deaths (1 million), and those who perished from disease due to the War (350,000), at least 3 million people died so that Lincoln could realize his dream of big government.[2837] This was 10 percent of the total population of America—about 30 million—at the time. Correlated in terms of America's population today (roughly 300 million), this would be the equivalent of 30 million deaths in 2013.

To put this in even better perspective, imagine if tomorrow a Southern leader launched a war against the North that killed every citizen of the states of New York and New Jersey? Or one that killed all the inhabitants of New England (Massachusetts, New Hampshire, Vermont, Rhode Island, Maine, and Connecticut), plus everyone living in Pennsylvania, Delaware, and Washington, D.C.? What kind of South-North conflict could ever justify this kind of mass bloodshed? None. Yet today the majority of Americans continue to worship a Northern president who committed this exact atrocity on the South.

The insensitivity, arrogance, hypocrisy, and ignorance of many 19th-Century Northerners concerning the South was encapsulated by longtime slave owner General Ulysses S. Grant who, after the War, recorded the following preposterous and offensive statements in his memoirs:

> There was no time during the rebellion when I did not think, and often say, that the South was more to be benefited by its defeat than the North. The latter had the people, the institutions, and the territory to make a great and prosperous nation. The former was burdened with an institution abhorrent to all civilized people not brought up under it, and one which degraded labor, kept it in ignorance, and enervated the governing class. With the outside world at war with this institution, they could not have extended their territory. The labor of the country was not skilled, nor allowed to become so. The whites could not toil without

---

2836. Zinn, p. 232. This is the standard Yankee figure, which means it is probably woefully underestimated.
2837. Timothy D. Manning Sr., personal correspondence. As mentioned earlier, President Jefferson Davis believed that Lincoln was responsible for killing at least half of the South's Negro population, which would be about 1,750,000 black men, women, and children. See F. Moore, pp. 278-279.

becoming degraded, and those who did were denominated 'poor white trash.' The system of labor would have soon exhausted the soil and left the people poor. The non-slaveholders would have left the country, and the small slaveholder must have sold out to his more fortunate neighbor. Soon the slaves would have outnumbered the masters, and, not being in sympathy with them, would have risen in their might and exterminated them. The war was expensive to the South as well as to the North, both in blood and treasure, but it was worth all it cost.[2838]

Not one word in this passage is true, the many reasons for which have been thoroughly discussed throughout this book. Yet Grant, a Yankee slaver, a war criminal, and the second most corrupt president in U.S. history, had the gall to call hardworking white Southerners "poor white trash," a phrase that has the same meaning to Southern Caucasians as the word "nigger" has to blacks.

But not all Northerners agreed with Grant. When it came to Reconstruction, Yankee General Carl Schurz posed questions few other Northerners would dare entertain, let alone speak. Did not Lincoln's War bring forth, Schurz asked,

> a greedy craving on the part of a great many to use the needs of the government and the public distress as an opportunity for making money by sharp practices, and did not the rapid accumulation of fortunes develop during and after the war a 'materialistic' tendency far worse than any we had known among us before? Is it really true that our war turned the ambitions of our people into the channels of lofty enthusiasms and aspirations and devotion to high ideals? Has it not rather left behind it an era of absorbing greed of wealth, a marked decline of ideal aspirations, and a dangerous tendency to exploit the government for private gain—a tendency which not only ran wild in the business world, but even tainted the original idealism of the war volunteers who had freely offered their lives to the Republic in obedience to patriotic impulse . . . ?[2839]

The "greedy craving," "sharp practices," and "materialistic tendency" of the Yankee did indeed leave their mark on the South. Sadly, their presence can still be felt and seen throughout Dixie into the present day—one of

---

2838. U. S. Grant, Vol. 2, pp. 39-40.
2839. Bancroft and Dunning, Vol. 3, pp. 135-136.

Lincoln's uglier and more incorrigible legacies.

Thankfully, 150 years after Reconstruction there are still thousands of Southerners who consider themselves "unreconstructed"; that is, who have refused to accept the defeat of the Old Confederacy and the Starry Cross; who still cherish the Jeffersonian ideals that their Southern ancestors fought and died for.[2840] For such individuals, numerous organizations exist today (for both men and women) that promote both the preservation of America's Confederate history and her Southern heritage.[2841] Long may they endure.

Victorian Southerners felt no guilt for seceding from the Union. Why should they have? The sole reason they had fought Lincoln was to maintain the government of their ancestors, the Southern Founding Fathers—or as Alexander H. Stephens put it, to "rescue the constitution from utter annihilation."[2842] Most could not accept defeat and Northernization. Even fewer could accept the dishonor many Yanks heaped on them after the War. And so they chose to remain unreconstructed.[2843]

The archetypal unreconstructed Southerner was Edmund Ruffin, Virginian, farmer, agricultural reformer, and ardent admirer of the Old South and her traditions. After being humiliated and defeated by Lincoln and his War, Ruffin loaded up his shotgun and made one last entry in his diary. The date was June 17, 1865:

> I here declare my unmitigated hatred to Yankee rule—to all political, social and business connections with the Yankees and to the Yankee race. Would that I could impress these sentiments, in their full force, on every living Southerner and bequeath them to every one yet to be born! May such sentiments be held universally in the outraged and down-trodden South, though in silence and

---

2840. Faust, s.v. "unreconstructed."
2841. Among the better known neo-Confederate, Southern nationalist, Southern heritage groups are: the Sons of Confederate Veterans (SCV), the United Daughters of the Confederacy (UDC), the League of the South, Order of Confederate Rose (OCR), the Military Order of the Stars and Bars (MOSB), and the Confederate Memorial Association, among many others. Please note that liberal hate groups like to call these and other pro-South organizations "racist." They are not, as their white, black, red, brown, and yellow members will readily testify. I myself belong to the racially-inclusive SCV, whose very constitution contains anti-racist, anti-defamation clauses. Like the vast majority of our members, I am proud of the multicultural, multiracial makeup of the SCV, and of the South herself.
2842. Seabrook, TAHSR, p. 212.
2843. Grissom, p. 164.

stillness, until the now far-distant day shall arrive for just retribution for Yankee usurpation, oppression and atrocious outrages, and for deliverance and vengeance for the now ruined, subjugated and enslaved Southern States! . . . And now with my latest writing and utterance, and with what will be near my latest breath, I here repeat and would willingly proclaim my unmitigated hatred to Yankee rule—to all political, social and business connections with Yankees, and the perfidious, malignant and vile Yankee race.[2844]

After setting down his pen, Ruffin put the gun barrel in his mouth and pulled the trigger. For the Virginia farmer, like hundreds of thousands of other loyal Southerners who fought the good fight against the Illinois dictator, death was preferable to living under the imperialistic thumb of Yankee domination.

Another unreconstructed Southerner of note was Confederate Major R. E. Wilson, a sharpshooter with the 1st North Carolina. Said Wilson:

If I ever disown, repudiate, or apologize for the cause for which Lee fought and Jackson died, let the lightnings of Heaven rend me, and the scorn of all good men and true women be my portion. Sun, moon, stars, all fall on me when I cease to love the Confederacy. 'Tis the cause, not the fate of the cause, that is glorious![2845]

Ruffin's and Wilson's unreconstructed sentiments were embodied in the song *The Good Old Rebel*, written in 1914 by a former Confederate officer:

O, I'm a good old Rebel, now that's just what I am
For this 'Fair Land of Freedom,' I don't care a damn
I'm glad I fit against it, I only wish we'd won
And I don't want no pardon for anything I done

I hates the Constitution, this great republic too
I hates the Freedman's Buro, in uniforms so blue
I hates the nasty eagle, with all the brag and fuss

2844. *Tyler's Quarterly Historical and Genealogical Magazine*, 1924, Vol. 5, pp. 193-195.
2845. Grissom, p. 164; Martin, p. 280.

> The lyin', thievin' Yankees, I hates 'em wuss and wuss
>
> I hates the Yankee nation and everything they do
> I hates the Declaration of Independence too
> I hates the glorious Union, 'tis dripping with our blood
> I hates their striped banner, I fit it all I could
>
> I followed old marse Robert for four year, near about
> Got wounded in three places, and starved at Pint Lookout
> I ketched the rheumatism a'campin' in the snow
> But I ketched a chance of Yankees, I'd like to ketch some mo'
>
> Three hundred thousand Yankees is stiff in Southern dust
> We got three hundred thousand before they conquered us
> They died of Southern fever, and Southern steel and shot
> I wish they was three million instead of what we got
>
> I can't take up my musket and fight 'em now no more
> But I ain't going to love 'em, now that is sarten sure
> And I don't want no pardon for what I was and am
> I won't be reconstructed, and I don't give a damn

As these lyrics intimate, Lincoln's victory over the South was merely a physical one, attained by sheer military might. While he subdued the Southerner's body, he never conquered his heart or mind—and never will. Loathing of liberal Lincoln lives on today among the conservative sons and daughters of the traditional South.

Though Reconstruction failed in its day, Lincoln's Northernization plans for the South eventually succeeded beyond his wildest dreams. Indeed, his very War thrust industrialization upon the South, whether she was ready for it or not.[2846] By the end of World War II (1945) the Old Agrarian South was dead, replaced by a "New Industrial South," one that would soon compete with the industrial North in production and economic power.

Industry, centralization, and finance—a result of Lincoln's violent political shift from the states to the Federal government, from small businesses to massive corporations—now dominated the national polity across the entire U.S. For better or for worse, it was Lincoln who gave

---

2846. Wiley, SN, p. 59.

birth to the idea of the "American mass market."[2847]

Today, Atlanta, Georgia, as just one example, is considered the most "Northern of the Southern cities," a thoroughly reconstructed town whose "disloyalty to Dixie" prompted Southerner John Shelton Reed to write:

> Every time I look at Atlanta, I see what a quarter million Confederate soldiers died to prevent.[2848]

As early as 1875, Yankee visitors to the city, men like Edward King of Hartford, Connecticut, were already observing that "there is but little that is distinctively Southern in Atlanta; it is the antithesis of Savannah."[2849]

With the South's industrialization, with her seduction to become a twin of the "greedy, materialistic North," Dixie lost her innocence. But America herself also lost something of incalculable value.

Large factories and power driven machinery were soon introduced to the South, aiding in the inevitable fragmentation of the Southern family.[2850] Then, in the 1950s South, along with the realization of Lincoln's anti-South dream of a completely industrialized nation, came a sharp increase in air and water pollution, the negligent destruction of green spaces, the selling off of great swaths of farmland, the creation of urban sprawl, and a concomitant, nationwide rise in mental illness, organized crime, and juvenile delinquency.[2851]

Dixie's youngest and brightest, trying to escape the grinding poverty and lack of financial opportunity that Reconstruction left in its wake, fled the South in an attempt to find jobs, further draining Dixie of her intellectual wealth. Meanwhile, more and more Northerners fled southward, from the Rust Belt to the Sun Belt, in search of the "perfect vacation."[2852] Many stayed. Soon Dixie started to become what every Southerner feared and what every Northerner hoped: a mirror image of Yankeedom.[2853]

2847. Palmer and Colton, p. 544.
2848. M. Phillips, p. 46; Horwitz, p. 283; Thompson, p. 23.
2849. King, p. 350.
2850. Dinnerstein and Jackson, p. 371.
2851. Weintraub, p. 143.
2852. Grissom, p. 11.
2853. K. C. Davis, p. 452.

Today, traditional Southerners cling to vestiges of the Old South, trying to preserve what little remains of a once incomparable culture. But this is becoming more difficult with each passing year. For the realization of Lincoln's dream included conformity (a decidedly Yankee trait), and so the South traded her agrarian identity for a strip-mall mentality; sold her farmer's soul to the Devil for the promise of industrial treasure.[2854]

But as the brilliant agrarian Andrew Nelson Lytle observed, industry is not the answer to America's problems. It is the land, farming, cultivating the soil,[2855] a return to the Great Mother, whom ancient Europeans called Erda (from whence we get the word earth);[2856] the same deity who Native-Americans have long worshiped as "the Mother of All."[2857] It is impossible, Lytle correctly affirmed, for a society to be happy and healthy without a respectful connection to the land.[2858] What will happen when that connection is completely severed by the adoption of "modern conveniences"?

While there are still two distinct Americas, one South and one North,[2859] thanks in large part to Lincoln, the spirit-enriching differences that once existed between cities like Nashville and Detroit are fast disappearing, especially since the close of World War II, when the South emerged as a true industrial region for the first time.[2860]

Lincoln's political nemesis, Stephen A. Douglas, once admonished America about what he called "Lincoln's doctrine of uniformity." During a public debate at Ottawa, Illinois, on August 21, 1858, Douglas said:

> Why should Illinois be at war with Missouri, or Kentucky with Ohio, or Virginia with New York, merely because their institutions differ? Our fathers [the Founders] intended that our institutions should differ. They knew that the North and South having different climates, productions, and interests, required different institutions.
> This doctrine of Mr. Lincoln of uniformity among the institutions of the different States, is a new doctrine never dreamed of by Washington, Madison, or the framers of this government.

2854. See Simpson, p. 199.
2855. Simpson, p. 203.
2856. Seabrook, BR, p. 45; Walker, s.v. "Earth."
2857. Deloria, p. 107.
2858. Simpson, p. 203.
2859. Kennedy and Kennedy, NT, pp. 187-199.
2860. Weintraub, p. 143.

> Mr. Lincoln and the Republican party set themselves up as wiser than these men who made this government, which has flourished for seventy years under the principle of popular sovereignty, recognizing the right of each State to do as it pleased. . . . why can we not adhere to the great principle of self government upon which our institutions were originally based? I believe that this new doctrine preached by Mr. Lincoln and his party will dissolve the Union if it succeeds. They are trying to array all the Northern States in one body against the South, to excite a sectional war between the Free States and the Slave States, in order that the one or the other may be driven to the wall.[2861]

Douglas' prophecy was correct: Lincoln did indeed drive the South "to the wall," afterward imposing his "doctrine of uniformity" upon the "conquered province" formerly known as the Southern Confederacy.

Now, with a large push from Lincoln, America is rapidly losing a region that is unique in all the world, his own original homeland: Dixie. How tragic. Marshall McLuhan noted decades ago that the agrarian, traditional, chivalric South remains the last defense against the industrial, modern, corrupt influences of the commercial-minded North.[2862] When this is gone, what will we do?

One of Lincoln's sworn enemies, Confederate Vice President Alexander H. Stephens,[2863] had warned the nation years earlier about the dangers that would result if a regional imbalance was created within the Union, for the conservative agricultural South has always acted as a vital counterweight to the liberal mechanized North.[2864] If the South becomes fully Northernized, however, what will become of America's political, social, spiritual, and cultural equilibrium?

Douglas' accusation that Lincoln wanted "to impose on the nation a uniformity of local laws and institutions and a moral homogeneity dictated by the central government" still holds true of the North.[2865] But do Americans today really want their country to be identical from coast to coast? What of the uniqueness of the South, the North, the East, and the

---

2861. M. M. Miller, Vol. 5, pp. 128-129.
2862. Ashdown and Caudill, pp. 118-119.
2863. Though Stephens seems to have had some admiration for Lincoln as a person (the two had been political antebellum colleagues), he detested Lincoln's wartime policies and came out vehemently against him after the Battle of Fort Sumter. See Seabrook, TAHSR, passim; Seabrook, TQAHS, passim.
2864. M. Davis, p. 81.
2865. Napolitano, p. 65.

West? Are we all to become a single, homogenized, amorphous mass, lacking even a shred of individuality? Northerners and New South scallywags may desire this, but traditional Southerners are as much against this idea now as they were before and during Lincoln's War, if not more so.

What will happen if we ignore the Southern agrarian's gospel that industrialism is the destroyer of Nature, beauty, and chivalry, that "modern science is the enemy of faith,"[2866] and that liberalism and big government are the adversaries, not the friends, of the confederate ideals of the Founding generation?

In the early 1900s, Southerners were already noting, with evident sorrow, the Northernization process as it swept across Dixie. Wrote Virginian Lyon Gardiner Tyler in the 1920s:

> What we have [now] is a great Northern Nation, controlled by Northern majorities to which the South has had to conform all its policy and sacrifice all its ideals for sixty years. The national authority is only Northern authority. The South, growing every day more commercialized, is little more than a neglected part of the Great North. The old Union was one of consent, the present Nation is one of force, imperialistic in every sense and masquerading under the name of Union.[2867]

As for himself, Tyler said unhappily:

> I accept the results of the war and have tried to make the best of conditions. I am commercialized, industrialized, and Northernized.[2868]

From what we have examined it would appear that Lincoln won his War to kill off Dixie's Southernness. But did he really? On the surface, yes—and the U.S. flag, not the C.S. flag, now flies over the Southern states to prove it.

What he did not defeat, however, was Dixie's soul: her sense of independence, her natural pugnaciousness, her "rebelliousness," her

---

2866. Bledsoe, AT, p. 23.
2867. *Tyler's Quarterly Historical and Genealogical Magazine*, 1929, Vol. 10, "General Lee's Birthday," p. 17.
2868. *Tyler's Quarterly Historical and Genealogical Magazine*, 1929, Vol. 10, "General Lee's Birthday," p. 19.

passion for freedom, her love of self-determination.[2869] These traits were, after all, the real core of the Confederacy. And they still are. For it was not a place, a region on a map that could be overthrown and subdued, as even some Northerners once recognized. In the late 1800s a wise man from Massachusetts wrote:

> Such character and achievement were not all in vain; that though the Confederacy fell as an actual physical power, it lives eternally in its just cause—the cause of constitutional liberty.[2870]

Southerners could not have agreed more.

On November 7, 1864, the same day he advocated the official start of Southern emancipation[2871] and six months before the end of Lincoln's War, President Davis stood before the Confederate Congress and said:

> . . . if the campaign against Richmond had resulted in success instead of failure; if the valor of the army, under the leadership of its accomplished commander, had resisted in vain the overwhelming masses which were, on the contrary, decisively repulsed; if we had been compelled to evacuate Richmond as well as Atlanta, the Confederacy would have remained as erect and defiant as ever. Nothing could have been changed in the purpose of its Government, in the indomitable valor of its troops, or in the unquenchable spirit of its people. The baffled and disappointed foe would in vain have scanned the reports of your proceedings, at some new legislative seat, for any indication that progress had been made in his gigantic task of conquering a free people. The truth so patent to us must ere long be forced upon the reluctant Northern mind. There are no vital points on the preservation of which the continued existence of the Confederacy depends. There is no military success of the enemy which can accomplish its destruction. Not the fall of Richmond, nor Wilmington, nor Charleston, nor Savannah, nor Mobile, nor of all combined, can save the enemy from the constant and exhaustive drain of blood and treasure which must continue until he shall discover that no peace is attainable unless based on the recognition of our indefeasible rights.[2872]

2869. For the Southern view from 1863, see Durden, p. 37.
2870. Christian, p. 3.
2871. Long and Long, pp. 593-594.
2872. *ORA*, Ser. 4, Vol. 3, p. 792.

Davis' words, though 145 years old, explain why, to this day, traditional Southerners are "still fightin' the War." Not the "Civil War." But the war to reclaim America's true political heritage, the very one Lincoln destroyed on April 9, 1865, at Appomattox;[2873] the one he promised our nation in his Gettysburg Address on November 19, 1863; the same Jeffersonian heritage that, two years later, he overturned and caused to "perish from the earth"; namely, a constitutional government "of the people, by the people, for the people."[2874]

Northerners created Lincoln, Northerners elected Lincoln, Northerners supported Lincoln, Northerners worshiped Lincoln, Northerners murdered Lincoln, and Northerners fabricated his mythology after his death. Perhaps then it takes a Northerner to truly get to the heart of the matter.

Here is what one of them, Maryland journalist, H. L. Mencken, had to say about Lincoln's most famous declamation:

> The Gettysburg speech was at once the shortest and the most famous oration in American history. . . the highest emotion reduced to a few poetical phrases. Lincoln himself never even remotely approached it. It is genuinely stupendous. But let us not forget that it is poetry, not logic; beauty, not sense. Think of the argument in it. Put it into the cold words of everyday. The doctrine is simply this: that the Union soldiers who died at Gettysburg sacrificed their lives to the cause of self-determination—that government of the people, by the people, for the people, should not perish from the earth. It is difficult to imagine anything more untrue. The Union soldiers in the battle actually fought against self-determination; it was the Confederates who fought for the right of their people to govern themselves.[2875]

British journalist Alistair Cooke agreed, calling Lincoln's Gettysburg Address a classic work of oratory of highly questionable reasoning.[2876]

2873. Napolitano, p. 8; Palmer and Colton, p. 543.
2874. Thornton and Ekelund, pp. 98-99.
2875. Website: www.lewrockwell.com/orig/mencken2.html.
2876. A. Cooke, ACA, p. 214. Contrary to Northern mythology, Lincoln's Gettysburg Address was not received with rapt attention, constant cheers, tear swollen eyes, and thunderous applause. Lincoln's own reaction to its reception tells it all: ". . . that speech fell on the audience like a wet blanket. I am distressed about it." Lamon, RAL, p. 173. "It is a flat failure and the people are disappointed," Lincoln told his friend Ward Hill Lamon. Christian, p. 27. Neither was it of much interest to either the media or the public at large. Indeed, "at the time almost no attention was paid to this address, it being relegated to the inner pages

The great irony of Lincoln is that during his lifetime he was voted America's worst president, and the direct cause of disunion, America's bloodiest and most expensive war, and the unnecessary deaths of thousands. He was also denounced as the leader of our nation's most corrupt and diabolical administration, and the man responsible for the loss of the Founding Father's Confederate government, the destruction of the original Constitution, increased racial strife, and the near annihilation of much of what was good, beautiful, noble, and unique about the South. Yet *after* death, thanks to the diligent and overly imaginative work of Lincoln hagiographers, eulogists, and mythologists, he was recast as the Nation's Healer, the Great Emancipator, the Great Peacemaker, the Great Preserver, the Greatest of all Presidents: "Honest Abe."[2877]

However, only one of these two legacies can be authentic, not both. The traditional South will adhere to the former, for as true Americans we believe it is more important to be historically accurate than politically correct.[2878]

Despite this, Lincoln continues to be idolized by many in the South today—primarily scallywags, who choose to adhere to the latter legacy.[2879] Why? It is because the truth about Lincoln and his War has been aggressively falsified and suppressed by pro-North, South-loathing writers, publishers, educators, administrators, magazines, newspapers, Websites, editors, screenwriters, scriptwriters, TV producers, film producers, book distributors, libraries, schools, universities, museums, gift shops, and bookstores, many of them located in Dixie herself.[2880]

Southern Truth, which is based on facts, is called a "myth," a "falsehood," a "lie," "subjective," "revisionist," "biased," "slanted," and "inaccurate," while Northern "Truth," which is founded on distortion,

---

of the newspapers." Encyc. Brit., s.v. "Lincoln, Abraham."
2877. M. Davis, p. 170.
2878. By "true Americans" I am referring to Conservatives and Libertarians, for they are the only political groups which continue to adhere (however loosely in some cases) to the Jeffersonian concepts upon which the U.S. was originally constructed by the Founders, particularly the Southern Founding Fathers.
2879. See Meriwether, pp. 1-2.
2880. If you are a parent, check with your child's school or college. You may be surprised to learn that books of a pro-South (conservative) nature are not allowed in the institution's library (very common across the U.S.), that they are not taught by any teacher, that students are actively prevented from being exposed to them, that they are strictly censored on campus, and that students are probably even prohibited, or at least discouraged, from reading them. It is for this very reason that I wrote *Honest Jeff and Dishonest Abe: A Southern Children's Guide to the Civil War*. Since few schools would ever allow this book into their libraries or curriculum, it is particularly useful for home-schooling families.

misrepresentation, wishful thinking, opinion, emotion, 19th-Century propaganda, and overt disinformation, is called "scholarly," "objective," "factual," and "impartial." Nowhere is this unjust dichotomy more true than when dealing with the life and figure of Abraham Lincoln.

Fortunately, there are many educated and enlightened Southerners today who would agree with the words of the Honorable George L. Christian, concerning America's sixteenth president. In 1920 Christian wrote:

> . . . we are unable to find in his career any substantial basis for the great name and fame now claimed for him by his admirers both at the North and at the South, and certainly nothing either in his character, career or conduct to engender veneration, admiration and love for his memory on the part of the people of the South.[2881]

On February 22, 1861, nearly two months before he inaugurated war on the South, in a speech delivered at Independence Hall, Philadelphia, Pennsylvania, Lincoln told his audience that he would rather be assassinated than give up his commitment to his socialist, big government agenda.[2882] The world had no way of knowing then that four years later Lincoln would pay for his anti-South liberalism in this exact manner.

But Lincoln himself knew, and he spoke often to his associates of the many dark premonitions he experienced pertaining to his premature demise, even regarding the unfinished U.S. Capitol building in Washington, D.C., as a foreshadowing of evil to come.[2883]

Admittedly highly superstitious, with an obsessive interest in omens, signs, and portents, even before he became president Lincoln seemed to psychically know what lay ahead.[2884] Addressing his supporters at Springfield, Illinois, Lincoln spoke the following startling words on August 14, 1860, three months *prior* to his election:

> I am profoundly grateful for this manifestation of your feelings. I am grateful, because it is a tribute such as can be paid to no man as

---

2881. Christian, p. 27.
2882. Nicolay and Hay, ALCW, Vol. 1, p. 691.
2883. W. B. Garrison, CWTFB, p. 171.
2884. Encyc. Brit., s.v. "Lincoln, Abraham."

a man; it is the evidence that four years from this time you will give a like manifestation to the next man who is the representative of the truth on the questions that now agitate the public; and it is because you will then fight for this cause as you do now, or with even greater ardor than now, though I be dead and gone, that I most profoundly and sincerely thank you.[2885]

During his Farewell Address at Springfield, Illinois, on February 11, 1861, the day on which he was to leave for his inauguration at Washington, D.C., he noted that he might not ever return:

> My Friends: No one, not in my situation, can appreciate my feeling of sadness at this parting. To this place, and the kindness of these people, I owe everything. Here I have lived a quarter of a century, and have passed from a young to an old man. Here my children have been born, and one is buried. I now leave, not knowing when or whether ever I may return, with a task before me greater than that which rested upon Washington. Without the assistance of that Divine Being who ever attended him, I cannot succeed. With that assistance, I cannot fail. Trusting in Him who can go with me, and remain with you, and be everywhere for good, let us confidently hope that all will yet be well. To His care commending you, as I hope in your prayers you will commend me, I bid you an affectionate farewell.[2886]

Clairvoyantly, Lincoln began to realize that although he *would* return to Springfield one day, he would not be alive at the time. He would be in a casket.

He had another one of these strange prognostications in April 1865, just days before he was assassinated.[2887] Here is how the president described the uncannily prophetic dream to his wife:

> About ten days ago, I retired very late. I had been up waiting for important dispatches from the front. I could not have been long in bed when I fell into a slumber, for I was weary. I soon began to dream. There seemed to be a death-like stillness about me. Then I heard subdued sobs, as if a number of people were weeping. I thought I left my bed and wandered downstairs. There the silence

---

2885. Nicolay and Hay, ALCW, Vol. 1, p. 648.
2886. Nicolay and Hay, ALCW, Vol. 1, p. 672.
2887. W. B. Garrison, LNOK, pp. 246-253.

was broken by the same pitiful sobbing, but the mourners were invisible. I went from room to room; no living person was in sight, but the same mournful sounds of distress met me as I passed along. It was light in all the rooms; every object was familiar to me; but where were all the people who were grieving as if their hearts would break? I was puzzled and alarmed. What could be the meaning of all this? Determined to find the cause of a state of things so mysterious and so shocking, I kept on until I arrived at the East Room [of the White House], which I entered. There I met with a sickening surprise. Before me was a catafalque, on which rested a corpse wrapped in funeral vestments. Around it were stationed soldiers who were acting as guards; and there was a throng of people, some gazing mournfully upon the corpse, whose face was covered, others weeping pitifully. 'Who is dead in the White House?' I demanded of one of the soldiers. 'The President,' was his answer; 'he was killed by an assassin!' Then came a loud burst of grief from the crowd, which awoke me from my dream. I slept no more that night; and although it was only a dream, I have been strangely annoyed by it ever since.[2888]

Mary, Lincoln's wife, was mortified. "That was horrid," she cried to her husband. "I wish you had not told it." "Well, it is only a dream," he replied calmly.

Despite the eerie nature of the augury, Lincoln was unruffled—and for good reason.

He had been aware long before 1865 that the occupation of U.S. president was one for which he was not qualified; one that he should not pursue. In 1864, for example, when he was asked what he thought of the anti-Lincoln Wade-Davis Bill, as well as a scathing speech given by his arch critic Wendell Phillips, Lincoln replied:

> No, I have not seen them, nor do I care to see them. I have seen enough to satisfy me that I am a failure, not only in the opinion of the people in rebellion, but of many distinguished politicians of my own party.[2889]

Far earlier, in 1858, when—despite the fact that he had had only

---

2888. Lamon, RAL, pp. 115-116.
2889. Lamon, RAL, pp. 189-190.

one year of formal education[2890]—he was repeatedly advised to run for the nation's highest office by Northern newspapers, he jokingly disqualified himself, saying: "Just think of such a sucker as me as President."[2891]

When an appointed select committee finally excitedly notified Lincoln of his election in November 1860, he replied listlessly:

> With deep gratitude to my countrymen for this mark of their confidence, with a distrust of my own ability to perform the required duty under the most favourable circumstances . . .[2892]

This weak, self-negating, ungracious, and unmanly attitude had not prevented his fellow party members from nominating him in the first place, however; even when he made remarks like the following, which he sent in a letter to a newspaper editor on April 16, 1859: "I must in candor say I do not think myself fit for the Presidency."[2893]

Here is the most honorable, and honest, statement Lincoln ever made—and we the in the South agree with it. We only wish that the North had listened to him.

If she had, the United States would be an even wealthier, stronger, happier, less racially divided, more fully developed country than it is today, and Virginian George L. Christian would not have had to sum up the Southern view of America's sixteenth president this way:

> Was the character of Abraham Lincoln such as to make him an ideal and exemplar for our children, and were the methods employed by him such as to excite and command the reverence, admiration and emulation of those who come after us? We answer, No; a thousand times, No.[2894]

2890. DeGregorio, s.v. "Abraham Lincoln" (p. 228).
2891. Villard, Vol. 1, p. 96.
2892. Hopley, Vol. 1, p. 219.
2893. Nicolay and Hay, ALCW, Vol. 1, p. 533.
2894. Christian, p. 30.

APPENDIX A
LINCOLN, WASHINGTON, & NERO

Excerpted from Henry Clay Dean's 1869 book
Crimes of the Civil War and Curse of the Funding System

ABRAHAM LINCOLN has been compared to George Washington; herein they differed.

Washington was modest, reticent, dignified. Lincoln was familiar, garrulous and clownish.

Washington was wise, sincere and determined. Lincoln was cunning, treacherous and fickle.

Washington refused presents, pay for his services, and emoluments for his sacrifices. Lincoln kept each member of his family as beggars for presents, silent partners in contracts, and grew wealthy from the spoils of office.

Washington established constitutional liberty among men, upon the sure foundations of law. Lincoln tore up that very Constitution, and set up his arbitrary will instead.

Washington was religiously careful in the selection of the ablest, purest men of the country to administer the government; choosing those who differed with him in opinion, for the good of the country. Lincoln selected the weakest, worst and most corrupt men of the country, because they agreed with him in opinion, and served him cheerfully as instruments of usurpation.

Washington moulded chaos into order, stability and legitimate government. Lincoln dissolved the government, and left the country in anarchy.

Washington received the spontaneous devotion of his countrymen through the press which he had made free, and the people who were secure in their liberty. Lincoln enforced the most extravagant adulation from his own hired presses, his officers who were plundering the country, and the pulpit bribed to chant his praises.

Washington went to every part of the land, unattended by military array, except those crowds of old volunteers of liberty, who came to pay their respect to his person, and congratulate the country upon the success of constitutional government. Women, with woven garlands, met him wherever he went. Beautiful maidens and sweet little children, strewed his walks with flowers.

From the day of the inauguration to the hour of his tragical death, Lincoln was never out of the reach of the sound of artillery; was surrounded by soldiers to guard his person; flatterers and courtiers to corrupt his heart; and female sycophants begging favors, dispensing praises, and making merry in his court.

After his term of office, Washington retired to his farm, to open the hospitable door of his mansion to his old confreres in arms, and entertain visitors who sought his company to learn more of manly liberty. In the strength of his mind and the vigor of a green old age, surrounded by friends who loved him, he surrendered his soul to God, to be mourned by his countrymen and honored by mankind. Lincoln closed his life as stated above.

There *was* a singular resemblance between the Roman Emperor Claudius Nero, and Abraham Lincoln.

In early life, Nero was remarkable for his jovial habit of illustration. Lincoln's whole field of logic, illustration, ridicule and satire, was anecdote and stories.

Nero proposed many reforms under Seneca and Burrhus, and grew in popularity among the people, until he was accounted a god. Lincoln commenced his administration as a benevolent reformer, under the auspices of all the reformers of the country.

Nero's subjects rebelled against his usurpation. Lincoln's subjects anticipated his usurpation. Such rulers always create rebellions and excite resistance.

Nero played the drama of the destruction of Troy, during the seven days' burning of Rome. Lincoln attended balls and engaged in festivities during the five years' conflagration of the country, and the wanton, bloody slaughter of his countrymen; and had vile songs sung among his dying armies.

Nero rebuilt Rome at his own expense, by extortion and robbery, and the tyrant was liberal to the sufferers. In this Nero excelled Lincoln, who repaired no damages of burning cities.

Nero threw prisoners to wild beasts. Lincoln kept prisoners confined in cold prisons, where their limbs were frozen; in filthy prisons where they were eaten up with vermin; starved them until they died of scurvy and other loathesome diseases, after months of terror, torture and cruelty.

Nero put Christians to death under false pretence, to gratify the worshippers of the Pantheon. Lincoln corrupted one part of the Church to engage in warfare with the other part, and burned twelve hundred houses of worship; mutilated grave-yards; and left whole cities, churches and all in ashes; dragged ministers from their knees in the very act of worship; tied them up by their thumbs; had their daughters stripped naked by negro soldiers, under the command of white officers.

Suetonius, under Nero, butchered eighty thousand Britons, defended by Queen Boadicea. His officers flogged Boadicea and ravished her daughters; and lost thousands of Romans in the attempt to subdue the Britons, who were defending their homes, altars and grave-yards.

Lincoln let loose Turchin to ravish the women of Athens, Alabama; Banks and Butler to rob New Orleans; Sheridan to burn up Virginia; Sherman to ravage the South with desolating fires; Payne and Burbridge to murder in Kentucky; Neil, Strachan and the vagabond thieves, to murder, rob and destroy Missouri, until one million of his murdered countrymen butchered each other by his command.

Every department of Nero's government was signalized by licentiousness and debauchery, nameless and loathesome. Lincoln's court was the resort of debauchees; the Treasury Department was a harem; the public officers were one great unrestrained multitude who yielded to the coarsest appetites of nature, stimulated by strong drinks and inflamed by the indulgence of every other vice.

In this did Nero, to his credit, differ from Lincoln. The generals of Nero respected the works of arts, the paintings, poems and manuscripts of the learned, and the discoveries of genius.

Upon the other hand, Lincoln destroyed everything that indicated superior civilization. In one instance, a general officer of scientific pretension, arrayed his daughter in the stolen garments of the wife of C. C. Clay, an old Senator of Alabama. During the invasion of Huntsville, Mr. Clay's house was robbed of its jewelry, the heir-looms of three generations, taken against the tearful prayers of his black servant. The exquisitely beautiful statue of his dead babe, was ground to powder before his eyes. An appeal to Lincoln's men, that any object was of scientific value, only hastened its destruction; his wars were directed against civilization.

Nero fled before the judgment of the Senate, and died by his own hand. Lincoln could not have survived his crimes, so unrelenting is the retributive justice of God.[2895]

[2895]. H. C. Dean, pp. 171-174.

APPENDIX B
MARX'S 1864 LETTER TO LINCOLN
ORIGINAL SOURCE OF MARX'S LETTER: *BEEHIVE*, LONDON, UK, JANUARY 7, 1865

Introductory Notes by Lochlainn Seabrook

Naturally, Karl Marx, the founder of modern communism, saw the world through the eyes of a communist. But it was not the easy-going bohemian communism often peddled by left-wing propagandists today. Marx's form of communism was so ruthless and radical that it has been placed in its own category: Marxism.

We may define Marxism as a rigid and literal interpretation of communism according to the specific words and ideas of Marx. This includes *dialectical materialism* (an essentially atheistic view that sees humans as only capable of progress through—often violent—class and economic struggle) and *revolutionary socialism* (the achievement of a communist society by any means necessary, including bloodshed). On the political spectrum this places Marxism to the left of communism, which is left of socialism.[2896]

In a word, Karl Marx was one of the most extreme left-wing revolutionaries the world has ever known.

Why then was he a staunch champion of Abraham Lincoln, a man he took so seriously that in November 1864 he wrote the president a fawning two-page letter brimming with cloying superlatives, undisguised adoration, and near fanatical sycophancy?

As I believe this question has been aptly answered in this book, I need not go into detail here, other than to state that South-hating communist Marx would not have penned this missive unless he saw in big government Liberal Lincoln a kindred spirit, one who was not only receptive to socialist views, but one who actually supported many of them. And indeed, not only was Lincoln known to speak before socialist gatherings (even once "gratefully" accepting an honorary membership from a socialist organization), but he also filled his administration and armies with socialists and communists—many, like Charles A. Dana, who were personal friends of Marx.[2897] As noted on page 184, Marx even authored a reverential book on the Union president. Thus we can be sure that Lincoln received the famous communist's note with a willing and appreciative smile.

2896. Heilbroner, p. 40.
2897. See Seabrook, ALWALJDWAC, passim; Seabrook, LW, passim.

What of Marx's letter? How does the Conservative South view it?

It is a shining example of socialist and communist propaganda, written by a nihilistic anti-American extremist who saw life through the lense of economic, racial, sexual, and class warfare—"the struggle," as radical left-wingers still refer to it. Though they themselves fabricate and escalate "the struggle" through political agitation and social divisiveness, this communist artifice is presented to the public as resulting from a wide variety of "inequalities" and "injustices" brought on primarily by capitalism and all its alleged "attendant evils." Most importantly for students of Lincoln and his war, Marx's letter portrays the entire "Civil War" as one directly related to labor, socialism, and race; the "American Anti-slavery War," as he refers to it.

Karl Marx: founder of modern communism, anti-American, atheist, South-hater, revolutionary, anti-capitalist, coauthor of *The Communist Manifesto*, supporter of Abraham Lincoln.

Comrade Marx does not stop there. The South is cast in a most absurd and dishonest light as a "pro-slavery" region—a "slave power," in fact, while rich upperclass Southern whites, the always reviled "Confederate gentry," are described as traitorously launching a "slaveholders' rebellion." Actually, the South was altogether nonaggressive ("all we ask is to be let alone," said President Davis), and only took up arms to protect its homeland from Lincoln's illegal and unnecessary invasion.[2898]

Surprisingly, Marx references Northern slavery. But he does not acknowledge that both the American slave trade and American slavery began in the North and that the latter was only later pushed Southward on a reluctant populace when cold-weather Yankees found slavery unprofitable and the intimate presence of blacks repugnant.[2899]

Throughout Marx's letter I have highlighted these and other communist lies, myths, and fairy tales in bold text, along with informational footnotes.

Let us now examine this important historical document. The opening two paragraphs were written by the German socialist author Herman Schlüter, and are not part of Marx's letter. Rather they are Schlüter's introduction to it. Marx's indented letter follows. LOCHLAINN SEABROOK

[2898]. For more on this topic see my book, *All We Ask is to be Let Alone: The Southern Secession Fact Book*.
[2899]. For more on this topic see my book, *Everything You Were Taught About American Slavery is Wrong, Ask a Southerner!*

Letter from Karl Marx to Abraham Lincoln

IN THE BEGINNING of November, 1864, Lincoln was elected for the second time to the Presidency of the United States. Under the direct influence and upon the suggestion of the General Council of the International Workingmen's Association, the workingmen of London arranged a new series of meetings to protest against the anti-Union attitude of the manufacturers and the Government of their country. *It was [Karl] Marx who furnished the initiative for this renewal of agitation* [emphasis by L.S.].

In one of the following meetings of the General Council, one of its members, Dick, made a motion, which was seconded by G. Howell, to draft an address to the American people congratulating them upon **their struggles and sacrifices in behalf of the principles of freedom**[2900] and upon **their re-election of Lincoln** to the Presidency of the United States.[2901] A committee was appointed to formulate this address, and this committee submitted its draft, the author of which was Marx, to the General Council at its meeting on November 29th [1864]. The draft was accepted, and a resolution was adopted to forward it by a committee to Charles Francis Adams [Sr.], the American Minister at London, for transmission to his Government. The following is the text of the address [by Marx]:

> To Abraham Lincoln, President of the United States of America.
> Sir—We congratulate the American people upon your **re-election by a large majority**.[2902] If resistance to the **Slave Power**[2903] was the watchword of your first election, **the triumphal war-cry of your re-election is Death to Slavery**.[2904]
> From the commencement of the titanic American

[2900]. It was not the Liberal North, the Union, that "struggled and sacrificed in behalf of the principles of freedom," it was the Conservative South, the Confederacy.
[2901]. As discussed in this very book, Lincoln was not "re-elected," he was *re-installed* by way of numerous criminalities and illegalities.
[2902]. As I have discussed, none of the Southern states participated in the 1864 U.S. presidential election. Lincoln's reelection then could hardly be considered having been won "by a large majority." Vide supra, pp. 273-274.
[2903]. The Old South never came close to being a "Slave Power." The Old North, where both the American slave trade and American slavery were born, was America's one and only true slave power. See my book, *Everything You Were Taught About American Slavery is Wrong, Ask a Southerner!*
[2904]. As I have shown in detail, Lincoln's reelection in 1864 was in no way connected to the communists' "Death to Slavery" movement. This is just more communist gaslighting.

strife the workingmen of Europe felt distinctively that the Star Spangled Banner carried the destiny of their class. **The contest for the territories which opened the *dire epopèe* ["terrible epic"], was it not to decide whether the virgin soil of immense tracts should be wedded to the labor of the immigrant or be prostituted by the tramp of the slavedriver?**[2905]

When an **oligarchy of 300,000 slaveholders**[2906] dared to inscribe for the first time in the annals of the world **"Slavery"**[2907] on the banner of **armed revolt,**[2908] when on the very spots where hardly a century ago the idea of one great **Democratic Republic**[2909] had first sprung up, whence the first declaration of the Rights of Man was issued, and the first impulse given to the European Revolution of the eighteenth century, when on those very spots counter-revolution, with systematic thoroughness, gloried in rescinding **"the ideas entertained at the time of the formation of the old constitution"** and maintained **"slavery to be a beneficial institution,"** indeed, the only solution of the great problem of the "relation of capital to labor," and cynically proclaimed property in man **"the cornerstone of the new edifice,"**[2910]—then the working classes of Europe

---

2905. From the South's perspective the War had nothing to do with slavery, neither its maintenance, its expansion, or its extinction. It was about preserving the original Constitution as perceived and penned by the Founding Fathers. This included the idea of states' rights, tacitly laid out in the Ninth and Tenth Amendments, which gave the states the right to choose whether to allow slavery within their borders or prohibit it. This is far from the "pro-slavery" position that Marx fraudulently ascribes to the South, the birthplace of the American abolition movement. In point of fact, the Conservative South—which was in the midst of working out plans for complete abolition across the South in 1861—was pro-choice on slavery, the Liberal North was anti-choice.
2906. There has never been an "oligarchy of 300,000 slaveholders" in the South at any time in America's history.
2907. Confederate President Davis, like many other Southern leaders, was clear on this point. The South did not fight for the preservation of slavery. Marx's comment therefore is nothing but communist disinformation, meant to confuse and mislead. For more on this topic see my book, *The Quotable Jefferson Davis*.
2908. The South did not "revolt." It peacefully separated from the Union in accordance with constitutional law. See my book, *All We Ask is to be Let Alone: The Southern Secession Fact Book*.
2909. The U.S.A. is not a "democratic republic." Washington and Jefferson, as well as many other Founders very deliberately labeled it a "confederate republic." See my books, *Lincoln's War: The Real Cause, the Real Winner, the Real Loser*; *Confederacy 101*; and *The Great Yankee Coverup*.
2910. Pertaining to these quotes by my cousin Confederate Vice President Alexander H. Stephens: 1) They are taken out of context; 2) they did not represent the sentiment of the majority of white Southerners at the time; 3) Stephens was echoing the earlier words of a Yankee who had stated that slavery was the foundation of the U.S. Constitution. For more on these and related topics see my book *The Alexander H. Stephens Reader*

understood at once, even before the fanatic partisanship of the upper classes, for the **Confederate gentry** had given its dismal warning, that the **slaveholders' rebellion** was to sound the tocsin for **a general holy war of property against labor**,[2911] and that for the men of labor, with their hopes for the future, even their past conquests were at stake in that tremendous conflict on the other side of the Atlantic. Everywhere they bore therefore patiently the hardships imposed upon them by the cotton crisis, opposed enthusiastically the **pro-slavery intervention**[2912]—importunities of their betters—and from most parts of Europe contributed their quota of blood to the good of the cause.

While the workingmen, the true political power of the North, allowed slavery to defile their own republic, while before the Negro, mastered and sold without his concurrence, they boasted it the highest prerogative of the white-skinned laborer to sell himself and choose his own master, they were unable to attain the true freedom of labor, or to support their European brethren in their struggle for emancipation; but **this barrier to progress**[2913] has been swept off by the red sea of **civil war**.[2914]

The workingmen of Europe felt sure that, as the American War of Independence [1775] initiated **a new era of ascendency for the middle class**,[2915] so the **American Anti-slavery War**[2916] will do for **the**

---

and *The Quotable Alexander H. Stephens*.

2911. As noted, the so-called "Confederate gentry" did not initiate the War, it did not fight for the preservation of slavery, the War was not a "slaveholders' rebellion," and the War had little or nothing to do with "property" or "labor." These are all communist fantasies. See my book, *Everything You Were Taught About the Civil War is Wrong, Ask a Southerner!*

2912. There was no "pro-slavery intervention" in the South, in Europe, or anywhere else between 1861 and 1865.

2913. Marx, using communist myth and language, describes the Yankee's inability to "attain the true freedom of [white] labor" in the Northern states as a "barrier to progress." Progress toward what? A socialist-communist state, which the vast majority of Americans have never desired and never will desire.

2914. According to the official definition of the phrase, Lincoln's War was not a "civil war" (that is, a conflict between states of the *same* country). It was a regular war, with *two separate countries* pitted against one another.

2915. America's middle class did not enter a "new era of ascendency" due to the Revolutionary War. Marx, like other communists, hated the middle class and wanted to believe this.

2916. This is certainly one of the most purposely misleading, most disingenuous phrases ever used to describe Lincoln's War. Union General Ulysses S. Grant himself asserted that: "The sole object of the war is to restore the Union. Should I be convinced it has any other object, or that our [U.S.] government designs using its soldiers to execute the wishes of abolitionists, I pledge to you as a man and a soldier, I would resign my working classes.²⁹¹⁷ They consider it an earnest sign of the epoch to come that it fell to the lot of **Abraham Lincoln, the single-minded son of the working class,**²⁹¹⁸ to lead his country through the **matchless struggle**²⁹¹⁹ for the rescue of **the enchained race**²⁹²⁰ and **the reconstruction of a social world.**²⁹²¹

Signed on behalf of the International Workingmen's Association, the Central Council:

Longmaid, Worley, Whitlock, Blackmore, Hartwell, Pidgeon, Lucraft, Weston, Dell, Nicars, Shaw, Lake, Buckley, Osborn, Howell, Carter, Wheeler, Starnsby, Morgan, Grossmith, Dick, Denoual, Jourdain, Morissot, Leroux, Bor. dage, Bosquet, Talandier, Dupont, L. Wolf, Aldrovandi, Lama, Solustri, Nuspert, Eccarius, Wolf, Lessner, Pfänder, Lochner, Taub, Balliter, Rypcrynski, Hansen, Schantzenbeck, Smales, Cornelius, Peterson, Otto, Bagnagatti, Setocri; George Odgers, President of the Council; P. V. Lubez, Corresponding Secretary for France; Karl Marx, Corresponding Secretary for Germany; C. P. Fontana, Corresponding Secretary for Italy; J. E. Holtorp, Corresponding Secretary for Poland; H. F. Jung, Corresponding Secretary for Switzerland; William Cremer, Hon. General Secretary, 18 Greek Street, Soho, London W.²⁹²²

---

commission and carry my sword to the other side." See Meriwether, p. 219; Stonebraker, p. 70.
2917. Lincoln's War did not appreciably alter the position of the "working classes"—and was never intended to.
2918. Marx guilefully paints Lincoln as being raised in a socialistic home, which, in Marx's view, qualifies the Yankee demagogue to "lead his country through the matchless struggle . . ." toward socialism.
2919. Only an inveterate socialist-communist could see Lincoln's War as a "matchless struggle for the rescue of the enchained race." It was a conflict over constitutional interpretation, which is why Confederate General Robert E. Lee called it "the War of the Constitution." The abolition of slavery only came eight months after Lincoln's death, and was a result, not of the War, but of the radicals (socialists and communists) in Lincoln's party, who illegally pushed through the Thirteenth Amendment in December 1865.
2920. Southern black servants were never chained, except during punishment (and even that was rare)—the same penalty inflicted on white criminals. See my book, *Everything You Were Taught About American Slavery is Wrong, Ask a Southerner!*
2921. No one on either side, South or North, took up arms in order to "reconstruct a social world"; and by "social world" Marx means a *socialist* world.
2922. Schlüter, pp. 187-191.

BIBLIOGRAPHY

Note: My pro-South readers are to be advised that the majority of the books listed here are anti-South in nature (some extremely so), and were written primarily by liberal elitist, socialist, and Marxist authors who loath the South, and typically the United States and the U.S. Constitution as well. Despite this, as a scholar I find these titles indispensable, for an honest evaluation of Lincoln's War is not possible without studying both the Southern and the Northern versions. Still, it must be said that the material contained in these works is largely the result of a century and a half of Yankee myth, falsehoods, cherry-picking, disinformation, slander, anti-South propaganda, and junk research, as modern pro-North writers merely copy one another's errors without ever looking at the original 19th-Century sources. This type of literature pro-North advocates call "scholarly" and "objective." In the process, the mistakes and lies in these fault-ridden, historically inaccurate works have been magnified over the years, and the North's version of the "Civil War" has come to be accepted as the only legitimate one. Indeed, it is now the only one known by most people. That over 95 percent of the titles in my bibliography fall into the anti-South category is simply a reflection of the enormous power and influence that the pro-North movement—our nation's cultural ruling class—has long held over America's educational system, libraries, publishing houses, and media (paper and electronic). My books serve as a small rampart against the overwhelming tide of anti-South Fascists and liberal political elites, all who are working hard to make sure you never learn the Truth about Lincoln and his War.

Abanes, Richard. *Inside Today's Mormonism*. Eugene, OR: Harvest House, 2004.
Abbott, John Stevens Cabot. *The Life of General Ulysses S. Grant*. Boston, MA: B. B. Russell, 1868.
Adams, Charles. *When in the Course of Human Events: Arguing the Case for Southern Secession*. Lanham, MD: Rowman and Littlefield, 2000.
Adams, Francis D., and Barry Sanders. *Alienable Rights: The Exclusion of African Americans in a White Man's Land, 1619-2000*. 2003. New York, NY: Perennial, 2004 ed.
Adams, Henry (ed.). *Documents Relating to New-England Federalism, 1800-1815*. Boston, MA: Little, Brown, and Co., 1877.
Adams, Nehemiah, Rev. *A South-side View of Slavery: Three Months at the South, in 1854*. Boston, MA: T. R. Marvin, 1855.
Alexander, William T. *History of the Colored Race in America*. Kansas City, MO: Palmetto Publishing, 1887.
Alotta, Robert I. *Civil War Justice: Union Army Executions Under Lincoln*. Shippensburg, PA: White Mane, 1989.
An Appeal From the Colored Men of Philadelphia to the President of the United States. Philadelphia, PA, 1862.
Anderson, John Q. (ed.). *Brokenburn: The Journal of Kate Stone, 1861-1868*. 1955. Baton Rouge, LA: Louisiana State University Press, 1995 ed.
Andrewes, Antony. *The Greeks*. 1967. New York, NY: W. W. Norton and Co., 1978 ed.
Andrews, Elisha Benjamin. *The United States in Our Own Time: A History From Reconstruction to Expansion*. 1895. New York, NY: Charles Scribner's Sons, 1903 ed.
Andrews, Sidney. *The South Since the War: As Shown by Fourteen Weeks of Travel and Observation*. Boston, MA: Ticknor and Fields, 1866.
Angle, Paul M. (ed.). *The Complete Lincoln-Douglas Debates of 1858*. Chicago, IL: University of Chicago Press, 1991.
Annunzio, Frank (chairman). *The Capitol: A Pictorial History of the Capitol and of the Congress*. Washington, D.C.: U.S. Joint Committee on Printing, 1983.

Anonymous. *Life of John C. Calhoun: Presenting a Condensed History of Political Events, From 1811 to 1843.* New York, NY: Harper and Brothers, 1843.
Appleman, Roy Edgar (ed.). *Abraham Lincoln: From His Own Words and Contemporary Accounts.* Washington, D.C.: U.S. Department of the Interior, National Park Service, 1942.
Ariès, Philippe, and George Duby (eds.). *A History of Private Life: From Pagan Rome to Byzantium.* Cambridge, MA: Belknap Press, 1987.
Arnold, Isaac Newton. *The History of Abraham Lincoln, and the Overthrow of Slavery.* Chicago, IL: Clarke and Co., 1866.
Ashdown Paul, and Edward Caudill. *The Myth of Nathan Bedford Forrest.* 2005. Lanham, MD: Rowman and Littlefield, 2006 ed.
Ashe, Captain Samuel A'Court. *A Southern View of the Invasion of the Southern States and War of 1861-1865.* 1935. Crawfordville, GA: Ruffin Flag Co., 1938 ed.
Ashworth, John. *Slavery, Capitalism, and Politics in the Antebellum Republic.* 2 vols. New York, NY: Cambridge University Press, 2007.
Astor, Gerald. *The Right to Fight: A History of African Americans in the Military.* Cambridge, MA: Da Capo, 2001.
Baepler, Paul (ed.). *White Slaves, African Masters: An Anthology of American Barbary Captivity Narratives.* Chicago, IL: University of Chicago Press, 1999.
Bailey, Anne C. *African Voices of the Atlantic Slave Trade: Beyond the Silence and the Shame.* Boston, MA: Beacon Press, 2005.
Bailey, Hugh C. *Hinton Rowan Helper: Abolitionist-Racist.* Tuscaloosa, AL: University of Alabama Press, 1965.
Bailey, Thomas A. *A Diplomatic History of the American People.* 1940. New York, NY: Appleton-Century-Crofts, 1970 ed.
Bailyn, Bernard, Robert Dallek, David Brion Davis, David Herbert Donald, John L. Thomas, and Gordon S. Wood. *The Great Republic: A History of the American People.* 1977. Lexington, MA: D. C. Heath and Co., 1992 ed.
Baker, George E. (ed.). *The Works of William H. Seward.* 5 vols. 1861. Boston, MA: Houghton, Mifflin and Co., 1888 ed.
Ballagh, James Curtis. *White Servitude in the Colony of Virginia: A Study of the System of Indentured Servitude in the American Colonies.* Whitefish, MT: Kessinger Publishing, 2004.
Bancroft, Frederic. *The Life of William H. Seward.* 2 vols. New York, NY: Harper and Brothers, 1900.
——. *Slave-Trading in the Old South.* Baltimore, MD: J. H. Furst, 1931.
Bancroft, Frederic, and William A. Dunning (eds.). *The Reminiscences of Carl Schurz.* 3 vols. New York, NY: McClure Co., 1909.
Banks, Noreen. *Early American Almanac.* New York, NY: Bantam, 1975.
Bark, William Carroll. *Origins of the Medieval World.* Garden City, NY: Anchor, 1958.
Barnes, Gilbert H., and Dwight L. Dumond (eds.). *Letters of Theodore Dwight Weld, Angelina Grimké Weld and Sarah Grimké, 1822-1844.* 2 vols. New York, NY: D. Appleton-Century Co., 1934.
Barney, William L. *Flawed Victory: A New Perspective on the Civil War.* New York, NY: Praeger Publishers, 1975.
Barrow, Charles Kelly, J. H. Segars, and R. B. Rosenburg (eds.). *Black Confederates.* 1995. Gretna, LA: Pelican Publishing Co., 2001 ed.
——. *Forgotten Confederates: An Anthology About Black Southerners.* Saint Petersburg, FL: Southern Heritage Press, 1997.
Bartlett, Irving H. *John C. Calhoun: A Biography.* New York, NY: W. W. Norton, 1994.
——. *Wendell Phillips: Brahmin Radical.* Boston, MA: Beacon Press, 1961.
Barton, William E. *The Soul of Abraham Lincoln.* New York, NY: George H. Doran, 1920.
Basler, Roy Prentice (ed.). *Abraham Lincoln: His Speeches and Writings.* 1946. New York, NY: Da Capo Press, 2001 ed.
—— (ed.). *The Collected Works of Abraham Lincoln.* 9 vols. New Brunswick, NJ: Rutgers University Press, 1953.
Bateman, William O. *Political and Constitutional Law of the United States of America.* St. Louis,

MO: G. I. Jones and Co., 1876.
Baxter, Maurice G. *Henry Clay and the American System.* Lexington, KY: University Press of Kentucky, 2004.
Beard, Charles A., and Birl E. Schultz. *Documents on the State-Wide Initiative, Referendum and Recall.* New York, NY: Macmillan, 1912.
Beard, Charles A., and Mary R. Beard. *The Rise of American Civilization.* 1927. New York, NY: MacMillan, 1930 ed.
Beck, Glenn. *Glenn Beck's Common Sense: The Case Against an Out-of-Control Government, Inspired by Thomas Paine.* New York, NY: Threshold, 2009.
Becker, Carl L., and Frederic Duncalf. *Story of Civilization.* 1938. New York, NY: Silver Burdett Co., 1944 ed.
Bede, Saint. *A History of the English Church and People.* (Original work written in 731.) 1955. Harmondsworth, UK: Penguin, 1974 ed.
Bedford, Henry F., and Trevor Colbourn. *The Americans: A Brief History.* 1972. New York, NY: Harcourt Brace Jovanovich, 1980 ed.
Benedict, Michael Les. *The Impeachment and Trial of Andrew Johnson.* New York, NY: W. W. Norton and Co., 1973.
Bennett, Lerone, Jr. *Before the Mayflower: A History of Black America.* 1961. Harmondsworth, UK: Penguin, 1993 ed.
——. *Forced Into Glory: Abraham Lincoln's White Dream.* Chicago, IL: Johnson Publishing Co., 2000.
Benns, F. Lee, and Mary Elisabeth Seldon. *Europe: 1914-1939.* 1949. New York, NY: Appleton-Century-Crofts, 1965 ed.
Benson, Al, Jr., and Walter Donald Kennedy. *Lincoln's Marxists.* Gretna, LA: Pelican Publishing Co., 2011.
Benton, Thomas Hart. *Thirty Years View; or A History of the Working of the American Government for Thirty Years, From 1820 to 1850.* 2 vols. New York, NY: D. Appleton and Co., 1854.
Bergh, Albert Ellery (ed.). *The Writings of Thomas Jefferson.* 20 vols. Washington, D.C.: Thomas Jefferson Memorial Association of the U.S., 1905.
Bernhard, Winfred E. A. (ed.). *Political Parties in American History - Vol. 1: 1789-1828.* New York, NY: G. P. Putnams' Sons, 1973.
Berry, Wendell. *The Unsettling of America: Culture and Agriculture.* San Francisco, CA: Sierra Club Books, 1996.
Berwanger, Eugene H. *The Frontier Against Slavery: Western Anti-Negro Prejudice and the Slavery Extension Controversy.* 1967. Urbana, IL: University of Illinois Press, 1971 ed.
Beschloss, Michael R. *Presidential Courage: Brave Leaders and How They Changed America, 1789-1989.* New York, NY: Simon and Schuster, 2007.
Beveridge, Albert Jeremiah. *Abraham Lincoln: 1809-1858.* 2 vols. Boston, MA: Houghton Mifflin, 1928.
Black, Chauncey F. *Essays and Speeches of Jeremiah S. Black.* New York, NY: D. Appleton and Co., 1886.
Black, Robert W., Col. *Cavalry Raids of the Civil War.* Mechanicsburg, PA: Stackpole, 2004.
Blackerby, Hubert R. *Blacks in Blue and Gray.* New Orleans, LA: Portals Press, 1979.
Blassingame, John W. *The Slave Community: Plantation Life in the Antebellum South.* 1972. New York, NY: Oxford University Press, 1974 ed.
Bledsoe, Albert Taylor. *An Essay on Liberty and Slavery.* Philadelphia, PA: J. B. Lippincott and Co., 1856.
——. *A Theodicy; or a Vindication of the Divine Glory, as Manifested in the Constitution and Government of the Moral World.* New York, NY: Carlton and Porter, 1856.
——. *Is Davis a Traitor; or Was Secession a Constitutional Right Previous to the War of 1861?* Richmond, VA: Hermitage Press, 1907.
Blee, Kathleen M. *Women of the Klan: Racism and Gender in the 1920s.* 1991. Berkeley, CA: University of California Press, 1992 ed.
Blight, David W. *Frederick Douglass' Civil War: Keeping Faith in Jubilee.* 1989. Baton Rouge, LA: Louisiana State University Press, 1991 ed.

Bliss, William Dwight Porter (ed.). *The Encyclopedia of Social Reform.* New York, NY: Funk and Wagnalls, 1897.
Boardman, John, Jasper Griffin, and Oswyn Murray. *The Roman World.* 1986. Oxford, UK: Oxford University Press, 1988 ed.
Boatner, Mark Mayo. *The Civil War Dictionary.* 1959. New York, NY: David McKay Co., 1988 ed.
Bode, Carl, and Malcolm Cowley (eds.). *The Portable Emerson.* 1941. Harmondsworth, UK: Penguin, 1981 ed.
Bone, Robert Gehlmann. *Ancient History.* Ames, IA: Littlefield, Adams and Co., 1955.
Boorstin, Daniel J. *The Discoverers: A History of Man's Search to Know His World and Himself.* 1983. New York, NY: Vintage, 1985 ed.
Boren, Henry C. *The Roman Republic.* Princeton, NJ: D. Van Nostrand Co., 1965.
Bowen, Catherine Drinker. *John Adams and the American Revolution.* 1949. New York, NY: Grosset and Dunlap, 1977 ed.
Bowers, John. *Chickamauga and Chattanooga: The Battles that Doomed the Confederacy.* New York, NY: HarperCollins, 1994.
Bowman, John S. (ed.). *The Civil War Day by Day: An Illustrated Almanac of America's Bloodiest War.* 1989. New York, NY: Dorset Press, 1990 ed.
———. *Encyclopedia of the Civil War* (ed.). 1992. North Dighton, MA: JG Press, 2001 ed.
Bowman, Virginia McDaniel. *Historic Williamson County: Old Homes and Sites.* 1971. Franklin, TN: Territorial Press, 1989 ed.
Bradford, James C. (ed.). *Atlas of American Military History.* New York, NY: Oxford University Press, 2003.
Bradford, Ned (ed.). *Battles and Leaders of the Civil War.* 1-vol. ed. New York, NY: Appleton-Century-Crofts, 1956.
Bradley, Michael R. *Nathan Bedford Forrest's Escort and Staff.* Gretna, LA: Pelican Publishing Co., 2006.
Brady, Cyrus Townsend. *Three Daughters of the Confederacy.* New York, NY: G. W. Dillingham, 1905.
Brady, James S. (ed.). *Ronald Reagan: A Man True to His Word - A Portrait of the 40th President of the United States In His Own Words.* Washington D.C.: National Federation of Republican Women, 1984.
Brandt, Robert S. *Touring the Middle Tennessee Backroads.* 1995. Winston-Salem, NC: John F. Blair, 2005 ed.
Breasted, James Henry. *Ancient Times: A History of the Early World.* 1916. Boston, MA: Ginn and Co., 1944 ed.
———. *The Conquest of Civilization.* New York, NY: Harper and Brothers, 1926.
Brent, Linda. *The Deeper Wrong; or Incidents in the Life of a Slave Girl, Written by Herself.* London, UK: W. Tweedie, 1862.
Brinkley, Alan. *The Unfinished Nation: A Concise History of the American People.* 1993. Boston, MA: McGraw-Hill, 2000 ed.
Brockett, Linus Pierpont. *The Life and Times of Abraham Lincoln, Sixteenth President of the United States.* Philadelphia, PA: Bradley and Co., 1865.
Brodie, Fawn M. *Thomas Jefferson: An Intimate History.* 1974. New York, NY: Bantam, 1981 ed.
Bronowski, J., Bruce Mazlish. *The Western Intellectual Tradition: From Leonardo to Hegel.* 1960. New York, NY: Harper and Row, 1975 ed.
Brooks, Gertrude Zeth. *First Ladies of the White House.* Chicago, IL: Charles Hallberg and Co., 1969.
Brooksher, William R., and David K. Snider. *Glory at a Gallop: Tales of the Confederate Cavalry.* 1993. Gretna, LA: Pelican Publishing Co., 2002 ed.
Browder, Earl. *Lincoln and the Communists.* New York, NY: Workers Library Publishers, Inc., 1936.
Brown, Dee. *Bury My Heart at Wounded Knee: An Indian History of the American West.* 1970. New York, NY: Owl Books, 1991 ed.
Brown, Rita Mae. *High Hearts.* New York, NY: Bantam, 1987.

Brown, William Wells. *The Black Man: His Antecedents, His Genius, and His Achievements*. New York, NY: Thomas Hamilton, 1863.
Browne, Ray B., and Lawrence A. Kreiser, Jr. *The Civil War and Reconstruction*. Westport, CT: Greenwood Publishing, 2003.
Bruce, Philip Alexander. *The Plantation Negro As a Freeman*. New York, NY: G. P. Putnam's Sons, 1889.
Brunner, Borgna (ed.). *The Time Almanac* (1999 ed.). Boston, MA: Information Please, 1998.
Bryan, William Jennings. *The Commoner Condensed*. New York, NY: Abbey Press, 1902.
Buchanan, James. *The Works of James Buchanan*. 12 vols. Philadelphia, PA: J. B. Lippincott Co., 1911.
Buchanan, Patrick J. *A Republic, Not an Empire: Reclaiming America's Destiny*. Washington, D.C.: Regenry, 1999.
Buckingham, James Silk. *The Slave States of America*. 2 vols. London, UK: Fisher, Son, and Co., 1842.
Buckley, Gail. *American Patriots: The Story of Blacks in the Military from the Revolution to Desert Storm*. New York, NY: Random House, 2001.
Bultman, Bethany. *Redneck Heaven: Portrait of a Vanishing Culture*. New York, NY: Bantam, 1996.
Burgess, John William. *Reconstruction and the Constitution: 1866-1876*. New York, NY: Charles Scribner's Sons, 1903.
Burlingame, Michael. *The Inner World of Abraham Lincoln*. Champaign, IL: University of Illinois Press, 1997.
Burns, Andrew Robert. *The Pelican History of Greece*. 1965. Harmondsworth, UK: Penguin, 1968 ed.
Burns, James MacGregor. *The Vineyard of Liberty*. New York, NY: Alfred A. Knopf, 1982.
Burns, James MacGregor, and Jack Walter Peltason. *Government by the People: The Dynamics of American National, State, and Local Government*. 1952. Englewood Cliffs, NJ: Prentice-Hall, 1964 ed.
Burns, James MacGregor, Jack Walter Peltason, Thomas E. Cronin, David B. Magleby, and David M. O'Brien. *Government by the People* (National Version). 1952. Upper Saddle River, NJ: Prentice Hall, 2001-2002 ed.
Burrell, Sidney A. *Handbook of Western Civilization: Beginnings to 1700*. 1965. New York, NY: Wiley and Sons, 1972 ed.
Burton, Robert. *The Anatomy of Melancholy*. 3 vols. 1621. London, UK: George Bell and Sons, 1896 ed.
Bushnell, Horace. *The Census and Slavery, Thanksgiving Discourse, Delivered in the Chapel at Clifton Springs, New York, November 29, 1860*. Hartford, CT: L. E. Hunt, 1860.
Butler, Benjamin Franklin. *Butler's Book (Autobiography and Personal Reminiscences of Major-General Benjamin F. Butler: A Review of His Legal, Political, and Military Career)*. Boston, MA: A. M. Thayer and Co., 1892.
Butler, Lindley S., and Alan D. Watson (eds.). *The North Carolina Experience: An Interpretive and Documentary History*. Chapel Hill, NC: University of North Carolina Press, 1984.
Butler, Trent C. (ed.). *Holman Bible Dictionary*. Nashville, TN: Holman Bible Publishers, 1991.
Cahill, Thomas. *How the Irish Saved Civilization: The Untold Story of Ireland's Heroic Role From the Fall of Rome to the Rise of Medieval Europe*. New York, NY: Doubleday, 1995.
Calvert, Thomas H. *The Federal Statutes Annotated*. 10 vols. Northport, NY: Edward Thompson, 1905.
Cannon, Devereaux D., Jr. *The Flags of the Confederacy: An Illustrated History*. Memphis, TN: St. Luke's Press, 1988.
Cappelluti, Frank J., and Ruth H. Grossman. *The Human Adventure: A History of Our World*. San Francisco, CA: Field Educational Publications, 1970.
Carey, Matthew, Jr. (ed.). *The Democratic Speaker's Hand-Book*. Cincinnati, OH: Miami Print and Publishing Co., 1868.
Carlton, Frank Tracy. *Organized Labor in America*. New York, NY: D. Appleton and Co., 1920.
Carman, Harry J., and Harold C. Syrett. *A History of the American People - Vol. 1: To 1865*. 1952. New York, NY: Alfred A. Knopf, 1958 ed.

Carpenter, Stephen D. *Logic of History: Five Hundred Political Texts, Being Concentrated Extracts of Abolitionism.* Madison, WI: Stephen D. Carpenter, 1864.
Carr, Curtis. *Mormonism: Will It Stand the Test?* 1996. Indianapolis, IN: Dog Ear, 2012 ed.
Carruth, Gorton (ed.). *The Volume Library: A Modern, Authoritative Reference for Home and School Use.* 1917. Nashville, TN: The Southwestern Co., 1988 ed.
Cartmell, Donald. *Civil War 101.* New York, NY: Gramercy, 2001.
Cash, W. J. *The Mind of the South.* 1941. New York, NY: Vintage, 1969 ed.
Catton, Bruce. *The Coming Fury* (Vol. 1). 1961. New York, NY: Washington Square Press, 1967 ed.
———. *Terrible Swift Sword* (Vol. 2). 1963. New York, NY: Pocket Books, 1967 ed.
———. *A Stillness at Appomattox* (Vol. 3). 1953. New York, NY: Pocket Books, 1966 ed.
Celeste, Sister Mary. *The Old World's Gifts to the New.* 1932. Long Prairie, MN: Neumann Press, 1999 ed.
Chambers, Mortimer, Raymond Grew, David Herily, Theodore K. Rabb, and Isser Woloch. *The Western Experience - Vol. 2: the Early Modern Period.* 1974. New York, NY: Alfred A. Knopf, 1987 ed.
Chambers, Robert (ed.). *The Book of Days: A Miscellany of Popular Antiquities in Connection with the Calender.* 2 vols. London, UK: W. & R. Chambers, 1883.
Channing, Steven A. *Confederate Ordeal: The Southern Home Front.* 1984. Morristown, NJ: Time-Life Books, 1989 ed.
Chesnut, Mary. *A Diary From Dixie: As Written by Mary Boykin Chesnut, Wife of James Chesnut, Jr., United States Senator from South Carolina, 1859-1861, and afterward an Aide to Jefferson Davis and a Brigadier-General in the Confederate Army.* (Isabella D. Martin and Myrta Lockett Avary, eds.). New York, NY: D. Appleton and Co., 1905 ed.
———. *Mary Chesnut's Civil War.* 1860-1865 (Woodward, Comer Vann, ed.). New Haven, CT: Yale University Press, 1981 ed.
Childe, Gordon. *What Happened in History.* 1942. Harmondsworth, UK: Penguin, 1964 ed.
Chodes, John. *Destroying the Republic: Jabez Curry and the Re-Education of the Old South.* New York, NY: Algora, 2005.
Christian, George L. *Abraham Lincoln: An Address Delivered Before R. E. Lee Camp, No. 1 Confederate Veterans at Richmond, VA, October 29, 1909.* Richmond, VA: L. H. Jenkins, 1909.
Cimprich, John. *Fort Pillow, a Civil War Massacre, and Public Memory.* Baton Rouge, LA: Louisiana State University Press, 2005.
Cisco, Walter Brian. *States Rights Gist: A South Carolina General of the Civil War.* 1991. Gretna, LA: Pelican Publishing Co., 2008 ed.
———. *War Crimes Against Southern Civilians.* Gretna, LA: Pelican Publishing Co., 2007.
Civil War Book of Lists, The. 1993. Edison, NJ: Castle Books, 2004 ed.
Civil War Society, The. *Civil War Battles: An Illustrated Encyclopedia.* 1997. New York, NY: Gramercy, 1999 ed.
———. *The Civil War Society's Encyclopedia of the Civil War.* New York, NY: Wings Books, 1997.
Clark, Grahame. *From Savagery to Civilization.* New York, NY: Henry Schuman, 1953.
Clark, Kenneth. *Civilization: A Personal View.* New York, NY: Harper and Row, 1969.
Clark, L. Pierce. *Lincoln: A Psycho-Biography.* New York, NY: Charles Scribner's Sons, 1933.
Clarke, James W. *The Lineaments of Wrath: Race, Violent Crime, and American Culture.* 1998. New Brunswick, NJ: Transaction, 2001 ed.
Clough, Shepard B. *The Rise and Fall of Civilization: An Inquiry Into the Relationship Between Economic Development and Civilization.* 1951. New York, NY: Columbia University Press, 1957 ed.
Clough, Shepard B., Nina G. Garsoian, and David L. Hicks. *A History of the Western World: Ancient and Medieval.* Boston, MA: D. C. Heath and Co., 1964.
Cluskey, Michael W. (ed.). *The Political Text-Book, or Encyclopedia.* Philadelphia, PA: Jas. B. Smith, 1859 ed.
Cmiel, Kenneth. *Democratic Eloquence: The Fight Over Popular Speech in Nineteenth-Century America.* Berkeley, CA: University of California Press, 1990.
Coe, Joseph. *The True American.* Concord, NH: I. S. Boyd, 1840.

Coffin, Charles Carleton. *Abraham Lincoln*. New York, NY: Harper and Brothers, 1893.
Coit, Margaret L. *John C. Calhoun: American Portrait*. Boston, MA: Sentry, 1950.
Collier, Christopher, and James Lincoln Collier. *Decision in Philadelphia: The Constitutional Convention of 1787*. 1986. New York, NY: Ballantine, 1987 ed.
Collins, Elizabeth. *Memories of the Southern States*. Taunton, UK: J. Barnicott, 1865.
Collins, John A. (ed.). *The Anti-Slavery Picknick: A Collection of Speeches, Poems, Dialogues and Songs Intended for Use in Schools and Anti-Slavery Meetings*. Boston, MA: H. W. Williams, 1842.
Commager, Henry Steele, and Erik Bruun (eds.). *The Civil War Archive: The History of the Civil War in Documents*. 1950. New York, NY: Black Dog and Leventhal, 1973 ed.
Compton's Encyclopedia. 1922. Chicago, IL: William Benton, 1969 ed.
Conner, Frank. *The South Under Siege, 1830-2000: A History of the Relations Between the North and the South*. Newnan, GA: Collards Publishing Co., 2002.
Conway, Moncure Daniel. *Testimonies Concerning Slavery*. London, UK: Chapman and Hall, 1865.
Cooke, Alistair. *Alistair Cooke's America*. 1973. New York, NY: Alfred A. Knopf, 1984 ed.
Cooke, John Esten. *A Life of General Robert E. Lee*. New York, NY: D. Appleton and Co., 1871.
Cooley, Henry S. *A Study of Slavery in New Jersey*. Baltimore, MD: Johns Hopkins University Press, 1896.
Cooper, William J., Jr. *Jefferson Davis, American*. New York, NY: Vintage, 2000.
——. (ed.). *Jefferson Davis: The Essential Writings*. New York, NY: Random House, 2003.
Cornford, Francis MacDonald. *The Republic of Plato*. 1941. New York, NY: Oxford University Press, 1964 ed.
Cornish, Dudley Taylor. *The Sable Arm: Black Troops in the Union Army, 1861-1865*. 1956. Lawrence, KS: University Press of Kansas, 1987 ed.
Coulter, Ann. *Guilty: Liberal "Victims" and Their Assault on America*. New York, NY: Three Rivers Press, 2009.
Countryman, Edward. *The American Revolution*. 1985. New York, NY: Hill and Wang, 1993 ed.
Cousins, Norman (ed.). *In God We Trust: The Religious Beliefs and Ideas of the American Founding Fathers*. New York, NY: Harper and Brothers, 1958.
Craig, Albert M., William A. Graham, Donald Kagan, Steven Ozment, and Frank M. Turner. *The Heritage of World Civilizations - Vol.1: To 1600*. 1986. New York, NY: Macmillan College Publishing Co., 1994 ed.
Crallé, Richard Kenner. (ed.). *The Works of John C. Calhoun*. 6 vols. New York: NY: D. Appleton and Co., 1853-1888.
Crane Brinton, John B. Christopher, and Robert Lee Wolff. *A History of Civilization - Vol. 1: Prehistory to 1715*. Englewood Cliffs, NJ: Prentice Hall, 1955.
——. *A History of Civilization - Vol. 2: 1715 to the Present*. 1955. Englewood Cliffs, NJ: Prentice Hall, 1962 ed.
Craven, John J. *Prison Life of Jefferson Davis*. New York: NY: Carelton, 1866.
Crawford, Samuel Wylie. *The Genesis of the Civil War: The Story of Sumter, 1860-1861*. New York, NY: Charles L. Webster and Co., 1887.
Crocker, H. W., III. *The Politically Incorrect Guide to the Civil War*. Washington, D.C.: Regnery, 2008.
Cromie, Alice Hamilton. *A Tour Guide to the Civil War: The Complete State-by-State Guide to Battlegrounds, Landmarks, Museums, Relics, and Sites*. 1964. Nashville, TN: Rutledge Hill Press, 1990 ed.
Cromwell, John Wesley. *The Negro in American History: Men and Women Eminent in the Evolution of the American of African Descent*. Washington, D.C.: American Negro Academy, 1914.
Cross, F. L., and F. A. Livingston (eds.). *The Oxford Dictionary of the Christian Church*. 1957. London, UK: Oxford University Press, 1974 ed.
Crutchfield, James A. *Franklin: A Photographic Recollection*. 2 vols. Franklin, TN: Canaday Enterprises, 1996.

Crutchfield, James A., and Robert Holladay. *Franklin: Tennessee's Handsomest Town.* Franklin, TN: Hillsboro Press, 1999.
Cummins, Joseph. *Anything For a Vote: Dirty Tricks, Cheap Shots, and October Surprises in U.S. Presidential Campaigns.* Philadelphia, PA: Quirk, 2007.
Current, Richard N. *The Lincoln Nobody Knows.* 1958. New York, NY: Hill and Wang, 1963 ed.
———. (ed.) *The Confederacy (Information Now Encyclopedia).* 1993. New York, NY: Macmillan, 1998 ed.
Curry, Leonard P. *Blueprint for Modern America: Nonmilitary Legislation of the First Civil War Congress.* Nashville, TN: Vanderbilt University Press, 1968.
Curti, Merle, Willard Thorpe, and Carlos Baker (eds.). *American Issues: The Social Record.* 1941. Chicago, IL: J. B. Lippincott, 1960 ed.
Curtin, Philip D. *The Atlantic Slave Trade: A Census.* Madison, WI: The University of Wisconsin Press, 1969.
———. *The Rise and Fall of the Plantation Complex: Essays in Atlantic History.* 1990. Cambridge, UK: Cambridge University Press, 1999 ed.
Curtis, George Ticknor. *Life of James Buchanan: Fifteenth President of the United States.* 2 vols. New York, NY: Harper and Brothers, 1883.
Curtis, William Eleroy. *Abraham Lincoln.* Philadelphia, PA: J. B. Lippincott Co., 1902.
Cushman, Horatio Bardwell. *History of the Choctaw, Chickasaw and Natchez Indians.* Greenville, TX: Headlight Printing House, 1899.
Custer, George Armstrong. *Wild Life on the Plains and Horrors of Indian Warfare.* St. Louis, MO: Excelsior Publishing, 1891.
Dabney, Robert Lewis. *A Defense of Virginia and the South.* Dahlonega, GA: Confederate Reprint Co., 1999.
Daniel, John M. *The Richmond Examiner During the War.* New York, NY: John M. Daniel, 1868.
Daniel, John W. *Life and Reminiscences of Jefferson Davis by Distinguished Men of His Time.* Baltimore, MD: R. H. Woodward, and Co., 1890.
Darwin, Charles. *On the Origin of Species By Means of Natural Selection.* London, UK: John Murray, 1866.
Daugherty, James. *Abraham Lincoln.* 1943. New York, NY: Scholastic Book Services, 1966 ed.
Davidson, Basil. *The African Slave Trade.* 1961. Boston, MA: Back Bay Books, 1980 ed.
———. *The Black Man's Burden: Africa and the Curse of the Nation-State.* New York, NY: Times Books, 1992.
Davis, David Brion. *The Problem of Slavery in Western Culture.* 1966. Ithaca, NY: Cornell University Press, 1969 ed.
Davis, Jefferson. *The Rise and Fall of the Confederate Government.* 2 vols. New York, NY: D. Appleton and Co., 1881.
———. *A Short History of the Confederate States of America.* New York, NY: Belford, 1890.
Davis, Kenneth C. *Don't Know Much About the Civil War: Everything You Need to Know About America's Greatest Conflict But Never Learned.* 1996. New York, NY: HarperCollins, 1997 ed.
Davis, Michael. *The Image of Lincoln in the South.* Knoxville, TN: University of Tennessee Press, 1971.
Davis, Varina. Jefferson Davis: *Ex-President of the Confederate States of America - A Memoir by His Wife.* 2 vols. New York, NY: Belford Co., 1890.
Davis, William C. *Jefferson Davis: The Man and His Hour.* New York, NY: HarperCollins, 1991.
———. *An Honorable Defeat: The Last Days of the Confederate Government.* New York, NY: Harcourt, 2001.
———. *Look Away: A History of the Confederate States of America.* 2002. New York, NY: Free Press, 2003 ed.
Davenport, Robert R. *Roots of the Rich and Famous: Real Cases of Unlikely Lineage.* Dallas, TX: Taylor Publishing Co., 1998.
Dawood, N. J. (trans.). *The Koran.* 1956. New York, NY: Penguin, 1990 ed.
Dawson, Sarah Morgan. *A Confederate Girl's Diary.* London, UK: William Heinemann, 1913.
Dean, Henry Clay. *Crimes of the Civil War, and Curse of the Funding System.* Baltimore, MD:

William T. Smithson, 1869.
Dean, Vera Micheles. *The Nature of the Non-Western World*. 1957. New York, NY: Mentor, 1962 ed.
De Angelis, Gina. *It Happened in Washington, D.C.* Guilford, CT: Globe Pequot Press, 2004.
DeCaro, Louis A., Jr. *Fire From the Midst of You: A Religious Life of John Brown*. New York, NY: New York University Press, 2002.
Decker, Ed, and Dave Hunt. *The God Makers*. Eugene, OR: Harvest House, 1984.
Decker, Ed, and Caryl Matrisciana. *The God Makers II*. Eugene, OR: Harvest House, 1993.
Deems, Edward Mark. *Holy-Days and Holidays: A Treasury of Historical Material, Sermons in Full and Brief, Suggestive Thoughts, and Poetry*. New York, NY: Funk and Wagnalls, 1902.
De Forest, John William. *A Volunteer's Adventures: A Union Captain's Record of the Civil War*. 1946. North Haven, CT: Archon, 1970 ed.
DeGregorio, William A. *The Complete Book of U.S. Presidents*. 1984. New York, NY: Barricade, 1993 ed.
Delbanco, Andrew. *The Portable Abraham Lincoln*. New York, NY: Penguin, 1992.
Deloria, Vine, Jr. *Custer Died For Your Sins: An Indian Manifesto*. 1969. New York, NY: Avon, 1973 ed.
Denney, Robert E. *The Civil War Years: A Day-by-Day Chronicle of the Life of a Nation*. 1992. New York, NY: Sterling Publishing, 1994 ed.
Denson, John V. (ed.). *Reassessing the Presidency: The Rise of the Executive State and the Decline of Freedom*. Auburn, AL: Mises Institute, 2001.
DeRosa, Marshall L. *The Confederate Constitution of 1861: An Inquiry into American Constitutionalism*. Columbia, MO: University of Missouri Press, 1991.
De Rosa, Peter. *Vicars of Christ: The Dark Side of the Papacy*. New York, NY: Crown, 1988.
Desty, Robert. *The Constitution of the United States*. San Francisco, CA: Sumner Whitney and Co., 1881.
Diamond, Jared. *Guns, Germs, and Steel: The Fate of Human Societies*. 1997. New York, NY: W. W. Norton, 1999 ed.
Dicey, Edward. *Six Months in the Federal States*. 2 vols. London, UK: Macmillan and Co., 1863.
DiLorenzo, Thomas J. "The Great Centralizer: Abraham Lincoln and the War Between the States." *The Independent Review*, Vol. 3, No. 2, Fall 1998, pp. 243-271.
——. *The Real Lincoln: A New Look at Abraham Lincoln, His Agenda, and an Unnecessary War*. Three Rivers, MI: Three Rivers Press, 2003.
——. *Lincoln Unmasked: What You're Not Supposed to Know About Dishonest Abe*. New York, NY: Crown Forum, 2006.
——. *Hamilton's Curse: How Jefferson's Archenemy Betrayed the American Revolution—and What It Means for America Today*. New York, NY: Crown Forum, 2008.
Dimont, Max I. *Jews, God and History*. New York, NY: Signet, 1962.
Dinkins, James. *1861 to 1865: Personal Recollections and Experiences in the Confederate Army, by an "Old Johnnie"*. Cincinnati, OH: Robert Clarke, 1897.
Dinnerstein, Leonard, and Kenneth T. Jackson. *American Vistas: 1877 to the Present*. New York, NY: Oxford University Press, 1979.
Doddridge, Joseph. *Notes on the Settlement and Indian Wars of the Western Parts of Virginia and Pennsylvania, From 1763 to 1783, Inclusive*. Albany, NY: Joel Munsell, 1876.
Donald, David Herbert. *Lincoln Reconsidered: Essays on the Civil War Era*. 1947. New York, NY: Vintage Press, 1989 ed.
——. (ed.). *Why the North Won the Civil War*. 1960. New York, NY: Collier, 1962 ed.
——. *Lincoln*. New York, NY: Simon and Schuster, 1995.
Dormon, James H., and Robert R. Jones. *The Afro-American Experience: A Cultural History Through Emancipation*. New York, NY: John Wiley and Sons, 1974.
Dorward, David. *Scottish Surnames: A Guide to the Family Names of Scotland*. Glasgow, Scotland: HarperCollins, 1995.
Doubleday's Encyclopedia. 1931. New York, NY: Doubleday, Doran and Co., 1939 ed.
Douglas, Henry Kyd. *I Rode With Stonewall: The War Experiences of the Youngest Member of Jackson's Staff*. 1940. Chapel Hill, NC: University of North Carolina Press, 1968 ed.

Douglass, Frederick. *Narrative of the Life of Frederick Douglass: An American Slave.* 1845. New York, NY: Signet, 1997 ed.
——. *The Life and Times of Frederick Douglass, From 1817 to 1882.* London, UK: Christian Age Office, 1882.
Dowley, Tim (ed.). *The History of Christianity.* 1977. Oxford, UK: Lion, 1990 ed.
Drescher, Seymour, and Stanley L. Engerman (eds.). *A Historical Guide to World Slavery.* New York, NY: Oxford University Press, 1998.
Du Bois, William Edward Burghardt. *Darkwater: Voices From Within the Veil.* New York, NY: Harcourt, Brace and Howe, 1920.
DuBose, John Witherspoon. *General Joseph Wheeler and the Army of Tennessee.* New York, NY: Neale Publishing Co., 1912.
Duff, Mountstuart E. Grant. *Notes From a Diary, 1851-1872.* 2 vols. London, UK: John Murray, 1897.
Duke, Basil W. *Reminiscences of General Basil W. Duke, C.S.A.* New York, NY: Doubleday, Page and Co., 1911.
Dumond, Dwight Lowell. *Antislavery Origins of the Civil War in the United States.* 1939. Ann Arbor, MI: University of Michigan Press, 1960 ed.
Dunbar, Rowland (ed.). *Jefferson Davis, Constitutionalist: His Letters, Papers, and Speeches.* 10 vols. Jackson, MS: Mississippi Department of Archives and History, 1923.
Dunner, Joseph (ed.). *Handbook of World History: Concepts and Issues.* New York, NY: Philosophical Library, 1967.
Durant, Will and Ariel. *The Age of Reason Begins: A History of European Civilization in the Period of Shakespeare, Bacon, Montaigne, Rembrandt, Galileo, and Descartes, 1558-1648.* New York, NY: Simon and Schuster, 1961.
Durden, Robert F. *The Gray and the Black: The Confederate Debate on Emancipation.* Baton Rouge, LA: Louisiana State University Press, 1972.
Early, Jubal A. *A Memoir of the Last Year of the War for Independence in the Confederate States of America.* Lynchburg, VA: Charles W. Button, 1867.
Easton, Stewart C. *The Heritage of the Past: From the Earliest Times to the Close of the Middle Ages.* 1955. New York, NY: Rinehart and Co., 1957 ed.
Eaton, Clement. *A History of the Southern Confederacy.* 1945. New York, NY: Free Press, 1966 ed.
——. *Jefferson Davis.* New York, NY: Free Press, 1977.
Eaton, John, and Ethel Osgood Mason. *Grant, Lincoln and the Freedmen: Reminiscences of the Civil War, With Special Reference to the Work of the Contrabands and Freedmen of the Mississippi Valley.* New York, NY: Longmans, Green, and Co., 1907.
Edmonds, Franklin Spencer. *Ulysses S. Grant.* Philadelphia, PA: George W. Jacobs and Co., 1915.
Elliot, Jonathan. *The Debates in the Several State Conventions on the Adoption of the Federal Constitution, As Recommended by the General Convention at Philadelphia in 1787.* 5 vols. Philadelphia, PA: J. B. Lippincott, 1891.
Elliott, E. N. *Cotton is King, and Pro-Slavery Arguments: Comprising the Writings of Hammond, Harper, Christy, Stringfellow, Hodge, Bledsoe, and Cartwright, on this Important Subject.* Augusta, GA: Pritchard, Abbott and Loomis, 1860.
Ellis, Joseph J. *American Sphinx: The Character of Thomas Jefferson.* 1996. New York, NY: Vintage, 1998 ed.
——. *Founding Brothers: The Revolutionary Generation.* 2000. New York, NY: Vintage, 2002 ed.
Eltis, David. *The Rise of African Slavery in the Americas.* Cambridge, UK: Cambridge University Press, 2000.
Emerson, Bettie Alder Calhoun. *Historic Southern Monuments: Representative Memorials of the Heroic Dead of the Southern Confederacy.* New York, NY: Neale Publishing Co., 1911.
Emerson, Ralph Waldo. *The Complete Works of Ralph Waldo Emerson.* 12 vols. 1878. Boston, MA: Houghton, Mifflin and Co., 1904 ed.
——. *Journals of Ralph Waldo Emerson.* 10 vols. Edward Waldo Emerson and Waldo Emerson Forbes, eds. Boston, MA: Houghton, Mifflin and Co., 1910.

———. *The Journals and Miscellaneous Notebooks of Ralph Waldo Emerson*. 16 vols. Cambridge, MA: Belknap Press, 1975.
Emison, John Avery. *Lincoln Über Alles: Dictatorship Comes to America*. Gretna, LA: Pelican Publishing Co., 2009.
Encyclopedia Britannica: A New Survey of Universal Knowledge. 1768. Chicago, IL/London, UK: Encyclopedia Britannica, 1955 ed.
Escott, Paul D. (ed.). *North Carolinians in the Era of the Civil War and Reconstruction*. Chapel Hill, NC: University of North Carolina Press, 2008.
Essah, Patience. *A House Divided: Slavery and Emancipation in Delaware, 1638-1865*. Charlottesville, VA: University Press of Virginia, 1996.
Evans, Clement Anselm (ed.). *Confederate Military History: A Library of Confederate States History, in Twelve Volumes, Written By Distinguished Men of the South*. 12 vols. Atlanta, GA: Confederate Publishing Co., 1899.
Evans, David. *Sherman's Horsemen: Union Cavalry Operations in the Atlanta Campaign*. Bloomington, IN: Indiana University Press, 1996.
Evans, Eli N. *Judah P. Benjamin: The Jewish Confederate*. 1988. New York, NY: Free Press, 1989 ed.
Evans, Lawrence B. (ed.). *Writings of George Washington*. New York, NY: G. P. Putnam's Sons, 1908.
Faragher, John Mack. *Sugar Creek: Life on the Illinois Prairie*. New Haven, CT: Yale University Press, 1986.
Farrar, Victor John. *The Annexation of Russian America to the United States*. Washington D.C.: W. F. Roberts, 1937.
Farrow, Anne, Joel Lang, and Jennifer Frank. *Complicity: How the North Promoted, Prolonged, and Profited From Slavery*. New York, NY: Ballantine, 2005.
Faulkner, Harold Underwood. *American Political and Social History*. 1937. New York, NY: Appleton-Century-Crofts, 1948 ed.
Faulkner, William. *The Unvanquished*. 1934. New York, NY: Vintage, 1966 ed.
Faust, Patricia L. (ed.). *Historical Times Illustrated Encyclopedia of the Civil War*. New York, NY: Harper and Row, 1986.
Fay, Edwin Hedge. *This Infernal War: The Confederate Letters of Edwin H. Fay*. Austin, TX: University of Texas Press, 1958.
Fehrenbacher, Don E. (ed.). *Abraham Lincoln: A Documentary Portrait Through His Speeches and Writings*. New York, NY: Signet, 1964.
———. *Lincoln in Text and Context: Collected Essays*. Stanford, CA: Stanford University press, 1987.
———. (ed.) *Abraham Lincoln: Speeches and Writings, 1859-1865*. New York, NY: Library of America, 1989.
———. *The Slaveholding Republic: An Account of the United States Government's Relations to Slavery*. New York, NY: Oxford University Press, 2002.
Fehrenbacher, Don E., and Virginia Fehrenbacher (eds). *Recollected Works of Abraham Lincoln*. Stanford, CA: Stanford University Press, 1996.
Ferguson, Wallace K., and Geoffrey Bruun. *A Survey of European Civilization - Part 1: To 1660*. 1936. Boston, MA: Houghton Mifflin Co., 1947 ed.
———. *A Survey of European Civilization - Part 2: Since 1660*. 1936. Boston, MA: Houghton Mifflin Co., 1947 ed.
Ferris, Marcie Cohen, and Mark I. Greenberg (eds.). *Jewish Roots in Southern Soil: A New History*. Waltham, MA: Brandeis University Press, 2006.
Fields, Annie (ed.) *Life and Letters of Harriet Beecher Stowe*. Cambridge, MA: Riverside Press, 1897.
Findlay, Bruce, and Esther Findlay. *Your Rugged Constitution: How America's House of Freedom is Planned and Built*. 1950. Stanford, CA: Stanford University Press, 1951 ed.
Finkelman, Paul. *Dred Scott v. Sanford: A Brief History With Documents*. Boston, MA: Bedford Books, 1997.
Fite, Emerson David. *Social and Industrial Conditions in the North During the Civil War*. New York, NY: Macmillan, 1910.

——. *The Presidential Election of 1860*. New York, NY: MacMillan, 1911.
Fleming, Walter Lynwood. *Civil War and Reconstruction in Alabama*. New York, NY: Macmillan, 1905.
Flood, Charles Bracelen. *1864: Lincoln At the Gates of History*. New York, NY: Simon and Schuster, 2009.
Fogel, Robert William. *Without Consent or Contract: The Rise and Fall of American Slavery*. New York, NY: W. W. Norton, 1989.
Fogel, Robert William, and Stanley L. Engerman. *Time On the Cross: The Economics of American Negro Slavery*. Boston, MA: Little, Brown, and Co., 1974.
Foley, John P. (ed.). *The Jeffersonian Cyclopedia*. New York, NY: Funk and Wagnalls, 1900.
Foner, Eric. *Free Soil, Free Labor, Free Men: The Ideology of the Republican Party Before the Civil War*. New York, NY: Oxford University Press, 1970.
——. *Reconstruction: America's Unfinished Revolution, 1863-1877*. 1988. New York, NY: Harper and Row, 1989 ed.
Foner, Philip S., and Robert James Branham (eds.). *Lift Every Voice: African American Oratory, 1787-1900*. Tuscaloosa, AL: University of Alabama Press, 1998.
Foote, Shelby. *The Civil War: A Narrative, Fort Sumter to Perryville, Vol. 1*. 1958. New York, NY: Vintage, 1986 ed.
——. *The Civil War: A Narrative, Fredericksburg to Meridian, Vol. 2*. 1963. New York, NY: Vintage, 1986 ed.
——. *The Civil War: A Narrative, Red River to Appomattox, Vol. 3*. 1974. New York, NY: Vintage, 1986 ed.
Ford, Paul Leicester (ed.). *The Works of Thomas Jefferson*. 12 vols. New York, NY: G. P. Putnam's Sons, 1904.
Ford, Worthington Chauncey (ed.). *A Cycle of Adams Letters*. 2 vols. Boston, MA: Houghton Mifflin, 1920.
Forman, S. E. *The Life and Writings of Thomas Jefferson*. Indianapolis, IN: Bowen-Merrill, 1900.
Förster, Stig, and Jörg Nagler (eds.). *On the Road to Total War: The American Civil War and the German Wars of Unification, 1861-1871*. 1997. Cambridge, UK: Cambridge University Press, 2002 ed.
Foster, John W. *A Century of American Diplomacy*. Boston, MA: Houghton, Mifflin and Co., 1901.
Fowler, John D. *The Confederate Experience Reader: Selected Documents and Essays*. New York, NY: Routledge, 2007.
Fowler, William Chauncey. *The Sectional Controversy; or Passages in the Political History of the United States, Including the Causes of the War Between the Sections*. New York, NY: Charles Scribner, 1864.
Fox-Genovese, Elizabeth. *Within the Plantation Household: Black and White Women of the Old South (Gender and American Culture)*. Chapel Hill, NC: University of North Carolina Press, 1988.
Fox, Gustavus Vasa. *Confidential Correspondence of Gustavus Vasa Fox, Assistant Secretary of the Navy, 1861-1865* (Vol. 1). 1918. New York, NY: Naval History Society, 1920 ed.
Franklin, Benjamin. *The Life and Writings of Benjamin Franklin*. 2 vols. Philadelphia, PA: McCarty and Davis, 1834.
——. *The Complete Works of Benjamin Franklin*. 10 vols. New York, NY: G. P. Putnam's Sons, 1887.
Franklin, John Hope. *Reconstruction After the Civil War*. Chicago, IL: University of Chicago Press, 1961.
Fredrickson, George M. *The Black Image in the White Mind: The Debate on Afro-American Character and Destiny, 1817-1914*. New York, NY: Harper and Row, 1971.
Fremantle, Arthur James. *Three Months in the Southern States, April-June, 1863*. New York, NY: John Bradburn, 1864.
Friedman, Saul S. *Jews and the American Slave Trade*. New Brunswick, NJ: Transaction, 2000.
Frost, Frank J. *Greek Society*. 1971. Lexington, MA: D. C. Heath, 1980 ed.
Furguson, Ernest B. *Freedom Rising: Washington in the Civil War*. 2004. New York, NY: Vintage,

2005 ed.
Furnas, J. C. *The Americans: A Social History of the United States, 1587-1914*. New York, NY: G. P. Putnam's Sons, 1969.
Galenson, David W. *White Servitude in Colonial America*. New York, NY: Cambridge University Press, 1981.
Gamoran, Mamie G. *The New Jewish History: From the Discovery of America to Our Own Day*. 1957. New York, NY: The Union of American Hebrew Congregations, 1959 ed.
Garland, Hugh A. *The Life of John Randolph of Roanoke*. New York, NY: D. Appleton and Co., 1874.
Garraty, John A. (ed.). *Historical Viewpoints: Notable Articles From American Heritage - Vol. 1: To 1877*. 1970. New York, NY: Harper and Row, 1979 ed.
Garraty, John A., and Robert A. McCaughey. *A Short History of the American Nation*. 1966. New York, NY: HarperCollins, 1989 ed.
Garrison, Webb B. *Civil War Trivia and Fact Book*. Nashville, TN: Rutledge Hill Press, 1992.
———. *The Lincoln No One Knows: The Mysterious Man Who Ran the Civil War*. Nashville, TN: Rutledge Hill Press, 1993.
———. *Civil War Curiosities: Strange Stories, Oddities, Events, and Coincidences*. Nashville, TN: Rutledge Hill Press, 1994.
———. *The Amazing Civil War*. Nashville, TN: Rutledge Hill Press, 1998.
Garrison, Wendell Phillips, and Francis Jackson Garrison. *William Lloyd Garrison, 1805-1879*. 4 vols. New York, NY: Century Co., 1889.
Garrison, William Lloyd. *Thoughts on African Colonization*. Boston, MA: Garrison and Knapp, 1832.
Gates, Henry Louis, Jr. (ed.) *The Classic Slave Narratives*. New York, NY: Mentor, 1987.
Genovese, Eugene D. *Roll, Jordan, Roll: The World the Slaves Made*. New York, NY: Pantheon, 1974.
Gerster, Patrick, and Nicholas Cords (eds.). *Myth and Southern History*. 2 vols. 1974. Champaign, IL: University of Illinois Press, 1989 ed.
Gilmore, James Roberts. *Personal Recollections of Abraham Lincoln and the Civil War*. Boston, MA: L. C. Page and Co., 1898.
Golay, Michael. *A Ruined Land: The End of the Civil War*. New York, NY: John Wiley and Sons, 1999.
Goldschmidt, Arthur, Jr. *A Concise History of the Middle East*. 1979. Boulder, CO: Westview Press, 1988 ed.
Gordon, Armistead Churchill. *Figures From American History: Jefferson Davis*. New York, NY: Charles Scribner's Sons, 1918.
Gordon, Irving L. *World History: Review Text*. 1965. New York, NY: Amsco School Publications, 1969 ed.
Goubert, Pierre. *Louis XIV and Twenty Million Frenchman*. 1966. New York, NY: Vintage, 1972 ed.
Gower, Herschel, and Jack Allen (eds.). *Pen and Sword: The Life and Journals of Randal W. McGavock*. Nashville, TN: Tennessee Historical Commission, 1959.
Gragg, Rod. *The Illustrated Confederate Reader: Extraordinary Eyewitness Accounts by the Civil War's Southern Soldiers and Civilians*. New York, NY: Gramercy Books, 1989.
Graham, John Remington. *A Constitutional History of Secession*. Gretna, LA: Pelican Publishing Co., 2003.
———. *Blood Money: The Civil War and the Federal Reserve*. Gretna, LA: Pelican Publishing Co., 2006.
Grant, Arthur James. *Greece in the Age of Pericles*. London, UK: John Murray, 1893.
Grant, Michael. *The World of Rome*. 1960. New York, NY: Mentor, 1964 ed.
Grant, Ulysses Simpson. *Personal Memoirs of U. S. Grant*. 2 vols. 1885-1886. New York, NY: Charles L. Webster and Co., 1886.
Gray, Robert, Rev. (compiler). *The McGavock Family: A Genealogical History of James McGavock and His Descendants, from 1760 to 1903*. Richmond, VA: W. E. Jones, 1903.
Gray, Thomas R. *The Confessions of Nat Turner: The Leader of the Late Insurrection in Southampton,*

Virginia. Richmond, VA: Thomas R. Gray, 1831.
Greeley, Horace (ed.). *The Writings of Cassius Marcellus Clay*. New York, NY: Harper and Brothers, 1848.
———. *A History of the Struggle for Slavery Extension or Restriction in the United States From the Declaration of Independence to the Present Day*. New York, NY: Dix, Edwards and Co., 1856.
———. *The American Conflict: A History of the Great Rebellion in the United States, 1861-1865*. 2 vols. Hartford, CT: O. D. Case and Co., 1867.
Green, Constance McLaughlin. *Eli Whitney and the Birth of American Technology*. Boston, MA: Little, Brown, and Co., 1956.
———. *Washington: A History of the Capital, 1800-1950*. 1962. Princeton, NJ: Princeton University Press, 1976 ed.
Green, John Richard. *A Short History of the English People*. 2 vols. London, UK: Macmillan and Co., 1892.
Greenberg, Martin H., and Charles G. Waugh (eds.). *The Price of Freedom: Slavery and the Civil War - Vol. 1: The Demise of Slavery*. Nashville, TN: Cumberland House, 2000.
Greene, Lorenzo Johnston. *The Negro in Colonial New England, 1620-1776*. New York, NY: Columbia University Press, 1942.
Greenhow, Rose O'Neal. *My Imprisonment and the First Year of Abolition Rule at Washington*. London, UK: Richard Bentley, 1863.
Greer, Thomas H. *A Brief History of Western Man: To 1650*. New York, NY: Harcourt Brace Jovanovich, 1972.
Grimsley, Mark. *The Hard Hand of War: Union Military Policy Toward Southern Civilians, 1861-1865*. 1995. Cambridge, UK: Cambridge University Press, 1997 ed.
Grissom, Michael Andrew. *Southern By the Grace of God*. 1988. Gretna, LA: Pelican Publishing Co., 1995 ed.
Groom, Winston. *Shrouds of Glory - From Atlanta to Nashville: The Last Great Campaign of the Civil War*. New York, NY: Grove Press, 1995.
Guelzo, Allen C. *Abraham Lincoln As a Man of Ideas*. Carbondale, IL: Southern Illinois University Press, 2009.
Gwatkin, H. M., and J. P. Whitney (eds.). *The Cambridge Medieval History - Vol. 2: The Rise of the Saracens and the Foundation of the Western Empire*. New York, NY: Macmillan, 1913.
Hacker, Louis Morton. *The Shaping of the American Tradition*. New York, NY: Columbia University Press, 1947.
Haggard, Dixie Ray (ed.). *African Americans in the Nineteenth Century: People and Perspectives*. Santa Barbara, CA: ABC-Clio, 2010.
Haines, C. Grove, and Warren B. Walsh. *The Development of Western Civilization*. 2 vols. 1941. New York, NY: Henry Holt and Co., 1947 ed.
Hale, John. *The Civilization of Europe in the Renaissance*. New York, NY: Atheneum, 1994.
Hall, B. C., and C. T. Wood. *The South: A Two-step Odyssey on the Backroads of the Enchanted Land*. New York, NY: Touchstone, 1996.
Hall, Kermit L. (ed.). *The Oxford Companion to the Supreme Court of the United States*. New York, NY: Oxford University Press, 1992.
Hall, Walter Phelps, Robert Greenhalgh Albion, and Jennie Barnes Pope. *A History of England and the Empire-Commonwealth*. 1937. Waltham, MA: Blaisdell, 1965 ed.
Haller, William. *The Rise of Puritanism*. 1938. New York, NY: Harper Torchbooks, 1957 ed.
Hamblin, Ken. *Pick a Better Country: An Unassuming Colored Guy Speaks His Mind About America*. New York, NY: Touchstone, 1997.
Hamilton, Alexander, James Madison, and John Jay. *The Federalist: A Collection of Essays by Alexander Hamilton, James Madison, and John Jay*. New York, NY: The Co-operative Publication Society, 1901.
Hamilton, Neil A. *Rebels and Renegades: A Chronology of Social and Political Dissent in the United States*. New York, NY: Routledge, 2002.
Handlin, Oscar (ed.). *Readings in American History - Vol. 1: From Settlement to Reconstruction*. 1957. New York, NY: Alfred A. Knopf, 1970 ed.

Hannity, Sean. *Let Freedom Ring: Winning the War of Liberty Over Liberalism.* New York, NY: HarperCollins, 2002.
Hansen, Harry. *The Civil War: A History.* 1961. Harmondsworth, UK: Mentor, 1991 ed.
Harding, Samuel Bannister. *The Contest Over the Ratification of the Federal Constitution in the State of Massachusetts.* New York, NY: Longmans, Green, and Co., 1896.
Harper, William, James Henry Hammond, William Gilmore Simms, and Thomas Roderick Dew. *The Pro-Slavery Argument, As Maintained by the Most Distinguished Writers of the Southern States.* Charleston, SC: Walker, Richards and Co., 1852.
Harrell, David Edwin, Jr., Edwin S. Gaustad, John B. Boles, Sally Foreman Griffith, Randall M. Miller, and Randall B. Woods. *Unto a Good Land: A History of the American People.* Grand Rapids, MI: William B. Eerdmans, 2005.
Harris, Joel Chandler. *Stories of Georgia.* New York, NY: American Book Co., 1896.
Harris, Norman Dwight. *The History of Negro Servitude in Illinois.* Chicago, IL: A. C. McClurg and Co., 1904.
Harrison, Peleg D. *The Stars and Stripes and Other American Flags.* 1906. Boston, MA: Little, Brown, and Co., 1908 ed.
Hartman, Gertrude, and Lucy S. Saunders. *Builders of the Old World.* 1946. Boston, MA: Little, Brown and Co., 1959 ed.
Hartzell, Josiah. *The Genesis of the Republican Party.* Canton, OH: n.p., 1890.
Harwell, Richard B. (ed.). *The Confederate Reader: How the South Saw the War.* 1957. Mineola, NY: Dover, 1989 ed.
Hattaway, Herman, and Archer Jones. *How the North Won: A Military History of the Civil War.* 1983. Champaign, IL: University of Illinois Press, 1991 ed.
Hawthorne, Julian (ed.). *Orations of American Orators.* 2 vols. New York, NY: Colonial Press, 1900.
Hawthorne, Julian, James Schouler, and Elisha Benjamin Andrews. *United States, From the Discovery of the North American Continent Up to the Present Time.* 9 vols. New York, NY: Co-operative Publication Society, 1894.
Hayes, Carlton J. H., Marshall Whited Baldwin, and Charles Woolsey Cole. *History of Europe.* 1949. New York, NY: Macmillan Co., 1950 ed.
Haygood, Atticus G. *Our Brother in Black: His Freedom and His Future.* Nashville, TN: M. E. Church, 1896.
Hedrick, Joan D. (ed.). *The Oxford Harriet Beecher Stowe Reader.* New York, NY: Oxford University Press, 1999.
Heer, Friedrich. *The Medieval World - Europe: 1100-1350.* 1961. New York, NY: Mentor, 1962 ed.
Heilbroner, Robert L. *The Worldly Philosophers.* 1965. Lincoln, NE: Cliffs Notes, 1974 ed.
Helper, Hinton Rowan. *The Impending Crisis of the South: How to Meet It.* New York, NY: A. B. Burdick, 1860.
———. *Compendium of the Impending Crisis of the South.* New York, NY: A. B. Burdick, 1860.
———. *Nojoque: A Question for a Continent.* New York, NY: George W. Carleton, 1867.
———. *The Negroes in Negroland: The Negroes in America; and Negroes Generally.* New York, NY: George W. Carlton, 1868.
———. *Oddments of Andean Diplomacy and Other Oddments.* St. Louis, MO: W. S. Bryan, 1879.
Hendelson, William H. (ed.). *Funk and Wagnalls New Encyclopedia.* New York, NY: Funk and Wagnalls, 1973 ed.
Henderson, George Francis Robert. *Stonewall Jackson and the American Civil War.* 2 vols. London, UK: Longmans, Green, and Co., 1919.
Henry, Robert Selph (ed.). *The Story of the Confederacy.* 1931. New York, NY: Konecky and Konecky, 1999 ed.
———. *As They Saw Forrest: Some Recollections and Comments of Contemporaries.* 1956. Wilmington, NC: Broadfoot Publishing Co., 1991 ed.
———. *First with the Most: Forrest.* New York, NY: Konecky and Konecky, 1992.
Henson, Josiah. *Father Henson's Story of His Own Life.* Boston, MA: John P. Jewett and Co., 1858.

Herm, Gerhard. *The Celts: The People Who Came Out of the Darkness.* New York, NY: St. Martin's Press, 1975.
Herndon, William H., and Jesse W. Weik. *Abraham Lincoln: The True Story of a Great Life.* 2 vols. New York, NY: D. Appleton and Co., 1892.
Herring, Hubert. *A History of Latin America: From the Beginnings to the Present.* 1955. New York, NY: Alfred A. Knopf, 1968 ed.
Herskovits, Melville J. *The Myth of the Negro Past.* 1941. Boston, MA: Beacon Press, 1969 ed.
Hertz, Emanuel. *Abraham Lincoln: A New Portrait.* 2 Vols. New York, NY: H. Liveright, 1931.
——. *The Hidden Lincoln.* New York, NY: Blue Ribbon Works, 1940.
Hervey, Anthony. *Why I Wave the Confederate Flag, Written By a Black Man: The End of Niggerism and the Welfare State.* Oxford, UK: Trafford Publishing, 2006.
Hesseltine, William B. *Lincoln and the War Governors.* New York, NY: Alfred A. Knopf, 1948.
Hey, David. *The Oxford Guide to Family History.* Oxford, UK: Oxford University Press, 1993.
Hickey, William. *The Constitution of the United States.* Philadelphia, PA: T. K. and P. G. Collins, 1853.
Highsmith, Carol M. and Ted Landphair. *Civil War Battlefields and Landmarks: A Photographic Tour.* New York, NY: Random House, 2003.
Hildreth, Richard. *The White Slave: Another Picture of Slave Life in America.* Boston, MA: Adamant Media Corp., 2001.
Hinkle, Don. *Embattled Banner: A Reasonable Defense of the Confederate Battle Flag.* Paducah, KY: Turner Publishing Co., 1997.
Hinnells, John R. *Dictionary of Religions: From Abraham to Zoroaster.* 1984. Harmondsworth, UK: Penguin, 1986.
Hitler, Adolf. *Mein Kampf.* 2 vols. 1925, 1926. New York: NY: Reynal and Hitchcock, 1941 English translation ed.
Hoffman, Michael A., II. *They Were White and They Were Slaves: The Untold History of the Enslavement of Whites in Early America.* Dresden, NY: Wiswell Ruffin House, 1993.
Hofstadter, Richard. *The American Political Tradition, and the Men Who Made It.* New York, NY: Alfred A. Knopf, 1948.
——. (ed.) *Great Issues in American History: From Reconstruction to the Present Day, 1864-1969.* 1958. New York, NY: Vintage, 1969 ed.
Holland, Jesse J. *Black Men Built the Capitol: Discovering African-American History in and Around Washington, D.C.* Guilford, CT: The Globe Pequot Press, 2007.
Holland, Josiah Gilbert. *The Life of Abraham Lincoln.* Springfield, MA: Gurdon Bill, 1866.
Holland, Rupert Sargent (ed.). *Letters and Diary of Laura M. Towne: Written From the Sea Islands of South Carolina, 1862-1884.* Cambridge, MA: Riverside Press, 1912.
Holzer, Harold (ed.). *The Lincoln-Douglas Debates: The First Complete, Unexpurgated Text.* 1993. Bronx, NY: Fordham University Press, 2004 ed.
Hood, John Bell. *Advance and Retreat: Personal Experiences in the United States and Confederate States Armies.* New Orleans, LA: G. T. Beauregard, 1880.
Hopley, Catherine Cooper. *Life in the South; From the Commencement of the War, By a Blockaded British Subject.* 2 vols. London, UK: Chapman and Hall, 1863.
Horn, Stanley F. *Invisible Empire: The Story of the Ku Klux Klan, 1866-1871.* 1939. Montclair, NJ: Patterson Smith, 1969 ed.
——. *The Decisive Battle of Nashville.* 1956. Baton Rouge, LA: Louisiana State University Press, 1991 ed.
Horwitz, Tony. *Confederates in the Attic: Dispatches From the Unfinished Civil War.* 1998. New York, NY: Vintage, 1999 ed.
House Documents, 64th Congress, 1st Session, December 6, 1915, to September 8, 1916, Vol. 145. Washington, D.C.: Government Printing Office, 1916.
Howe, Daniel Wait. *Political History of Secession.* New York, NY: G. P. Putnam's Sons, 1914.
Howe, Henry. *Historical Collections of Virginia.* Charleston, SC: William R. Babcock, 1852.
Howe, M. A. DeWolfe (ed.). *Home Letters of General Sherman.* New York, NY: Charles Scribner's Sons, 1909.
Howells, William. *Back of History: The Story of Our Own Origins.* 1954. Garden City, NY:

Doubleday, 1963 ed.
Hubbard, John Milton. *Notes of a Private*. St. Louis, MO: Nixon-Jones, 1911.
Hunt, John Gabriel (ed.). *The Essential Abraham Lincoln*. Avenel, NJ: Portland House, 1993.
Hurmence, Belinda (ed.). *Before Freedom, When I Can Just Remember: Twenty-seven Oral Histories of Former South Carolina Slaves*. 1989. Winston-Salem, NC: John F. Blair, 2002 ed.
Hurst, Jack. *Nathan Bedford Forrest: A Biography*. 1993. New York, NY: Vintage, 1994 ed.
Ingersoll, Thomas G., and Robert E. O'Connor. *Politics and Structure: Essential of American national Government*. North Scituate, MA: Duxbury Press, 1979.
Isaacson, Walter (ed.). *Profiles in Leadership: Historians on the Elusive Quality of Greatness*. New York, NY: W. W. Norton and Co., 2010.
Jahoda, Gloria. *The Trail of Tears: The Story of the American Indian Removals, 1813-1855*. 1975. New York, NY: Wings Book, 1995 ed.
Jaquette, Henrietta Stratton (ed.). *South After Gettysburg: Letters of Cornelia Hancock, 1863-1868*. Philadelphia, PA: University of Pennsylvania Press, 1937.
Jefferson, Thomas. *Notes on the State of Virginia*. Boston, MA: H. Sprague, 1802.
———. *Thomas Jefferson's Farm Book*. (Edwin Morris Betts, ed.). Charlottesville, VA: Thomas Jefferson Memorial Foundation, 1999.
Jenkins, John S. *The Life of James Knox Polk, Late President of the United States*. Auburn, NY: James M. Alden, 1850.
Jensen, Merrill. *The New Nation: A History of the United States During the Confederation, 1781-1789*. New York, NY: Vintage, 1950.
———. *The Articles of Confederation: An Interpretation of the Social-Constitutional History of the American Revolution, 1774-1781*. Madison, WI: University of Wisconsin Press, 1959.
Jimerson, Randall C. *The Private Civil War: Popular Thought During the Sectional Conflict*. Baton Rouge, LA: Louisiana State University Press, 1988.
Johannsen, Robert Walter. *Lincoln, the South, and Slavery: The Political Dimension*. Baton Rouge, LA: Louisiana State University Press, 1991.
Johnson, Adam Rankin. *The Partisan Rangers of the Confederate States Army*. Louisville, KY: George G. Fetter, 1904.
Johnson, Allen W., and Timothy Earle. *The Evolution of Human Societies: From Foraging Group to Agrarian State*. Stanford, CA: Stanford University Press, 1987.
Johnson, Benjamin Heber. *Making of the American West: People and Perspectives*. Santa Barbara, CA: ABC-Clio, 2007.
Johnson, Clint. *The Politically Incorrect Guide to the South (and Why It Will Rise Again)*. Washington, D.C.: Regnery, 2006.
Johnson, Ludwell H. *North Against South: The American Iliad, 1848-1877*. 1978. Columbia, SC: Foundation for American Education, 1993 ed.
Johnson, Michael, and James L. Roark. *Black Masters: A Free Family of Color in the Old South*. New York, NY: W.W. Norton, 1984.
Johnson, Oliver. *William Lloyd Garrison and His Times*. 1879. Boston, MA: Houghton Mifflin and Co., 1881 ed.
Johnson, Paul. *A History of the American People*. 1997. New York, NY: HarperCollins, 1999 ed.
Johnson, Robert Underwood (ed.). *Battles and Leaders of the Civil War*. 4 vols. New York, NY: The Century Co., 1884-1888.
Johnson, Thomas Cary. *The Life and Letters of Robert Lewis Dabney*. Richmond, VA: Presbyterian Committee of Publication, 1903.
Jones, Gwyn. *A History of the Vikings*. 1968. Oxford, UK: Oxford University Press, 1984 ed.
Jones, John Beauchamp. *A Rebel War Clerk's Diary at the Confederate States Capital*. 2 vols. in 1. Philadelphia, PA: J. B. Lippincott and Co., 1866.
Jones, John William. *Personal Reminiscences, Anecdotes, and Letters of Gen. Robert E. Lee*. New York, NY: D. Appleton and Co., 1874.
Jones, Prudence, and Nigel Pennick. *A History of Pagan Europe*. London, UK: Routledge, 1995.
Jones, Wilmer L. *Generals in Blue and Gray*. 2 vols. Westport, CT: Praeger, 2004.
Jordan, Don, and Michael Walsh. *White Cargo: The Forgotten History of Britain's White Slaves in America*. New York, NY: New York University Press, 2008.

Jordan, Ervin L. *Black Confederates and Afro-Yankees in Civil War Virginia*. Charlottesville, VA: University Press of Virginia, 1995.
Jordan, Robert Paul. *The Civil War*. Washington, D.C.: National Geographic Society, 1969.
Jordan, Thomas, and John P. Pryor. *The Campaigns of General Nathan Bedford Forrest and of Forrest's Cavalry*. New Orleans, LA: Blelock and Co., 1868.
Julian, George Washington. *Speeches on Political Questions*. New York, NY: Hurd and Houghton, 1872.
Kagan, Donald. *Problems in Ancient History - Vol. 1: The Ancient Near East and Greece*. 1966. New York, NY: Macmillan, 1975 ed.
Kane, Joseph Nathan. *Facts About the Presidents: A Compilation of Biographical and Historical Data*. 1959. New York, NY: Ace, 1976 ed.
Katcher, Philip. *The Civil War Source Book*. 1992. New York, NY: Facts on File, 1995 ed.
———. *Brassey's Almanac: The American Civil War*. London, UK: Brassey's, 2003.
Kautz, August Valentine. *Customs of Service for Non-Commissioned Officers and Soldiers (as Derived from Law and Regulations and Practised in the Army of the United States)*. Philadelphia, PA: J. B. Lippincott and Co., 1864.
Keckley, Elizabeth. *Behind the Scenes, or Thirty Years a Slave, and Four Years in the White House*. New York, NY: G. W. Carlton and Co., 1868.
Kelly, Alfred H., Winfred A. Harbison, and Herman Belz. *The American Constitution: Its Origins and Development* (Vol. 2). 1965. New York, NY: W.W. Norton, 1991 ed.
Kennedy, James Ronald, and Walter Donald Kennedy. *The South Was Right!* Gretna, LA: Pelican Publishing Co., 1994.
———. *Why Not Freedom!: America's Revolt Against Big Government*. Gretna, LA: Pelican Publishing Co., 2005.
———. *Nullifying Tyranny: Creating Moral Communities in an Immoral Society*. Gretna, LA: Pelican Publishing Co., 2010.
Kennedy, Walter Donald. *Myths of American Slavery*. Gretna, LA: Pelican Publishing Co., 2003.
Kennett, Lee B. *Sherman: A Soldier's Life*. 2001. New York, NY: HarperCollins, 2002 ed.
Kettell, Thomas Prentice. *History of the Great Rebellion*. Hartford, CT: L. Stebbins, 1865.
Kinder, Hermann, and Werner Hilgemann. *The Anchor Atlas of World History: From the French Revolution to the American Bicentennial*. 2 vols. Garden City, NY: Anchor, 1978.
King, Charles R. (ed.). *The Life and Correspondence of Rufus King*. 6 vols. New York, NY: G. P. Putnam's Sons, 1897.
King, Edward. *The Great South: A Record of Journeys*. Hartford, CT: American Publishing Co., 1875.
Kinshasa, Kwando Mbiassi. *Black Resistance to the Ku Klux Klan in the Wake of the Civil War*. Jefferson, NC: McFarland and Co., 2006.
Kirkland, Edward Chase. *The Peacemakers of 1864*. New York, NY: Macmillan, 1927.
Kishlansky, Mark, Patrick Geary, and Patricia O'Brien. *Civilization in the West - Vol. 2: Since 1555*. New York, NY: HarperCollins, 1995.
Klingaman, William K. *Abraham Lincoln and the Road to Emancipation, 1861-1865*. 2001. New York, NY: Penguin, 2002 ed.
Knox, Thomas Wallace. *Camp-Fire and Cotton-Field: Southern Adventure in Time of War - Life With the Union Armies, and Residence on a Louisiana Plantation*. New York, NY: Blelock and Co., 1865.
Koger, Larry. *Black Slaveowners: Free Black Slave Masters in South Carolina, 1790-1860*. Columbia, SC: University of South Carolina Press, 1995.
Kramer, Samuel Noah. *Cradle of Civilization*. New York, NY: Time-Life Books, 1967.
Lamon, Ward Hill. *The Life of Abraham Lincoln: From His Birth to His Inauguration as President*. Boston, MA: James R. Osgood and Co., 1872.
———. *Recollections of Abraham Lincoln: 1847-1865*. Chicago, IL: A. C. McClurg and Co., 1895.
Lancaster, Bruce, and J. H. Plumb. *The American Heritage Book of the Revolution*. 1958. New York, NY: Dell, 1975 ed.
Lang, J. Stephen. *The Complete Book of Confederate Trivia*. Shippensburg, PA: Burd Street Press, 1996.

Langer, William L. (ed.). *Perspectives in Western Civilization*. New York, NY: American Heritage, 1972.
Lanning, Michael Lee. *The African-American Soldier: From Crispus Attucks to Colin Powell*. 1997. New York, NY: Citadel Press, 2004 ed.
Lapsley, Arthur Brooks (ed.). *The Writings of Abraham Lincoln*. 8 vols. New York, NY: The Lamb Publishing Co., 1906.
Lau, Theodora. *The Handbook of Chinese Horoscopes*. 1979. New York, NY: Harper and Row, 1988 ed.
Lawrence, William. *Life of Amos A. Lawrence*. Boston, MA: Houghton, Mifflin, and Co., 1899.
Leech, Margaret. *Reveille in Washington, 1860-1865*. 1941. Alexandria, VA: Time-Life Books, 1980 ed.
Lee, Robert E., Jr. *Recollections and Letters of General Robert E. Lee*. New York, NY: Doubleday, Page and Co., 1904.
Lemay, J. A. Leo, and P. M. Zall (eds.). *Benjamin Franklin's Autobiography: An Authoritative Text, Backgrounds, Criticism*. 1791. New York, NY: W. W. Norton and Co., 1986 ed.
Lemire, Elise. *Black Walden: Slavery and Its Aftermath in Concord, Massachusetts*. Philadelphia, PA: University of Pennsylvania Press, 2009.
Leonard, Jonathan Norton. *Ancient America*. New York, NY: Time, 1967.
Lerner, Max. *America as a Civilization - Vol. 2: Culture and Personality*. 1957. New York, NY: Simon and Schuster, 1961 ed.
Lerner, Robert E., Standish Meacham, and Edward McNall Burns. *Western Civilizations: Their History and Their Culture - Vol. 2*. 1941. New York, NY: W. W. Norton and Co., 1988 ed.
Lester, Charles Edwards. *Life and Public Services of Charles Sumner*. New York, NY: U.S. Publishing Co., 1874.
Lester, John C., and D. L. Wilson. *Ku Klux Klan: Its Origin, Growth, and Disbandment*. 1884. New York, NY: Neale Publishing, 1905 ed.
Lewis, Joseph. *Atheism and Other Addresses*. New York, NY: The Freethought Press, Association, 1941.
———. *Lincoln the Atheist*. Austin, TX: American Atheist Press, 1979.
Lewis, Lloyd. *Myths After Lincoln*. 1929. New York, NY: The Press of the Reader's Club, 1941 ed.
LeVert, Suzanne (ed.). *The Civil War Society's Encyclopedia of the Civil War*. New York, NY: Wings Books, 1997.
Levin, Mark R. *Liberty and Tyranny: A Conservative Manifesto*. New York, NY: Threshold, 2009.
Lincoln, Abraham. *The Autobiography of Abraham Lincoln* (selected from the *Complete Works of Abraham Lincoln*, 1894, by John G. Nicolay and John Hay). New York, NY: Francis D. Tandy Co., 1905.
Lincoln, Abraham, and Stephen A. Douglas. *Political Debates Between Abraham Lincoln and Stephen A. Douglas*. Cleveland, OH: Burrows Brothers Co., 1894.
Lind, Michael (ed.). *Hamilton's Republic: Readings in the American Democratic Nationalist Tradition*. New York, NY: Free Press, 1997.
Littell, Eliakim (ed.). *The Living Age*. Seventh Series, Vol. 30. Boston, MA: The Living Age Co., 1906.
Litwack, Leon F. *North of Slavery: The Negro in the Free States, 1790-1860*. Chicago, IL: University of Chicago Press, 1961.
———. *Been in the Storm So Long: The Aftermath of Slavery*. New York, NY: Vintage, 1980.
Livermore, Thomas L. *Numbers and Losses in the Civil War in America, 1861-65*. 1900. Carlisle, PA: John Kallmann, 1996 ed.
Livingstone, E. A. *The Concise Oxford Dictionary of the Christian Church*. 1977. Oxford, UK: Oxford University Press, 1980 ed.
Livingstone, William. *Livingstone's History of the Republican Party*. 2 vols. Detroit, MI: William Livingstone, 1900.
Locke, John. *Two Treatises of Government* (Mark Goldie, ed.). 1924. London, UK: Everyman, 1998 ed.

Lodge, Henry Cabot (ed.). *The Works of Alexander Hamilton*. 12 vols. New York, NY: G. P. Putnam's Sons, 1904.
Logan, John Alexander. *The Great Conspiracy: Its Origin and History*. New York, NY: A. R. Hart, 1886.
Logsdon, David R. (ed.). *Eyewitnesses at the Battle of Franklin*. 1988. Nashville, TN: Kettle Mills Press, 2000 ed.
——. *Tennessee Antebellum Trail Guidebook*. Nashville, TN: Kettle Mills Press, 1995.
Long, Everette Beach, and Barbara Long. *The Civil War Day by Day: An Almanac, 1861-1865*. 1971. New York, NY: Da Capo Press, 1985 ed.
Lonn, Ella. *Foreigners in the Confederacy*. 1940. Chapel Hill, NC: University of North Carolina Press, 2002 ed.
Lott, Stanley K. *The Truth About American Slavery*. 2004. Clearwater, SC: Eastern Digital Resources, 2005 ed.
Lowry, Don. *Dark and Cruel War: The Decisive Months of the Civil War, September-December 1864*. New York, NY: Hippocrene, 1993.
Lubbock, Francis Richard. *Six Decades in Texas, or Memoirs of Francis Richard Lubbock, Governor of Texas in War-Time, 1861-1863*. 1899. Austin, TX: Ben C. Jones, 1900 ed.
Ludlow, Daniel H. (ed.). *Encyclopedia of Mormonism: The History, Scripture, Doctrine, and Procedure of the Church of Jesus Christ of Latter-Day Saints*. New York, NY: Macmillan, 1992.
Lyman, Darryl. *Civil War Wordbook, Including Sayings, Phrases, and Expletives*. Conshohocken, PA: Combined Books, 1994.
Lytle, Andrew Nelson. *Bedford Forrest and His Critter Company*. New York, NY: G. P. Putnam's Sons, 1931.
MacDonald, William. *Select Documents Illustrative of the History of the United States 1776-1861*. New York, NY: Macmillan, 1897.
Mackay, Charles. *Life and Liberty in America, or Sketches of a Tour in the United States and Canada in 1857-58*. New York, NY: Harper and Brothers, 1859.
MacQuarrie, Kim. *The Last Days of the Incas*. New York, NY: Simon and Schuster, 2007.
Madison, James. *Letters and Other Writings of James Madison, Fourth President of the United States*. 4 vols. Philadelphia, PA: J. B. Lippincott and Co., 1865.
Magoffin, Ralph V. D., and Frederic Duncalf. *Ancient and Medieval History: The Rise of Classical Culture and the Development of Medieval Civilization*. Morristown, NJ: Silver Burdett Co., 1959.
Maihafer, Harry J. *War of Words: Abraham Lincoln and the Civil War Press*. Dulles, VA: Brassey's, 2001.
Main, Jackson Turner. *The Anti-Federalists: Critics of the Constitution, 1781-1788*. 1961. New York, NY: W. W. Norton and Co., 1974 ed.
Malone, Laurence J. *Opening the West: Federal Internal Improvements Before 1860*. Westport, CT: Greenwood Press, 1998.
Mandel, Bernard. *Labor, Free and Slave: Workingmen and the Anti-Slavery Movement in the United States*. New York, NY: Associated Authors, 1955.
Manning, Timothy D., Sr. (ed.) *Lincoln Reconsidered: Conference Reader*. High Point, NC: Heritage Foundation Press, 2006.
Marshall, Jessie Ames. *Private and Official Correspondence of General Benjamin F. Butler During the Period of the Civil War*. 5 vols. Norwood, MA: The Plimpton Press, 1917.
Marten, James. *The Children's Civil War*. Chapel Hill, NC: University of North Carolina Press, 1998.
Martin, Iain C. *The Quotable American Civil War*. Guilford, CT: Lyons Press, 2008.
Martineau, Harriet. *Retrospect of Western Travel*. 3 vols. London, UK: Saunders and Otley, 1838.
Martinez, James Michael. *Carpetbaggers, Cavalry, and the Ku Klux Klan: Exposing the Invisible Empire During Reconstruction*. Lanham, MD: Rowman and Littlefield, 2007.
Marx, Karl, and Frederick Engels. *Manifesto of the Communist Party*. (Engels, ed. and translator.) Chicago, IL: Charles H. Kerr and Co., 1908.
Masur, Louis P. *The Real War Will Never Get In the Books: Selections From Writers During the Civil*

War. New York, NY: Oxford University Press, 1993.
Mathes, Capt. J. Harvey. *General Forrest*. New York, NY: D. Appleton and Co., 1902.
Maury, Dabney Herndon. *Recollections of a Virginian in the Mexican, Indian, and Civil Wars*. New York, NY: Charles Scribner's Sons, 1894.
Mayer, David N. *The Constitutional Thought of Thomas Jefferson*. Charlottesville, VA: University of Virginia Press, 1995.
Mayer, Henry. *All on Fire: William Lloyd Garrison and the Abolition of Slavery*. New York, NY: St. Martin's Press, 1998.
Mbiti, John S. *African Religions and Philosophy*. 1969. Nairobi, Kenya: Heinemann Kenya Limited, 1988 ed.
McAfee, Ward M. *Citizen Lincoln*. Hauppauge, NY: Nova History Publications, 2004.
McCabe, James Dabney. *Our Martyred President: The Life and Public Services of Gen. James A. Garfield, Twentieth President of the United States*. Philadelphia, PA: National Publishing Co., 1881.
McCarty, Burke (ed.). *Little Sermons In Socialism by Abraham Lincoln*. Chicago, IL: The Chicago Daily Socialist, 1910.
McClure, Alexander Kelly. *Abraham Lincoln and Men of War-Times: Some Personal Recollections of War and Politics During the Lincoln Administration*. Philadelphia, PA: Times Publishing Co., 1892.
——. *Our Presidents and How We Make Them*. New York, NY: Harper and Brothers, 1900.
McCullough, David. *John Adams*. New York, NY: Touchstone, 2001.
McDonald, Forrest. *States' Rights and the Union: Imperium in Imperio, 1776-1876*. Lawrence, KS: University Press of Kansas, 2000.
McDonough, James Lee, and Thomas L. Connelly. *Five Tragic Hours: The Battle of Franklin*. 1983. Knoxville, TN: University of Tennessee Press, 2001 ed.
McElroy, Robert. *Jefferson Davis: The Unreal and the Real*. 1937. New York, NY: Smithmark, 1995 ed.
McFeely, William S. *Yankee Stepfather: General O. O. Howard and the Freedmen - The Story of a Civil War Promise to Former Slaves Made—and Broken*. 1968. New York, NY: W. W. Norton, 1994.
McGehee, Jacob Owen. *Causes That Led to the War Between the States*. Atlanta, GA: A. B. Caldwell, 1915.
McGuire, Hunter, and George L. Christian. *The Confederate Cause and Conduct in the War Between the States*. Richmond, VA: L. H. Jenkins, 1907.
McHenry, George. *The Cotton Trade: Its Bearing Upon the Prosperity of Great Britain and Commerce of the American Republics, Considered in Connection with the System of Negro Slavery in the Confederate States*. London, UK: Saunders, Otley, and Co., 1863.
McIlwaine, Shields. *Memphis Down in Dixie*. New York, NY: E. P. Dutton, 1848.
McKay, John P., Bennett D. Hill, and John Buckler. *A History of Western Society - Vol. 1: From Antiquity to the Enlightenment*. Boston, MA: Houghton Mifflin, 1987.
——. *A History of Western Society - Vol. 2: Since 1500*. Boston, MA: Houghton Mifflin, 1988.
McKenzie, John L. *Dictionary of the Bible*. New York, NY: Collier, 1965.
McKissack, Patricia C., and Frederick McKissack. *Sojourner Truth: Ain't I a Woman?* New York: NY: Scholastic, 1992.
McManus, Edgar J. *A History of Negro Slavery in New York*. Syracuse, NY: Syracuse University Press, 1966.
——. *Black Bondage in the North*. Syracuse, NY: Syracuse University Press, 1973.
McMaster, John Bach. *Our House Divided: A History of the People of the United States During Lincoln's Administration*. 1927. New York, NY: Premier, 1961 ed.
McMurry, Richard M. *John Bell Hood and the War For Southern Independence*. 1982. Lincoln, NE: University of Nebraska Press, 1992 ed.
McNeill, William H. *The Rise of the West: A History of the Human Community*. 1963. New York, NY: Mentor, 1965 ed.
McPherson, Edward. *The Political History of the United States of America, During the Great Rebellion (From November 6, 1860, to July 4, 1864)*. Washington, D.C.: Philp and Solomons,

1864.

——. *The Political History of the United States of America, During the Period of Reconstruction, (From April 15, 1865, to July 15, 1870,) Including a Classified Summary of the Legislation of the Thirty-ninth, Fortieth, and Forty-first Congresses*. Washington, D.C.: Solomons and Chapman, 1875.

McPherson, James M. *The Struggle for Equality: Abolitionists and the Negro in the Civil War and Reconstruction*. 1964. Princeton, NJ: Princeton University Press, 1992 ed.

——. *The Negro's Civil War: How American Negroes Felt and Acted During the War for the Union*. 1965. Chicago, IL: University of Illinois Press, 1982 ed.

——. *Battle Cry of Freedom: The Civil War Era*. Oxford, UK: Oxford University Press, 2003.

——. *The Atlas of the Civil War*. Philadelphia, PA: Courage Books, 2005.

McPherson, James M., and the staff of the *New York Times*. *The Most Fearful Ordeal: Original Coverage of the Civil War by Writers and Reporters of the New York Times*. New York, NY: St. Martin's Press, 2004.

McWhiney, Grady, and Judith Lee Hallock. *Braxton Bragg and Confederate Defeat*. 2 vols. Tuscaloosa, AL: University of Alabama Press, 1991.

McWhiney, Grady, and Perry D. Jamieson. *Attack and Die: Civil War Military Tactics and the Southern Heritage*. Tuscaloosa, AL: University of Alabama Press, 1982.

Melish, Joanne Pope. *Disowning Slavery: Gradual Emancipation and 'Race' in New England 1780-1860*. Ithaca, NY: Cornell University Press, 1998.

Meltzer, Milton. *Slavery: A World History*. 2 vols. in 1. 1971. New York, NY: Da Capo Press, 1993 ed.

Meriwether, Elizabeth Avery. *Facts and Falsehoods Concerning the War on the South, 1861-1865*. (Originally written under the pseudonym "George Edmonds.") Memphis, TN: A. R. Taylor, 1904.

Message of the President of the United States and Accompanying Documents to the Two Houses of Congress at the Commencement of the Third Session of the 40th Congress. Washington, D.C.: Government Printing Office, 1868.

Metzger, Bruce M., and Michael D. Coogan (eds.). *The Oxford Companion to the Bible*. New York, NY: Oxford University Press, 1993.

Miller, Francis Trevelyan. *Portrait Life of Lincoln*. Springfield, MA: Patriot Publishing Co., 1910.

Miller, John Chester. *The Wolf By the Ears: Thomas Jefferson and Slavery*. 1977. Charlottesville, VA: University Press of Virginia, 1994 ed.

Miller, Marion Mills (ed.). *Great Debates in American History*. 14 vols. New York, NY: Current Literature, 1913.

Miller, Nathan. *Star-Spangled Men: America's Ten Worst Presidents*. New York, NY: Touchstone, 1998.

Min, Pyong Gap (ed.). *Encyclopedia of Racism in the United States*. 3 vols. Westport, CT: Greenwood Press, 2005.

Minor, Charles Landon Carter. *The Real Lincoln: From the Testimony of His Contemporaries*. Richmond, VA: Everett Waddey Co., 1904.

Mirabello, Mark. *Handbook for Rebels and Outlaws*. Oxford, UK: Mandrake of Oxford, 2009.

Mish, Frederick C. (ed.). *Webster's Ninth New Collegiate Dictionary*. 1984. Springfield, MA: Merriam-Webster.

Mitchell, Margaret. *Gone With the Wind*. 1936. New York, NY: Avon, 1973 ed.

Mitgang, Herbert (ed.). *Lincoln As They Saw Him*. 1956. New York, NY: Collier, 1962 ed.

Mode, Peter George. *Source Book and Bibliographical Guide for American Church History*. Menasha, WI: Collegiate Press, 1921.

Mode, Robert L. (ed.). *Nashville: Its Character in a Changing America*. Nashville, TN: Vanderbilt University, 1981.

Montefiore, Simon Sebag. *Stalin: The Court of the Red Star*. 2003. New York, NY: Vintage, 2004 ed.

Montgomery, David Henry. *The Leading Facts of English History*. 1887. Boston, MA: Ginn and Co., 1900 ed.

——. *The Student's American History*. 1897. Boston, MA: Ginn and Co., 1905 ed.

Moore, Clark D., and Ann Dunbar (eds.). *Africa Yesterday and Today.* 1968. New York, NY: 1970 ed.
Moore, Frank (ed.). *The Rebellion Record: A Diary of American Events.* 12 vols. New York, NY: G. P. Putnam, 1861.
Moore, George Henry. *Notes on the History of Slavery in Massachusetts.* New York, NY: D. Appleton and Co., 1866.
Moorhead, James H. *American Apocalypse: Yankee Protestants and the Civil War, 1860-1869.* New Haven, CT: Yale University Press, 1971.
Morgan, Edmund S. *The Birth of the Republic, 1763-89.* 1956. Chicago, IL: University of Chicago Press, 1967 ed.
Morison, Samuel Eliot, and Henry Steele Commager. *The Growth of the American Republic.* 2 vols. 1930. New York, NY: Oxford University Press, 1965 ed.
Morris, Benjamin Franklin (ed.). *The Life of Thomas Morris: Pioneer and Long a Legislator of Ohio, and U.S. Senator from 1833 to 1839.* Cincinnati, OH: Moore, Wilstach, Keys and Overend, 1856.
Morris, Thomas D. *Free Men All: The Personal Liberty Laws of the North, 1780-1861.* Baltimore, MD: Johns Hopkins University Press, 1974.
Morton, John Watson. *The Artillery of Nathan Bedford Forrest's Cavalry.* Nashville, TN: The M. E. Church, 1909.
Moses, John. *Illinois: Historical and Statistical, Comprising the Essential Facts of Its Planting and Growth as a Province, County, Territory, and State* (Vol. 2). Chicago, IL: Fergus Printing Co., 1892.
Mullen, Robert W. *Blacks in America's Wars: The Shift in Attitudes From the Revolutionary War to Vietnam.* 1973. New York, NY: Pathfinder, 1991 ed.
Muller, Herbert J. *The Uses of the Past: Profiles of Former Societies.* 1954. New York, NY: Mentor, 1960 ed.
Munford, Beverly Bland. *Virginia's Attitude Toward Slavery and Secession.* 1909. Richmond, VA: L. H. Jenkins, 1914 ed.
Murphy, Jim. *A Savage Thunder: Antietam and the Bloody Road to Freedom.* New York, NY: Margaret K. McElderry, 2009.
Muzzey, David Saville. *The American Adventure: A History of the United States - Vol. 2: From the Civil War.* 1924. New York, NY: Harper and Brothers, 1927 ed.
Myers, Philip Van Ness. *Ancient History.* 1904. Boston, MA: Ginn and Co., 1916 ed.
Napolitano, Andrew P. *The Constitution in Exile: How the Federal Government has Seized Power by Rewriting the Supreme Law of the Land.* Nashville, TN: Nelson Current, 2006.
Neely, Mark E., Jr. *The Fate of Liberty: Abraham Lincoln and Civil Liberties.* New York, NY: Oxford University Press, 1991.
Neilson, William Allan (ed.). *Webster's Biographical Dictionary.* Springfield, MA: G. and C. Merriam Co., 1943.
Neufeldt, Victoria (ed.). *Webster's New World Dictionary of American English* (3rd college ed.). 1970. New York, NY: Prentice Hall, 1994 ed.
Nevins, Allan. *The Evening Post: A Century of Journalism.* New York, NY: Boni and Liveright, 1922.
Nevins, Allan, and Henry Steele Commager. *A Pocket History of the United States.* 1942. New York, NY: Pocket Books, 1981 ed.
Nicolay, John G., and John Hay (eds.). *Abraham Lincoln: A History.* 10 vols. New York, NY: The Century Co., 1890.
——. *Complete Works of Abraham Lincoln.* 12 vols. 1894. New York, NY: Francis D. Tandy Co., 1905 ed.
——. *Abraham Lincoln: Complete Works.* 12 vols. 1894. New York, NY: The Century Co., 1907 ed.
Nivola, Pietro S., and David H. Rosenbloom (eds.). *Classic Readings in American Politics.* New York, NY: St. Martin's Press, 1986.
Norwood, Thomas Manson. *A True Vindication of the South.* Savannah, GA: Citizens and Southern Bank, 1917.

Norton, Mary Beth, David M. Katzman, Paul D. Escott, Howard P. Chudacoff, Thomas G. Paterson, and William M. Tuttle Jr. *A People and a Nation: A History of the United States - Vol. 2: Since 1865*. Boston, MA: Houghton Mifflin, 1986.
Nye, Russel B. *William Lloyd Garrison and the Humanitarian Reformers*. Boston, MA: Little, Brown and Co., 1955.
Oates, Stephen B. *Abraham Lincoln: The Man Behind the Myths*. New York, NY: Meridian, 1984.
———. *The Approaching Fury: Voices of the Storm, 1820-1861*. New York, NY: Harper Perennial, 1998.
O'Brien, Arthur. *Europe Before Modern Times: An Ancient and Mediaeval History*. Chicago, IL: Loyola University Press, 1943.
O'Brien, Cormac. *Secret Lives of the U.S. Presidents: What Your Teachers Never Told You About the Men of the White House*. Philadelphia, PA: Quirk, 2004.
———. *Secret Lives of the Civil War: What Your teachers Never Told You About the War Between the States*. Philadelphia, PA: Quirk, 2007.
Oglesby, Thaddeus K. *Some Truths of History: A Vindication of the South Against the Encyclopedia Britannica and Other Maligners*. Atlanta, GA: Byrd Printing, 1903.
Oliver, Edmund Henry. *Roman Economic Conditions to the Close of the Republic*. Toronto, CAN: University of Toronto Library, 1907.
Olmsted, Frederick Law. *A Journey in the Seaboard Slave States, With Remarks on Their Economy*. New York, NY: Dix and Edwards, 1856.
———. *A Journey Through Texas; or a Saddle-Trip on the Western Frontier*. New York, NY: Dix and Edwards, 1857.
———. *A Journey in the Back Country*. New York, NY: Mason Brothers, 1860.
———. *The Cotton Kingdom: A Traveler's Observations on Cotton and Slavery in the American Slave States*. 2 vols. London, UK: Sampson Low, Son, and Co., 1862.
Olson, Ted (ed.). *CrossRoads: A Southern Culture Annual*. Macon, GA: Mercer University Press, 2004.
ORA (full title: *The War of the Rebellion: A Compilation of the Official Records of the Union and Confederate Armies*. 128 vols. Washington, D.C.: Government Printing Office, 1880.
ORN (full title: *Official Records of the Union and Confederate Navies in the War of the Rebellion*). 31 vols. Washington, D.C.: Government Printing Office, 1894.
Owsley, Frank Lawrence. *King Cotton Diplomacy: Foreign Relations of the Confederate States of America*. 1931. Chicago, IL: University of Chicago Press, 1959 ed.
Oxford English Dictionary. 1928. Oxford, UK: Oxford University Press, 1979 ed.
Page, Thomas Nelson. *Robert E. Lee, Man and Soldier*. New York, NY: Charles Scribner's Sons, 1911.
Palin, Sarah. *Going Rogue: An American Life*. New York, NY: HarperCollins, 2009.
Palmer, R. R., and Joel Colton. *A History of the Modern World*. 1950. New York, NY: Alfred A. Knopf, 1965 ed.
Parker, Bowdoin S. (ed.). *What One Grand Army Post Has Accomplished: History of Edward W. Kinsley Post, No. 113*. Norwood, MA: Norwood Press, 1913.
Parry, J. H. *The Establishment of the European Hegemony, 1415-1715: Trade and Exploration in the Age of the Renaissance*. 1949. New York, NY: Harper Torchbooks, 1966 ed.
Parry, Melanie (ed.). *Chambers Biographical Dictionary*. 1897. Edinburgh, Scotland: Chambers Harrap, 1998 ed.
Patrick, Rembert W. *Jefferson Davis and His Cabinet*. Baton Rouge, LA: Louisiana State University Press, 1944.
Paul, Ron. *The Revolution: A Manifesto*. New York, NY: Grand Central Publishing, 2008.
Pearson, Henry Greenleaf. *The Life of John A. Andrew, Governor of Massachusetts, 1861-1865*. 2 vols. Boston, MA: Houghton, Mifflin and Co., 1904.
Pendleton, Louis Beauregard. *Alexander H. Stephens*. Philadelphia, PA: George W. Jacobs and Co., 1907.
Penrose, Boies. *Travel and Discovery in the Renaissance, 1420-1620*. 1952. New York, NY: Atheneum, 1962 ed.
Perkins, Henry C. *Northern Editorials on Secession*. 2 vols. D. Appleton and Co., 1942.

Perry, James M. *Touched With Fire: Five Presidents and the Civil War Battles That Made Them.* New York, NY: Public Affairs, 2003.
Perry, John C. *Myths and Realities of American Slavery: The True History of Slavery in America.* Shippenburg, PA: Burd Street Press, 2002.
Perry, Mark. *Lift Up Thy Voice: The Grimké Family's Journey From Slaveholders to Civil Rights Leaders.* New York, NY: Penguin, 2001.
Persuitte, David. *Joseph Smith and the Origins of the Book of Mormon.* Jefferson, NC: McFarland and Co., 2000.
Peter, Laurence J., and Raymond Hull *The Peter Principle: Why Things Always Go Wrong.* New York, NY: William Morrow and Co., 1969.
Peters, F. E. *The Harvest of Hellenism: A History of the Near East From Alexander the Great to the Triumph of Christianity.* New York, NY: Touchstone, 1970.
Peterson, Merrill D. (ed.). *James Madison, A Biography in His Own Words.* (First published posthumously in 1840.) New York, NY: Harper and Row, 1974 ed.
——. (ed.). *Thomas Jefferson: Writings, Autobiography, A Summary View of the Rights of British America, Notes on the State of Virginia, Public Papers, Addresses, Messages and Replies, Miscellany, Letters.* New York, NY: Literary Classics, 1984.
Peterson, Paul R. *Quantrill of Missouri: The Making of a Guerilla Warrior, The Man, the Myth, the Soldier.* Nashville, TN: Cumberland House, 2003.
Phillips, Michael. *White Metropolis: Race, Ethnicity, and Religion in Dallas, 1841-2001.* Austin, TX: University of Texas Press, 2006.
Phillips, Robert S. (ed.). *Funk and Wagnalls New Encyclopedia.* 1971. New York, NY: Funk and Wagnalls, 1979 ed.
Phillips, Ulrich Bonnell. *American Negro Slavery: A Survey of the Supply, Employment and Control of Negro Labor as Determined by the Plantation Régime.* New York, NY: D. Appleton and Co., 1929.
Phillips, Wendell. *Speeches, Letters, and Lectures.* Boston, MA: Lee and Shepard, 1894.
Piatt, Donn. *Memories of the Men Who Saved the Union.* New York, NY: Belford, Clarke, and Co., 1887.
Piatt, Donn, and Henry V. Boynton. *General George H. Thomas: A Critical Biography.* Cincinnati, OH: Robert Clarke and Co., 1893.
Pickett, George E. *The Heart of a Soldier: As Revealed in the Intimate Letters of General George E. Pickett, CSA.* 1908. New York, NY: Seth Moyle, 1913 ed.
Pickett, William Passmore. *The Negro Problem: Abraham Lincoln's Solution.* New York, NY: G. P. Putnam's Sons, 1909.
Pike, James Shepherd. *The Prostrate State: South Carolina Under Negro Government.* New York, NY: D. Appleton and Co., 1874.
Pollard, Edward A. *Southern History of the War.* 2 vols. in 1. New York, NY: Charles B. Richardson, 1866.
——. *The Lost Cause.* 1867. Chicago, IL: E. B. Treat, 1890 ed.
——. *The Lost Cause Regained.* New York, NY: G. W. Carlton and Co., 1868.
——. *Life of Jefferson Davis, With a Secret History of the Southern Confederacy, Gathered "Behind the Scenes in Richmond."* Philadelphia, PA: National Publishing Co., 1869.
Post, Lydia Minturn (ed.). *Soldiers' Letters, From Camp, Battlefield and Prison.* New York, NY: Bunce and Huntington, 1865.
Potter, David M. *The Impending Crisis: 1848-1861.* New York, NY: Harper and Row, 1976.
Powell, Edward Payson. *Nullification and Secession in the United States: A History of the Six Attempts During the First Century of the Republic.* New York, NY: G. P. Putnam's Sons, 1897.
Powell, William S. *North Carolina: A History.* 1977. Chapel Hill, NC: University of North Carolina Press, 1988 ed.
Pratt, Harry E. *Concerning Mr. Lincoln: As He Appeared to Letter Writers of His Time.* Springfield, IL: The Abraham Lincoln Association, 1944.
Pritchard, Russ A., Jr. *Civil War Weapons and Equipment.* Guilford, CT: Lyons Press, 2003.
Putnam, Samuel Porter. *400 Years of Free Thought.* New York, NY: Truth Seeker Co., 1894.
Quarles, Benjamin. *The Negro in the Civil War.* 1953. Cambridge, MA: Da Capo Press, 1988 ed.

Quintero, José Agustín, Ambrosio José Gonzales, and Loreta Janeta Velazquez (Phillip Thomas Tucker, ed.). *Cubans in the Confederacy*. Jefferson, NC: McFarland and Co., 2002.
Rabb, Theodore K. *The Struggle for Stability in Early Modern Europe*. 1975. New York, NY: Oxford University Press, 1980 ed.
Rable, George C. *The Confederate Republic: A Revolution Against Politics*. Chapel Hill, NC: University of North Carolina Press, 1994.
Radzinsky, Edvard. *Stalin: The First In-depth Biography Based on Explosive New Documents From Russia's Secret Archives*. New York, NY: Anchor, 1996.
Ramage, James A. *Rebel Raider: The Life of General John Hunt Morgan*. Lexington, KY: University Press of Kentucky, 1986.
Randall, James Garfield. *Lincoln: The Liberal Statesman*. New York, NY: Dodd, Mead and Co., 1947.
Randall, James Garfield, and Richard N. Current. *Lincoln the President: Last Full Measure*. 1955. Urbana, IL: University of Illinois Press, 2000 ed.
Randolph, Thomas Jefferson (ed.). *Memoir, Correspondence, and Miscellanies, from the Papers of Thomas Jefferson*. 4 vols. Charlottesville, VA: F. Carr and Co., 1829.
Ransom, Roger L. *Conflict and Compromise: The Political Economy of Slavery, Emancipation, and the American Civil War*. Cambridge, UK: Cambridge University Press, 1989.
Rawle, William. *A View of the Constitution of the United States of America*. Philadelphia, PA: Philip H. Nicklin, 1829.
Rayfield, Donald. *Stalin and His Hangmen: The Tyrant and Those Who Killed For Him*. New York, NY: Random House, 2004.
Rayner, B. L. *Sketches of the Life, Writings, and Opinions of Thomas Jefferson*. New York, NY: Alfred Francis and William Boardman, 1832.
Reaney, P. H., and R. M. Wilson. *A Dictionary of English Surnames*. 1958. Oxford, UK: Oxford University Press, 1997 ed.
Reid, Richard M. *Freedom for Themselves: North Carolina's Black Soldiers in the Era of the Civil War*. Chapel Hill, NC: University of North Carolina Press, 2008.
Reid, Whitelaw. *After the War: A Southern Tour - May 1, 1865, to May 1, 1866*. Cincinnati, OH: Moore, Wilstach and Baldwin, 1866.
Remsburg, John B. *Abraham Lincoln: Was He a Christian?* New York, NY: The Truth Seeker Co., 1893.
Reports of Committees of the Senate of the United States (for the Thirty-eighth Congress). Washington, D.C.: Government Printing Office, 1864.
Report of the Joint Committee on Reconstruction (at the First Session, Thirty-ninth Congress). Washington, D.C.: Government Printing Office, 1866.
Reports of Committees of the Senate of the United States (for the Second Session of the Forty-second Congress). Washington, D.C.: Government Printing Office, 1872.
Report of the Joint Select Committee to Inquire into the Condition of Affairs in the Late Insurrectionary States. Washington, D.C.: Government Printing Office, 1872.
Reuter, Edward Byron. *The Mulatto in the United States*. Boston, MA: Gorham Press, 1918.
Reyes, E. Christopher. *In His Name*. Bloomington, IN: AuthorHouse, 2010.
Rhodes, James Ford. *History of the United States from the Compromise of 1850 to the Final Restoration of Home Rule at the South in 1877*. 7 vols. 1895. New York, NY: Macmillan Co., 1907 ed.
Rice, Allen Thorndike (ed.). *The North American Review*, Vol. 227. New York, NY: D. Appleton and Co., 1879.
——. *Reminiscences of Abraham Lincoln, by Distinguished Men of His Time*. New York, NY: North American Review, 1888.
Richardson, James Daniel (ed.). *A Compilation of the Messages and Papers of the Confederacy*. 2 vols. Nashville, TN: United States Publishing Co., 1905.
Rickard, J. A. *History of England*. 1933. New York, NY: Barnes and Noble, 1957 ed.
Riedel, Eunice, Thomas Tracy, and Barbara D. Moskowitz. *The Book of the Bible*. New York, NY: William Morrow and Co., 1979.
Riley, Franklin Lafayette (ed.). *Publications of the Mississippi Historical Society*. Oxford, MS: The

Mississippi Historical Society, 1902.
——. *General Robert E. Lee After Appomattox*. New York, NY: MacMillan Co., 1922.
Riley, Russell Lowell. *The Presidency and the Politics of Racial Inequality*. New York, NY: Columbia University Press, 1999.
Rives, John (ed.). *Abridgement of the Debates of Congress: From 1789 to 1856* (Vol. 13). New York, NY: D. Appleton and Co., 1860.
Roberts, Paul M. *United States History: Review Text*. 1966. New York, NY: Amsco School Publications, 1970 ed.
Roberts, R. Philip. *Mormonism Unmasked: Confronting the Contradictions Between Mormon Beliefs and True Christianity*. Nashville, TN: Broadman and Holman, 1998.
Robertson, James I., Jr. *Soldiers Blue and Gray*. 1988. Columbia, SC: University of South Carolina Press, 1998 ed.
Rockwell, Llewellyn H., Jr. "Genesis of the Civil War." Website: www.lewrockwell.com/rockwell/civilwar.html.
Rogers, Joel Augustus. *Africa's Gift to America: The Afro-American in the Making and Saving of the United States*. St. Petersburg, FL: Helga M. Rogers, 1961.
——. *The Ku Klux Spirit*. 1923. Baltimore, MD: Black Classic Press, 1980 ed.
Rosen, Robert N. *The Jewish Confederates*. Columbia, SC: University of South Carolina Press, 2000.
Rosenbaum, Robert A. (ed). *The New American Desk Encyclopedia*. 1977. New York, NY: Signet, 1989 ed.
Rosenbaum, Robert A., and Douglas Brinkley (eds.). *The Penguin Encyclopedia of American History*. New York, NY: Viking, 2003.
Rothschild, Alonzo. *"Honest Abe": A Study in Integrity Based on the Early Life of Abraham Lincoln*. Boston, MA: Houghton Mifflin Co., 1917.
Rouse, Adelaide Louise (ed.). *National Documents: State Papers So Arranged as to Illustrate the Growth of Our Country From 1606 to the Present Day*. New York, NY: Unit Book Publishing Co., 1906.
Rowland, Dunbar (ed.). *Jefferson Davis, Constitutionalist: His Letters, Papers, and Speeches*. 10 vols. Jackson, MS: Mississippi Department of Archives and History, 1923.
Rozwenc, Edwin Charles (ed.). *The Causes of the American Civil War*. 1961. Lexington, MA: D. C. Heath and Co., 1972 ed.
Rubenzer, Steven J., and Thomas R. Faschingbauer. *Personality, Character, and Leadership in the White House: Psychologists Assess the Presidents*. Dulles, VA: Brassey's, 2004.
Ruffin, Edmund. *The Diary of Edmund Ruffin: Toward Independence: October 1856-April 1861*. Baton Rouge, LA: Louisiana State University Press, 1972.
Rutherford, Mildred Lewis. *Four Addresses*. Birmingham, AL: The Mildred Rutherford Historical Circle, 1916.
——. *A True Estimate of Abraham Lincoln and Vindication of the South*. N.p., n.d.
——. *Truths of History: A Historical Perspective of the Civil War From the Southern Viewpoint*. Confederate Reprint Co., 1920.
——. *The South Must Have Her Rightful Place In History*. Athens, GA, 1923.
Rutland, Robert Allen. *The Birth of the Bill of Rights, 1776-1791*. 1955. Boston, MA: Northeastern University Press, 1991 ed.
Sachsman, David B., S. Kittrell Rushing, and Roy Morris, Jr. (eds.). *Words at War: The Civil War and American Journalism*. West Lafayette, IN: Purdue University Press, 2008.
Salley, Alexander Samuel, Jr. *South Carolina Troops in Confederate Service*. 2 vols. Columbia, SC: R. L. Bryan, 1913 and 1914.
Salzberger, Ronald P., and Mary C. Turck (eds.). *Reparations For Slavery: A Reader*. Lanham, MD: Rowman and Littlefield, 2004.
Samuel, Bunford. *Secession and Constitutional Liberty*. 2 vols. New York, NY: Neale Publishing, 1920.
Sancho, Ignatius. *Letters of the Late Ignatius Sancho, an African*. 1782. New York, NY: Cosimo Classics, 2005 ed.
Sandburg, Carl. *Abraham Lincoln: The War Years*. 4 vols. New York, NY: Harcourt, Brace and

World, 1939.

———. *Storm Over the Land: A Profile of the Civil War*. 1939. Old Saybrook, CT: Konecky and Konecky, 1942 ed.

Sargent, F. W. *England, the United States, and the Southern Confederacy*. London, UK: Sampson Low, Son, and Co., 1863.

Scharf, John Thomas. *History of the Confederate Navy, From Its Organization to the Surrender of Its Last Vessel*. Albany, NY: Joseph McDonough, 1894.

Schauffler, Robert Haven. *Our American Holidays: Lincoln's Birthday - A Comprehensive View of Lincoln as Given in the Most Noteworthy Essays, Orations and Poems, in Fiction and in Lincoln's Own Writings*. 1909. New York, NY: Moffat, Yard and Co., 1916 ed.

Schlüter, Herman. *Lincoln, Labor and Slavery: A Chapter from the Social History of America*. New York, NY: Socialist Literature Co., 1913.

Schrier, Arnold, Harry J. Carroll Jr., Ainslie T. Embree, Knox Mellon Jr., and Alastair M. Taylor. *Modern European Civilization*. 1961. Chicago, IL: Scott, Foresman and Co., 1963 ed.

Schurz, Carl. *Life of Henry Clay*. 2 vols. 1887. Boston, MA: Houghton, Mifflin and Co., 1899 ed.

Schwartz, Barry. *Abraham Lincoln and the Forge of National Memory*. Chicago, IL: University of Chicago Press, 2000.

Scott, Emmett J., and Lyman Beecher Stowe. *Booker T. Washington: Builder of a Civilization*. Garden City, NY: Doubleday, Page, and Co., 1916.

Scott, James Brown. *James Madison's Notes of Debates in the Federal Convention of 1787, and Their Relation to a More Perfect Society of Nations*. New York, NY: Oxford University Press, 1918.

Scruggs, *The Un-Civil War: Truths Your Teacher Never Told You*. Hendersonville, NC: Tribune Papers, 2007.

Seabrook, Lochlainn. *Britannia Rules: Goddess-Worship in Ancient Anglo-Celtic Society - An Academic Look at the United Kingdom's Matricentric Spiritual Past*. 1999. Franklin, TN: Sea Raven Press, 2007 ed.

———. *The Caudills: An Etymological, Ethnological, and Genealogical Study - Exploring the Name and National Origins of a European-American Family*. 2003. Franklin, TN: Sea Raven Press, 2010 ed.

———. *Nathan Bedford Forrest: Southern Hero, American Patriot*. 2007. Franklin, TN, 2010 ed.

———. *Abraham Lincoln: The Southern View*. 2007. Franklin, TN: Sea Raven Press, 2013 ed.

———. *The McGavocks of Carnton Plantation: A Southern History - Celebrating One of Dixie's Most Noble Confederate Families and Their Tennessee Home*. 2008. Franklin, TN, 2011 ed.

———. *A Rebel Born: A Defense of Nathan Bedford Forrest*. 2010. Franklin, TN: Sea Raven Press, 2011 ed.

———. *A Rebel Born: The Screenplay* (for the film). 2011. Franklin, TN: Sea Raven Press.

———. *Everything You Were Taught About the Civil War is Wrong, Ask a Southerner!* 2010. Franklin, TN: Sea Raven Press, revised 2019 ed.

———. *The Quotable Jefferson Davis: Selections From the Writings and Speeches of the Confederacy's First President*. Franklin, TN: Sea Raven Press, 2011.

———. *The Quotable Robert E. Lee: Selections From the Writings and Speeches of the South's Most Beloved Civil War General*. Franklin, TN: Sea Raven Press, 2011 Sesquicentennial Civil War Edition.

———. *Lincolnology: The Real Abraham Lincoln Revealed In His Own Words*. Franklin, TN: Sea Raven Press, 2011.

———. *The Unquotable Abraham Lincoln: The President's Quotes They Don't Want You To Know!* Franklin, TN: Sea Raven Press, 2011.

———. *Honest Jeff and Dishonest Abe: A Southern Children's Guide to the Civil War*. Franklin, TN: Sea Raven Press, 2012.

———. *Encyclopedia of the Battle of Franklin - A Comprehensive Guide to the Conflict that Changed the Civil War*. Franklin, TN: Sea Raven Press, 2012.

———. *The Quotable Nathan Bedford Forrest: Selections From the Writings and Speeches of the Confederacy's*

———. *Most Brilliant Cavalryman*. Spring Hill, TN: Sea Raven Press, 2012.
———. *Forrest! 99 Reasons to Love Nathan Bedford Forrest*. Spring Hill, TN: Sea Raven Press, 2012.
———. *Give 'Em Hell Boys! The Complete Military Correspondence of Nathan Bedford Forrest*. Spring Hill, TN: Sea Raven Press, 2012.
———. *The Constitution of the Confederate States of America Explained: A Clause-by-Clause Study of the South's Magna Carta*. Spring Hill, TN: Sea Raven Press, 2012 Sesquicentennial Civil War Edition.
———. *The Great Impersonator: 99 Reasons to Dislike Abraham Lincoln*. Spring Hill, TN: Sea Raven Press, 2012.
———. *The Old Rebel: Robert E. Lee As He Was Seen By His Contemporaries*. Spring Hill, TN: Sea Raven Press, 2012 Sesquicentennial Civil War Edition.
———. *The Quotable Stonewall Jackson: Selections From the Writings and Speeches of the South's Most Famous General*. Spring Hill, TN: Sea Raven Press, 2012 Sesquicentennial Civil War Edition.
———. *Saddle, Sword, and Gun: A Biography of Nathan Bedford Forrest for Teens*. Spring Hill, TN: Sea Raven Press, 2013.
———. *The Alexander H. Stephens Reader: Excerpts From the Works of a Confederate Founding Father*. Spring Hill, TN: Sea Raven Press, 2013.
———. *The Quotable Alexander H. Stephens: Selections From the Writings and Speeches of the Confederacy's First Vice President*. Spring Hill, TN: Sea Raven Press, 2013 Sesquicentennial Civil War Edition.
———. *Give This Book to a Yankee! A Southern Guide to the Civil War for Northerners*. Spring Hill, TN: Sea Raven Press, 2014.
———. *The Articles of Confederation Explained: A Clause-by-Clause Study of America's First Constitution*. Spring Hill, TN: Sea Raven Press, 2014.
———. *Confederate Blood and Treasure: An Interview With Lochlainn Seabrook*. Spring Hill, TN: Sea Raven Press, 2015.
———. *Nathan Bedford Forrest and the Battle of Fort Pillow: Yankee Myth, Confederate Fact*. Spring Hill, TN: Sea Raven Press, 2015.
———. *Everything You Were Taught About American Slavery War is Wrong, Ask a Southerner!* Spring Hill, TN: Sea Raven Press, 2015.
———. *Confederacy 101: Amazing Facts You Never Knew About America's Oldest Political Tradition*. Spring Hill, TN: Sea Raven Press, 2015.
———. *The Great Yankee Coverup: What the North Doesn't Want You to Know About Lincoln's War!* Spring Hill, TN: Sea Raven Press, 2015.
———. *Slavery 101: Amazing Facts You Never Knew About America's "Peculiar Institution."* Spring Hill, TN: Sea Raven Press, 2015.
———. *Confederate Flag Facts: What Every American Should Know About Dixie's Southern Cross*. Spring Hill, TN: Sea Raven Press, 2016.
———. *Nathan Bedford Forrest and the Ku Klux Klan: Yankee Myth, Confederate Fact*. Spring Hill, TN: Sea Raven Press, 2016.
———. *Seabrook's Bible Dictionary of Traditional and Mystical Christian Doctrines*. Spring Hill, TN: Sea Raven Press, 2016.
———. *Everything You Were Taught About African-Americans and the Civil War is Wrong, Ask a Southerner!* Spring Hill, TN: Sea Raven Press, 2016.
———. *Nathan Bedford Forrest and African-Americans: Yankee Myth, Confederate Fact*. Spring Hill, TN: Sea Raven Press, 2016.
———. *Women in Gray: A Tribute to the Ladies Who Supported the Southern Confederacy*. Spring Hill, TN: Sea Raven Press, 2016.
———. *Lincoln's War: The Real Cause, the Real Winner, the Real Loser*. Spring Hill, TN: Sea Raven Press, 2016.
———. *The Unholy Crusade: Lincoln's Legacy of Destruction in the American South*. Spring Hill, TN: Sea Raven Press, 2017.
———. *Abraham Lincoln Was a Liberal, Jefferson Davis Was a Conservative: The Missing Key to Understanding the American Civil War*. Spring Hill, TN: Sea Raven Press, 2017.

———. *All We Ask is to be Let Alone: The Southern Secession Fact Book*. Spring Hill, TN: Sea Raven Press, 2017.
———. *The Ultimate Civil War Quiz Book: How Much Do You Really Know About America's Most Misunderstood Conflict?* Spring Hill, TN: Sea Raven Press, 2017.
———. *Rise Up and Call Them Blessed: Victorian Tributes to the Confederate Soldier, 1861-1901*. Spring Hill, TN: Sea Raven Press, 2017.
———. *Victorian Confederate Poetry: The Southern Cause in Verse, 1861-1901*. Spring Hill, TN: Sea Raven Press, 2018.
———. *Confederate Monuments: Why Every American Should Honor Confederate Soldiers and Their Memorials*. Spring Hill, TN: Sea Raven Press, 2018.
———. *The God of War: Nathan Bedford Forrest as He Was Seen by His Contemporaries*. Spring Hill, TN: Sea Raven Press, 2018.
———. *The Battle of Spring Hill: Recollections of Confederate and Union Soldiers*. Spring Hill, TN: Sea Raven Press, 2018.
———. *I Rode With Forrest! Confederate Soldiers Who Served With the World's Greatest Cavalry Leader*. Spring Hill, TN: Sea Raven Press, 2018.
———. *The Battle of Nashville: Recollections of Confederate and Union Soldiers*. Spring Hill, TN: Sea Raven Press, 2018.
———. *The Battle of Franklin: Recollections of Confederate and Union Soldiers*. Spring Hill, TN: Sea Raven Press, 2018.
———. (ed.) *A Short History of the Confederate States of America* (Jefferson Davis, Belford Company, NY, 1890). A Sea Raven Press Reprint. Spring Hill, TN: Sea Raven Press, 2020.
———. (ed.) *Prison Life of Jefferson Davis: Embracing Details and Incidents in his Captivity, With Conversations on Topics of Public Interest* (John J. Craven, Sampson, Low, Son, and Marston, London, UK, 1866). A Sea Raven Press Reprint. Spring Hill, TN: Sea Raven Press, 2020.
———. (ed.) *What the Confederate Flag Means to Me: Americans Speak Out in Defense of Southern Honor, Heritage, and History*. Spring Hill, TN: Sea Raven Press, 2021.
———. *Heroes of the Southern Confederacy: The Illustrated Book of Confederate Officials, Soldiers, and Civilians*. Spring Hill, TN: Sea Raven Press, 2021.
———. (ed.) *Support Your Local Confederate: Wit and Humor in the Southern Confederacy*. Spring Hill, TN: Sea Raven Press, 2021.
———. *America's Three Constitutions: Complete Texts of the Articles of Confederation, Constitution of the United States of America, and Constitution of the Confederate States of America*. Spring Hill, TN: Sea Raven Press, 2021.
Segal, Charles M. (ed.). *Conversations with Lincoln*. 1961. New Brunswick, NJ: Transaction, 2002 ed.
Segars, J. H., and Charles Kelly Barrow. *Black Southerners in Confederate Armies: A Collection of Historical Accounts*. Atlanta, GA: Southern Lion Books, 2001.
Seligmann, Herbert J. *The Negro Faces America*. New York, NY: Harper and Brothers, 1920.
Semmes, Admiral Ralph. *Service Afloat, or the Remarkable Career of the Confederate Cruisers Sumter and Alabama During the War Between the States*. London, UK: Sampson Low, Marston, Searle, and Rivington, 1887.
Sewall, Samuel. *Diary of Samuel Sewall*. 3 vols. Boston, MA: The Society, 1879.
Sewell, Richard H. *John P. Hale and the Politics of Abolition*. Cambridge, MA: Harvard University Press, 1965.
Shenkman, Richard. *Legends, Lies and Cherished Myths of American History*. New York, NY: Perennial, 1988.
Shenkman, Richard, and Kurt Edward Reiger. *One-Night Stands with American History: Odd, Amusing, and Little-Known Incidents*. 1980. New York, NY: Perennial, 2003 ed.
Sheppard, Eric William. *Bedford Forrest, The Confederacy's Greatest Cavalryman*. 1930. Dayton, OH: Morningside House, 1981 ed.
Sherman, Dennis (ed.). *Western Civilization: Sources, Images, and Interpretation - Vol. 2: Since 1660*. 1983. New York, NY: McGraw-Hill, 1995 ed.
Sherman, William Tecumseh. *Memoirs of General William T. Sherman*. 2 vols. 1875. New York,

NY: D. Appleton and Co., 1891 ed.
Shillington, Kevin. *History of Africa*. 1989. New York, NY: St. Martin's Press, 1994 ed.
Shirer, William L. *The Rise and Fall of the Third Reich: A History of Nazi German*. New York, NY: Simon and Schuster, 1960.
Shorto, Russell. *Thomas Jefferson and the American Ideal*. Hauppauge, NY: Barron's, 1987.
Shotwell, Walter G. *Life of Charles Sumner*. New York, NY: Thomas Y. Crowell and Co., 1910.
Siepel, Kevin H. *Rebel: The Life and Times of John Singleton Mosby*. New York, NY: St. Martin's Press, 1983.
Simkins, Francis Butler. *A History of the South*. New York, NY: Random House, 1972.
Simmons, Henry E. *A Concise Encyclopedia of the Civil War*. New York, NY: Bonanza Books, 1965.
Simon, Paul. *Lincoln's Preparation for Greatness: The Illinois Legislative Years*. 1965. Chicago, IL: University of Illinois Press, 1971 ed.
Simons, Gerald. *Barbarian Europe*. 1968. New York, NY: Time-Life Books, 1975 ed.
Simpson, Lewis P. (ed.). *I'll Take My Stand: The South and the Agrarian Tradition*. 1930. Baton Rouge, LA: University of Louisiana Press, 1977 ed.
Skidmore, Max J. *Presidential Performance: A Comprehensive Review*. Jefferson, NC: McFarland and Co., 2004.
Slotkin, Richard. *No Quarter: The Battle of the Crater, 1864*. New York, NY: Random House, 2009.
Smelser, Marshall. *American Colonial and Revolutionary History*. 1950. New York, NY: Barnes and Noble, 1966 ed.
——. *The Democratic Republic, 1801-1815*. New York, NY: Harper and Row, 1968.
Smith, Emma Peters, David Saville Muzzey, and Minnie Lloyd. *World History: The Struggle for Civilization*. Boston, MA: Ginn and Co., 1946.
Smith, Hedrick. *Reagan: The Man, The President*. Oxford, UK: Pergamon Press, 1980.
Smith, John David (ed.). *Black Soldiers in Blue: African American Troops in the Civil War Era*. Chapel Hill, NC: University of North Carolina Press, 2002.
Smith, Joseph. *The Pearl of Great Price*. Salt Lake City, UT: George Q. Cannon and Sons, 1891.
Smith, Mark M. (ed.). *The Old South*. Oxford, UK: Blackwell Publishers, 2001.
Smith, Page. *Trial by Fire: A People's History of the Civil War and Reconstruction*. New York, NY: McGraw-Hill, 1982.
Smith, Philip. *A History of the World: From the Creation to the Fall of the Western Roman Empire*. 3 vols. New York, NY: D. Appleton and Co., 1885.
Smith, William. *A Dictionary of the Bible*. 1893. Nashville, TN: Thomas Nelson, 1986 ed.
Smucker, Samuel M. *The Life and Times of Thomas Jefferson*. Philadelphia, PA: J. W. Bradley, 1859.
Snider, Denton J. *Lincoln at Richmond: A Dramatic Epos of the Civil War*. St. Louis, MO: Sigma, 1914.
Sobel, Robert (ed.). *Biographical Directory of the United States Executive Branch, 1774-1898*. Westport, CT: Greenwood Press, 1990.
Sorrel, Gilbert Moxley. *Recollections of a Confederate Staff Officer*. New York, NY: Neale Publishing Co., 1905.
Spaeth, Harold J., and Edward Conrad Smith. *The Constitution of the United States*. 1936. New York, NY: HarperCollins, 1991 ed.
Sparks, Jared. *The Works of Benjamin Franklin*. 10 vols. Chicago, IL: Townsend Mac Coun, 1882.
Speer, Albert. *Inside the Third Reich*. 1969. New York, NY: Avon, 1971 ed.
Spence, James. *On the Recognition of the Southern Confederation*. Ithaca, NY: Cornell University Library, 1862.
Spooner, Lysander. *No Treason* (only Numbers 1, 2, and 6 were published). Boston, MA: Lysander Spooner, 1867-1870.
Stampp, Kenneth M. *The Peculiar Institution: Slavery in the Antebellum South*. New York, NY: Vintage, 1956.
Stanford, Peter Thomas. *The Tragedy of the Negro in America*. Boston, MA: published by author,

1898.

Stanton, Elizabeth Cady, Susan B. Anthony, and Matilda Joslyn Gage (eds.). *History of Woman Suffrage*. 2 vols. New York, NY: Fowler and Wells, 1881.

Starr, John W., Jr. *Lincoln and the Railroads: A Biographical Study*. New York, NY: Dodd, Mead and Co., 1927.

Staudenraus, P. J. *The African Colonization Movement, 1816-1865*. New York, NY: Columbia University Press, 1961.

Stavrianos, Leften Stavros. *The World Since 1500: A Global History*. 1966. Englewood Cliffs, NJ: Prentice Hall, 1991 ed.

Stebbins, Rufus Phineas. *An Historical Address Delivered At the Centennial Celebration of the Incorporation of the Town of Wilbraham, June 15, 1863*. Boston, MA: George C. Rand and Avery, 1864.

Stedman, Edmund Clarence, and Ellen Mackay Hutchinson (eds.). *A Library of American Literature From the Earliest Settlement to the Present Time*. 10 vols. New York, NY: Charles L. Webster and Co., 1888.

Steele, Joel Dorman, and Esther Baker Steele. *Barnes' Popular History of the United States of America*. New York, NY: A. S. Barnes and Co., 1904.

Steele, Shelby. *White Guilt: How Blacks and Whites Together Destroyed the Promise of the Civil Rights Era*. New York, NY: Harper Perennial, 2007.

Stein, Ben, and Phil DeMuth. *How To Ruin the United States of America*. Carlsbad, CA: New Beginnings Press, 2008.

Steiner, Bernard. *The History of Slavery in Connecticut*. Baltimore, MD: Johns Hopkins University Press, 1893.

Steiner, Lewis Henry. *Report of Lewis H. Steiner: Inspector of the Sanitary Commission, Containing a Diary Kept During the Rebel Occupation of Frederick, MD, September, 1862*. New York, NY: Anson D. F. Randolph, 1862.

Stephens, Alexander Hamilton. *Speech of Mr. Stephens, of Georgia, on the War and Taxation*. Washington, D.C.: J & G. Gideon, 1848.

———. *A Constitutional View of the Late War Between the States; Its Causes, Character, Conduct and Results*. 2 vols. Philadelphia, PA: National Publishing, Co., 1870.

———. *Recollections of Alexander H. Stephens: His Diary Kept When a Prisoner at Fort Warren, Boston Harbour, 1865*. New York, NY: Doubleday, Page, and Co., 1910.

Stephenson, Nathaniel Wright. *Lincoln: An Account of His Personal Life, Especially of Its Springs of Action as Revealed and Deepened by the Ordeal of War*. Indianapolis, IN: Bobbs-Merrill, 1922.

Sterling, Dorothy (ed.). *Speak Out in Thunder Tones: Letters and Other Writings by Black Northerners, 1787-1865*. 1973. Cambridge, MA: Da Capo, 1998 ed.

Stern, Philip Van Doren (ed.). *The Life and Writings of Abraham Lincoln*. 1940. New York, NY: Modern Library, 2000 ed.

Stonebraker, J. Clarence. *The Unwritten South: Cause, Progress and Results of the Civil War - Relics of Hidden Truth After Forty Years*. Seventh ed., n.p., 1908.

Stovall, Pleasant A. *Robert Toombs: Statesman, Speaker, Soldier, Sage*. New York, NY: Cassell Publishing, 1892.

Strain, John Paul. *Witness to the Civil War: The Art of John Paul Strain*. Philadelphia, PA: Courage, 2002.

Strayer, Joseph R. *Western Europe in the Middle Ages: A Short History*. New York, NY: Appleton-Century-Crofts, 1955.

Strayer, Joseph R., and Hans W. Gatzke. *The Mainstream of Civilization - Vol. 2: Since 1660*. 1969. New York, NY: Harcourt Brace Javonovich, 1984 ed.

Strode, Hudson. *Jefferson Davis: American Patriot*. 3 vols. New York, NY: Harcourt, Brace and World, 1955, 1959, 1964.

Sturge, Joseph. *A Visit to the United States in 1841*. London, UK: Hamilton, Adams, and Co., 1842.

Summers, Mark W. *The Plundering Generation: Corruption and the Crisis of the Union, 1849-1861*. New York, NY: Oxford University Press, 1988.

Sumner, Charles. *The Crime Against Kansas: The Apologies for the Crime - The True Remedy.* Boston, MA: John P. Jewett, 1856.
Swain, Joseph Ward. *The Harper History of Civilization.* New York, NY: Harper and Brothers, 1958.
Swint, Henry L. (ed.) *Dear Ones at Home: Letters From Contraband Camps.* Nashville, TN: Vanderbilt University Press, 1966.
Sword, Wiley. *The Confederacy's Last Hurrah: Spring Hill, Franklin, and Nashville.* New York, NY: HarperCollins, 1992.
——. *Southern Invincibility: A History of the Confederate Heart.* New York, NY: St. Martin's Press, 1999.
Tagg, Larry. *The Unpopular Mr. Lincoln: The Story of America's Most Reviled President.* New York, NY: Savas Beatie, 2009.
Tarbell, Ida Minerva. *The Life of Abraham Lincoln.* 4 vols. New York, NY: Lincoln History Society, 1895-1900.
Tatalovich, Raymond, and Byron W. Daynes. *Presidential Power in the United States.* Monterey, CA: Brooks/Cole, 1984.
Taylor, Richard. *Destruction and Reconstruction: Personal Experiences of the Late War in the United States.* New York, NY: D. Appleton, 1879.
Taylor, Susie King. *Reminiscences of My Life in Camp With the 33rd United States Colored Troops Late 1st S. C. Volunteers.* Boston, MA: Susie King Taylor, 1902.
Taylor, Walter Herron. *General Lee: His Campaigns in Virginia, 1861-1865, With Personal Reminiscences.* Norfolk, VA: Nusbaum Book and News Co., 1906.
Tenney, William Jewett. *The Military and Naval History of the Rebellion in the United States.* New York, NY: D. Appleton and Co., 1865.
Terkel, Studs. *Hard Times: An Oral History of the Great Depression.* New York, NY: Avon, 1970.
Testimony Taken By the Joint Select Committee to Inquire Into the Condition of Affairs in the Late Insurrectionary States. 13 vols. Washington, D.C.: Government Printing Office, 1872.
Thackeray, William Makepeace. *Roundabout Papers.* Boston, MA: Estes and Lauriat, 1883.
Thatcher, Marshall P. *A Hundred Battles in the West: St. Louis to Atlanta, 1861-1865.* Detroit, MI: Marshall P. Thatcher, 1884.
The American Annual Cyclopedia and Register of Important Events of the Year 1861. New York, NY: D. Appleton and Co., 1868.
The American Annual Cyclopedia and Register of Important Events of the Year 1862. New York, NY: D. Appleton and Co., 1869.
The American Annual Cyclopedia and Register of Important Events of the Year 1863. New York, NY: D. Appleton and Co., 1864.
The Collegiate Encyclopedia. 1963. New York, NY: Grolier, 1970 ed.
The Congressional Globe, Containing Sketches of the Debates and Proceedings of the First Session of the Twenty-Eighth Congress (Vol. 13). Washington, D.C.: The Globe, 1844.
The Great Issue to be Decided in November Next: Shall the Constitution and the Union Stand or Fall, Shall Sectionalism Triumph? Washington, D.C.: National Democratic Executive Committee, 1860.
The National Almanac and Annual Record for the Year 1863. Philadelphia, PA: George W. Childs, 1863.
The Oxford English Dictionary. Compact edition, 2 vols. 1928. Oxford, UK: Oxford University Press, 1979 ed.
The Quarterly Review (Vol. 111). London, UK: John Murray, 1862.
The Standard American Encyclopedia. 1916. Chicago, IL: Standard American Corp., 1937 ed.
The World Book Encyclopedia. 1928. Chicago, IL: Field Enterprises Educational Corp., 1966 ed.
Thomas, Emory M. *The Confederate Nation: 1861-1865.* New York, NY: Harper and Row, 1979.
Thomas, Gabriel. *An Account of Pennsylvania and West New Jersey.* 1698. Cleveland, OH: Burrows Brothers Co., 1903 ed.
Thompson, Frank Charles (ed.). *The Thompson Chain Reference Bible* (King James Version). 1908.

Indianapolis, IN: B. B. Kirkbride Bible Co., 1964 ed.
Thompson, James Westfall, and Edgar Nathaniel Johnson. *An Introduction to Medieval Europe: 300-1500.* New York, NY: W. W. Norton and Co., 1937.
Thompson, Neal. *Driving With the Devil: Southern Moonshine, Detroit Wheels, and the Birth of NASCAR.* Three Rivers, MI: Three Rivers Press, 2006.
Thompson, Robert Means, and Richard Wainwright (eds.). *Confidential Correspondence of Gustavus Vasa Fox, Assistant Secretary of the Navy, 1861-1865.* 2 vols. 1918. New York, NY: Naval History Society, 1920 ed.
Thorndike, Rachel Sherman (ed.). *The Sherman Letters.* New York, NY: Charles Scribner's Sons, 1894.
Thornton, Brian. *101 Things You Didn't Know About Lincoln: Loves and Losses, Political Power Plays, White House Hauntings.* Avon, MA: Adams Media, 2006.
Thornton, Gordon. *The Southern Nation: The New Rise of the Old South.* Gretna, LA: Pelican Publishing Co., 2000.
Thornton, John. *Africa and Africans in the Making of the Atlantic World, 1400-1800.* 1992. Cambridge, UK: Cambridge University Press, 1999 ed.
Thornton, Mark, and Robert B. Ekelund, Jr. *Tariffs, Blockades, and Inflation: The Economics of the Civil War.* Wilmington, DE: Scholarly Resources, 2004.
Tilley, John Shipley. *Lincoln Takes Command.* 1941. Nashville, TN: Bill Coats Limited, 1991 ed.
———. *Facts the Historians Leave Out: A Confederate Primer.* 1951. Nashville, TN: Bill Coats Limited, 1999 ed.
Tocqueville, Alexis de. *Democracy in America.* 2 vols. 1836. New York, NY: D. Appleton and Co., 1904 ed.
Toland, John. *Adolf Hitler.* 1976. New York, NY: Ballantine, 1987 ed.
Tourgee, Albion W. *A Fool's Errand By One of the Fools.* London, UK: George Routledge and Sons, 1883.
Toynbee, Arnold J. *Greek Civilization and Character: The Self-Revelation of Ancient Greek Society.* New York, NY: Mentor, 1953.
Tracy, Gilbert A. (ed.). *Uncollected Letters of Abraham Lincoln.* Boston, MA: Houghton Mifflin Co., 1917.
Traupman, John C. *The New College Latin and English Dictionary.* 1966. New York, NY: Bantam, 1988 ed.
Trevelyan, George Macaulay. *History of England.* 1926. Garden City, NY: Doubleday Anchor, 1952 ed.
Trumbull, Lyman. *Speech of Honorable Lyman Trumbull, of Illinois, at a Mass Meeting in Chicago, August 7, 1858.* Washington, D.C.: Buell and Blanchard, 1858.
Truth, Sojourner. *Sojourner Truth's Narrative and Book of Life.* 1850. Battle Creek, MI: Sojourner Truth, 1881 ed.
Tucker, St. George. *On the State of Slavery in Virginia, in View of the Constitution of the United States, With Selected Writings.* Indianapolis, IN: Liberty Fund, 1999.
Turner, Edward Raymond. *The Negro in Pennsylvania, Slavery, Servitude, Freedom, 1639-1861.* Washington, D.C.: American Historical Association, 1911.
Tyler, Lyon Gardiner. *The Letters and Times of the Tylers.* 3 vols. Williamsburg, VA: N.P., 1896.
———. *Propaganda in History.* Richmond, VA: Richmond Press, 1920.
———. *The Gray Book: A Confederate Catechism.* Columbia, TN: Gray Book Committee, SCV, 1935.
Unger, Irwin. *These United States: The Questions of Our Past - Vol. 2: Since 1865.* 1978. Englewood Cliffs, NJ: Prentice Hall, 1992 ed.
Upshur, Abel Parker. *A Brief Enquiry Into the True Nature and Character of Our Federal Government.* Philadelphia, PA: John Campbell, 1863.
Vallandigham, Clement Laird. *Speeches, Arguments, Addresses, and Letters of Clement L. Vallandigham.* New York, NY: J. Walter and Co., 1864.
Vaillant, George C. *The Aztecs of Mexico: Origin, Rise and Fall of the Aztec Nation.* 1944. Harmondsworth, UK: Penguin, 1960 ed.
Vanauken, Sheldon. *The Glittering Illusion: English Sympathy for the Southern Confederacy.* Washington, D.C.: Regnery, 1989.

Van Buren, G. M. *Abraham Lincoln's Pen and Voice: Being a Complete Compilation of His Letters, Civil, Political, and Military*. Cincinnati, OH: Robert Clarke and Co., 1890.
Van Loon, Hendrik Willem. *The Story of America*. 1927. Cleveland, OH: The World Publishing Co., 1942 ed.
Van Nostrand, John J., and Paul Schaeffer. *Western Civilization: A Political, Social, and Cultural History - Vol. 1, to 1660*. 1949. Princeton, NJ: D. Van Nostrand Co., 1956 ed.
Varhola, Michael O. *Life in Civil War America*. Cincinnati, OH: Family Tree Books, 1999.
Vaux, Roberts. *Memoirs of the Life of Anthony Benezet*. London, UK: Darton, Harvey, and Co., 1817.
Ver Steeg, Clarence Lester, and Richard Hofstadter. *A People and a Nation*. New York, NY: Harper and Row, 1977.
Villard, Henry. *Memoirs of Henry Villard, Journalist and Financier, 1835-1900*. 2 vols. Boston, MA: Houghton, Mifflin and Co., 1904.
Voegeli, Victor Jacque. *Free But Not Equal: The Midwest and the Negro During the Civil War*. Chicago, IL: University of Chicago Press, 1967.
Wade, Wyn Craig. *The Fiery Cross: The Ku Klux Klan in America*. 1987. New York, NY: Touchstone, 1988 ed.
Walker, Barbara G. *The Woman's Encyclopedia of Myths and Secrets*. New York, NY: Harper and Row, 1983.
Wallcut, R. F. (pub.). *Southern Hatred of the American Government, the People of the North, and Free Institutions*. Boston, MA: R. F. Wallcut, 1862.
Wallechinsky, David, Irving Wallace, and Amy Wallace. *The People's Almanac Presents The Book of Lists*. New York, NY: Morrow, 1977.
Walsh, George. *"Those Damn Horse Soldiers": True Tales of the Civil War Cavalry*. New York, NY: Forge, 2006.
Ward, John William. *Andrew Jackson: Symbol for an Age*. 1953. Oxford, UK: Oxford University Press, 1973 ed.
Waring, George Edward, Jr. *Whip and Spur*. New York, NY: Doubleday and McClure, 1897.
Warner, Ezra J. *Generals in Gray: Lives of the Confederate Commanders*. 1959. Baton Rouge, LA: Louisiana State University Press, 1989 ed.
——. *Generals in Blue: Lives of the Union Commanders*. 1964. Baton Rouge, LA: Louisiana State University Press, 2006 ed.
Warnock, Robert, and George K. Anderson. *The Ancient Foundations*. 1950. Glenview, IL: Scott, Foresman and Co., 1967 ed.
Warren, Robert Penn. *Who Speaks for the Negro?* New York, NY: Random House, 1965.
Washington, Booker T. *Up From Slavery: An Autobiography*. 1901. Garden City, NY: Doubleday, Page and Co., 1919 ed.
Washington, Henry Augustine. *The Writings of Thomas Jefferson*. 9 vols. New York, NY: H. W. Derby, 1861.
Watkins, Samuel Rush. *"Company Aytch," Maury Grays, First Tennessee Regiment; or, A Side Show of the Big Show*. 1882. Chattanooga, TN: Times Printing Co., 1900 ed.
Watson, Harry L. *Andrew Jackson vs. Henry Clay: Democracy and Development in Antebellum America*. New York, NY: St. Martin's Press, 1998.
Watts, Peter. *A Dictionary of the Old West*. 1977. New York, NY: Promontory Press, 1987 ed.
Waugh, John C. *Surviving the Confederacy: Rebellion, Ruin, and Recovery - Roger and Sara Pryor During the Civil War*. New York, NY: Harcourt, 2002.
Weintraub, Max. *The Blue Book of American History*. New York, NY: Regents Publishing Co., 1960.
Welles, Gideon. *Diary of Gideon Welles, Secretary of the Navy Under Lincoln and Johnson* (Vol. 1). Boston, MA: Houghton Mifflin, 1911.
Wells, H. G. *The Outline of History: Being a Plain History of Life and Mankind*. 2 vols. 1920. Garden City, NY: Garden City Books, 1961 ed.
Westermann, William L. *The Story of Ancient Nations*. New York, NY: D. Appleton and Co., 1912.
White, Charles Langdon, Edwin Jay Foscue, and Tom Lee McKnight. *Regional Geography of*

616 ABRAHAM LINCOLN: THE SOUTHERN VIEW

  Anglo-America. 1943. Englewood Cliffs, NJ: Prentice-Hall, 1985 ed.
White, Henry Alexander. *Robert E. Lee and the Southern Confederacy, 1807-1870*. New York, NY: G. P. Putnam's Sons, 1897.
White, Jon Manchip. *Everyday Life in Ancient Egypt*. 1963. New York, NY: Perigee, 1980 ed.
White, Reginald Cedric. *A. Lincoln: A Biography*. New York, NY: Random House, 2009.
White, R. J. *The Horizon Concise History of England*. New York, NY: American Heritage, 1971.
Whitman, Walt. *Leaves of Grass*. 1855. New York, NY: Modern Library, 1921 ed.
———. *Complete Prose Works*. Boston, MA: Small, Maynard, and Co., 1901.
Wilbur, Henry Watson. *President Lincoln's Attitude Towards Slavery and Emancipation: With a Review of Events Before and Since the Civil War*. Philadelphia, PA: W. H. Jenkins, 1914.
Wilder, Craig Steven. *A Covenant With Color: Race and Social Power in Brooklyn*. New York, NY: Columbia University Press, 2000.
Wiley, Bell Irvin. *Southern Negroes: 1861-1865*. 1938. New Haven, CT: Yale University Press, 1969 ed.
———. *The Life of Johnny Reb: The Common Soldier of the Confederacy*. 1943. Baton Rouge, LA: Louisiana State University Press, 1978 ed.
———. *The Plain People of the Confederacy*. 1943. Columbia, SC: University of South Carolina, 2000 ed.
———. *The Life of Billy Yank: The Common Soldier of the Union*. 1952. Baton Rouge, LA: Louisiana State University Press, 2001 ed.
Wilkens, J. Steven. *America: The First 350 Years*. Monroe, LA: Covenant Publications, 1998.
Wilkerson, Lyn. *Roads Less Traveled: Exploring America's Past on Its Back Roads*. San Jose, CA: Writers Club Press, 2000.
Williams, Charles Richard. *The Life of Rutherford Birchard Hayes, Nineteenth President of the United States*. 2 vols. Boston, MA: Houghton Mifflin Co., 1914.
Williams, George Washington. *History of the Negro Race in America: From 1619 to 1880, Negroes as Slaves, as Soldiers, and as Citizens*. New York, NY: G. P. Putnam's Sons, 1885.
———. *A History of the Negro Troops in the War of the Rebellion 1861-1865*. New York, NY: Harper and Brothers, 1888.
Williams, James. *The South Vindicated*. London, UK: Longman, Green, Longman, Roberts, and Green, 1862.
Williams, William H. *Slavery and Freedom in Delaware, 1639-1865*. Wilmington, DE: Scholarly Resources, 1996.
Willis, F. Roy. *World Civilizations - Vol. 1: From Ancient Times Through the Sixteenth Century*. 1982. Lexington, MA: D. C. Heath and Co., 1986 ed.
Wills, Brian Steel. *The Confederacy's Greatest Cavalryman: Nathan Bedford Forrest*. Lawrence, KS: University Press of Kansas, 1992.
Wilson, Charles Reagan, and William Ferris. *Encyclopedia of Southern Culture* (Vol. 1). New York, NY: Anchor, 1989.
Wilson, Clyde N. *Why the South Will Survive: Fifteen Southerners Look at Their Region a Half Century After I'll Take My Stand*. Athens, GA: University of Georgia Press, 1981.
———. (ed.) *The Essential Calhoun: Selections From Writings, Speeches, and Letters*. New Brunswick, NJ: Transaction Publishers, 1991.
———. *A Defender of Southern Conservatism: M.E. Bradford and His Achievements*. Columbia, MO: University of Missouri Press, 1999.
———. *From Union to Empire: Essays in the Jeffersonian Tradition*. Columbia, SC: The Foundation for American Education, 2003.
———. *Defending Dixie: Essays in Southern History and Culture*. Columbia, SC: The Foundation for American Education, 2005.
Wilson, Henry. *History of the Rise and Fall of the Slave Power in America*. 3 vols. Boston, MA: James R. Osgood and Co., 1877.
Wilson, Joseph Thomas. *The Black Phalanx: A History of the Negro Soldiers of the United States in the Wars of 1775-1812, 1861-'65*. Hartford, CT: American Publishing Co., 1890.
Wilson, Woodrow. *Division and Reunion: 1829-1889*. 1893. New York, NY: Longmans, Green, and Co., 1908 ed.

———. *A History of the American People*. 5 vols. 1902. New York, NY: Harper and Brothers, 1918 ed.
Winks, Robin W., Crane Brinton, John B. Christopher, and Robert Lee Wolff. *A History of Civilization - Vol. 1: Prehistory to 1715*. 1955. Englewood Cliffs, NJ: Prentice Hall, 1988 ed.
Wood, W. J. *Civil War Generalship: The Art of Command*. 1997. New York, NY: Da Capo Press, 2000 ed.
Woodard, Komozi. *A Nation Within a Nation: Amiri Baraka (LeRoi Jones) and Black Power Politics*. Chapel Hill, NC: University of North Carolina Press, 1999.
Woodburn, James Albert. *The Life of Thaddeus Stevens*. Indianapolis, IN: Bobbs-Merrill, 1913.
Woods, Thomas E., Jr. *The Politically Incorrect Guide to American History*. Washington, D.C.: Regnery, 2004.
Woodson, Carter G. (ed.). *The Journal of Negro History* (Vol. 4). Lancaster, PA: Association for the Study of Negro Life and History, 1919.
Woodward, William E. *Meet General Grant*. 1928. New York, NY: Liveright Publishing, 1946 ed.
Woodworth, Steven E. *Jefferson Davis and His Generals: The Failure of Confederate Command in the West*. Lawrence, KS: University Press of Kansas, 1990.
Wright, John D. *The Language of the Civil War*. Westport, CT: Oryx, 2001.
Wu, Shelly. *Chinese Astrology: Exploring the Eastern Zodiac*. Franklin, Lakes, NJ: Career Press, 2005.
Wyeth, John Allan. *Life of General Nathan Bedford Forrest*. 1899. New York, NY: Harper and Brothers, 1908 ed.
Young, John Russell. *Around the World With General Grant*. 2 vols. New York, NY: American News Co., 1879.
Zaehner, R. C. (ed.) *Encyclopedia of the World's Religions*. 1959. New York, NY: Barnes and Noble, 1997 ed.
Zall, Paul M. (ed.). *Lincoln on Lincoln*. Lexington, KY: University Press of Kentucky, 1999.
Zavodnyik, Peter. *The Age of Strict Construction: A History of the Growth of Federal Power, 1789-1861*. Washington, D.C.: Catholic University of America Press, 2007.
Zinn, Howard. *A People's History of the United States: 1492-Present*. 1980. New York, NY: HarperCollins, 1995.

INDEX

Note: Unlike typical indexes, this one has been compiled using an indexer: a combination of laborious manual entry work and an automated program. The result, a literary search engine of sorts, has produced some peculiarities, but should prove to be of benefit to the reader.

abolition, 8, 15, 59, 64, 67, 68, 72, 73, 75, 76, 105, 129, 144, 153, 172, 176, 177, 183, 188, 189, 191, 193, 194, 196-199, 204, 206, 207, 209, 211, 215-217, 226, 228, 250, 267, 271, 272, 297, 298, 315, 324, 341, 365, 378, 380, 382, 409, 423, 430, 464, 467, 469, 470, 478, 479, 481, 578, 580, 594, 601, 610
abolition movement, 8, 153, 194, 196, 197, 206, 215, 267, 578
abolition movement, American, began in the South, 194, 578
abolition of slavery, 105, 176, 380, 464, 580, 601
abolitionism, 257, 532, 586
abolitionist sentiment, 207
abolitionists, 7, 8, 59, 74, 131, 134, 143, 152, 157, 177, 182, 188, 191, 193, 194, 198, 199, 201, 206-208, 210, 226, 238, 244, 248, 257, 259, 265, 267-270, 276, 315, 321, 322, 332, 360, 367, 416, 427, 462, 477, 481, 518, 523, 525, 533, 579, 602
Abraham Lincoln, The Southern View (Seabrook), 27
Abraham Lincoln's white dream, 252, 583
ACS, 252, 253, 256, 528
Acton, Lord, 511
Adams, Charles F., Jr., 143
Adams, Charles F., Sr., 143, 577
Adams, John, 21, 36, 55, 99, 107, 143, 196, 469
Adams, John Quincy, 61, 88, 210
Adams, Samuel, 19, 47, 99
administrators, South-hating, 568
Adverse Action Medal of Honor Board, 306
Africa, 2, 9, 11, 13, 15, 31, 32, 56, 59, 76, 122, 126-129, 134, 135, 144, 151, 158, 161, 163-168, 170-176, 178-180, 190, 191, 195-197, 211, 218, 219, 221, 228-232, 235, 236, 239, 240, 244, 245, 248, 249, 252-254, 256, 257, 259, 261, 268, 269, 312, 315, 316, 320, 323, 332, 335, 336, 338, 339, 341, 344, 345, 347, 349, 356, 357, 359, 362-364, 366, 377, 381-385, 387, 392, 402-410, 413, 414, 416, 418-423, 431, 465-467, 479-481, 483-485, 487, 493, 517, 518, 550, 552, 581, 582, 587, 588, 590, 592-594, 596, 599, 601, 603, 607, 609, 611, 612, 614, 650
African domestic slavery, 405, 406
African Iron Age, 406
African Methodist Episcopal Church, 176
African peoples, 165
African servitude, 163, 190
African slave trade, 164, 195, 406, 410, 588
African slavery, 15, 144, 163, 164, 167, 403, 404, 406, 590
African slavery, indigenous, 164-167, 405-409
African slavery, the start of in Mediterranean Europe, 402
African-American slave owners, 161, 382
African-American war effort, 335
Africans, who practiced slavery, 164-167, 405, 407, 409
African-American culture, 151
African-Americans, 2, 9, 13, 31, 32, 76, 122, 126-129, 170, 172, 175, 178, 191, 218, 219, 229, 230, 236, 239, 245, 252, 256, 257, 259, 269, 312, 315, 316, 320, 332, 338, 341, 344, 345, 349, 356, 357, 359, 363, 377, 416, 418, 419, 421, 422, 483, 485, 609
Afro-European slave trade, 167
Agassiz, Louis, 127
agrarianism, 51, 186, 298
Agricultural Revolution, 406
Akoa pa, 166
Akyere, 166
Alabama, 11, 58, 60-62, 79, 150, 201, 234, 236, 311, 317, 335, 337, 383, 450, 472, 533, 539, 542, 549, 574, 582, 592, 602, 610
Albania, white slaves from, 391
Albany, New York, 271
Alcott, Louisa May, 192
Alexandria, Virginia, 227
Alien and Sedition Acts, 54, 55

All We Ask is to be Let Alone (Seabrook), 576, 578
all-black state in U.S., proposed by Lincoln, 252
allegiance to nation, 98
allegiance to state, 98
Alton, Illinois, 424
amalgamation, 245, 247, 253
America, 2, 3, 5-13, 16, 18, 20-25, 27, 29-33, 37-42, 44-57, 61, 64, 66, 68-72, 76, 79, 80, 83, 85-87, 89, 91-94, 97-100, 102-104, 109, 113-115, 121-123, 125-130, 134, 139, 142, 143, 145, 148, 150, 151, 153, 156, 158-162, 164, 166-168, 170-176, 178-180, 183-185, 187, 191, 193-197, 199, 202, 204, 206, 212, 213, 215, 217-223, 226, 228-233, 235, 236, 239, 240, 243, 245-247, 249, 250, 252, 253, 256, 257, 259-261, 267, 269-275, 277, 284, 285, 288, 289, 291, 293-296, 298, 301-303, 306, 307, 310, 312, 314-323, 325, 332, 335-341, 343-345, 347, 349, 356-359, 362-364, 371, 376, 377, 379, 381-385, 387, 391, 395, 402-404, 406-410, 412-414, 416-423, 427, 429-431, 433, 438, 445, 449, 451, 452, 455-458, 460-462, 465, 468-470, 472, 477, 479, 481, 483-485, 487, 488, 494, 495, 506-517, 519, 520, 525-527, 536, 537, 544, 546-548, 550, 552, 553, 556, 557, 559, 562-564, 567-569, 572, 576-617, 649, 653
American abolition movement, 8, 194, 206, 215, 578
American Anti-slavery War myth, 579
American Anti-slavery War, Marxist term, 576
American Anti-Slavery Society, 227
American apartheid, 8, 245, 525
American Caesar, nickname for Lincoln, 456
American Colonization Society, 9, 31, 170, 245, 252, 479, 481
American Confederacy, 47, 49, 51, 55, 86
American Confederacy, the U.S. as the, 48
American expansionism, 509
American imperialism, 509, 513
American mass market, 562
American Nebuchadnezzar, nickname for Lincoln, 456
American Party, 24, 270, 550
American protectionism, 509
American Revolutionary War, 85, 125, 579
American slave trade, 576
American slavery, 2, 8, 139, 167, 172, 178, 270, 376, 408, 412, 462, 576, 577, 580, 592, 598, 600, 605, 609, 653
American System, 49-51, 57, 76, 121, 134, 301, 451, 455, 511, 583
American-African slave trade, 406
America's bloated military despotism, 509
America's central banking system, 509
America's corporate welfare system, 509
America's enormous standing army, 509
America's internal revenue program, 509
America's nation-building agenda, 509
Ames, Fisher, 21
ammunition runners, 345, 346
anaconda (snake), 304
Anaconda Plan, 291, 304
Andersonville prison, 300, 303, 506
Andrew, John A., 227, 362
Andrews, Elisha B., 540
Andrews, Sidney, 443, 530
Angles' Land, 399
Anglo-Saxons, and white slavery, 399
Anglo-African, 240
Annapolis, Maryland, 173
Anneke, Fritz, 510
anti-choice on slavery, the North, 578
anti-Semitism, and Lincoln, 182, 495
Anti-Slavery Society, 406
anti-Union attitudes, 577
Antifederalism, 18, 19, 22
Antifederalism, defined, 18
Antifederalist, defined, 18
Antifederalists, 18, 19, 21, 23, 41, 50, 54, 86, 98
Antigua, 169
antislavery leaders, Southern, 198
anti-abolitionists, 248
anti-Semitism, 495
Anti-Slavery International, 261
anti-South folklore, 156
anti-South partisans, 194
anti-South propaganda, 29, 427, 581
anti-South proponents, 213
anti-South writers, 154
apartheid, 8, 245, 252, 261, 525
Appomattox, North Carolina, 150
Appomattox, Virginia, 429, 506, 512, 521, 525, 567
apportionment of representatives, 105
apprentices, Southern slaves as, 139
apprenticeship, Southern slavery similar to, 139
Aquinas, Saint Thomas, 410
Arab slave traders, 405
Arabia, and white slavery, 401
architects, 141
Argentina, 462
Aristotle, 399, 409
Arizona, 12
Arkansas, 12, 58, 303, 311, 317, 333, 533, 549

Arlington House, 339
Arlington National Cemetery, 339, 340
Army of Tennessee, 590
Arthur, Chester A., 66
Articles of Confederation, 3, 18, 44, 47, 54, 86, 90, 92, 100, 101, 118, 514, 597, 609, 610
artillerymen, 345
Asante, slavery among the, 166
Ashanti, slavery among the, 166
Ashe, Samuel A., 93, 205, 494, 507
Asia, 13, 56, 177, 201, 213, 245, 248, 358, 387-391, 401-403, 406, 555, 558
Asia Minor, white slaves from, 391
Assyrian slavery, 387, 405
Astor, John Jacob, and slavery, 172
astrology, Chinese, and Lincoln, 112
atheism, 426, 498, 501, 502, 504, 506, 575, 599
Athenian culture, 398
Athens, white slavery in ancient, 396
Atlanta campaign, 591
Atlanta, Georgia, 435, 436, 517, 562
Atlantic slave trade, 167, 409, 582, 588
atrocities, committed by Lincoln, 300
Attica, white slavery in, 389
Attucks, Crispus, 126
Augusta, Alexander T., 359, 360
Augusta, Georgia, 526
Augustin Guards, 382
Augustine, Saint, 410
Austria, 462
Autobiography of Abraham Lincoln, The (Lincoln), 272
Awowa, 166
Aztec slavery, 387
Babylonian slavery, 387, 405
Bachman, John, 441, 442
Back to Africa movement, 245
Balkans, white slavery in the, 390, 402
Baltimore American, 294
Baltimore Sun, 461
Baltimore, Maryland, 173, 278, 359, 649
Bancroft, Frederic, 309
Banks, Nathaniel P., 227, 228, 361, 485, 574
baptism, 129
barbers, 345
Barksdale, Ethelbert, 342
Barnett, T. J., 532
barracoons, 165
Bartlett, Josiah, 99
Bateman, Newton, 504
Bateman, William O., 103
Battle of Antietam, 319
Battle of Atlanta, 273
Battle of Baton Rouge, 39
Battle of Bethel Church, 346

Battle of Chickamauga, 39
Battle of First Manassas, 121, 342
Battle of Fort Pillow, 2, 67, 449, 609
Battle of Fort Sumter, 113, 117, 202, 333
Battle of Franklin II, 433
Battle of Gettysburg, 334
Battle of Lexington (American Revolution), 126
Battle of New Orleans, 125
Battle of Pydna, 392
Battle of Second Manassas, 365
Battle of Sharpsburg, 319, 365, 488
Battle of Shiloh, 39
Battle of the Crater, 358, 359, 611
Battle of Yorktown, 346
Battle of Yorktown (American Revolution), 126
battle reenactments, 472
Beaufort, South Carolina, 439
Beauregard, Pierre G. T., 114
Bedford, Gunning, 186, 187
Beecher, Henry Ward, 266, 526, 532
Beecher, Lyman, 170
Beehive, London, UK, 575
beggary, 471
Behind the Scenes (Keckley), 162
Belarus, 476
Belcher, Jonathan, 169
Belchers, New England slaving family, 169
Belgium, 462
Belknap Bribery, 547
Belknap, William W., 547
Bell, Alfred, 27
Bell, John, 273
Bellamy, Francis, 510
Belmont, August, 495
Benedict, Augustus C., 229
Benjamin, Judah, 335, 378, 515
Bennett, Lerone, Jr., 423
Benton, Thomas Hart, 43, 48, 53
Bertonneau, Arnold, 485
Bible, 3, 9, 127, 128, 322, 409, 497-502, 504, 585, 601, 602, 606, 609, 611, 613, 614, 651
Big Brother, 7, 509
big government, 7, 22, 24, 30-32, 38, 57, 184, 310, 316, 509, 510, 512, 515, 526, 557, 565, 569, 575, 598
Bight of Benin, 166
Bight of Biafra, 167
Bill of Rights, 10, 30, 51, 53, 54, 87, 89, 100, 105, 282, 515, 554, 607
Billy Yank, 616
Binis, slavery among the, 165
black citizenship, 9, 132, 134, 481-483
black civil rights, 31, 32, 59, 74, 130, 134, 170, 226, 239, 241, 242, 260, 267, 313, 315, 323, 330, 341, 342, 373, 377, 378, 416, 470, 484, 494

Black Codes, 170, 175, 238, 239
black colonization, 9, 107, 129, 170, 249, 255, 259, 267, 328, 414, 417, 418, 479, 525
black colonization program, 328
black colonizationists, 245, 338
black commissioned officers, 361
black committee, at the White House, 416
black Confederate, 332, 335, 340, 343, 346, 382
black Confederate soldiers, 330, 332, 333, 336-338, 343, 345
black Confederate troops, 335
black Confederates, 336, 338, 343, 582, 598
black deportation, 15, 144, 177, 243, 255, 256, 259, 416
black enlistment, 123, 124, 130, 298, 324, 329, 342, 350, 352, 362, 370, 371, 378, 384, 477, 481
black enlistment, and Lincoln, 125
black enlistment, reasons CSA stalled official, 343
black equality, 267, 271
black female Confederate soldiers, 346
Black Hawk War, 112
black labor, 480, 524
black land giveaways, 470
black leaders, 134, 418, 477
Black Leagues, 552
black nationalism, 245
black officers, 361, 362, 486
black pride, 245
black racism, 230, 245
black racism (African-American), 249
black racists, 245
Black Sea region, white slavery in, 396, 401
black separatism, 245
black separatists, 245
black servitude, 153, 205, 242
black skin, and black racism, 245
black slave owners, 9, 125, 151, 159, 381-384, 471
black soldiers, 32, 329, 335, 336, 343, 349, 350, 355, 356, 358-364, 367, 368, 371, 377, 485-487, 606, 611
black soldiers, under Lincoln, 364
black soldiers' children, enslaved by Lincoln, 485
black soldiers' wives, enslaved by Lincoln, 485
black suffrage, 9, 134, 220, 276, 481-483, 485, 486, 539, 548
black support, of the Confederacy, 331
Black Terror, 192
black troops, 229, 357, 361, 368, 378, 587
black Union soldiers, 349
black Yankee officers, 230, 361
Black, Jeremiah S., 308
black-only state in Africa, proposed by Western blacks, 245
black-only state in U.S., proposed by Lincoln, 252
blacks, 8, 9, 16, 32, 59, 64, 72, 76, 122-134, 140, 142, 143, 146-154, 156, 158, 159, 162, 168-170, 173-175, 177, 178, 191, 193, 194, 200-202, 206-208, 212, 218-240, 242-245, 247-250, 252-261, 267-269, 271, 272, 275, 276, 288, 297-299, 312-314, 316, 319-321, 323, 328-334, 336-363, 366-368, 371, 373, 377, 379-382, 384, 404, 413, 414, 416-423, 427, 428, 432, 437, 439, 440, 442, 466, 468, 470, 471, 477-487, 494, 508, 531, 534, 538, 539, 541, 542, 544, 547, 550, 551, 558, 576, 583, 585, 603, 612
blacks (Southern), number killed by Lincoln, 299, 557
blacks, number of that fought for Confederacy, 337, 338
blacksmiths, 141, 356
Blackwell, Hardin, 332
Blair, Montgomery, 116, 251
Bledsoe, Albert Taylor, 60, 426
Blind Tom, 332
Boadicea, 574
bodyguards, 345
Bolivia, 462
bond, between Southern whites and blacks, 345
bondage, 142, 146-148, 156, 164, 166, 177, 283, 324, 388, 391, 393, 399, 400, 405, 407, 412, 480, 601
bondservants, 168
book distributors, South-hating, 568
bookstores, South-hating, 568
Booth, John Wilkes, 258, 259, 482, 521, 649
Bornu, slavery among the, 166
Bosnia, 391, 476
Bosnia, white slaves from, 391
Boston Massacre, 126
Boston Post, 220
Boston, Massachusetts, 77, 126, 168-170, 175, 206, 218, 223, 234, 252, 270, 271, 428, 530, 549
Bostonians, 270, 530
Bourne, George, 198
Bradford, Augustus, 281
branding, 161
branding, of ancient white slaves, 389
Brannigan, Felix, 124
Braxton, Carter, 100
Brazil, 410, 462
Brazil, African slavery in, 410
Breckinridge, John Cabell, 102, 273, 347
Brentwood, Tennessee, 430

brickmakers, 141
Brierfield, 260
Briggs, George, 332
Bristol, England, white slavery at, 399
Britain, 46, 77, 85, 86, 97-99, 101, 104, 108, 143, 144, 171, 196, 297, 353, 460, 462, 601
British Empire, 88
Britons, white slavery among, 399
Brookline, Massachusetts, 169
Brooks, Preston S., 429, 467
Brotherhood Organization of a New Destiny, 339
Browder, Earl, 546
brown racism (Hispanic-American), 249
Brown University, 169, 208, 540
Brown University, connected to slavery, 169, 208
Brown, J. N., 241
Brown, John, 192, 193, 234, 427
Brown, William, 585
Browne, Charles Farrar (Artemus Ward), 491
Browne, William Hand, 36
Browns, New England slaving family, 169
Bryce, James, 460
Buchanan, James, 90, 109, 111, 205, 308, 458
Buchanan, Patrick J., 68
Buckingham, James S., 223, 234
Buell, Don Carlos, 442
buglers, 345
bummers, 437
Bureau of Printing and Engraving, 514
Burke, Joseph F., 182
Burns, Robert, 499, 502
Burnside, Ambrose E., 358
Burr, Aaron, 108
Burrhus, 574
Bush, George W., 54
Bushnell, Horace, 127
Butler, Andrew Pickens, 429
Butler, Benjamin F., 124, 258, 309, 357, 359, 371, 433, 443, 545, 574
Butler, Evan, 502
Butler, Pierce, 309
butternut, 344
C.S.A., 37, 38, 65, 113, 190, 291, 303, 590
Cabots, New England slaving family, 169
Caesar, Julius, 391, 392
Cain, mark of, 127
Calhoun, John C., 36, 43, 44, 51, 53, 55, 61, 185, 199, 204, 457, 463
California, 178, 431, 552, 583, 586
Cambyses, nickname for Lincoln, 456
Camden, South Carolina, 353
Cameron, Simon, 122, 123, 275, 276, 304, 309, 313
Camp Stanton, Maryland, 360

Campbell, John A., 120
Canaan, 128
Canada, 12, 56, 462, 587, 600
Canby, Edward R. S., 340
Canterbury, Connecticut, 271
capitalism, 51, 186, 470, 576, 582
capitalism, and Marxism, 576
Carlyle, Thomas, 323
Carnton Plantation, 3, 231, 608
Carpenter, F. B., 486
carpenters, 141, 356
carpetbag rule, 551-553
carpetbaggers, 228, 531, 537, 539, 550, 551, 555, 600
Carroll, Charles (of Carrollton), 99
Carter, Hattie, black female Confederate soldier, 346
Carter, Jimmy, 23, 160, 556
Carter, Littleberry Walker, 556
Carthage, white slaves from, 391
Cartright, Peter, 501
Cass, Lewis, 48
casualty rate, of black Union soldiers, 364
Catalans, and slavery, 405
Catholicism, 409, 410
Catholicism, and slavery, 409
Caucasian, 177, 245, 248, 388, 390, 391, 403, 406, 555
Caucasians, 201, 245, 387, 389, 402, 558
cavalrymen, 345
Celts, ancient, and white slavery, 400, 406
Celts, enslaved by Romans, 392
censorship, of pro-South books by school libraries, 568
Central America, 246, 417, 418
central banking system, 509
central government, 18-22, 26, 40, 44, 45, 51-55, 71, 78, 86, 100, 284, 301, 316, 452, 457, 475, 476, 510
Central Park, New York, 145
centralism, 512
centralization, 65, 452, 510, 513, 539, 561
chaining, 161, 389
Chaldean slavery, 387
Chambersburg, Pennsylvania, 436
Champlains, New England slaving family, 169
Channing, William Ellery, 170, 208
chaplains, 337
Charles IX, nickname for Lincoln, 456
Charleston Mercury, 217, 294, 455, 493
Charleston, Illinois, 131, 415
Charleston, South Carolina, 27, 79, 113, 346, 348, 382, 531, 566
Chase, Salmon P., 176, 266, 285, 325, 463, 465, 483
Chase, Samuel, 19, 99
Chasseboeuf, C. F. de, 497

chattel slavery, 189, 261
Cheever, George B., 266
Cherokee, 384, 385
Chesnut, James, Jr., 335
Chesnut, Mary, 161, 210, 234, 335, 345, 356, 442, 491
Chicago Daily Times, 285
Chicago Times, 294
Chicago Tribune, 341
Chicago, Illinois, 178, 240, 265, 271, 301, 510
Chickasaw, 384, 385, 588
chickens, 162
child labor, 316
children, 2, 9, 10, 14, 59, 62, 108, 127, 128, 140, 145, 146, 151, 152, 160, 164, 166, 167, 177, 178, 187, 200, 202, 212, 214, 218, 231, 233, 234, 237, 243, 254, 268, 299, 301, 315, 316, 338, 348, 352-355, 388-391, 393, 400-402, 406, 408, 417, 420, 432, 436-439, 442, 443, 445, 450, 485, 495, 512, 517, 537, 540, 542, 549, 557, 570, 572, 573
Children's Crusade, and white slavery, 401
Chile, 462
Chinese astrology, and Lincoln, 112
Choctaw, 384, 385, 588
Christ, 3, 9, 14, 128, 192, 411, 497, 498, 500, 501, 516, 526, 589, 600
Christian clergy, as slave owners, 409
Christian Observer, 285
Christian Recorder, 269
Christian, George L., 14, 37, 276, 326, 448, 524, 569, 572
Christianity, 3, 254, 498-500, 502, 504, 505, 590, 605, 607
Christianity, and slavery, 409
Christians, 390, 401, 410, 499, 503, 574
Christmas, 3, 12, 142, 162, 435, 549
Church of Jesus Christ of Latter-Day Saints, 128, 600
Church of Lincoln, 29
Cincinnati Commercial, 347
Cincinnati Gazette, 540, 548
Cincinnati, Ohio, 123, 151, 174
citizenship, 9, 131, 132, 134, 479, 481-483, 556
City Point, Virginia, 447
civil rights, 9, 31, 32, 55, 59, 63, 74, 76, 102, 126, 130, 134, 164, 167, 170, 220, 226, 239, 241, 242, 248, 249, 257, 260, 267, 285, 288, 291, 305, 310-316, 323, 330, 341, 342, 363, 365, 371, 373, 377, 378, 380, 381, 413, 416, 470, 478, 482, 484, 487, 494, 527, 536, 549, 605, 612
Civil War, 2, 3, 9, 25, 29, 30, 37, 38, 41, 58, 83, 105, 111, 114, 120, 121, 151-153, 174, 184, 186, 197, 206, 209, 227, 268, 288, 298, 299, 304, 310, 316, 320, 323, 332, 345, 435, 446, 458, 460, 472, 512, 519, 546, 567, 568, 573, 579, 581-612, 614-617, 651, 653
Civil War amendments, 316
Civil War disqualification and debt, 105
Civil War Sesquicentennial, 29
Civil War, England's, 460
civilian deaths, Southern, 299, 432, 472
Clark, Abraham, 99
Clark, L., 586
class struggle, 575
class warfare, and Marx, 576
Clay, C. C., 574
Clay, Cassius M., 59
Clay, Henry, 36, 42, 49, 50, 57, 59, 134, 219, 252, 254, 301, 479
cleaning, 6, 230, 355
Cleburne, Patrick R., 481, 518, 519
Clement V, Pope, 409
clergymen, 131, 297, 301, 303, 477, 478
Cleveland, Ohio, 271
cliometric research, on tariffs, 46
Clymer, George, 99
Coit, Margaret L., 199, 467
Coldstream Guards, 334
Coles, Edward, 224
Colfax, Schuyler, 547
collective slavery, 261
Colonial Period, 172
colonization, 9, 31, 107, 129, 170, 177, 218, 245, 246, 249, 251, 252, 254-256, 258-260, 267, 328, 380, 414, 416, 418, 419, 479-481, 487, 525, 593, 612
colonization of America, 487
colonization, black, Lincoln's plan for, 249
colonizationist, 153, 182, 315, 483
colonizationists, 177, 245, 259, 338
Colored Brigades, Confederate, 342
Columbia, South Carolina, 348, 443, 472
Columbus, Christopher, 387, 402
Committee on the Conduct of the War, 39
common law suits, 105
communism, 575
communism, and Lincoln, 546
communist gaslighting, 577
Communist Party Convention (1939), and Lincoln, 510
communist propaganda, and Lincoln, 576
communist society, 575
communists, and Lincoln, 510
communists, in Lincoln's administration and armies, 510

communists, in the Republican Party, 176, 259
comparative slavery, 406
compensated emancipation, 313, 380, 469, 524, 525
compensation of members of Congress, 105
Complete Works of Abraham Lincoln (Nicolay and Hay), 272
Compromise of 1877, 553
Comptroller of the Currency, 514
Concord, Massachusetts, slavery in, 169
confeder, defined, 18
Confederacy, 2, 3, 6, 8, 11, 15, 17-20, 22, 32, 37, 44, 47-49, 51, 55, 57, 58, 61, 64-69, 71, 76, 77, 80, 83, 86, 87, 100, 101, 107-111, 113-118, 120, 122, 126, 143, 153, 179, 181, 182, 185, 186, 190, 193, 203, 204, 212, 213, 247, 274, 277, 291, 292, 295, 296, 298, 301-305, 311, 312, 317, 318, 327, 329, 330, 332, 333, 335, 337-339, 343-346, 349, 350, 354, 355, 358, 361, 364, 372, 383, 384, 391, 430, 433, 438, 455, 459, 461, 462, 478, 495, 510, 514, 520, 522, 533, 556, 559, 560, 564, 566, 577, 578, 584, 585, 588, 590, 595, 600, 605, 606, 608-610, 614-616, 651
Confederacy 101 (Seabrook), 578
confederacy, defined, 18
confedral government, 18-20, 50, 86
confedral, defined, 18
confederalism, defined, 19
Confederalist, 18, 19, 21, 22, 52
confederalist, defined, 19
Confederalists, 19, 44, 50, 53, 54, 65, 86, 87
confederalization, defined, 19
confederalize, defined, 19
confederance, defined, 19
Confederate army, 32, 39, 68, 117, 160, 279, 331, 334-337, 341, 346, 347, 382, 586, 589
Confederate Battle Flag, 55, 56, 596
Confederate bonds, 332
Confederate Capitol, 48
Confederate Cause, 39, 66, 296, 332, 347, 348, 382, 601
Confederate Congress, 68, 77, 203, 311, 352, 566
Confederate Constitution, 179
Confederate flag, 2, 179, 274, 331, 333, 596, 609, 610, 653
Confederate gentry, a Marxist term, 576
Confederate House of Representatives, 66
Confederate Jews, 182
Confederate Mary, 346
Confederate Memorial Association, 559
Confederate military, 8, 334, 335, 340, 343, 346, 591
Confederate Monument, Arlington National Cemetery, 339
Confederate navy, 346, 608
Confederate Southern Memorial Association, 517
Confederate States of America, 3, 6, 13, 18, 38, 44, 47, 49, 69, 85, 89, 100, 274, 296, 303, 338, 438, 588, 590, 604, 609, 610
Confederate troops, 335
Confederate veterans, 56, 347, 559, 586, 651
Confederate White House, 260
confederate, defined, 20, 55
confederated, defined, 20
confederately, defined, 20
confederateship, defined, 20
confederating, defined, 20
confederation, 3, 15, 18-20, 22, 35, 44-49, 52, 54, 55, 57, 68, 72, 86, 90, 92, 100, 101, 110, 118, 512, 514, 597, 609-611
Confederation of Tennessee Native Tribes, 68
Confederation of the American States, the U.S. as the, 48
confederation, defined, 20
confederatism, defined, 20
confederator, defined, 20
confedery, defined, 20
Confiscation Acts, 380, 478
conformity, 563
Congress, 6, 46, 52, 60, 66, 68, 73, 77, 81, 82, 85, 86, 99, 105, 109-112, 126, 135, 155, 157, 174, 177, 179, 184, 187, 203, 242, 243, 246, 255, 256, 279, 281, 283, 284, 286, 300, 303, 307, 309-311, 315, 316, 352, 356, 357, 364, 375, 376, 447, 458, 470, 478-480, 483, 491, 492, 495, 501, 503, 504, 521, 524, 533, 547, 551, 555, 566, 581, 588, 596, 602, 606, 607, 613
Conkling, James C., 370, 371
Connecticut, 39, 41, 97, 99, 103, 127, 168, 220, 233, 271, 285, 467, 537, 552, 557, 562, 612
conservatism, 24, 25, 209, 306, 616
conservatives, 23-25, 39, 247, 273, 274, 527, 551, 568
consolidation, 52, 65, 94, 102, 452, 510, 511
consolidationism, 512
Constantinople, and white slavery, 402
Constitution Day, 70
Constitution of the Confederate States, 3, 609, 610
Constitutional Convention, 41, 51, 70, 86, 98, 100, 186, 204, 281, 587

Constitutional Convention of 1787, 51, 70, 86, 100, 587
constitutional law, 91, 285, 305, 307, 310, 376, 426, 463, 578, 582
Constitutionalism, 68, 202, 589
construction of Constitution, 105
Continental Army, 157
contraband, 227, 228, 300, 303, 516, 613
contraband camps, 228, 613
contrabands, 590
Contract Labor Act, 514
Conway, Moncure D., 123
Cooke, Alistair, 63, 567
cooking, 230, 355, 398, 540
cooks, 335, 341, 345, 347
coopers, 141
copperhead, 112, 190, 287, 482, 649
Cornett, Rachel, 433
Coroticus, King, 406
corporate welfare, 50
corporate welfare system, 509
Corwin Amendment, 8, 375, 376, 481
Corwin, Thomas, 376
cotton, 43, 46, 89, 90, 157, 158, 172, 200, 210, 211, 221, 232, 233, 352, 408, 431, 435, 444, 465-468, 541, 579, 590, 598, 601, 604
cotton gin, 211, 467
Cotton Triangle, 465, 466
Cotton Triangle, English, 465
Cotton Triangle, Yankee, 465, 466
counter-Reconstruction, 551
Courier des États-Unis, 294
coverers, 584
craftsmen, 141
Crandall, Prudence, 271
Crawford, William, 95
Credit Mobilier, 547
Creek, 384, 385, 426, 591, 614
Cremer, William, 580
Creoles, 333
Creswell, John A. J., 523, 525
Crete, 401
Crete, white slavery in, 401
Crimea, the, white slavery in, 401
criminal prosecutions, 105
criminals, 112, 156, 158, 161, 166, 175, 206, 250, 401, 433, 434, 437, 580
Croatia, 476
Cromwell, Oliver, 460
Crowninshield Island, 169
Crowninshields, New England slaving family, 169
crucifixes, display of prohibited by Mormons, 128
cruel and unusual punishment, 105
Cuba, 462, 606

Cuffe, Paul, 245
Czar, nickname for Lincoln, 456
czars, governmental, 54
Dabney, Robert Lewis, 117
Dahomeans, 165
Daily Conservative, 341, 343
Daily Courier, 348
Daily Express, 294
Daily Picayune, 294
Daily True Delta, 228
Dallas Herald, 294
Dallas, Texas, 538
Dana, Charles A., 510, 575
Dana, Richard H., 266
Danish slave traders, 405
Danish slaves, 401
DAR, 542
Dare, Virginia, 385
dark lantern tactics, 550
Darwin, Charles, 127
Davis, David, 248, 275, 285
Davis, Henry Winter, 266
Davis, Jefferson, 7, 14, 22, 29, 48, 61, 62, 65, 66, 70, 71, 77, 95, 98, 109, 118-120, 134, 155, 158, 190, 199, 203, 204, 219, 260, 261, 277, 280, 291, 298-300, 307, 311, 312, 320, 327, 334, 340, 343, 346, 352, 353, 374, 384, 447, 450, 451, 456, 458, 463, 481, 487, 493, 506, 515, 518, 519, 522, 525, 534, 548, 556, 557, 566, 567, 576, 578
Davis, Jefferson C. (Yankee), 158
Davis, Varina (Howell), 260
Davis, William C., 333
Dawson, Nathaniel, 524
De Forest, John W., 130
de Wolfs, New England slaving family, 169
death, 3, 29, 48, 66, 121, 126, 129, 146, 148, 154, 180, 193, 195, 196, 199, 222, 227, 228, 233, 237, 256, 259, 260, 270, 271, 284, 299, 300, 304, 314, 315, 329, 363, 365, 366, 393-395, 397, 406, 442, 449, 452, 457, 461, 477, 483, 521-529, 543, 544, 553, 555, 557, 560, 567, 568, 570, 573, 574, 577, 580, 650
DeBow, James D. B., 214
Declaration of Independence, 60, 82, 85, 86, 90, 95, 98-101, 118, 196, 279, 301, 404, 508, 515, 561, 594
Deep South, 151, 156, 382, 468, 535, 556
defeatism, 121
defection, 121
Deism, 498
Delany, Martin, 245
Delaware, 79, 97, 99, 103, 123, 186, 480, 491,

557, 591, 616
demagoguism, 241, 522
Democracy in America (Tocqueville), 93
Democrat, defined, 20
Democratic party, 21-23, 25, 42, 273
Democratic-Republican party, 23
Denmark, 141, 192, 462
Denmark Vesey Rebellion, 192
Dent, Julia Boggs, 257
Department of Agriculture, 513
deportation, 15, 31, 129, 144, 177, 239, 243, 249, 251, 252, 255, 256, 258, 259, 288, 299, 323, 328, 408, 416, 418, 436, 479-481, 650
Depression, 27, 28, 489, 511, 613
depression, and Lincoln, 28, 489
desertion, 121, 157, 299, 311, 312
desertion rates, Yankee, 121
desertion, under Washington, 157
Destruction and Reconstruction (Taylor), 63
Detroit, Michigan, 178, 271, 563
dialectical materialism, 575
diaries, 331, 385
Dicey, Edward, 225
Dickens, Charles, 80
DiLorenzo, Thomas J., 513
disease, 51, 121, 228, 353, 364, 403, 471, 557
dishonest historians, 481
District of Columbia Emancipation Act, 176, 177
disunion, 80, 91, 184, 475, 476, 568
Division and Reunion: 1829-1889 (Wilson), 142
Dixie, 3, 30, 38, 42, 44, 55, 64, 67, 71, 72, 80, 81, 98, 114, 129, 141, 148, 150-152, 167, 185, 203, 207-209, 211, 212, 220-222, 228, 232, 237, 260, 273, 276, 296, 305, 311, 330-332, 339, 344, 346, 347, 350, 351, 354, 428-430, 434, 438, 443, 444, 460, 461, 469, 472, 480, 488, 492, 493, 517, 519, 520, 530-533, 535-537, 539, 540, 544, 545, 551, 553-555, 558, 562, 564, 565, 568, 586, 594, 601, 616, 649
Dixie (song), 221
doctrine of uniformity, Lincoln's, 563
Dodge, William E., 69
Dodson, Jacob, 122
Doroughty, Lee, 449
double jeopardy, 105
Douglas, Stephen A., 31, 49, 64, 125, 132, 241, 242, 253, 256, 273, 414, 415, 424, 432, 482, 563, 564
Douglass, Frederick, 9, 74, 141, 170, 192, 226, 245, 249, 266, 267, 315, 341, 342, 360, 362, 418, 421, 422
Douglass' Monthly, 341, 363, 418, 494

Dred Scott case, 482
drivers, black, 159
drummers, 345
Du Bois, W. E. B., 413, 470
due process, 105, 279, 299, 306, 309, 310
Duncan, James, 198
Durden, Robert F., 232
Durnford, Andrew, 383
Dutch slave traders, 405
Earl of Oxford, 651
Early, Jubal, 436, 438, 439
East Coast Elites, 30
Ebony magazine, 423
economic struggle, 575
economic warfare, and Marx, 576
economics, 71, 77, 80, 161, 592, 614
Ecuador, 462
editors, South-hating, 568
educational system, the modern South's, 472
educators, South-hating, 568
efficiency, slave labor vs. free labor, 468
Efiks, slavery among the, 165
Egyptian slavery, 387
Eighteenth Amendment, 105
Eighteenth Amendment repealed, 105
Eighth Amendment, 105
election of 1860, 247, 273, 274, 276, 303, 379
election of 1864, 273, 288, 289, 303, 319
election of 1868, 545
election of 1876, 553
election of 1976, 556
election of president and vice president, 105
Electoral College, 273, 274, 292
Eleventh Amendment, 105
Ellery, William, 99
Ellerys, New England slaving family, 169
Ellis, John Willis, 115
Ellison, William, black slave owner, 383
emancipation organizations, 198
Emancipation Proclamation, 7, 8, 10, 32, 64, 67, 76, 122, 130-134, 144, 164, 173, 177, 199, 216, 220, 227, 237, 244, 253, 256, 257, 259, 269, 276, 296-298, 301, 312-314, 317-322, 324-330, 350, 355, 356, 364-366, 370, 371, 374, 375, 377, 381, 463, 467, 469, 477-479, 481, 491, 541, 650
emancipation proclamations, nullified by Lincoln, 304
Emerson, Ralph Waldo, 169, 192, 427, 428, 430, 492
empire, 24, 42, 49-51, 88, 266, 322, 389-391, 394, 401, 402, 452, 455, 456, 460, 515, 585, 594, 596, 600, 611, 616
Encyclopedia of Mormonism (Ludlow), 129
Engels, Friedrich, 184

engineers, 141
England, 38, 43, 77, 79, 98, 107-109, 143, 148, 156, 168-171, 181, 184, 192, 196, 200, 208, 211, 246, 252, 270, 271, 294, 296, 304, 321, 366, 399, 402, 404, 428, 465, 517, 532, 557, 581, 594, 602, 606, 608, 614, 616
England, white slaves from, 399, 402
England's Civil War, 460
English, 18, 20, 40, 63, 80, 98, 117, 127, 145, 156, 160, 223-225, 233, 236, 267, 296, 298, 374, 376, 385, 399, 401, 403, 405, 406, 410, 460, 465, 468, 517, 583, 594, 596, 602-604, 606, 613, 614
English slave traders, 405
English, white slavery among, 399
Epirus, 392
equal protection, 105
equal rights, 239, 315, 316, 370, 479
Equal Rights Amendment, 315
Equal Rights Party, 315
Erda, 563
Esclavon, Jacques, 332
esoteric signals, 550
Estonia, 476
Ethelwulf, King, 399
Europe, 3, 13, 18, 40, 54, 56, 61, 68, 77, 79, 129, 148, 161, 164-167, 184, 206, 219, 222, 231, 232, 249, 256, 294-298, 302, 321-324, 345, 358, 364, 385, 388, 389, 391, 400-404, 407-409, 416, 469, 491, 520, 525, 537, 563, 578, 579, 583, 585, 590, 591, 594, 595, 597, 604, 606, 608, 611, 612, 614, 651
European Enlightenment, 54, 469
European slavery, 404
European support, 129, 520
European support of the Confederacy, 296
Europeans, 77, 164, 296-298, 322, 323, 345, 389, 400, 402, 404, 407-409, 563
European-American hegemony, 249
European-Americans, 13, 206, 358, 385, 416, 537
Evarts, Jeremiah, 170
Everything You Were Taught About the CW is Wrong (Seabrook), 579
Ex parte Milligan, 483
excessive bail or fines, 105
execution of black soldiers, by Lincoln, 363
Executive Order 9981, 357
expansion of slavery, 242, 375
expansionism, 509
Ezekiel, Moses Jacob, 182, 184, 340
Facts & Falsehoods Concerning the War on the South (Meriwether), 516

Fair Labor Standards Act, 316
Fairfax, Fernando, 197
Fall of Man, 410
Faneuil Hall, 169, 270
Faneuil, Peter, 270
Faneuils, New England slaving family, 169
Fantins, slavery among the, 165
Farewell Address, Washington's, 451, 452
farmers, 45, 64, 157, 212, 213, 220, 396, 432, 468
Farragut, David G., 182
farriers, 345
Father-God, 129
Faulkner, William, 234
Fay, Edwin, 433
fear of his father, Lincoln's, 490
federacy, defined, 20
federal government, 17, 20, 21, 43, 50, 88-90, 92-94, 102, 109, 110, 119, 181, 204, 287, 376, 448, 511, 513, 536, 561, 603, 614
federal, defined, 20
Federalism, 19, 21, 22, 39, 581
federalism, defined, 21
federalist, defined, 21
Federalists, 18, 21, 23, 24, 50-55, 57, 65, 86, 87, 600
federalization, defined, 21
federalize, defined, 21
federate, 17, 20-22, 55, 57, 186, 510
federate, defined, 21, 55
federation, defined, 21
felons, 437
Ferdinand the Catholic of Aragon, 410
Ferguson, Tom, 347
Fernandina, Florida, 79, 363
Field, Stephen J., 285
fifers, 345
Fifteenth Amendment, 105, 316, 554
Fifth Amendment, 105
fifty-dollar bill, 548
Fillmore, Millard, 404
film producers, South-hating, 568
Final Emancipation Proclamation, 67, 122, 133, 216, 269, 317, 318, 330, 364, 381, 479, 481
Finley, Robert, 252
firemen, 345
fire-eater, 114, 217
First Amendment, 105
First Inaugural Address, Davis', 61
First Inaugural Address, Hayes', 553
First Inaugural Address, Jefferson's, 46, 88, 96
First Inaugural Address, Lincoln's, 58, 75, 101, 312, 342, 376, 379, 461, 478, 556
First Inaugural Address, Pierce's, 48
First Inaugural Address, Polk's, 48

First Punic War, 392
Fitzhugh, George, 146, 147
Five Civilized Tribes, 384
Fleming, Walter L., 335
Flemings, and slavery, 405
Florentines, and slavery, 405
Florentines, sold into slavery by the Catholic Church, 409
Florida, 11, 12, 58, 60, 79, 81, 201, 311, 317, 363, 461, 533, 549
Floyd, William, 99
Fon, 165
Fon, slavery among the, 165
Fontana, C. P., 580
forced African labor, 487
forced enlistment, 353
forced labor, 322
Ford Theater, Washington, D.C., 649
foreign alliances, 451, 509
Forrest, Nathan Bedford, 67, 71, 118, 158, 160, 261, 347, 383, 449, 552
Forrest! (Seabrook), 449, 552
Fort Hamilton, 308
Fort Lafayette, 277, 308
Fort McHenry, 280, 445
Fort Monroe, 119, 227
Fort Smith, 333
Fort Sumter, 15, 58, 68, 107, 113, 114, 117, 119, 202, 375, 376, 529, 535, 555, 564, 592
forty acres and a mule, 470
Forty-Eighters, the, 510
Foster, Augustus J., 186
Founders, 43-45, 51, 68-71, 87, 93, 210, 256, 284, 302, 475, 476, 509, 515, 568, 578
Founding documents, 70, 82, 93
Founding Fathers, 17, 24, 39, 46, 47, 69, 103, 118, 251, 455, 469, 475, 510, 514, 568, 578, 587
Founding Generation, 56, 508, 565
Fourier, Charles, 532
Fourierism, 532
Fourteenth Amendment, 105, 316, 554
Fourth Amendment, 105
Fox, Gustavus, 116, 117
France, 38, 96, 171, 294, 296, 297, 398, 462, 580
Francis, Newton, 502
Franklin, Benjamin, 64, 70, 99, 218
Franklin, Tennessee, 30, 32, 231, 433
free blacks, 126, 140, 146-148, 154, 170, 175, 206, 207, 224, 229, 239, 248, 249, 252, 253, 255, 275, 328, 330, 337, 346, 348, 382, 421, 471, 481
free enterprise, 513
free labor, 155, 230, 243, 396, 398, 468, 532, 592
free labor, efficiency of vs. slave labor, 468
free laborers, 147
free schools, 200
free trade, 77, 182, 186
free trade system, 77
Free Urban mail delivery, 514
Freedman's Village, 177
freedmen, 150, 159, 217, 227, 228, 237, 345, 356, 362, 470, 480, 553, 590, 601
freedmen, used by the North instead of freemen, 371
Freedmen's Bureau, 541, 551
freedom of religion, 54, 105, 287
freedom of speech, 10, 279
freedom of the press, 7, 10, 282, 287, 311, 460
freedwomen, 150, 470
Freeman's Journal, 285, 493
freemen, as opposed to freedmen, 371
free-loveism, 532
Free-Soil party, 219, 404
Fremantle, Arthur J., 334
Frémont, John C., 266, 304, 313, 380, 554
French and Indian War, 125
French colonial commerce, and slavery, 398
French slave traders, 405
Fugitive Slave Law, 74, 174, 342
Gabriel Prosser Rebellion, 192
Gallic Wars, 391
Gambia, slavery in, 165
Gardner, Isabella Stewart, 169
Gardners, New England slaving family, 169
Garfield, James A., 66
Garret, Richard, 649
Garrison, William Lloyd, 152, 153, 170, 173, 205-208, 227, 234, 267, 270, 272, 315, 343, 366, 469, 478, 492
Garvey, Marcus, 245
gaslighting, communist, 577
Gaul, white slaves from, 391
Gauls, enslaved by Romans, 392
General Order No. 11, 494, 495
General Order No. 3, 74
Geneva Convention, 10, 299, 440, 446
genocide-at-law, and Lincoln, 126
Genoese, and slavery, 405
Genoese, and white slavery, 401
George II, nickname for Lincoln, 456
George III, 46, 97, 98, 171, 196
Georgia, 43, 48, 58, 60, 97, 100, 103, 119, 157, 172, 186, 194, 201, 228, 260, 311, 317, 332, 340, 434, 435, 440, 444, 446, 459, 517, 526, 531, 533, 549, 554, 556, 562, 595, 612, 616
Germans, ancient, and white slavery, 400, 406
Germans, white slavery among, 399
Germany, 38, 301, 306, 402, 580

Gerry, Elbridge, 19, 99
Gettysburg Address, 100, 320, 567
gift shops, South-hating, 568
Gilmer, John A., 176, 424
Give 'Em Hell Boys! (Seabrook), 449, 552
gladiators, Roman, and white slavery, 396
God, 2, 3, 31, 44, 45, 89, 96, 128, 129, 150, 162, 180, 187, 193, 241, 244, 246, 289, 320, 382, 410, 411, 429, 442, 461, 469, 487, 497-501, 505, 506, 527, 573, 574, 587, 589, 594, 610
gold, 2, 3, 5, 166, 203, 222, 442, 651
Gold Coast, 166
Gone With the Wind (Mitchell), 149, 273
Good Friday, 526
Goodlow, Daniel Reaves, 198
GOP.gov, 511
Gordon, John B., 187
Gordon, Nathaniel, 180
Goudy, William, 53
governmental centralization, 513
Gracie, Archibald, and slavery, 172
Grady, Henry W., 531
Graham, Levin, 332
grand jury, 105
Grand Rapids, Michigan, 477
Grant, Ulysses S., 66, 149, 182, 189, 216, 244, 257, 290, 328, 330, 338, 340, 355, 356, 367, 404, 433, 435, 444, 445, 447, 467, 487, 494, 495, 507, 521, 534, 548, 557, 558, 579
Grantism, 547
Grappe, Gabriel, 332
Great Britain, 46, 97-99, 143, 144, 171, 196, 297, 353, 460, 462, 601
Great Emancipator, 11, 37, 298, 568
Great Mother, 563
Greece, ancient, and white slavery, 396
Greece, white slaves from, 391
Greek slavery, 388, 405
Greek slaves, paid a salary, 140
Greeley, Horace, 89, 153, 266, 267, 343, 366, 368, 380, 381, 516, 526, 548
Greenhow, Rose O'Neal, 183, 184
Greenmount Cemetery, 649
Gregory, Saint of Nazianzus, 410
Gregory, Saint, the Great, 399
Grey, Adeline, 148
Grimké, Angelina, 152, 198
Grimké, Sarah, 198, 315
gunpowder, 407
Gwinnett, Button, 100
habeas corpus, 10, 31, 277, 280, 286, 310, 311, 547
Hacker, Louis M., 44, 379
hagiographers, 568
Hahn, Michael, 485

Haiti, 177, 201, 256, 481
Haitian Revolution, 201
Haley, Alex, 173
Hall, Lyman, 100
Hall, Thomas, 471
Halleck, Henry W., 74, 356, 446, 447, 495, 496
Halstead, Murat, 548
Ham, 128
Hamilton, Alexander, 21, 22, 48, 50, 64, 107, 186, 457
Hamiltonianism, 21, 22
Hamiltonianism, defined, 22
Hamiltonians, 23, 50, 51
Hamlin, Hannibal, 133, 266, 330, 529, 547
Hammond, James H., 148
Hammurabi, Law of, 388
Hampton Roads Conference, 67, 115, 258, 374, 375, 525
Hampton, Wade, 14, 443, 551
handclasps, 270, 550
Hanks, Nancy, 39, 515
Hanks, Tom, 515
Hardin Co., Kentucky, 556
Hardscrabble farm, 384
Harper's Ferry, Virginia, 192, 193
Harris, Isham G., 343
Harrison, Benjamin, 66, 100
Harrison, William H., 265
Hart, John, 99
Hartford Convention, 108
Hartford, Connecticut, 562
Harvard Law School, 169
Harvard University, 169, 529, 610
Hatch, Edward, 299, 433
Hausas, slavery among the, 165
Hawthorne, Nathaniel, 193
Hay, John, 115, 272, 385, 486
Hayes, Rutherford B., 66, 553, 556
Hayne, Robert Young, 223
headright system, 404
Hebrew slavery, 387, 388
Hebrews, early, 411
Hedrick, Benjamin Sherwood, 198
Helm, Ben Hardin, 39
Helm, Emilie (Todd), 39
Helots, white slaves, 393, 396
Helper, Hinton Rowan, 143, 250, 251
Hemings, Sally, 239
Henry the Lion, 401
Henry VIII, King, 410
Henry, Patrick, 14, 19, 194, 195
Henry, Robert Selph, 461
Henson, Josiah, 151
Herndon, W. D., 501
Herndon, William H., 284, 490, 491, 499, 500, 502

Herzegovina, 476
Hewes, Joseph, 100
Heyward, Thomas, Jr., 100
Higginson, Thomas Wentworth, 192, 378
Higher Law, 7, 306, 308
Hill, Samuel, 498, 500
Hill, Thomas, 529
Hilton Head, South Carolina, 352
Himmler, Heinrich, 403
Hitler, Adolf, 126, 295, 301, 306, 402, 403
Hittite slavery, 387
Hodges, Silas, 449
hog story, and Lincoln, 516
hogs, 436, 516
Holtorp, J. E., 580
homelessness, 146, 147, 230, 436, 471
Homer, 406
Homestead Act, 277, 513
Homeward Passage, 465
Honest Jeff and Dishonest Abe (Seabrook), 519, 568
Hood, John Bell, 273, 435, 437
Hooker, Joseph, 365, 456
Hooper, William, 100
Hopkins, Stephen, 99
Hopkinson, Francis, 99
Hotze, Henry, 221
House of Burgesses, Virginia, 126
House of Representatives, 39, 66, 111, 112, 285, 376, 532, 551
house servants, 230
Howe, Samuel Gridley, 192
Howell, G., 577
Howell, Varina, 260
Hughes, John, 366
Humphreys, Dan, 332
Hungary, white slaves from, 391
Hunt, John, 597
Hunter, David, 76, 266, 304, 313, 380, 433, 438, 439, 446
Huntington, Samuel, 99
Hurst, Fielding, 449
hypochondriasm, and Lincoln, 490
Ibos, slavery among the, 165
Iliad, the, 389
Illinois, 12, 24, 27, 30, 31, 39, 49, 57, 64, 74, 93, 125, 129, 131, 178, 224, 239-242, 244-246, 249, 252, 253, 255, 256, 265, 271, 285, 294, 315, 317, 325, 350, 366, 370, 414, 415, 424, 426, 431, 432, 467, 482, 489, 496, 498, 503, 504, 510, 520, 527, 552, 560, 563, 569, 570, 583, 585, 591, 593-595, 602, 603, 606, 611, 614
Illinois Journal, 520
Illinois Staats-Anzeiger, 520

Illinois State Register, 294
Illinoisans, 39, 239, 240, 325
imperialism, 509, 513
Inca, 387
Inca slavery, 387
income tax, 50, 105, 284, 302, 303, 513
Independence Hall, 49, 569
Independent party, 25
India, 9, 39, 68, 112, 123, 125, 126, 138, 159, 164, 168, 211, 244, 275, 276, 295, 315, 343, 379, 384, 385, 387, 405, 428, 462, 467, 547, 550, 552, 584, 586, 588, 589, 591, 592, 597, 601, 612, 614, 617
India, white slavery in, 405
Indian slave owners, 9, 384
Indiana, 39, 138, 275, 276, 379, 467, 550, 552, 586, 591, 592, 612, 614, 617
individual rights, 515
Industrial Revolution, 200, 468
industrial slavery, 189, 322
industrialism, 51, 186, 298, 565
industrialization, 539, 561, 562
inequality, and communism, 576
infantrymen, 345
inflation, 203, 535, 614
injustice, and communism, 576
Innocent VIII, Pope, 410
insurrection, Southern black, planned by Yanks, 133
integration, 177, 228, 240, 249, 267, 357, 358, 361
internal improvements, 509
internal revenue, 509
International Law, 60, 205, 300, 304
International Workingmen's Association, 577, 580
interracial marriage, 9, 230, 237, 238, 241, 245, 250, 416
intertribal raids, and slavery in Africa, 407
involuntary enlistment, of blacks into U.S. military, 351
involuntary servitude, defined, 139
Iowa, 350
Iranian slavery, 394
Iraq, ancient, and white slavery, 388
Ireland, 3, 402, 406, 536
Ireland, white slaves from, 402
Irish, 231, 286, 321, 322, 399, 406, 585
Irish House of Commons, 286
Irish, purchase white English slaves, 399
IRS, 284, 302, 509
Irwinville, Georgia, 119
Isabella Stewart Gardner Museum, 169
Iscariot, Judas, 515
Islam, 391
Islam, and slavery, 391

Islamic slavery, 412
Israel, Moses Jacob, 184
Italian slavery, 401
Italians, enslaved by Nazis, 403
Italy, 79, 391-393, 396, 401, 580
Italy, and white slavery, 396
Italy, Southern, white slavery in, 401
Italy, white slaves from, 391
Jackson, Andrew, 23, 25, 42, 237, 286, 509
Jackson, Claiborne F., 115
Jackson, Thomas Stonewall, 14, 199, 260, 336, 519, 560
Jacksonian Republicans, 23
Jamestown, Virginia, 9, 419
Japheth, 128
Jay, John, 44, 48, 64
Jefferson, Thomas, 18, 19, 22, 24, 36, 38, 41, 42, 44-48, 50, 53, 54, 64, 69, 70, 85, 88, 90, 95-98, 100, 104, 107, 108, 139, 142, 181, 186, 195, 196, 203, 235, 238, 251, 302, 303, 383, 452, 455, 493, 508, 509, 514, 515, 567, 578
Jeffersonianism, 19, 22, 50, 56, 288
Jeffersonianism, defined, 22
Jent, Elias, Sr., 433
Jesuits, and slavery, 410
Jesus, 3, 128, 129, 410, 411, 497-501, 504, 505, 515, 516, 600
Jesus, and Satan are brothers according to Mormons, 129
Jew peddlers, 495
Jewish Confederate soldiers, 340
Jewish slavery, 388
Jews, enslaved by Nazis, 403
Jim Crow states, 239
Johnny Reb, 67, 152, 344, 366, 526, 616
Johnson, Andrew, 318, 404, 444, 457, 523, 529, 533, 535, 544, 545, 554
Johnson, Anthony, 381
Johnson, Clint, 27-29
Johnson, Robert, 363
Johnson, William, 384
Johnston, Albert Sydney, 14, 199
Johnston, Joseph E., 14
Jones, John, 240, 333, 597
Joseph, 411
Journal of Commerce, 285
journals, 331, 353, 385, 590, 591, 593
Journey in the Seaboard Slave States, A (Olmsted), 145
Jubilee, day of (emancipation), 149
Judean slavery, 405
judicial limits, 105
Julian, George W., 138, 379
Jung, H. F., 580
jury trial, 105

Kansas, 12, 42, 220, 253, 292, 341, 343, 581, 587, 601, 613, 616, 617
Kansas-Nebraska Act, 42
Kaskel, Caesar J., 495
Kautz, August V., 337, 338
Keckley, Elizabeth, 141, 162, 354
Kendael, Hiram, 332
Kennan, T. R., 429
Kentucky, 11, 39, 55, 59, 64, 102, 123, 198, 292, 294, 433, 485, 515, 556, 563, 574, 583, 606, 617, 651
Kentucky and Virginia Resolutions, 55
Kenya, slavery in, 165
Key, Francis Scott, 252
King John, nickname for Lincoln, 456
King, Edward, 562
King, Horace, black slave owner, 383
King, nickname for Lincoln, 456
King, Rufus, 107
Kings, New York, 172
Kinte, Kunta, 173
Kirkwood, Samuel J., 350
Kitchell, Joseph, 239
KKK, 129, 270, 549-552, 554
KKK, and Mormons, 129
Know-Nothing party, 270
Koran, 412, 588
Korean War, 357
Krus, slavery among the, 165
Ku Klux Klan, 2, 270, 549, 550, 596, 598-600, 609, 615
Ku Klux Klan, New England version, 270
La Patrie, 294
labor colonies, 227, 228
labor productivity, 468
labor, Marxism, and Lincoln, 576
labor, white, 579
laborers, 124, 131, 147, 200, 210, 252, 261, 314, 337, 341, 343, 345, 356, 369, 390, 397, 479, 480
Lafayette, Marquis de la, 308
laissez-faire economy, 25, 26, 46, 77
Lake Champlain, 169
Lamon, Ward H., 266, 280, 310, 498, 500, 503, 526, 567
landscapers, 141
Lane, Jim, 304
Lansing, John, 19
larceny, 448, 542
large scale farming, 210
Larue Co., Kentucky, 556
Latin America, 256, 257, 596
Latinos, 494
Latin-Americans, 13, 126, 358
Latvia, 476
laundry, 355
Laurium, Greece, 397

Lawrence, Amos A., 529
LDS, 128
League of the South, 430, 559
Leaves of Grass (Whitman), 527
Lee, Francis Lightfoot, 100
Lee, Richard Henry, 19, 100, 199
Lee, Robert E., 14, 69, 71, 72, 98, 134, 149, 199, 202, 203, 211, 212, 298, 311, 319, 339, 358, 429, 447, 458, 471, 481, 506, 511, 512, 519, 521, 543, 560, 580
left-wing propagandists, 575
left-wingers, radical, 576
Lehman Brothers, and slavery, 172
Lenin, Vladimir, 510
Lenoir, William, 53
Lester, Charles Edward, 188
Lester, Julius, 423
Letcher, John, 438
Lewis, Francis, 99
Lexington, Virginia, 433
Liberal Establishment, 30
liberal Northerners, 452
liberalism, 25, 47, 301, 565, 569, 595
liberals, 24, 29, 50, 54, 86, 288, 301, 306, 510, 527, 529, 539, 545, 554
Liberia, 177, 245, 253, 256, 271, 414, 417
libertarian, 18, 25, 26, 30, 39, 311, 322, 510, 515
Libertarian party, 25
libertarianism, 18, 19, 22-24, 51
libertarians, 23, 50, 568
liberty, 24, 44, 78, 85, 89, 92, 120, 140-142, 146, 147, 187, 189, 196, 198, 202, 203, 219, 220, 224, 250, 254, 279, 285-289, 378, 422, 451, 457, 459, 460, 463-465, 468, 469, 477, 485, 507, 510, 512, 515, 522, 566, 573, 583, 585, 595, 599, 600, 603, 607, 614
libraries, South-hating, 568
Limber, Jim, 260
Lincoln Memorial, 76, 488
Lincoln Monument, 488
Lincoln Myth, the, 30
Lincoln, Abraham, 7-9, 14, 22, 27, 28, 30-32, 36, 37, 39, 42-44, 46, 47, 49, 52, 57, 59, 67, 70, 71, 75, 79, 82, 89, 91, 93, 96, 100-102, 104, 109, 111, 114, 117, 120, 121, 129-132, 135, 138, 141, 143-145, 148, 153, 164, 167, 170, 173, 177, 178, 180, 181, 188, 199, 204, 205, 208, 209, 212, 218-220, 226, 228, 232, 237, 238, 240-242, 244-254, 256, 258-261, 266-268, 274, 276, 281, 283, 285-287, 291, 292, 295, 296, 298, 299, 301, 302, 305, 306, 309, 311, 312, 315, 317, 318, 320, 322, 328-330, 332-334, 338, 341, 342, 346, 349, 350, 354, 355, 357, 362-364, 367, 368, 371, 373-379, 381, 384, 385, 408, 413-415, 421, 422, 424, 429-435, 437-439, 441, 444, 446, 448-450, 452, 453, 455-459, 461, 462, 465, 467, 469, 471, 472, 475-477, 480, 487, 489, 492, 495, 497, 502, 506-508, 511-513, 515-519, 521, 524-527, 532, 535, 538, 544-549, 551, 553-557, 560, 562-565, 567, 569, 571, 573-575, 577, 579, 580, 649, 650
Lincoln, Abraham, and Karl Marx, 575
Lincoln, Mary (Todd), 39, 160, 570, 649
Lincoln, Thomas, 39
Lincolndom, 530
Lincolnian apologists, 526
Lincolnian mythology, 222, 527
Lincolnian myths, 63
Lincolnites, 59, 144, 526, 546
Lincolnology (Seabrook), 38, 144
Lincoln's War, 2, 3, 9, 16, 26, 27, 29, 37, 40, 43, 55, 62, 63, 66, 67, 69, 72, 73, 79, 80, 83, 109, 112, 117, 118, 121, 123, 134, 148, 150, 153, 157-159, 172, 181, 182, 184, 192, 193, 199, 200, 202, 203, 205, 211, 217, 220, 230-232, 235, 238, 284, 299, 304, 316, 337, 340, 342, 343, 348, 361, 421, 427, 429, 449, 450, 458, 459, 461, 467, 468, 470, 508, 512, 519, 538, 543, 546, 548, 551, 554, 556, 558, 565, 566, 578-581, 609, 653
Lincoln's War (Seabrook), 578
Linconia, 257
Linder, Usher F., 265
liquor abolished, 105
little bell, Seward's, 308, 309
livestock, 140, 228, 332, 399, 402, 412, 537, 551
Livingston, Philip, 99
Livingstone, David, 166
Locke, David R., 416
Locke, John, 87, 468
Lodge, Henry Cabot, Jr., 169
Lodge, Henry Cabot, Sr., 169
Logan, John A., 350
logbooks, 331
London Spectator, 321
London Standard, 294, 321
London Telegraph, 350
London Times, 294, 321, 459

London, UK, 577
Long Island, New York, 419
Longstreet, James, 334
Los Angeles, California, 178
Lost Cause, 114, 605
Louisiana, 11, 58, 60, 79, 107, 149, 154, 200, 201, 239, 294, 303, 317, 324, 331, 336, 355, 361, 368, 382-384, 482, 485, 531, 533, 538, 549, 553, 581, 583, 586, 590, 596-598, 604, 607, 611, 615, 616, 650
Louisiana Native Guards, 361
Louisiana Purchase, 107
Louisville Journal, 294
Love, Henry, 332
Lovejoy, Elijah, 271, 275, 481
Lubez, P. V., 580
Ludlow, Daniel H., 129
Lundy, Benjamin, 193
Luther, Martin, 410
Lutz, Charles, 332
Lynch, Thomas, Jr., 100
Lynchburg, Virginia, 438
Lyons, Lord, 309
Lytle, Andrew Nelson, 72, 563
Macedonia, white slaves from, 391
Mackay, Charles, 267
Maddison, John, 404
Madeira, 462
Madison, James, 14, 36, 43-45, 54, 55, 64, 70, 88, 90, 96, 103, 110, 187, 195, 224, 286, 404, 455, 508, 515, 563
magazines, South-hating, 568
maiming, 448
Maine, 52, 271, 285, 294, 306, 491, 538, 557
Majorca, African slavery on, 402
Malbones, New England slaving family, 169
Malcolm X, 423
Mali, slavery in, 165
Mallory, Stephen R., 71
mammy, the, 159, 230
Manassas, Virginia, 341
Manchester Guardian, 117
Mandingos, slavery among the, 165
Manigault, Louis, 232
manumission societies, 198
marble, 396
Marblehead, Massachusetts, 168
Marching Through Georgia (Work), 444
Marfan Syndrome, and Lincoln, 28, 487
Marius, Gaius, 392
Marshall, John, 21
martial law, 277, 278, 304, 305, 318, 533
Martin, Luther, 19
Martineau, Harriet, 224
Marx, Karl, 184, 575-577, 579, 580
Marx, Karl, and Lincoln, 575

Marx, Karl, his letter to Lincoln, 576
Marxism, 575
Marxists, and Lincoln, 7, 510
Maryland, 6, 97, 99, 103, 123, 173, 258, 277, 278, 280-283, 287, 294, 319, 359, 360, 480, 523, 567, 649
Mason, George, 19, 52-54, 70, 181, 197, 204, 455, 463
Mason, James M., 297, 463
Mason, Jeremiah, 170
Masonry and Mormonism, 129
Masonry, Mormonism based on, 128
masons, 141, 356
Mason-Dixon Line, 508
Massachusetts, 11, 41, 52, 61, 97, 99, 103, 104, 107, 109, 126, 159, 167-171, 175, 210, 218, 225, 227, 237, 245, 252, 265, 270, 280, 314, 362, 371, 378, 404, 429, 467, 529, 531, 537, 538, 549, 557, 566, 595, 599, 603, 604
Massachusetts Bay, 97, 404
Massachusetts Bay Colony, 404
Matheny, James H., 500, 501
May, Samuel J., 210
Mayan slavery, 387
McCarty, Burke, 546
McClellan, George B., 74, 274, 342, 366, 378, 491, 492
McConnell, Lewis, 332
McGavock family, 204, 231
McGavock, Randal, 213, 214
McGavocks, 3, 231, 608
McKean, Thomas, 99
McKinley, William, 66
McLuhan, Marshall, 564
Medal of Honor, 306
Mediterranean Europe, and white and black slavery, 402
megalomania, and Lincoln, 28
Meigs, Montgomery C., 340
Mein Kampf (Hitler), 301
melancholia, and Lincoln, 490
Melchizedek, 515
Melting Pot, U.S. as a, 257
Memoir of the Last Year of the War for Independence, A (Early), 438
Memphis, Tennessee, 332
Mencken, H. L., 567
merchants, 64, 78, 107, 168, 210, 275, 400, 431
Meridian, Mississippi, 434
Meriwether, Elizabeth Avery, 516
Merryman, John, 280
Mesopotamian slavery, 405
Metoyer family, black slave owners, 382
Metoyer, Augustin, 383
Mexicans, 8, 125, 556

Mexican-American War, 125, 243, 247, 556
Mexico, 243, 296, 462, 614
Michigan, 12, 48, 178, 220, 477, 590
Middle Ages, 396, 402, 590, 612
middle class, American, 579
middle class, Marx's hatred of the, 579
Middle Passage, 158, 409, 465
Middle Tennessee, 584, 651
Middleton, Arthur, 100
middle-class mulattos, 64
Military Department of the West, 74
military despotism, 287, 302, 509
military draft, 268, 303
military executions, Yankee, under Lincoln, 298
military measure, 323
military necessity, 102, 304, 379, 483, 505
military necessity, Lincoln's imagined theory, 483
Military Order of the Stars and Bars, 559
Mill, John Stuart, 298
millers, 141
Milroy, Robert H., 433
Minor, Berkeley, 461
miscegenation, 253, 254
Mississippi, 11, 58, 60, 157, 167, 201, 203, 231, 311, 317, 377, 384, 434, 446, 468, 495, 516, 533, 545, 548, 549, 553, 590, 606, 607
Mississippi River, 468
Missouri, 41, 42, 48, 64, 115, 123, 128, 174, 188, 200, 220, 236, 242, 285, 292, 318, 446, 563, 574, 589, 605, 616
Missouri Compromise of 1820, 41, 42
Missouri River, 128
Mitchell, James, 416
Mitchell, Margaret, 149, 273
mob boss, Lincoln as a, 277
Mobile Register, 40, 62
Mobile, Alabama, 79, 335, 337, 566
Mohr, Clarence, 344
monarchical empire, 452
monarchism, 21, 22
Monarchists, 50, 51, 57, 526
monarchy, 46, 287, 452, 455, 460
money order system, 514
Monroe, James, 14, 19
Montana, 12
Montgomery convention, 118
Montgomery, Alabama, 61
Montgomery, Augustus S., 133
Monticello, 452
monument, Southern, to black Confederate soldiers, 338
Morehead, Charles S., 375
Morgan, Pierpont, and slavery, 172
Morgan, Sarah, 144, 145, 149
Morgan, T. J., 124

Mormon beliefs, 128
Mormon groups, 129
Mormon law, and slavery, 128
Mormon laws, 128
Mormon ministers, 129
Mormon priesthood, 129
Mormon slave owners, 128
Mormon slaves, 128
Mormonism and Curse of Ham, 129
Mormonism and Goddess-worship, 129
Mormonism and Masonry, 129
Mormonism and white racism, 128
Mormonism Unmasked (Roberts), 129
Mormons, 128, 129
Mormons, and KKK, 129
Morning News, 285, 552
Morrill Land-Grant College Act, 513
Morrill Tariff, 513
Morris, Lewis, 99
Morris, Robert, 99
Morris, Thomas, 466
Morton, John, 99
MOSB, 559
Mosby, John Singleton, 71, 200, 232, 445
Moses, 14, 128, 182, 325, 340, 388, 515, 603
mother fixation, and Lincoln, 490
Mother-Goddess, 129
Mother-Goddess, and Mormonism, 129
Mott, Lucretia, 314
Mount Rushmore, 488
mountaineers, 64
Mozambique, slavery in, 165
Mudd, Roger, 649
Mudd, Samuel, 649
Muhammad, prophet, 391
mulattoes, 237, 253
murderers, 189, 442
museum managers, 255
museums, South-hating, 568
musicians, 335, 345
Muslim slaves, 412
mutilation, 161
Mycenaean slavery, 387
Myers, Thomas J., 353
NAACP, 338, 339
nanny state, 510
Nantes, France, 398
Napoleon III, 297
narcissism, and Lincoln, 490
Nash, Beverly, 236, 542
Nashville, Tennessee, 5, 318, 333, 430, 472, 548, 563
Nat Turner Rebellion, 192, 206
Natchez National Historical Park, 384
Natchez, Mississippi, 384
Nathan Bedford Forrest (Seabrook), 449, 552
National Academy of Science, 514

National Association for the Advancement of Colored People, 338
National Banking Acts, 514
National Colored Republican Convention, 541
national debt, 81, 82, 511, 543
national government, 17, 52, 87, 90, 452, 475, 514, 597
National Intelligencer, 182, 478
National Park Service, 582
national Republican convention, 1860, 275
National Women's Rights Convention, 314
nationalism, 21, 22, 245
nationalism, defined, 22
nationalists, and Lincoln, 510
nationalized banking system, 455
nation-building agenda, 509
nation-states, 18, 20, 44, 68, 90, 97, 98, 100, 103, 512
Native Guards, 361
Native-Americans, make slaves of early white settlers, 385
Native-Americans, poor treatment of by U.S. government, 126
Native-American rights, 315
Native-American slave owners, 9, 151, 384, 468
Native-Americans, 8, 10, 13, 68, 123, 126, 159, 168, 213, 275, 289, 295, 315, 358, 384, 385, 410, 494, 563
natural law, 468
natural rights, 78, 146, 200, 301, 468, 514
natural selection, 127, 588
naval blockade, 10, 304, 327, 449, 471
Nazi Germany, 306, 402
Nazi Slave Labor Program, 403
Nazi slavery, 403
Nebraska, 42, 244, 429, 601
Nebraska Territory, 429
necessity, theory of, Lincoln's, 483
negative stereotypes, of the South, 430
Negro, 76, 108, 123, 125, 127, 130, 131, 144-147, 163, 193, 208, 209, 222-224, 229, 233, 236, 240, 241, 243, 244, 246-248, 268, 299, 325, 329, 334, 335, 340, 341, 346, 353, 357, 359, 361, 366, 370, 371, 407, 416, 424, 438, 439, 444, 471, 483, 493, 517, 541-543, 557, 574, 579, 583, 585, 587, 592, 594-596, 599, 601, 602, 605, 610, 611, 614-617
Negro Convention, 150
Negro Digest, 236
Negro enlistment, 357
Negro kings, and African slavery, 407
Negroes, 63, 122-124, 143, 145, 147, 159, 170, 179, 186, 197, 211, 222-224, 231, 235, 237, 239, 240, 246-248, 250, 251, 258, 272, 279, 329, 334, 336, 341, 343, 346-350, 353, 361, 363, 370, 371, 380, 383, 408, 415, 416, 439, 445, 517, 518, 595, 602, 616
Negrophobia, 218, 482
Nelson, Thomas, Jr., 100
neo-Confederate, 56, 559
Nero, 573-575
Netherlands, 404, 462
neutrality, European, 297
Nevada, 11, 292
New Bedford, Massachusetts, 170
New Bern, North Carolina, 79
New Deal, 7, 513
New England, 43, 98, 107-109, 156, 168-171, 181, 192, 208, 211, 246, 252, 270, 271, 366, 428, 465, 557, 594, 602
New England secession movement, 107
New Englanders, 22, 193, 270, 271, 465, 530
New Hampshire, 48, 97, 99, 103, 104, 145, 168, 285, 458, 466, 538, 557
New Jersey, 97, 99, 103, 108, 172, 215, 252, 418, 467, 557, 602
New Orleans, Louisiana, 149, 333, 485
New South, 38, 71, 130, 149, 153, 156, 194, 234, 249, 268, 340, 344, 427, 448, 531, 565
New South Southerners, 38, 71
New South writers, 234
New Testament, 3, 410, 411, 501
New Testament, and slavery, 410
New World, 401, 603
New York, 11, 49, 59, 69, 77, 82, 89, 95-97, 99, 103, 108, 119, 124, 145, 149, 172, 173, 178, 180, 181, 206, 210, 215, 223, 225, 229, 234, 251, 267-269, 271, 277, 283, 285, 294, 308, 309, 324, 336, 359, 362, 363, 365, 380, 404, 419, 467, 476, 488, 516, 522, 538, 547, 548, 550, 552, 557, 563, 581-608, 610-617
New York City, New York, 77, 172, 173, 178, 206, 223, 225, 234, 547
New York Daily News, 294
New York Evening Day-Book, 294
New York Evening Post, 82, 359
New York Herald, 294
New York Tribune, 89, 267, 363, 522
New York World, 285, 294, 324, 488
Newburyport, Massachusetts, 270
newspapers, South-hating, 568
Newsweek, 149, 472
Nicolay, John G., 115, 272, 385, 486
Nigeria, slavery in, 166
Nigger Hill, Boston, Massachusetts, 175
Nigger Hill, Washington, D.C., 175
Nightingale, the, 180

Nineteenth Amendment, 105, 315
Ninth Amendment, 105, 578
Noah, 127
non-enumerated rights, 105
Nordhoff, Charles, 220
Norfolk, Virginia, 79, 440
North Carolina, 28, 41, 58, 79, 93, 97, 100, 103, 115, 150, 186, 198, 215, 317, 363, 477, 533, 549, 551, 560, 585, 589, 591, 592, 600, 605, 606, 611, 617, 651
North Carolina Manumission Society, 198
North pushes slavery South, 211
Northern abolition movement, 267
Northern abolitionists, 152, 188, 201, 226, 244, 259, 276, 427
Northern blacks, 220, 221, 225, 226, 249, 268, 487
Northern businessmen, 77, 158, 174, 178, 196, 530, 535
Northern historians, 268, 269
Northern history, 204, 537
Northern industrialism, 186, 298
Northern Ireland, 536
Northern literature, 163, 537
Northern merchants, 78, 209, 210
Northern myth, 11, 134, 149, 161, 162, 176, 178, 203, 204, 213, 215, 316, 476, 649
Northern mythologists, 71, 160, 197, 229, 527
Northern mythology, 32, 37, 67, 154, 158, 164, 231, 419, 538, 567
Northern Nero, nickname for Lincoln, 456
Northern newspapers, 31, 119, 182, 284, 354, 442, 572
Northern plantations, and slavery, 465
Northern ports, 77, 178
Northern prejudice, 364
Northern progressivism, 186
Northern propaganda, 538
Northern racism, 15, 191, 217, 227, 271, 349, 359, 360, 371
Northern slave owners, 197, 215
Northern slavery, 7, 167, 171-173, 177, 178, 180, 181, 230, 481, 576
Northern states, 48, 62, 96, 107, 126, 193, 197, 201, 223, 224, 237, 247, 277, 283, 288, 290, 305, 467, 517, 518, 538, 548, 564, 579
Northern textbooks, 537
Northern whites, 175, 220, 269, 271, 319, 354, 360, 361, 371, 404
Northerners, 2, 8, 24, 25, 29, 31, 38-40, 43, 48, 52, 58, 61, 66, 72, 80, 89, 91, 98, 114, 121, 127, 131, 134, 139, 140, 143, 149, 153, 159, 170, 181, 182, 192, 194, 200, 208, 210, 213, 214, 216-218, 228, 239, 242, 245, 249, 253, 257, 267-271, 274, 277, 284, 285, 298, 299, 305, 306, 323, 324, 329, 333, 338, 340, 344, 345, 351, 359, 364, 367, 371, 428, 442, 448, 450, 452, 465, 470, 472, 477, 491, 508, 515, 529, 530, 533, 535, 537, 550, 551, 553, 557, 558, 562, 565-567, 609, 612
Northernization, 9, 521, 559, 561, 565
North's Great Emancipators, 481
Norway, 476
Notes on the State of Virginia (Jefferson), 104, 203
Nova Scotia, 108
Nubian slaves, 391
nullification, 447, 605
nurses, 234, 343, 345, 347
Oak Ridge Cemetery, 527
Oath of Allegiance, 279, 280, 300, 303, 378, 537
Obama, Barack Hussein, 29, 54, 70, 511, 513
Occidental Slave Trade, 164
Oceania, 56
Odgers, George, 580
Odonko, 166
Odyssey, the, 389
Office of Immigration, 514
Official Records, 133, 134, 351, 440, 604
Official Records of the War of the Rebellion, 440
Ohio, 123, 151, 174, 182, 219, 220, 272, 284, 285, 288, 294, 309, 375, 437, 466, 467, 529, 540, 553, 555, 563, 603
Ohio River, 437
Oklahoma, 12
Old Agrarian South, 561
Old North, 57, 231, 481, 577
Old South, 2, 57, 98, 140, 142, 146, 149, 164, 167, 231, 237, 395, 413, 481, 512, 531, 559, 563, 577, 582, 586, 592, 597, 611, 614
Old South abolitionists, 481
Old Testament, 128, 388, 411
Old Testament, and slavery, 388, 411
olive oil, 396
Olmsted, Frederick Law, 145, 198, 233, 234
On Agriculture (Cato the Elder), 390
Ord, Edward O. C., 533
Order of Confederate Rose, 559
Order of the Sons of Liberty, 285
Oregon, 11, 552
Oriental Slave Trade, 164
Original Sin, 410
Osborne, Charles, 198
Ottawa, Illinois, 241, 256, 414, 432, 482, 563
Ottoman Empire, and white slavery, 402

Our American Cousin (Taylor), 649
outlaws, 437, 602
Outward Passage, 465
overdeveloped super-ego, Lincoln's, 490
overseers, black, 159
Owens, Mary, 504
Owsley, Frank Lawrence, 44, 179, 193, 538
O'Hara, Scarlett, 273
Paca, William, 99
Paine, Robert Treat, 99
Paine, Thomas, 45, 497, 499
paleoconservatives, 23
paleoconservativism, 23
Palestinian slavery, 388
Palmerston, Lord, 297
Panama, 256, 258, 259
Panama plan, Lincoln's colonization, 259
Papacy, and slavery, 409
Paris, France, 96, 171
Parker, Theodore, 192, 499
Patrick, Saint, 406
patronage, 7, 94, 542, 554
Paul III, Pope, 409
Paul, Saint, 129, 410, 499
Paullus, Lucius Aemilius, 392
Payne, Daniel A., 176
peace advocates, 311
peace party, 274, 285
peace societies, 311
peculiar institution, 172, 383, 405, 430, 611
Pendleton, George H., 274
Penn, John, 100
Pennsylvania, 49, 86, 91, 97, 99, 103, 108,
    111, 156, 173, 178, 187, 243, 276,
    285, 308, 334, 419, 436, 466, 487,
    495, 532, 557, 569, 589, 597, 599,
    613, 614
Pensacola, Florida, 79
pension applications, 331
Peoria, Illinois, 244, 246, 414
Pepperell, Massachusetts, 169
Pepperells, New England slaving family, 169
Persian slavery, 387, 394
personal letters, 331
Perth Amboy, New Jersey, 215
Petersburg, Virginia, 358
Peterson, Jesse Lee, 339
Phelps, John W., 266, 304
Phelps, Thomas A., 336
Philadelphia Evening Journal, 285
Philadelphia, Pennsylvania, 41, 49, 77, 86, 98,
    173, 178, 204, 206, 223, 224, 227,
    234, 309, 569
Philip II, nickname for Lincoln, 456
Phillips, Wendell, 74, 266, 267, 315, 478, 571
Phoenician slavery, 387, 405
physical force, and slavery, 161

Piatt, Don, 491, 528
Picayune Butler (song), 488
Pickens, Francis W., 348
Pickering, Timothy, 107, 108
Pickett, George E., 91
Pierce, Franklin, 48, 264, 458
Pierce, William, 168
Pierre-August, Jean Baptiste, 332
Pierre-August, Lufray, 332
Pillsbury, Parker, 315
Pinckney, Charles, 44, 70, 204, 455
pirate, defined, 304
Plains, Georgia, 556
plantation, 3, 143-145, 150-152, 154, 155, 226,
    231, 235, 237, 260, 322, 323, 331,
    381, 384, 391, 441, 465, 541, 583,
    585, 588, 592, 598, 605, 608
plantation belts, 151
plantation books, 331
plantation manuals, 154
plantation slavery, 322, 323
plantations, 97, 103, 132, 143, 149, 150, 154,
    155, 158, 159, 161, 162, 169, 171,
    191, 211, 215, 228, 236, 331, 346,
    351, 355, 401, 402, 431, 439, 446,
    465, 468, 530, 531, 537, 541
planters, wealthiest, 214
Plato, 399
Pleasants, M. F., 545
Pleasants, Robert, 195
Pledge of Allegiance, 510
Plutarch, 391
Poles, enslaved by Nazis, 403
political agitation, and communists, 576
politically correct, 71, 427, 568
Polk, James K., 48
poll taxes barred, 105
Pollard, Edward A., 102, 114, 115, 119, 142,
    163
polygamy, 129
Pomeroy, Samuel, 257
poor white trash, 558
poor whites, 64
Pope, John, 366, 433, 533, 539
Porter, Fitz John, 365
Portland, Maine, 52
Portugal, 462
Portuguese slave traders, 405
Portuguese, first European slaver traders in
    Africa, 164
Postal Service, 513
postwar reunion notes, 331
Potomac River, 174
Potter, Charles Francis, 516
poverty, 227, 235, 471, 541, 562
Preliminary Emancipation Proclamation, 133,
    134, 144, 256, 259, 320, 324, 330,

355, 381, 479, 650
presentism, 146
presidential disability and succession, 105
presidential term and succession, 105
presidential vote for District of Columbia, 105
prisoners, Lincoln's treatment of, 506
private soldier, defined, 337
privateer, defined, 304
privileges and immunities, 105
pro-choice on slavery, the South, 578
pro-North Civil War writers, 30
pro-slavery intervention myth, 579
pro-South groups, 30
Prohibition, 105, 157, 179, 197
promiscuity, alleged, among Southern whites and blacks, 237
proslavery amendment, Lincoln's, 376
Prosser, Gabriel, 192
prostitutes, 437
prostitution, 3, 388, 471
protectionism, 50, 509
protective tariff, 57, 61
proto-peasants, Southern black slaves as, 141
Providence Plantations, 97, 103, 171
Providence Post, 354
provision grounds, 140
Provisional Congress of the Confederacy, 66
pro-Lincoln mythology, 427
pro-North historians, 9, 423
Prussia, 462
psychopathology, and slavery, 161
publishers, South-hating, 568
Puerto Rico, 462
Pulaski, Tennessee, 549
Punch, 294
Puritan stock, Yankees from, 127
Puritans, 168
Purvis, Robert, 420
Quarles, Benjamin, 347
quartering of soldiers, 105, 286
Queens, New York, 172
Quetzalcoatl, Pagan god and Mormonism, 129
race, and Marxism, 576
racial separatism, 245
racial warfare, and Marx, 576
racism, 10, 15, 56, 127, 129, 137, 147, 171, 177, 191, 209, 217, 222, 225, 227, 229, 230, 238, 245, 249, 271, 338, 349, 357, 359, 360, 362, 363, 367, 369, 371, 387, 414, 416, 418, 466, 481, 487, 508, 549, 550, 552, 583, 602
racism, black (African-American), 249
racism, brown (Hispanic-American), 249
racism, in the North, 222, 223
racism, white (European-American), 249
racism, yellow (Asian-American), 249

racist military policies, Lincoln's, 363
racists, non-white, 245
Radicals, 176, 259, 328, 478, 524, 525, 531, 533, 535, 539, 544, 545, 552, 580
railway mail service, 514
Randolph, George Wythe, 41
Randolph, John, 98, 198, 431
Rankin, John, 198
rape, 231, 299, 322, 438, 440, 448, 450, 531, 539
rape of black females, by Yankee soldiers, 440
rape of white females, by Yankee soldiers, 438
Rawle, William, 91, 94
Read, George, 99
Reagan, Ronald, 23, 512
Rebel Born, A (Seabrook), 449, 552
Rebels, 74, 77, 116, 117, 330, 336, 337, 340, 341, 346, 355, 380, 383, 429, 432, 488, 506, 529, 594, 602
Reconstruction, 9, 16, 63, 110, 184, 236, 304, 309, 425, 508, 521-525, 528-531, 533-536, 538-541, 544, 545, 548-555, 558, 559, 561, 562, 580, 581, 585, 591, 592, 594, 596, 600, 602, 606, 611, 613, 649
red racism (Native-American), 249
red slave owners, 213, 385, 413
Reddick, Maria, 231
redistribution, of Southern land and wealth by Lincoln, 9, 355
Reed, John S., 562
Reed, W. M., 449
refugeeing, 231
refugees, 9, 436, 437, 470
refugees, Southern, 436
Reich government, Hitler and Lincoln, 302
Reid, Whitelaw, 530, 540
reign of terror, Lincoln's, 283, 543
reign of terror, Obama's, 29
reign of terror, Stalin's, 402
Remsburg, John E., 498
Rennolds, Fielding, 332
reparationists, 381
reparations, for slavery, 381
republic, defined, 49
Republican party, 19, 22, 23, 25, 42, 43, 246, 523, 541, 546, 564, 592, 595, 599
Republican Watchman, 285
Republican, defined, 22
republicanism, 18, 22, 51
reunion, 142, 162, 331, 347, 374, 475, 616
Reuter, Edward B., 237, 253
Revenue Act of 1861, 284
revisionist historians, 536
revolutionary socialism, 575
Revolutionary War, 42, 55, 85, 125, 126, 157, 357, 579, 603, 651

Rhett, Robert B., 217
Rhode Island, 95-97, 99, 104, 168, 169, 171, 467, 538, 557
Rhodes, James Ford, 127, 325
Richmond Dispatch, 293, 295
Richmond Enquirer, 294
Richmond Examiner, 119, 312, 588
Richmond Sentinel, 208, 294
Richmond Whig, 294
Richmond, New York, 172
Richmond, Virginia, 14, 48, 276, 333, 346, 538, 540, 566
right to bear arms, 54, 105
right to confront and to counsel, 105
rights reserved to states, 105
rituals, 270, 550
Rives, William C., 375
robber barons, 77
Roberts, R. Philip, 129
Robinson, Charles D., 130, 377
Robinson, Daniel, 332
Robinson, Marius, 198
Robinsons, New England slaving family, 169
Roche, Sir Boyle, 286
Rochester Negro Leader, 341
Rock, John S., 225
Rodney, Caesar, 99
Roman imperial system, 398
Roman pirates, and white slavery, 392
Roman slavery, 388, 405
Romania, white slaves from, 391
Rome, Georgia, 440
Roosevelt, Franklin Delano, 54, 513
Roosevelt, Theodore, 477
root, pig, or perish emancipation plan, Lincoln's, 470, 471
Roots (Haley), 173
Rosa, Robert, 510
Roseboom, Eugene H., 548
Ross, George, 99
Roswell, Georgia, 434
Rothschilds, the, 495
Roudanez, Jean Baptiste, 485
Royall family crest, 169
Royalls, New England slaving family, 169
Ruffin, Edmund, 71, 202, 559, 560
Ruffner, Henry, 207
rum, traded for slaves in Africa, 407
Rush, Benjamin, 99
Russell County, Alabama, 383
Russell, John, 183
Russia, 283, 401, 403, 406, 462, 476, 510, 591, 606
Russia, white slavery in, 401
Russians, enslaved by Nazis, 403
Rutherford, Mildred Lewis, 517, 519
Rutledge, Edward, 100

sadism, and slavery, 161
Saffins, New England slaving family, 169
Saint Andrew's Cross, 56
Saint Patrick's Cross, 56
Salem, Massachusetts, 168
Salt Lake Valley, and Mormon slavery, 128
Sanborn, Franklin B., 192
Sangamo Journal, 520
Sangamo, the, 520
Sangamon Journal, 490, 520
Sangamon, the, 520
Sardinians, as slaves, 393
Sartoris, Bayard, 234
Satan, and Jesus are brothers, according to Mormons, 129
Saulsbury, Willard, 491
Savannah Republican, 493
Savannah, South Carolina, 79, 562, 566
Saxton, Rufus, 351, 439
scalawag, defined, 22
scalawag, etymology of, 551
Scalloway, Scotland, 551
scallywag, defined, 22
scallywag, etymology of, 551
scallywags, 22, 29, 71, 149, 194, 213, 340, 351, 448, 472, 531, 537, 550, 551, 565, 568
Schenck, Robert C., 278, 279
Schenectady, New York, 149
Schlüter, Herman, 576
Schofield, John, 533
school administrators, 255
schools, South-hating, 568
Schurz, Carl, 443, 444, 510, 535, 558
Scotland, 40, 402, 462, 536, 589, 604
Scotland, white slaves from, 402
Scott, Dred, 219, 482
Scott, Winfield, 116, 182, 304
screenwriters, South-hating, 568
Screven County, Georgia, 157
scriptwriters, South-hating, 568
SCV, 30, 32, 559, 614
Scythian slavery, 387
Seabrook, Lochlainn, 27, 29, 30, 32, 575, 576, 651, 653
search and seizure, 105
secession, 2, 7, 15, 29, 35, 41, 44, 55, 63, 67, 71, 76, 77, 80-83, 85, 86, 88-96, 100, 104, 105, 107-109, 111, 112, 118, 119, 171, 187, 189, 292, 305, 430, 447, 475, 476, 509, 512, 514, 520, 534, 554, 576, 578, 581, 583, 593, 596, 603-605, 607, 610, 653
secession, legal right of established, 85, 86, 88-92, 95
Second Amendment, 105, 304
Second Annual Message to Congress, Lincoln's,

255, 479
Second Inaugural Address, Grant's, 548
Second Inaugural Address, Lincoln's, 117, 461, 506
Secret Six, 192
sectionalism, 56, 613
Seddon, James A., 134
segregation, 126, 170, 177, 231, 252, 358
self-incrimination, 105
self-government, 42, 62, 64, 71, 202, 204, 209, 302, 408, 452, 460, 514
Seminole, 384
senators elected by popular vote, 105
Seneca, 298, 574
Seneca Falls Woman's Rights Convention, 314
Senegambia, 166
Sengalese, slavery among the, 165
separation of powers, 44, 90, 277, 514
servant, 11, 128, 141, 142, 147-150, 154, 155, 162, 167, 202, 225, 231-233, 340, 348, 356, 367, 370, 381, 383, 393, 396, 404, 468, 477, 492, 532, 574
servants, 9, 43, 128, 139-142, 144-149, 152, 154, 155, 160-162, 164, 167, 168, 177, 179, 191, 202, 204, 207, 209, 213, 214, 225, 230, 231, 233, 235, 237, 240, 260, 321, 323, 331, 332, 335, 337, 339, 341, 342, 345, 347, 356, 381, 383, 389, 399, 400, 402-404, 419, 421, 441, 471, 475, 522, 531, 542, 580
servants, expense of keeping, 202
servitude, 125, 128, 139, 140, 142, 145, 146, 148, 149, 151, 153, 156, 161, 163, 165, 190, 199, 200, 205, 212, 215, 222, 242, 243, 318, 403, 410, 422, 468, 471, 582, 593, 595, 614
servitude, defined, 139
Seventeenth Amendment, 105
Seventh Amendment, 105
Sewall, Samuel, 404
Seward, William H., 73, 113, 120, 244, 247, 251, 252, 266, 295, 296, 307-309, 319, 324, 328, 375, 463, 476
sexual warfare, and Marx, 576
Seymour, Horatio, 172, 268
sharecropping, 150
sharpshooters, 345
Shem, 128
Shenandoah Holocaust, 445
Shenandoah Valley, 433, 436, 438, 444, 446
Shenandoah Valley Campaign, 444
Shepherd, Heyward, 193
Sheridan, Philip H., 299, 300, 433, 443-445, 447, 450, 533, 574
Sherman, John, 529
Sherman, Roger, 99

Sherman, Thomas W., 159
Sherman, William T., 27, 124, 126, 290, 299, 300, 338, 353, 433-437, 440-443, 445-448, 450, 472, 487, 517, 574
Shetland Islands, 551
Shields, James A., 504
shoemakers, 141
shoemen, 345
Sicily, 393-396, 401, 402
Sicily, African slavery in, 402
Sicily, slavery in, 393
Sicily, white slavery in, 396, 401
Sickles, Daniel E., 533
sideburns, 358
Sierra Leone, 166, 167, 245, 462
silver, 396
Sioux Indians, 295
Sixteenth Amendment, 105
Sixth Amendment, 105
Sixtus IV, Pope, 409
Slav, etymology of, 400
slave catchers, professional, Roman, 392
slave gangs, white, 395
slave insurrection, 133, 192, 193, 323, 393
slave labor, 171, 246, 383, 400, 403, 466, 468
slave labor, efficiency of vs. free labor, 468
slave labor, in preconquest Africa, 406
Slave Narratives, 162, 593
slave owners, black, 151
slave owners, correct number of, 213
slave owners, skewing number of by anti-South movement, 213
slave pens, 174
slave power, the South as a, 577
slave power, the South as a, Marxist term, 576
slave revolt, 317, 330, 393
slave revolts, 132, 147, 304
slaveholders' rebellion myth, 579
slaveholders' rebellion, a Marxist term, 576
slavery, 2, 7, 8, 15, 16, 32, 37, 40, 42, 59, 62-68, 71-76, 80, 105, 122, 127-129, 131, 135, 137, 139-148, 152-154, 156, 162-169, 171-173, 175-179, 181-184, 186-190, 192-197, 199-219, 222-228, 230, 236, 238-251, 253, 254, 256, 257, 259-261, 265, 267, 269, 270, 272, 282, 296-298, 304, 312, 313, 317, 318, 320, 322-324, 328, 334, 342, 344, 354, 365, 366, 368, 371-381, 383, 387-392, 394-416, 419, 422-424, 427-432, 462-471, 478, 481, 487, 494, 518, 520, 534, 544, 556, 576-583, 585, 587, 588, 590-592, 594, 595, 597-609, 611, 612, 614-616, 653
slavery as cornerstone of C.S.A. myth, 578

slavery figures, skewing by anti-South advocates, 213
slavery in Africa, 405
slavery scholars, 154, 166, 322, 406
slavery statistics, in the South, 213
slavery to be a beneficial institution myth, 578
slavery, as "cornerstone" of Confederacy, 67
slavery, defined, 139
slavery, in ancient Islam, 412
slavery, Northern, 576
slavery, Southern, 576
slavery, white, 387
slaves, 7-9, 12, 32, 59, 63, 66, 68, 74-76, 78, 124, 126-128, 132-134, 140-152, 154, 155, 158-161, 164-168, 172, 174-179, 181-183, 188, 192-195, 197, 198, 200-203, 209, 210, 212-216, 218, 220, 222, 224, 229, 232, 234, 235, 237, 242, 248, 249, 253, 257, 275, 282, 297, 299, 304, 305, 312, 314, 317, 318, 321, 324-326, 330, 333, 335, 338-340, 343, 344, 347, 350, 351, 354, 355, 365-367, 374, 375, 377, 380-385, 387-405, 407-414, 416, 421, 424, 427, 443, 456, 462, 463, 465-469, 471, 472, 477, 478, 481, 485, 487, 508, 509, 517, 518, 523, 524, 534, 536, 538, 540, 551, 558, 582, 593, 596, 597, 601, 616
slaves, as butlers, 162
slaves, as domestics, 162
slaves, as hands, 162
slaves, as maids, 162
slaves, as servants, 162
Slavic people, 400
Slavonic languages, 400
Slavs, enslaved by Nazis, 403
Slidell, John, 297
Slovakia, 400
Slovaks, 400
Slovenes, 400
Slovenia, 400, 476
Smith, Caleb B., 275, 276
Smith, Gerrit, 192, 234, 249, 548
Smith, James, 99
Smith, John, 611
Smith, Joseph, 128, 129
Smith, William Sooy, 449
Smithsonian Institution, 174
social divisiveness, and communists, 576
social inequality, African, caused by indigenous slavery, 167
Social media, and the traditional South, 30
socialism, 21, 51, 513, 546, 575, 576, 580, 601
socialism, and Lincoln, 546
socialist propaganda, and Lincoln, 576

socialist views, Lincoln's, 575
socialists and communists, in Lincoln's party, 580
socialists, and Lincoln, 264, 510
socialists, in Lincoln's administration and armies, 510
socialists, in the Republican Party, 176, 259
Sons of Confederate Veterans, 56, 559
South America, 56, 250, 406
South Carolina, 12, 27, 44, 58, 60, 61, 79, 97, 100, 103, 113, 116, 119, 148, 161, 186, 187, 198, 201, 204, 214, 217, 223, 225, 229, 232, 236, 294, 317, 322, 338, 343, 348, 351, 353, 382-384, 429, 431, 439-441, 443, 467, 472, 531, 533, 537, 542, 543, 549, 553, 586, 596-598, 605, 607, 616
South-hating writers, 568
Southern abolition movement, 196, 197
Southern abolitionists, 59
Southern agrarianism, 186, 298
Southern blacks, 32, 132, 133, 140, 148, 150, 151, 158, 191, 206, 220, 221, 223, 231, 232, 235-238, 319, 321, 328, 330-334, 338, 341, 343-348, 350-354, 357, 358, 362, 367, 371, 432, 440, 470, 479, 480, 531, 551
Southern Confederacy, 2, 3, 15, 22, 32, 37, 48, 55, 58, 61, 69, 71, 107, 111, 126, 185, 186, 204, 337, 338, 354, 430, 433, 459, 462, 564, 590, 605, 608-610, 614, 616
Southern families, 125, 204, 213, 525, 536
Southern Illustrated News, 283, 294
Southern Literary Messenger, 120
Southern nationalism, 559
Southern plans for complete abolition, 578
Southern plantations, 155, 161, 191, 531
Southern ports, 77, 82, 304
Southern slave owners, 191, 202, 206, 209, 213-215, 383, 413, 414, 524
Southern slavery, 231
Southern slaves, paid a salary, 140
Southern states, 29, 37, 41, 48, 58, 64, 70, 73, 75, 78, 80, 98, 107, 109, 115, 121, 134, 154, 155, 172, 179, 183, 193, 199-201, 209, 214, 225, 237, 239, 273, 274, 276, 291, 292, 301, 303-305, 317, 325, 373, 374, 376, 379, 428, 446, 459, 465, 475, 476, 481, 486, 518, 525, 533, 534, 549, 552, 553, 555, 560, 565, 577, 582, 587, 592, 595
Southern traditionalism, 186
Southern Truth, 146, 197, 234, 517, 519, 568
Southern whites, 76, 132, 155, 201, 212-214,

229, 232, 236, 237, 245, 261, 432, 551, 553, 576
Southerners, 8, 23-25, 29, 32, 38, 39, 44, 46, 48, 53, 55, 61, 63, 65, 67, 69, 71, 75, 80, 82, 98, 117, 118, 121, 126, 132, 133, 142, 150, 153-155, 161, 193-195, 198-204, 206-217, 228, 232, 233, 235, 237, 238, 250, 259, 261, 270, 274, 276, 285, 288, 296, 298, 299, 306, 316, 321-324, 337, 343, 345, 391, 429, 430, 434, 436, 445, 456-458, 461, 468, 469, 471, 472, 477, 491, 508, 509, 511, 512, 515-517, 519-521, 529-531, 535-537, 539, 544, 545, 549-552, 554, 558-560, 563, 565-567, 569, 578, 582, 610, 616
Southerners, percentage of who owned servants, 213
Southrons, 40
South's Great Emancipators, 481
Spain, 391, 401, 462
Spain, white slavery in, 401
Spain, white slaves from, 391
Spanish slave traders, 405
Sparta, white slavery in ancient, 396
Spartans, and white slave rebellion, 393
Spartiates, 396
Speed, Joshua F., 490, 500
spies, 8, 293, 306, 345, 346, 356, 378
Spooner, Lysander, 78, 189, 265, 322, 378, 433, 455, 456, 463, 465
Spring Hill, Tennessee, 6
Springfield, Illinois, 24, 64, 241, 253, 255, 370, 501, 504, 520, 527, 569, 570
St. Andrew's Cross, 56
St. Patrick's Cross, 56
Stalin, Joseph, 402, 510
Stampp, Kenneth M., 213
Standard, the, 321
standing army, 80, 509
Stanley, John, black slave owner, 383
Stanly, Edward, 477, 478
Stanton, Edwin M., 266, 294, 339, 370, 439, 446, 490, 506, 545
Stanton, Elizabeth C., 314
starry cross, 55, 559
Stars and Bars, 179, 559
Stars and Stripes, 178, 595
starvation, 300, 353, 389, 409, 445, 470, 471
state slaves, 396
state sovereignty, 66, 76, 97, 301
states' rights, 15, 24, 31, 35, 38, 42, 44-46, 56, 65, 76, 82, 85-87, 89, 90, 105, 182, 187, 192, 202, 276, 301, 302, 310, 332, 414, 431, 452, 458, 460, 475, 477, 509, 511, 514, 532, 578,

601
states' rights movements, 532
status of income tax clarified, 105
Stearns, George L., 192
Stephens, Alexander H., 29, 67, 71, 219, 283, 374, 459, 514, 543, 554, 559, 564, 578, 579
stevedores, 437
Stevens, Matthew, 537
Stevens, Thaddeus, 266, 522, 531, 532, 539, 554
stewards, 345
Stockdale, Fletcher, 543
stocks, decline of due to Grant, 547
stocks, decline of due to Lincoln, 547
Stockton, Richard, 99
Stone, Kate, 324, 650
Stone, Thomas, 99
Stoughton, Edwin H., 488
Stowe, Harriet Beecher, 148, 151, 153, 154, 163, 170, 205, 217, 267, 526
Strong, George T., 492
struggle, the, and the Left, 576
Stuart, Alexander H., 185
Stuart, Jeb (James Ewell Brown), 14, 443
Stuart, John T., 500-502
Sturge, Joseph, 224
sugar plantations, 402, 465
sugar plantations, West Indies, 465
suits against a state, 105
Sumerian slavery, 387
Sumner Tunnel, 428
Sumner, Charles, 176, 188, 266, 428-430, 463-465, 481, 522, 531
Supreme Court, 119, 120, 303, 306, 308, 310, 483, 554, 594
survival of the fittest, 127
sutlers, 337
Swahili, slavery among the, 165
Sweden, 462, 476
Swedish slave traders, 405
Syrian slavery, 388
Tam O'Shanter (Burns), 502
Taney, Roger B., 280, 310
Tappan, Lewis, 271
Tariff of Abominations, 61
tax-and-spend government, 510
Taylor, George, 99
Taylor, James, 99
Taylor, Richard, 63, 335
Taylor, Susie King, 360
Taylor, Tom, 649
Taylor, Zachary, 335, 556
teamsters, 335, 337, 343, 345, 347
Ten Percent Plan, Lincoln's, 378
Tennesseans, 152
Tennessee, 3, 5, 6, 11, 30, 32, 58, 68, 152,

158, 231, 303, 311, 318, 343, 346, 430, 432, 449, 472, 529, 533, 538, 549, 584, 588, 590, 593, 600, 601, 608, 615, 651
Tennessee, first American state to enlist blacks, in June 1861, 343
Tennessee's black soldiers, 343
Tenth Amendment, 87, 93, 95, 105, 483, 515, 554, 578
Texas, 12, 58, 60, 81, 216, 294, 304, 317, 468, 512, 533, 543, 549, 553, 591, 600, 604, 605
textiles, 407
Thackeray, William M., 145, 202
Thanksgiving Day, 290, 291
The Alexander H. Stephens Reader (Seabrook), 578
The American Commonwealth (Bryce), 460
The Communist Manifesto (Marx and Engels), 576
The Cotton Kingdom (Olmsted), 233
The Crisis, 294, 418, 612
The Day-Book, 285
The Democrat, 39, 285, 294
The Farmer, 45, 51, 285
The Federalist, 17, 25, 44, 45, 47, 594
The Good Old Rebel, 560
The Great Yankee Coverup (Seabrook), 578
The Herald, 285
The Impending Crisis of the South (Helper), 250
The Liberator, 170, 173, 205, 206, 208, 226, 363, 422
The Lost Cause (Pollard), 114
The McGavocks of Carnton Plantation (Seabrook), 231
The Memoirs of Uncle Tom (Henson), 151
The Missourian, 285
The New York World, 285, 324, 488
The North Star, 315
The Order of the Star Spangled Banner, 270, 549, 550
The Quotable Alexander H. Stephens (Seabrook), 579
The Quotable Jefferson Davis (Seabrook), 578
The Quotable Nathan Bedford Forrest (Seabrook), 449, 552
The Rise and Fall of the Confederate Government (Davis), 95, 307, 522
The Second Treatise of Government (Locke), 468
The Sentinel, 209, 285
The South, 6-9, 11-14, 26, 30, 32, 37-43, 46, 51, 55, 56, 58, 60-72, 76-83, 89, 96, 108, 109, 112-120, 129, 131, 132, 134, 139-143, 145, 146, 150, 151, 153, 155, 157, 159, 161, 163, 164, 167, 171, 172, 179, 181, 184-186, 191, 193, 194, 197, 199-218, 220-225, 227, 228, 230-232, 234-238, 247, 248, 250, 251, 253, 258, 260, 261, 272, 274-276, 282, 289-291, 293-300, 304, 305, 311, 312, 317, 319, 323, 324, 329-334, 337-345, 348, 351, 353, 354, 358, 364, 367, 372, 373, 375, 376, 378, 381, 384, 421, 423, 424, 427-434, 436, 437, 439, 443, 444, 446, 448, 456, 459-461, 464, 466-468, 471, 472, 476, 477, 483, 487, 488, 495, 506-508, 516-518, 520-526, 528-545, 548-559, 561-565, 568, 569, 572, 574, 576, 578, 579, 581, 586-588, 591, 594-598, 602-604, 606, 607, 611, 616, 649, 650
The South Since the War (Andrews), 443
the South, positive aspects of, 430
The Southern Cross (poem), 280
The Star-Spangled Banner (Key), 252
The Unvanquished (Faulkner), 234
theory of necessity, Lincoln's faulty, 483
thievery, 471, 542, 543
Third Amendment, 105
Thirteenth Amendment, 105, 140, 182, 197, 216, 259, 316, 326, 343, 375, 469, 580
Thirteenth Kentucky Cavalry, CSA, 433
Thomas, Gabriel, 156
Thomas, George H., 182, 435
Thomas, Lorenzo, 341, 367
Thome, James, 198
Thoreau, Henry David, 192
Thornton, Matthew, 99
Thrace and white slavery, 396, 402
thralls, white English slaves, 399
thugocracy, Lincoln's, 8, 277
Tiffany, Charles, and slavery, 172
Tilton, Theodore, 266
Tocqueville, Alexis de, 49, 93, 222, 223
Todd, Alexander H., 39
Todd, David H., 39
Todd, Elodie, 524
Todd, Francis, 270
Todd, George Rogers Clark, 39
Todd, Mary (Lincoln's wife), 39, 182, 491, 503, 524, 649
Todd, Samuel Briggs, 39
Toombs, Robert A., 48, 71
Torah, and slavery, 388
torture, 8, 10, 229, 231, 299, 305, 311, 389, 397, 406, 438, 441, 442, 448, 449, 531, 543, 574
torture, of ancient white slaves, 389
totalitarians, and Lincoln, 510

Tourgee, Albion W., 555
Towne, Laura, 429
Transcontinental Railroad land grants, 514
Travel & Leisure, 430
treason, 10, 39, 279, 280, 286, 465, 493, 611
Treaty of Ghent, 109
Treaty of Washington, 181
Treaty with Great Britain, 97, 171
trial by jury in civil cases, 105
Tri-Weekly Telegraph, 294
Trollope, Frances, 42
True, B. H., 228
Truman, Harry, 357, 522, 523
Trumbull, Lyman, 246, 247, 249, 266, 315
Truth Is Stranger Than Fiction (Henson), 151
Truth, Sojourner, 8, 178, 315, 342, 421, 462, 477
Tucker, St. George, 92, 93, 197
Turchin, John B., 450
Turkey, 390, 406
Turkey, and white slavery, 390
Turner, Nat, 192, 206, 343
Tuskegee, Alabama, 150
TV producers, South-hating, 568
Tweed Ring, 547
Twelfth Amendment, 105
Twentieth Amendment, 105
Twenty-Fifth Amendment, 105
Twenty-First Amendment, 105
Twenty-Fourth Amendment, 105
Twenty-Second Amendment:, 105
Twenty-Seventh Amendment, 105
Twenty-Sixth Amendment, 105
Twenty-Third Amendment, 105
two-term limit on president, 105
Tyler, Erastus B., 280
Tyler, John, 48, 66, 94, 185
Tyler, Lyon Gardiner, 66, 300, 430, 528, 565
tyrannical proclivities, 475
Tyrant, nickname for Lincoln, 456
U.S. army, 82, 177, 284, 319, 366, 482
U.S. Capitol, 32, 174, 485, 569
U.S. Capitol, constructed by black slaves, 174, 485
U.S. Census, 173, 213
U.S. Confederacy, 87, 462
U.S. Congress, 73, 85, 174, 184, 255, 356, 364, 447, 470, 478, 491, 495, 521
U.S. Constitution, 7, 10, 18, 22, 29, 41, 49, 70, 89, 95, 100, 103, 112, 118, 171, 179, 216, 283, 301, 431, 463, 505, 508, 554, 578, 581
U.S. flag, 178
U.S. government, 29, 42, 66, 70, 77, 96, 119, 126, 140, 180, 227, 276, 288, 300, 310, 359, 360, 376, 455, 463, 511, 513, 536, 549, 551, 553

U.S. military, 357, 363, 384
U.S. News & World Report, 472
U.S. Supreme Court, 120, 308
U.S. threatens war on Great Britain, for aiding Confederacy, 143, 296
U.S. Treasury, 461, 536
U.S.A., 13, 37, 38, 44, 49, 90, 190, 291, 301, 578
UDC, 559
Ullmann, Daniel, 368, 369
Uncle Tom's Cabin (Stowe), 151-153, 155, 217, 267
Underground Railroad, 149
Underhill, John, 198
unforced labor, 322
Union, 2, 6, 7, 12, 16, 18, 20, 22, 27, 37, 39, 41, 42, 47, 61, 64-74, 76, 77, 79-82, 87, 88, 90-93, 95-97, 100-105, 107-111, 113-115, 118, 121, 122, 124, 129-131, 133, 134, 143, 149, 157-159, 182, 184, 187-189, 192, 210, 219, 222, 223, 227, 228, 230, 236, 247, 251, 258, 260, 261, 269, 283, 288-291, 298, 300-302, 314, 318, 323, 325, 331, 336-343, 349, 351, 352, 354, 356, 357, 359-361, 363, 365-368, 372-381, 384, 424, 429, 431, 433, 439-441, 446, 449, 451, 455-459, 461, 463, 475-477, 481, 483, 485, 486, 489, 494, 495, 506, 508, 516, 518, 520, 525, 531, 532, 534, 535, 539, 541, 549, 553, 554, 556, 559, 561, 564, 565, 567, 575, 577-579, 581, 587, 589, 591, 593, 594, 598, 601, 602, 604, 605, 610, 612, 613, 615, 616
Union army, 261, 331, 341, 365, 384, 486, 495, 581, 587
Union officers, 290, 361, 365, 367
Unionizing process, Yankee, 537
Unionville, South Carolina, 537
United Confederate Veterans, 347
United Daughters of the Confederacy, 193, 330, 337, 358, 559
United States Colored Troops, 358, 487, 613
United States of America, 3, 10, 18, 20, 69, 85-87, 91, 99, 100, 103, 134, 179, 180, 302, 303, 318, 462, 494, 507, 577, 582, 601, 602, 606, 610, 612
universities, South-hating, 568
universities, Southern, 472
University of Alabama, 472, 582, 592, 602
Unmelted Pot, U.S. as an, 257
Upshur, Abel Parker, 94
Ural Mountains, 403
urbanization, 466

Uruguay, 462
USCT, 358, 487
Utah, 128, 129
Uzbekistan, white slavery in, 401
Vallandigham, Clement L., 284-288
Van Buren, Cornelius M., 404
Van Buren, Martin, 45, 404, 482
Vanderbilt University, 472, 548, 588, 602, 613
Vanderbilt, Cornelius, 548
Varro, Marcus Terentius, 400
Vassa, Gustavus, 141
Venetians, and slavery, 405
Venezuela, 462
Venice, and the white slave trade, 401
Verdun, France, and white slavery, 398
Vermont, 12, 431, 466, 531, 538, 557
Vertrees, Peter, 332
Vesey, Denmark, 141, 192
Vest, George G., 157
Victorian Southern children, 160
Vietnam War, 357
View of the Constitution of the US of America, A (Rawle), 91
Virgil, 393
Virgin Mary, 515
Virginia, 9, 11, 14, 39, 41, 43, 44, 46, 48, 52, 55, 58, 66, 68, 72, 74, 79, 94-98, 100, 103, 104, 108, 115, 119, 126, 139, 145, 146, 185, 187, 192-195, 197, 198, 201, 203, 204, 206, 207, 216, 224, 227, 231-233, 235, 274, 276, 292, 294, 303, 304, 317, 326, 333, 334, 336, 338, 339, 346, 347, 358, 359, 367, 368, 381, 384, 385, 419, 431, 433, 440, 447, 506-508, 521, 533, 540, 549, 553, 559, 560, 563, 565, 572, 574, 582, 584, 588, 589, 591, 594, 596-598, 601-603, 605, 613, 614, 649, 651
Virginia Convention, 52
Virginia Declaration of Rights, 197
Virginia Military Institute, 433
Vohburg, Diepold von, 401
Volney, Count, 497
Voltaire, 497
voting age set to eighteen years, 105
Voting Rights Act, 316
Wade, Benjamin F., 266, 481
Wade-Davis Bill, 521, 522, 571
Wadsworth, James, 486
Wait, Thomas, 52
Wakefield, John A., 504
Walden Pond, 169
Waldos, New England slaving family, 169
Waldrop, R. W., 526
Wales, 536
Walker, David S., 461

Wall Street Boys, 7, 77, 78, 81, 82, 189, 275, 455
Walton, George, 100
Wanton, Joseph, 169
war crimes, Lincoln's, 299, 303, 305, 311
war crimes, of Sherman, 436
war crimes, Southern, fabricated by the North, 448
war crimes, Yankee, 438-441
War Department, 123, 173, 329, 350, 361
War for Southern Independence, 17, 23, 29, 66, 192, 288, 295, 339, 461, 556, 601
war measure, 32, 189, 301, 317, 322, 328, 371, 374
War of 1812, 107, 109, 125
War of Rebellion, 71, 72, 112
war powers, and Lincoln, 483, 484, 535
Ward, Artemus, 491
Ward, James, 367
Warren, Joe, 332
warrior-pharaohs, and Egyptian slavery, 388
Washburne, Elihu B., 116, 257, 496
Washington College, 207, 438
Washington Post, 509
Washington, Booker T., 150, 235, 236
Washington, D.C., 6, 12, 32, 50-52, 66, 69, 76, 78, 115, 123, 159, 173, 175, 177, 178, 182, 186, 217, 252, 266, 293, 307, 315, 375, 422, 435, 443, 476, 485, 487, 488, 493, 501, 527, 544, 557, 569, 570, 581-583, 585, 587, 589, 596-598, 601, 602, 604, 606, 612-614, 617, 649
Washington, George, 14, 36, 45, 64, 70, 88, 91, 107, 126, 157, 195, 197, 204, 308, 342, 383, 438, 451, 452, 455, 493, 508, 509, 563, 570, 573, 578
Watie, Stand, 384
Watkins, Sam, 433
Wayland, Francis, 208
wealthy blacks, 64, 382
weavers, 141
Weber, Max, 510
Websites, South-hating, 568
Webster, Alexander H., 459
Webster, Daniel, 170, 183, 186, 252
Webster, Massachusetts, 252
Weld, Theodore, 271
Welles, Gideon, 116, 117, 133, 307, 329
Welling, James C., 478
Wells, H. G., 168
West Africa, 167, 173
West Central Africa, 167
West Coast Elites, 30
West Indies, 168, 465
West Indies, and Yankee slavery, 168
West Virginia, 74, 274, 292, 317

Westchester, New York, 172
Western states, 22, 220, 245, 274
Western Territories, 139, 245, 246, 248, 375, 384
Whigs, 23, 25
whip, 15, 139, 153-156, 158-161, 173, 206, 346, 516, 518, 615
whipping, 151, 154-157, 160, 161, 229, 240
whipping post, 151, 154
whipping, and slavery, 156, 157
whipping, in England, 156
Whipple, William, 99
Whiskey Ring, 547
White House, 29, 42, 54, 69, 111, 122, 131, 174, 189, 258, 260, 266, 316, 354, 370, 416, 418, 420, 421, 456, 476-478, 481-483, 485, 489, 496, 529, 549, 571, 584, 598, 604, 607, 614
White House, Confederate, 260
White House, constructed by black slaves, 174, 485
white labor, 59, 243, 246, 251, 479, 480
white racism, 230
white racism (European-American), 249
white racism and the Bible, 127
white racism in Illinois, 239, 240
white racism, worst in North, 222
white servitude, 582, 593
white sharecroppers, 150
white slave owners, 9, 128, 152, 212, 323, 381, 382, 385
white slavery, 8, 388, 389, 392, 395-402, 404-406
white slaves, 381, 388, 389, 391-398, 401-405, 582, 597
white slaves, owned by American blacks, 381
white supremacy, 241, 248, 249, 251, 270, 272, 481, 550
white supremacy, built into Lincoln's platform, 248
whites, 8, 59, 64, 76, 124, 126, 132, 140, 141, 143, 150, 154-156, 159, 161, 162, 168, 170, 174, 175, 177, 192, 201, 206, 207, 212-214, 218, 220, 222, 223, 226, 227, 229, 230, 232, 235-245, 247, 248, 250, 253, 259, 261, 268, 269, 271, 273, 299, 316, 319, 329, 331, 335, 337-339, 344, 354, 357, 358, 360, 361, 364, 367, 371, 377, 382, 385, 387, 388, 391, 392, 398, 401, 403, 404, 407, 408, 413, 419, 421, 423, 432, 471, 480, 486, 508, 537-539, 542, 544, 550, 551, 553, 557, 576, 596, 612
Whitman, George, 527
Whitman, Walt, 527

Whitney, Eli, 211, 467
Wiggins, Thomas, 332
Wilder, C. B., 227
Wilfrid I, Bishop, 399
Wilkinson, James, 286
Williams, William, 99
Willich, August, 510
Willis, Jesse, 198
Wilmington, Delaware, 79
Wilmot Proviso, 243, 244
Wilmot, David, 243, 244
Wilson, Henry, 369, 404, 463
Wilson, James, 44, 99
Wilson, R. E., 560
Wilson, Woodrow, 109, 142, 185, 257, 340, 423, 549
Winthrop, Theodore, 345
Wisconsin, 123, 220, 588, 597
Witherspoon, John, 99
Wolcott, Oliver, 99
women, 2, 3, 9, 10, 105, 145, 146, 164, 187, 214, 220, 224, 233, 244, 253, 268, 275, 299, 301, 314-316, 322, 338, 353-355, 383, 399, 400, 406, 407, 421, 436-439, 442, 443, 450, 489, 491, 494, 495, 516, 517, 540, 557, 559, 560, 573, 574, 583, 584, 587, 592, 609
women given the vote, 105
women's suffrage, 220
women's rights, 314, 315
Wood, Fernando, 172
Woodhull, Victoria C., 314
Woods, Thomas E., Jr., 24
Woods, William B., 554
Woodward, Comer Vann, 345
Worcester, Massachusetts, 314
Work, Henry C., 444
workingmen of Europe, and communism, 579
World War II, 79, 148, 178, 511, 536, 561, 563
wounds, 44, 121, 158, 339, 461, 522, 537
writers, South-hating, 568
Wythe County, Virginia, 231
Wythe, George, 100
Xenophon, 400
Yancey, William L., 273
Yankee crimes, against Southern blacks, 439
Yankee Doodle, 114
Yankee folklore, 37, 149, 164
Yankee greed, 558
Yankee industrialists, 77
Yankee materialism, 558
Yankee myth, 2, 68, 155, 192, 219, 222, 234, 310, 311, 407, 469, 552, 581, 609
Yankee mythology, 29, 209, 267, 345, 549
Yankee propaganda, 152, 518, 649

Yankee propaganda machine, 518
Yankee racism, 225, 229, 238, 369, 466, 487
Yankee rule, 202
Yankee slave traders, 174, 197, 200, 405
Yankee slave trading, 181
Yankee war crimes, 440
Yankee war criminals, 433
Yankee, defined, 22
Yankee, racism, 576
Yankeedom, 43, 218, 238, 530, 539, 562
Yankees, 25, 80, 107, 127, 153, 159, 169, 172, 179, 192, 207-209, 215, 216, 218, 220, 226, 242, 244, 252, 253, 266, 267, 273, 285, 305, 308, 332, 335, 336, 345, 346, 354, 366, 370, 371, 382, 407, 409, 421, 427, 434, 439, 465, 466, 480, 506, 526, 529-531, 534, 535, 539, 540, 543, 544, 548, 553, 559-561, 576, 598
Yates, Richard, 240
Yates, Robert, 19
yellow racism (Asian-American), 249
York, England, 399
York, Pennsylvania, 108, 187
Yoruba, 165, 166
Yoruba, slavery among the, 165
Yosemite nature reserve land grant, 514
Young, Brigham, 128
Yugoslavia, 400, 476
Yugoslavians, 400
Zeus, 488

A Note On
JOHN WILKES BOOTH

Above, disillusioned Copperhead John Wilkes Booth flees across the stage of the Ford Theater in Washington, D.C. after shooting Lincoln on April 14, 1865. Lincoln and his wife Mary Todd had been enjoying Tom Taylor's theatrical comedy, *Our American Cousin*, when Booth surprised the president from behind, shooting him in the back of the head with a Deringer .44 caliber. Lincoln can be seen slumped over in the presidential box, upper middle, with his wife Mary reaching out to him. He never regained consciousness and died the next day.

Jumping from the balcony, Booth, a popular actor, broke his leg when it got caught in a decorative flag sitting on the stage. As he limped hurriedly from the theater, he cried out, "*sic semper tyrannis!*" ("thus always to tyrants") and "the South is avenged!" Booth went on the run for nearly two weeks, finding little sympathy along the way. He stopped at the home of Dr. Samuel Mudd (a relative of TV host and journalist Roger Mudd), where his injured leg was set and bandaged.

On April 26, Booth was caught hiding in a tobacco barn on the property of Richard Garret, located near Port Royal, Virginia. U.S. soldiers set the structure on fire, and in the ensuing gun battle Booth was shot through the neck. He was dragged from the smoking barn and laid out on the porch of the Garrets' farmhouse, where, according to Yankee legend, he died. The twenty-six year old's last words were "useless, useless." He was buried in the Booth family plot at Greenmount Cemetery, Baltimore, Maryland.

Booth's act did nothing to help the South. Instead it magnified the horrors of Lincoln' War, stiffened Northern resolve to punish Dixie, and aggravated Reconstruction. Worst of all, it immortalized Lincoln, allowing his image to be forever glorified, sentimentalized, and romanticized. His figure now cloaked in a shroud of Northern myth, pious Yankee propaganda, self-serving folklore, and flagrant disinformation, today Lincoln's crimes have largely been forgotten.

But here in the South we will always remember.

Epitaph

"I wonder what will be the result of this diabolical move? Surely not as bad for us as they intended it to be. I think that there is little chance for a happy hereafter for President Lincoln. A thousand years of repentance would be but brief time to wipe out his sins against the South. How can he even sleep with the shades of thousands he has consigned to a bloody death darkening his soul?"

> Kate Stone, diary entry, October 1, 1862, Louisiana, on hearing of Lincoln's Preliminary Emancipation Proclamation (issued September 22, 1862), in which he called for both a murderous slave rebellion in the South and the deportation of all "persons of African descent . . . upon this continent or elsewhere."

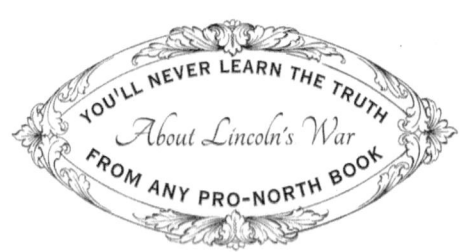

MEET THE AUTHOR

NEO-VICTORIAN SCHOLAR LOCHLAINN SEABROOK, a descendant of the families of Alexander Hamilton Stephens, John Singleton Mosby, Edmund Winchester Rucker, and William Giles Harding, is a 7th generation Kentuckian and the most prolific pro-South writer in the world today. Known by literary critics as the "new Shelby Foote" and by his fans as the "Voice of the Traditional South," he is a recipient of the prestigious Jefferson Davis Historical Gold Medal. As a lifelong writer he has authored and edited books ranging in topics from history, politics, science, religion, and biography, to nature, music, humor, gastronomy, and the paranormal; books that his readers describe as "game changers," "transformative," and "life altering."

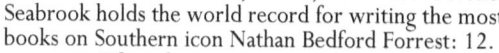

One of the world's most popular living historians, he is a 17th generation Southerner of Appalachian heritage who descends from dozens of patriotic Revolutionary War soldiers and Confederate soldiers from Kentucky, Tennessee, North Carolina, and Virginia. A proud member of the Sons of the Confederate Veterans, he is a true Renaissance Man. Besides being an accomplished and well respected author-historian and Bible authority, he is also a Kentucky Colonel, eagle scout, screenwriter, nature, wildlife, and landscape photographer, artist, graphic designer, songwriter (3,000 songs), film composer, multi-instrument musician, vocalist, session player, music producer, genealogist, former history museum docent, and a former ranch hand, zookeeper, and wrangler.

His (currently) 76 adult and children's books contain some 60,000 well-researched pages that have earned him accolades from around the globe. His works, which have sold on every continent except Antarctica, have introduced hundreds of thousands to vital facts that have been left out of our mainstream books. He has been endorsed internationally by leading experts, museum curators, award-winning historians, bestselling authors, celebrities, filmmakers, noted scientists, well regarded educators, TV show hosts and producers, renowned military artists, esteemed heritage organizations, and distinguished academicians of all races, creeds, and colors. Colonel Seabrook holds the world record for writing the most books on Southern icon Nathan Bedford Forrest: 12.

Of northern, western, and central European ancestry, he is the 6th great-grandson of the Earl of Oxford and a descendant of European royalty. His modern day cousins include: Johnny Cash, Elvis Presley, Lisa Marie Presley, Billy Ray and Miley Cyrus, Patty Loveless, Tim McGraw, Lee Ann Womack, Dolly Parton, Pat Boone, Naomi, Wynonna, and Ashley Judd, Ricky Skaggs, the Sunshine Sisters, Martha Carson, Chet Atkins, Patrick J. Buchanan, Cindy Crawford, Bertram Thomas Combs (Kentucky's 50th governor), Edith Bolling (second wife of President Woodrow Wilson), Andy Griffith, Riley Keough, George C. Scott, Robert Duvall, Reese Witherspoon, Lee Marvin, Rebecca Gayheart, and Tom Cruise.

A constitutionalist and avid outdoorsman and gun advocate, Colonel Seabrook is the author of the international blockbuster, *Everything You Were Taught About the Civil War is Wrong, Ask a Southerner!* He lives with his wife and family in beautiful historic Middle Tennessee, the heart of the Confederacy.

For more information on author Mr. Seabrook visit

LOCHLAINNSEABROOK.COM

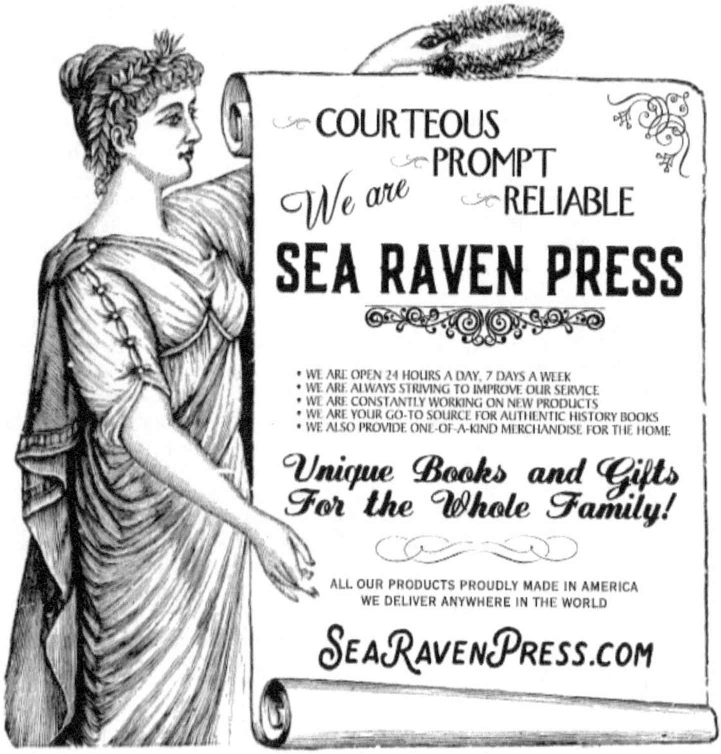
COURTEOUS
PROMPT
We are
RELIABLE
SEA RAVEN PRESS
• WE ARE OPEN 24 HOURS A DAY, 7 DAYS A WEEK
• WE ARE ALWAYS STRIVING TO IMPROVE OUR SERVICE
• WE ARE CONSTANTLY WORKING ON NEW PRODUCTS
• WE ARE YOUR GO-TO SOURCE FOR AUTHENTIC HISTORY BOOKS
• WE ALSO PROVIDE ONE-OF-A-KIND MERCHANDISE FOR THE HOME
Unique Books and Gifts For the Whole Family!
ALL OUR PRODUCTS PROUDLY MADE IN AMERICA
WE DELIVER ANYWHERE IN THE WORLD
SeaRavenPress.com

If you enjoyed this book you will be interested in Colonel Seabrook's popular related titles:

- ABRAHAM LINCOLN WAS A LIBERAL, JEFFERSON DAVIS WAS A CONSERVATIVE
- EVERYTHING YOU WERE TAUGHT ABOUT THE CIVIL WAR IS WRONG, ASK A SOUTHERNER!
- ALL WE ASK IS TO BE LET ALONE: THE SOUTHERN SECESSION FACT BOOK
- EVERYTHING YOU WERE TAUGHT ABOUT AMERICAN SLAVERY IS WRONG, ASK A SOUTHERNER!
- CONFEDERATE FLAG FACTS: WHAT EVERY AMERICAN SHOULD KNOW ABOUT DIXIE'S SOUTHERN CROSS
- LINCOLN'S WAR: THE REAL CAUSE, THE REAL WINNER, THE REAL LOSER

Available from Sea Raven Press and wherever fine books are sold

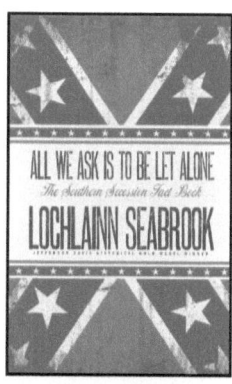

ALL OF OUR BOOK COVERS ARE AVAILABLE AS 11" X 17" COLOR POSTERS, SUITABLE FOR FRAMING

SeaRavenPress.com

www.ingramcontent.com/pod-product-compliance
Lightning Source LLC
Chambersburg PA
CBHW021412300426
44114CB00010B/469